Money, Interest, and Banking
in Economic Development

The Johns Hopkins Studies in Development
Vernon W. Ruttan and T. Paul Schultz,
Consulting Editors

Money, Interest, and Banking in Economic Development

Second Edition

Maxwell J. Fry
University of Birmingham

The Johns Hopkins University Press
Baltimore and London

The first edition was published in hardcover and paperback by
The Johns Hopkins University Press in 1988.

The Johns Hopkins University Press
2715 North Charles Street
Baltimore, Maryland 21218–4319
The Johns Hopkins Press Ltd., London

A catalog record for this book is available from the British Library.

Library of Congress Cataloging-in-Publication Data

Fry, Maxwell J.
   Money, interest, and banking in economic development /
Maxwell J. Fry. – 2nd ed.

      p.   cm. — (The Johns Hopkins studies in development)
   Includes bibliographical references (p.   ) and index.
   ISBN 0-8018-5026-6 (alk. paper) — ISBN 0-8018-5027-4
(pbk.: alk. paper)
      1. Money — Developing countries — Econometric models.
   2. Monetary policy — Developing countries — Econometric
   models.   3. Interest rates — Developing countries —
   Econometric models.   4. Banks and banking — Developing
   countries — Econometric models.   I. Title.   II. Series.
   HG1496.F79   1995
   332.1′09172′4–dc20   94-3466
                                                   CIP

Contents

Figures

Tables

Acronyms

2SLS	Two-stage least squares
3SLS	Three-stage least squares
ASEAN	Association of South East Asian Nations
CCI	Costs of credit intermediation
CD	Certificate of deposit
CUSUM	Cumulative sum
DFI	Development finance institution
DIS	Deposit insurance scheme
DMB	Deposit money bank
EDI	Economic Development Institute (World Bank)
EU	European Union
FDI	Foreign direct investment
GDP	Gross domestic product
GNP	Gross national product
ICOR	Incremental capital/output ratio
IDA	International Development Association
IDPS	Implicit deposit protection scheme
IFC	International Finance Corporation
IMF	International Monetary Fund
IOCR	Incremental output/capital ratio
LDC	Less developed country
LIBOR	London Inter-Bank Offered Rate
LTV	Loan-to-value
NCD	Negotiable certificate of deposit
OECD	Organisation for Economic Co-operation and Development
OLS	Ordinary least squares
SE	Standard error
SEE	Standard error of the estimate
UMM	Unorganized money market
VAR	Vector autoregression

Preface and Acknowledgements

THE RESPONSE TO THE FIRST EDITION OF *Money, Interest, and Banking in Economic Development* encouraged me to embark on a second edition over two years ago. The task took far longer than I had expected because thousands of articles and hundreds of books have been written in this field since 1988. The second edition contains new chapters on finance in endogenous growth models, financial repression and capital flows, foreign direct investment and the accumulation of foreign debt, and fiscal activities of central banks in developing countries. All other chapters have been rewritten to amend and extend the analysis in the light of the literature explosion over the past seven years. The second edition contains over 400 new bibliographical entries.

New features of the second edition include the presentation of stylized facts on finance and financial systems in economic development supported by cross-country data from 110 countries; adverse selection, principal-agent problems, and moral hazard treated in greater depth; the Diamond-Dybvig banking model explained and used in the presentation of finance in endogenous growth models; borrowing constrained consumption behavior analyzed within a three-period intertemporal utility-maximizing model; analysis of foreign debt accumulation and the impact of foreign direct investment; evaluation of new micro data sets enabling more rigorous examination of the link between finance and business activity; new empirical evidence suggesting that borrowing constrained households in Japan, Korea, and Taiwan do save more; new data on curb market interest rates in Korea and Taiwan; and the link between financial repression and deficit finance explored in depth.

This book still provides the only comprehensive overview of financial development since the path-breaking work of Ronald McKinnon and Edward Shaw in 1973. It surveys, analyzes, and criticizes the literature on financial development that has mushroomed since 1973. It also presents some of my own work in this field. The book is divided into four more or less self-contained parts, starting with theory, then examining the evidence, and ending with some policy evaluation. The first part analyzes the theoretical controversy between the McKinnon-Shaw school and the neostructuralists as well as the new literature on finance in endogenous growth models. To do this, I dissect several models of financial development to discover what makes them tick. Vicious editorial cuts made some of these models that appeared as journal articles particularly difficult to understand. Numerous typographical errors created difficulties with others. I hope therefore to meet two objectives in the first part: to make the extant financial development models more accessible than they have been to date, and to show exactly how they produce their major results. In some cases, I examine what happens when key assumptions of the model are changed. This also helps to illuminate just how they work.

The second part reviews all the econometric evidence that I have been able to find on the effects of financial conditions in developing countries. Specifically, I examine the influence of the level of real institutional interest rates and the proximity of bank branches on saving behavior, the ratio of investment to gross national product, and the rate of economic growth. One chapter is devoted to the effects of financial conditions on portfolio allocation, income distribution, and industrial concentration. The effects of stabilization policies, with and without a financial liberalization component, on inflation and short-run growth are simulated in another. The next chapter in this part analyzes the causes and effects of different monetary policy regimes using pooled time-series data for a large number of developing countries. The final chapter examines the effects of foreign debt accumulation and foreign direct investment inflows on the recipient developing countries.

The analysis of money and banking requires a mixture of micro- and macroeconomics. The third part, therefore, covers microeconomic and institutional aspects of financial development. In the first chapter of this part, important new ideas on equilibrium credit rationing, adverse selection in the credit market, and the allocative efficiency of financial intermediation are explored. I examine increasingly problematic institutional issues, such as the high delinquency and default rates suffered by financial institutions in many developing countries, financial layering, universal banking, and conglomeration, in the next chapter. The final chapter in this part analyzes various types of government intervention in the financial sector. The objective here is to delineate necessary and benign intervention, such as prudential regulation and supervision, from financial repression. Much of the material in this part helps in the analysis of the recently failed financial liberalization programs in Latin America.

The final part deals with monetary and financial policies in economic development. It starts with an analysis of the macroeconomic environment and macroeconomic policies conducive to or necessary for successful financial development. I then explore the fiscal activities of central banks in developing countries, using Argentina in the late 1980s as a case study. A chapter on interest rate and selective credit policies in a sample of Asian developing countries follows. The final chapter pulls together the strings and proposes some elements for what might constitute a successful financial development program.

My thanks go to the many individuals who have responded to requests for material for both the first and second editions of the book, who have helped provide information during my field trips, and who have read and commented on material used in this book: Graham Abbott (Tasmania), Dale Adams (Ohio State University), Tony Addison (University of Warwick), Ramgopal Agarwala (World Bank), Pierre-Richard Agénor (International Monetary Fund), Myrvin Anthony (University of Strathclyde), Philip Arestis (University of East London), José Arellano (CIEPLAN, Santiago), Heinz Arndt (Australian National University), Mukul Asher (National University of Singapore), Edmar Bacha (Columbia University), Roger Backhouse (University of Birmingham), Bela Balassa, Tomás Baliño (International Monetary Fund), Jean-Claude Berthélemy (OECD Development Centre), Jagdish Bhagwati (Columbia University), Mario Blejer (International Monetary Fund), Emma Bonoan (Asian Development Bank), Frits Bouman (Wageningen Agricultural University), Compton Bourne (University of the West Indies), William Branson (Princeton University), Maja Bresslauer (World Bank), Philip Brock (University of Washington), Udo Broll (University of Osnabrück), Edward Buffie (Indiana University), Terrence Canavan (Chemical Bank), Gerard Caprio, Jr. (World Bank), Richard Caves (Harvard University), Anand Chandavarkar (Washington, D.C.), Yoon Je Cho (Korea Tax Institute), Emil-Maria Claassen (University of Paris-Dauphine), Stijn Claessens (World Bank), Margaret Clarke (University of Birmingham), Warren Coats, Jr. (International Monetary Fund), David Cobham (University of St Andrews), David Cole (Harvard Institute for International Development), Anthony Courakis (Brasenose College, Oxford University), Tyler Cowen (George Mason University), John Cuddington (Georgetown University), William Darity (University of North Carolina), Dilip Das (International Management Institute, New Delhi), José De Gregorio (International Monetary Fund), Aristóbulo de Juan (Madrid), Jaime de Melo (World Bank), Martha de Melo (World Bank), David Demery (University of Bristol), Panicos Demetriades (Keele University), Jean-Jacques Deschamps (World Bank), Michael Devereux (Keele University), Carlos Diaz-Alejandro, Edward Dommen (United Nations Conference on Trade and Development), John Donnelly (Manufacturers Hanover), Michael Dooley (University of California at Santa Cruz), Rudiger Dornbusch (Massachusetts Institute of Technology), Peter Drake (Australian Catholic University), William Easterly (World Bank), Jonathan Eaton (Boston University), Liam Ebrill (International Monetary Fund), Sebastián Edwards (University of California at Los Angeles), Robert Emery (Chevy Chase), Antonio Estache (World Bank), Shakil Faruqi (World Bank), John Fender (University of Birmingham), Bernhard Fischer (Hamburg Institut für Wirtschaftsforschung), Stanley Fischer (Massachusetts Institute of Technology), Michael Foot (Bank of England), James Ford (University of Birmingham), Jeffrey Frankel (University of California at Berkeley), Cynthia Franklin (University of Birmingham), Celia Fry (Birmingham), Sandra Frydman (Agency for International Development), Ricardo

Ffrench-Davis (CIEPLAN, Santiago), Milton Friedman (Hoover Institution), Vicente Galbis (International Monetary Fund), Alan Gelb (World Bank), Hafez Ghanem (World Bank), Ejaz Ghani (World Bank), Prabhu Ghate (New Delhi), David Gill (International Finance Corporation), Michael Gilroy (University of St. Gall), Alberto Giovannini (Columbia University), Eric Girardin (University of Bordeaux I), Marcelo Giugale (World Bank), Amihai Glazer (University of California at Irvine), Reuven Glick (Federal Reserve Bank of San Francisco), Claudio González-Vega (Ohio State University), Michael Gould (World Bank), Douglas Graham (Ohio State University), Jeremy Greenwood (University of Rochester), David Groves (World Bank), Jack Guenther (Citibank), Kanhaya Gupta (University of Alberta), Stephan Haggard (University of California at San Diego), James Hanson (World Bank), Karen Hanson (University of Birmingham), Ann Harrison (World Bank), Thomas Havrilesky (Duke University), Hal Hill (Australian National University), David Holland (London), Wontack Hong (Seoul National University), Patrick Honohan (Economic and Social Research Institute, Dublin), Charles Horioka (Osaka University), Jocelyn Horne (International Monetary Fund), Michael Hutchison (University of California at Santa Cruz), Alain Ize (International Monetary Fund), Y. C. Jao (University of Hong Kong), Ronald Johannes (World Bank), Joseph Joyce (Wellesley College), Kwang Jun (World Bank), Woo Jung (University of Kansas), Basant Kapur (National University of Singapore), Peter Kenen (Princeton University), Denis Kessler (Fondation pour la Recherche Economique et Financière, Paris), Mohsin Khan (International Monetary Fund), Homi Kharas (World Bank), Miguel Kiguel (World Bank), Tony Killick (Overseas Development Institute, London), Young-ja Kim (International Monetary Fund), Malcolm Knight (International Monetary Fund), Peter Knight (World Bank), Akira Kohsaka (Kyoto University), Shirley Kuo (Council for Economic Planning and Development, Taipei), Timur Kuran (University of Southern California), Ashok Lahiri (International Monetary Fund), David Laidler (University of Western Ontario), Mario Lamberte (Philippine Institute for Development Studies), Prem Laumas (Northern Illinois University), Chung Lee (East-West Center, Honolulu), Jungsoo Lee (Asian Development Bank), Sheng-Yi Lee (Singapore), Nathaniel Leff (Columbia University), Danny Leipziger (World Bank), Kui Wai Li (City Polytechnic of Hong Kong), Yvonne Liem (International Monetary Fund), Sándor Ligeti (Karl Marx University, Budapest), Leslie Lipschitz (International Monetary Fund), Richard Lipsey (Simon Fraser University), Millard Long (World Bank), Alan Lowe (Morgan Guaranty), Ross McLeod (Australian National University), Anne McGuirk (International Monetary Fund), Ronald McKinnon (Stanford University), Sandy Mackenzie (International Monetary Fund), Jesús Marcos Yacaman (Banco de México), Jaime Marquez (Federal Reserve System), Paul Masson (International Monetary Fund), Donald Mathieson (International Monetary Fund), Richard Mattione (Morgan Guaranty), Arnaldo Mauri (FINAFRICA,

Milan), Allan Meltzer (Carnegie-Mellon University), Richard Meyer (Ohio State University), Chris Milner (Loughborough University), Basil Moore (Wesleyan University), Jacques Morisset (World Bank), Giovanna Mossetti (Torino), Andrew Mullineux (University of Birmingham), James Nash (Morgan Guaranty), Anwar Nasution (University of Indonesia), Somanathan Nayar (National Institute of Public Finance and Policy, New Delhi), Gordon Nelson (Morgan Guaranty), Andrew Nickson (University of Birmingham), William Norton (Macquarie University), Jeffrey Nugent (University of Southern California), José Ocampo (FEDESARROLLO, Bogota), Ashok Parikh (University of East Anglia), Yung Chul Park (Korea University), Jonathan Parker (World Bank), Hugh Patrick (Columbia University), WenSheng Peng (International Monetary Fund), Eric Pentecost (Loughborough University), Dwight Perkins (Harvard Institute for International Development), John Pencavel (Stanford University), Guy Pfeffermann (International Finance Corporation), Arturo Porzecanski (Morgan Guaranty), Robert Pringle (*Central Banking,* London), Rati Ram (Illinois State University), Edward Ray (Ohio State University), Helmut Reisen (OECD Development Centre), Clark Reynolds (Stanford University), David Robinson (International Monetary Fund), Sherman Robinson (University of California at Berkeley), Alan Roe (University of Warwick), Paul Romer (University of California at Berkeley), Nouriel Roubini (Hoover Institution), Gilles Saint-Paul (DELTA, Paris), Xavier Sala-i-Martin (Yale University), John Samuels (University of Birmingham), Andreas Savvides (Oklahoma State University), Susan Schadler (International Monetary Fund), Fabio Schiantarelli (Boston University), Christian Schmidt (World Bank), Tibor Scitovsky (Stanford), Henry Scott (University of Birmingham), Dieter Seibel (Universität zu Köln), Tharman Shanmugaratnam (Monetary Authority of Singapore), Edward Shaw (Stanford), Andrew Sheng (Hong Kong Monetary Authority), Kumiharu Shigehara (Organisation for Economic Cooperation and Development), Peter Sinclair (University of Birmingham), Sukh Singh (Asian Development Bank), Tanys Sirivedhin (Bank of Thailand), Michael Skully (University of New South Wales), Betty Slade (Harvard Institute for International Development), Joseph Stiglitz (Stanford University), Venkataraman Sundararajan (International Monetary Fund), Oren Sussman (Hebrew University, Jerusalem), Alan Tait (International Monetary Fund), Augustine Tan (National University of Singapore), Aysit Tansel (Middle East Technical University, Ankara), Vito Tanzi (International Monetary Fund), Juro Teranishi (Hitotsubashi University), Henry Terrell (Federal Reserve System), Jim Thomas (London School of Economics), Grace Tsiang (University of Chicago), Sho-chieh Tsiang, Christopher Towe (International Monetary Fund), David Turnham (OECD Development Centre), James Tybout (Georgetown University), Antoine van Agtmael (International Finance Corporation), Sweder van Wijnbergen (University of Amsterdam), Aristomène Varoudakis (Université Robert Schuman, Strasbourg), George Viksnins (Georgetown University), Delano Villanueva (International Monetary Fund), Robert Vogel (University of Miami), George von Furstenberg (Indiana University), John D. Von Pischke (World Bank), Hercules Voridis (Athens), Richard Wada (Asian Development Bank), Wilima Wadhwa (University of California at Irvine), Rodney Wagner (Morgan Guaranty), U Tun Wai (Bethesda), Jean Wakefield (University of Birmingham), Andrew Warner (World Bank), Maxwell Watson (International Monetary Fund), John Williamson (Institute for International Economics, Washington, D.C.), Stuart Wilson (University of Hull), Alan Winters (World Bank), Wing Woo (University of California at Davis), Jang Hee Yoo (Korea Institute for International Economic Policy), and Zainal Aznam Yusof (Bank Negara Malaysia).

Typesetting the second edition of this book using Leslie Lamport's LaTeX, a set of macros that simplifies the use of Donald Knuth's TeX typesetting software, has been greatly facilitated by technological advances over the past seven years. I used David Lilien's *EViews,* his new version of *MicroTSP* for *Windows,* to prepare all the data-based graphs. The *EViews* graphs were edited and all the other graphs drawn in *CorelDraw. MicroTSP* was used to run most of the regressions and all the simulations reported in this book. As with the first edition, I have enjoyed working with members of the Johns Hopkins University Press: Douglas Armato, Jack Goellner, Anita Scott, Henry Tom, Gregg Wilhelm, and especially Barbara Lamb. Jack Ray copyedited the manuscript and Maria Coughlin again prepared the index with incredible accuracy and speed.

The second edition contains revised material from work that was originally sponsored by the Asian Development Bank, the Bank of England, the Bank of Japan, the International Monetary Fund, the Institute of Southeast Asian Studies, the OECD Development Centre, the Reserve Bank of India, and the World Bank. The Tokai Bank's endowment to the University of Birmingham and the Bank of England's support to the International Finance Group have been invaluable in facilitating my research. I would like to acknowledge the financial support provided by these organizations while making the usual disclaimer that the analysis, opinions, and policy recommendations contained herein are not necessarily those of these or any other organization or individual mentioned here. Finally, I am grateful to the American Economic Association, the Asian Development Bank, Blackwell, Butterworth-Heinemann, Macmillan, and the Royal Economic Society for their permission to use material previously published by them.[1]

---

[1] The relevant articles listed in the bibliography are Fry (1979b, 1989a, 1991a, 1991b, 1992a, 1993a, 1993c, 1993d) and Fry and Lilien (1986).

Part I

Theoretical Models of Financial Development

Chapter 1

Keynesian Monetary Growth Models and the Rationale for Financial Repression

1.1 Introduction

A S ITS TITLE INDICATES, this book is about the effects of money, interest rates, and banking systems on the rate of economic growth in developing countries. To understand the relationships between financial and real variables it is necessary to understand the way in which financial markets operate and how they differ from other markets. It is also necessary to understand the process of economic growth and how financial variables can affect that process. To that end Part I of this book explores the theoretical literature on finance, financial policies, and their effects on the rate of economic growth. Part II surveys the econometric evidence on the practical importance of these effects. Part III analyzes some institutional aspects of financial liberalization and development. Finally, Part IV examines monetary and financial policies and their effects on rates of economic growth in developing countries.

All financial systems in market economies, whether they are developed or developing, perform two basic functions: (a) administering the country's payments mechanism; and (b) intermediating between savers and investors.[1] Even at this stage, however, one might well ask two simple questions: (a) Is one function more important than the other with respect to economic growth? (b) Is performance in one function related to performance in the other?

There is little disagreement that hyperinflation impairs the domestic currency's attributes not only of a store of value but also of a means of payment. As James Tobin (1992, 772) states: "A society's money is necessarily a store of value. Otherwise it could not be an acceptable means of payment." Finan-

---

[1]Mark Gertler and Andrew Rose (1994) provide a nontechnical exposition of the theory of financial intermediation. Gertler (1988) offers a more technical analysis.

cial systems are impeded in performing both of their basic functions under hyperinflation. Society turns to substitute means of payment (foreign currencies or barter trade), thereby bypassing the domestic financial system. This substitution is one manifestation of the law of demand. As the opportunity cost of holding money rises, the demand for money expressed at constant prices or in real terms falls.

In the simplest balance sheet of the banking system, the banks hold loans L and reserves R as their assets and deposits D as their liabilities:

Assets		Liabilities	
Reserves	R	Deposits	D
Loans	L		

The balance sheet identity implies $R + L = D$. Naturally, this balance sheet identity is still preserved if one divides both assets and liabilities by nominal GNP Y:

Assets		Liabilities	
Reserves	R/Y	Deposits	D/Y
Loans	L/Y		

Ceteris paribus, the ratio D/Y falls as inflation accelerates because households and firms choose to hold smaller money balances in relation to their expenditure levels due to the rising cost of holding money. Therefore, the ratio $(R+L)/Y$ must also fall. If the ratio R/L remains roughly constant, then both R/Y and L/Y fall as D/Y falls. Since L/Y is the ratio of bank loans to the nominal value of output, business firms find themselves facing a credit squeeze as inflation rises. Unable to obtain the necessary loans to cover the costs of their working capital, some firms may be unable to stay in business. The aggregate level of output in real terms would then fall. In this case, therefore, the deterioration of money reduces the extents to which the banking system administers the country's payments mechanism and intermediates between savers and investors; performance in both functions is related. Perhaps the former effect reduces income levels while the latter effect reduces income growth.

The first stylized fact about financial systems in developing economies is that they are dominated by commercial banks. Assets of insurance and pension companies are minuscule in most developing countries. Development finance institutions such as agricultural and development banks are also small compared with the commercial banks. Commercial bond markets are typically thin and government bond markets are often used only by captive buyers obliged to hold such bonds to satisfy liquidity ratio requirements or to bid for government contracts. Although equity markets are sizable in several developing countries, their role in the process of financial intermediation remains small. Indeed, the relatively large Taiwanese equity market produces a transfer of resources from the business sector to the household sector in the form of dividends that exceeds the transfer from the household sector to the business sector in the form of new issue purchases.

The second stylized fact about financial systems in developing countries is that they tend to be heavily taxed. Inflation has long been analyzed as a tax and hence as a source of government revenue (Bailey 1956, Friedman 1971). The tax collector is the central bank, the tax base is reserve or high-powered money, and the tax rate is the inflation rate. Holders of currency pay the tax through the erosion in the purchasing power of their currency. Banks also pay the tax by holding reserves, invariably in the form of required reserves. For a sample of 26 developing countries, I find that the inflation tax yielded revenue for the government equal to 2.8 percent of GNP on average in 1984; this represented over 17 percent of the government's current revenue (Fry 1993b, Table 1, 11).

In 1969, inflation averaged 5.9 percent in developing countries compared with 4.9 percent in the industrial countries.[2] With the gap widening after 1974, developing country inflation reached 30 percent in 1982 compared with 7.6 percent in the industrial countries. By 1990, the average inflation rate in developing countries had reached 98.6 percent compared with 5 percent in the industrial countries (*International Financial Statistics Yearbook* 1992, 105). Evidently, the inflation tax rate has increased rapidly in the developing countries over the past two decades.

The third stylized fact of financial systems in developing countries is that their banking systems face high required reserve ratios. Indeed, substantial use of the inflation tax tends to be accompanied by high required reserve ratios. Data from *International Financial Statistics* CD-ROM (September 1993) show that, over the period 1978–1987, the ratio of bank reserves (reserve money minus currency in circulation) to bank deposits (including saving and time deposits) averaged 21.2 percent in 91 developing countries compared with 7.1 in 19 industrial countries. In other words, the ratio of reserves to deposits was three times higher in developing countries than in industrial countries. Comparing the ratio of the central government's domestic credit to aggregate domestic credit tells a similar story. The proportion of domestic credit expropriated by central governments averaged 52.6 percent in these 91 developing countries compared with 18.1 percent in the 19 industrial countries.

In contrast to the textbook discussion of higher required reserve ratios as a monetary policy instrument to restrict monetary growth, a cross-country comparison indicates that monetary growth or inflation and the ratio of bank reserves to deposits are positively correlated. There is also a significantly positive relationship between the period-average inflation rate and the reserve

---

[2]These figures represent geometric means for 113 developing countries and 23 industrial countries.

ratio in these 111 countries (91 developing and 19 industrial countries).[3] Evidently countries using the inflation tax tend to combine higher tax rates with a larger tax base in the form of higher required reserve ratios.

The fourth stylized fact about financial systems in developing countries is the prevalence of ceilings on deposit and loan rates of interest. The extraction of the inflation tax from the banking system through high reserve requirements is a form of financial repression. However, the term financial repression more commonly refers to interest rate ceilings. Financial repression can also be analyzed as a tax and hence as another source of government revenue. The tax is imposed directly on depositors when deposit rate ceilings are set by government fiat. In the absence of deposit rate ceilings, the financial repression tax may still be borne by depositors to the extent that banks are required to use their own resources to acquire nonreserve assets that yield net returns below the world market interest rate. The tax is also imposed on any other private sector agents that are obliged to hold such assets, for example, as a precondition for bidding on government contracts.

Alberto Giovannini and Martha de Melo (1993, Table 1, 959) estimate the tax revenue from financial repression in the form of private sector holdings of government bonds at yields below the world market rate. They calculate average tax revenue from financial repression equal to 1.8 percent of GDP for 22 developing countries over various periods spanning the years 1972–1987. Giovannini and de Melo (1993, 961) state that "the revenue from financial repression is, at least for half of the countries in the sample, of approximately the same size as the revenue from seigniorage."

The term seigniorage applied originally to the mint's charges for coinage. Subsequently it meant the difference between the face value and the intrinsic value of a monopoly-supplied money. Under a paper standard, seigniorage virtually equals the face value of the note issue. Seigniorage revenue, therefore, accrues from increasing the note issue or the issue of reserve money. Hence, Giovannini and de Melo measure seigniorage revenue as the change in reserve money divided by GDP.

Revenue from the inflation tax will be lower than revenue from seigniorage in a growing economy, because economic growth enables the central bank to issue some more reserve money without causing inflation. The inflation tax starts when the central bank issues so much more reserve money that the general price level starts to rise. For 16 of the countries in the Giovannini-de Melo sample for which I collected inflation tax data (Fry 1993b), the average tax revenue from financial repression of 1.9 percent of GDP can be compared with average tax revenue from the inflation tax of 2 percent of GNP.[4]

---

[3]Similar correlations are presented by Philip Brock (1989, Table 1, 116) and Pierre-Richard Agénor and Peter Montiel (1994, Table 5.1).

[4]The observation periods and the denominators differ, so the figures are not strictly comparable.

In broad terms, therefore, it appears that financial repression is as important a source of government revenue in developing countries as the inflation tax. The effect of financial repression on saving, investment, and growth is a major point of disagreement between current theories of the role of financial systems in the process of economic development. The effect of the required reserve ratio on saving, investment, and growth is another of the main points of disagreement between these theories.

The fifth stylized fact is that there is a positive link between financial and economic development. Financial systems that are stunted and repressed are typically found in stagnant economies with low per capita incomes. Real interest rates averaged over several years to provide a proxy for the degree of financial repression are positively associated with rates of economic growth (World Bank 1989, Table 2.3, 31). As discussed in Part II, higher growth in countries with higher real interest rates is the result of higher output/capital ratios rather than higher investment ratios. In other words, growth rates in the countries with strongly negative real interest rates are lower than growth rates in countries with positive real interest rates because investment is less productive in the former group of countries.

1.2   The Keynesian Liquidity Trap

Critics of capitalism place considerable emphasis on the pernicious role of the financial system that forms the hub of the capitalist economy (Hilferding 1910). Karl Marx recognized the importance of the financial system in the process of capitalist economic development over a century ago. Lenin, impressed by the powerful political and economic influence of the European banks in the eighteenth and nineteenth centuries, also understood the crucial role of the financial system. He nationalized all Russian banks immediately after the 1917 revolution as the fastest and most effective way of ending capitalism and assuming control over the entire Russian economy.

John Maynard Keynes was also wary of the potential damage that could be wrought by financial systems in capitalist economies. He believed that without careful management money could disrupt economic activity quite seriously. Keynes's liquidity trap sets a floor to the nominal rate of interest. When the trap is binding, the real interest rate exceeds its equilibrium level consistent with full employment. In a liquidity trap, planned saving at the full-employment level of income exceeds planned investment. This disequilibrium is resolved by a fall in real income that, in turn, reduces planned saving.

The simplest money demand function in use before the Keynesian Revolution was the Cambridge equation:

$$M^d = k \cdot y \cdot P, \tag{1.1}$$

where M^d is the aggregate demand for money, k is the public's desired ratio of money balances to income, y is real income or income expressed at constant prices, and P is the price level. This specification of the demand for money does not consider explicitly the factors that affect k. One such factor is the interest rate: the cost or opportunity cost of holding money balances is the forgone earnings from holding alternative assets. Since the money demand function describes the demand to hold a stock of money balances, yields on assets that can be held as substitutes for money should have a significant effect on money demand.

Keynes criticized the Cambridge equation precisely because it neglects the role of interest rates in determining the demand for money. Keynes offers an alternative formulation of the demand for money which he calls liquidity preference. According to Keynes, people hold money balances for three basic reasons. They hold transactions balances in order to bridge the gap between planned receipts and expenditures. They hold precautionary balances to meet unexpected bills. Finally, they may hold speculative balances if they expect the market value of alternative assets to fall.

Keynes suggests that the speculative demand for money arises from decisions about the allocation of wealth. Instead of considering all forms of wealth, Keynes assumes for simplicity that the choice is between holding money and holding consols—government bonds that pay a fixed coupon or dividend each year forever.[5] Consols always yield the market interest rate i. Since the coupon or dividend D remains constant, the market price of the consol P_c fluctuates inversely with changes in the market interest rate: $P_c = D/i$, where i is expressed as a proportion rather than as a percentage. If D is \$10 and i is 0.1 or 10 percent, P_c is \$100. If i rises to 0.12, P_c falls to \$83.33.

The speculative motive for holding money arises from the desire to maximize wealth. As long as expected capital losses are not sufficient to offset the coupon income from the consol, individuals continue to keep all their investment portfolios in consols. However, if capital losses are expected to be large enough to more than wipe out the coupon income, money is clearly more attractive than consols as a form in which to hold one's wealth. This means that the demand for speculative money balances is produced by an expectation or fear that the percentage fall in the market price of consols will exceed the current market rate of interest. When the interest rate is low, a relatively small percentage drop in the market price of consols will wipe out interest earnings. With higher interest rates, the percentage fall in the market price of consols has to be more substantial for interest earnings to be completely offset. Thus, the incentive for individuals to hold speculative money balances as opposed to consols is greater the lower is the interest rate.

---

[5] A financial claim of this kind is called an annuity in perpetuity.

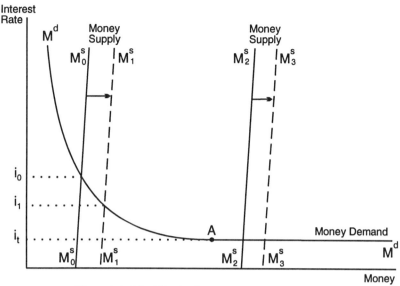

Figure 1.1. Liquidity Preference and the Interest Rate

In Keynes's theory, there is some interest rate that individuals consider to be "normal" at each particular moment. When interest rates rise above this normal level, there is a tendency for people to expect interest rates to fall. On the other hand, when the interest rate lies below this normal level, it is expected to rise. The lower the interest rate relative to the normal level, the greater will be the expected capital loss from an expected rise in the interest rate if wealth is held in consols.

Since individuals have different expectations about future changes in bond prices, the switch in the aggregate from bonds to money as the interest rate declines will be gradual. However, the lower the current interest rate relative to the level generally considered to be normal, the larger is the number of people who expect a future fall in the market price of consols to wipe out interest earnings. Hence more people prefer to hold their wealth in the form of money balances. Summing everyone's speculative demand for money produces the relationship between interest rates and the aggregate demand for speculative money balances shown in Figure 1.1. This money demand function can be expressed:

$$M^d = \beta_0 + \beta_1/(i - i_t), \qquad (1.2)$$

where i_t is the liquidity-trap interest rate.

Figure 1.1 shows a money demand curve that becomes perfectly interest elastic at the low rate of interest i_t. If the money supply increases from M_0^s to M_1^s, some people find that they are holding more money than they wish. Their reaction is to buy bonds, which raises bond prices and so lowers the interest rate. At point A, however, the interest rate has fallen so far below its normal level that virtually everyone has the same expectation that the interest rate will rise sufficiently in the future for capital losses to wipe out all interest earnings on bonds (Keynes 1936, 172). If the money supply increases from M_2^s to M_3^s, therefore, no one would want to buy more bonds. Everyone would prefer to hold the additional money rather than risk capital losses by holding bonds.

From another perspective, a very small change in the interest rate elicits a huge switch in desired portfolio composition at point A. The massive dumping of bonds when the interest rate falls as low as i_t ensures that bond prices rise no further and hence that the market interest rate can no longer fall. This phenomenon is now known as the liquidity trap. If it exists, monetary policy could become impotent: a change in the money supply would have no effect on the market rate of interest. Equilibrium in the money market would persist at the same interest rate i_t no matter how much the money supply was increased. In terms of equation 1.1, the Cambridge equation, the liquidity trap implies that any given increase in M would produce a proportional change in k. Hence, $y \cdot P$ would remain unaffected.

This floor to the interest rate has a crucial implication for the equilibrium level of output in an economy. In the simple Keynesian model, saving S is determined solely by the level of income Y, while desired or planned investment I_p is determined solely by the real interest rate or the nominal interest rate adjusted for inflation r.[6] Suppose, for example, that $S = -20 + 0.2Y$ and that $I_p = 190 - 1000i$, where S, Y, and I_p are expressed in billions of dollars, and i is the nominal interest rate expressed as a proportion. With zero inflation, i equals r. If the full-capacity or full-employment level of income were \$1000 billion, saving would be \$180 billion. Planned or desired investment I_p, however, would equal saving at \$180 billion only when the interest rate was 0.01 or 1 percent, as illustrated in Figure 1.2 by I_{pf}. At any interest rate above 0.01 or 1 percent, desired investment would be less than \$180 billion.

If the liquidity trap sets a floor to the interest rate at 0.02 or 2 percent, desired investment would be \$170 billion, \$10 billion less than saving at the full-employment level of income. In this situation, illustrated by I_{pt} in Figure 1.2, planned expenditures on goods and services fall short of production by \$10 billion and there is unintended inventory accumulation of \$10 billion. If the interest rate remains at 2 percent, production and income will eventually fall to \$950 billion, \$50 billion below its full-capacity or full-employment level. At this level of income saving will fall to \$170 billion.

In a liquidity trap, therefore, planned saving at the full-employment level of income exceeds planned investment. This disequilibrium is resolved by

---

[6]Frederic Mishkin (1992, ch. 24) provides a clear derivation of the Keynesian model.

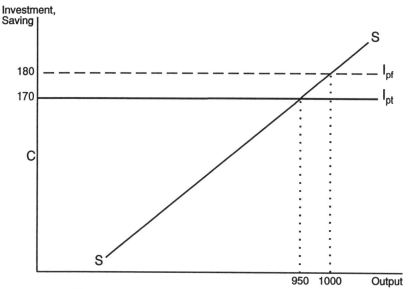

Figure 1.2. Saving and Investment in a Liquidity Trap

a fall in real income that, in turn, reduces planned saving. Were there no money and hence no liquidity trap in the economy, the interest rate could fall to 0.01 or 1 percent, investment would rise to $180 billion and saving would be equated with planned or desired investment at the full-capacity or full-employment level of income.

Keynes (1936, 351) argues that historically there has been a natural tendency for the real interest rate to rise above its full-employment equilibrium level:

> The destruction of the inducement to invest by an excessive liquidity-preference was the outstanding evil, the prime impediment to the growth of wealth, in the ancient and medieval worlds. And naturally so, since certain of the risks and hazards of economic life diminish the marginal efficiency of capital whilst others serve to increase the preference for liquidity. In a world, therefore, which no one reckoned to be safe, it was almost inevitable that the rate of interest, unless it was curbed by every instrument at the disposal of society, would rise too high to permit of an adequate inducement to invest.

The substitution of "developing world" for Keynes's "ancient and medieval worlds" seems natural.

The relative attractiveness of holding money as an asset instead of holding productive capital is the cause of the inadequate level of investment. The simple Keynesian model resolves the disequilibrium through a reduction in income. In the quotation above, however, Keynes recognizes an alternative adjustment mechanism—a change in the relative returns on the two competing assets, money and capital. If the price level is fixed and expectations about the future price level are therefore static, expansionary monetary policy could reduce the interest rate and at the same time satisfy the increase in liquidity preference. Were an interest rate ceiling imposed by the authorities, investment could still be stimulated by the lower imposed interest rate, provided that an accommodative monetary policy were pursued. This Keynesian solution has strong appeal but ignores the inflationary consequences of monetary expansion or accommodation.

Another strategy is to discourage the demand for liquidity by raising the opportunity cost of holding money without raising the interest rate. Silvio Gesell (1911, ch. IV–1) was the first to advocate stamped money for precisely this purpose. Currency stamps obtainable at post offices would have to be attached to currency notes every Wednesday. Gesell (1911, 273) suggests a charge for the stamps of 1 per mil, equivalent to 5.2 percent a year. Keynes (1936, 357), stating that the idea was sound, proposes that the stamp tax on money should equal the difference between the actual interest rate and the equilibrium rate at which full-employment saving and investment plans would be equated.

1.3   The Production Function

The welfare-enhancing effects of taxing money and hence repressing financial development received further attention in the postwar period. However, analysis of the effects of finance on economic growth depends crucially on the choice of growth model. For example, the neoclassical growth model uses a production function with diminishing marginal returns to each factor of production. The Cobb-Douglas production function provides a convenient example:

$$Y = K^\alpha \cdot L^{1-\alpha}, \tag{1.3}$$

where Y is output, K is the capital stock, L is the labor force, and α is a parameter or coefficient. Equation 1.3 can be expressed in per capita terms:

$$y = k^\alpha, \tag{1.4}$$

where $y = Y/L$ and $k = K/L$.

Equation 1.4 indicates that a steady state with constant per capita output would exist in this economy provided capital per worker remained constant ($\Delta k = 0$). If the labor force is growing at a rate n, then aggregate output must also grow at the same rate in the steady state: $\Delta L/L = \Delta Y/Y = n$. This would happen only if the capital stock was also growing at the rate n: $\Delta Y/Y = \Delta L/L = \Delta K/K = n$. Otherwise, capital per worker would not remain constant.

For simplicity assume that the capital stock does not depreciate, that saving is a fixed proportion of output s, and that all saving increases the capital stock ($\Delta K = sY$). In other words, this is a closed economy. The condition for a steady state requires the rate of increase in the capital stock sY/K to equal n. Suppose that s now rises so that $sY/K > n$. In such case, capital per worker will start to rise, as will output per worker. Because the Cobb-Douglas production function exhibits diminishing marginal returns to capital, however, output rises less than proportionally to capital. Hence, the ratio of capital to output also rises.

As this process continues over time, the rate at which the capital stock increases declines because the same proportion of output saved represents a smaller and smaller proportion of the capital stock; the capital stock is rising in relation to output. Eventually, the rate of growth in the capital stock will fall to equal the rate of growth in both output and the labor force. In the long run, therefore, a higher saving-investment ratio raises the level of income but has no effect on the rate of economic growth. Under such circumstances, financial conditions that affect the quantity of saving and investment have only a temporary effect on the rate of economic growth.

The specific Cobb-Douglas production function $K^{0.33} \cdot L^{0.67}$ illustrates this characteristic of neoclassical growth models. In year 0 the labor force and the capital stock are both 1; hence output is also 1. The labor force increases annually at 5 percent, while the capital stock increases by sY. In the first example with s set at 0.3, the rate of growth in output is 13.8 percent in year 1, 12.3 percent in year 2, and thereafter declines steadily to 5.0 percent (to one decimal place) in year 104. In the steady state, per capita income is 2.476. Had s been 0.4 instead of 0.3, output growth would have been 17.3 percent in year 1, 14.5 percent in year 2, and 12.7 percent in year 3. Thereafter, growth would have declined steadily to 5.0 percent in year 106. With the higher saving ratio, per capita income reaches 2.853 in the steady state.

In a Harrod-Domar growth model based on fixed proportions and constant marginal returns to capital, any influence of financial conditions on the saving-investment ratio produces a permanent effect on the long-run rate of economic growth. The standard Harrod-Domar model used in development economics is based on the assumption of surplus labor. Hence, it can be expressed $Y = \sigma K$, where Y is output, σ is the constant output/capital ratio, and K is the capital stock. Taking first differences and dividing both sides by Y gives the growth rate relationship $\gamma = \sigma(I/Y)$, where γ is the rate of economic growth $\Delta Y/Y$ and I is investment (ΔK). An increase in the saving-investment ratio I/Y raises the growth rate γ permanently. For example, with s equal to 0.3 and σ equal to 0.25, the rate of growth is 7.75 percent. At a saving ratio of 0.4 percent, the growth rate rises to 10 percent.

The assumption of constant marginal returns to capital in the early financial development models was regarded as undesirable but necessary for analytical tractability when they appeared in the 1970s. However, endogenous growth models developed since the mid-1980s provide a theoretical justification for assuming that the marginal product of capital does not diminish for the economy as a whole. As Paul Krugman (1993, 17) notes: "The basic idea of this literature is that there may be external economies to capital accumulation, so that the true elasticity of output with respect to capital greatly exceeds its share of GNP at market prices." The aggregate production function in a typical endogenous growth model takes the form $Y = K^\alpha X^\beta$, where K is capital, X is some factor like land or labor that has a fixed supply per capita, and $\alpha \geq 1$. The variable K represents a combination of physical capital and knowledge.

To be compatible with the existence of competitive markets, individual firms face declining returns to scale and diminishing marginal productivity of their own capital. However, positive production externalities from the knowledge component or learning process of K, which is a public good, increase returns and raise the marginal productivity of capital at the aggregate level. This is modelled by making the efficiency of an individual firm a function of the aggregate capital stock. For an individual firm using k and x inputs combined with the aggregate stock of knowledge, the production function could take the form $y = K^\varphi k^\nu x^\beta$, where $\nu + \beta \leq 1$ and $\varphi + \nu = \alpha \geq 1$ (Romer 1991, 92–93). In this model, as in the Harrod-Domar model, an increase in the investment ratio raises the growth rate permanently.

Capital as broadly defined in endogenous growth models need not suffer from diminishing marginal returns due to learning-by-doing, human capital, research and development, or public infrastructure. One group of endogenous growth models (Scott 1989, 1992) sets the elasticity of output with respect to the aggregate capital stock at one, implying increasing returns to capital and labor together. Another group (Lucas 1988, Romer 1990) introduces a specific growth factor which raises the total productivity of the other factors of production; one such growth factor is human capital. Empirically, it is much easier to broaden the concept of capital and posit a learning externality than it is to identify and estimate any specific growth factor.

Neoclassical growth models imply that capital flows from the capital-rich countries to capital-poor countries with higher marginal returns to capital. However, this flow can exert only a small and temporary effect on poor countries' growth rates. Endogenous growth models provide a much more important role for capital in the growth process. Without diminishing marginal productivity of capital, however, there is no incentive to transfer it from capital-rich to capital-poor countries (Krugman 1993, 18–19).

1.4 Tobin's Portfolio Allocation Model

James Tobin (1965) develops one of the earlier models linking financial conditions and economic growth using Robert Solow's (1956) neoclassical growth model. The Keynesian liquidity trap is based on a particular money demand function in which only one component of money holdings is affected by the opportunity cost consisting of the expected return on bonds, the alternative asset. The standard approach today is to treat money as a durable asset yielding a stream of services to money holders. This stream of services can be expressed as an implicit rate of return to money holding. The law of diminishing marginal utility ensures that the higher is the value of money held, the lower will be its implicit rate of return.

The derived demand for money can, therefore, be analyzed in exactly the same way as the demand for anything else. Other things equal, the quantity demanded will vary inversely with its price or cost because utility maximization requires money holders to increase their money holdings only up to the point at which the marginal utility or implicit service derived from an extra unit of money equals its opportunity cost. The demand to hold money, therefore, will be related inversely to the opportunity cost of holding money. As with all other applications of demand theory, consumption of money services is limited by a budget constraint. In the case of a durable asset, the appropriate budget constraint is total wealth.

In Tobin's (1965) model of money and economic growth, economic units allocate their wealth between two assets, money M and productive capital K. In this economy, the economic units are all small household producers. Hence, the business sector is identical to the household sector. The demands for money and productive capital can be expressed in the following form:

$$M^d = [b_{10} + b_{11}r + b_{12}\pi]W, \qquad (1.5)$$

$$K^d = [b_{20} + b_{21}r + b_{22}\pi]W, \qquad (1.6)$$

where M^d and K^d are demands for money and productive capital, respectively, r is the real return on productive capital, and π is the inflation rate.[7] In this case, $r + \pi$ equals the nominal interest rate i and constitutes the opportunity cost of holding money, while r is the real return to productive capital. The opportunity cost of holding money is the forgone return which could have been obtained from holding productive capital.

The coefficients b_{10}, b_{11}, b_{12}, b_{20}, b_{21}, and b_{22} are subject to two restrictions derived from the fact that equations 1.5 and 1.6 represent a complete

---

[7]All growth, inflation, and interest rates in this book are continuously compounded rates of change ($\Delta \log$). Hence the real interest rate r equals exactly the nominal interest rate i minus the expected inflation rate π^e. Using simple interest rates, the real rate r equals $(1+i)/(1+\pi^e) - 1$ or $(i - \pi^e)/(1 + \pi^e)$, where r, i, and π^e are all expressed in proportional rather than percentage form.

system of demand equations. First, the coefficients b_{10} and b_{20} must add up to 1. If r and π were both zero, the demand for money would be $b_{10}W$ and the demand for productive capital would be $b_{20}W$. If an individual's wealth is \$100 and must all be allocated between money and productive capital ($W = M + K$), a value for b_{10} of 0.4 implies that b_{20} must equal 0.6. In this case, \$40 is held in the form of money and \$60 is held in the form of productive capital. The total value of money and productive capital equals the amount of wealth to be allocated.

Second, the sum of b_{11} and b_{21} must equal zero, as must the sum of b_{12} and b_{22}. Suppose that b_{11} equals –3 and that the real interest rate rises from zero to 0.02 or 2 percent. In this case, the demand for money will fall from \$40 to \$34 ($40 - 3 \cdot 0.02 \cdot 100$). If the demand for money falls by \$6, then the demand for productive capital must rise by \$6 to satisfy the requirement that all wealth be allocated between money and capital. In this case, b_{21} must equal 3. The same argument applies for the equal and opposite values of b_{12} and b_{22}.

If the return on capital relative to money rises in Tobin's model, households increase the ratio of capital to money in their portfolios. This portfolio shift produces a higher capital/labor ratio, higher labor productivity, and hence greater per capita incomes. The rate of economic growth accelerates during the transition from a lower to a higher capital/labor ratio that occurs after the relative yield on money falls. Hence reducing the return on money increases welfare. This can be accomplished either by reducing deposit rates of interest, or by taxing money as proposed by Gesell, or simply by accelerating the rate of growth in the money stock, thereby raising the inflation rate.

Miguel Sidrauski (1967) shows that the steady-state capital/labor ratio in Tobin's model is invariant to the relative return on capital when individuals optimize over an infinite horizon. However, Allan Drazen (1981b) replicates Tobin's results in a finite horizon optimizing framework. Stanley Fischer (1979a) presents a dynamic model incorporating the Tobin effect. Elsewhere, Fischer (1979b) demonstrates that, even in Sidrauski's model, the speed with which the economy approaches the steady state can be affected by the rate of monetary growth and hence the relative yield on money in the way asserted by Tobin. Drazen (1981a) shows that the properties of the steady state itself may depend on the transition path if technical progress takes the form of learning-by-doing. Indeed, with an endogenous growth model rather than a neoclassical model, Tobin's portfolio shifts produce permanent growth rate effects.

The money analyzed by Gesell, Keynes, and Tobin is deadweight money. Gold specie and fiat money exemplify this kind of money. To a large extent, credit money has now displaced commodity and fiat money everywhere, a fact that has been ignored by some of Tobin's followers (Carmichael 1982; Drazen 1981b; Fischer 1979a, 1979b, 1981; Stockman 1981). In the terminology of

John Gurley and Edward Shaw (1960, 72–73), however, a choice between inside and outside money is still required.

Money created as loans to the private sector is termed inside money because it is based on the internal debt of the private sector. Any change in either the nominal or real amount of inside money leaves private sector wealth unchanged; the asset change is matched exactly by a corresponding liability change in the private sector's consolidated balance sheet. Outside money is backed by loans to the government. A change in outside money does change private wealth as conventionally measured because the increased money held by the private sector is not matched by any change in private sector liabilities. Outside money is not available to finance private sector investment. If money is entirely outside money, banks hold government bonds and make no loans to the private sector.

Even with outside money, Tobin's conclusions can be reversed if the real money stock is included in the aggregate production function (Kapur 1986, chs. 1–2; Khan and Ahmad 1985; Levhari and Patinkin 1968). More strikingly, Yang-Pal Lee (1980) modifies Tobin's model, as extended by Sidrauski (1966), by substituting inside for outside money and irreproducible tangible assets held as inflation hedges (such as gold, jewelry, unfinished buildings, antique furniture, artwork, jade carvings, postage stamps) for productive capital in household portfolios. In this model inside money is backed entirely by loans for productive investment purposes by the private business sector.

With these changes, a lower relative return on money caused by higher inflation reduces real money demand and hence also reduces funds available to finance productive investment. The same conclusion is reached using rational (Sidrauski 1967) and life-cycle saving functions. In all cases the portfolio shift from money to inflation hedges reduces productive investment and hence the rate of economic growth during the transition from higher to lower capital/labor ratios. Tobin's results concerning the relationship between inflation and economic growth are simply reversed by substituting inside money for outside money and inflation hedges for productive capital in household portfolios.

Using a broad definition of money, most of it is inside rather than outside money in industrial countries and about half of it is inside money in developing countries. Inflation hedges such as gold, jewelry, and uncompleted buildings are important repositories of savings in many developing countries (Bouman 1989, 1994). If households hold inside money and inflation hedges (or outside money and productive capital), the substitution effects are unambiguous. If they hold inside money and productive capital, the substitution effects depend on the relative productivity of household-financed and business-financed investment. However, if households hold inside money, inflation hedges, and informal financial instruments referred to as curb market loans, the substitution effects are ambiguous. A higher return on money could produce substitution from curb market loans instead of inflation hedges. More complexities and ambiguities are introduced when households hold equities or productive physical capital as well as money, curb market loans, and inflation hedges.

1.5 Rationale for Financial Repression

The writings of Marx, Keynes, and Tobin have influenced monetary and financial policies pursued in many countries throughout the world. There are also well-known political and religious objections to high, usurious, or even nonzero interest rates. Many industrialized countries have pursued low interest rate policies from time to time. Institutional interest rates in most developing countries have indeed been "curbed by every instrument at the disposal of society." However, the relatively low and uniform institutional interest rate structures found in many developing countries today do not replicate the experience of the industrialized countries in their early stages of development.

The prevalence of interest rate ceilings has a number of other economic rationales in addition to Keynes's liquidity preference and Tobin's monetary growth model. Development planning models based on fixed input-output coefficients constitute another economic rationale for low interest rate policies. Many developing countries use or have used selective or directed credit policies to implement planned sectoral investment programs derived from an input-output matrix. Institutional loan rate ceilings are a key element of directed credit policies. The ceilings are set deliberately below the equilibrium interest rate so that credit can be allocated on nonprice criteria. In this way the private sector can be encouraged to undertake the planned investment even though these projects might well be unprofitable at the competitive free-market equilibrium rate of interest. In particular, loan rate ceilings have been used in conjunction with import restrictions to encourage industrialization through import substitution.

Structuralists and neostructuralists argue that raising interest rates increases inflation in the short run through a cost-push effect and lowers the rate of economic growth at the same time by reducing the supply of credit in real terms available to finance investment. Hence, their models provide an intellectual justification for financial repression.

In practice, however, the predominant rationale for financial repression lies in its fiscal implications. Interpreted as a discriminatory tax on the financial system, financial repression comprises inflation, reserve requirements, and interest rate ceilings. If institutional constraints prevent the government from collecting enough normal tax revenue to finance the level of government expenditure it regards as optimal, financial repression may be justified as a second-best strategy. Given disadvantages of high inflation and high reserve requirements, the government may turn to interest rate ceilings. Government deficits can be financed at a lower inflation rate and a lower required reserve ratio the more the private sector is hindered from competing for available funds (Fry 1973, Giovannini and de Melo 1993, Nichols 1974).

1.6 Summary

Financial systems in most developing countries face discriminatory taxation in the form of high reserve requirements combined with high inflation rates. At the same time, many developing country banking systems are subject to interest rate ceilings on deposits and loans. Governments in developing countries use both forms of financial repression to finance their deficits. Since commercial banks tend to dominate financial systems in developing countries, measures that repress and so reduce the size of the banking system in relation to the rest of the economy stifle financial intermediation.

Although interest rate ceilings tend to be used as a way of reducing government expenditure on interest payments, there are a number of justifications for maintaining low interest rates. The Keynesian liquidity trap can be used to rationalize taxing money holdings so that full employment can be attained. Tobin's portfolio allocation model shows that capital/labor ratios and per capita incomes may be raised through financial repression that reduces the attractiveness of holding money vis-à-vis productive capital. Analysis indicating that financial liberalization and development could promote economic growth is reviewed in the next two chapters.

Chapter 2

The McKinnon-Shaw Financial Development Framework

2.1 Introduction

THE MAIN INTELLECTUAL BASIS for financial sector analysis and policy advice over the past 21 years lies in the work of Ronald McKinnon (1973) and Edward Shaw (1973). McKinnon and Shaw analyze developing economies that are financially repressed. Their central argument is that financial repression—indiscriminate "distortions of financial prices including interest rates and foreign-exchange rates"—reduces "the real rate of growth and the real size of the financial system relative to nonfinancial magnitudes. In all cases this strategy has stopped or gravely retarded the development process" (Shaw 1973, 3–4). Their prescription is the removal of these distortions imposed by so many governments in developing countries.

This chapter presents the basic elements of the McKinnon-Shaw framework. Section 2.2 describes the transition from financial restriction to financial repression in the archetypal developing economy. Section 2.3 presents the essential elements of the McKinnon-Shaw financial development model. Section 2.4 analyzes the key difference between McKinnon and Shaw's formal models, namely McKinnon's use of outside money and Shaw's choice of inside money. The chapter ends with a discussion of financial repression and economic dualism.

2.2 Financial Restriction and Financial Repression

Many developing countries appear to have slipped into financial repression inadvertently. The original policy was aimed not at indiscriminate repression but rather at financial restriction (Fry 1973, Giovannini and de Melo 1993, Nichols 1974). Financial restriction encourages financial institutions and financial instruments from which government can expropriate significant seigniorage; it discourages others. For example, money and the banking system are favored and protected because reserve requirements and obligatory holdings of government bonds can be imposed to tap this source of saving at zero- or low-interest cost to the public sector. Private bond and equity markets are suppressed through transaction taxes, stamp duties, special tax rates on income from capital, and an unconducive legal framework, because seigniorage cannot be extracted so easily from private bonds and equities. Interest rate ceilings are imposed to stifle competition to public sector fund raising from the private sector. Measures such as the imposition of foreign exchange controls, interest rate ceilings, high reserve requirements, and the suppression or nondevelopment of private capital markets can all increase the flow of domestic resources to the public sector without higher tax, inflation, or interest rates (Fry 1973, Nichols 1974).

Successful financial restriction is exemplified by a higher proportion of funds from the financial system being transferred to the public sector and by three effects on the demand for money: a rightward shift in the function, a higher income elasticity, and a lower cost elasticity. Successful financial restriction produces a low and falling income velocity of circulation. This allows a greater public sector deficit to be financed at a given rate of inflation and a given level of nominal interest rates.

Selective or sectoral credit policies are common components of financial restriction. The techniques employed to reduce the costs of financing government deficits can also be used to encourage private investment in what the government regards as priority activities. Interest rates on loans for such approved investment are subsidized. Selective credit policies necessitate financial restriction, since financial channels would otherwise develop expressly for rerouting subsidized credit to uses with highest private returns. For selective credit policies to work at all, financial markets must be kept segmented and restricted.

The following quotation referring to Portugal describes a typical case of financial restriction: "To finance its deficit, the government has largely preempted the supply of domestic savings by preserving a 'sheltered' market for its own bond issues. Recourse of the private sector to the domestic bond market was, moreover, effectively curtailed by maintaining the maximum interest rate for bond issues at 5 percent" (Lundberg 1964, 40). The ceiling on after-tax returns from private bonds in Portugal was lower than the rate offered on government bonds. Even with these interest rate ceilings on competitive financial instruments, returns on government securities were so low that virtually no voluntary purchases took place: "In actual fact, the vast majority of the public debt bonds were taken up by the welfare institutions, the commercial banks, the Caixa Geral de Depósitos and insurance companies" (Banco de Portugal 1963, 52). However, the seigniorage base in the form of the money supply (broadly defined to include currency in circulation, sight deposits, and time deposits—*M2*) was large and growing. Velocity of circulation in Portugal fell smoothly from 1.46 in 1962 to 1.09 in 1973.

Financial restriction was also successful in Turkey during the 1960s. Velocity of circulation (again using *M2*) fell from 5.26 to 3.66 between 1963 and 1970, a period of price stability and rapid economic growth. Interest rate ceilings protected banking, the government's golden goose, from outside competition (Fry 1972, chs. 3, 6). As soon as private bonds showed signs of becoming a serious competitive threat in the early 1970s, controls were tightened up. Similar phenomena have been detected in Korea since 1965 (Min 1976).

Nominal interest rate ceilings established to limit competition under policies of financial restriction are highly destabilizing in the face of inflationary shocks. Just as deposit rate ceilings in the United States and other industrial countries caused disruptive disintermediation in periods of rising inflation and rising free-market interest rates, so all-embracing interest rate ceilings in developing countries cause destabilizing portfolio shifts from financial to tangible assets when inflation accelerates (Lee 1980, Shaw 1975). Clearly such reaction magnifies the initial inflationary shock. Typically, it seems, financial repression is the unintended consequence of low, fixed nominal interest rates combined with high and rising inflation.

2.3   McKinnon and Shaw

Liberal attitudes to finance can be traced back at least to the seventeenth century. Among the earlier writers who stressed the importance of sound money and unfettered financial intermediation were John Locke (1695), Adam Smith (1776), Jeremy Bentham (1787), and Joseph Schumpeter (1912). Schumpeter (1912) stresses the importance of finance in the process of development. The pure entrepreneur who embodies development by trying out new techniques requires credit: "He can only become an entrepreneur by previously becoming a debtor" (Schumpeter 1912, 102). Finance and development are related as follows: "Granting credit in this sense operates as an order on the economic system to accommodate itself to the purposes of the entrepreneur, as an order on the goods which he needs: it means entrusting him with productive forces. It is only thus that economic development could arise from the mere circular flow in perfect equilibrium" (Schumpeter 1912, 107).

Finally, Schumpeter (1912, 74) views the banker as the key agent in this process:

> The banker, therefore, is not so much primarily the middleman in the commodity 'purchasing power' as a *producer* of this commodity. However, since all reserve funds and savings to-day usually flow to him, and the total demand for free purchasing power, whether existing or to be created, concentrates on him, he has either replaced private capitalists

or become their agent; he has himself become the capitalist par excellence. He stands between those who wish to form new combinations and the possessors of productive means. He is essentially a phenomenon of development, though only when no central authority directs the social process. He makes possible the carrying out of new combinations, authorises people, in the name of society as it were, to form them. He is the ephor of the exchange economy.

Other more recent precursors include Alexander Gerschenkron (1962, 1968), who examines of the role of banks in German economic development, and Rondo Cameron, who coordinates and contributes several historical analyses of banking and economic development in Europe, Japan, Louisiana, and Russia in the nineteenth century (Cameron, Crisp, Patrick, and Tilly 1967, Cameron 1972). Nevertheless, for 60 years from the onset of World War I, advocates of financial liberalization were a rare breed. During this period the bulk of theoretical work relating financial conditions to economic development detected possibilities for negative or, at best, neutral effects of financial development on income levels or growth rates.

In 1973 the dominant theoretical position was forcefully challenged. McKinnon and Shaw both develop models of economic development in which financial liberalization and development accelerate the rate of economic growth. They also highlight some of the deleterious effects of financial repression—interest rate ceilings, high reserve requirements, directed credit policies, and discriminatory taxation of financial intermediaries—on economic growth.

McKinnon and Shaw reject the monetary models of Keynes, Keynesians, and structuralist economists. Both argue that crucial assumptions in these paradigms are erroneous in the context of developing countries. Both provide theoretical frameworks for analyzing the role of financial development in the process of economic growth. McKinnon and Shaw challenge the case for low controlled interest rates and financial repression. They advocate financial liberalization and development as growth-enhancing economic policies. Much of the empirical support for their policy recommendations is derived from the financial reforms in Taiwan (early 1950s) and Korea (mid-1960s).

The essential common elements of the McKinnon-Shaw inside money model, in which financial institutions intermediate between savers and investors, are illustrated in Figure 2.1. Saving S_{g_0} at a rate of economic growth g_0 is a positive function of the real rate of interest (McKinnon 1973, 67; Shaw 1973, 73, 77–78). The line FF represents financial repression, taken here to consist of an administratively fixed nominal interest rate that holds the real rate r below its equilibrium level (McKinnon 1973, 71–77; Shaw 1973, 81–87). Actual investment is limited to I_0, the amount of saving forthcoming at the real interest rate r_0.

One reason why saving may fall when inflation accelerates or the nominal interest is lowered can be analyzed by considering nondepreciating assets in fixed supply. Suppose that inflation hedges take the form of a fixed supply of

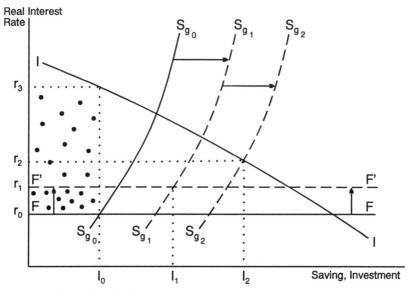

Figure 2.1. Saving and Investment under Interest Rate Ceilings

land. Land prices are expected to increase at least as fast as the general price
level. Hence, as real interest rates fall, land becomes an increasingly attractive
repository for savings compared with deposits. Clearly, however, buying land
does not constitute investment for the economy as a whole; by assumption,
the amount of land is fixed. As the real interest rate falls, more households
will remove savings from the banks to buy land. In this process the price of
land will be bid up faster than the increase in the general price level. With
higher real land prices and no change in real incomes, the household sector's
wealth/income ratio rises. All saving theories based on intertemporal utility
maximization show that greater wealth raises consumption both now and in
the future. It therefore induces a decline in saving out of current income (Fry
and Williams 1984, 286–288).

   If the interest rate ceiling applied only to savers' interest rates (only to
deposit but not to loan rates of interest), the investor/borrower would face an
interest rate of r_3, the rate that clears the market with the constrained supply of
saving I_0, in Figure 2.1. The spread r_3-r_0 would be spent by a regulated but
competitive banking system on nonprice competition (advertising and opening
new bank branches). These nonprice services, however, may not be valued
at par with interest payments; real money demand invariably declines with a
decrease in the explicit real deposit rate of interest.

   To the extent that the real deposit rate is reduced by a higher inflation rate
rather than a lower nominal deposit rate of interest, this phenomenon could
be caused by the implicit tax imposed on financial intermediation through

the reserve requirement. This tax rises in step with inflation. Provided loan demand is not completely interest inelastic, depositors will bear some of the increased tax burden. This will take the form of reduced nonprice services offered by banks.[1]

In fact, there are loan rate ceilings as well as deposit rate ceilings in most financially repressed economies. Furthermore, there are very few competitive banking systems in the developing world. Although private commercial banks can evade loan rate ceilings through compensating balances, they seem to be observed by some state-owned banks and for most public sector borrowing. To the extent that banks do observe loan rate ceilings, nonprice rationing of loanable funds must occur. Credit is allocated not according to expected productivity of the investment projects but according to transaction costs and perceived risks of default.[2] Quality of collateral, political pressures, "name," loan size, and covert benefits to loans officers may also influence allocation. The investments that are financed under such conditions are illustrated by the dots in Figure 2.1.

Even if credit allocation is random, the average efficiency of investment is reduced as the loan rate ceiling is lowered because investments with lower returns now become profitable. Entrepreneurs who were previously deterred from requesting bank loans now enter the market. Hence, adverse selection in terms of social welfare occurs when interest rates are set too low and so produce disequilibrium credit rationing of the type described here. As discussed in Part III, adverse selection also occurs when interest rates rise too high because equilibrium credit rationing is not working properly.

Loan rate ceilings discourage financial institutions from taking any risks; risk premia cannot be charged when ceilings are binding and effective. This itself may ration out a large proportion of potentially high-yielding investments. In the financially repressed economy there is, therefore, a tendency for the investments that are financed to yield returns barely above the ceiling interest rate r_0. These are shown in Figure 2.1 by the dots lying just above FF but below $F'F'$.[3]

McKinnon (1973, 9) emphasizes this dispersion in rates of return to investment in financially repressed economies: "In the face of great discrepancies in rates of return, it is a serious mistake to consider development as simply the accumulation of homogeneous capital of uniform productivity. Let us de-

---

[1] See Anthony Courakis (1984, 1986) and Chapter 7.

[2] See Yoon Je Cho (1984, 16), Courakis (1981a, 236–256; 1981b, 220–228), and section 13.5 for an analysis of credit rationing in the absence of interest rate ceilings.

[3] Christophe Chamley and Patrick Honohan (1993) pinpoint another drawback of loan rate ceilings in that they tend to deter bank spending on loan assessments. Since even in an unrepressed situation banks are likely to underspend on screening, this additional deterrence may be worse for social welfare than another form of repression that affects the financial system at a margin which is initially undistorted.

fine 'economic development' as the reduction of the great dispersion in social
rates of return to existing and new investments under domestic entrepreneurial
control."

Interest rate ceilings distort the economy in four ways. First, low interest rates produce a bias in favor of current consumption and against future
consumption. Therefore, they may reduce saving below the socially optimum level. Second, potential lenders may engage in relatively low-yielding
direct investment instead of lending by way of depositing money in a bank.
Third, bank borrowers able to obtain all the funds they want at low loan rates
will choose relatively capital-intensive projects. Fourth, the pool of potential
borrowers contains entrepreneurs with low-yielding projects who would not
want to borrow at the higher market-clearing interest rate. To the extent that
banks' selection process contains an element of randomness, some investment
projects that are financed will have yields below the threshold that would be
self-imposed with market-clearing interest rates.

Under selective or directed credit programs, banks are required to allocate
minimum percentages of their asset portfolios for loans to priority sectors of
the economy at subsidized loan rates of interest. Part of the critical problem of
loan delinquency encountered in virtually all directed credit programs is due
to the fact that these subsidized loan rates, which are typically negative in real
terms, discourage prompt loan repayment. High delinquency and default rates
reduce the flexibility (less credit available for new investment) and increase
the fragility of financial systems, an issue taken up again in Part III.

Raising the interest rate ceiling from FF to $F'F'$ (from r_0 to r_1) in Figure 2.1 increases saving and investment. Changes in the real interest rate trace
out the saving function in this disequilibrium situation. Raising the interest
rate ceiling also deters entrepreneurs from undertaking all those low-yielding
investments illustrated by the dots below $F'F'$. They are no longer profitable
at the higher interest rate r_1. Hence the average return to or efficiency of
aggregate investment increases. The rate of economic growth rises in this
process and shifts the saving function to S_{g_1}.

Thus the real rate of interest as the return to savers is the key to a higher
level of investment, and as a rationing device to greater investment efficiency.
The increased quantity and quality of investment interact in their positive
effects on the rate of economic growth. Growth in the financially repressed
economy is constrained by saving; investment opportunities abound here (Mc-
Kinnon 1973, 59–61; Shaw 1973, 81).

The policy prescription for the financially repressed economy examined
by McKinnon and Shaw is to raise institutional interest rates or to reduce
the rate of inflation. Abolishing interest rate ceilings altogether produces the
optimal result of maximizing investment and raising still further investment's
average efficiency. This is shown in Figure 2.1 by the equilibrium I_2, r_2, and
the higher rate of economic growth g_2.

McKinnon (1982, 160; 1984, 1–2) stresses fiscal discipline as a prerequisite for successful financial liberalization, because government deficits are invariably financed by taxing the domestic monetary system in one way or another. Use of the inflation tax on domestic financial intermediation leads to foreign exchange controls to prevent circumvention of the taxed domestic financial intermediaries (Berger 1980). Both capital outflows and inflows need to be controlled. In turn, foreign exchange controls necessitate a fixed exchange rate system (McKinnon 1982, 161). Hence large public sector deficits tend to be incompatible with financial liberalization and development.

2.4 McKinnon's Complementarity Hypothesis and Shaw's Debt-Intermediation View

McKinnon follows Tobin in developing a model based on commodity or outside money, although he switches to an inside-money model in much of his verbal exposition. McKinnon's formal analysis of how the real deposit rate of interest affects saving, investment, and growth is based implicitly on an outside money model. It rests on two assumptions: (a) all economic units are confined to self-finance; and (b) indivisibilities in investment are of considerable importance—investment expenditures are lumpier than consumption expenditures. Potential investors must accumulate money balances prior to their investment; this is Keynes's finance motive (Keynes 1937, 246–247; Tsiang 1980a). The lower the opportunity cost of accumulating real money balances or the higher the real deposit rate of interest, the greater is the incentive to invest. In this situation, the relative lumpiness of investment expenditures implies that aggregate demand for money will be greater the larger the proportion of investment in total expenditures. Since firms cannot borrow to finance investment, McKinnon is using implicitly an outside money model here.

McKinnon formalizes his complementarity hypothesis, "the basic complementarity between money and physical capital" (McKinnon 1973, 59), which he applies to "semi-industrial LDCs" (McKinnon 1973, 2). Complementarity is reflected in the demand for money function

$$M/P = f(Y, \ I/Y, \ d-\pi^e), \tag{2.1}$$

where M is the money stock (broadly defined to include saving/time deposits as well as demand/sight deposits and currency in circulation—*M2*), P is the price level, Y is real GNP, I/Y is the ratio of gross investment to GNP, and $d-\pi^e$ is the real deposit rate of interest (d is the nominal deposit rate and π^e is expected inflation, both continuously compounded).

Complementarity works both ways: "The conditions of money supply have a first-order impact on decisions to save and invest" (McKinnon 1973, 60).

Hence McKinnon's complementarity can also be expressed in an investment function of the form

$$I/Y = f(\bar{r},\ d-\pi^e), \tag{2.2}$$

where $\bar{r}$ is the average return to physical capital (McKinnon 1973, 61). Complementarity appears in the partial derivatives

$$\frac{\partial(M/P)}{\partial(I/Y)} > 0; \quad \frac{\partial(I/Y)}{\partial(d-\pi^e)} > 0.$$

Shaw discards Keynes's finance motive and neoclassical monetary growth models in favor of the debt-intermediation view that he himself pioneered in the 1950s (Gurley and Shaw 1955, 1960). John Gurley and Shaw (1955) stress the great difference in financial systems in developed and developing countries. In sharp contrast to the developing countries, the industrialized countries possess sophisticated and elaborate systems of financial institutions which facilitate intermediation between savers and investors. In the Gurley-Shaw model, the role of financial intermediaries in improving resource allocation is an important determinant of different levels of per capita income. That a positive relationship between the level of per capita income and the degree of financial sophistication exists is not disputed; Raymond Goldsmith (1969) confirms this association in great detail. The debate concerns the direction of causality.

Shaw constructs a monetary model in which money is backed by productive investment loans to the private sector. The larger is this money stock in relation to the level of economic activity, the greater is the extent of financial intermediation between savers and investors through the banking system. Shaw maintains that expanded financial intermediation between savers and investors resulting from financial liberalization (higher real institutional interest rates) and financial development increases the incentives to save and invest; it also raises the average efficiency of investment. Financial intermediaries raise real returns to savers and at the same time lower real costs to investors by accommodating liquidity preference, reducing risk through diversification, reaping economies of scale in lending, increasing operational efficiency, and lowering information costs to both savers and investors through specialization and division of labor.

Financial intermediation is repressed and suboptimal when interest rates are administratively fixed below their equilibrium levels. When interest rates are employed as rationing devices (allowed to find their equilibrium levels), financial intermediaries can use their expertise to allocate efficiently the larger volume of investible funds which is then forthcoming. Extensions of the debt-intermediation view stress the importance of free entry into and competition within the banking system as prerequisites for successful financial liberalization along the lines spelt out by Shaw (Cho 1984, 7; Fry 1980b, 543).

The debt-intermediation view is based firmly on an inside money model. It produces a demand for money function that can be characterized as follows (Shaw 1973, 62):

$$M/P = f(Y, \nu, d-\pi^e), \qquad (2.3)$$

where ν is a vector of opportunity costs in real terms of holding money. Shaw expects real yields on all forms of wealth, including money, to have a positive effect on the saving ratio (Shaw 1973, 73). Complementarity has no place here precisely because investors are not constrained to self-finance. Where institutional credit is unavailable, noninstitutional markets invariably appear. In fact, McKinnon also recognizes the importance of financial intermediation.

Lazaros Molho (1986a) argues that the models of McKinnon and Shaw need not be viewed as incompatible with one another, even though McKinnon's formal analysis uses outside money:

> McKinnon's complementarity hypothesis, on the one hand, emphasizes the role of deposits in encouraging self-financed investment. A rise in the deposit rate stimulates demand for capital by making savings accumulation more rewarding and by increasing the amount of internally financed investment. Shaw's debt-intermediation view, on the other hand, focuses on the role of deposit accumulation in expanding the lending potential of financial intermediaries. Higher deposit rates encourage the inflow of deposits to banks, which in turn can increase lending, thereby stimulating externally financed investment. Although the Shaw and McKinnon theses emphasize different aspects of the process of accumulation of financial assets and liabilities, it is clear from the discussion so far that these theses should be viewed as complementary rather than competing theories ... The two approaches complement each other because most projects are financed in part with own funds and in part with borrowings. (Molho 1986a, 102, 111)

For this compatibility, however, McKinnon's model has to be interpreted as an inside money model in which there are borrowing constraints and indivisibilities that prevent *some* investors from borrowing *all* they wish to borrow for particular lumpy investments. McKinnon (1973, 56) states that "*all* economic units are confined to self-finance, with no useful distinction to be made between savers (households) and investors (firms). These firm-households do not borrow from, or lend to, each other" (emphasis added). Molho actually modifies McKinnon's model in a sensible and realistic way. However, his view that this is simply the correct interpretation of the complementarity hypothesis is hardly compatible with McKinnon's own statement of his model.

Molho (1986a, 91) suggests that house purchase is an obvious example in industrial countries of a lumpy investment, where some investors (households) cannot borrow all they wish to borrow and must accumulate deposits or other financial assets in advance. In such cases, deposits accumulated in period 1 may be complementary to physical capital in period 2, an intertemporal complementarity. At the same time, deposits and physical capital in the same period may be substitutes (Molho 1986a, 95). Molho then shows that financial liberalization can reduce investment in the short run by causing substitution from capital into deposits, but increase investment in the medium run through intertemporal complementarity. In other words, the current substitution into deposits occurs in part because accumulating money for *future* investment expenditure has become more attractive.

Paul Burkett and Robert Vogel (1992) reconstitute McKinnon's complementarity hypothesis in the case of a borrowing-constrained firm that holds bank deposits with which to finance operating costs. In this model, a higher real deposit rate raises the return to working capital. Hence, the firm increases the ratio of working to fixed capital and its deposits. Since one firm's deposit is another firm's credit, the expanded loan supply made possible by the higher deposit rate may increase the optimum size of a firm's capital stock as well as its deposit holdings. Hence, complementarity can be achieved even with an inside-money model. Using a similar model, Michael Samson (1992) shows that credit subsidies can decrease output if they are financed through a fall in real deposit rates.

2.5   Financial Repression and Dualism

McKinnon (1973) argues that financial repression fosters economic dualism in developing economies. Traditional techniques with low productivities are found in operation alongside modern techniques with high productivities. The traditional techniques generate low incomes, while modern techniques produce high incomes. Yoon Je Cho (1984), Paul Krugman (1978), and Richard Sines (1979) all use a diagram based on Irving Fisher's (1930) two-period analysis to illustrate this dualism.

Fisher analyzes an individual's saving decision using indifference curves in the two-period framework illustrated in Figure 2.2. Here the individual's indifference curves U_i each represent a constant utility level. The aim is to reach the highest level of utility, which is achieved by being on the highest attainable indifference curve. In Figure 2.2 the individual has an endowment Y which provides income Y_1 in period 1 and Y_2 in period 2. The market borrowing-lending line M drawn through Y shows that consumption can differ from income in each period to the extent that an individual borrows or lends.

Since utility is maximized when the highest possible indifference curve is reached, the individual moves from Y to C, the point of tangency between the borrowing-lending line and an indifference curve. In this example, consuming less than income in period 1 involves moving up the borrowing-lending line from Y to C. At C, the individual consumes C_1 in period 1 and C_2 in

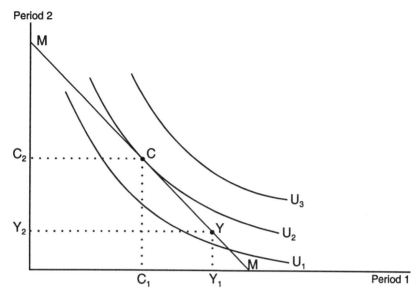

Figure 2.2. Intertemporal Maximization of Consumption through Borrowing or Lending

period 2. Because the borrowing-lending line incorporates a positive real interest rate of say, 10 percent, saving of $10 in period 1 enables consumption to exceed income by $11 in period 2. Hence, Y_1-C_1 is smaller than Y_2-C_2.

Fisher's next step is to introduce investment. Part of the endowment can be invested along the investment opportunity curve I, illustrated with diminishing marginal returns to investment in Figure 2.3. The slope of the investment curve I measures the yield of each extra dollar of current investment. The volume of investment is measured leftward from Y_1 and can exceed Y_1 through borrowing. The fact that the investment opportunity curve extends to the left of the vertical line indicates simply that profitable investment opportunities exceed the current period's endowment Y_1.

To maximize utility, the individual invests this period's endowment Y_1 plus a loan of L_1 to produce at point P where the investment opportunity curve is tangential to the borrowing-lending line. This is the highest borrowing-lending line that the individual can reach, given the investment opportunities. From P the individual can transact along the borrowing-lending line to reach the point of tangency with the highest indifference curve. In this case, the individual borrows the entire current-period consumption C_1 as well as L_1. In period 2 total loans are repaid with interest from output P_2-Y_2 produced by the investment plus Y_2 endowment in period 2, leaving C_2 for consumption (Hirshleifer 1970, chs. 2, 3). The distance P_2-C_2 representing the loan

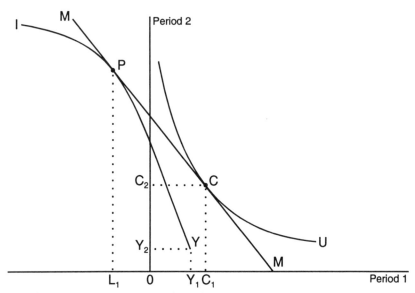

Figure 2.3. Intertemporal Maximization of Consumption through Investment

repayment equals $(C_1 + L_1) \cdot (1 + i)$, where i is the market interest rate
expressed in proportional rather than percentage form.

Fisher's analytical framework can be used to show what happens to individuals living under conditions of financial repression. McKinnon (1973,
20) demonstrates the biases and duality in capital formation created by interest rate ceilings in Figure 2.4. Here individuals or firms face two distinct
technologies. I_t is the traditional technology with continuously diminishing
marginal returns to investment. I_n is the new technology that requires a
large initial investment before there is any output. Once this investment is
made, however, returns are high and rising until well to the left of the vertical
axis. Everywhere to the right of the vertical line, the traditional technology
produces more than the new technology.

The point Y is the individual's endowment representing Y_1 in period 1
and Y_2 in period 2. If the entrepreneur is restricted to self-financed investments, the optimal strategy is to invest in the traditional technology. Hence
the borrowing-constrained investor would choose point P_t tangential to the
highest attainable indifference curve. This enables consumption levels of C_{t_1}
in period 1 and C_{t_2} in period 2. The internal rate of return of the investment
in the traditional technology at P_t is given by the slope of the investment
curve at that point.

Were some investors able to borrow at an interest rate given by the slope of
the borrowing line B, the new technology could be adopted and investment in
it would be continued up to point P_n. In this case the entrepreneur's utility is

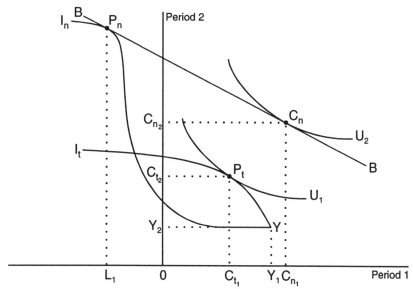

Figure 2.4. Choice of Technique with and without Borrowing

maximized by a consumption pattern given by point C_n. The new technology allows more consumption both in the current period at C_{n_1} and in the second period at C_{n_2} than does the traditional technology.

Figure 2.4 might suggest that differential access to credit produced by financial repression causes economic dualism, the coexistence of both modern and traditional production techniques. McKinnon (1973, 19–21) states that providing low-cost credit to some and denying it to other entrepreneurs induces less than optimal investment efficiency. There is no mechanism for equating marginal rates of return to investment across the economy. The differential access to credit also produces income inequality.

Krugman (1978) shows that financial repression does indeed cause income inequality and investment inefficiency but not necessarily economic dualism. Even if all individuals had identical tastes, endowments, and access to both technologies, some would choose the traditional technology and others the modern technology. Indifference in this choice springs from the fact that both yield exactly the same levels of consumption when interest rates are market-determined.

In the absence of interest rate restrictions and credit rationing, the market borrowing-lending line would ensure that those adopting the traditional technology would also lend to those adopting the modern technology. Figure 2.5 shows that individuals would be indifferent between borrowing and investing in the new technology at P_n and investing P_t in the old technology and lending from P_t to C at the market rate of interest. In either case, every individual

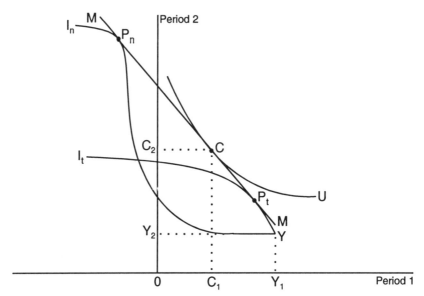

Figure 2.5. Market Borrowing-Lending Line with Identical Individuals

has the same consumption levels, C_1 and C_2, in periods 1 and 2. The market-equilibrating process ensures that the interest rate adjusts to elicit a sufficient lending response from traditional investors to satisfy the borrowing demand of investors in the modern technology. Without a sufficiently high rate of interest, everyone would prefer the modern technology and there would be no lenders. Figure 2.5 shows that financial repression is not responsible for the coexistence of both modern and traditional production techniques. Both are used to the optimal extents when all individuals face the same market borrowing-lending line.

When borrowing possibilities are available to some but not to others at an interest rate administratively fixed below the market-determined rate as in Figure 2.4, those who can borrow increase their consumption in both periods from C_1 and C_2 in Figure 2.5 to C_{n_1} and C_{n_2} in Figure 2.4, while nonborrowers have to reduce consumption in both periods to C_{t_1} and C_{t_2}. Hence Krugman's extension shows explicitly the possibility that financial repression can worsen the distribution of income. When the interest rate is set below its market equilibrium rate and credit is rationed in this nonequilibrium fashion, money holders are implicitly taxed to subsidize favored borrowers. This particular tax and subsidy scheme worsens income distribution.

Cho (1984, 34–41) also shows that deposit and loan rate ceilings are likely to worsen the distribution of income. First, most of the economic rent goes to large borrowers rather than small savers/lenders when deposit and loan rates are held well below their market equilibrium levels. Income distribution is likely to worsen most where the borrowing firms are predominantly family-owned companies. Second, capital-intensive production methods reduce the demand for labor. Consequently, wages of unskilled labor will fall. Duality, taking the form of inefficient small-scale direct investments on the one hand and excessively capital-intensive large-scale investments on the other hand, creates greater dispersion in wages. In practice, bank loans tend to become concentrated to a small number of large and well-established customers when finance is repressed. Greater economic concentration tends to reduce economic efficiency.

In contrast to studies of financial repression based on neoclassical production functions with declining marginal returns to capital, Vicente Galbis (1977) shows that financial repression fosters economic dualism in a model based on Harrod-Domar production functions. Galbis (1977) constructs a two-sector model to analyze the effect of financial repression on the average efficiency of investment in the economy. Sector 1 is the traditional economy with a low constant return to its capital r_1, while sector 2 is the modern economy with a higher constant return to capital r_2. The coexistence of both techniques of production in the Galbis economy with constant but different rates of return in both sectors is inefficient. This coexistence is not necessarily inefficient in a dualistic economy with declining marginal returns to capital in both sectors/techniques.

Depreciation rates are identical and output is produced competitively in both sectors of Galbis's economy:

$$Y = Y_1 + Y_2 = r_1 K_1 + w_1 N_1 + r_2 K_2 + w_2 N_2, \qquad (2.4)$$

where r_i is the return to capital K_i and w_i is the return (wage) to labor N_i in sector i. An increase in K_2 at the expense of K_1 (leaving the total capital stock constant) raises Y by increasing the average output/capital ratio σ, since $r_2 > r_1$.

Investment in sector 1 is entirely self-financed; this traditional sector has no access to bank credit. The level of this investment is determined by r_1 and the return $d - \pi^e$ on deposits, the only available financial asset:

$$I_1 = H_1(\overset{+}{r}_1, \, \overset{-}{d - \pi^e})Y_1. \qquad (2.5)$$

Given the self-finance constraint,

$$S_1 = I_1 + \Delta(M_1/P), \qquad (2.6)$$

where M_1/P are the real money balances held by sector 1. Saving is simply a constant fraction of income: $S_1 = s_1 Y_1$.

Sector 2 borrows from the banking system. Banks use deposits entirely to extend loans to sector 2. Hence

$$I_2 = S_2 + \Delta(M_1/P). \qquad (2.7)$$

Sector 2 also holds money balances but borrows them all back again, thereby netting them out exactly as either a saving leakage or an additional source of investment finance. Sector 2's investment equals its saving plus incremental bank borrowing in excess of its increased deposit holdings. Investment opportunities abound in this sector (Galbis 1977, 63). Sector 2's investment function takes the form

$$I_2 = H_2(r_2, \ \ell - \pi^e)Y_2, \tag{2.8}$$

where ℓ is the loan rate of interest.

Galbis's subsequent analysis can be greatly simplified by adopting a zero-cost, competitive banking system subject to effective deposit but not loan rate ceilings. The government fixes the deposit rate of interest below its equilibrium level. Therefore, the loan rate is above its competitive free-market equilibrium level as shown in Figure 2.1. A decrease in $d - \pi^e$ reduces real money demand by sector 1 (and, albeit irrelevantly, by sector 2) and so the real increase in credit $\Delta(M_1/P)$ for sector 2; hence I_2 is reduced.

Supply is brought into equilibrium with demand (equation 2.7) by whatever increase in $\ell - \pi^e$ is needed to adjust demand (equation 2.8) to equal the predetermined supply $S_2 + \Delta(M_1/P)$. A wider gap between d and ℓ is absorbed by transfer payments or more nonprice competition by the banks. Evidently σ is positively related to $d - \pi^e$, since a rise in $d - \pi^e$ reduces I_1 and raises I_2, thus increasing the average productivity of investment. Indeed, the higher real deposit rate may improve average investment efficiency through financial intermediation not only of intersectoral but also of intrasectoral saving.

Suppose that economic agents in sector 1 face the choice of holding money balances with a return of 4 percent or investing in physical capital with a risk-adjusted return of 5 percent. Suppose that with these relative rates of return, economic agents in sector 1 allocate $10 to increased money balances and $90 to physical investment. Economic agents in sector 2 can borrow $10 from the banks at an interest rate of 9 percent, which they do because their investments yield a risk-adjusted return of 10 percent. They also contribute their total saving of $100 to their investment.[4] The average rate of return to the additional capital stock in this economy is 7.75 percent: $(5 \cdot \$90 + 10 \cdot \$110)/\$200$.

Now suppose that the deposit rate of interest is increased to 6 percent, but that the competitively determined loan rate remains at 9 percent. Rational economic agents in sector 1 increase their money balances by the full amount of their total $100 saving and sector 2 borrows $100 for a total investment of $200. The average return to the new capital stock in the economy rises

---

[4] Any increased demand for money by agents in sector 2 is simply borrowed back by other agents in this sector.

from 7.75 to 10 percent. In this case the old deposit rate of 4 percent was so far below the market clearing equilibrium that it produced an inefficient mix of investment in both traditional and modern techniques. The new higher deposit rate of 6 percent deterred investment yielding only 5 percent. This beneficial self-selection process is also illustrated in Figure 2.1.

Gilles Saint-Paul (1992b) converts this deterministic two-sector model into a stochastic two-sector model in which consumers choose between holding shares in high-risk high-return firms and low-risk low-return firms. If financial markets are undeveloped and consumers cannot diversify, their choice will favor the low-risk low-return firms. An improvement in financial markets that enables more diversification reduces the size of the low-risk low-return sector and increases the size of the high-risk high-return sector. The rate of growth rises as a result of this substitution.[5]

Jeremy Greenwood and Boyan Jovanovic (1990) also address the issue of financial development and income distribution. They show that the process of financial development can produce greater inequality even in the absence of financial repression. If using financial intermediaries involves a fixed cost, then those who happen to have less wealth and lower incomes may prefer lower-yielding self-financed projects, while those with more wealth and higher incomes find it more profitable to obtain the higher returns offered by financial intermediaries. Financial intermediaries can offer higher returns because they collect and analyze information which facilitates "the migration of funds to the place in the economy in which they have the highest social return" (Greenwood and Jovanovic 1990, 1085).

If saving ratios are constant across levels of per capita income but returns are higher for richer individuals who use financial intermediaries, then wealth and income distributions will become more unequal over time. As incomes of poorer individuals rise, however, at some point they find it profitable to use financial intermediaries. They then enjoy the same higher rates of return as the rich do.[6] Eventually, when the entire population is rich enough to benefit from financial intermediation, everyone's wealth rises at the same rate and the distribution of wealth stabilizes (Greenwood and Jovanovic 1990, 1091–1098).

By increasing the costs of financial intermediation, financial repression prolongs the transition process from zero to full financial intermediation. Indeed, it could exclude some individuals from using financial intermediaries indefinitely. Hence, financial repression could be incorporated into the Greenwood-Jovanovic model as a cause of additional income inequality. By

---

[5]The endogenous growth literature discussed in section 1.3 and Chapter 4 provides a theoretical justification for the assumption of constant returns.

[6]Note that the fixed cost of using financial intermediaries resembles the cost of installing a telephone line. The cost of connecting to the network of telephone users is an initial one-off membership fee.

retarding growth and also by subsidizing some users of financial intermediaries while taxing or deterring others, financial repression causes even more income inequality than occurs in the unfettered process of financial development and economic growth.

2.6   Summary

Financial repression consists of various measures, such as interest rate ceilings, high reserve requirements, and directed credit policies, that impose discriminatory taxes on financial intermediation. These measures, which are often introduced under fiscal exigencies, reduce the incentive to hold money and other financial assets, and so reduce the overall availability of loanable funds to investors. Not only may the credit shortage encourage more low-yielding self-financed investment, but low subsidized interest rates to priority borrowers may also reduce the average return on credit-financed investment.

The McKinnon-Shaw model formalizes these ideas, showing that financial repression reduces both the quantity and the quality of investment in the economy as a whole. Hence McKinnon and Shaw conclude that financial liberalization can increase economic growth by increasing investment and its productivity. Since 1973 the McKinnon-Shaw financial repression paradigm has exerted considerable influence on macroeconomic policy in developing countries, particularly through the recommendations of the IMF and the World Bank. Some of the policy experience is examined in Part IV.

McKinnon also suggests that financial repression encourages economic dualism. Krugman shows that financial repression can worsen income distribution, but need not necessarily cause economic dualism. However, Galbis constructs a model in which financial repression not only worsens income distribution but also maintains economic dualism. As Greenwood and Jovanovic demonstrate, even an unrepressed process of financial development can produce a transitional phase of worsening income distribution. Financial repression could prolong and deepen such a phase.

Chapter 3

The McKinnon-Shaw School

3.1 Introduction

F IRST GENERATION EXTENSIONS of the McKinnon-Shaw framework consist of formal macroeconomic models in which the key instrument of financial repression is a deposit rate of interest fixed by government authorities below its free-market competitive equilibrium level. Reserve requirements are sometimes included, but no attention is paid to the nature of banking or financial markets. While stabilization issues are considered in some of the extensions, inflation is not placed in a fiscal context. The first generation financial repression models are represented by, among others, Yoon Je Cho (1984), Vicente Galbis (1977), Basant Kapur (1976a), Yang-Pal Lee (1980), Donald Mathieson (1980) and myself (Fry 1978, 1980a, 1980b).

In all the first generation financial repression models, money demand is a function of the real deposit rate of interest $d-\pi^e$. With d fixed, higher expected inflation π^e (equal to actual inflation π in the steady state) reduces demand for money in real terms $(M/P)^d$, where M is money and P is the price level.[1] As the liabilities of the banking system contract in real terms, so too must its assets; hence the supply of bank loans L for investment finance dries up. In a portfolio framework, a lower real deposit rate of interest encourages households to hold unproductive inflation hedges rather than deposits that would be used to finance productive investment. Hence, the accumulation of productive capital slows down, so reducing the rate of economic growth.

Even if deposit and loan rates of interest were allowed to be freely determined in a competitive environment, financial repression could be exerted through reserve requirements, as illustrated in Chapter 1. If the public holds only deposit money D and banks hold all the reserve or high-powered money

---

[1] In fact, the same results are produced when the loan rate rather than the deposit rate is set below its competitive equilibrium level by government fiat.

H issued as a transfer payment by the government through the central bank, the simplified consolidated balance sheet of the banking system can be written $H + L = M$ instead of the expression $R + L = D$ used in Chapter 1.

Inflation intensifies financial repression caused by reserve requirements. Given the inflation rate, however, a lower required reserve ratio has two effects: (a) it enables the banks to increase lending to finance productive private sector investment from a given volume of deposits; (b) for any given loan rate, it raises the competitive deposit rate of interest, thereby increasing money demand. The resulting larger real size of the banking system implies more bank lending in real terms.

Among the first generation financial repression models, the most elaborate are those of Kapur and Mathieson. The Kapur-Mathieson model applies to a labor-surplus developing economy characterized by the following Harrod-Domar aggregate production function:

$$Y = \sigma K, \tag{3.1}$$

where Y is real output (GNP at constant prices), and K is total utilized capital. Capital consists of both fixed and working capital, but there is always some excess or unutilized fixed capital. Utilized fixed capital is combined in constant ratio with working capital. Since the proportion of utilized fixed capital in total utilized capital is α, the ratio of working capital to total utilized capital is $1-\alpha$. Hence an increase in working capital of \$1 increases total utilized capital by the multiplied amount $\$1/(1-\alpha)$.

Both Kapur and Mathieson assume that the output/capital ratio σ is constant. The Kapur-Mathieson model allows financial conditions to affect solely the quantity of investment ΔK. Unfortunately, the available empirical evidence reviewed in Chapter 8 suggests that financial liberalization and development have much greater impacts on the quality of investment as measured by σ than on the quantity of investment ΔK. Nevertheless both Kapur and Mathieson do capture various dynamic regularities of the typical stabilization process.

3.2 Kapur

Kapur (1976a) assumes that there is unused fixed capital in the economy. Hence working capital constitutes the binding constraint on the level of output. Banks provide credit to finance a fixed fraction θ of the cost of replacing *depleted* working capital (in real terms). Bank credit is used to finance all net *additions* (again in real terms) to working capital. In the next period, however, entrepreneurs repay only the fraction θ of bank loans used to finance the now-depleted net *additions* to working capital before taking out new loans to finance replacement working capital. Hence the fraction $1-\theta$ of loans acquired for expansion is never repaid, although entrepreneurs could apparently pay a fully competitive interest rate on this outstanding balance.

For simplicity assume that all working capital is used up every time period. Then the additional nominal value of bank credit needed to maintain working capital at a constant level in real terms is $\Delta P \theta (1-\alpha) K$, where ΔP is the change in the price level. Therefore, the net increase in total utilized capital in real terms in Kapur's model is

$$\Delta K = \frac{1}{(1-\alpha)} \left[\frac{\Delta L - \Delta P \theta (1-\alpha) K}{P} \right], \tag{3.2}$$

where ΔL is the nominal increase in bank loans. Equations 3.1 and 3.2 indicate that changes in the supply of bank credit in real terms affect the rate of economic growth.

Kapur assumes that the money stock is backed by loans L and high-powered money (cash base or reserve money) H held by both the banks and the public. High-powered money is issued as a transfer payment by the government. The analysis can be simplified with no loss of generality to Kapur's model by assuming that the public holds only deposit money (Bailey 1956). Bank assets consist of required reserves (equal to H when the public holds no currency in circulation) and loans. Deposits are the banks' only liabilities.

The supply of bank credit can now be linked to the money stock. With a fixed required reserve ratio H/M equal to $1-q$ and no excess reserve holdings, the ratio of bank credit to money L/M is q. The central bank controls the rate of growth of nominal high-powered money and through this the rate of growth of bank loans and deposit money: $\Delta H/H = \Delta L/L = \Delta M/M = \mu$.

Substituting π for $\Delta P/P$, μ for $\Delta M/M$, and qM for L, equation 3.2 can be rewritten

$$\Delta K = \frac{1}{(1-\alpha)} \left[\mu q \frac{M}{P} - \pi \theta (1-\alpha) K \right]. \tag{3.3}$$

Since Y/K equals σ and $\Delta K/K$ equals the rate of economic growth $\Delta Y/Y$ or γ, equation 3.3 can be expressed in terms of γ by dividing both sides by K:

$$\gamma = \mu \frac{M}{P \cdot Y} \cdot \frac{\sigma q}{(1-\alpha)} - \pi \theta. \tag{3.4}$$

Equation 3.4 shows that the rate of economic growth is affected positively by the rate of monetary growth μ, the output/capital ratio σ, the ratio of loans to money q, and the ratio of utilized fixed capital to total utilized capital α (and so also the ratio of utilized fixed capital to working capital). Economic growth is reduced by an increase in the income velocity of circulation $P \cdot Y/M$, the number of times that money circulates on average over a year in payment for final goods and services and hence measured as the ratio of nominal GNP to money. Economic growth is also reduced by a higher fraction of bank-financed replacement working capital θ. A higher required reserve ratio $1-q$ reduces the ratio of loans to the money stock q and so also lowers the rate of economic growth in Kapur's model.

The term $\mu(M/P)$ is the standard expression for real revenue from inflation (Friedman 1971). Equation 3.4 is, therefore, an elaborate form of the inflation tax expression converted into a relationship between monetary expansion and growth.[2] This is achieved by assuming that a fixed proportion q of the inflation tax is used to finance working capital investment. Working capital creates economic growth through a combination of the output/capital ratio σ and the ratio of working capital to total utilized capital $1-\alpha$. Finally, $\pi\theta$ represents the cost of inflation to the banking system in terms of additional finance it provides to replace depleted working capital.

The key variable influencing the rate of economic growth is the supply of bank credit in real terms available for net additions to working capital. This is determined by the rate of monetary expansion, the ratio of loans to money q, the financing proportion θ, and real money demand $(M/P)^d$. Kapur chooses a variant of Phillip Cagan's (1956) money demand function frequently used in the inflation tax literature:

$$(M/P)^d = Y \cdot e^{a(d-\pi^e)}, \tag{3.5}$$

where $(M/P)^d$ represents the desired holdings of real money balances, π^e is expected inflation, and d is the deposit rate of interest. Dividing both sides of equation 3.5 by Y gives

$$M^d/(P \cdot Y) = e^{a(d-\pi^e)}. \tag{3.6}$$

Since the coefficient a is positive, equation 3.6 indicates that a rise in expected inflation reduces $M^d/(P \cdot Y)$ and so raises velocity of circulation $(P \cdot Y)/M$ in equilibrium when money demand M^d equals money supply M^s.

The coefficients of d and π^e are constrained to be equal and opposite to each other in equation 3.5. This is clearly appropriate in a two-asset portfolio model of deposits and tangible assets that are held as inflation hedges. Cournot aggregation requires an increase in deposits to be offset by a reduction in holdings of inflation hedges, and vice versa. In a portfolio model of more than two assets (for example, currency, deposits, and inflation hedges), this coefficient constraint is not necessarily appropriate (Burkner 1982). However, it is correct in a portfolio model with more than two assets if all assets possess just two attributes, namely return and liquidity (Fry 1981b, 264–265).[3]

---

[2] See Robert Mundell (1965) for the original analysis of growth through the inflation tax.

[3] Of course, constraining income elasticity of money demand to equal 1 is extremely unrealistic. It does not, however, affect the qualitative results of the model.

In the steady state, expected inflation π^e equals actual inflation π and income velocity of circulation V is constant, given Kapur's assumption of unit income elasticity of money demand.[4] Hence π and π^e both equal $\mu - \gamma$ from the logarithmic differentiation of the quantity equation $MV \equiv PY$ when V is constant.

In combination, equations 3.4 and 3.6 show that a faster rate of monetary growth has both a positive and a negative effect on the rate of economic growth. While the direct effect of μ in equation 3.4 is positive, the indirect effect through the reduction in $M^d/(P \cdot Y)$ caused by higher inflation is negative. The upshot is that there is a finite value of μ which maximizes γ.

Money is nonneutral in its effect on the rate of economic growth in Kapur's model for three reasons: (a) the fixed nominal deposit rate of interest d ensures that real money demand and hence real credit supply both change when the inflation rate changes; (b) the required reserve ratio imposes an effective tax on financial intermediation which increases as inflation increases; and (c) all net working capital investment is financed by bank credit, while only a fraction of replacement working capital is financed by banks.

Since money demand in real terms is determined in part by the real deposit rate of interest, real money demand declines when inflation rises (due to accelerated monetary growth or reduced real economic growth) and the nominal deposit rate of interest remains unchanged. In this model, an increase in the deposit rate of interest d increases real money demand and hence the real supply of bank credit. One growth-enhancing policy is, therefore, to increase the nominal deposit rate of interest d towards its competitive free-market level.

The real deposit rate of interest and hence real money demand can decline with an increase in the inflation rate even with a competitively determined nominal deposit rate of interest when a required reserve ratio is imposed. If banking costs are zero and no interest is paid on bank reserves, the competitive relationship between the nominal deposit d and loan rate ℓ rate of interest is

$$d = q\ell, \tag{3.7}$$

where $1-q$ is the required reserve ratio.[5] For example, with a required reserve ratio of 0.2 or 20 percent and \$100 of deposits, \$20 must be set aside as reserves, leaving \$80 for lending. A loan rate of 10 percent yields \$8 that has to be spread over \$100 of deposits. Hence the deposit rate cannot exceed 8 percent. Higher inflation increases the wedge between deposit and loan rates. With 20 percent inflation and a loan rate of 30 percent, equation 3.7 shows that the deposit rate cannot exceed 24 percent, implying a fall in the real deposit rate from 8 to 4 percent.

---

[4]Throughout this chapter, the term *steady state* refers to the equilibrium of a dynamic model rather than to the long-run equilibrium of an actual economy. None of the models discussed here attempts to describe the latter.

[5]The more realistic condition of positive bank operating cost ratios is considered in Chapter 14.

The real return on working capital investment r^* is invariant to the quantity of working capital in Kapur's model. Hence demand for credit is infinitely elastic at a nominal loan rate of $r^* + \pi$ in the steady state where π equals π^e. At lower loan rates there is an infinitely large demand for credit. The competitive loan rate of interest ℓ is therefore $r^* + \pi^e$.

Setting the nominal deposit rate at $q(r^* + \pi^e)$ maximizes real money demand (the tax base), the real supply of bank credit, and hence the real rate of economic growth for any given required reserve ratio and rate of monetary expansion. Financial liberalization, taking the form of the abolition of interest rate ceilings when the banking system is competitive, will produce this optimal result automatically in Kapur's model. When the banking system is cartelized and oligopolistic, conditions fostered by financial repression, the appropriate deposit rate will have to be imposed by the monetary authorities as a minimum rate the banks may offer (Fry 1980b, 543).[6]

A second growth-enhancing policy suggested by Kapur's model and advocated by McKinnon (1977, 15; 1981, 382; 1982, 162) is a reduction in the required reserve ratio $1-q$ or payment of the market clearing loan rate on required reserves. The rate of growth is maximized when reserve requirements are abolished completely. This conclusion concurs with neostructuralist models that compare unfavorably the efficiency of financial intermediation through the banking system with the efficiency of financial intermediation through the curb or unregulated financial markets because of the imposition of reserve requirements on the former.[7]

Suppose that the government issues high-powered money H not as a transfer payment but as loans at an interest rate of r^*. The government then transfers this interest to the banks as payment on required reserves (H is still held solely by the banks as reserves). In terms of the loan volume and the competitive equilibrium deposit rate, this is equivalent to abolishing the reserve requirement altogether. Effectively, q equals 1 and growth is maximized. In Kapur's model, therefore, the optimal value of $d - \pi$ is r^* and depositors receive a constant real deposit rate of interest, irrespective of the inflation rate. In other words, they do not bear the inflation tax. In this case, the rate of economic growth always rises with faster monetary growth because real money demand (the tax base) no longer falls to offset faster monetary growth (the tax rate).

The third source of money's nonneutrality lies in the financing arrangements embodied in θ. Equation 3.2 shows that all net *additional* working capital in real terms is financed by bank credit, while only a fraction of replacement capital is. Note again that entrepreneurs never repay the fraction $1 - \theta$ of the original loan for net working capital investment, although they

---

[6]The issue of equilibrium credit rationing by banks is explored in Part III.

[7]The reserve requirement is considered again in Chapter 7.

could pay a competitive interest rate to be passed on to depositors on the outstanding balance. With no inflation, the unpaid balance of the loan for net working capital investment can be combined with a new bank loan equal to the fraction θ of the original loan to meet exactly the replacement cost of this net working capital investment. With inflation, however, the unpaid balance is not sufficient to cover that part of the replacement cost to be met by the entrepreneur. Additional funds have to be found or generated from revenue. The entrepreneur, therefore, bears the rising burden of inflation-induced increases in the replacement cost of working capital.

On the other hand, since banks finance only the fraction θ of inflation-induced increases in the replacement cost of working capital, the central bank can enable commercial banks to expand lending for net additional working capital investment indefinitely through monetary expansion, provided real money demand remains constant. When prices are stable, the banks have a fraction θ of revolving one-year loans and a fraction $1-\theta$ of undated loans or consols on their books. For example, with θ equal to 0.7, banks might have $70 in revolving loans and $30 in consols matching $90 in deposits and $10 in reserves. Each period the working capital revolving loans are repaid and lent out again with no funds to spare to finance additional working capital.

Now money and prices rise by 10 percent. On the liability side, banks hold $99 in deposits and $11 in reserves. On the asset side, revolving loans must rise to $77, but the nominal value of consols remains unchanged. Therefore, the banks have $3 ($2.73 at constant prices) to spare for loans to finance net additional working capital investment. Faster monetary expansion always increases the resources that banks have available to finance net additional working capital; a doubling of money and prices enables banks to provide $60 ($30 at constant prices) for financing additional working capital investment.

This third source of nonneutrality highlights the main defect of Kapur's model—the absence of a behavioral saving function or supply constraints. Investment can be increased indefinitely, even exceeding the total value of output. Kapur provides no indication of where the extra saving comes from to finance the extra investment. Clearly, however, it need not be forced saving extracted from depositors. Indeed, Kapur (1976a, n. 7, 789) anticipates this criticism: "The persistence of this higher growth rate over time presupposes the existence of some mechanism which ensures that the availability of fixed-capital services expands at an adequate rate, since otherwise at some point the fixed capacity would become fully utilized. Since our concern in this paper is primarily with short-run analysis, we shall not pursue this matter further, except to point out that an obvious candidate for such a mechanism is an increase in fixed investment out of the higher level of business profits that results from a higher level of capacity utilization." Such a mechanism is specified in Kapur (1974, ch. 4). In that model, money is neutral in the absence of interest rate ceilings and a reserve requirement tax.

Kapur's (1976a) model can be salvaged by eliminating this peculiar source of nonneutrality. The easiest way is to assume that banks finance the same proportion of net and replacement working capital investment. Now there is no longer any relationship between μ and γ. The indeterminacy of the rate of growth in the steady state, however, once again highlights the critical lacuna of Kapur's model, the absence of a saving function and hence any constraint on investment.

McKinnon and Shaw both discuss dynamic aspects of financial repression and liberalization programs. However, neither of them constructs a formal dynamic model. McKinnon makes the important point that stabilization programs implemented through monetary contraction invariably produce an initial rise in velocity of circulation (using the broad *M2* definition of money) and hence a credit squeeze in real terms. Only later does declining inflation raise real money demand and so reduce velocity. There is little dispute that a credit squeeze is contractionary from the supply side as well as from the demand side (Blinder 1987).

Kapur (1976a) includes two sources of dynamic adjustment, adaptive expectations of the inflation rate and money market disequilibrium, in his model. Adaptive expectations can be expressed:

$$\frac{d\pi^e}{dt} = \beta(\pi - \pi^e), \tag{3.8}$$

where π^e is expected inflation and π is the actual inflation rate. Mainstream macroeconomics has now dropped adaptive expectations in favor of rational expectations. People form their expectations rationally if they make efficient use of the available information on past inflation and other variables to avoid making systematic mistakes (Barro 1987, 171). In deterministic models, the incorporation of rational expectations is equivalent to perfect foresight. In this case, therefore, using adaptive expectations is a convenient way of allowing expected inflation to differ from actual inflation, at least in the short run. Provided part of any reduction in the inflation rate is unexpected, the contractionary effects of monetary deceleration follow. For estimation purposes, the stochastic versions of all the dynamic models reviewed in this chapter can easily include rational expectations.

Kapur uses an expectations-augmented Phillips curve to introduce money market disequilibrium:

$$\pi = h\left(\frac{M^s}{PY} - \frac{M^d}{PY}\right) + \pi^e, \tag{3.9}$$

where M^s is money supply, M^d is money demand, P is the price level, and Y is real GNP. In a two-market economy, excess supply of money equals excess demand for goods. Hence equation 3.9 is a transformation of the standard expectations-augmented Phillips curve, in which excess demand for goods proxied by the gap between actual and trend output is used in place of excess supply of money. Equation 3.9 indicates that markets do not clear instantaneously. Rather, excess demand for goods causes producers to raise prices faster than the expected inflation rate until excess demand is *eventually* eliminated. Equation 3.9 could also incorporate a stock adjustment mechanism for the gap between desired and actual holdings of real money balances. Equation 3.9 is a Phelpsian version of the expectations-augmented Phillips curve (Laidler 1978).

Defining W as the logarithm of velocity of circulation V, Kapur's model can be reduced to two equations of motion:

$$\Delta W = -\mu \left(1 - \tfrac{\sigma q}{1-\alpha}e^{-W}\right) + (1-\theta)\pi^e$$
$$+ (1-\theta)\left[e^{-W} - e^{a(d-\pi^e)}\right];$$

(3.10)

$$\frac{d\pi^e}{dt} = \beta h \left[e^{-W} - e^{a(d-\pi^e)}\right].$$

(3.11)

Kapur simulates two alternative stabilization policies introduced when the economy is experiencing excessive inflation and, hence, low growth; simulation is necessary because an analytical solution is intractable. The first policy reduces the rate of monetary growth μ. This produces a phase of rising velocity W and falling expected inflation π^e, followed by a phase of falling W and falling π^e, followed possibly by cyclical convergence to the new equilibrium—falling W, rising π^e; rising W, rising π^e; rising W, falling π^e; falling W, falling π^e (Kapur 1976a, 787). In other words, monetary deceleration produces the initial velocity acceleration stressed by McKinnon.

Kapur's growth equation can be expressed in terms of the logarithm of velocity W:

$$\gamma = \mu \frac{\sigma q}{(1-\alpha)}e^{-W} - \pi\theta.$$

(3.12)

The initial fall in the money growth rate μ reduces the rate of economic growth γ, as does the rising velocity W of the first phase. The rising W produces a declining rate of inflation, as shown by equation 3.11. The reduction in μ cuts the net flow of real bank credit, which immediately reduces γ. Then falling actual and expected inflation (π and π^e) partly, completely, or more than offset the negative effects of the rising W on γ. When W and π are both falling, γ will be above its long-run equilibrium level, to which it then converges.

The second policy raises the deposit rate of interest d towards its equilibrium level. In this case, the logarithm of velocity W and expected inflation π^e both fall in the initial phase. The increase in d raises real money demand immediately and so initially lowers the inflation rate π, since there is no jump in W or π^e. Equation 3.12 shows that the initial fall in π raises γ. The falling W and π of the first phase raise γ until it overshoots its new higher equilibrium value, to which it then converges. An upward shift in d has favorable effects on γ and π in both the short run and in the steady state (Kapur 1976a, 792).

The optimal policy with respect to d is to set it at, or allow it to rise through competitive market forces to, its upper bound, which would equal $r^* + \pi^e$ when bank intermediation costs and reserve requirements are both zero (q equal to 1). When $q = 1$, $d = r^* + \pi^e$, and $\theta < 1$, the growth-maximizing value of μ is ∞, as already pointed out earlier. Despite this, Kapur's model portrays vividly the dynamics of two alternative stabilization policies and illustrates clearly the superiority of financial liberalization, taking the form of the abolition of interest rate ceilings, over monetary contraction alone as a stabilization device.

In subsequent papers, Kapur (1982, 1983) applies control theory techniques to solve the optimal stabilization problem. The government's loss function includes target values for π and W. In most cases, the nominal deposit rate d is set at its upper bound ($r^* + \pi^e$ when q equals 1 and banking costs are zero) throughout the transition period. However, Kapur (1983) finds that the deposit rate may have to be set below its upper bound during the transition period to deter excessive capital inflows in his open economy model (in which expectations are formed rationally). In all cases, the optimal solution entails setting d at its upper bound in the steady state.

The optimal transition path invariably necessitates initial discrete changes in μ and d, which may then be followed by smooth convergence to steady state values. However, the optimal transition can require discrete changes from minimum to maximum, intermediate to minimum or maximum, minimum or maximum to intermediate, and maximum to minimum values of μ and d. Such changes occur in some instances of cyclical convergence. While such switches in policy instruments from one extreme to the other are fairly typical of dynamic control model solutions, they highlight the practical limitations of this technique for practical economic policy implementation.

3.3 Mathieson

Mathieson (1980) adopts Kapur's production function and the assumption of the fixed ratio of working to total utilized capital $1-\alpha$. Mathieson parts company with Kapur by assuming that fixed capital is fully utilized and that a fixed proportion θ of all investment—fixed capital, net working capital, and replacement working capital—is financed by bank loans. Total real loan demand is

$$L/P = \theta K. \tag{3.13}$$

Mathieson now explains the rate of capital accumulation by firms' saving behavior. This is determined by the fixed real return on capital r' (which differs from r^*, Kapur's fixed real return to working capital investment) and the real loan rate of interest $\ell - \pi^e$:

$$\Delta K = s(r' - \ell + \pi^e)Y. \qquad (3.14)$$

Equation 3.14 gives the investment ratio which creates the demand for bank loans.

Mathieson's growth rate function is derived from equation 3.14 by dividing both sides by K and substituting σ for Y/K:

$$\gamma = s(r' - \ell + \pi^e)\sigma. \qquad (3.15)$$

As in Kapur's model, $\Delta K/K = \Delta Y/Y = \gamma$. Growth is greater the higher the real return to investment, the lower the nominal loan rate, the higher the expected inflation rate, and the higher the output/capital ratio σ.

The supply of loans is determined by the demand for deposits and the required reserve ratio, provided that high-powered money is not backed by loans but is created through transfer payments. Using Kapur's definition, the reserve ratio is $1-q$. Hence,

$$L/P = q(D/P), \qquad (3.16)$$

where D is the level of deposits. Demand for deposits takes the form

$$D/P = f(d - \pi^e)Y. \qquad (3.17)$$

Mathieson assumes that the currency/money ratio is constant, as does Kapur. Again setting the currency/money ratio at zero sacrifices no loss in generality. Hence, for a constant required reserve ratio, $\Delta H/H = \Delta D/D = \Delta L/L = \Delta M/M = \mu$.

In the steady state, with a competitive banking system incurring zero costs, ℓ equals d/q and so the demand for loans from equation 3.13 and the supply of loans derived from equation 3.17 will determine the equilibrium deposit rate. Using Kapur's money demand function gives

$$Y \cdot e^{a(d - \pi^e)} = (\theta/q)K \qquad (3.18)$$

as the equilibrium condition. When π^e equals π, which in turn equals $\mu - \gamma$, equation 3.18 yields

$$d = \pi + (1/a)\log(\theta/q\sigma) \qquad (3.19)$$

or

$$d = \mu - \gamma + (1/a)\log(\theta/q\sigma). \qquad (3.20)$$

In fact, for any money demand function with the coefficients of d and π^e constrained to be equal and opposite to each other, the competitive free-market equilibrium real deposit rate $d - \pi^e$ is invariant to the rate of inflation in the steady state when π^e equals π. Mathieson's model produces this invariancy because loan demand is completely interest inelastic. In contrast, loan demand is perfectly elastic in Kapur's model. A higher required reserve ratio in Mathieson's model raises d and so increases real money demand. It also raises the equilibrium loan rate ℓ, which in turn reduces investment and growth.

The sharp difference in loan demand elasticities in the models of Kapur and Mathieson springs from the difference in loan use. Kapur has bank loans used solely for working capital. Working capital is used up and the loans are repaid each time period. Since the real return to working capital investment is fixed at r^*, demand for bank loans to finance working capital is infinitely interest elastic at r^*. Mathieson assumes that the demand for bank loans in real terms is simply a fixed fraction of the capital stock. The loan rate influences the rate of change of that stock (investment), but cannot affect its *level* at any instant in time. Hence the stock of loans outstanding is invariant to the current loan rate.

Equations 3.19 and 3.20 show that the equilibrium deposit rate will be higher the larger the proportion of bank-financed investment, the higher the reserve ratio, and the lower the output/capital ratio. In this equilibrium situation a higher deposit rate raises the loan rate, which in turn reduces the rate of economic growth.[8]

Money is not neutral in Mathieson's model if d or ℓ is fixed below its competitive market equilibrium level, or if $q < 1$. If $d-\pi^e$ falls when inflation accelerates because d or ℓ is fixed, the real supply of loans must also decline. If $q < 1$, the real loan rate will rise as inflation accelerates. Both a fall in the real supply of loans and a rise in the real loan rate must reduce investment and growth. With d and ℓ free to find their equilibrium levels and either no required reserves or a competitive interest rate paid on required reserves, money is neutral in the steady state.

Mathieson assumes that the government fixes deposit and loan rates. If the loan rate alone is fixed and if the banking system is competitive, the deposit rate would still bear the relationship to the loan rate $d = q\ell$. However, d would be suboptimal were ℓ held below its competitive equilibrium level. Hence the real supply of credit L/P and the capital stock K (from equation 3.13) would be lower than they would be when both loan and deposit rates find their competitive equilibrium levels. With ℓ kept low, there would be a high desired rate of capital accumulation in equation 3.14. In other words, demand for bank loans would exceed the supply. Equation 3.14 cannot be satisfied in this disequilibrium situation.

---

[8] See Anthony Courakis (1984, 1986) and Chapter 7 for a more realistic analysis of the reserve requirement tax when the demand for loans is neither perfectly interest elastic nor perfectly inelastic.

In conjunction with the abolition of interest rate ceilings, paying a competitive return on bank reserves would make money neutral in Mathieson's model and also neutral in a slightly modified version of Kapur's model in which banks finance the same proportion of net and replacement working capital investment. In both models, financial liberalization raises investment and the rate of economic growth.

Mathieson (1980) incorporates adaptive expectations of the inflation rate and a decaying stock of fixed-interest bank loans as two sources of dynamic adjustment in his model. Mathieson assumes that loan rates on bank loans are fixed for the duration of the loan. Hence it takes time for banks to replace low interest rate loans with higher interest rate loans after financial liberalization. Indeed, Mathieson shows that financial liberalization can bankrupt established financial institutions holding a portfolio of loans yielding low pre-reform returns. New entrants could attract deposits away from existing institutions with earnings from portfolios consisting solely of higher-yielding post-reform loans. Competing with new entrants could completely erode existing institutions' net worth.

Mathieson (1980) specifies the government's loss function in terms of target inflation π^t and target growth γ^t rates:

$$U = \delta_1(\pi - \pi^t)^2 + \delta_2(\gamma - \gamma^t)^2, \tag{3.21}$$

where δ_1 and δ_2 are both positive. This loss function is minimized by employing the policy instruments μ, d, and ℓ, subject to two constraints: (a) money and credit markets must remain in continuous equilibria; and (b) no bankruptcies of established financial institutions may occur. Equations 3.16 and 3.17 indicate that money and credit market equilibria can be maintained if and only if Δd equals $\Delta \pi^e$. In other words, the real deposit rate of interest must be held constant.

Initially, the real loan rate needs to be set above its steady state value to compensate for the existing stock of low-yielding loans. It is reduced gradually as these pre-reform loans are repaid; the average real loan rate remains constant at the zero profit level for existing institutions. Since the wider gap between deposit and loan rates during the transition will attract new entrants, the monetary authorities must prevent them from engaging in price competition.

If the economy starts from a financially repressed, high inflation, low growth condition, the optimal strategy necessitates initial discrete increases in both d and ℓ, provided that the loan rate was held below its market clearing level, as Mathieson assumes. A discrete decrease in μ to a rate below its long-run value will also be required. During the transition d and ℓ are gradually reduced, d in step with π^e, ℓ somewhat more rapidly, and μ is gradually raised to its steady state value consistent with $\pi = \pi^t$. The growth rate γ jumps to a higher level and then rises towards γ^t. At the same time π declines monotonically towards π^t. There is no cyclical convergence in Mathieson's model.

Mathieson's (1980) model is needlessly complicated by the incorporation of low fixed-interest loans in bank portfolios. As suggested earlier, the effective loan rate is actually likely to be above rather than below its competitive market equilibrium level under conditions of financial repression. In any case, government-fixed bank loan rates in a number of financially repressed developing economies are subject to automatic adjustment whenever the official interest rate structure is changed. In other words, banks only offer variable rate loans with the loan rate pegged to the official rate. In Korea and Taiwan simple alternative techniques have been used to prevent bankruptcies after upward revisions of the institutional interest rate structure.

The growth rate target is achieved as soon as the real loan rate $\ell - \pi^e$ is set at its steady state value in Mathieson's model. This can be done immediately at the beginning of the stabilization program, provided that bank loan rates are variable or adjustable and that a competitive nominal return is paid on bank reserves (so making q effectively equal to 1). With no interest paid on required reserves, the real loan rate will decline and the growth rate will rise as the inflation rate falls.

The adaptive expectations mechanism affects only the path of the actual inflation rate when there is no required reserve ratio or when required reserves earn a competitive return. In this case money is neutral even during the transition period. With rational expectations and a preannounced credible stabilization program, μ, d, and ℓ can all be set at their steady state values at the start of the program, provided there are no low fixed-interest rate loans in bank portfolios.

The essential differences between the Kapur and Mathieson models lie in the growth rate functions and Kapur's market disequilibrium mechanism. These provide Kapur with possibilities of cyclical convergence and discrete switches in the values of policy instruments. After initial discrete changes, policy instruments are always changed monotonically during the transition period in Mathieson's model since cyclical convergence never occurs.

Setting an independent inflation target in either the Kapur or Mathieson model must be based on considerations that are not incorporated in the models. Provided $q < 1$, growth maximization requires an inflation rate of $-\infty$ in Mathieson's model and a positive finite value in Kapur's model. With q equal to 1 or a competitive return paid on required reserves, money is neutral in Mathieson's model, whereas growth is then maximized when inflation is ∞ in Kapur's model.

3.4 Open-Economy Extensions

As part of its financial and fiscal reforms of 1964–1965, Korea devalued its currency from 130 won to 270 won to the dollar. The new exchange rate was supported in part by liberal government exchange rate guarantees. There was general confidence in the sustainability of the new rate. Under such conditions, the high nominal interest rates provided a strong incentive for short-term capital inflows. The resulting increase in net foreign assets jeopardized monetary control.

McKinnon and Shaw both have a good deal to say about balance-of-payments and exchange rate policies in the light of the Korean experience. However, neither provides any formal framework for the analysis. McKinnon (1973, ch. 11) and Shaw (1973, ch. 7) both view a flexible exchange rate policy as a crucial element in the optimal financial stabilization and liberalization program. Since inflation, or at least expected inflation, does not decline immediately after a reform, nominal interest rates must be set at relatively high levels at the outset of the transition period. To deter undesired and disruptive capital inflows, McKinnon (1973, 166–167) advocates the adoption of a crawling peg to maintain both interest rate and purchasing power parity during the deflationary process. Shaw (1973, 221–226) prefers a floating exchange rate and its concomitant of full convertibility. In a less than perfect world, he also advocates a crawling peg (Shaw 1976).

Kapur (1983) and Mathieson (1979a) both develop open economy models of a financially repressed economy. The exchange rate becomes an additional policy instrument. The extension to an open economy adds considerably to the models' complexity, in large part because the exchange rate is allowed to deviate from purchasing power parity.

Kapur adds to his closed economy model a production function for working capital K_w:

$$K_w = K_{wd}^a \cdot K_{wf}^{1-a}, \tag{3.22}$$

where K_{wd} is domestic working capital inputs and K_{wf} is the imported flow of working capital inputs. K_{wd} and K_{wf} are combined in their cost-minimizing ratio:

$$\frac{K_{wf}}{K_{wd}} = \frac{(1-a)}{a} \cdot \frac{P}{e_n} = \frac{(1-a)}{a} \cdot \frac{1}{e_r}, \tag{3.23}$$

where e_n is the nominal exchange rate, e_r is the real exchange rate, and the foreign currency price of K_{wf} is 1. The price of K_w at the cost-minimizing combination of K_{wd} and K_{wf} is P_w:

$$P_w = a^{-a}(1-a)^{a-1} \cdot P^a \cdot e_n^{1-a}. \tag{3.24}$$

P_w is substituted for P in equation 3.2.

With rational expectations (π^e equal to π and $[\Delta e_n / e_n]^e$ equal to $\Delta e_n / e_n$) and the money demand function of equation 3.5, the growth rate for this open economy is

$$\gamma = \mu \frac{\sigma q}{(1-\alpha)} a^a (1-a)^{1-a} \cdot e^{-W} \cdot e_r^{(a-1)}$$

$$- \theta \left[\pi + (1-a) \frac{\Delta e_n}{e_n} \right]. \tag{3.25}$$

The balance of payments involves imports of K_{wf} given by equation 3.23, exports E as a function of the real exchange rate and the level of output $E = E(e_r)Y$, and short-term capital inflows FI:

$$FI = f \left[d - d_w - (\frac{\Delta e_n}{e_n})^e \right] P \cdot Y, \tag{3.26}$$

where d_w is the nominal interest rate abroad. The complete balance of payments can be expressed

$$\Delta R = P \cdot E - e_n K_{wf} + FI, \tag{3.27}$$

where ΔR is the nominal change in net foreign assets.

Money is backed by domestic cash C, net foreign assets R, and loans L. As before, C is created as a transfer payment and can be manipulated to control monetary expansion: $L/M = q$, $(C+R)/M = 1-q$, and $(\Delta C + \Delta R)/(C+R) = \Delta M/M = \mu$. This assumption about monetary control is clearly at variance with the reality of many developing countries.

Kapur's open economy model has three target variables, e_r, W, and π, and three policy instruments for their achievement, d, μ, and v, where v is $\Delta \log(e_r)$. The government's objectives are to create a nonnegative trade balance, to lower inflation, and to raise the rate of economic growth. The economy is found initially in a situation of trade deficit, high inflation, and low growth. The transition process to minimize the loss function G,

$$G = \int_0^\infty e^{-\rho t} \left[m_1 (W - W^t)^2 + m_2 (\pi - \pi^t)^2 \right] dt, \tag{3.28}$$

where ρ is the social discount rate, involves discrete and continuous changes in d, μ, and v.

The main additional economic insight gleaned from Kapur's model is that the real exchange rate (the nominal exchange rate adjusted for relative inflation rates at home and abroad) may well have to depreciate during the transition from repressed to liberalized states. Kapur shows that it is not necessarily optimal to devalue the nominal exchange rate initially by the full extent required for trade balance in the new steady state. In fact, such a devaluation could well produce excessive short-term capital inflows, a problem faced by Korea in the 1960s and Chile in the 1970s. On the one hand, a high real rate of depreciation during the transition period reduces γ, as can be seen from equation 3.25. On the other hand, a high value for v permits a high value for d, since the real exchange rate now starts below its target value and the rate of return on working capital r^* is inversely related to e_r:

$$r^* = [P \cdot Y - P_w K_w]/P_w K_w$$
$$= \tfrac{\sigma}{(1-\alpha)} a^a (1-a)^{1-a} \cdot e_r^{a-1} - 1. \tag{3.29}$$

For some initial conditions, the optimal value of v lies somewhere between its arbitrarily imposed lower bound of zero and its upper bound, at which capital flight occurs. In this case, the positive value of v supports strong deflationary measures at some cost in terms of forgone growth.

Mathieson's (1979a) open economy model is an extension of his closed economy model (Mathieson 1980). The low fixed-interest loan portfolio problem, which features prominently in his closed economy model, does not appear in the open economy model. In addition to balance-of-payments considerations, the open economy model contains a Phillips curve:

$$\pi = \phi \log(Q/Y), \tag{3.30}$$

where Q is aggregate demand and Y is aggregate supply in real terms. As Mathieson adopts rational expectations here ($\pi^e = \pi$ and $x^e = x$, where x is the rate of change in the nominal exchange rate), this is the sole source of dynamic adjustment in the model. Here π refers to the rate of change in the price of domestic goods. Aggregate demand for domestic output is a function of domestic income Y, foreign income Y_f, expected inflation π^e, and the relative price of domestic goods P to foreign goods P_f converted through the exchange rate e_n into domestic currency units:

$$\log(Q) = \tau_0 - \tau_1 \log(P/e_n P_f) + \tau_2 \log(Y)$$
$$+ \tau_3 \pi^e + \tau_4 \log(Y_f), \tag{3.31}$$

where τ_1, τ_2, τ_3, and τ_4 are all positive.

The general price level P_g is defined as

$$P_g = P^\epsilon (e_n P_f)^{1-\epsilon}, \tag{3.32}$$

where ϵ is the weight attached to the price of domestic goods. The demand for loans is given by equation 3.13: $L/P_g = \theta K$. The rate of capital accumulation is the same as equation 3.14: $\Delta K = s(r' - \ell + \pi_g^e)Y$, where π_g^e is the general inflation rate. The demand for deposits, however, differs from equation 3.17 in that a substitute financial asset in the form of foreign deposits with a yield d_w is introduced:

$$D/P_g = f(d - \pi_g^e, \; d_w + x^e - \pi_g^e)Y. \tag{3.33}$$

All money is held as deposits. The ratio of deposits to high-powered money H is fixed: $D = (1-q)H$. High-powered money H equals $C+R$, as in Kapur's open economy model. In fact, Mathieson misleadingly defines H equal to domestic credit DC plus reserves. However, DC is not credit since it is not added to L. Rather, Mathieson appears to create DC as a transfer payment in the same way that Kapur creates C.

In contrast to Kapur's model, here the government can control μ or x but not both. If x is chosen as the policy instrument, then D is determined solely by demand and C affects only the overall balance-of-payments position.

Mathieson's model would collapse were purchasing power parity imposed. It is therefore curious that μ and x cannot be used as independent policy instruments. The technical explanation for this lies in the fact that disequilibrium in Mathieson's money market does not affect the domestic price level directly (equations 3.30 and 3.31). The only equilibrating mechanism is a change in e_n, which affects Q, which in turn affects π. Clearly, therefore, if e_n is chosen as the policy instrument, equilibrium in the money market can be achieved only through corresponding changes in H.

Mathieson provides no equilibrating mechanism in his open economy model. Furthermore, balance-of-payments equilibrium can be achieved only through C policy (the simplest monetary approach to the balance of payments), despite less than perfect substitutability between domestic and foreign goods and financial assets. This is due to the requirement that $C+R$ "must" equal the demand-determined $D/(1-q)$. The absence of any behavioral determinants of the balance-of-payments position in this model is a disturbing lacuna.

The most serious problem with Mathieson's (1979a) model is the lack of any equilibrating mechanism in the money market. Independent monetary and exchange rate policies could be permitted simply by allowing money market disequilibrium to spill over directly, as seems eminently reasonable for any developing economy, into the domestic goods market. Mathieson actually assumes that the monetary authority adjusts the deposit rate to prevent money market disequilibrium at all times. Hence no spillover effects can occur. In such case, it is unnecessary to model any equilibrating mechanism. It seems rather anomalous, however, to construct a model in which interest rates are constrained to take their market clearing values to analyze the transition from financial repression to financial liberalization. Indeed, Mathieson's model does not purport to describe the financially repressed economy, but rather a developing economy under the benign influence of equilibrating financial policies.

With rational expectations, imposing equilibrium in the money and credit markets as a prerequisite for the optimal stabilization program necessitates

$$\mu - \epsilon\pi - (1-\epsilon)x = \gamma, \tag{3.34}$$

since D/P_g equals $\theta(K/q)$ and π_g equals $\epsilon\pi + (1-\epsilon)x$. In other words, velocity of circulation has to be kept constant.

Logarithmic differentiation of equation 3.33 with respect to time gives

$$\mu - \epsilon\pi - (1-\epsilon)x = \tfrac{f_1}{f} \left[\Delta d - \epsilon\Delta\pi - (1-\epsilon)\Delta x\right]$$
$$+ \tfrac{f_2}{f} \left[\Delta x - \epsilon\Delta\pi - (1-\epsilon)\Delta x\right] + \gamma,$$
(3.35)

when d_w is constant. Hence the nominal deposit rate of interest has to be changed as follows:

$$\Delta d = \epsilon(1+\eta)\Delta\pi + [1 - \epsilon(1+\eta)]\Delta x,$$
(3.36)

where η equals f_2/f_1, to maintain velocity constant.

Mathieson (1979a, 458) illustrates a dynamic solution of his model by assuming that the economy starts from a position of "rapid inflation, low or zero growth, and a balance-of-payments deficit." Using equation 3.30, Mathieson shows that price stability can be approached through an initial discrete increase in d and ℓ, an *overdepreciation* of e_n, and a decline in the growth rate of C. The instantaneous effect is an upward jump in γ as a result of financial liberalization.

After these discrete changes, the economy can approach its steady state through a gradual appreciation in the exchange rate,[9] gradual reductions in d and ℓ, and a gradual increase in C at a rate lower than μ. It turns out that γ may *decline* gradually to its steady state value during the transition period. The inflation rate will fall and the balance of payments will return to equilibrium after capital inflows generated by appropriate control over C have occurred during the transition period.

The reason why economic growth can be above its steady state value during the transition period lies in the exchange rate policy. The initial overdepreciation of the domestic currency produces expectations of subsequent appreciation in e_r. Given levels of d and d_w, a decline in the expected nominal depreciation raises the demand for deposits, as shown in equation 3.33. *Ceteris paribus*, the more e_r is expected to appreciate, the less e_n will be expected to depreciate. Hence the greater the initial overdepreciation, the lower is the value for $d-\pi_g^e$ required to generate a given demand for deposits. In turn, a lower real deposit rate permits a lower real loan rate $\ell-\pi_g^e$, and this encourages more rapid capital accumulation and so a higher rate of economic growth. Basically, the overdepreciation deters capital flight by reducing the attractiveness of foreign financial assets.

The greater the overdepreciation, the higher is the domestic inflation rate (equations 3.30 and 3.31), due to greater aggregate demand for domestic goods. Higher inflation reduces growth by increasing the spread between d and ℓ, due to the inflation tax levied through noninterest-earning bank reserves.

---

[9]Mathieson refers only to the nominal exchange rate e_n, but presumably he means the real exchange rate e_r since inflation is eliminated only gradually.

There is, therefore, an optimal extent of overdepreciation at which the effect of a lower value of x^e on d is exactly offset by the effect of a higher π^e on both d and ℓ, such that $\ell-\pi_g^e$ is minimized.

Demand for loans is infinitely elastic at a nominal loan rate ℓ, which is equal to $r^*+\pi^e$ in Kapur's model. Hence the inflation tax levied through bank reserves is borne entirely by depositors. In Mathieson's model, demand of loans is not infinitely elastic. A higher value of $\ell-\pi_g^e$ reduces capital accumulation and hence economic growth. However, the equilibrium deposit rate is invariant to the rate of economic growth and must be set at the level needed to generate a deposit/income ratio equal to $\theta/\sigma q$ (since $L/P_g = \theta K$, $D/P_g = f \cdot Y = f \cdot \sigma K$, and $L = qD$). Hence the higher is the required reserve ratio $1-q$, the higher will be the market equilibrating value of d. The inflation tax is borne entirely by borrowers. Far from being able to raise growth as in Kapur's model, inflation always reduces growth in Mathieson's model, since in both these open economy models expectations are rational (hence π^e always equals π).

Mathieson's (1979a) open economy model warrants a number of comments. First, if π^e deserves a place in the demand function for goods (equation 3.31) then so do d, d_w, and x^e. As with π^e, the signs of their coefficients are ambiguous in theory. Empirical evidence suggests that higher real deposit rates reduce aggregate demand in a number of countries (Boskin 1978, Fry 1978, 1979a). The inclusion of d in equation 3.31 could produce a sharp deflationary impact at the outset of the stabilization program. This might more than counteract the inflationary impulse of the devaluation.

Second, it seems logical and consistent to include d_w and x^e in the saving/investment function. Entrepreneurs might also buy foreign bonds rather than invest domestically. Perhaps the major problem here is the lack of separate saving and investment functions, a defect that can be traced back to McKinnon's (1973, ch. 6) self-finance model. As already pointed out, Kapur specifies neither a saving nor an investment function. Separate saving and investment functions are clearly required for an inside money economy in which money itself enables decisions to save to be taken independently from decisions to invest.

Finally, the trick of overdepreciation to obtain a rate of economic growth above equilibrium during the transition could be repeated. A series of discrete devaluations followed by subsequent gradual currency appreciation would, it might seem, make foreign financial assets always less attractive to domestic deposit holders. Growth could always be kept above its steady state rate. Of course, this happy outcome would be possible only if depositors irrationally failed to anticipate future devaluations. It appears that they must rationally anticipate the irrational policy of government until the rational stabilization program is initiated as a complete surprise. That is, a big devaluation is not anticipated. From then on, government policy strives and is expected to strive to reach the steady state.

Mathieson's (1979a) model leads to the opposite conclusion to Kapur's with respect to devaluation strategy. Mathieson shows that an initial overdepreciation of the real exchange rate followed by gradual appreciation maintains the rate of economic growth above its steady state value during the transition period. This is because expected appreciation of the domestic currency in real terms reduces the incentive towards currency substitution and so lowers the real deposit rate required to generate any given demand for real money balances. In turn, a lower real deposit rate permits a lower real loan rate, and this encourages more rapid capital accumulation and so a higher rate of economic growth. Basically, the initial overdepreciation deters capital flight by reducing the attractiveness of foreign financial assets.

The fundamental difference in exchange rate policies in the open economy models of Kapur and Mathieson springs from several sources. First, the real rate of return on working capital r^* is negatively related to the real exchange rate in Kapur's model. A higher r^* allows a higher $d-\pi^e$, which is deflationary as well as growth-accelerating. Second, money demand is not affected by returns on foreign financial assets adjusted for exchange rate changes, so faster depreciation during the transition period does not reduce real money demand in Kapur's model.

In contrast, money demand is affected by the exchange-rate-adjusted return on foreign financial assets in Mathieson's model. Furthermore, investment and growth are raised in Mathieson's model by the lower real loan rate, concomitant with the lower real deposit rate made possible during transition by an appreciation of the real exchange rate.

3.5 Summary

In the first generation financial repression models, money demand is a function of the real deposit rate of interest $d-\pi^e$. With d fixed, a higher inflation rate (equal to expected inflation in the steady state) reduces demand for money in real terms. As the liabilities of the banking system contract in real terms, so too must its assets and hence the supply of credit for investment finance dries up. In a portfolio framework, a lower real deposit rate of interest encourages households to hold unproductive inflation hedges rather than deposits that would be used to finance productive investment. Hence, the accumulation of productive capital slows down, so reducing the rate of economic growth.

A common feature of the first generation financial repression models is that the growth-maximizing deposit rate of interest is the competitive free-market equilibrium rate. Even if deposit and loan rates of interest were allowed to be freely determined in a competitive environment, however, financial repression could be exerted in the Kapur-Mathieson models through reserve requirements. Evidently, inflation worsens financial repression caused by reserve requirements. The competitive free-market equilibrium deposit rate of interest may be raised, so increasing the real supply of credit and hence the rate of economic growth, without affecting the loan rate by reducing reserve requirements or by paying the competitive loan rate on required reserves.

The policy implications of these models are that economic growth can be increased by abolishing institutional interest rate ceilings, by abandoning selective or directed credit programs, by eliminating the reserve requirement tax, and by ensuring that the financial system operates competitively under conditions of free entry. Where competitive conditions cannot be achieved immediately, minimum deposit rates may be imposed to simulate the competitive outcome. Some of the practical problems involved in implementing these policy changes are considered in Parts III and IV.

The dynamic extensions illustrate the benign effects of interest rate policy as a stabilization device, when the economy is financially repressed. Although the first generation financial repression models find no benefit from financial repression under any conditions, there is a double advantage in initiating financial liberalization as part of a stabilization program. It avoids or at least ameliorates the contractionary effects of deflation produced solely through monetary deceleration. It must be stressed, however, that the advocacy of interest rate policy as a stabilization device is simply the advice to stop hitting one's head against a wall.

Kapur and Mathieson introduce the exchange rate as an additional policy instrument in their open economy models. Neither Kapur nor Mathieson discusses the reserve requirement as a fourth policy instrument in an open economy setting. In fact, reserve requirement policy may be more important when the economy is more open. The reserve requirement tax provides negative effective protection to the domestic banking industry. Foreign exchange and trade liberalization in the presence of a high required reserve ratio could destroy the domestic banking system by encouraging financial intermediation to take place abroad, where the tax can be avoided (Berger 1980). The reserve requirement is taken up again in Chapter 7.

Chapter 4

Financial Development in Endogenous Growth Models

4.1 Introduction

THE LITERATURE ON FINANCE and economic development has taken on a new lease of life over the past decade. A second generation of more complex financial growth models has emerged that incorporates both endogenous growth and endogenous financial institutions. Among the earlier contributions that provide building blocks for the work considered here are John Boyd and Edward Prescott (1986), Douglas Diamond (1984), Diamond and Philip Dybvig (1983), Robert Lucas (1988), Paul Romer (1986, 1990), and Robert Townsend (1983a, 1983b). Typically, financial intermediation is modelled explicitly rather than taken for granted or treated in simple deterministic terms, as it is in the first generation financial repression models. Various techniques, such as externalities and quality ladders, are used to model endogenous growth. However, the precise cause of endogenous growth does not affect the role of finance. Hence, it is possible to select alternative financial models for use with alternative endogenous or even nonendogenous growth models.

Second generation financial growth models include, among others, Valerie Bencivenga and Bruce Smith (1991, 1992, 1993), Jeremy Greenwood and Boyan Jovanovic (1990), Greenwood and Smith (1993), José De Gregorio (1992a, 1992b, 1993), Robert King and Ross Levine (1993a, 1993b), Levine (1993), Marco Pagano (1993), Nouriel Roubini and Xavier Sala-i-Martin (1992a, 1992b), Gilles Saint-Paul (1992a, 1992b), and Oren Sussman (1993). None of them attempts to combine short-run stabilization with long-run growth. All these financial development models using endogenous growth ignore the dynamic process of financial liberalization or stabilization.

4.2   Asymmetric Information and Uncertainty

To understand the second generation financial growth models, one must start first with an explanation of why financial markets differ from markets for apples, carrots, or rice. The fundamental reason why financial markets are special is because they involve delivery in the future and the future is always uncertain. In principle, financial contracts could be written to deal with all future contingencies. Such a set of state-contingent securities is known as Arrow-Debreu securities (Arrow 1953, Debreu 1959). Essentially these are a set of insurance policies, one for each possible future state of the world. In this case, there is a set of prices for insurance cover against all forms and types of uncertainty. With such insurance possibilities, everyone would be able to borrow and lend unlimited amounts at the market rate of interest. Furthermore, the interest rate would ensure optimal allocation of income between saving and consumption, as well as optimal allocation of investible funds across all potential investment projects.

For example, a farmer wishes to borrow funds to buy seed. With full and costless information about all possible future weather conditions and the probabilities attached to them, the farmer and lender can enter into a contract that specifies the payoffs under all possible future states of the world. Under competitive conditions, the lender will be able to obtain an expected return equal to the riskless interest rate. The farmer would borrow to the point at which the marginal expected return from extra investment in seed or fertilizer exactly equals the marginal cost of borrowing. Hence, the farmer invests to the point at which the marginal expected return to the investment equals the riskless interest rate.

With all potential investors bidding for funds to the point at which their marginal expected returns equal the marginal cost of borrowing, all investments would yield the same marginal expected rate of return. In this situation, there would be no higher-yielding investment projects unexploited. Hence, the allocation of investible funds would be optimal because no reallocation of funds between actual or potential investment projects could increase total income; allocation is Pareto efficient.

An additional feature of the Arrow-Debreu world is that the source of funds and the types of financial contracts are irrelevant, as is the farmer's balance sheet position. The farmer can expect to be just as well off by issuing equity, borrowing, or using internal funds. If the farmer borrows, this can free up internal funds for lending at the same expected rate of return as the cost of borrowing. In this world, transaction costs are zero.

The Arrow-Debreu solution involving a complete set of financial markets for each possible state of the world can exist only if information about all possible future states of the world is freely available and easily interpretable; monitoring must also be costless. Since this is never the case, financial markets fail to provide insurance against all possible future states of the world.

Because some risks are uninsurable, borrowing possibilities are not unlimited for everyone. Hence, marginal expected returns to different investments will not all be equated. Furthermore, some high-yielding investment opportunities may not be exploited because information is too costly to obtain.

One problem of costly information involves monitoring costs. To ensure that all conditions of a state-contingent contract are observed, the lender must monitor the behavior of the borrower. In the previous example, the farmer agrees to exert a given amount of effort and resources to the investment project. However, the farmer has an incentive to use less labor and resources than agreed and to blame the lower output on bad weather. Hence, the lender must monitor the farmer to ensure that all terms and conditions of the contract are honored. In some circumstances, monitoring costs may be so high that the borrower and lender will be unable to reach a mutually beneficial agreement. Hence, marginal expected returns to investment need not be equated.

Finance and financial institutions become relevant in a world of positive information, transaction, and monitoring costs. If monitoring costs are high, a simple debt instrument may dominate a more complicated state-contingent contract that resembles equity. By ignoring all contingencies, however, debt can lead to insolvency, a situation in which the borrower's net worth is no longer positive. The lender may reduce risk from default by considering a potential borrower's balance sheet and taking collateral, rationing the borrower by providing less than requested, or restricting the maturity of the loan.

4.3   Effects of Financial Intermediaries on Portfolio Choice

One way of showing how financial intermediaries can offer higher expected returns is to construct a model in which individuals can choose between unproductive assets (consumer goods or commodity money) and an investment in a firm. The investment in a firm takes time to become productive and so is illiquid. However, the expected return from a two-period investment in a firm is greater than the return from an inventory of consumer goods or currency. Uncertainty may force some individuals to liquidate or abandon their investments in firms after only one period. In such case, they would be worse off than had they held solely an inventory of consumer goods or currency (Bencivenga and Smith 1991, 1992; Greenwood and Smith 1993; Levine 1993). Individuals may also be deterred from investing in a firm by productivity risk; some firms do better than others (King and Levine 1993b).

Without banks, individuals must allocate their portfolios between capital and currency to maximize expected utility. Although they know the probability of the event which could make a productive investment worthless, their choice will also be affected by their degree of risk aversion. Those with greater risk aversion will choose a higher proportion of currency than those with less risk aversion. Any productive investment bears some risk of becoming worthless.

Suppose that individuals start with an endowment of $100 and face the choice of holding currency or investing in a firm which will produce $4 for each $1 invested after two periods but zero if liquidated after one period. If the probability of premature liquidation or abandonment is 0.5, the expected return from each $1 invested in a firm is $2 or 100 percent. Since there is a 50 percent chance of getting nothing, however, any risk aversion would dictate that some currency should be held to reduce the degree of possible destitution. Exactly how much currency to hold depends on the individual's utility function. Unless the entire portfolio is held in the form of currency, there is a risk that some productive capital will be wasted.

Bencivenga and Smith (1991, 1992), Greenwood and Smith (1993), and Levine (1993) embed the Diamond-Dybvig (1983) model of financial intermediation in an overlapping generations model with production and capital accumulation. Here young individuals work only in the first period of their lives for a real wage w_t and consume only in periods 2 and 3. All young individuals have utility functions of the form:

$$u(c_1, c_2, c_3, \phi) = -\frac{(c_2 + \phi c_3)^{-\varepsilon}}{\varepsilon}, \qquad (4.1)$$

where $\varepsilon > -1$ and ϕ equals 1 with probability π and 0 with probability $1-\pi$.[1] Under these assumptions, young individuals allocate their total earnings in period 1 between currency, capital, and deposits. This implies that the saving ratio is constant and invariant to changing financial conditions.

Type A individuals live three periods, while type B individuals live only two periods. At the beginning of age 2, individuals discover whether they are type A individuals and will live to operate firms for two periods; the probability is π. Type B individuals maximize their utilities by consuming all their wealth before the end of age 2. Since type B investors can operate their firms for only one period, they lose any capital investments they may have made.

With the introduction of banks, individuals can hold deposits which banks then invest in currency and capital. As cooperative institutions, banks choose their deposit rates in the form of payments to be made per unit of deposit, r_1 and r_2 for deposits of one- and two-period maturity, and their reserve ratio $1-q$ to maximize the expected utility of a representative depositor. Provided the return on capital exceeds the return on currency, young individuals hold all their initial wealth in the form of bank deposits. Type B individuals withdraw all their deposits at the beginning of age 2 to consume all their savings during their last period. Type A individuals choose to keep all their deposits in the bank for the higher level of consumption this will allow at age 3.

---

[1] Greenwood and Smith (1993) specify $u(c_1, c_2, c_3, \phi) = -[(1-\phi)c_2 + \phi c_3]^{-\varepsilon}/\varepsilon$ as the utility function rather than $u(c_1, c_2, c_3, \phi) = -(c_2 + \phi c_3)^{-\varepsilon}/\varepsilon$.

Production at age 3 is the culmination of a two-step process. First, each unit of investment at time t yields R units of capital at time $t+2$. An individual entrepreneur holding k_t of capital at time t then produces consumer goods by combining capital and labor in the production function:

$$y_t = \bar{k}_t^\lambda k_t^\theta L_t^{1-\theta}, \tag{4.2}$$

where $\bar{k}_t$ is the average capital stock per entrepreneur and is responsible for the externality effect enabling endogenous growth (Bencivenga and Smith 1991, 197–198).

Under competitive conditions, labor demand by each firm can be expressed:

$$L_t = k_t[(1 - \theta)\bar{k}_t^\lambda / w_t]^{1/\theta}, \tag{4.3}$$

while labor supply to each firm is $1/\pi$, since only the fraction π of the population survives to operate firms. As all firms are identical, the market equilibrium wage is

$$w_t = \bar{k}_t(1 - \theta)\pi^\theta. \tag{4.4}$$

Finally, the expected return to capital is $\theta\bar{k}_t^\lambda k_t^\theta L_t^{1-\theta} = \theta\bar{k}_t^\lambda k_t[(1-\theta)\bar{k}_t^\lambda / w_t]^\omega$, where $\omega = (1 - \theta)/\theta$.

The banks' maximization problem can be illustrated in the simplest case of logarithmic preferences ($\varepsilon = 0$). In this case $u(c_1, c_2, c_3) = \ln(c_2 + \phi c_3)$. Although banks must recognize that more capital investment raises wages as well as profits, w_t is treated here as exogenous. If the price level is constant, the real return from holding currency is zero. Now the banks' maximization problem can be expressed:

$$\text{Maximize} \quad (1 - \pi) \ln r_1 + \pi \ln r_2, \tag{4.5}$$

$$\text{subject to} \quad (1 - \pi)r_1 = 1 - q; \tag{4.6}$$

$$\pi r_2 = Rq. \tag{4.7}$$

Since type A individuals will postpone all their consumption to period 3, expected utility of young depositors is simply the sum of the logarithms of expected consumption in period 2 and expected consumption in period 3. The resource constraints indicate that banks can pay out to type B individuals who want to withdraw their deposits after one period an amount equal to their holdings of currency reserves. Premature liquidation of capital is pointless because it does not increase the resources available for distribution to type B depositors. Funds that are not held as reserves are invested in capital yielding R. The solution to this particular constrained maximization problem is $q = \pi$, implying $r_1 = 1$ and $r_2 = R$. In other words, type B depositors simply get their deposits back, while type A depositors obtain the return R on the banks' capital investment.

Neither type A nor type B individuals could do better by holding any combination of currency and capital rather than by holding deposits. Individuals holding 100 percent of their wealth in reserves would achieve r_1 if they turn out to be type B, but less than r_2 if they turn out to be type A. Conversely, individuals holding 100 percent of their wealth in capital would receive zero if they turn out to be type B and r_2 if they turn out to be type A. All diversified portfolios yield returns less than r_1 for individuals who turn out to be type B and less than r_2 if they turn out to be type A.

By exploiting the law of large numbers, banks ensure that they never have to liquidate capital prematurely. They can guarantee returns of r_1 and r_2 because they know exactly what proportion of depositors will withdraw deposits after one and after two periods. Hence banks avoid the uncertainty which leads to resource misallocation by individuals. By ensuring that capital is never wasted, financial intermediation may produce higher capital/labor ratios and higher rates of economic growth.

Whether or not this happens depends on individuals' degree of risk aversion. As ε approaches -1 individuals become increasingly risk neutral. With completely risk neutral depositors, banks would invest all deposits in capital (Greenwood and Smith 1993, 14). If ε is sufficiently high, implying sufficient risk aversion, individuals would hold a higher proportion of their wealth in the form of currency $1-q^*$ than the banks' reserve ratio $1-q$. Clearly, this would ensure that growth was lower in the absence of financial intermediaries. The condition for faster growth from intermediation is less restrictive than $q > q^*$, where q^* is the ratio of capital to wealth held by individuals in the absence of banks. Because capital held by type B individuals is wasted, the condition for higher growth with a banking system is $q/\pi > q^*$.

Greenwood and Smith (1993, 19) show that the existence of a stock market increases the growth rate in comparison to a situation with no financial intermediation. This is simply because stock markets can prevent premature capital liquidation by enabling individuals to sell firms that they will be unable to operate in period 3. However, when a stock market is compared to a banking system, relative growth rates again depend on the degree of risk aversion. With risk aversion greater than that given by the logarithmic utility function, banks would hold a higher proportion of reserves than individuals would in the absence of banks ($1-q > 1-q^*$ or $q < q^*$). In this case, a stock market provides higher growth than a banking system. Once stock markets and banks are allowed to coexist, the growth rate can be higher than it would be with only banks or a stock market.

Banks rely on the law of large numbers to estimate deposit withdrawals which are unpredictable individually but deterministic for the economy as a whole. By engaging in maturity intermediation, financial institutions offer liquidity to savers and, at the same time, longer-term funds to investors. In so doing, they stimulate productive investment by persuading savers to switch from unproductive investment in tangible assets to productive investment in firms. Levine (1991) and Saint-Paul (1992a) demonstrate that stock markets can also encourage a higher proportion of productive investment by enabling individuals to diversify away idiosyncratic risk of individual projects, so encouraging capital ownership and investment in firms.

One of the more unrealistic assumptions in the Diamond-Dybvig models developed by Bencivenga and Smith (1991, 1992, 1993) and Greenwood and Smith (1993) is that banks are established by and deal with only one generation of individuals. Overlapping generations make it unnecessary for banks to hold any currency at all. Maturing capital from deposits placed by generation 0 could be used to pay out withdrawals of type B individuals of generation 1. Alternatively, the introduction of a stock market would enable banks of one generation to trade with banks of another generation, so releasing them from the obligation to hold reserves for type B individuals.

In the Diamond-Dybvig model liquidity risk manifests itself in period 2. Type B individuals now find that they want to consume all their remaining wealth in this period because they will not survive after period 2. Stock markets enable type B individuals to sell shares in period 2 to type A individuals who now realize that they hold unnecessarily large amounts of currency. Within some bounds, therefore, shares can be traded without any removal of physical resources from firms. However, each financial transaction incurs a fixed cost. If this fixed transaction cost is high enough, no one will use the stock market and the economy returns to financial autarky. "Thus, public policies that raise transactions costs could inhibit the formation and functioning of capital markets" (Levine 1993, 122–123).

Those who live two periods may make two financial transactions, while those who live three periods may make three (one to buy some shares in period 1, a second to buy more shares in period 2, and a third to sell shares in period 3). If individuals could place their savings in a bank instead of holding shares and stocks of consumer goods, the number of financial transactions can be reduced; all individuals need now make only two financial transactions, as in the Diamond-Dybvig model. The bank now diversifies its portfolio across firms, enabling it to offer a positive return on deposits in both periods 2 and 3. If banks offer a return in period 2 that is exactly the same as the expected return from equities in the economy with only a stock market, they can offer a net return in period 3 that exceeds the expected return in the simpler economy because fewer financial transactions are needed (Levine 1993, 124). Because transaction costs are reduced on average, more individuals make financial transactions, excess inventories of currency or consumer goods are reduced, and the growth rate is increased by the greater volume of resources invested in firms.

Stock markets, banks, and mutual funds reduce liquidity and productivity risks. Stock markets enable individuals to sell shares in a firm to other individuals rather than having to remove physical resources from the firm. Banks and mutual funds diversify their portfolios and hence reduce productivity risk. Individuals can also use stock markets directly to diversify, but financial institutions can reduce the transaction costs of this. Reduced liquidity and productivity risks encourage individuals to invest more in firms. In various ways, therefore, financial institutions can encourage individuals to invest more resources, either directly or indirectly, in firms. More investment in firms raises the rate of economic growth.

Those who do not use the Diamond-Dybvig model of financial intermediation find other ways in which banks can stimulate endogenous growth. For example, Greenwood and Jovanovic (1990) stress the role of financial intermediaries in pooling funds and acquiring information that enables them to allocate capital to its highest valued use, so raising the average return to capital. Specifically, Greenwood and Jovanovic (1990) allow capital to be invested in safe, low-yielding investments or risky, high-yielding investments. Risk is created by both aggregate and project-specific shocks. Individuals cannot differentiate between the two types of shock.

With large portfolio holdings, however, financial intermediaries can experiment with a small sample of high-yielding projects to determine the state of the world. With this expenditure on the collection and analysis of information, financial intermediaries determine their investment strategies in the knowledge of the current-period aggregate shock. Were a negative shock to make the high-risk investments less profitable than the low-risk investments, financial intermediaries would invest only in the low-risk projects. Provided the costs of information collection and analysis are sufficiently small, the ability to choose the appropriate set of projects in the knowledge of a given aggregate shock raises the expected return on the intermediaries' portfolios above that of individuals who must choose one or the other technology without any information about the aggregate shock.

King and Levine (1993b) suggest that financial institutions play a key role in evaluating prospective entrepreneurs and financing the most promising ones: "Better financial systems improve the probability of successful innovation and thereby accelerate economic growth" (King and Levine 1993b, 513). Following Joseph Schumpeter (1912), they stress that "financial institutions play an active role in evaluating, managing, and funding the entrepreneurial activity that leads to *productivity growth*. Indeed, we believe that our mechanism is the channel by which finance must have its dominant effect, due to the central role of productivity growth in development" (King and Levine 1993b, 515).

4.4 Financial Development and Endogenous Growth

In a typical endogenous growth model, more resources kept in firms during the two-period production process increase the human capital of each worker "independently of that individual's own investment of resources" (Levine

1993, 114–115). An individual's accumulation of human capital depends on (a) interaction with others in a firm; (b) the amount of resources the individual invests; and (c) the average amount of resources invested and retained in the firm for two periods.

The externality implies that liquidation of an investment by an individual member of a firm after one period reduces the rate of human capital accumulation and hence slows down the rate of technological progress; the rate of economic growth declines. The externality also implies that the amount of resources invested in firms in competitive equilibrium is less than optimal. Although individuals find it prohibitively expensive to identify externalities and to mobilize resources, such an activity could be profitable for an investment bank (Bencivenga and Smith 1991, 199). By encouraging investment in firms, such an institution would accelerate the rate of economic growth.

Authors using the Diamond-Dybvig framework develop a two-stage production process outlined in section 4.3. The simple story is that inventors, enjoying free access to the technical information on all existing designs, discover new designs or techniques in stage 1. This is the externality effect. Patents enable designers to sell the exclusive rights for the production of their new design. Machines incorporating the new design are then rented by producers of consumer goods. Growth occurs by increasing the range of machinery in use.

The main feature of endogenous growth models is that a broadly defined concept of the economy's capital stock does not suffer from diminishing returns; hence growth is a positive function of the investment ratio. One approach is to broaden the concept of capital to include human capital or the state of knowledge. Equation 4.2 provides an externality effect through the average capital stock per entrepreneur that can eliminate diminishing returns in the economy as a whole. For the economy as a whole, the production function can be expressed:

$$y = Ak, \tag{4.8}$$

where y is per capita output, k is per capita capital, and A is the level of technology. With this production function, steady-state growth γ in a closed economy equals

$$\gamma = sA - \delta, \tag{4.9}$$

where s is the saving ratio and δ is the rate of capital depreciation. Here an increase in the saving-investment ratio raises the rate of economic growth.

Another of the more unrealistic assumptions in the Diamond-Dybvig models is the absence of financial intermediation costs. Pagano (1993) rectifies this by introducing costly financial development into the endogenous growth model characterized by equation 4.8. He specifies that a fraction $1-\mu$ of saving is lost in the intermediation process. Hence, equation 4.9 can be rewritten:

$$\gamma = s\mu A - \delta. \tag{4.10}$$

Hence, financial development could affect growth by influencing A, s, or μ.

King and Levine (1993b) provide an alternative way of including finance in endogenous growth models by separating the economy into households, financial institutions, and firms. In the King-Levine model, potential entrepreneurs possess the capability to manage an innovative project leading to productivity growth with probability α. Whether or not an entrepreneur is capable of managing an innovative project can be ascertained for a fixed cost f. Financial institutions invest f for this information, provided the expected return from the evaluation strategy exceeds the expected return from financing the investment blind; the blind investment strategy involves financing both capable and incapable entrepreneurs. Assuming that this condition holds, the financial institution now provides capable entrepreneurs with funds to finance x hours of labor for the project.

Even if the entrepreneur is capable, there is still only a probability ϖ that the project will succeed. Success or failure is revealed after these x hours of labor have been devoted to the project. Finance of these innovative activities is provided by financial institutions rather than by the entrepreneur for two reasons. First, the labor requirement x could involve a minimum number of employees that would cost more than the entrepreneur's wealth. Second, the risk of innovation failure can be completely diversified. Hence, a large financial intermediary can provide incomes with certainty to all members of the innovation team including the entrepreneur (King and Levine 1993b, 519).

Financial intermediaries in this model could be investment banks or venture capital firms that hold equity stakes in firms. Whatever their precise form, these financial institutions provide "research, evaluative, and monitoring services more effectively and less expensively than individual investors; they also are better at mobilizing and providing appropriate financing to entrepreneurs than individuals. Overall, the evaluation and sorting of entrepreneurs lowers the cost of investing in productivity enhancement and stimulates economic growth" (King and Levine 1993b, 515). In competitive equilibrium, the expected value from rating prospective entrepreneurs will equal its cost.

King and Levine (1993b) adopt the productivity model of Gene Grossman and Elhanan Helpman (1991). Innovations reduce production costs and involve moving up a product's technology ladder. Each successful innovation gives the entrepreneur a stream of monopoly rents, but inflicts a capital loss on the previous market leader. The current leader in each industry sets the price of its product equal to its rival's unit costs. The probability of innovation in any particular industry Π is proportional to the number of entrepreneurs trying to improve this product. With e entrepreneurs, $\Pi = \varpi e$. Since productivity growth depends on innovation, the productivity growth rate is a function of the number of entrepreneurs, since more entrepreneurs increases the probability of an innovation. "Better financial services expand the scope and improve the efficiency of innovative activity; they thereby accelerate economic growth" (King and Levine 1993b, 517). Roubini and Sala-i-Martin (1992b, 11) reach a similar conclusion with a production function of the form $Y_t = \phi(A)K_t$, where Y is output, K is a broad measure of capital that includes human capital, and A is related to the level of financial development.

In general equilibrium, King and Levine (1993b, 523–527) show that there is an ambiguous relationship between the real interest rate r and growth γ on the production side; in Romer's (1990) model it is negative. Using common elements in the King-Levine and Romer models, immortal households possess a time-separable utility function $U = \int_0^\infty u(c_{t+s})e^{-\nu s}ds$ and a momentary utility function $u(c_t) = (c_t^{1-\sigma} - 1)/(1 - \sigma)$, where $1/\sigma$ is the intertemporal elasticity of substitution in consumption or σ is the coefficient of relative risk aversion ($\sigma > 0$). Households maximize utility subject to their common rate of time preference ν.

This preference-side relationship produces a positive relationship between γ and r: $\gamma = (r - \alpha)/\sigma$. The market equilibrium growth rate that satisfies both the production and preference sides of the model is raised by higher values of the monopoly markup, the invention productivity parameter, and the total stock of human capital. The growth rate is also increased by lower values of ν and σ.

Figure 4.1 shows the interaction between the preference-side or upward-sloping Ramsey curve (Ramsey 1928) and the production-side or downward-sloping Romer curve (Romer 1990).[2] A higher degree of impatience ν shifts the Ramsey curve upward, while greater relative risk aversion σ steepens this curve by rotating it around its vertical intercept. In both cases, the equilibrium interest rate is raised and the equilibrium growth rate reduced.

The cost of financial intermediation is introduced by the dashed or net Romer curve which is flatter than the zero-cost or gross Romer curve. This cost produces a wedge W between the return to savers r_d and the cost to investors r_ℓ as shown in Figure 4.1. Households can save only in the form of bank deposits and firms borrow from the banks to buy innovation blueprints or to finance investment. The intermediation cost reduces growth from γ^* to γ_w. Both Pagano (1993) and Sussman (1993) model financial development as a process of reducing this wedge, so accelerating the rate of economic growth by steepening the Romer curve.

The cost of financial intermediation is not necessarily a deadweight loss. Indeed, Angel de la Fuente and José Maria Marin (1993) show that better monitoring increases the probability that the banks obtain correct information. With a continuous cost function of this kind, monitoring costs are increased to the point at which the marginal benefit from the better information equals the marginal cost of additional monitoring. Figure 4.2 shows the impact of extra monitoring costs on the gross and net Romer curves. In this case, a greater intermediation wedge ($X > W$) actually increases the growth rate because

---

[2]I am grateful to Peter Sinclair for providing his lecture notes on this topic.

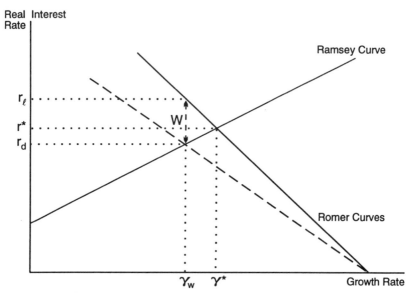

Figure 4.1. Interest and Growth in Ramsey-Romer Model

the gross Romer curve is steepened through additional monitoring by more than the net curve. Hence the net Romer curve with higher costs of financial intermediation lies above the net Romer curve with lower intermediation costs.

The Fuente-Marin model makes the optimal amount of monitoring depend on relative factor prices. The optimal intensity of monitoring increases as the capital/labor ratio rises and labor becomes relatively more expensive. This change in relative factor prices is associated with an increase in the rate of innovation which tends to offset any tendency for growth to slow down as capital accumulates. "Hence, real growth feeds upon and contributes to a smooth process of financial development which takes the form of a gradual improvement in the operation of capital markets, rather than the sudden jump from nonexistent to fully developed banks or stock markets that we find in some of the literature" (Fuente and Marin 1993, 2).

De Gregorio (1992a) develops a third way of introducing finance into endogenous growth models by making the cost of delivering a unit of goods by firms a decreasing function of real money balances. For consumers, intertemporal utility maximization involves a choice between consumption, leisure, and shopping. Shopping time is reduced by higher money balances. In this way, changing financial conditions can affect both the demand for and the supply of labor, which in turn affects the productivity of capital through an externality effect.

In all these models, growth rate comparisons can be made between economies with and without banks. "Relative to the situation in the absence of

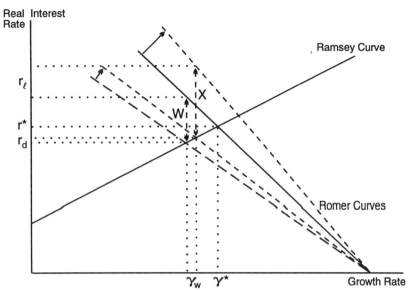

Figure 4.2. Optimum Intermediation Wedge in Ramsey-Romer Model

banks (financial autarky), banks reduce liquid reserve holdings by the economy as a whole, and also reduce the liquidation of productive capital. Then, with an externality in production ... higher equilibrium growth rates will be observed in economies with an active intermediary sector" (Bencivenga and Smith 1991, 196).

4.5 Financial Repression in Endogenous Growth Models

In the King-Levine (1993b) model, financial sector taxation always reduces the real interest rate for any given growth rate on the production side. The higher cost of evaluating and financing entrepreneurs lowers the rate of return for each growth rate, so making the net Romer curve flatter in Figure 4.1 (King and Levine 1993b, 527). It follows that financial repression in the form of discriminatory taxes on financial intermediation reduces the growth rate. Financial sector taxes are equivalent to taxes on innovative activity, since they reduce the net returns that financial intermediaries gain from financing successful entrepreneurs. The growth rate is also reduced by the imposition of credit ceilings. More generally, "financial repression ... reduces the services provided by the financial system to savers, entrepreneurs, and producers; it thereby impedes innovative activity and slows economic growth" (King and Levine 1993b, 517). Figure 4.1 also suggests that, while monopoly profit speeds innovation by firms and so increases the growth rate, monopoly in the banking sector reduces growth by increasing the wedge between borrowing and lending rates of interest.

Other government interventions such as an increase in corporate profits tax or weakened property rights also reduce the size of the financial sector: "With a lower return to innovation, less evaluation of entrepreneurs and external finance of projects is required. Specifically, lower returns to innovation cause entrepreneurs to demand fewer financial services" (King and Levine 1993b, 527).

Inflation itself can also be classified as a manifestation of financial repression in that it constitutes a tax on money holders. De Gregorio (1992a) shows that higher inflation raises nominal interest rates and reduces real money balances, which increases shopping time and so increases the effective cost of consumption. The consequent substitution from consumption to leisure reduces labor supply. Labor demand is also reduced by inflation because firms have to use more inputs on transactions rather than on production and this lowers their rate of return. The reduction in employment reduces the productivity of capital even if the rate of investment remains constant (De Gregorio 1992a, 421–422). Hence, the growth rate is reduced by higher inflation. It could also be portrayed as increasing the costs of financial intermediation in Figure 4.1 for any banking system that holds currency reserves. An increased required reserve ratio has a similar effect.

After constructing their endogenous growth model, Roubini and Sala-i-Martin (1992b, 17) conclude: "In order to increase the revenue from money creation, short sighted governments may choose to increase per capita real money demand by repressing the financial sector. As a side effect this policy will tend to reduce the amount of services the financial sector provides to the whole economy and, given the total stock of inputs, the total amount of output will be reduced. This will reduce the asymptotic marginal product of the inputs that can be accumulated (such as private physical, private human or public capital) and, consequently, the steady-state rate of growth." This is the growth-reducing impact of financial restriction discussed in Chapter 2 that also flattens the net Romer curve in Figure 4.1.

While financial repression and financial restriction flatten the net Romer curve, discriminatory taxation of the financial system is unlikely to steepen the gross Romer curve. An increased wedge produced by such taxation would only steepen the gross Romer curve if the government used the revenue more productively than the private sector. If this possibility is ruled out, the increased wedge created by financial repression and restriction cannot increase the growth rate.

Endogenous growth in all these models magnifies and prolongs the effects of financial conditions. If financial development improves overall productivity, discriminatory taxation of commercial banks, investment banks, mutual funds, and stock markets through high reserve requirements, interest and credit ceilings, directed credit programs, and inflation reduces the growth rate by impeding financial development. Indeed, the existence of externalities implies that welfare may be improved through some public subsidy of financial intermediation.

4.6   Emergence and Development of Financial Structures

Financial institutions emerge to reduce liquidity and productivity risks for savers. Individuals can reduce the number of transactions, so economizing on transaction costs, by holding their savings in a bank rather than in a diversified portfolio of direct financial instruments (equities and bonds). At the same time, they may achieve a preferred tradeoff between liquidity and return. Financial intermediaries also exploit economies of scale in evaluating and monitoring borrowers. Financial intermediaries are the only source of external funds for many small- and medium-sized businesses because information costs are prohibitively high for them to issue equity or bonds.

The literature on finance in endogenous growth models suggests various rationales for the existence of financial institutions. The main ingredients are some form of uncertainty, costly information, transaction costs, and economies of scale in information collection. However, none of these can explain the emergence and spread of financial intermediaries during the process of economic development. Something else is needed to show how rising incomes can stimulate financial intermediation while simultaneously financial intermediaries can stimulate growth by raising the saving ratio and the productivity of investment.

Greenwood and Jovanovic (1990), Greenwood and Smith (1993), and Levine (1993) adopt the simple device of a fixed entry fee or fixed transaction cost reminiscent of the early work on demand for money by William Baumol (1952) and employed more recently by Townsend (1978). This enables financial development to occur as per capita incomes and per capita wealth rise. Because there are fixed entry costs to individuals who wish to use financial intermediaries, individuals use them only after their incomes and wealth reach some minimum level. Hence, in the early stages of economic development there are virtually no financial institutions.

At some intermediate stage of development, however, richer individuals find it worthwhile to pay the entry fee in order to reap the higher returns offered by the financial intermediaries. Over time, an increasing proportion of the population finds that income levels have risen to the point at which it becomes profitable to use financial institutions. Eventually everyone is rich enough to benefit from financial intermediary services and the financial sector no longer grows faster than other parts of the economy. Levine (1993) extends this idea by introducing fixed entry fees or transaction costs of increasing magnitude for more sophisticated financial services. In this way, a simple financial system becomes more elaborate as per capita incomes and wealth rise.

Finally, Levine (1993, 125) shows that more sophisticated financial institutions such as investment banks may form to "research production processes and mobilize resources to take full advantage of profitable production opportunities." There is a critical level of per capita income at which such financial institutions emerge: "If per capita income is sufficiently high, agents choose to purchase services that involve researching firms, certifying the existence of worthy projects, and mobilizing resources to exploit fully investment opportunities. If per capita income is not sufficiently high, agents find that the additional returns generated by these financial services are not worth the cost" and so they stick to the financial institutions that simply reduce transaction costs (Levine 1993, 126). Hence, Levine's model augments the Greenwood-Jovanovic (1990) model to explain not only how financial intermediation affects growth but also how income levels can affect the structure of the financial system.

4.7 Summary

In contrast to the McKinnon-Shaw models, the endogenous growth models surveyed in this chapter provide a rationale for financial intermediation and explain how financial intermediaries emerge. Financial systems can encourage individuals to release their savings for productive investment by reducing their holdings of unproductive tangible assets and can also improve the allocation of investible funds in several ways: pooling funds and acquiring information that enables them to allocate capital to its highest valued use, so raising the average return to capital; providing maturity intermediation by offering liquidity to savers and, at the same time, longer-term funds to investors, so stimulating productive investment; enabling individuals to diversify away idiosyncratic risk of individual projects, so encouraging capital ownership and productive investment; evaluating investment projects and valuing the expected profits from specific innovative activities. In these ways, financial systems can encourage portfolio allocation in favor of productive investment, so increasing both the quality and quantity of productive investment.

Not only do endogenous financial growth models provide rigorous analysis of household portfolio behavior under uncertainty, they also demonstrate how financial intermediation resulting from this portfolio behavior can accelerate the rate of economic growth. Here, the insights from endogenous growth models are combined with the behavior of financial intermediaries to show that increased quality or quantity of investment in firms resulting from financial intermediation can produce externalities that make all firms more productive. Because these externalities ensure that capital is not subject to diminishing marginal returns for the economy as a whole, improved financial intermediation increases the rate of economic growth. However, since these models only investigate steady states, they cannot provide any guidance about the dynamic transition paths that might occur when financial conditions are deliberately changed.

Chapter 5

Financial Repression and Capital Inflows

5.1 Introduction

IF FINANCIAL REPRESSION INCREASES the current account deficit, it may well accelerate the buildup of foreign debt. Some of my own work adapts the McKinnon-Shaw framework to analyze the destructive effects of foreign debt accumulation experienced by several developing countries since the mid-1970s (Fry 1989a, 1993a, 1993c). Financial repression can also exacerbate the growth-inhibiting effects of foreign debt accumulation in developing countries for reasons discussed in previous chapters.

The effect of the real deposit rate of interest on national saving is ambiguous, given possible counteracting income and substitution effects. In an open economy, however, financial repression may affect *measured* national saving through unambiguous portfolio shifts rather than true saving effects. If illegal capital flight takes place through underinvoicing exports and overinvoicing imports, the measured balance-of-payments deficit on current account rises when capital flight increases. Since national saving is measured by subtracting the current account deficit from domestic investment, it will fall when the measured current account deficit rises. If such illegal capital flight is influenced in part by relative yields on domestic and foreign financial assets, measured national saving or national saving actually available to finance domestic investment would be affected positively by an increase in the domestic real interest rate.

After some of the negative consequences of excessive foreign debt accumulation emerged in the early 1980s, many developing countries took a fresh look at their policies towards foreign direct investment (FDI). Inflows of FDI can offer an alternative way of financing a current account deficit. Since 1982 foreign capital inflows to developing countries have declined and world real interest rates have increased. It is against this background that FDI has been viewed by some as a panacea for declining domestic investment and higher costs of borrowing abroad.

Foreign direct investment appears attractive because it involves a risk-sharing relationship with investors from the source country. Such risk-sharing does not exist in the formal contractual arrangements for foreign loans. Foreign direct investment appears particularly attractive when existing stocks are low. Low stocks of foreign-owned capital imply low flows of repatriated profits. Over time, however, success in attracting FDI increases this counterflow, which could exceed the alternative flow of interest payments in the longer run. Clearly, therefore, the question of the cost of FDI to reduce risk must be addressed in any evaluation of the benefits to be derived from substituting FDI for foreign borrowing.

The framework used here to analyze the impact of foreign debt accumulation in developing countries can be adapted to analyze the effects of FDI. The macroeconomic model presented in this chapter focuses on the role of saving and investment in determining the current account. It also examines the feedback effects of foreign debt accumulation and FDI flows on saving and investment. Section 5.2 outlines the small-scale macroeconomic model of a small semi-open financially repressed developing country. The subsequent sections examine the constituent behavioral equations that determine saving, investment, export supply, import demand, economic growth, inflation, and a monetary policy reaction function. While the models presented so far in this book are designed to provide theoretical rather than empirical insights, the model developed in this chapter is designed explicitly for empirical testing.

5.2 A Model of Foreign Debt Accumulation

The balance-of-payments accounts show that current account deficits are financed by capital inflows or decreases in official reserves. One way of presenting this identity is:[1]

$$CAY + KAY \equiv \Delta RY, \qquad (5.1)$$

where CAY is the current account as a proportion of GNP, KAY is the capital account ratio, and ΔRY is the change in official reserves also expressed as a ratio of GNP. If the change in official reserves is unaffected, an increased capital inflow is matched by a smaller current account surplus or a larger current account deficit.

Capital inflows allow domestic investment to exceed national saving when they finance a current account deficit. Domestic investment equals national saving plus the current account deficit or foreign saving, as shown by the national income definition of the balance of payments on current account:

$$IY = SNY + SFY \qquad (5.2)$$

---

[1]This identity ignores errors and omissions.

or

$$CAY = SNY - IY, \tag{5.3}$$

where SFY is foreign saving, which equals the current account deficit and so is equal but of opposite sign to CAY, the balance of payments on current account, SNY is national saving, and IY is domestic investment, all divided by GNP.[2] Hence, capital inflows that finance the current account deficit can increase investment and the rate of economic growth.

The current account ratio can also be defined as the export ratio XY plus the ratio of net factor income from abroad to GNP $NFIY$ minus the import ratio IMY:

$$CAY \equiv XY + NFIY - IMY. \tag{5.4}$$

If capital inflows increase capital formation in the host country, the increased investment could involve increased imports of raw materials or capital equipment. Alternatively, it could reduce exports by diverting them into the additional investment. In either case, the current account must deteriorate in equation 5.4 by exactly the same amount as it does in equations 5.1 and 5.3.

The extent and financing of a current account deficit depend both on a country's desire to spend more than its income and on the willingness of the rest of the world to finance the deficit from its saving. In other words, a current account deficit is determined simultaneously by both the demand for and the supply of foreign saving. My saving-investment model of a semi-open developing economy attempts to capture the essential determinants of this interactive process.

With the assumption that foreign saving takes the form of foreign loans, my model also permits the ratio of foreign debt to GNP to converge to a constant and hence sustainable steady state. A steady state exists if a higher level of foreign indebtedness improves the current account. If foreign indebtedness reduces investment by more than it reduces saving, or raises investment by less than it raises saving, rising foreign indebtedness improves the current account and so slows down the buildup of foreign debt. Hence the model contains an informal error-correction process. The model also specifies a monetary policy reaction function, since domestic credit expansion usually worsens a current account.

The key components of this open-economy model are represented in Figure 5.1. This figure echoes Lloyd Metzler (1968) in viewing the current account deficit as the difference between domestic investment and national saving. It shows the planned levels of national saving, foreign saving, and domestic investment at different levels of real interest rates r. The domestic

---

[2]This definition of the current account ratio is derived from the national income rather than the balance-of-payments accounts. It differs from the balance-of-payments definition by excluding unrequited transfers.

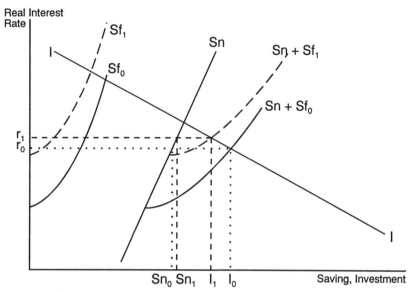

Figure 5.1. Saving, Investment, and the Current Account Deficit

investment function I slopes downwards indicating that there is more investment at lower interest rates. The national saving function Sn is nearly vertical indicating that national saving does not vary greatly with changes in the domestic real interest rate.

Most developing countries face an upward-sloping supply curve of foreign saving Sf_0. However, the effective cost at which foreign saving begins to be supplied in any particular year depends on the country's foreign debt position inherited from past borrowing. In this model, the effective cost of foreign borrowing is also the effective domestic real interest rate. At an effective interest rate of r_0, domestic investment I_0 exceeds national saving Sn_0. Hence, the inflow of foreign saving is positive and the country runs a current account deficit on its balance of payments equal to $I_0 - Sn_0$.

The accumulation of foreign debt resulting from the current account deficit in year 0 raises the foreign saving curve to Sf_1 in the next year. This change produces an effective cost of foreign borrowing of r_1 in year 1. In this case, foreign debt accumulation reduces domestic investment and raises national saving through a higher domestic real interest rate. As this process continues in subsequent years, the current account deficit declines until it reaches a steady-state equilibrium in which the foreign debt/GNP ratio is constant. This is the stabilizing financial effect of foreign debt accumulation.

Figure 5.2 illustrates the situation in a semi-open financially repressed developing economy. Here the supply of national saving is not influenced at all by the effective real interest rate r_0 or r_1 because the ceiling facing

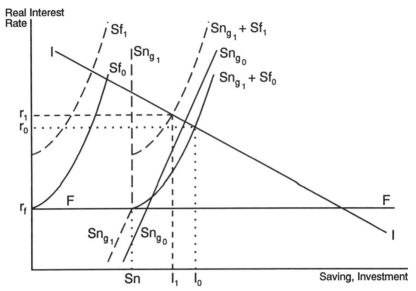

Figure 5.2. Saving, Investment, and the Current Account Deficit under Interest Rate Ceilings

savers is fixed at r_f. In this situation, the effective interest rate is higher and domestic investment is lower than they are in Figure 5.1. Furthermore, any given rise in the effective interest rate reduces the current account deficit by a smaller amount than it does in Figure 5.1. Hence, the accumulation of foreign debt builds up at a faster pace under financial repression than it does when institutional interest rates are freely determined by competitive market forces. Nevertheless, the rising effective cost of investible funds still produces the stabilizing financial effect of foreign debt accumulation illustrated in Figure 5.1.

Financial repression is shown in Figure 5.2 by a low fixed real deposit rate r_f that reduces national saving. This in turn reduces domestic investment by creating a larger current account deficit which can be financed only at a higher effective interest rate. Because the effective cost at which foreign saving begins to be supplied in any particular year depends on the country's foreign debt position inherited from past foreign borrowing, a long history of financial repression will deter domestic investment by more than a recent deterioration into that condition.

In practice, financial repression is more likely to reduce national saving by lowering the growth rate from g_0 to g_1, as shown in Figure 5.2. For reasons discussed in previous chapters, financial repression reduces the average productivity of investment which in turn reduces growth. Lower growth reduces the saving ratio. Slower growth shifts the national saving function leftwards in Figure 5.2 (as it does in Figure 2.1), so increasing the current account deficit and raising the effective interest rate. This leftward shift in the national saving function occurs whether or not national saving is influenced by the real deposit rate of interest. Whenever financial repression causes a higher effective interest rate, investment and growth decline.

Much foreign debt in developing countries takes the form of government and government-guaranteed foreign debt. The level of this type of foreign debt accumulated from past current account deficits may itself affect the position of the saving functions in Figures 5.1 and 5.2. Presumably the modern Ricardian equivalence view would hold that if households expect the existence of government-guaranteed foreign loans to necessitate government expenditure and hence higher taxation in the future, private saving would rise as more guarantees were extended. Hence the Ricardian equivalence hypothesis suggests that more foreign debt could actually raise the national saving ratio, since this *future* contingent government liability does not reduce the *current* level of government saving.

While rising government and government-guaranteed foreign debts could well lead households to anticipate higher future tax burdens for debt service and repayment, they may respond in the alternative way suggested by David Ricardo (1817, 338):

> A country which has accumulated a large debt is placed in a most artificial situation; and although the amount of taxes, and the increased price of labour, may not, and I believe does not, place it under any other disadvantage with respect to foreign countries, except the unavoidable one of paying those taxes, yet it becomes the interest of every contributor to withdraw his shoulder from the burthen, and to shift this payment from himself to another; and the temptation to remove himself and his capital to another country, where he will be exempted from such burthens, becomes at last irresistible, and overcomes the natural reluctance which every man feels to quit the place of his birth, and the scene of his early associations. A country which has involved itself in the difficulties attending this artificial system, would act wisely by ransoming itself from them, at the sacrifice of any portion of its property which might be necessary to redeem its debt.

Savers could also perceive that a high and rising foreign debt ratio may goad the government into stimulating exports, which would involve a devaluation in the real exchange rate. Indeed, a steady-state equilibrium necessitates a depreciation in the real exchange rate. In this case, the real returns on assets held abroad could be higher than the real returns on domestic assets.

Most developing countries prohibit capital outflows. Hence the removal of capital abroad takes place through overinvoicing imports and underinvoicing exports (Cuddington 1986, 38; Dooley 1986, 1988; Khan and Haque 1985; Watson et al. 1986). Typically, an exporter submits an invoice for a smaller sum than that actually received for the exports when surrendering foreign exchange to the central bank; the difference can then be deposited in the exporter's bank account abroad. Conversely, an importer submits an invoice for an amount exceeding the true cost of the imports in order to siphon the difference into his or her foreign bank account.

This method of removing capital from a country reduces measured national saving, even in the unlikely event that the true level of saving remains constant. Hence one might expect a higher value of government plus government-guaranteed foreign debt to reduce measured national saving, implying leftward shifts in the saving functions in Figure 5.1 and 5.2. Here, therefore, is an explanation of a *negative* effect of foreign debt on the current account; an increase in foreign debt can worsen the current account. This is the destabilizing fiscal effect of foreign debt accumulation which may or may not outweigh the stabilizing financial effect of foreign debt accumulation discussed above.

The magnitude of capital flight caused by a buildup of foreign debt can be, and in several developing countries has been, destabilizing. Instead of an increase in foreign debt *reducing* domestic investment and *increasing* national saving, the foreign debt buildup shifts the national saving function to the left; hence the current account deficit *increases*. Real interest rates can reach, and in several developing countries have reached, astronomical levels without reducing the current account deficit.

The variable representing this foreign debt factor $DETY_{t-1}$ is last year's stock of government plus government-guaranteed foreign debt converted from dollars to local currency divided by last year's GNP. In addition to its effect on the position of the national saving function, $DETY_{t-1}$ also affects the supply of foreign saving. By reducing foreign saving from Sf_0 to Sf_1, a higher debt ratio produces a higher domestic real interest rate and hence a movement up the saving function in Figure 5.1. This financial or interest rate effect on saving (a movement up the saving function) can be of opposite sign to the fiscal effect of $DETY_{t-1}$ (a leftward shift in the saving function). To allow for these conflicting and possibly nonlinear influences of debt on saving, the debt/GNP ratio is used in quadratic form; the debt ratio $DETY_{t-1}$ and the debt ratio squared $DETY_{t-1}^2$ are both included to explain saving behavior.

An increase in government and government-guaranteed foreign debt may also deter domestic investment because it raises the probability of higher taxes on domestic assets in the future (Ize and Ortiz 1987). This would shift the investment function in Figures 5.1 and 5.2 to the left. Anne Krueger (1987, 163) concludes: "When debt-service obligations are high, increasing public resources to service debt will be likely to reduce incentives and resources available to the private sector sufficiently to preclude the necessary investment response." Jeffrey Sachs (1986, 1989, 1990) documents the deleterious effects of the foreign debt buildup on investment in Latin America.

In its early stages, however, foreign debt buildup could actually stimulate investment. Entrepreneurs may perceive that there would be profitable investment opportunities in export activities as debt service mounts and the government is forced to intensify its drive to raise foreign exchange earnings. Because there could again be conflicting effects of debt on investment, the foreign debt ratio $DETY_{t-1}$ and the foreign debt ratio squared $DETY_{t-1}^2$ are both included as determinants of investment behavior.

An alternative measure of a country's foreign indebtedness can be estimated by cumulating the current account deficit over time. In this case, the balance-of-payments definition of the current account, which subtracts unrequited transfers from the measured deficit, must be used. The dollar stock of *net* foreign liabilities derived in this way can then be converted into domestic currency and expressed as a ratio of GNP. Perhaps these foreign liabilities exert the stabilizing influence of foreign debt buildup illustrated in Figures 5.1 and 5.2. Furthermore, as net foreign liabilities increase and net wealth declines, higher cumulated net foreign liabilities could reduce consumption and so shift the national saving function to the right (Winters 1987). In other words, these foreign liabilities could have the opposite effect to government and government-guaranteed foreign debt on the current account. The variable representing these net foreign liabilities FLY_{t-1} is last year's stock of cumulated *net* foreign liabilities converted into domestic currency and divided by last year's GNP.

The main problem in estimating the model sketched in Figures 5.1 and 5.2 is that effective costs of foreign borrowing or domestic shadow interest rates r_0 and r_1 are unobservable. As Vassilis Hajivassiliou (1987, 205) points out: "The spread over the London interbank offer rate (LIBOR) does not perform the key role of clearing the market for international loans. Instead allocation of scarce credit among third world countries is fundamentally carried out through quantity offers and requests." To overcome this difficulty, a reduced-form equation for r can be derived from simple demand and supply functions for foreign saving. The demand for foreign saving equals the saving-investment gap, which depends on all the determinants of national saving and domestic investment, including the effective cost of foreign borrowing:

$$Sf^d = \xi(\bar{r}). \tag{5.5}$$

An increase in r decreases Sf^d by deterring domestic investment.

The supply of foreign saving is determined by the world real interest rate RW plus a country-specific risk premium, the *effective* premium which produces the effective cost of foreign borrowing and hence the domestic shadow interest rate. Among other factors, this premium is determined by previous debt buildup (Dooley 1986, Edwards 1986) and the ratio of public sector credit to total domestic credit $DCGR$. The variable $DCGR$ is a proxy for fiscal performance (Harberger 1981, 40). This ratio may also indicate the general state of macroeconomic management. A government that extracts high seigniorage from the banking system may well be following a variety of other growth-inhibiting macroeconomic policies. Foreign lenders are doubly deterred from lending to countries whose governments exhibit weak fiscal discipline (so eroding confidence in their guarantees) and poor macroeconomic management which stalls the growth process. The supply function, therefore, can be specified:

$$Sf^s = \zeta(\overset{+}{r}, \overset{-}{RW}, \overset{-}{DETY}_{t-1}, \overset{-}{FLY}_{t-1}, \overset{-}{DCGR}). \qquad (5.6)$$

While a rise in r increases Sf^s, increases in RW, $DETY_{t-1}$, FLY_{t-1}, and $DCGR$ reduce Sf^s.

Equating demand and supply provides a reduced-form expression for the domestic shadow interest rate or the effective cost of foreign borrowing:

$$r = \varphi(\overset{+}{RW}, \overset{+}{DETY}_{t-1}, \overset{+}{FLY}_{t-1}, \overset{+}{DCGR}). \qquad (5.7)$$

Hence, RW, $DETY_{t-1}$, FLY_{t-1}, and $DCGR$ can be substituted for r in the saving and investment functions derived below.

While foreign debt accumulation could either improve or worsen a country's current account through financial and fiscal effects, FDI inflows could affect a country's current account in a more direct way by increasing capital formation. As Michael Dooley (1990) points out, however, FDI constitutes a flow-of-funds concept and records a financial flow. Financial flows from saving to investment can take many forms, some of which are virtually perfect substitutes. For example, debt flows can become equity flows when tax reforms change incentives without affecting capital formation in any way. In the same way, foreign debt flows can become FDI flows without causing any change in capital formation.

Because of the high degree of substitutability and fungibility in such financial flows, flow-of-funds data are seldom useful for economic analysis (Dooley 1990, 75). In other words, FDI may be autonomous or accommodating, either increasing capital formation or providing additional balance-of-payments financing, or providing neither because an increase in FDI simply offsets a reduction in another type of capital flow.

In an attempt to discriminate between these possibilities, FDI can be used as an explanatory variable in a five-equation macroeconomic model which also incorporates the effects of foreign debt buildup to explain saving, investment, exports, imports, and the rate of growth. Since causation could run both ways and FDI could well be determined simultaneously with saving and investment, it is treated as an endogenous variable. The components of this model are presented in Table 5.1.

Table 5.1. Foreign Debt Accumulation and Foreign Direct Investment in a Financially Repressed Economy

$$SNY = b_{10} + \overset{+}{b}_{11}\widehat{INCG} + (\overset{-}{b}_{12} + \overset{?}{b}_{13}\widehat{INCG}) \cdot DEPR$$

$$+ (\overset{?}{b}_{14} + \overset{?}{b}_{15}\widehat{INCG}) \cdot \widehat{DCPY} + (\overset{?}{b}_{16} + \overset{?}{b}_{17}\widehat{INCG}) \cdot RD$$

$$+ (\overset{?}{b}_{18} + \overset{?}{b}_{19}\widehat{INCG}) \cdot RW + (\overset{?}{b}_{20} + \overset{?}{b}_{21}\widehat{INCG}) \cdot DETY_{t-1}$$

$$+ (\overset{?}{b}_{22} + \overset{?}{b}_{23}\widehat{INCG}) \cdot DETY_{t-1}^2 + (\overset{?}{b}_{24} + \overset{?}{b}_{25}\widehat{INCG}) \cdot FLY_{t-1} \quad (5.8)$$

$$+ (\overset{?}{b}_{26} + \overset{?}{b}_{27}\widehat{INCG}) \cdot FLY_{t-1}^2 + (\overset{-}{b}_{28} + \overset{?}{b}_{29}\widehat{INCG}) \cdot DCGR$$

$$+ (\overset{?}{b}_{30} + \overset{?}{b}_{31}\widehat{INCG}) \cdot GBOND + (\overset{?}{b}_{32} + \overset{?}{b}_{33}\widehat{INCG}) \cdot \widehat{FDIY}$$

$$+ (\overset{+}{b}_{34} + \overset{?}{b}_{35}\widehat{INCG}) \cdot SNY_{t-1}.$$

$$IKY = b_{40} + \overset{+}{b}_{41}\widehat{YG} + \overset{+}{b}_{42}YG_{t-1} + \overset{+}{b}_{43}TTL + \overset{+}{b}_{44}\widehat{REXL}$$

$$+ \overset{-}{b}_{45}\widehat{DCPY} + \overset{-}{b}_{46}\widehat{DDCPY} + \overset{+}{b}_{47}RW + \overset{-}{b}_{48}DCGR$$

$$+ \overset{?}{b}_{49}DETY_{t-1} + \overset{?}{b}_{50}DETY_{t-1}^2 + \overset{?}{b}_{51}FLY_{t-1} \quad (5.9)$$

$$+ \overset{?}{b}_{51}FLY_{t-1}^2 + \overset{+}{b}_{52}\widehat{FDIY} + \overset{+}{b}_{53}IKY_{t-1}.$$

$$IMKY = b_{60} + \overset{+}{b}_{61}\widehat{REXL} + \overset{+}{b}_{62}TTL + \overset{+}{b}_{63}\widehat{IKY} + \overset{+}{b}_{64}\widehat{XY}$$

$$+ \overset{-}{b}_{65}IDETY + \overset{+}{b}_{66}\widehat{FDIY} + \overset{+}{b}_{67}IMKY_{t-1}. \quad (5.10)$$

$$XKY = b_{70} + \overset{-}{b}_{71}\widehat{REXL} + \overset{?}{b}_{72}\widehat{FDIY} + \overset{+}{b}_{73}XKY_{t-1}. \quad (5.11)$$

$$YGN = b_{80} + (\overset{+}{b}_{81} + \overset{+}{b}_{82}RD) \cdot \widehat{IKY} + \overset{+}{b}_{83}LG + \overset{+}{b}_{84}\widehat{XKG}$$

$$+ \overset{+}{b}_{85}\widehat{XKGY} + \overset{-}{b}_{86}VM + \overset{?}{b}_{87}\widehat{FDII} + \overset{+}{b}_{88}YGW + \overset{+}{b}_{89}RW. \quad (5.12)$$

Note: Hats denote endogenous variables.

Table 5.1. Foreign Debt Accumulation and Foreign Direct Investment in a Financially
Repressed Economy *(Continued)*

		Endogenous Variables
SNY	–	National saving/GNP (current prices)
$INCG$	–	Rate of growth in aggregate real income (constant prices, continuously compounded)
$DCPY$	–	Domestic credit to the private sector/GNP (current prices)
$DDCPY$	–	Change in real domestic credit to private sector/real GNP (constant prices)
$FDIY$	–	Net inflow of foreign direct investment/GNP (dollar values converted to domestic currency, current prices)
IKY	–	Domestic investment/GNP (constant prices)
YG	–	Rate of growth in GNP (constant prices, continuously compounded)
$REXL$	–	Real exchange rate in natural logarithms [(domestic GNP deflator/U.S. wholesale price index)/domestic currency per U.S. dollar]
$IMKY$	–	Imports/GNP (constant prices)
XY	–	Exports/GNP (current prices)
XKY	–	Exports/GNP (constant prices)
YGN	–	Normal or long-run rate of growth in GNP (constant prices, continuously compounded)
XKG	–	Rate of growth in exports (constant prices, continuously compounded)
$XKGY$	–	Rate of growth in exports divided by the lagged export/GNP ratio (constant prices, continuously compounded)
$FDII$	–	Net inflow of foreign direct investment/domestic investment (dollar values converted to domestic currency, current prices)

5.3 Saving

Equation 5.8 in Table 5.1 is a saving function SNY expressed as the ratio
of national saving to GNP (both in current prices). It is based on a life-
cycle model that incorporates the variable rate-of-growth effect developed by
Andrew Mason (1981, 1987). The standard life-cycle saving model assumes
that young, income-earning households save to finance consumption when
they become old, nonearning households. Figure 5.3 illustrates these life-
cycle patterns of income and consumption. Income $E(a)$ and consumption
$C(a)$ of a household aged a are expressed as a fraction of lifetime income.

The simplest life-cycle model assumes that each household consumes all
its resources over its lifetime. If each household consumes all its resources
over its lifetime, the level of household consumption L over its lifetime

$$L = \int C(a)da \qquad (5.13)$$

Table 5.1. Foreign Debt Accumulation and Foreign Direct Investment in a Financially Repressed Economy *(Concluded)*

Exogenous or Predetermined Variables	
DEPR	– Population aged under 15 and over 64 divided by the population aged 15 to 64
RD	– Real deposit rate of interest rate (12-month deposit rate minus inflation, continuously compounded)
RW	– World real interest rate (6-month LIBOR deposit rate minus U.S. inflation, continuously compounded)
DETY	– End-of-year government plus government-guaranteed foreign – debt/GNP (dollar values converted to domestic currency, current prices)
FLY	– Cumulated end-of-year net foreign liabilities/GNP (dollar values converted to domestic currency, current prices)
DCGR	– Net domestic credit to government/domestic credit (average of beginning and end-of-year figures, current prices)
GBOND	– End-of-year government domestic debt/GNP (current prices)
TTL	– Terms of trade in natural logarithms (export price index/import price index)
IDETY	– Interest cost of foreign debt/GNP (current prices)
LG	– Rate of growth in population aged 15 to 64
YGW	– Rate of growth in OECD output (constant prices, continuously compounded)
VM	– Country-specific variance in money growth shocks.

is equal to 1. Even if no household saves over its lifetime, this life-cycle model shows that aggregate saving can still be positive, provided that there is positive growth in aggregate real income. With positive growth, the lifetime resources of young savers exceed those of old dissavers and there will be positive aggregate saving. Because incomes of younger, earning households are higher than were incomes of older, nonearning households, saving exceeds dissaving in the society as a whole.

The aggregate saving ratio is determined by the age profile of the average household's saving $S(a) = E(a) - C(a)$ and by the lifetime resources that each age group can mobilize. If $V(a)$ is the ratio of lifetime resources of all households aged a to aggregate real income, then $V(a)S(a)$ is the total saving of age group a as a fraction of aggregate real income. The aggregate saving ratio s is derived by summing across all age groups:

$$s = \int V(a)S(a)da. \qquad (5.14)$$

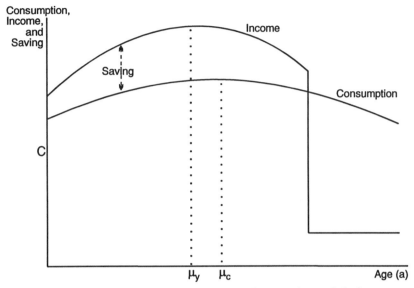

Figure 5.3. Life-Cycle Patterns of Income, Consumption, and Saving

With steady-state growth, $V(a)$ is independent of time and given by

$$V(a) = V(0)e^{-ga}, \qquad (5.15)$$

where $V(0)$ is the ratio of lifetime resources of newly formed households to aggregate real income and g is the rate of growth in aggregate real income. If g is zero

$$s = V(0)(1 - L) = 0. \qquad (5.16)$$

All aggregate real income is consumed because $V(a)$ is a constant, L equals 1, and $\int S(a)da$ is $1-L$.

With positive growth in aggregate real income, the lifetime resources $V(a)$ of young savers exceed those of old dissavers and there can be positive aggregate saving. This is the rate-of-growth effect. The rate-of-growth effect is itself determined by the relationship between income and consumption over the household's lifetime. Mason (1987) shows that the timing of household saving can be defined in terms of the mean ages of consumption μ_c and income μ_y, as shown in Figure 5.3. These are the average ages (weighted by the values of consumption expenditure and income at each age) at which half lifetime consumption and income are reached.

The higher is the rate of economic growth, the richer is the current generation compared with the previous generation. The rate-of-growth effect can be positive only to the extent that households on average accumulate wealth when they are younger in order to dispose of these assets when they are older.

In countries where households can borrow against future income, households may have spent more than they have earned, in cumulative terms, for a large part of their lifetime. In this case, the rate-of-growth effect can be negative.

When the restrictive assumption of zero lifetime saving is discarded, the life-cycle model can incorporate both a level effect as well as the rate-of-growth effect discussed above. The level effect, which includes the bequest motive for saving, refers to the ratio of lifetime consumption to lifetime income. Any factor that increases this consumption ratio reduces the ratio of lifetime saving to lifetime income. It also reduces the ratio of current saving to current income.

The aggregate saving ratio can be represented approximately as a function of g, L, μ_c, and μ_y. All factors that influence the aggregate saving ratio must enter through one of these four variables (Fry and Mason 1982, 430):

$$s \approx -\log(L) + (\mu_c - \mu_y)g. \tag{5.17}$$

Equation 5.17 allows factors that influence the timing of consumption or income over the life cycle to enter the saving function interactively with the rate of growth in income.

The level of household consumption can be approximated by a log-linear function in a vector of independent variables z:

$$L = e^{-\alpha z}. \tag{5.18}$$

The difference between the mean ages of consumption and income is represented by a linear function in the same vector of independent variables z:

$$\mu_c - \mu_y = \beta z. \tag{5.19}$$

Substituting equations 5.18 and 5.19 into equation 5.17 gives

$$s \approx \alpha z + \beta z g. \tag{5.20}$$

Hence all the explanatory variables in equation 5.8, except the rate of growth in real income, should be included twice. They should appear as αz and also interacted with the growth rate as $\beta z g$.

The rate-of-growth effect in the life-cycle saving model refers to the rate of growth in aggregate real income. Typically, empirical tests use the rate of growth in aggregate real output or real GNP defined here as YG. In an open economy, however, the rate of growth in gross national income $INCG$ differs from the rate of growth in real GNP YG due to terms-of-trade changes. An improvement in the terms of trade raises national saving and so improves the current account (Harberger 1950, Laursen and Metzler 1950, Svensson and Razin 1983).

Real gross national income can be defined as $y + x(P_x/P_m - 1)$, where y is real GNP, x is exports measured at constant prices, and P_x/P_m is the price of exports divided by the price of imports or the gross barter terms of trade. Here, I use the rate of change in real income derived from this measure of real gross national income. Real income growth $INCG$ can be decomposed into income growth due to real output growth YG and real income growth due to terms-of-trade changes TTG to test for differential effects. The terms of trade expressed in logarithms TTL could also exert an independent effect on saving by affecting income distribution.

A higher population dependency ratio $DEPR$ (measured as the population under 15 and over 64 divided by the population aged 15 to 64) could reduce the national saving ratio; a large body of empirical evidence suggests that more children in a household raises consumption in relation to income (Fry and Mason 1982). Indeed, one might expect that total consumption over the household's entire lifetime would be higher when it raises more children. In other words, households may not save more when their children have become independent to offset completely the lower saving during the child-rearing period. In the terminology of the life-cycle saving theory, this is known as the level effect.

Although a higher population dependency ratio may reduce the level of saving over the household's lifetime, more children could increase a household's desire to leave a larger bequest, so increasing the level effect. Hence, the level effect of household size on saving behavior is ambiguous in theory. The level effect, which can be influenced by any explanatory variable, incorporates the bequest motive for saving.

Mason (1981) shows that a rise in the population dependency ratio is likely to reduce the mean age of consumption but to have a relatively small effect on the mean age of earning. Hence an increase in the population dependency ratio $DEPR$ reduces the rate-of-growth effect in the aggregate saving function (Mason 1981, 1987; Fry and Mason 1982).

When the population dependency ratio is held constant, the life-cycle theory indicates that growth in per capita real income and in population should have identical effects on the aggregate saving ratio. In other words, it is irrelevant whether younger, saving households have more weight in the aggregate because they are richer or because they are more numerous. Empirical tests by Fry and Mason (1982) on a sample of seven Asian developing countries were unable to reject this implication of the life-cycle theory.

Credit rationing is endemic throughout the developing world. Even where interest rates are relatively free for investment lending, there may be restrictions on consumer lending. If some households are liquidity constrained, credit availability could affect consumption and saving behavior. For a liquidity-constrained consumer, an increase in credit availability will raise consumption, lower saving and hence worsen the current account. In this case, domestic credit to the private sector scaled by nominal GNP $DCPY$ is used as a proxy for credit availability.

An increase in the real rate of return on financial assets raises the relative price of current to future consumption. If the substitution effect outweighs the income effect as posited by Mancur Olson and Martin Bailey (1981, 1), then the saving ratio rises with an increase in both domestic and foreign real interest rates, RD and RW, provided capital outflows are not prevented completely. This implies an increase in the mean age of consumption. Lawrence Summers (1981) also pinpoints circumstances in which a rise in the rate of interest shifts consumption towards older age, raising the mean age of consumption.

The saving ratio could be affected by the domestic real shadow interest rate r, for which $\varphi(RW, DETY_{t-1}, FLY_{t-1})$ can be substituted. For many households, the real deposit rate of interest may be the relevant variable. The real deposit rate of interest $d-\pi^e$ or RD is measured by subtracting domestic inflation estimated from the GNP deflator from the 12-month deposit rate (both continuously compounded). The world real rate of interest RW is proxied by the 6-month LIBOR (London Inter-Bank Offered Rate) deposit rate minus U.S. inflation (both continuously compounded).

Theoretically, it is possible that the income effect could outweigh the substitution effect, so causing a decline in the mean age of consumption, provided the income elasticity of current consumption substantially exceeds the income elasticity of future consumption. There is, however, no plausible basis for expecting such a preference structure (Olson and Bailey 1981). The interest rate effect on the mean age of earning is ambiguous but probably negligible. Consequently, one anticipates that a rise in the domestic or foreign real interest rates would increase the rate-of-growth effect.

The real rate of interest also influences the relative price of bequests. Thus a rise in the real rate of interest may reduce the level of lifetime consumption. There is no reason, however, why the elasticity of substitution between present and future consumption should be the same as the elasticity of substitution between present consumption and bequests (Olson and Bailey 1981, 17).

Any observed association between real interest rates and saving ratios may indicate only that there is substitution between saving embodied in physical goods that are not recorded as investment in the national income accounts and saving embodied in financial assets that does finance investment as defined by national income accountants (Brown 1973, 202; Fry 1978, 99). In this case, a higher real interest rate may not raise the true saving ratio, but rather free more resources for productive investment. Its true effect may be on the average efficiency of investment, not on its volume.

Net inflows of FDI expressed as a ratio to GNP $FDIY$ could also be accompanied by a decline in the measured national saving ratio. As in the case of a decline in measured national saving induced by an increase in the world real interest rate, any negative effect of FDI on national saving ratios may be a statistical artifact. If some residents realize that terms and conditions for FDI are more favorable than they are for locally financed investment, they have an incentive to remove capital from their country and to bring it back again in the form of FDI. To the extent that these individuals wish to conceal the capital outflow, they will also overinvoice imports and underinvoice exports. In such case, an increase in FDI would be accompanied by a reduction in recorded national saving (Fry 1994). If this roundtrip capital flow does not occur, FDI would have no direct impact on the measured national saving ratio.

In effect, the saving function derived here is the private sector saving function $SNPY$ to which the government saving ratio $SNGY$ has been added: $SNY = SNPY + SNGY$. Unfortunately, disaggregated saving data are rarely available for developing countries.[3] Therefore, the effect of the government's domestic budgetary position on national saving in developing countries can be tested only by including some proxy for government saving. The one chosen here is the ratio of net domestic credit to the government sector to total domestic credit $DCGR$. This variable should reflect fiscal stance, since governments in most developing countries tend to rely heavily, if not exclusively, on the banking system for their domestic borrowing requirements. Total domestic credit, instead of GNP, is used as the denominator to offset the differential effect of inflation on the values of financial stock variables compared to flow variables.

In any case, inflation badly distorts the measurement of disaggregated private and public saving because of the failure to account correctly for the inflation tax revenue. Fortunately, however, including components of public saving that are not substitutes for private saving affects only the intercept, provided they are independent of the explanatory variables (Fry and Mason 1982, 433).

The Ricardian equivalence hypothesis states that the effect of higher government expenditure is the same whether financed by borrowing or by higher lump-sum taxes. If individuals perceive that they will have to pay higher lump-sum taxes in the future to meet the interest payments on the newly issued government debt, they will consume less now as well as in the future. Higher private sector saving completely offsets this lower public sector saving or increased public sector dissaving. Hence national saving remains unchanged. Even if taxes do not take the form of lump-sum taxes, there is still no wealth effect under Ricardian equivalence. However, there could then be attempts to avoid tax through intertemporal substitution of labor for leisure.

Government deficits and the debt they produce may have no impact on national saving if households are not borrowing constrained, foresee the future interest payments on that debt, recognize that their disposable income in the future will be reduced to that extent, and therefore reduce their present consumption appropriately, hence raising their saving ratios. This Ricardian equivalence argument seems particularly implausible for developing countries

---

[3]Indeed, not even government deficit or government revenue and consumption expenditure data are available for many developing countries.

with only rudimentary financial markets, in which many households face borrowing constraints. Furthermore, to the extent that a government deficit results in socially productive investment, household disposable income would not be reduced in the future.

The Ricardian equivalence theory applies to a closed economy model, although Jacob Frenkel and Assaf Razin (1986) adapt it for an open economy. In an open economy, however, households may evade future taxation by removing their savings abroad illegally. Hence measured national saving may fall, even in the unlikely event that the true level of saving remains constant. In such case, the measured national saving ratio would fall as government domestic debt *GBOND*, and hence the expected future tax burdens, rise. An analogous case has already been made for the effect of the government's foreign debt *DETY*.

5.4   Investment

Equation 5.9 in Table 5.1 is the investment function *IKY* specified here as the ratio of investment to GNP measured at constant prices. This equation is derived from the flexible accelerator model. Mario Blejer and Mohsin Khan (1984, 382–383) describe some of the difficulties of estimating neoclassical investment functions for developing countries. In particular, there are no readily available measures of the capital stock or its rate of return. There is, therefore, little choice in practice but to use some version of the accelerator model, particularly for pooled time series analysis on data from several developing countries (Fry 1986a, 62–64; Fry 1989a, 321–323).

The accelerator model sets the desired capital stock K^* proportional to real output y:

$$K^* = \alpha y. \tag{5.21}$$

This can be expressed in terms of a desired ratio of investment to output $(I/Y)^*$:

$$(I/Y)^* = \alpha\gamma, \tag{5.22}$$

where γ is the rate of growth in output.

The adjustment mechanism allows the actual investment ratio to adjust partially in any one period to the difference between the desired investment ratio and the investment ratio in the previous period:

$$\Delta(I/Y) = \lambda[(I/Y)^* - (I/Y)_{t-1}] \tag{5.23}$$

or

$$I/Y = \lambda(I/Y)^* + (1-\lambda)(I/Y)_{t-1}, \tag{5.24}$$

where λ is the coefficient of adjustment. The flexible accelerator model allows economic conditions to influence the adjustment coefficient λ. Specifically,

$$\lambda = \beta_0 + \left[\frac{\beta_1 z_1 + \beta_2 z_2 + \beta_3 z_3 + \cdots}{(I/Y)^* - (I/Y)_{t-1}} \right], \qquad (5.25)$$

where z_i are the variables (including an intercept term for the depreciation rate) that affect λ.

The partial adjustment mechanism specified for the investment *ratio* is somewhat more complicated than the equivalent mechanism for the *level* of investment. Specifically, there could be a lag in achieving the same investment ratio this year as last year if output rose rapidly last year; this year's desired investment *level* will be higher than last year's, despite a constant desired *ratio* of investment to output. To incorporate this adjustment lag, last year's growth rate γ_{t-1} can be included as an additional explanatory variable.

The speed of adjustment in this flexible accelerator investment function is determined by the terms of trade expressed in natural logarithms TTL, the natural logarithm of the real exchange rate $REXL$, credit availability $DCPY$, the FDI ratio $FDIY$, the world real interest rate RW, the ratio of net domestic credit to the government sector to total domestic credit $DCGR$, and the foreign debt ratios used in the saving function.

Torsten Persson and Lars Svensson (1985) construct a model in which the investment ratio could be influenced positively or negatively by changes in the terms of trade. In their overlapping-generations model, a permanent improvement in the terms of trade expressed in natural logarithms TTL raises the investment ratio by increasing the return to capital. However, a temporary improvement in the terms of trade can reduce investment because stocks of inventories are run down to benefit from the temporary improvement in the relative price of these exports. If terms-of-trade changes are perceived to be permanent, the investment effect on the current account is opposite to the saving effect. On the other hand, if the terms-of-trade changes are expected to be temporary, the investment effect strengthens the saving effect and improves the current account.

The price of intermediate imports may affect the profitability of investment projects in developing countries. Hence, the real exchange rate expressed in natural logarithms $REXL$ is included as a proxy for the price of nontradable goods in relation to import prices. I measure the real exchange rate REX as: (domestic GNP deflator/U.S. wholesale price index)/domestic currency per U.S. dollar. Therefore, a higher value of $REXL$ implies a lower relative price of imports. By appreciating the real exchange rate, capital inflows may stimulate investment.

The availability of institutional credit can be an important determinant of the investment ratio, for the reasons discussed by Alan Blinder and Joseph Stiglitz (1983), Fry (1980b), and Peter Keller (1980). Banks specialize in acquiring information on default risk. Such information is highly specific to each client and difficult to sell. Hence the market for bank loans is a customer market, in which borrowers and lenders are very imperfect substitutes. A credit squeeze rations out some bank borrowers who may be unable to find loans elsewhere and so be unable to finance their investment projects (Blinder and Stiglitz 1983, 300). Here, therefore, the investment ratio is influenced by domestic credit to the private sector scaled by GNP $DCPY$ or the change in the real volume of private sector credit divided by real GNP $DDCPY$.

If all institutional credit consisted of short-term loans, the ratio of private sector credit to GNP $DCPY$ would be the more appropriate variable, whereas for long-term loans $DDCPY$ should be used. For loans of intermediate maturity or for a portfolio of short- and long-term loans, both the level and the change might influence the investment ratio. Blejer and Khan (1984, 389) use the change in real private sector domestic credit $DDCP$ in their investment function. This is equivalent to $DDCPY$ in a model using the investment ratio as the dependent variable.

Domestic costs of borrowing are extraordinarily difficult to measure in almost all developing countries because of selective credit policies and disequilibrium institutional interest rates. This is why the quantity rather than the price of domestic credit is included in the investment function. The domestic investment ratio would, however, be affected negatively by the world real interest rate RW, provided there were some international capital mobility. Furthermore RW has a positive effect on the domestic real shadow interest rate r.

The weaker is fiscal performance, as proxied by the ratio of public or government credit to total domestic credit $DCGR$, the greater is the probability of increased asset taxation in the future (Hamilton and Flavin 1986, King and Plosser 1985, Plosser 1982). For this reason, a higher value of $DCGR$ would deter domestic investment. This variable may also act as a proxy for the general state of macroeconomic management. A government that extracts high seigniorage from the banking system may well be following a variety of other macroeconomic policies that impair the investment climate.

The ratio of government plus government-guaranteed foreign debt to GNP $DETY$ is used again here. This variable as well as FLY may also serve as proxies for the country-specific risk premium (Dooley 1986, Edwards 1986). Therefore, these foreign debt ratios may affect the investment ratio negatively either because they reduce the expected net return to domestic investment or because they reflect a higher cost of investible funds.

Whether or not substitutability and fungibility are so high in the case of developing countries that FDI flows provide no relevant economic information is an empirical question. Hence FDI is included as an endogenous explanatory variable in the investment equation. A coefficient of 1 would suggest both that FDI is an autonomous capital inflow and that FDI does not crowd out domestically financed investment. An insignificant coefficient would imply that FDI inflows were either accommodating, and so simply financing an increased current account deficit, or that they constituted a close substitute for other types of capital flows.

5.5 Economic Growth

The normal or long-run rate of economic growth YGN in this model is derived from an endogenous growth production function. The first explanatory variable therefore is the investment ratio IKY expressed in constant prices, included here as a proxy for the rate of growth in the capital stock. The investment ratio is interacted with the real deposit rate RD to enable changes in the real deposit rate to affect investment productivity. The second variable affecting the rate of economic growth is the rate of growth in the labor force LG. I assume that the unemployment rate remains constant, since employment data are unavailable for most developing countries.

Gershon Feder (1982) detects two channels—higher marginal productivities and externalities—through which rapid export growth could affect the rate of economic growth in excess of the contribution of *net* export growth to GNP growth. If exports affect the production of nonexports with a constant elasticity θ, the rate of growth in *gross* exports at constant prices XKG captures solely the externality effect. However, the rate of growth in exports scaled by the lagged export/GNP ratio $XKGY$ captures any differential marginal productivity δ as well as the externality effect. Hence, $YG = [\delta/(1+\delta) - \theta] \cdot XKGY + \theta \cdot XKG$ (Feder 1982, 67).[4]

The growth rate may be affected negatively by the variance of money growth shocks VM, as measured by the variance of innovations to the time-series process of money growth. The innovations are residuals of country-specific regressions of the money growth rate on its own lagged value and a constant. Among others, Constantine Glezakos (1978) and Axel Leijonhufvud (1981) show that greater uncertainty with respect to the future price level reduces output growth. Fry and David Lilien (1986) find that VM has a negative effect on the rate of economic growth in pooled time-series analysis of 55 developed and developing countries.

If FDI is not a perfect substitute for other capital inflows, the proportion of FDI in aggregate domestic investment $FDII$ could affect the average efficiency of investment or total factor productivity. If FDI either augments domestic investment or crowds out domestically financed investment, it could affect the average efficiency of domestic investment provided its efficiency differs on average from the efficiency of domestically financed investment. Although the average efficiency of FDI might be higher than the efficiency of domestically

---

[4]Only XKG is significant in my own empirical work, implying that $\delta/(1+\delta) = \theta$.

financed investment under conditions of financial repression, other distortions in the economy might reverse the relative efficiencies (Fry 1993e). In an endogenous growth context, the externalities of FDI may be smaller than the externalities of domestically financed and managed investment.

Finally, growth of the OECD economies YGW and the real 6-month LIBOR deposit rate RW are included to capture external demand effects on growth not picked up by export growth (Callier 1984).

5.6 Trade Equations

The import demand equation $IMKY$ expressed as the ratio of imports to GNP (both in constant prices) is given by equation 5.10 in Table 5.1. Since developing countries face an infinitely elastic supply of imports, their import volume is determined solely by demand. This demand is affected by the prices of exports, imports, and nontradable goods. The price variables actually used here are the real exchange rate in natural logarithms $REXL$, as a proxy for the relative price of nontraded goods to imports, and the terms of trade in natural logarithms TTL, which is of course the ratio of export to import prices.

After several empirical tests, I find the assumption of unit income elasticity of import demand is not rejected for several samples of developing countries.[5] However, the composition of GNP does affect imports. Specifically, investment is more import intensive than consumption. Hence, the ratio of imports to GNP is determined in part by the ratio of investment to GNP IKY.

Adjustment to the desired level of imports may be constrained by the availability of foreign exchange earned by exporters. Many developing countries impose quantitative restrictions on imports of consumer goods. Typically, licenses to import these restricted items are rationed not on the basis of total foreign exchange availability but rather on the availability of nonborrowed foreign exchange or foreign exchange earned by exporters. The ratio of nominal exports to nominal GNP XY is used to proxy this rationing constraint. Since export earnings must also be used to service foreign debt, quantitative restrictions on imports may also be tightened as debt service obligations rise. For this reason, the ratio of interest cost of foreign debt to GNP $IDETY$ is included as the final explanatory variable in the import demand function.

If FDI increases domestic investment but has no effect on national saving, it worsens the current account. Equation 5.4 indicates that a worsened current account must be accompanied by an increase in imports, a decrease in exports, or by some combination of increased imports and decreased exports. Hence the final explanatory variable in the import equation is FDI expressed as a

---

[5] The logarithm of per capita real GNP, the reciprocal of the logarithm of per capita real GNP, and the rate of economic growth are all insignificant in both the import demand and export supply functions.

ratio to GNP *FDIY*. An inflow of FDI could influence imports directly were it accompanied by an increase in imports for investment that would not have occurred in the absence of this FDI. In this case, FDI inflows are tied to the import of raw materials and capital equipment that would otherwise have not taken place. However, an inflow of FDI could also influence imports indirectly by appreciating the real exchange rate to stimulate unrelated imports and effect the transfer by increasing the current account deficit. For this reason, I estimate the import function with and without the real exchange rate *REXL* in order to test the extent to which FDI exerts an indirect rather than a direct effect on imports. If FDI is simply a substitute for other types of capital inflows, it would have no effect either directly or indirectly on imports.

For a small open developing economy, export demand is likely to be infinitely elastic. Therefore, the volume of exports in this model is determined by supply. Export supply expressed as the ratio of exports to GNP *XKY* (both in constant prices) is determined by the relative prices of exports and nontraded goods *REXL* as well as by *FDIY*. Hence, the export equation estimated here takes the form of equation 5.11 in Table 5.1.

Many developing countries impose a requirement that FDI be concentrated in their foreign trade sectors. Therefore, even if FDI has no impact on total domestic investment, it might change the composition of investment in a way that increased exports at some point in the future. Were the FDI concentrated in import-substitution activities, such a compositional shift could also decrease imports in the future. To test for these delayed effects of FDI on exports and imports, I also estimate equations 5.10 and 5.11 with the average ratio of FDI to GNP over the previous five years *FDIYL* instead of the concurrent and 1-year lagged FDI ratio.

5.7 Inflation and Cyclical Growth

As in the models of Basant Kapur and Donald Mathieson, but in sharp contrast to the neostructuralist models, inflation is determined explicitly in my model as the difference between growth rates in per capita nominal money supply and per capita real money demand. Provided that the money market clears within the time period under consideration, inflation can be explained proximately by the rate of change in nominal money supply and the determinants of the rate of change in real money demand. The equilibrium condition in the money market can be expressed:

$$M^s = M^d \tag{5.26}$$

or

$$M^s = P \cdot N \cdot m^d, \tag{5.27}$$

where M^s is nominal money supply (as usual defined broadly to include saving/time deposits as well as currency in circulation and demand deposits

—M2), M^d is nominal money demand, P is the price level, N is population, and m^d is per capita demand for real money balances $(M^d/P)/N$. It seems reasonable to expect the market clearing or equilibrium condition—short-run demand equal to supply—to hold for annual models applied to most developing economies because of the prevalence of auction markets.

Equation 5.27 can be expressed in first difference logarithmic form:

$$\Delta \log(M^s) = \Delta \log(P) + \Delta \log(N) + \Delta \log(m^d), \qquad (5.28)$$

which can be rearranged:

$$\pi = \Delta \log(M^s/N) - \Delta \log(m^d), \qquad (5.29)$$

where π is the continuously compounded rate of change in the price level $\Delta \log(P)$.

The inflationary process can be understood fully only through an analysis of the determinants of both nominal money supply and real money demand. However, provided that any feedback from inflation to money supply growth occurs with a lag, the model is recursive (Aghevli and Khan 1977). In such case, changes in the nominal money supply can be treated as if they were exogenous for the purpose of estimating inflation.

Real money demand is invariably specified as a function of one or more price (interest rate) variables and a budget constraint. Here the price variable is the real deposit rate of interest $d-\pi^e$, and the budget constraint is per capita permanent or expected real income y_p. The long-run or desired money demand function takes the standard form:

$$m^* = cy_p^b e^{a(d-\pi^e)}, \qquad (5.30)$$

where m^* is the long-run or desired level of real money balances and a, b, and c are constants.

The actual level of real money balances may be adjusted with a lag to changes in the determinants of money demand. To allow for this, short-run or actual money demand is specified:

$$\log(m^d) = \log(m_{t-1}) + \theta[\log(m^*) - \log(m_{t-1})]. \qquad (5.31)$$

Some fraction θ of the gap between desired money balances and money balances held in the previous time period is eliminated in the current period. Equations 5.30 and 5.31 can be combined and expressed in first difference logarithmic form:

$$\Delta \log(m^d) = \theta b \Delta \log(y_p) + \theta a \Delta(d-\pi^e) + (1-\theta)\Delta \log(m_{t-1}). \qquad (5.32)$$

Now defining γ^e as the rate of change in per capita permanent income $\Delta \log(y_p)$ and substituting equation 5.32 into equation 5.29,

$$\pi = \Delta \log(M^s/N) - \theta b \gamma^e - \theta a \Delta(d-\pi^e) - (1-\theta)\Delta\log(m_{t-1}). \qquad (5.33)$$

This model includes the same sources of dynamic adjustment as Kapur's —adaptive expectations of the inflation rate, the price level, and the rate of growth in per capita real permanent income, and an expectations-augmented Phillips curve—in addition to the various adjustment lags specified in Table 5.1 (Fry 1978, 1979a, 1980a, 1980b, 1981a, 1982b, 1982c, 1986a, 1988). The adaptive mechanisms are somewhat more general than those used by Kapur and Mathieson:

$$\pi^e = \sum_{i=0}^{m} \alpha_i \pi_{t-i};$$ (5.34)

$$\gamma^e = \sum_{j=0}^{n} \beta_j \gamma_{t-j}^{pc},$$ (5.35)

where γ^{pc} is per capita actual income growth and γ^e is per capita permanent income growth. The lag coefficients α_i and β_j are constrained to sum to 1 and to decline monotonically or exhibit an inverted U pattern.

The response lags specified in equations 5.34 and 5.35 provide a dynamic adjustment mechanism for the inflation equation 5.33, which already incorporates a stock adjustment lag for real money balances. Equation 5.33 can be rewritten in the terms of the Kapur-Mathieson symbols:

$$\pi = \mu - \nu - b\gamma^e - a\Delta(d - \pi^e) - c(\mu - \pi - \nu)_{t-1},$$ (5.36)

where ν is the population growth rate. In terms of the symbols used in this chapter, the inflation equation can be written:

$$INF = a_{10} + \overset{+}{a}_{11} MNG + \overset{+}{a}_{12} \widehat{YNGE} + \overset{+}{a}_{13} DRD,$$ (5.37)

where INF is the inflation rate, MNG is the rate of growth in the per capita stock of money, $YNGE$ is expected growth in per capita income, and DRD is the change in the real deposit rate of interest RD.

Equation 5.37 is derived from the equilibrium condition in the money market; demand equals supply. The credit market, on the other hand, remains in a disequilibrium condition whenever there is financial repression. Walras's law states that disequilibrium in one market must be matched by an equal and opposite disequilibrium in one or more other markets. It is natural to think of an excess demand for credit matched by an excess supply of money. However, credit market disequilibrium can be viewed as an excess supply of bonds at the administratively fixed interest rate. This is matched by planned investment exceeding planned saving at that interest rate. In this case, however, planned investment does not represent *effective* investment demand since it is contingent upon obtaining investible funds at the fixed interest rate. Effective investment demand is curtailed by the lack of credit to equal saving forthcoming at the fixed interest rate. Demand for and supply of money can be equilibrated through price changes. Hence money market equilibrium can coexist with disequilibrium in the credit market.

Prices may adjust in disequilibrium more rapidly in most developing economies than they do in industrialized countries because of the preponderance of auction markets or faster expectations responses in the former (Lucas 1973). Hence it may be reasonable to expect equilibrium in the money market to hold, at least for models intended for estimation using annual observations. Furthermore, velocity of circulation tends to fall back after a rise following the introduction of monetary deceleration within 12 months. In other words, money market disequilibrium, although important, appears to be eliminated through price adjustment within the time period of this model.

Money market equilibrium in my model contrasts with Kapur's dynamic mechanism that relies in part on money market disequilibrium. Mathieson, on the other hand, specifies his optimal stabilization strategy as one that establishes immediately and then maintains money and credit market equilibria.

Consistent with the argument used above to justify the assumption of market equilibrium in the money market is my choice of a Fisherian Phillips curve in preference to a Phelpsian Phillips curve (Laidler 1978). This Fisherian Phillips curve determines the cyclical rate of economic growth YGC. The first determinant of YGC is the ratio of the actual to the expected price level P/P^e or, alternatively, the difference between actual and expected inflation $\pi - \pi^e$. The expected price level P^e is $e^{\pi^e} \cdot P_{t-1}$. If actual price or inflation exceeds expected price or inflation, entrepreneurs interpret the difference to reflect a real increase in the demand for their products. Their response is to raise the rate of capacity utilization of existing capital to increase output in the short run, and to invest more to increase capacity in the longer run. The higher is P/P^e or $\pi - \pi^e$, the better the investment outlook appears and the greater is the rate of economic growth.

Expected inflation also affects short-run growth through the real deposit rate of interest $d - \pi^e$. Under the disequilibrium interest rate and foreign exchange control systems found in financially repressed developing economies, real money demand determines to a large extent the real supply of domestic credit; domestic credit is the primary asset backing the monetary liabilities of the banking system. As inflation accelerates and real deposit rates of interest fall, an increasing proportion of the declining supply of real domestic credit is expropriated by government to finance current expenditures (Aghevli and Khan 1977, 1978; Dutton 1971; Ness 1972; Uluatam 1973). Hence funds for both working and fixed capital are doubly squeezed.

The traditional link between credit and output is through demand—the increase in credit created by monetary expansion is accompanied by an increase in demand which stimulates real output. Since 1973, however, a number of economists have focused on the link between credit and real output through the supply side (Blinder 1987; Buffie 1984; Cavallo 1977; Fry 1980b; Kapur 1976a, 1976b; Keller 1980; Mathieson 1980; Taylor 1983; van Wijnbergen

1982, 1983a, 1983b). This Wicksellian view holds that the availability of working capital determines, *ceteris paribus*, the volume of production that can be financed. In particular, as Keller (1980, 455) argues, "production *expansion* may depend, entirely or in part, on credit availability and/or the cost of credit." This supply link between credit availability and real economic growth springs from the ratio of credit to output, or from the real rather than the nominal volume of credit.

Faster expansion of money and nominal credit raises the inflation rate. If the nominal deposit rate is fixed, the ensuing increase in expected inflation reduces the real deposit rate of interest. This in turn reduces real money demand or decreases the ratio of money to nominal output. The ratio of domestic credit to nominal output may also fall even if domestic credit expansion is the cause of monetary acceleration. This could happen if domestic credit expansion reduced net foreign assets by less than the amount of the credit expansion. Thus, an acceleration in nominal domestic credit and hence in the money supply may reduce credit availability in real terms.

As inflation accelerates, and as real deposit rates, real money demand, and real credit supply all decline, the gap between conventional tax receipts and public expenditure tends to widen. This bigger gap is then financed by heavier reliance on seigniorage or the inflation tax. The government extracts greater seigniorage by increasing the proportion of domestic credit allocated to the public sector, and thus reduces the ratio of private sector credit to total domestic credit. It levies an inflation tax by creating more money than the public wishes to hold at the current price level. This produces a double squeeze on credit available for private sector working capital. In Turkey, for example, velocity of circulation (using $M2$) rose by 70 percent and the ratio of public sector domestic credit to the money supply increased from 20 to 229 percent as the expected real deposit rate of interest fell from 0.2 percent in 1970 to −22.7 percent in 1980.

Turkey's private sector was starved of credit as the real supply of domestic credit declined and government extracted a higher seigniorage from the money supply. Funds to finance working capital dried up, and the credit squeeze reduced the rate of capacity utilization of the existing fixed capital stock (Fry 1979a, 1980b). The growth rate declined. In a reduced-form equation, therefore, $d-\pi^e$ has a positive effect on YGC. This variable determines credit availability and also allocative efficiency of loanable funds.

Finally, actual growth is affected by the normal growth rate YGN, as analyzed in section 5.5. In practice, normal or noncyclical growth is affected by fluctuations in agricultural output, which is determined in part by variations in weather conditions. Fluctuations in the level of imports (mainly raw materials, semi-finished products, and capital equipment that act as factor constraints to output in the short run) are also exogenous or noncyclical phenomena in financially repressed economies that maintain disequilibrium foreign trade regimes subject to tight government control (Hemphill 1974, Krueger 1974, 48–50).

Normal growth $YGNA$, redefined to include fluctuations around the long-run trend in agricultural output, exerts a positive effect on the actual growth rate YG. However, above-average growth in agricultural output depresses growth in other sectors of the economy due to another credit effect. Credit requirements of agricultural price support programs that are positively related to growth in agricultural output typically crowd out credit demands of other sectors. Hence other sectors suffer a credit squeeze in real terms when more of the fixed real supply of domestic credit is allocated to agriculture.

All this implies that the effect of $YGNA$ on YG is positive but that the coefficient of $YGNA$ is somewhat less than 1, despite the fact that on average YG equals $YGNA$. Above-average growth in agricultural output imposes a credit squeeze on the other sectors of the economy, which reduces their rates of capacity utilization and so produces below-average growth there. Hence

$$YG = a_{20} + \overset{+}{a}_{21}YGNA + \overset{+}{a}_{22}(\hat{\pi} - \pi^e) + \overset{+}{a}_{23}RD \qquad (5.38)$$

or

$$YG = a_{20} + \overset{+}{a}_{21}YGNA + \overset{+}{a}_{22}\widehat{PPE} + \overset{+}{a}_{23}RD, \qquad (5.39)$$

where PPE is P/P^e.

This section can be summarized by comparing the short- and long-run inflation and growth tradeoffs implied by the Phillips curve models of Kapur (1976a), Mathieson (1980), and myself (Fry 1980b). Figure 5.4 shows short- and long-run Phillips curves under conditions of financial repression. The nominal deposit rate d is fixed below its competitive market equilibrium level. All three models agree that an increase in d towards its equilibrium raises the growth rate γ and reduces the inflation rate π at the same time.

5.8 Monetary Policy Reaction Function

Following earlier work on monetary policy reaction functions by Grant Reuber (1964) and Richard Froyen (1974), central bank objectives have typically been taken to include a balance-of-payments target, an inflation target or an inflation target relative to U.S. inflation and possibly some response to exogenous shocks such as oil price inflation. Here, an attempt is also made to determine the extent to which the central bank accommodates the credit requirements of the government sector without squeezing private sector credit availability and reacts to foreign debt accumulation.

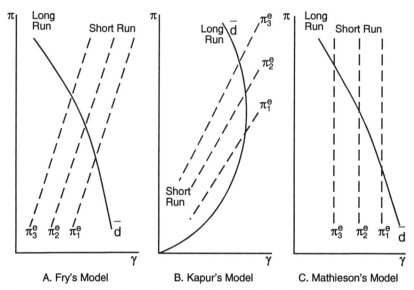

A. Fry's Model   B. Kapur's Model   C. Mathieson's Model

Figure 5.4.   Short- and Long-Run Phillips Curves in Three Financial Repression Models

To examine the inflationary process in developing countries, I specify a monetary policy reaction function in the form of the change in domestic credit scaled by GNP *DDCY*. It is designed to discover whether or not monetary authorities in developing countries pursue systematic monetary policies. Specifically, the monetary authorities might tighten monetary policy when foreign indebtedness $DETY_{t-1}$ or FLY_{t-1} was high.[6] The reaction function also includes the change in net foreign assets of the banking system scaled by GNP *DNFAY* to detect any systematic sterilization of the effects of such asset acquisition on the money supply. The monetary authorities might squeeze domestic credit in response to a widening gap between domestic inflation and inflation in the United States *INFGAP*. The monetary authorities might also squeeze domestic credit when oil price inflation *OILINF* was high. Alternatively, the monetary authorities might accommodate higher oil prices by increasing domestic credit.

In general, devaluations are effective in improving the current account only when accompanied by monetary policy designed to reduce absorption. Hence, an effective devaluation necessitates a restrictive credit policy. On the other hand, however, a devaluation increases the domestic currency cost of

---

[6] Any fiscal policy response to foreign debt buildup is already included in the effects of FLY_{t-1}, $DETY_{t-1}$ and $DETY_{t-1}^2$ on *SNY* and *IKY*, since fiscal policy directly affects either national saving or domestic investment.

servicing foreign debt. Hence, devaluations tend to increase the demand for credit, particularly by the public sector. A depreciation in the *real* exchange rate raises debt service costs in relation to other domestic currency expenditures and income. Hence, I include the lagged real exchange rate expressed in natural logarithms $REXL_{t-1}$ in this monetary policy reaction function. The variable $REXL_{t-1}$ would have a positive coefficient were a restrictive monetary stance pursued after a devaluation. A negative coefficient of $REXL_{t-1}$ would suggest that the monetary authorities accommodated price increases caused specifically by the devaluation.

Finally, the monetary authorities might squeeze domestic credit to the private sector when the credit requirements of the government, as measured by the change in net domestic credit to the government scaled by GNP $DDCGY$, increase. A complete neutralization of the public sector's credit requirements would imply a coefficient of zero for $DDCGY$. A partial offset would produce a coefficient greater than zero but less than 1.

This monetary policy reaction function is specified for estimation in the form:

$$
\begin{aligned}
DDCY = {} & a_{30} + \bar{a}_{31}\, FLY_{t-1} + \bar{a}_{32}\, DETY_{t-1} \\[4pt]
& + \bar{a}_{33}\, \widehat{DNFAY} + \overset{?}{a}_{34}\, DNFAY_{t-1} + \bar{a}_{35}\, \widehat{INFGAP} \\[4pt]
& + \overset{?}{a}_{36}\, INFGAP_{t-1} + \overset{?}{a}_{37}\, OILINF + \overset{?}{a}_{38}\, OILINF_{t-1} \\[4pt]
& + \overset{?}{a}_{39}\, REXL_{t-1} + \overset{+}{a}_{40}\, DDCGY + \overset{?}{a}_{41}\, DDCGY_{t-1}.
\end{aligned}
\tag{5.40}
$$

5.9 Summary

The model presented in this chapter incorporates disequilibrium interest rate effects in the saving, investment, and normal growth rate functions, as well as in the inflation equation and the short-run expectations-augmented Phillips curve containing a credit availability effect. An increase in the nominal deposit rate that raises the real deposit rate towards its competitive free-market equilibrium level may reduce the inflation rate, increase the saving ratio, raise the average efficiency of the greater volume of investment that can then be undertaken, and accelerate the rate of economic growth. Chapters 8 and 10 provide some empirical tests of these effects.

Under conditions of financial repression, developing countries may turn to foreign capital inflows to finance a level of domestic investment that exceeds national saving. This model is designed to examine the effects of foreign debt accumulation and FDI inflows on the recipient economy. It also includes a monetary policy reaction function to detect any policy responses to the buildup of foreign debt. Chapter 11 examines monetary policy, while Chapter 12 presents an empirical test of the effects of foreign debt accumulation and FDI inflows in a sample of developing countries.

Chapter 6

Critics of Financial Liberalization

6.1 Introduction

NEOSTRUCTURALISTS, REPRESENTED BY Edward Buffie (1984), Akira Kohsaka (1984), Lance Taylor (1983), and Sweder van Wijnbergen (1982, 1983a, 1983b), mounted an assault on the McKinnon-Shaw school in the early 1980s. Using a markup pricing framework, a cost-push inflation model, and Keynesian adjustment mechanisms, the neostructuralist models predict the opposite effects of financial development and liberalization to those derived from the McKinnon-Shaw models. In the neostructuralist models, the nominal interest rate, which is determined in the curb or noninstitutional credit market, adjusts to equate demand for and supply of money and credit. Income adjusts to equilibrate demand and supply in the goods market.

Joseph Stiglitz (1994) has criticized financial liberalization on different grounds. His argument focuses on the prevalence of market failures in financial markets. He suggests that "there exist forms of government intervention that will not only make these markets function better but will also improve the performance of the economy" (Stiglitz 1994, 20).

Other critics of the McKinnon-Shaw school employ a variety of models to demonstrate that financial liberalization may have negative effects on saving, investment, output, or economic growth. One group shows that corporate saving may decline by more than household sector saving would rise in the wake of a rise in real institutional interest rates. A second group demonstrates that household saving will decline if credit-constrained households are able to borrow after financial liberalization. A third line of attack is to show that, provided subsidized credit is available at the margin, higher real institutional interest rates deter investment. A fourth group adopts the neostructuralist position that higher real interest rates increase production costs, lower real wages, and cause stagflation. A fifth group combines a Cobb-Douglas production function with a portfolio allocation model and Keynesian demand equations to demonstrate that financial liberalization could reduce both prices and output. Finally, Paul Burkett (1987) disagrees with the explanation rather than the effects of financial repression.

6.2   Neostructuralist Models

Neostructuralist models are based on five assumptions that differ fundamentally from the basic assumptions of the McKinnon-Shaw school: (a) wages are determined institutionally or exogenously through class conflict; (b) inflation is determined by the relative power of capitalists and workers (who may themselves be influenced by the state of the economy); (c) saving takes place only out of profits, not wages; (d) the price level is determined by fixed markups over costs of labor, imports, and working capital finance (the interest rate); and (e) developing countries have a critical need for imports of raw materials, capital equipment, and intermediate goods (Taylor 1983). Assumptions (d) and (e) imply that a restrictive monetary policy that raises interest rates and a devaluation that raises the price of imports can produce stagflation—an acceleration in the inflation rate and a reduction in the rate of economic growth at the same time.

Neostructuralists treat curb markets, in which moneylenders and indigenous banks intermediate between savers and investors, as a crucial feature of their models of developing economies. Neostructuralists view these markets as "often competitive and agile" (Taylor 1983, 92). Since reserve requirements constitute a leakage in the process of financial intermediation through commercial banks, neostructuralists claim that banks cannot intermediate as efficiently as curb markets between savers and investors.

All neostructuralist models base household asset allocation on James Tobin's portfolio framework. Households face three categories of assets: gold or currency, bank deposits, and curb market loans. The McKinnon-Shaw models specify only two assets (gold or other inflation hedges and money) in household portfolios. Hence substitution into money must come from substitution out of inflation hedges. Taylor (1983, 101) and van Wijnbergen (1982) point out that whether higher deposit rates do increase the total real supply of credit depends on the required reserve ratio and on whether the increased holdings of real money balances come mainly at the expense of inflation hedges or mainly from direct lending in the curb market. Buffie (1984), Kohsaka (1984), Taylor, and van Wijnbergen conclude that, in practice, financial liberalization is likely to reduce the rate of economic growth by reducing the total real supply of credit available to business firms.

The neostructuralists assume that funds flow freely between the banking system and the curb market; savers and investors can use either market, at least to some extent. Hence the relevant interest rate in the structuralist models is the curb market rate: it represents the marginal cost of borrowing on the one hand, and enters the money demand function on the other hand, since curb market loans constitute an alternative to holding money balances.

Any increase in the curb market rate raises the price level because a rise in the curb market rate increases the cost of working capital; prices are determined by fixed markups over costs in all the neostructuralist models. A rise in the curb market rate also reduces output by deterring investment. An increase in the deposit rate of interest may raise the curb market rate and so depress growth if it reduces the total supply of working capital—working capital supplied by both the banking system and the curb market.

Commercial banks are subject to a fixed required reserve ratio $1-q$. Since the central bank does not extend credit to the private sector, the cash base (reserve money or high-powered money) is entirely outside money. An increase in the deposit rate of interest raises demand for deposits and reduces demand for currency and curb market loans. If substitution of deposits for curb market loans is more important than substitution of deposits for currency holdings, the total supply of working capital can fall and the curb market interest rate can rise (van Wijnbergen 1983a, 440–444). The same conclusion is reached by Buffie (1984, 320): "Once we allow for repercussions in the curb market, financial liberalization becomes a perilous undertaking."

6.3 Van Wijnbergen

Van Wijnbergen (1982, 1983a, 1983b, 1985) stresses the importance of incorporating the curb or unorganized money markets in monetary models of developing countries. His first published article applies the model to Korea, the only developing economy for which time-series data on both the volume of curb market loans as well as curb market interest rates exist. Van Wijnbergen bases part of his model on the Wicksellian credit availability effect also used by Domingo Cavallo (1977), Fry (1980b), and Peter Keller (1980). He argues that the corporate sector in the typical developing economy relies on credit to finance almost all its working capital; debt/equity ratios tend to be extremely high in developing economies (Sundararajan 1985, 1986b).

The model van Wijnbergen uses to analyze the effects of financial liberalization starts with Tobin-type portfolio behavior on the part of the household sector (van Wijnbergen 1983a, 435–436). Households allocate their real wealth W between currency CC, time deposits TD, and direct loans to the business sector through the curb or unorganized money market L_h, all expressed in real terms:

$$CC = f^c(\pi,\ i,\ r_{td},\ y)W; \tag{6.1}$$

$$TD = f^{td}(\pi,\ i,\ r_{td},\ y)W; \tag{6.2}$$

$$L_h = f^\ell(\pi,\ i,\ r_{td},\ y)W, \tag{6.3}$$

where π is the inflation rate, i is the nominal curb market rate of interest, r_{td} is the real time deposit rate of interest, and y is income. Since demands for currency and time deposits are positively related to income, the household sector's supply of funds to the curb market is negatively related to income, given the level of wealth.

The cash base, consisting of currency in circulation and bank reserves (banks are subject to a required reserve ratio $1-q$ against time deposits), is not backed by any private sector assets but is created through transfer payments (van Wijnbergen 1983a, 436). Banks supply loans to the business sector depending on their demand for excess reserves, the level of deposits, and the required reserve ratio. The nominal bank lending rate is fixed by the government below its equilibrium level, in contrast to the curb market interest rate, which is free to find its market-clearing equilibrium level.

Firms' demand for loans is determined by the real product wage and their output. Loan demand is completely inelastic with respect to the curb market rate of interest here. A change in the time deposit rate has no effect on the goods market in van Wijnbergen's model. However, the money market is subject to two effects. On the one hand, a higher time deposit rate increases money demand. On the other hand, substitution out of currency and into time deposits increases the money supply (the money supply multiplier rises with the decline in the currency/deposit ratio).

The net effect in the money market depends on the required reserve ratio and the relative elasticities of demand for currency and curb market assets with respect to the time deposit rate. If people substitute mainly from curb market loans into time deposits after a rise in the time deposit rate, the total supply of funds to the business sector declines. This follows from the assumption that the curb market provides one-for-one intermediation, whereas banks provide only partial intermediation due to the reserve requirement (van Wijnbergen 1983a, 438–439). In this case, the curb market rate rises and output falls. If people substitute mainly from currency into time deposits after a rise in the time deposit rate, the total supply of funds to the business sector will increase, the curb market rate falls, and output goes up.

Neostructuralists expect households to substitute mainly out of curb market loans into time deposits when the time deposit rate is increased. Hence the total supply of loanable funds falls and the curb market rate rises. Even in the longer run, van Wijnbergen (1983a, 448–449) finds that "the initial decrease in financial deepening because of the higher curb market rate persists over time *and our indicator of financial depth declines in the new steady state*." Kohsaka (1984) replicates van Wijnbergen's results with an almost identical model.

Van Wijnbergen (1983b) shows that a tight monetary policy reduces the rate of economic growth by squeezing total credit availability. If the supply reducing effect of such policy is greater than the demand reducing impact, the balance of payments on current account will deteriorate after the introduction of the tight monetary policy; Keller (1980) makes a similar point. With perfect international capital mobility, domestic credit policy has no effect on investment since the real borrowing rate remains at the world level. However, a restrictive domestic credit policy does affect disposable income in this situation by increasing the country's debt service burden.

A one-shot increase in the cash base raises output through the credit availability effect and tends to slow inflation. Here van Wijnbergen repeats an old argument in favor of deficit finance. According to this view, accelerated monetary growth need not be inflationary if it is all spent on productive investment. Suppose, however, that there is a relatively stable velocity of circulation of, say, 4 and an incremental capital/output ratio (ICOR) of 3. Now an increase in the money supply of $3 solely to finance new investment would raise output by $1 but would increase demand by $12. Unless one believes that velocity of circulation is simply a will-o'-the-wisp, it is hard not to conclude that any serious use of monetary expansion to finance investment would be inflationary.[1]

Van Wijnbergen's ambiguous portfolio effects are inevitable in any model containing more than two assets. For example, Peter Montiel (1991) analyzes the short-run effects of financial liberalization in a monetary policy model for developing countries which includes curb and parallel foreign exchange markets.[2] Portfolio choice is extended in this model to include domestic currency, bank deposits, curb market loans, foreign exchange, and bank credit; bank credit is a liability, while the other portfolio components are assets. However, bank credit and curb market loans are perfect substitutes, and hence are treated as a single asset, while currency is ignored. This means that household portfolios consist of three components, bank deposits, bank credit, and foreign exchange.

Montiel includes the wealth effects created by financial repression. On the one hand, access to bank credit provides a subsidy in the form of below-market loan rates. On the other hand, depositors are taxed by below-market administered loan rates that force banks to offer below-market deposit rates. Since reserve requirements ensure that bank deposits exceed bank loans, an increase in financial repression reduces private wealth.

---

[1] After examining the relationship between money and nominal GNP in Britain and the United States during the first half of this century, Milton Friedman and Anna Schwartz (1982, 215) conclude: "A numerically constant velocity does not deserve the sneering condescension that has become the conventional stance of economists. It is an impressive first approximation that by almost any measure accounts for a good deal more than half of the phase-by-phase movements in money or income. Almost certainly, measurement errors aside, it accounts for a far larger part of such movements than the other extreme hypothesis—that velocity is a will-o'-the-wisp reflecting independent changes in money and income. Yet, for most of the period since the mid-1930s, the will-o'-the-wisp extreme has been nearly the orthodox view among economists!"

[2] A similar model is presented in Pierre-Richard Agénor and Peter Montiel (1994).

Changes in reserve requirements and administered interest rates produce both substitution and wealth effects. As in van Wijnbergen's model, the partial equilibrium effect of an increase in administered rates on the total supply of loans in Montiel's model is ambiguous precisely because it depends on the relative substitution out of foreign currency holdings and curb market loans. However, the general equilibrium result indicates that the overall impact of a higher administered interest rate is deflationary, regardless of its effect on the curb market loan rate. This deflationary effect accords with McKinnon-Shaw rather than neostructuralist models.

6.4 Taylor

Taylor (1983, 98–103) also analyzes the effect of an increase in the time deposit rate when households hold gold, bank deposits, and curb market loans. Although there is no multiplier effect working on the money supply, the same ambiguous results found by van Wijnbergen emerge. Taylor (1983, 100) has little doubt as to which outcome is the more likely one:

> The difference between the two extremes hinges on the degree of financial intermediation that the commercial banks can legally provide. The informal market operates with no reserve requirement, channeling resources toward firms with great efficiency. By contrast, a fraction of each new deposit in the commercial banks goes to reserves and cannot be loaned out. Thus, unless banks largely draw hoarded assets [gold] into deposits when i_d [the nominal deposit rate of interest] goes up, the overall effect of reform can be stagflationary.

In the medium run, the saving ratio may respond positively to an increase in the time deposit rate. In such case, real wealth could increase and the total supply of funds to the business sector might increase, even if there were more substitution from curb market loans than from currency in circulation into time deposits. However, if the initial response is a reduction in the total supply of funds to the business sector, inflation will surge because aggregate supply falls by more than demand, and international competitiveness will be reduced, so bringing down profits and investment. The resulting fall in the rate of economic growth may produce a smaller amount of wealth, despite an increase in the saving ratio, than would have existed had there been no increase in the time deposit rate (van Wijnbergen 1983a, 441–451).

In Taylor's model, an increase in the curb market rate will raise the price level through a working capital cost-push effect but lower the price level by reducing investment demand. Whichever price-level effect dominates, an increase in the interest rate reduces the rate of economic growth, provided an increase in the profit rate affects saving by more than it affects investment (the standard stability condition) (Taylor 1983, 91).

An increase in the price level raises the nominal value of firms' fixed capital. This windfall gain stimulates investment, and firms demand more loans. Resources are drawn into the curb market from deposits through a higher interest rate.

When a tight monetary policy is pursued or when the money demand function shifts upwards, the curb market interest rate increases, investment declines, and the rate of economic growth falls (Taylor 1983, 97). In the short run, monetary contraction drives up prices, reduces output, and increases unemployment. These results are identical to van Wijnbergen's, as are Kohsaka's (1984, 428).

In Taylor's full model, households hold bank deposits, curb market loans, and gold. Using a Tobin-type portfolio framework similar to that constructed by van Wijnbergen, Taylor (1983, 94) shows the effects of an increase in the deposit rate of interest which increases money demand when the increase comes mainly from substitution out of curb market loans. In this case, the general price level and the price of gold fall, and investment and growth decline.

Taylor's medium-run results are also similar to those derived by van Wijnbergen. If aggregate demand effects dominate supply effects after an increase in the deposit rate, the inflation rate declines but real wages rise due to a lagged indexing system. The rise in real wages reduces the profit rate, investment, and growth: "A strong saving response to higher deposit rates could salvage the growth rate, although empirical evidence [provided in one neo-structuralist article by Giovannini (1983b)] suggests little to hope for on this score. The conclusion is that unless coupled with expansionary monetary policy from some other source (perhaps a reduction in reserve requirements), financial liberalization will do little to benefit economic performance in the medium run" (Taylor 1983, 122). Buffie (1984) shows that, if saving responds substantially to higher real deposit rates, the long-run multipliers can be opposite in sign to the short-run multipliers. In other words, the curb market rate may rise in the short run because the total supply of credit falls with substitution from curb loans to bank deposits. In the long run, however, the curb market rate could fall if higher deposit rates stimulate a sufficient increase in saving to counteract the leakage through reserve requirements.

E. V. K. FitzGerald (1993) develops a Kaleckian macroeconomic model with several neostructuralist features. Although he includes a banking sector, he finds that money is essentially neutral in the aggregate. There is no role for interest rates in the model because "interest rates do not substantially affect the aggregate rate of saving or investment in developing countries" (FitzGerald 1993, 92). However, higher real interest rates do increase production costs, lower real wages, and cause stagflation. Furthermore, "higher interest rates will undoubtedly cause a shift in portfolio composition in the sense of encouraging capitalists to shift funds out of 'hoarding', or the informal sector into bank deposits. This is held to increase efficiency, although we would doubt that investment is really increased or channelled towards more productive uses by such a transfer" (FitzGerald 1993, 93).

6.5   Curb Markets

Doug Chang and Woo Jung (1984) extend van Wijnbergen's model by introducing two alternative curb markets, a competitive curb market with close links to the banking system on both the demand and supply side, and an uncompetitive, primitive, and fragmented curb market operating independently from the banking system.

Chang and Jung (1984, 6) distinguish between two types of households: small savers who regard time deposits as the only alternative asset to currency, and large savers who face a wide range of investment opportunities, the curb market being perhaps the most important. Chang and Jung (1984, 7) suggest that substitutability between time deposits and curb market loans may not be high for large savers because these assets have very different risk attributes. In such case, the response of small savers to an increase in the time deposit rate could overwhelm the response of large savers. If so, the effect of financial liberalization would be an increase in the total supply of credit to the business sector.

Using the impressionist evidence presented by U Tun Wai (1980, chs. 6, 7), Chang and Jung (1984, 8–16) characterize the uncompetitive curb market as follows:

> The latter, on the other hand, is non-competitive, less developed, and "fragmented." It operates with relatively small funds and a small number of customers. Its information is rather imperfect since the markets are much less homogeneous than the organized markets and are generally scattered over the rural sector. As Wai well puts it, "it is indeed questionable whether the existing arrangements should be referred to as 'markets.'" It works quite independently from the banking system and thus the asset transacted in it may not be regarded as a close substitute of that in the official bank.

However, in both the competitive and the uncompetitive curb markets, interest rates adjust to clear the market.

The combined competitive and uncompetitive curb markets can be analyzed as if they were unofficial private banks. Since such banks have no official backing, depositors can hardly expect the government to bail them out in the event of insolvency. Hence these unofficial private banks may have to hold substantial reserves to meet possible runs. They may also have to hold reserves to meet defaults, which are likely to be greater in the curb market than in the official banking sector; the same point is made by Yoon Je Cho (1990, 478–479). Hence they may not provide 100 percent financial intermediation. Their small scale and imperfect information may well prevent the unofficial private banks from allocating credit as efficiently as the official banks. Clearly, if the curb market is not the efficient allocator of resources that the neostructuralists claim, then their conclusion about the effects of financial liberalization does not hold (Chang and Jung 1984, 18).

Basant Kapur (1992) develops a more formal model of the curb market. In this model, individuals maximize expected utility by smoothing their consumption over time. Hence, they accumulate savings during their working years for consumption during retirement. They also face unpredictable expenses X, such as medical expenses and vehicle repairs, for which insurance is unavailable. These unpredictable expenses never exceed $\overline{X}$.

Individuals can hold bank deposits earning d and curb market deposits earning i. Curb market deposits are less liquid than bank deposits. In contrast to bank deposits, curb market deposits cannot be withdrawn prematurely to meet these unpredictable expenses. If bank deposits are insufficient to meet such expenses, individuals must borrow from banks at an interest rate of h. If $d < i < h$, the utility-maximizing holding of bank deposits lies between zero and $\overline{X}$; remaining wealth is placed in curb market deposits (Kapur 1992, 69). The optimal holding of bank deposits depends on d, i, and h, as well as on the probability density function $f(X)$ of X.

Banks lend not only to individuals confronted with unpredictable expenses but also to firms. The government pegs the interest rate on loans to firms at ℓ. Firms that are unable to obtain sufficient bank financing borrow from the curb market. Financial liberalization taking the form of an increase in ℓ enables banks to raise d. Higher d increases bank deposits and so reduces the demand by individuals for bank loans. Because individuals increase their bank deposits and so reduce their bank borrowing on average, curb market deposits fall on average by more than the average increase in deposits. This greater decline in curb market deposits would be exactly compensated by the smaller average size of individual bank loans were it not for bank reserves. Because banks hold reserves, however, this portfolio shift reduces total lending to firms from banks and curb markets.

Kapur (1992, 75) points out that if the government recycles this windfall seigniorage gain back to firms via development banks or even via the commercial banks the net change in total lending to firms will be zero. However, there is a welfare gain from such financial liberalization since it raises individuals' lifetime wealth; utility from liquidity is cheaper to obtain. Furthermore, the higher bank lending rate may reallocate bank loans to higher-yielding projects through the self-selection process described in Chapter 2.

Jia-Dong Shea (1992) constructs a two-asset portfolio model in which households also hold bank deposits and curb market loans. Large firms can borrow from three sources: abroad, banks, and curb markets. Small firms can borrow only from curb markets. Both types of firms produce exportables and importables. Saving is a function of deposit and curb market interest rates. The government sets import duties, bank deposit and loan rates, and a ceiling on foreign capital inflow. In this model an increase in the deposit rate raises saving, increases bank credit, reduces the curb market rate, and so stimulates capital formation by both large and small firms. Output and welfare rise (Shea 1992, 710–711).

Evidently curb markets can be incorporated into McKinnon-Shaw models without producing the neostructuralist policy conclusions. While curb markets can offer higher returns to depositors, they can also provide small-scale or high-risk loans that banks avoid. Hence, formal and informal financial markets play complementary roles. As Kapur (1992, 76) concludes: "It is not necessary, and indeed it is positively undesirable, to continue to subject the formal financial system to artificial repression in the mistaken belief that only by doing so can the economy reap the benefits offered by the informal financial system." Indigenous financial institutions and markets in developing countries are discussed again in Chapter 14.

6.6   Neostructuralist Dynamics

Both Taylor and van Wijnbergen specify the rational formation of expectations in their models. In a nonstochastic model this implies perfect foresight; expected inflation is actual inflation. Hence expectations cannot provide a source of dynamic adjustment.

Taylor's (1983, 32–36) first dynamic exercise involves a profit-squeeze model. Here the markup rate varies over time as a function of capacity utilization (or the level of unemployment). Should the level of capacity utilization respond positively to the markup rate, the profit squeeze that occurs as capacity utilization rises and unemployment falls would produce convergence to a stable growth path. This convergence may be monotonic or cyclical (Taylor 1983, 35).

For an inflationary economy, Taylor postulates a wage adjustment process as an additional source of dynamic adjustment. In equilibrium, wages are fully indexed to the price level. However, wages catch up with higher prices only at discrete intervals. The lagged adjustment means that the average real wage is related inversely to the inflation rate. The dynamic mechanism has actual money wages growing faster than inflation when real wages are high. Low unemployment (hence high real wages because profits are squeezed when unemployment is low) leads to faster than normal money wage increases.

Faster money growth produces lower inflation, higher growth, and higher real wages when the interest rate effect raising working capital costs dominates. Faster money growth produces higher inflation and higher growth, but lower real wages, when the interest rate effect that reduces investment dominates. The dynamic adjustment mechanism traces out the path from one steady state situation to another. Again convergence can be monotonic or cyclical.

Van Wijnbergen's (1983b) model analyzed in section 6.2 treats inflation as exogenous. For dynamic analysis later in that article and also in his model of the Korean economy (van Wijnbergen 1982), inflation is endogenous. Van Wijnbergen's (1982) model of the Korean economy contains two types of dynamic adjustment. The first is partial adjustment in consumption and investment demand, firms' price setting behavior, the unemployment rate, as well as financial asset and liability demands (modelled by including lagged dependent variables). The second is an expectations-augmented Phillips curve used to determine the nominal wage rate w. Workers set a target real wage w^*. At the end of each period they base their nominal wage demands on their current nominal wage and the price level anticipated in the coming time period P^e. If an inflationary shock previously eroded the real wage below w^*, workers exert additional pressure to catch up.

Van Wijnbergen's (1983b, 51) theoretical model contains an open economy version of the expectations-augmented Phillips curve. The domestic price level in the goods market is sticky, and hence disequilibrium between demand and supply is eliminated only gradually by price adjustments. Rational expectations imply that π^e always equals π, the actual inflation rate. Actual inflation can be decomposed into domestic and imported components.

Because prices do not jump instantaneously to their new equilibrium level, a monetary contraction has the initial effect of reducing credit in real terms, as stressed by McKinnon. The net effect on inflation depends on whether the credit squeeze reduces supply through the working capital channel by more than it reduces investment demand. In a simulation of his Korea model, van Wijnbergen (1982, 159–165) finds that inflation rises in the first quarter following a monetary contraction and then falls in the second and third quarters as demand effects overwhelm the initial supply effects.

Using the deposit rate as a stabilization instrument can produce equally perverse results (van Wijnbergen 1983a, 445). With substitution mainly out of curb market loans, the real credit supply is reduced by the interest rate reform. Cost push inflation occurs in the short run as higher interest rates are passed on in prices and output falls due to the credit availability effect. The benign policy instrument of the McKinnon-Shaw model becomes as malignant as monetary contraction in the neostructuralists' economy.

Van Wijnbergen's (1982, 165–166) solution to the growth-reducing effect of monetary deceleration is an initial increase in the money stock level, followed by a gradual reduction in its growth rate. This is identical to Kapur's (1982) optimal control solution. An initial monetary acceleration in conjunction with interest rate liberalization is also required to stabilize growth in Fry (1978; 1981a, 16). In addressing the credibility problem of such a strategy, van Wijnbergen (1982, 166) points out that an initial *reduction* in the deposit rate of interest would serve just as well as an increase in the money stock level.

6.7   Market Failures

Stiglitz (1994) argues that there is an important role for government intervention and even financial repression in financial markets due to pervasive market failures. An essential function of financial markets is collecting, processing, and conveying information for allocating funds and monitoring their use. Costly information creates market failures.

One market failure arising from costly information occurs because monitoring is a public good. If one individual conducts research to determine the solvency of a financial institution and then acts upon that information, others can benefit from copying his actions. Because information about the management and solvency of financial institutions is a public good, there is suboptimal expenditure on monitoring them. When financial institutions know that they are not adequately monitored by depositors, they have incentives to take greater risks with their deposits.

Costly information can also produce externalities. For example, when several banks fail, depositors may assume that there is an increased probability that other banks will fail. Their reaction in the form of deposit withdrawal may produce the predicted failure. Externalities can also be transmitted across markets. For example, the provision of a bank loan makes it easier for a firm to raise equity capital. The bank loan provides a signal that the firm is sound and prospective equity participants can also expect the bank to monitor the firm in which they will be investing. Naturally, financial institutions are rarely concerned about these externality effects. Hence, private interest can diverge from public interest.

Markets in which information is imperfect are likely to be inefficient even if they are competitive. However, costly information ensures that such markets are unlikely to be fully competitive. Hence, government intervention could improve welfare. In contrast to depositors, borrowers cannot switch easily from one bank to another. First, information about a prospective borrower involves a fixed cost. The borrower's current bank has already incurred this cost, while a new bank would have to incur a cost before extending a loan. Hence, the new bank would charge a higher interest rate or decline to lend. This produces an element of natural monopoly for the current bank. Second, the new bank may decline to lend because it faces an adverse selection problem: Has the current bank restricted credit because the borrower is no longer a good risk? (Stiglitz 1994, 29).

In any event, governments are involved in financial systems. Governments cannot ignore impending collapses of one or more major financial institutions precisely because of the externalities that such a collapse would produce. The government becomes an insurer and this alters behavior. Specifically, "banks, knowing that they are effectively insured, may take greater risks than they otherwise would. In particular, they may undertake risks similar to those undertaken by other banks, since they assume that although the government might ignore the problems of a single bank, it could not allow the entire financial system to go belly-up. So long as the bank does what other banks are doing, the probability of a rescue is extremely high" (Stiglitz 1994, 27).

Stiglitz (1994, 27) continues: "Once we recognize the role of government as an insurer (willing or unwilling), financial market regulations can be seen from a new perspective, as akin to the regulations an insurance company imposes. The effects of some versions of financial market liberalization are similar to an insurance company's deciding to abandon fire codes, with similar disastrous consequences."

Because the government can enforce membership in its insurance programs, it can avoid the adverse selection problem. It may also be able to mitigate moral hazard problems by compelling more disclosure of information and using a range of indirect instruments of control. But because of compulsion, the government cannot discriminate in the same way that private insurance companies can and do. Assessing risk is subjective but competitive markets convert many subjective evaluations into an objective market standard. If individuals object to their car insurance premiums, they can shop around. Banks cannot shop around for alternative deposit insurance programs (Stiglitz 1994, 28).

The existence of market failures justifies government intervention. Stiglitz (1994, 33–39) provides some principles for appropriate government intervention. On the one hand, governments have powers arising from compulsion and proscription that the private sector does not possess. On the other hand, governments have constraints and limitations that can make them less effective than private sector agents in various activities. The first set of appropriate interventions springs from the role of government as the implicit or explicit insurer of the financial system. Here the government can use incentives and restraints designed to reduce the moral hazard problem in ways similar to those used by private insurers. The simplest device to reduce moral hazard problems is to increase capital requirements. The risk-weighted capital-adequacy framework produced by the Bank for International Settlements has rapidly become the worldwide standard to achieve this.

Stiglitz argues that a second set of appropriate government interventions arises from the externalities created by information problems. Given information imperfections, Stiglitz (1994, 39–42) argues that financial repression can improve the efficiency with which capital is allocated. First, lowering interest rates improves the average quality of the pool of loan applicants. Second, financial repression increases firm equity because it lowers the cost of capital. Third, financial repression could be used in conjunction with an alternative allocative mechanism such as export performance to accelerate economic growth. Fourth, directed credit programs can encourage lending to sectors with high technological spillovers.

The importance of information imperfections and the role of government intervention in the area of prudential regulation and supervision can be accepted without accepting the case for financial repression. First, lowering interest rates does not necessarily increase the average efficiency of investment because lower interest rates can encourage entrepreneurs with lower-yielding projects to bid for funds, as pointed out in Chapter 2. Second, financial repression may not lower the marginal cost of capital. Third, using past performance as a criterion for allocating credit discriminates against new entrants and perpetuates monopoly power.

José De Gregorio (1993), Robert King and Ross Levine (1993b), and Nouriel Roubini and Xavier Sala-i-Martin (1992b) demonstrate that financial repression reduces growth both in theory and in practice. Therefore, they too disagree with Stiglitz over the efficacy of financial repression. Valerie Bencivenga and Bruce Smith (1993, 114–116) show that a government program designed to reduce the cost of credit to a particular group of borrowers has the opposite effect to that desired because it exacerbates the adverse selection problem that already exists. In their model, "the program reduces the availability of credit to the group that is its intended beneficiary" (Bencivenga and Smith 1993, 116).

6.8   Financial Repression and Household Borrowing Constraints

Most of the finance and endogenous growth models concentrate on the effect of financial intermediation between savers and investors. Following the McKinnon-Shaw school, they tend to ignore financial intermediation between savers and dissavers. This is consistent with a constant saving ratio which is typically assumed in the more recent literature. However, if easier access to consumer credit or higher returns on financial assets reduce the saving ratio, financial development may not have as great a positive impact on growth as implied by models based on a zero effect.

Tullio Jappelli and Marco Pagano (1994) adopt the three-period model used in Chapter 4. A logarithmic utility function with a discount factor β takes the form:

$$u(c_1, c_2, c_3 = \ln c_1 + \beta \ln c_2 + \beta^2 \ln c_3. \tag{6.4}$$

However, households in this model work only in period 2 for a wage w. Hence they maximize utility subject to:

$$c_1 + c_2/R_2 + c_3/(R_2 \cdot R_3) \leq w_2/R_2; \tag{6.5}$$

$$c_1 \leq \phi w_2/R_2, \tag{6.6}$$

where ϕ is the maximum fraction of their lifetime discounted income that households can borrow in period 1. If the borrowing constraint is not binding, utility-maximizing households consume $(w_2/R_2)/(1 + \beta + \beta^2)$ in period 1 (Jappelli and Pagano 1994, 85).

The inability of young households to consume as much as they would like in period 1 raises the mean age of consumption in the life-cycle model described in Chapter 5. Hence, for a given growth rate, the steady-state saving ratio rises. The larger rate-of-growth effect implies that increased growth has a bigger impact on the saving ratio.

The aggregate production function for endogenous growth takes the form:

$$Y = AK^{\alpha+\eta}. \tag{6.7}$$

If $\alpha + \eta = 1$ equation 6.7 can be expressed in first differences with both sides divided by Y:

$$\Delta Y/Y = \gamma = A(I/Y). \tag{6.8}$$

Since a higher saving ratio produces a higher investment ratio, the growth rate of a closed economy with a binding liquidity constraint is permanently higher than it is in an economy with perfect credit markets (Jappelli and Pagano 1994, 85).

Even without endogenous growth, a reduced saving ratio will lower the steady-state capital stock and so reduce growth during the transition. In a zero-growth economy, the transition occurs as the young generation increases consumption while the old generation continues to consume at a rate higher than the new steady-state level. The old generation was subject to borrowing constraints and so consumes more in periods 2 and 3. The young generation consumes more in period 1 and so less in periods 2 and 3. During the transition the national saving ratio falls (Bayoumi 1993, 1433–1434).

The externalities from endogenous growth imply that financial repression in the form of consumer borrowing constraints may improve welfare. The distortionary welfare loss created by the borrowing constraint is offset by faster growth that in turn increases the wage w. This welfare gain grows over time while the distortionary loss remains constant. Hence welfare loss is unlikely to outweigh welfare gain except for the initial generation. Indeed, Jappelli and Pagano (1994, 90–91) show that with $\alpha = 0.3$ and $\beta = 0.9$ young households would like to borrow 36.9 percent of their permanent income. If ϕ is now imposed at a value greater than 16.8 percent (but less than 36.9 percent), the welfare of all generations, including the present one, increases.

De Gregorio (1992a, 1992b) challenges this argument in favor of household borrowing constraints using the same three-period framework as Jappelli and Pagano. De Gregorio (1992b, 17–19) shows that borrowing constrained individuals are more concerned about present income than about maximizing human wealth. To accumulate human capital, individuals must devote more time to education and less to earning current income. When they are young, therefore, such individuals may reduce time spent in accumulating human capital through education in order to devote more time to earning.

This idea can be extended to an uncertain environment. Suppose that borrowing constraints produce a precautionary demand for nonhuman wealth (Scheinkman and Weiss 1986). Again, therefore, time has to be redirected from accumulating human wealth to accumulating nonhuman wealth. This change in the composition of wealth could reduce the rate of economic growth, despite the increase in physical investment.

6.9 Monitoring Costs as an Externality

Brian Hillier and Tim Worrall (1994) develop a model in which there is hidden information and costly monitoring. Here the existence of risky projects with returns randomly drawn from a normal probability distribution function means that entrepreneurs must first invest to discover the actual return on their projects. Each capitalist can choose between a safe project, a bank deposit, or a direct loan to an entrepreneur. Diversification is impossible and each capitalist faces a safe project with a return also drawn randomly from a normal probability distribution function. Returns on safe projects are generally lower than returns on risky projects but are known in advance.

Banks offer standard debt contracts under which borrowers/entrepreneurs repay capital plus interest R if income equals or exceeds this sum, total income otherwise. Banks monitor entrepreneurs who fail to pay R. Because banks reduce monitoring costs, financial intermediation dominates direct lending. Following Stiglitz and Andrew Weiss (1981), this setup ensures that there is a finite profit-maximizing loan rate above which increased defaults more than offset the higher loan rate on performing loans. It can also mean that at the profit-maximizing loan rate there is excess demand for loans.

Hillier and Worrall (1994, 355–357) show that the average monitoring cost is an increasing function of loan volume. Because the deposit rate must be raised in order to provide more loans, the loan rate must also be raised under competitive conditions. A higher loan rate, however, increases the probability of default and so increases the average monitoring cost. Clearly, marginal cost exceeds average cost.

Social welfare is maximized when the marginal social cost equals the marginal social return. In both rationing and some nonrationing equilibria, Hillier and Worrall (1994, 356–358) show that marginal social cost exceeds marginal social benefit because monitoring costs act as an externality. "Banks, driven by competition, equate expected repayments to expected average monitoring costs plus what must be paid to depositors to secure funds. The resulting equilibrium is not consistent with the condition for social efficiency that the expected return from the marginal project equal the marginal monitoring cost plus what must be paid to depositors. The market produces too many loans and excess monitoring costs" (Hillier and Worrall 1994, 358). In such case, therefore, total welfare can be improved by imposing a ceiling on the deposit rate of interest.

6.10   Sectoral Redistribution of Saving

Building on the work of Michael Kalecki (1939, 1971), Yilmaz Akyüz (1991) shows that changes in the real interest rate can alter income distribution. Specifically, higher real interest rates increase household incomes at the expense of business firms and the government; higher interest rates produce an income transfer from debtors (firms and the government) to creditors (households). If the corporate sector has a higher propensity to save than the household sector, an increase in the interest rate on corporate debt would lower private saving. An increased interest rate on government debt would increase the government's deficit. If the household sector failed to save the entire increase in this interest income, aggregate saving would fall.

Higher interest rates raise the stock of debt relative to aggregate income and so produce financial deepening in Akyüz's model. In this case, however, increased debt corresponds to lower profits rather than increased investment. Hence, Akyüz expects financial deepening produced by higher real interest rates to be accompanied by slower growth as a result of lower saving and investment ratios. Paul Burkett and Amitava Dutt (1991, 134–136) reach a similar conclusion from a Kaleckian model in which higher real deposit rates can reduce output, profits, and investment by reducing aggregate demand, even if the cost of credit is lowered.

David Currie and Michael Anyadike-Danes (1980) point out that if deposit and loan rates move in step under conditions of financial repression, an increase in deposit rates and hence in loan rates could reduce firms' internally generated funds for investment (undistributed profits) by more than it increases the supply of domestic credit in real terms. As in Akyüz's model, the burden of higher loan rates could therefore reduce investment. This raises the important but unanswered question of how undistributed profits might be affected by the loan rate of interest under differing market conditions.

However, consider the situation in which loan rate ceilings are always evaded through compensating balances and the effective or shadow loan rate (always higher than the fixed bank lending rate at the margin) clears the market. In terms of Figure 2.1, $d-\pi^e$ equals r_0 and $\ell-\pi^e$ equals r_3. With this assumption, business saving would be deterred in the Akyüz and Currie–Anyadike-Danes models when the real deposit rate is held below its competitive free-market market level because the real loan rate of interest is then *above* its competitive free-market equilibrium level. An increase in $d-\pi^e$ towards its competitive level lowers $\ell-\pi^e$ and so raises business saving, investment, and growth.

In practice, the private corporate sector typically pays an effective loan rate that clears the market at the margin (r_3 in Figure 2.1). Intramarginally, subsidized loans are often supplied to export industries and to agriculture. The public sector, however, pays the official fixed loan rate (that moves in step with the deposit rate) to government-owned financial institutions. Lower real loan rates increase the number of investments with low or negative yields which appear financially viable. Hence the public sector's investments may well become increasingly inefficient as real deposit and loan rates to the public sector fall.

As the gap between the real deposit rate and the effective real loan rate charged to the private sector widens, banks engage in a larger volume of low-yielding expenditures on nonprice competition. A higher real deposit rate lowers the effective real loan rate to the private corporate sector and so stimulates investment in this sector, reduces unproductive investment by banks on establishing new bank branches, and may curtail some of the worst public sector projects.

Currie and Anyadike-Danes (1980) provide no explanation of why corporate saving might be adversely affected by higher loan rates. Indeed, corporate sector saving could well be a positive function of both the real return to investment and the real cost of bank borrowing. Suppose that an increase in the real deposit rate towards its competitive free-market equilibrium level increases the real supply of bank credit and lowers its cost. The greater volume of investment that then occurs may lower the real return to investment. Corporate saving would fall because both the real loan rate and the real return to investment decline. However, the reduction in corporate saving could not offset completely the increase in household saving in financial assets if the return on investment falls: the lower return on investment occurs only because the level of investment rises.

In a related paper, Venkataraman Sundararajan (1986b, 20–22) specifies net corporate saving as a function of the level of real output, excess demand for money, real wages, and the real cost of capital. The opportunity cost of equity funds is the present and prospective yields on loans from noninstitutional markets (curb market loans), since entrepreneurs place spare funds on the curb market. The real cost of capital is a weighted sum of the real opportunity costs of equity and debt finance. In contrast to Akyüz and Currie and Anyadike-Danes, Sundararajan finds that higher administered deposit and loan rates of interest raise corporate saving.

Evidently the effect of loan rates on corporate saving depends on various assumptions on which the model is built. In any closed economy model, however, financial liberalization that increases productive investment necessarily increases saving in forms that enable this investment to occur. Corporate or household saving could increase, or households could reduce unproductive investment and release resources for productive investment by the corporate sector by holding more financial assets. Any reduction in public sector saving produced by financial liberalization would also have to be offset by higher private sector saving.

6.11 Higher Average Borrowing Costs

Philip Arestis and Panicos Demetriades (1993) also use a Kaleckian framework to suggest that higher real interest rates reduce aggregate demand because increased markups associated with increased interest costs reduce real wages. In turn, lower aggregate demand reduces investment. In an open economy, higher real interest rates also appreciate the real exchange rate. This reduces export competitiveness and so deters investment in this sector. Arestis and Demetriades (1994) also suggest that financial liberalization can enable banking systems to exploit monopoly power and increases income inequality.

Arestis and Demetriades (1992) construct a model in which firms finance investment from both banks and curb markets. Firms maximize shareholder wealth subject to three constraints: net revenue, capital depreciation, and the supply of bank credit at a subsidized interest rate rationed on the basis of the firm's capital stock. The third constraint implies that a firm's cost of capital depends on both the bank lending rate and the curb market rate. At the macroeconomic level, a higher bank loan rate could increase the proportion of credit supplied at this less subsidized rate. Hence, the overall effect of a higher bank lending rate is ambiguous.

Buffie (1991) also explores the effects of rationed and subsidized bank loans on capital accumulation. He shows that credit policies tend to have effects in an overlapping-generations model that are opposite to those produced in an infinite-horizon model. In the infinite-horizon model, policies that increase capital accumulation when unanticipated induce capital decumulation when anticipated. Here Buffie uses neoclassical models to show that the clear-cut effects of financial liberalization produced by McKinnon-Shaw models are far from robust.

Nicholas Snowden (1987) presents some simulations based on Korean data to examine the consequences of higher bank loan rates on returns to equity. He suggests that higher loan rates could reduce returns to equity sufficiently to deter innovation and entrepreneurship. This deterrent effect could be offset by an increased supply of bank loans. Whether higher deposit rates are accompanied by higher loan rates or by greater efficiency within the financial sector, Snowden (1987, 91) argues that financial liberalization increases risk facing the banking system.

None of these authors considers how the real supply of subsidized credit is affected by the administratively fixed interest rate structure. One remote possibility is for the government to increase taxes to finance the subsidy. Another is to rely on the central bank. Unless prices fail to respond to the concomitant monetary acceleration, this option can provide only a temporary solution. Eventually higher expected inflation will reduce real money demand and so the real size of the banking system.

6.12   Portfolio Reallocation in General Equilibrium

Montiel, Pierre-Richard Agénor, and Nadeem Ul Haque (1993, chs. 4, 5) extend Montiel's (1991) model by introducing a Cobb-Douglas production function in which capital, labor, and intermediate imports are combined to produce home and export goods. Hence, this model includes supply functions for home goods and exports. Competitive conditions determine the equilibrium wage rate, to which wage contracts converge with a partial adjustment. Dynamics are also introduced through forward-looking expectations and changes in asset stocks. Hence, anticipated future changes in interest rates produce immediate effects.

The existence of administered interest and exchange rates produce a curb market and a parallel foreign exchange market. A premium in the parallel foreign exchange market encourages underinvoicing of exports. The smuggling of exports from the country provides foreign exchange to meet import demand not satisfied by the rationed supply of foreign exchange at the official exchange rate.

In contrast to neostructuralist models, the price of home goods is determined by the competitive interaction of demand and supply. The demand for currency is a function of the level of transactions, while the demand for bank deposits is a function of the administered deposit rate, the curb market rate, and the expected return on foreign currency. Private sector demand is influenced not only by disposable income and real wealth, but also by the real curb market interest rate. Since this rate is affected by monetary conditions, the price of home goods and the inflation rate are also determined by monetary conditions. The central bank finances that part of the government's deficit not financed by a predetermined amount of foreign borrowing (Montiel, Agénor, and Haque 1993, 120–130).

Montiel, Agénor, and Haque (1993, ch. 5) simulate this model with parameter values selected, where possible, from available econometric estimates. A simulated increase in administered interest rates produces substitution out of both curb market loans and foreign exchange. This raises the curb market rate and appreciates the exchange rate in the parallel market. The exchange rate appreciation reduces private wealth, part of which is held in foreign exchange. This wealth effect could offset the relative price effect of the deposit rate increase and actually reduce deposit demand.

Three effects reduce both prices and output in this model. First, the exchange rate appreciation exerts a negative wealth effect on aggregate demand, since some wealth is held in the form of foreign exchange. Second, the exchange rate appreciation reduces export supply. Third, the higher curb market interest rate reduces aggregate demand. Evidently, financial liberalization in this model produces both deflationary and recessionary effects as in the neostructuralist models: "The short-run macroeconomic effects of McKinnon-Shaw financial liberalization policies may prove to be problematic" (Montiel, Agénor, and Haque 1993, 153).

Although the Montiel-Agénor-Haque model omits the essential credit-availability effect incorporated in the McKinnon-Shaw models, the increased curb market interest rate caused by higher administered deposit and loan rates indicates that aggregate loan supply is reduced by the portfolio reallocation, as suggested by the neostructuralists. However, the rise in the curb market rate is produced not by direct portfolio substitution effects but, given the particular parameter values used, by the wealth effect of the currency appreciation on the demand for deposits and curb market loans. With greater substitutability between curb loans and deposits or a required reserve ratio lower than the 40 percent chosen by Montiel, Agénor, and Haque (1993, 133), the curb market interest rate could be reduced by higher administered interest rates.

While a lower curb market rate does not affect output directly in the Montiel-Agénor-Haque model, it could offset the contractionary effect of the currency appreciation were a credit-availability effect incorporated into the model. Nevertheless, this model provides considerably more insight into the general equilibrium effects of financial liberalization, which neither the McKinnon-Shaw nor the neostructuralist models provide. As the authors claim, it demonstrates that "the existence of informal financial markets cannot be ignored in developing country macroeconomics. In each of four policy shocks considered, informal financial markets play a key role in determining the timing, direction, and magnitude of macroeconomic effects" (Montiel, Agénor, and Haque 1993, 157).

6.13 Alternative Explanations for Financial Repression

Burkett (1987) interprets the prevalence of financial repression in Marxist terms: "Financially repressive interest rate policies are rooted in the patronage relations between the state and domestic classes which develop as a result of the absence of a strong domestic bourgeoisie (itself a symptom of unequal development), and/or in the attempts of Third World states to alter the international division of labor" (Burkett 1987, 17). Financial liberalization, which may be part of a stabilization program supported by the International Monetary Fund, generally requires increased political repression. However, "the inability of repressive strategies of financial liberalization to promote economic development reflects the limitations of externally oriented accumulation in the context of the unequal international division of labor caused by the uneven development of capital accumulation on a global scale" (Burkett 1987, 17).

Burkett (1987, 17) concludes:

> The analysis in this paper points out the need for financial policies
> which work to facilitate the financing of industrial production and to
> increase the real return on the savings of workers and peasants in Third
> World countries, without being associated with the repression of these
> groups by the state. This must involve the development of financial
> institutions which, through their establishment and operation, effect a
> transfer of political and economic hegemony to workers and peasants, in
> the context of a revolutionary program for the self-generating economic
> development of Third World Countries. This is where the truly difficult
> problems of "financial policy" begin.

Wontack Hong (1986) reaches a rather similar political explanation for
financial repression. Hong (1986, 358) argues that governments enjoy possessing power such as credit rationing provides, even if the result is a lower
saving ratio. Thus, the government develops an institutionalized monopsonistic capital market in which workers who save in financial form have to accept
whatever deposit rate the financial system dictates. Benefits are distributed to
large firms. "The unprivileged small entrepreneurs will have extra hardships
in their investment activities and the workers will have to accept disincentives for their wealth accumulation activities, but these are the members of the
underdeveloped societies who have to follow as best they can" (Hong 1986,
358).

6.14 Summary

A significant insight that the neostructuralist work brings to financial development modelling is the importance of noninstitutional finance or the curb
market. The absence of curb markets in the McKinnon-Shaw models represents a serious lacuna. As Chang and Jung (1984) point out, however, curb
markets take different forms. They are not necessarily so "competitive and
agile" as Taylor believes them to be. After the brief review of the available
economic literature on indigenous finance provided in Chapter 14, one must
conclude that much more empirical work is needed before the efficiency of
curb markets and commercial banks can be compared. The same goes for the
comparative degrees of substitutability between curb loans, inflation hedges,
and inside money. Here, however, the literature on curb markets suggests that
curb market and bank loans are complementary rather than competitive.

Taylor specifies a markup pricing mechanism, whereas van Wijnbergen
(1983a, 435–441) treats inflation as exogenous for part of his analysis. Although van Wijnbergen specifies a portfolio model containing demand functions for both currency and time deposits, the velocity of circulation is inde-
terminate in this model; the same is true of Taylor's model. Only in this way,
it seems, can monetary expansion stimulate aggregate supply by more than

aggregate demand, hence reducing the price level. It is indeed hard to believe that sustained monetary expansion could have any such benign outcome. In fact, when inflation is treated as endogenous, van Wijnbergen (1982, 1983b) supports this conclusion.

Both the McKinnon-Shaw and neostructuralist models assume that the government uses all the revenue it raises from the reserve requirement tax for transfer payments. Had the government a fixed public sector borrowing requirement, however, any increase in real money demand could be met by a reduction in the required reserve ratio. Indeed, the McKinnon-Shaw school advocates a reduction in the required reserve ratio as part of a financial liberalization program. In this case, the marginal financial intermediation of the banking system is identical to the 100 percent marginal financial intermediation of the curb market.

The same would also be true were the cash base not entirely outside money. Consider a typical situation in which the cash base is backed by loans to both the government and to the private sector through the rediscount mechanism. Then, with a fixed government borrowing requirement, an increase in the demand for money would increase the ratio of private to public sector debt backing the cash base through increased rediscounts. Again, the marginal financial intermediation of the banking system would be 100 percent. Effectively, banks would borrow all their additional required reserves from the central bank. Kapur (1992, 75) suggests additional central bank lending to development banks as yet another way of recycling these additional required reserves back to the private sector.

Stiglitz employs microeconomic analysis to argue that credit markets are particularly prone to market failures. This justifies government intervention. Stiglitz presents a convincing case for government intervention in the area of prudential regulation and supervision due to the government's *de facto* role as an insurer of the financial system. However, his arguments that financial repression can improve the average quality of the pool of loan applicants, increase firm equity, reward good performance, and encourage lending to sectors with high technological spillovers can be challenged.

Chapter 7

The Required Reserve Ratio in Financial Development

7.1 Introduction

REQUIRED RESERVE RATIOS against banks' deposit liabilities feature in both the McKinnon-Shaw and the neostructuralist models. A reserve requirement is essential in Basant Kapur's model to prevent the growth-maximizing rate of monetary expansion being infinite when the nominal deposit rate of interest is free to find its competitive free-market equilibrium level. The neostructuralists view the reserve requirement in the same way as Kapur; it constitutes a leakage in the intermediation process. The existence of required reserves may therefore reduce the intended effects of financial liberalization or even produce perverse results.

Both the McKinnon-Shaw school and the neostructuralists expect higher reserve requirements to reduce funds available for investment by reducing the demand for deposits or reducing the fraction of a given volume of deposits that is available for investment. Anthony Courakis (1984, 1986) shows that under some circumstances higher reserve requirements actually generate a larger volume of deposits. This can occur if the demand for loans is sufficiently interest inelastic relative to the demand for deposits that the equilibrium deposit rate rises with an increase in the required reserve ratio. If the funds obtained from required reserves are channelled to specialized development finance institutions for lending that would not be undertaken by the commercial banks, the total volume of loanable funds can be increased.

This chapter examines reserve requirements from three perspectives. The first is Courakis's partial equilibrium model, in which there can exist a positive deposit-maximizing required reserve ratio. The second follows some of my own partial equilibrium work (Fry 1981b) on tapping consumer surplus through differential pricing of nonhomogeneous components of the money stock. That work is extended in section 7.3 to show that the monopolistic profit-maximizing or cost-minimizing deposit rate can be secured from a competitive banking system through the imposition of differential reserve requirements against different types of deposits.

Neither of these models is set in a general equilibrium framework. Hence the welfare implications of pursuing either a deposit-maximizing or differential pricing strategy with respect to setting required reserve ratios are unclear. Fortunately, this lacuna has been filled by Philip Brock (1989) and Valerie Bencivenga and Bruce Smith (1992), whose models are reviewed as a third perspective in section 7.4. However, this chapter does not cover payment of interest on reserve requirements as a monetary policy instrument analyzed by David Van Hoose (1986) nor how reserve requirements impede the transmission of asset quality information by banks to their depositors examined by Stuart Greenbaum and Anjan Thakor (1989).

7.2 The Deposit-Maximizing Required Reserve Ratio

The conventional analysis of a required reserve ratio shows that required reserves on which no interest is paid impose a tax on financial intermediation at all nonnegative inflation rates. The simplest illustration abstracts from all resource costs of banking and has banks holding a volume of loans that equals the total volume of deposits. In such case, the competitive deposit rate d equals the competitive loan rate ℓ. Now a 20 percent required reserve ratio $1-q$ is imposed. With a 10 percent market clearing loan rate, the competitive deposit rate of a zero-cost banking system is 8 percent, as shown by equation 3.7. Provided that deposit demand is not completely interest inelastic, the volume of deposits will decline. The volume of loans will fall even more, since the smaller volume of deposits now has to be spread between both loans and reserves. In this example loan demand is perfectly interest elastic.

Reducing the required reserve ratio raises the deposit rate that can be offered for any given loan rate in Kapur's model. Hence one growth-enhancing policy suggested by Kapur's model and advocated by Ronald McKinnon (1977, 15; 1982, 162) is a reduction in the required reserve ratio or the payment of the market clearing loan rate on required reserves. Kapur (1974, 147–149), Donald Mathieson (1980), and McKinnon (1981) imply that the growth-inhibiting feature of bank reserves can be alleviated only by reducing the required reserve ratio or the inflation rate. Another solution in the tradition of David Ricardo, Keynes of the *Treatise*, Dennis Robertson, Jacob Viner, and John Gurley and Edward Shaw (1960) is to pay interest on required reserves (Berger 1980, Fry 1979b).[1] Were the cash base backed entirely by rediscounts (central bank holdings of private sector liabilities), the money stock would

---

[1] Van Hoose (1986) shows that paying interest on required reserves could also be used to dampen the variability of the money stock.

be entirely inside money. In conjunction with the abolition of interest rate ceilings, paying a competitive return on bank reserves would make money neutral in Mathieson's model and in a slightly modified version of Kapur's model in which banks finance the same proportion of net and replacement working capital investment (Fry 1982b, 735–736).

All McKinnon-Shaw models, as well as neostructuralist models, assume that funds extracted through reserve requirements are spent on government consumption or transfer payments. They are not used for investment either directly by the government or indirectly through central bank lending to specialized development finance institutions. Hence the availability of investible funds from a given volume of deposits is reduced *pari passu* by an increase in required reserves held by the banks. Paying the market clearing loan rate on required reserves removes the reserve requirement tax completely and so eliminates the effect of inflation on the real deposit rate of interest. However, the reserve requirement still crowds out investment when required reserves are outside money used for government consumption or transfer payments. Only the complete elimination of reserve requirements maximizes the rate of economic growth in such case, except when the banking system faces a completely inelastic demand for loans, as Mathieson assumes.

Neostructuralist models feature the reserve requirement as the key to comparing the efficiency of financial intermediation through the banking system unfavorably with the efficiency of financial intermediation through the curb or unregulated financial markets. The negative effect of required reserves on financial intermediation in the neostructuralist models comes entirely from the assumption that reserves are not available for investment finance by either the private or public sector.

Martin Bailey (1956) claims that a competitive banking system subject to a required reserve ratio $1-q$ would offer a deposit rate of interest equal to $q\pi$, where π is the inflation rate, provided the competitive deposit rate in the absence of inflation were zero. Bailey's result is valid only if demand for bank loans is perfectly elastic at the competitive real loan rate of interest. Otherwise, bank borrowers would bear some of the inflation tax burden, and the competitive nominal deposit rate would be greater than $q\pi$ (Fry 1981b, 263).

Courakis (1984) shows that when the banking system faces loan demand that is not perfectly interest elastic the imposition of a required reserve ratio can actually raise the profit-maximizing deposit rate and hence the volume of deposits. The imposition of a reserve requirement raises the loan rate and reduces the volume of bank loans under both competitive and monopolistic conditions. If the loan demand function is sufficiently interest inelastic, the profit-maximizing strategy for both competitive and monopolistic banks is to raise deposit rates in order to attract more deposits.

More generally, the effect of a required reserve ratio on the deposit rate of interest depends on both the loan and deposit demand functions. Maximizing the volume of deposits may involve setting a positive level of required reserves. It will do so if the interest elasticity of loan demand is less in absolute magnitude than the interest elasticity of deposit demand (Courakis 1984, 346–349). Courakis notes that the relationship between deposit volume and the required reserve ratio is not monotonic. Hence, initially, raising the reserve ratio can raise both the deposit rate of interest and the volume of deposits as noted by David Romer (1985, 184).[2] Eventually, however, raising the reserve ratio can lower both the deposit rate and deposit volume. In such case, there is a positive deposit-maximizing required reserve ratio.

Specifically, Courakis (1986, 154) formulates loan L^d and deposit D^d demand functions and the banks' balance sheet identity:

$$L^d = a_0 + a_1\ell; \tag{7.1}$$

$$D^d = b_0 + b_1 d; \tag{7.2}$$

$$L = qD, \tag{7.3}$$

where ℓ is the loan rate, d is the deposit rate, and $1-q$ is the required reserve ratio. In the zero-cost banking case, competition ensures that d equals $q\ell$. Hence the required reserve ratio $1-q$ drives a wedge between d and ℓ. The competitive equilibrium condition sets average cost AC equal to average revenue AR.

Total revenue TR and cost TC functions can be derived in terms of deposits from equations 7.1 to 7.3:

$$TR = (q^2 D^2 - a_0 qD)/a_1; \tag{7.4}$$

$$TC = (D^2 - b_0 D)/b_1. \tag{7.5}$$

Average revenue and cost functions can be produced by dividing equations 7.4 and 7.5 by D. Equating average cost and revenue gives the competitive equilibrium level of deposits D_{rr} in terms of q:

$$D_{rr} = (a_0 b_1 q - b_0 a_1)/(b_1 q^2 - a_1). \tag{7.6}$$

Imposing a tax rate of t on interest paid on deposits under competitive conditions also drives a wedge between the deposit and loan rate. The banking system has to subtract the tax rate t from loan earnings before paying out the net deposit rate. In effect, the average revenue function becomes

$$L^d = a_0 + a_1(1-t)\ell. \tag{7.7}$$

---

[2]In Romer's (1985, 186) general equilibrium model, "the directions of movement of almost all relevant variables [induced by an increase in the required reserve ratio] are ambiguous. Deposits, loans, and seignorage can all either increase or fall. One can show that if there is a representative consumer, the increase in the reserve requirement necessarily reduces welfare."

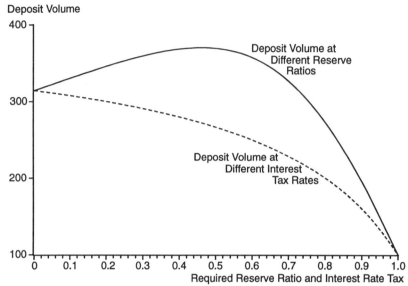

Figure 7.1. Deposit Volumes under a Required Reserve Ratio and a Deposit Interest Tax

Setting $\tau = 1 - t$, the competitive equilibrium level of deposits is

$$D_t = (a_0 b_1 \tau - b_0 a_1)/(b_1 \tau - a_1). \qquad (7.8)$$

Figure 7.1 shows deposit volumes from equations 7.6 and 7.8 with $a_0 = 400$, $a_1 = -2000$, $b_0 = 100$, and $b_1 = 5000$. The interest rates used in the equations are expressed as proportions rather than percentages. The deposit volume rises as the required reserve ratio is increased until the required reserve ratio equals 0.46. Thereafter the deposit volume declines. In contrast, a tax on the deposit rate of interest produces a monotonic decline in deposit volume. With zero reserve requirement and interest tax, the competitive equilibrium volume of deposits is 318. As the reserve requirement is increased, the competitive equilibrium produces an increase in the deposit rate of interest in order to attract additional resources into the banking system. Hence the deposit volume rises initially. An increasing tax on deposit interest always reduces the competitive deposit rate net of tax and hence lowers the deposit volume, while raising the competitive loan rate of interest. With a tax rate or a required reserve ratio of 100 percent, the deposit volume in both cases is 100, since in both cases the net deposit rate of interest is then zero.

One might well question the objective of deposit maximization. However, if required reserves are used to finance investments that otherwise would not be undertaken, using the required reserve ratio to maximize deposits is also using it to maximize investment. In particular, one could envisage the use of required reserves held by commercial banks to finance specialized development finance institutions (DFIs) that lend to investors who for one reason or another have no effective demand for commercial bank loans. The evidence presented in Chapters 13 and 14, however, shows that DFIs financed in this way have performed poorly throughout the developing world.[3]

Courakis (1986, 163–165) shows that if banks hold some other asset (in addition to bank loans), such as treasury bills, that is in elastic supply to the banking system, any increase in the required reserve ratio will lower the deposit rate of interest, the volume of deposits, and bank holdings of such bills. Broad treasury bill markets of the kind needed for a perfectly elastic supply of bills to the entire banking industry are characteristic of industrial rather than developing countries. Hence the traditional negative relationship between deposit volume and the required reserve ratio is more likely to be observed in industrial than in developing countries.

However, Courakis (1986, 165–167) also analyzes the case of a banking system facing a perfectly elastic supply of funds in a wholesale deposit market (market for certificates of deposit [CDs]), as well as an upward sloping supply of retail deposits. In this case, an increase in the required reserve ratio raises the loan rate, reduces the volume of loans, and may increase the volume of wholesale deposits taken in, while leaving the rate for and volume of retail deposits unchanged. Since the wholesale deposit market is a feature of industrial rather than developing countries, the presumption that industrial countries are more likely than developing countries to exhibit a negative relationship between the required reserve ratio and total deposit volume must be invalid.

Eugene Fama (1985) argues that in the United States the CD reserve requirement tax is borne by bank borrowers but that the reserve requirement tax on retail deposits is borne mainly by these depositors. That bank borrowers pay some of the reserve requirement tax implies that bank loans have no close substitutes. An explanation for this is provided in Chapter 13. Christopher James (1986) presents econometric evidence to support the claim that CD rates are unaffected by changes in reserve requirements. Furthermore, he finds that announcements of bank loan agreements raise the stock price of borrowing firms, whereas announcements of public debt offerings reduce stock prices. This finding also suggests that bank loans are special.

Money is not neutral when the banking system has to hold required reserves on which no interest is paid. Returning to the numerical example given at the beginning of this section, let inflation π now rise to 190 percent. Assume a perfectly elastic demand for loans. The nominal market clearing loan rate rises to 200 percent, since the market clearing real loan rate remains at

---

[3]McKinnon and Mathieson (1981, 7–15) and Alvin Marty (1990) use a rather similar model to analyze the choice of an inflation-minimizing required reserve ratio, given the government's financing requirement.

10 percent. With a 20 percent required reserve ratio, the competitive nominal deposit rate is now 160 percent. The real deposit rate of interest falls from +8 to –30 percent. The tax on deposits has increased dramatically.

In Kapur's model with a fixed return on working capital r^*, the competitive or optimal real deposit rate $d-\pi^e$ equals $q(r^*+\pi^e) - \pi^e$ or $qr^* - (1-q)\pi^e$. Evidently, the optimal real deposit rate of interest is inversely related to the expected inflation rate in the presence of reserve requirements and a perfectly elastic demand for loans. When all money is held in the form of bank deposits, the inflation tax is extracted entirely through reserve requirements (Bailey 1956; Brock 1982, 1984; Fry 1981b; Lee 1980; McKinnon 1981; McKinnon and Mathieson 1981; Remolona 1982).

The deposit-maximizing required reserve ratio also varies with expected inflation and hence with nominal interest rates (Courakis 1984, 356–359). As inflation rises, the deposit-maximizing required reserve ratio declines. Specifically, Courakis (1984, 368) rewrites the loan and deposit demand equations in terms of real rates of interest:

$$L^d = a_0 + a_1\ell - a_1\pi; \tag{7.9}$$

$$D^d = b_0 + b_1d - b_1\pi. \tag{7.10}$$

Now the competitive equilibrium deposit volume becomes

$$D_{r\pi} = [a_0b_1q - b_0a_1 + a_1b_1(1-q)\pi]/(b_1q^2 - a_1). \tag{7.11}$$

Differentiating equation 7.11 with respect to the required reserve ratio $1-q$ and setting the result equal to zero gives the deposit-maximizing reserve ratio k^* in terms of the inflation rate:

$$k^* = \left[2b_1(a_0b_1 - a_1b_0) - \{[2b_1(a_0b_1 - a_1b_0)]^2\right.$$

$$\left. - 4b_1^2(a_0-a_1\pi)[a_0b_1(b_1+a_1) - 2a_1b_0b_1 + b_1a_1(b_1-a_1)\pi]\}^{\frac{1}{2}}\right]$$

$$/ \left[2b_1^2(a_0 - a_1\pi)\right]. \tag{7.12}$$

Figure 7.2 shows that the deposit-maximizing reserve requirement falls monotonically from 1 at an inflation rate of –20 percent to zero at an inflation rate of 11.43 percent.

Given the inflation rate and the deposit-maximizing required reserve ratio, the competitive deposit volume can be calculated from equation 7.11. The loan volume can also be calculated from equation 7.3. These deposit and loan volumes are shown in Figure 7.3. Finally, equations 7.9 and 7.10 are inverted to give both the real and nominal deposit and loan rates of interest. Nominal and real deposit and loan rates are also related through the relationships

$$d = q\ell; \tag{7.13}$$

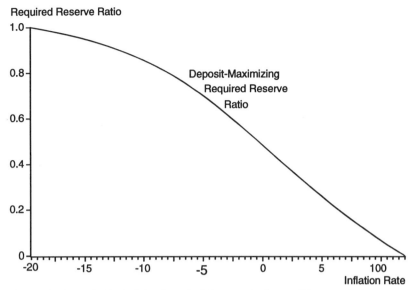

Figure 7.2. Deposit-Maximizing Required Reserve Ratio at Different Inflation Rates

$$d - \pi = q\ell - \pi. \qquad (7.14)$$

The nominal and real deposit and loan rates corresponding to the deposit-maximizing required reserve ratio at each inflation rate are shown in Figure 7.4.

Figures 7.2 to 7.4 indicate that the change in the required reserve ratio needed to maximize the deposit volume as inflation changes does not restore neutrality.[4] A lower inflation rate reduces the burden of required reserves because it decreases the gap between the zero return on reserves and the nominal loan rate of interest. The opportunity cost of holding reserves falls as inflation falls. At an inflation rate of –20 percent, required reserves incur no opportunity cost because there is no demand for loans at a nominal loan rate of zero and hence at a real loan rate of 20 percent. As the inflation rate rises, deposit maximization requires that some interest-earning loans be held in order to raise the nominal deposit rate of interest above zero. In turn, this involves reducing the required reserve ratio continuously from 1 to zero at an inflation rate of 11.43 percent.

---

[4]McKinnon and Mathieson (1981, 7–15) produce similar results in analyzing the inflation-minimizing required reserve ratio.

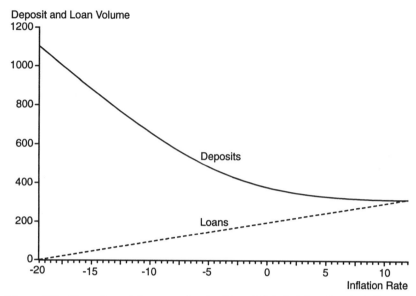

Figure 7.3. Deposits and Loans under the Deposit-Maximizing Required Reserve
Ratio at Different Inflation Rates

7.3   Differential Reserve Requirements

Suppose the government of a developing country is persuaded of the benefits
of financial liberalization. It realizes that this means giving up a crucial
revenue source, the inflation tax, and decides reluctantly that it cannot afford
to embark on any program of financial liberalization. Is there any second-best
solution?

The one explored here involves abandoning the price distorting tax at the
margin for a nondistortionary intramarginal tax. Specifically, it uses the reserve requirement to tap consumer surplus as an alternative source of revenue
for the government.

For simplicity, assume that wealth can be allocated among just three assets:
noninterest-earning components of the money stock D, interest-earning components of the money stock T, and tangible assets held as inflation hedges
A. Rodney Barrett, Malcolm Gray, and Michael Parkin (1975) develop a
stochastic cash requirement model in which assets possess just two attributes,
return and liquidity. Minor modifications of this model are made to derive the
following complete system of linear demand equations consistent with profit
maximization under uncertain cash requirements and positive liquidation costs
of converting T and A into D:

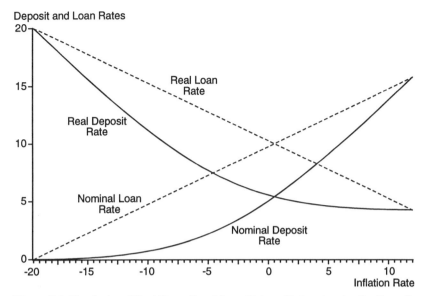

Figure 7.4. Nominal and Real Deposit and Loan Rates of Interest under the Deposit-Maximizing Required Reserve Ratio at Different Inflation Rates

$$D^* = [b_{10} + b_{11}i_D + b_{12}i_T + b_{13}i_A]W, \qquad (7.15)$$

$$T^* = [b_{20} + b_{21}i_D + b_{22}i_T + b_{23}i_A]W, \qquad (7.16)$$

$$A^* = [b_{30} + b_{31}i_D + b_{32}i_T + b_{33}i_A]W, \qquad (7.17)$$

where D^*, T^* and A^* are desired or long-run demands for D, T, and A, respectively, i_D is the nominal yield on noninterest-earning components of the money stock and is therefore always zero, i_T is the nominal rate of interest on time deposits, and i_A is the nominal yield on inflation hedges (the expected rate of inflation).

The ranking of these assets by return is identical to the ranking by illiquidity (the higher the return, the less liquid is the asset). Liquidation costs are greater for tangible assets than for deposits. The stochastic cash requirement model dictates the imposition of various restrictions on the coefficients of equations 7.15 to 7.17:

> The structure of these asset demand functions is very simple. The demand for the first asset depends only on its own rate of interest, the rate of interest on the next asset, and the upper limit of the probability distribution of cash requirements. Very sensibly, the function implies that the demand will rise if either the own rate rises or if the upper limit of the cash distribution rises and that demand will fall if the rate on the next asset rises. The "interior" asset demands depend only on three rates:

the own and two adjacent ones. Again, the response to a change in the own rate is positive and that to the other rates negative. The last asset demand depends in the usual way on its own rate and the rate on the next last asset, wealth, and the cash requirement upper limit. (Barrett, Gray, and Parkin 1975, 505)

The two modifications made here are to assume that the cash requirement distribution is proportional to wealth (making the asset demands homogeneous in wealth) and that the liquidation cost is also proportional to wealth rather than proportional to the value of the liquidation transaction (so adding a constant in each demand function).

Under these assumptions, the structure of these asset demand functions is very simple. The demand for the first asset depends only on its own rate of interest, the rate of interest on the next asset, and the upper limit of the cash requirement probability distribution. Demand for the interior asset (time deposits) is affected by all three rates of return. Demand for the last asset depends on its own rate, the rate on the next but last asset, and the cash requirement upper limit.

This system of demand equations satisfies the additivity constraints and the Slutsky symmetry conditions. While Cournot aggregation gives $\sum_{i=1}^{3} b_{ij} = 0$ for $j = 1, 2,$ and 3, Engels aggregation gives $\sum_{i=1}^{3} b_{i0} = 1$. Slutsky symmetry implies $b_{12} = b_{21}$, $b_{13} = b_{31}$, and $b_{23} = b_{32}$. Note that the Slutsky symmetry conditions are derived directly from profit maximization subject to stochastic cash requirements. In this case they apply to regular rather than to income-compensated demand functions.

Equations 7.15 to 7.17 can now be rewritten as follows (with the coefficients renamed):

$$D^* = [a_3 + a_1 i_D \qquad\qquad - a_1 i_T \qquad\quad]W, \qquad (7.18)$$

$$T^* = [a_4 - a_1 i_D + (a_1 + a_2)i_T - a_2 i_A]W, \qquad (7.19)$$

$$A^* = [a_5 \qquad\qquad\qquad - a_2 i_T + a_2 i_A]W. \qquad (7.20)$$

Evidently $a_2 > a_1 > 0$. One equation is redundant. Given wealth, demands for noninterest-earning components of the money stock D and time deposits T determine the demand for tangible assets as a residual.

Equations 7.18 to 7.20 represent long-run or desired demands. Short-run or actual demands adjust to long-run levels with a lag. Here I assume that a fixed proportion p of asset holders reviews its portfolios each year and adjusts its holdings to satisfy its demand functions, given the current rates of return, i_D, i_T, and i_A. The proportion $p(1-p)$ of asset holders reviewed and adjusted its portfolios last year, $p(1-p)^2$ the year before last, and so on. Hence,

$$D/W = p(D^*/W) + p(1-p)(D^*/W)_{t-1}$$

$$+ p(1-p)^2(D^*/W)_{t-2} + \cdots. \qquad (7.21)$$

Applying the Koyck transformation gives:

$$D/W = p(D^*/W) + (1-p)(D/W)_{t-1}. \tag{7.22}$$

Since i_D equals zero, short-run demand functions for currency and deposits are estimated in the form

$$D/W = b_{10} + b_{11}i_T \qquad\qquad + b_{13}(D/W)_{t-1}, \tag{7.23}$$

$$T/W = b_{20} + b_{21}i_T + b_{22}i_A + b_{23}(T/W)_{t-1}. \tag{7.24}$$

Two constraints for both the additivity and the Slutsky symmetry requirements can be imposed on this system from equations 7.18 to 7.20 in the estimation process:

$$b_{11} + b_{21} + b_{22} = 0, \tag{7.25}$$

$$b_{13} - b_{23} = 0. \tag{7.26}$$

Here is an empirical application of this model to Turkey over the period 1952–1978 using annual observations. Noninterest-earning money D is actually currency in circulation plus demand deposits (*M1*). Deposits T are time and saving deposits. Values for D and T are averages of beginning and end of year observations. The proxy for wealth W is permanent income calculated from weights estimated in Fry (1980b, 537) by applying a polynomial lag to past rates of change in per capita real GNP. Hence the previous year's real GNP is adjusted for expected growth. The expected rate of inflation i_A was estimated in the same way by applying a polynomial to past rates of change in the GNP implicit deflator. No regular econometric forecasts are published in Turkey, and the level of economic education is not high. Therefore, it seems reasonable to assume that expectations there regarding future inflation and income changes are formed on the sole basis of past values of the variables themselves. Only in special circumstances would such expectations be "rational." The deposit rate i_T is the return offered on 12-month time deposits. The inflation and deposit rates are continuously compounded and expressed in proportional rather than percentage form.

Using Kenneth White's (1978) maximum likelihood routine, the estimates of equations 7.23 and 7.24, subject to the constraints in equations 7.25 and 7.26, are (t values in parentheses):

$$
\begin{aligned}
D/W = \quad & 0.039 - 0.118i_T \qquad\quad + 0.847(D/W)_{t-1}, \\
& (2.913)(-2.248) \qquad\quad (15.524)
\end{aligned}
\tag{7.27}
$$

$$\overline{R}^2 = 0.64$$

$$T/W = -0.001 + 0.167i_T - 0.049i_A + 0.847(T/W)_{t-1}.$$
$$(-0.403) \quad (2.779) \quad (-3.043) \quad (15.524)$$

(7.28)

$$\overline{R}^2 = 0.95$$

The estimated demand for tangible assets can be derived from equations 7.27 and 7.28. The long-run or desired demand functions D^*, T^*, and A^* can be calculated by substituting the coefficients estimated in equations 7.27 and 7.28 into equations 7.18 to 7.20:

$$D^* = [\quad 0.255 + 0.769i_D - 0.769i_T \qquad]W, \qquad (7.29)$$

$$T^* = [-0.007 - 0.769i_D + 1.091i_T - 0.322i_A]W, \qquad (7.30)$$

$$A^* = [\quad 0.752 \qquad - 0.322i_T + 0.322i_A]W. \qquad (7.31)$$

Note that i_D has a coefficient, despite its observed value of zero throughout the regression period. Benjamin Klein (1974) stresses the importance of including the own rate of return, even if zero, in formulating a money demand function.

Now suppose that the competitive free-market equilibrium real time deposit rate i_T-i_A is 0.03 or 3 percent when reserve requirements against time deposits are zero, and that loan demand is infinitely elastic. The problem now is to determine the values of i_T and i_A that minimize the cost of generating the total real demand for money when i_T-i_A equals r^*, in this case 3 percent. The problem can be formulated in terms of setting deposit rates i_D and i_T to minimize cost C:

Minimize $\qquad C/W = i_D(D/W) + i_T(T/W)$ (7.32)

subject to $\qquad\qquad i_T - i_A \geq r^*;$ (7.33)

$$D/W = [a_3 + a_1 i_D - a_1 i_T];$$ (7.34)

$$T/W = [a_4 - a_1 i_D + (a_1 + a_2)i_T - a_2 i_A].$$ (7.35)

The cost-minimizing solution is bound to produce an equality in the second constraint. Hence this can be rewritten $i_T - i_A - r^* = 0$.

Since i_T is set in terms of i_A and r^*, the long-run cost-minimizing value of i_D can be obtained by taking the partial derivative of the following expression:

$$C/W = i_D[a_3 + a_1 i_D - a_1(i_A + r^*)]$$

$$+ (i_A + r^*)[a_4 - a_1 i_D + (a_1 + a_2)(i_A + r^*) - a_2 i_A].$$ (7.36)

The partial derivative of equation 7.36 with respect to i_D is

$$\frac{\partial(C/W)}{\partial i_D} = a_3 + 2a_1 i_D - 2a_1(i_A + r^*) = 0.$$ (7.37)

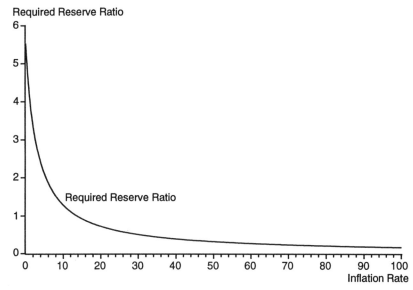

Figure 7.5. Required Reserve Ratio to Maintain a 16.6 Percentage Point Gap between Demand and Time Deposit Rates of Interest at Different Inflation Rates

The solution of equation 7.37 in terms of i_D is

$$i_D = i_A + r^* - a_3/2a_1. \tag{7.38}$$

With a_1 equal to 0.769 and a_3 equal to 0.255 from equation 7.29, the cost-minimizing deposit rate is $i_A + r^* - 0.166$. With zero inflation and r^* equal to 0.03, i_D should be set at -0.136 or -13.6 percent. If i_D is constrained to equal zero, then the inflation rate should be set at $a_3/2a_1 - r^*$, in this case 13.6 percent. The appropriate nominal time deposit rate would then be 0.166 or 16.6 percent.

To achieve this deposit rate structure in a competitive banking system using differential reserve requirements necessitates the imposition of a required reserve ratio against demand deposits equal to $a_3/2a_1(i_A + r^*)$, provided demand and time deposits incur the same administrative costs and possess identical characteristics as sources of loanable funds to the banks. This implies a required reserve ratio of 5.527 when inflation is zero. In other words, required reserves are a multiple, rather than a fraction, of demand deposits. With 13.6 percent inflation, the required reserve ratio is 1 (100 percent). When inflation rises to 80 percent, the required reserve ratio falls to 0.2 (20 percent). Figure 7.5 plots the nonlinear relationship between inflation and the required reserve ratio needed to maintain the cost-minimizing gap between demand and time deposit rates of interest.

Figure 7.5 illustrates the same feature of required reserve ratios as do Figures 7.2 to 7.4; namely, that the burden of required reserves is positively associated with the inflation rate. In this case the upper bound on the required reserve ratio need not be 1, since required reserves in excess of the volume of demand deposits can be met from time deposits.

Introducing some inelasticity in the demand for loans implies that the competitive real time deposit rate will no longer remain constant as the required reserve ratio on demand deposits varies. Hence the real time deposit rate will no longer be invariant to the inflation rate. Specifically, the real time deposit rate will fall as the inflation rate rises. In such case, the required reserve ratio needed to maintain the cost-minimizing gap between time and demand deposit rates of interest will fall more gradually than it would in the case of perfectly elastic loan demand as the inflation rate rises.

7.4 Optimal Reserve Requirements

The welfare cost of inflationary finance has been examined numerous times since Bailey's (1956) seminal analysis. The same technique can be applied to a combination of inflation rates and reserve requirements. Some of the welfare loss could be offset if the inflation and reserve requirement taxes are used to finance public sector investment (Mundell 1965). Then the higher growth rate from higher investment could offset some or all of the welfare loss from inflation. Alvin Marty (1990, 168) shows, however, that "the traditional argument against inflation as a tax, which rests on showing that welfare costs of the tax are excessive at moderate rates of inflation, remains intact even when the increase in the growth rate due to inflationary finance is brought into the picture."

Brock (1989) develops a model in which individuals hold both currency and deposits to illustrate the point that the government can choose a reserve requirement ratio as well as an inflation rate to maximize revenue from inflation. Individuals acquire consumption goods by shopping. Shopping time is reduced by a transactions technology that is a function of currency and deposit holdings in real terms.

The opportunity cost of holding currency is the nominal interest rate i and the deposit rate of interest is qi, where $1-q$ is the required reserve ratio. In other words, Brock adopts the assumption of a zero-cost competitive banking system used earlier. Brock (1989, 108) generates demands for currency and deposits in general functional form from the first-order conditions for utility maximization. By deriving indifference curves from the utility function for various combinations of inflation and reserve requirements, Brock (1989, 113–114) shows that there is a welfare-maximizing combination of inflation and reserve requirement for each government deficit. For some classes of transactions technology, welfare maximization involves raising the required reserve ratio and the inflation rate as the government's financing requirement increases.

Bencivenga and Smith (1992) also analyze the welfare effects of using financial repression in the form of a higher required reserve ratio when the government has to monetize its deficit. As usual, the government creates outside money or currency to finance its deficit. The Diamond-Dybvig (1983) model of financial intermediation is embedded in an overlapping generations model with production and capital accumulation. Bencivenga and Smith (1992) use this three-period model (described in Chapter 4) to show why individuals facing an uncertain future can benefit from the liquidity provided by banks. The two primary assets in the economy are capital and outside money. All other financial markets, except that for bank deposits, are suppressed for reasons explained in Chapter 1.

Young individuals work only in the first period of their lives for a real wage w_t and consume only in periods 2 and 3. All young individuals have utility functions of the form:

$$u(c_1, c_2, c_3) = \ln(c_2 + \phi c_3), \tag{7.39}$$

where ϕ equals 1 with probability π and 0 with probability $1-\pi$. Hence, they allocate their total earnings in period 0 between currency, capital, and deposits. This implies that the saving ratio is constant and invariant to changing financial conditions. Since bank deposits offer an expected return higher than currency, individuals hold deposits but not currency.

Banks accept deposits and invest them in capital and currency. As cooperative institutions, banks choose their deposit rates in the form of payments to be made per unit of deposit, r_1 and r_2 for periods 1 and 2, and their reserve ratio $1-q$ to maximize the expected utility of a representative depositor. Provided the return to capital exceeds the return to currency, young individuals hold all their initial wealth in the form of bank deposits.

Capital is produced by an investment technology such that one unit of the consumption good invested at t yields R units of capital at time $t+2$. The production function for all firms takes the form $k_t^\theta L_t^{1-\theta}$, where k is the quantity of capital and L the quantity of labor used. Firms operate competitively and maximize profits given a market real wage w_t, on which the government levies an income tax at a rate τ. Government expenditure g exceeds this tax revenue τw_t. The return to capital is $\theta k_t^\theta L_t^{1-\theta} = \theta k_t[(1 - \theta)/w_t]^\alpha$, where $\alpha = (1 - \theta)/\theta$. The market-clearing equilibrium wage is $w_t = (1 - \theta)\pi^\theta k_t^\theta$. The steady-state wage w^* turns out to equal $(1-\theta)[R\pi(1-\theta)(1-\tau)]^{1/\alpha}$. The value of the capital invested in a firm measured in terms of the consumption good is $R\theta[(1 - \theta)/w_{t+2}]^\alpha$.

Investors who do not operate their firms at $t+2$ lose all their capital investment. Type A individuals live three periods, while type B individuals live only two periods. At the beginning of age 2, individuals discover whether they are type A individuals and will live to operate firms at age 3; the probability is π. Type B individuals withdraw all their deposits at the beginning of age 2 to consume all their savings during their last period. Type A individuals choose to keep all their deposits in the bank for the higher level of consumption this will allow at age 3.

Young individuals have expected utility $(1 - \pi) \ln(c_2) + \pi \ln(c_3)$. To maximize this expected utility, banks maximize:

$$\ln[(1 - \tau)w_t] + (1 - \pi)\ln r_1 + \pi \ln\{r_2\theta[(1 - \theta)/w_2]\alpha\}, \qquad (7.40)$$

subject to their resource constraints

$$(1 - \pi)r_1 = (1 - q)(p_t/p_{t+1}) \qquad (7.41)$$

and

$$\pi r_2 = Rq. \qquad (7.42)$$

The banks' solution is to invest π of their total resources in the investment technology and $1-\pi$ in currency reserves. This allocation implies that banks offer a real deposit rate at time $t+1$ equal to the return on their currency reserves p_t/p_{t+1}, where p is the price level, and a deposit rate at time $t+2$ equal to R. This optimizing solution provides a relatively small amount of consumption for type B individuals and a relatively large amount for type A individuals. However, banks cannot pay more than p_t/p_{t+1} to type B individuals because they hold currency reserves exactly equal to type B individuals' deposits in order to maximize expected utility.

Even the return r_1 is better than the return that could be achieved by type B individuals who held some positive amount of capital in their portfolios. Because their capital investments are lost, their portfolio return is less than p_t/p_{t+1}. In other words, banks can eliminate entirely the potential loss from an unexploited capital investment.

The welfare-maximizing voluntary reserve ratio depends on the specific utility function chosen. For example, elsewhere Bencivenga and Smith (1991) give young individuals the utility function:

$$u(c_1, c_2, c_3, \phi) = -(1/\gamma)(c_2 + \phi c_3)^{-\gamma}. \qquad (7.43)$$

In this case, the optimal voluntary reserve ratio is

$$1 - q = 1 - \Phi/(1 + \Phi), \qquad (7.44)$$

where

$$\Phi = \left(\frac{\pi}{1 - \pi}\right)^{1/(1+\gamma)} \left[\frac{\pi n}{(1 - \pi)\theta\pi^{\theta-1}R}\right]^{\gamma/(1+\gamma)} \qquad (7.45)$$

and $n = p_t/p_{t+1}$. This utility function also makes the conditions under which financial intermediation will increase the growth rate somewhat more restrictive.

After calculating the steady-state demand for currency reserves by the banks, Bencivenga and Smith (1992, 243) show that:

$$\frac{p_t}{p_{t+1}} = \frac{(1-\pi)(1-\tau)w^* - (g - \tau w^*)}{((1-\pi)(1-\tau)w^*)}. \tag{7.46}$$

In other words, inflation is determined by the government's deficit $g - \tau w^*$ and variables that determine the banks' demand for currency reserves, π, τ, and w^*.

Suppose that the government sets a minimum reserve requirement $1 - \overline{q}$ that is greater than $1 - \pi$. Assuming that all investment continues to be intermediated, banks will increase r_1 and reduce r_2:

$$r_1 = (1 - \overline{q})(p_t/p_{t+1})/(1 - \pi) > p_t/p_{t+1}; \tag{7.47}$$

$$r_2 = R\overline{q}/\pi < R. \tag{7.48}$$

Under these conditions, banks have more resources in the form of currency reserves for type B individuals who withdraw their deposits at the start of period 2 and less in the form of capital for type A individuals who are residual claimants at the start of period 3.

Since banks invest less in capital with the deposits of young individuals, the steady-state capital stock is smaller and output lower. The corresponding lower steady-state wage rate reduces the real value of deposits. Hence, the overall effect on banks' demand for real currency reserves is ambiguous. If higher reserve requirements actually reduce banks' demand for real currency reserves, a higher reserve requirement *raises* the equilibrium inflation rate.

For given values of g and τ, Bencivenga and Smith (1992, 246–249) show when welfare can be improved by raising the required reserve ratio. *Ceteris paribus,* welfare is improved by lower inflation which raises r_1 and by a lower required reserve ratio which increases output. Hence, welfare cannot be improved by raising the required reserve ratio if this reduces banks' real currency reserve demand and so increases the inflation rate. Even if inflation is reduced by a higher required reserve ratio, welfare could be reduced by the lower level of output. Welfare will be increased by raising the required reserve ratio if the loss from reduced output is more than offset by the gain from reduced inflation. The optimal reserve requirement occurs where the marginal welfare loss from reduced output and poorer risk sharing just offsets the marginal welfare gain from lower inflation.

In establishing the precise conditions under which welfare will be increased by raising the required reserve ratio, Bencivenga and Smith (1992, 244) demonstrate that if the required reserve ratio is set such that $\overline{q} < \pi^2$ young individuals will place some of their savings directly into capital investment. In other words, a sufficient degree of financial repression will produce investment channels, such as curb markets, that avoid the reserve requirement. In this case, however, the capital investment of those not surviving into period 3 is lost.

Bencivenga and Smith (1992, 250–252) demonstrate that welfare is always increased by reducing reserve requirements to the point at which no young individuals choose to invest directly in capital and so place all their savings in the banks. They equate direct investment with curb markets or informal finance and conclude: "From a welfare perspective, it is desirable to draw resources into the banking system, where they are subject to the inflation tax, and where risk is shared more efficiently. Moreover, increasing $\bar{q}$ to its optimal value will eliminate the informal sector altogether" (Bencivenga and Smith 1992, 253). Because of the particular characteristics of this curb market, its existence is never welfare improving despite the fact that its existence eliminates the negative effect of higher reserve requirements on output. In this situation, therefore, financial liberalization is welfare improving but does not affect output.

Welfare is raised by increasing the reserve requirement in Bencivenga and Smith's model because it reduces inflation and so raises r_1. Although a single bank could redistribute consumption from type A to type B individuals by holding more reserves, this would not increase expected utility of young individuals. Only when higher reserve holdings are accompanied by lower inflation can there be a net welfare gain. This can be achieved through coercion or collusion. In either case, however, a higher reserve ratio reduces output. Since raising the income tax rate also reduces welfare, the optimal τ will not necessarily eliminate the government's deficit.

Using a different model, Alex Mourmouas and Steven Russell (1992) examine the alternative choice of raising government revenue through a required reserve ratio or a deposit tax. If the equilibrium solution involves a diversified portfolio containing both fiat money and physical capital, a binding required reserve ratio is broadly equivalent to raising the same revenue through a combination of seigniorage and deposit taxation. If the equilibrium solution does not involve a diversified portfolio, pure taxation of deposits Pareto-dominates the required reserve ratio.

7.5 Summary

The main upshot of section 7.2 is that the developmental effects of reserve requirements depend, not surprisingly, on the use to which the required reserves are put. In all extant financial development models, higher required reserve ratios against deposits reduce the volume of loans supplied by the commercial banks or other group of financial institutions subjected to the requirements. However, if the reserves are used to augment commercial bank loans with additional lending by development banks, the total volume of loans supplied by the financial system could be increased by a rise in the required reserve ratio.

Section 7.3 outlines a strategy of financial liberalization designed to minimize its negative impact on government finances. Specifically, the model uses the reserve requirement to make a competitive banking system engage in product discrimination. The monopoly profit obtained from this product discrimination accrues to the government as an alternative, albeit smaller, revenue source to the standard inflation tax extracted through uniform noninterest-earning reserve requirements. It must be emphasized again that both these models are based on partial equilibrium analysis and hence have no direct welfare implications. What they do show are the impacts of reserve requirement policies on the volume of deposits and the interest cost of attracting them to the banking system.

The general equilibrium model presented in section 7.4 does address the welfare issue of imposing binding reserve requirements. Within the restrictive assumptions of the model, Bencivenga and Smith show that the welfare-maximizing reserve requirement is not necessarily the inflation-minimizing one. This is because required reserves affect output as well as inflation. Hence, the welfare-maximizing reserve requirement occurs when the marginal gain from lower inflation just equals the marginal loss from reduced output and less efficient risk sharing.

Part II

Econometric Testing of Financial Development Models

Chapter 8

Effects of Financial Conditions on Saving, Investment, and Growth

8.1 Introduction

EMPIRICAL RESEARCH ON financial repression focused initially on its saving and investment effects. The worldwide inflation immediately following the publication of the books by Ronald McKinnon (1973) and Edward Shaw (1973) turned financial restriction into financial repression or worsened existing financial repression in many industrial and developing economies. Gaps between controlled and free-market interest rates widened, and institutional interest rates (loan as well as deposit rates) became negative in real terms almost everywhere. The result was disintermediation into direct financial claims where they existed or into inflation hedges (Cole and Patrick 1986, 39; Galbis 1979, 365).

In evaluating the experience of negative real institutional interest rates, Millard Long (1983, 22) enumerates the following effects: reduced national saving, more capital flight, worse misallocation of resources, excessive lending to prime borrowers, resurgence of noninstitutional money markets, increased use of foreign financial institutions, and increased problems of monetary control. Since then potential effects of financial conditions have been tested on numerous groups of countries with an array of alternative techniques. While few would disagree that financial development occurs in conjunction with rising per capita incomes, the issue of causality is hotly disputed. Does financial development cause economic growth or does it follow passively in the wake of economic growth? In econometric tests, one solution is to isolate exogenous financial variables, another is to conduct some form of causality test.

Since the mid-1970s financial deregulation and liberalization policies have been adopted by a large number of countries (Balassa 1989, Caprio et al. 1994, Cheng 1986b, Cho and Khatkhate 1989, Cole and Patrick 1986, Haggard,

Lee, and Maxfield 1993, McKinnon 1991, Tseng and Corker 1991). Real interest rates moved from negative levels to historically high positive levels in the industrial countries as well as in a number of developing countries. Hence the postwar period should offer enough variety in financial conditions to permit empirical investigation into some of their effects. Unfortunately, however, little consensus has emerged over the interpretation of the evidence. It appears that "good" financial conditions precede higher economic growth, but that radical financial reforms designed to produce these favorable financial conditions fail to deliver accelerated growth.

This chapter surveys the available quantitative empirical evidence on the effects of financial conditions on the volume of saving, the quantity and efficiency of investment, and the rate of economic growth in developing countries during the postwar period. Three quantitative measures of financial conditions considered here are the real deposit rate of interest, the rural population per rural bank branch, and a financial intermediation ratio. Section 8.2 surveys the evidence on the effects of financial conditions on national saving ratios. Sections 8.3 and 8.4 examine the quantity and quality of investment. Section 8.5 turns to the reduced-form evidence on the short- and medium-run impact of financial conditions on the rate of economic growth.

The three quantitative measures of financial conditions in developing countries may be proxies for the general state of an economy's financial conditions. If real deposit rates have been negative over substantial periods of time and if no efforts have been made to extend branches of depository institutions into rural areas, financial conditions in general are likely to be unconducive to domestic resource mobilization. Raising real deposit rates of interest and proliferating bank branches in rural areas do not in themselves constitute a general program of financial development. Hence it may well require more comprehensive financial reform and development to produce the effects on saving behavior and investment efficiency that these quantitative variables alone appear to yield. This caveat should be borne in mind throughout this chapter.

8.2   Saving Ratios

The proportion of GNP allocated to capital formation (the investment ratio) is one of the key determinants of sustained economic growth. Domestic investment can be financed from both national and foreign saving, but everywhere national saving provides the bulk of resources for investment. Hence saving behavior is a crucial element of the process of economic growth.

National saving flows to domestic investment via three channels: government appropriation, self-finance, and financial intermediation (both formal and informal). The relative importance of each channel depends, in the main, on the level of economic development and the roles ascribed to public and private sectors of the economy. Countries that rely more heavily on government appropriation place less emphasis on financial intermediation for the financing of investment.

Particularly since the collapse of the Soviet Union, developing countries have assigned a larger role to the private sector in the development process. In the face of contracting net inflows of external finance and a tendency for greater reliance on the private sector, the role of financial intermediation in the saving-investment process has become increasingly important for economic development. This section reviews the effects of financial conditions on domestic resource mobilization.

In an influential article written in the early 1970s, Raymond Mikesell and James Zinser (1973, 17) conclude that "it seems likely that interest rates are more significant in determining the channels into which savings will flow in the developed and developing countries than in altering saving propensities." However, most of the empirical studies published by that date had given little if any attention to modelling the formation of expectations about the inflation rate. Furthermore, real interest rates had not varied substantially in the industrial countries. Few empirical studies on the effect of financial conditions on saving in developing countries, with the exception of work on Taiwan and Korea, had been conducted.

The debate over the interest sensitivity of saving in developing and industrialized countries is still unsettled and continues to generate more heat than light. Franco Modigliani (1986, 304) asserts that "despite a hot debate, no convincing general evidence either way has been produced, *which leads me to the provisional view that* s [the saving ratio] *is largely independent of the interest rate.*" However, Mancur Olson and Martin Bailey (1981, 1) claim that "the case for positive time preference is absolutely compelling, unless there is an infinite time horizon with the expectation of unending technological advance combined with what we call 'drastically diminishing marginal utility.' This finding holds both in the positive and normative senses. *A corollary is that savings are interest elastic*" [emphasis added].

Michael Boskin (1978) finds a significantly positive interest rate coefficient in a saving function for the United States. My own empirical work reveals significantly positive interest rate effects on saving ratios in a sample of 14 Asian developing countries and Turkey (Fry 1978, 1979a, 1981c, 1984, 1991a). The empirical work of both authors has been subjected to considerable criticism. Those investigators looking for interest sensitivity find it, while those expecting no influence find none. For example, Rudiger Dornbusch and Alejandro Reynoso (1989, 205) state: "Evidence from the United States and other industrialized countries supports skepticism in that virtually no study has demonstrated a discernible net effect [of real deposit rates on saving ratios]." What is agreed, however, is that if an effect exists at all it is relatively small.

The disagreement over the empirical findings on the interest elasticity of saving springs from different measures of saving and real interest rates, different theoretical models, different econometric techniques, different samples of developing countries, and different time periods. As a broad generalization, positive interest rate effects are easier to find in Asia than in other parts of the developing world, but even in Asia the effects appear to have diminished over the past two decades, possibly because of financial liberalization.

For cross-country estimation, my preference is to use the gross national saving ratio SNY rather than other saving measures. The national saving ratio is defined as nominal gross national saving divided by nominal GNP. National saving is calculated by subtracting foreign saving from gross domestic investment (fixed investment plus changes in inventories). Foreign saving is defined as imports minus exports of goods and services minus net factor income from abroad ($SFY = IMY - XY - NFIY$).

Until the mid-1970s, the choice between national (including net factor income from abroad) and domestic saving (excluding net factor income) was fairly unimportant, because net factor incomes from abroad tended to be small in most developing countries. With the rapid rise in workers' remittances and foreign debt service (both components of net factor income from abroad) since the mid-1970s, the choice has become nontrivial. In part, national saving is chosen here as the dependent variable in preference to domestic saving because of the high degree of substitutability between domestic saving and workers' remittances. As household heads go abroad, their domestic household income and hence saving out of such income plunge. However, remittances sustain living standards of these households and saving out of domestic income plus remittances may actually increase. Hence, while domestic saving falls, national saving need not. One might reasonably anticipate that a drop in workers' remittances resulting from the return of household heads would be largely offset by a pickup in domestic saving. In other words, there is likely to be strong substitutability between domestic saving and the workers' remittance component of national saving.

In the second place, interest payments on foreign debt reduce national saving but not domestic saving. It seems irrational to ignore interest payments, while recognizing income from and expenditures on all other current-account transactions. Individuals ignore their interest payment obligations at their peril; so do nations. Furthermore, national saving measures the resources available locally to finance domestic investment. While domestic saving may indicate effort, national saving indicates the net result of that effort.

National saving also measures a country's own efforts, whether at home or abroad, to mobilize resources for investment. On the one hand, not all domestic saving is available to finance domestic investment when net factor income from abroad is negative. On the other hand, domestic saving will understate the funds generated by a country's own efforts (the country's own equity in its investment) when net factor income from abroad is positive. In this case, domestic saving presents an erroneously pessimistic picture of the national effort to mobilize resources.

The saving function developed in Chapter 5 focuses on determinants of household saving. On the one hand, private sector saving constitutes by far the largest component of national saving in most developing economies. On the other hand, the household sector uses the financial system extensively to channel its saving to investment. Since this book is concerned with domestic resource mobilization through financial development, its basic emphasis is necessarily on household saving behavior.

Household saving data are unavailable for most developing countries. There is therefore no choice but to examine household saving behavior indirectly through either national saving, which consists of household (including workers' remittances), business, and government saving, or private saving consisting of household and business saving. In fact, there is a strong argument against separating household from business saving. If business saving rises in the form of higher retained earnings, the real wealth of the households owning these firms also increases. Household saving might well decline as a result of this wealth effect. Conversely, if business saving falls, households owning firms would have to increase saving from other sources in order to achieve any particular wealth accumulation goals.

A similar case can be made against excluding government saving. Those households that are saving for retirement may treat government saving to finance pension programs as a substitute for their own efforts. An increase in government saving for higher pensions might therefore reduce household saving by a comparable amount. To the extent that business and government saving are close substitutes for household saving, it would be inappropriate to exclude them from an analysis of household saving behavior.

Indeed, all government saving or dissaving may be a substitute for household saving, since current government saving may imply lower future tax rates. With this expectation, households would consume more now and hence save less, in anticipation of higher disposable income in the future. Conversely, government dissaving now implies higher taxes later, and households may reduce their current consumption and hence save more in the expectation of lower future disposable income. In this Ricardian equivalence framework, therefore, household and government saving are virtually perfect substitutes. Household saving falls when government saving rises, and vice versa.

Were government saving not a close substitute for private saving, government and national saving ratios should be positively related. An examination of the relationship between government saving ratios and national saving ratios in 10 Asian developing economies for which data are available reveals no relationship at all between the direction of change in the government saving ratio and the direction of change in the national saving ratio between 1976 and 1981. In other words, the direction of change in the government saving ratio provides no prediction whatsoever of the direction of change in the national saving ratio. This finding is consistent with the substitutability hypothesis outlined above. It therefore supports the choice of national saving as the relevant variable for econometric analysis.

In any case, under inflationary conditions the disaggregation of saving between private and public saving invariably becomes badly distorted. One reason for this is that nominal interest payments are treated solely as current expenditure, rather than as part current expenditure and part principal repayment. The inflation premium in the nominal interest rate compensates for the erosion in the real value of financial claims and is, therefore, principal repayment in real terms.

I use current price rather than constant price data to calculate the national saving ratio for two reasons. First, the primary motive for saving is future consumption. Hence a constant price saving series should use the price of consumption goods as a deflator. In fact, however, constant price saving data are deflated implicitly by the investment price index, since national saving is derived by subtracting foreign saving from investment. Second, foreign saving measured at constant prices holds import and export prices constant. Hence it is quite possible to calculate negative foreign saving at constant prices when a deterioration in the terms of trade has produced a large balance-of-payments deficit on current account. In such case, the negative constant price measure of foreign saving is misleading and the relevant measure for the purposes of economic analysis is the positive current price measure of foreign saving corresponding to the actual, albeit current price, balance-of-payments deficit on current account.

Finally, I prefer gross rather than net saving because of the very arbitrary nature of depreciation allowances used to calculate net investment. These allowances differ from one country to another, so introducing even more problems of comparability.

The first major obstacle encountered by all macroeconomic studies of saving behavior lies in obtaining consistent and reliable saving data (Deaton 1990, 63–64; Gonzáles Arrieta 1988, 603). National saving is always obtained as a residual when it is derived from national income accounts; the only alternative is to use consumer income and expenditure data from sample surveys. National expenditure Y is the sum of $C + I + X + NFI - IM$, where C is consumption, I is investment, X is exports, NFI is net factor income from abroad, and IM is imports. Since saving S equals $Y - C$, it must also equal $I + X + NFI - IM$. In other words, national saving is calculated either by subtracting consumption from GNP or by subtracting foreign saving from gross domestic investment.

As discussed in Chapter 5, removing capital surreptitiously from a country can involve underinvoicing exports and overinvoicing imports. Higher recorded import costs and lower recorded export receipts reduce measured output Y by exactly the same amount as it affects the measured current account $X + NFI - IM$. By raising the cost of intermediate inputs (imports) and lowering the value of final output (exports), measured value added in each sector of the economy is also reduced. Similarly, higher measured import costs and lower measured export receipts reduce factor income by exactly the same amount as they reduce national output and expenditure by lowering recorded profits. Hence, whether national saving is calculated by subtracting consumption from income or by adding the current account to domestic investment, national saving will be underestimated.

Measurement errors in saving estimates arise from inaccuracies in both investment and balance-of-payments data. Gross domestic investment is usually estimated using the materials flow method. Annual additions to the fixed capital stock are estimated indirectly from figures for expenditures on commodities used for capital formation, such as steel and cement. Large margins of error arise from deriving total investment expenditure from a small number of constituent parts. Attempts to check these investment estimates from the expenditure side often run into the serious problem of income and output underreporting to evade taxation. Estimating inventory changes adds another major source of inaccuracy to the total investment figure.

Most of these errors tend to exert a downward bias on the investment estimate. By itself, a downward bias in an investment estimate would produce a downward bias in the corresponding national saving estimate. Frequently, however, this is partially offset by the underestimation of foreign saving that occurs when the exchange rate is overvalued and hence foreign exchange is undervalued. In this case, the conversion of foreign exchange receipts and payments into domestic currency will underestimate all balance-of-payments figures, including of course the gap between expenditures and receipts on the current account.

Despite these caveats regarding data inaccuracies, econometric analysis of the determinants of saving behavior in developing countries need not necessarily yield misleading results, provided that the saving data biases are constant over time and that the errors are random. The existence of large random errors reduces the ability of regression techniques to identify behavioral relationships. However, the greater the number of observations, the higher is the probability of detecting significant statistical relationships from poor data. For this reason, a good deal of the econometric analysis discussed here is based on pooled time-series data. A large number of observations permits behavioral relationships to be detected, despite the existence of substantial random errors in the data. The drawback of the pooled time-series approach lies in the possibility that important differences in behavior between countries may be concealed.

The first estimate of the variable rate-of-growth effect in the life-cycle saving model reported by Fry and Mason (1982, 435) includes the foreign saving ratio SFY or balance-of-payments deficit on current account as an explanatory variable, in addition to the variables discussed in section 5.3. Although foreign capital inflows might affect the timing of saving indirectly through their impact on the real rate of return on domestic financial assets, this effect is already captured by the inclusion of the real deposit rate of interest $d-\pi^e$ as an independent explanatory variable in the saving function. To the extent that foreign saving is a transfer (gift or heavily subsidized loan) to recipient countries, it constitutes an increase in real wealth not captured by GNP. As is the case for any increase in real wealth not captured by GNP, it should produce an increase in the level of consumption L.

The original Fry-Mason (1982) saving function was estimated on pooled time-series data for seven Asian countries (Burma, 1962–1969; India, 1962–1972; Korea, 1962–1972; Malaysia, 1963–1972; Philippines, 1962–1972; Singapore, 1965–1972; Taiwan, 1962–1972) using two-stage least squares (2SLS) with country dummy variables. A reestimate of this function for the same countries over the same time periods, but using the data definitions described above, by 2SLS with dummy country variables whose coefficients are not reported here gives (t values in parentheses):

$$SNY = 1.535(\widehat{YG}) - 8.157(DR) - 0.344(SFY)$$
$$(2.018)\phantom{(\widehat{YG})} (-2.281) (-3.333)$$

$$- 54.001(DR)\cdot\widehat{YG} + 4.197(d-\pi^e)\cdot\widehat{YG}, \qquad (8.1)$$
$$(-1.605)\phantom{(DR)\cdot\widehat{YG} + } (3.142)$$

$$\overline{R}^2 = 0.836$$

where d is the nominal 12-month time deposit rate of interest expressed as a continuously compounded proportional rather than percentage rate of change, π^e is the expected inflation rate estimated by applying polynomial distributed lags to current and past inflation rates, and $\widehat{YG}$ is the endogenous rate of growth in real GNP. Here the variable used for the population dependency ratio DR is a linear transformation of $DEPR$, the population under age 15 divided by the population aged 15 to 64: $DR = 0.0523(DEPR - 0.3082)$. This rescaling makes DR zero for zero population growth and 0.03 for a 3 percent population growth rate in long-run demographic equilibrium (Mason 1981).

All the coefficients in equation 8.1 are numerically slightly smaller than those in the original Fry-Mason estimate. The explanation for this is that the data sources differ, as do the expected inflation estimates and the instrumental variables used. Given these known differences, the coefficient values are reassuringly similar. Estimating the same function for a sample of 14 Asian developing countries (Bangladesh, Burma, Hong Kong, India, Indonesia, Korea, Malaysia, Nepal, Pakistan, Philippines, Singapore, Sri Lanka, Taiwan, and Thailand) over the period 1961–1983 yields:

$$SNY = 1.134(\widehat{YG}) - 9.188(DR) - 0.459(SFY)$$
$$\quad\quad (3.781) \quad\quad (-8.086) \quad\quad (-7.996)$$

$$- 25.967(DR)\cdot\widehat{YG} + 1.609(d-\pi^e)\cdot\widehat{YG}. \quad\quad (8.2)$$
$$\quad (-1.940) \quad\quad\quad (4.449)$$

$$\overline{R}^2 = 0.842$$

The rate-of-growth effect is somewhat smaller for this country sample. As a result, all three coefficients involving YG are numerically smaller in equation 8.2 than they are in equation 8.1.

Since the mid-1970s many developing countries have borrowed extensively on commercial terms from the international banking system. Treating foreign saving as exogenous is therefore no longer valid for the majority of these sample countries. In addition, terms-of-trade changes have become more pronounced in the past decade, making growth in real GNP an increasingly poor proxy for income growth. Hence the next saving function estimate for these 14 Asian developing countries drops SFY and includes TTG, income growth attributable to terms-of-trade changes:

$$SNY = 1.144(\widehat{YG}) + 0.266(TTG) + 0.122(d-\pi^e)$$
$$\quad\quad (4.440) \quad\quad (4.375) \quad\quad (7.105)$$

$$- 6.013(DR) - 25.967(DR)\cdot\widehat{YG}. \quad\quad (8.3)$$
$$\quad (-6.162) \quad\quad (-2.869)$$

$$\overline{R}^2 = 0.828$$

Finally, a more recent estimate for Bangladesh, India, Indonesia, Korea, Malaysia, Nepal, Pakistan, Philippines, Sri Lanka, Taiwan, and Thailand for the period 1961–1988 corrects for heteroscedasticity across countries using iterative weighted two-stage least squares (Fry 1991a, Table 1, 39):

$$SNY = 0.470(\widehat{INCG}) - 0.084(DEPR) - 0.853(DEPR)\cdot\widehat{YG}$$
$$\quad\quad (6.119) \quad\quad (-1.629) \quad\quad (-3.316)$$

$$+ 0.037(d-\pi^e) + 0.775(SNY)_{t-1}. \quad\quad (8.4)$$
$$\quad (3.916) \quad\quad (24.155)$$

$$\overline{R}^2 = 0.933$$

In this estimate the population dependency ratio $DEPR$ is not rescaled and includes the population aged 65 and over. Equation 8.4 combines income growth attributable to terms-of-trade improvements with output growth in the variable $INCG$.

On average, the national saving ratio is increased in the long run by about 0.1 percentage point for each 1 percentage point rise in the real deposit rate of interest. Although this effect is statistically significant, its magnitude is not large enough to warrant much policy significance. As a device for increasing saving, the real deposit rate is subject to an upper bound at its competitive free-market equilibrium level normally lying in the range of 0 to 5 percent. Hence only in countries where the real deposit rate is negative by a considerable margin can there be much scope for increasing saving *directly* by raising the deposit rate.

Equations 8.1 to 8.4 show that a 1 percentage point increase in the growth rate raises the long-run national saving ratio in these Asian developing countries by about 1 percentage point. This rate-of-growth effect is reduced substantially by high population dependency ratios (Bangladesh and Pakistan), as indicated by the interaction term $DR \cdot \widehat{YG}$ in equations 8.1 to 8.3 and $DEPR \cdot \widehat{YG}$ in equation 8.4. Equations 8.3 and 8.4 show that national saving ratios are increased, as one might expect, by improved terms of trade. An increase in the terms of trade makes the rate of growth in income higher than the rate of growth in output.

The second financial variable examined here is the proximity or accessibility of depository institutions' branches in rural areas, as proxied by the rural population per branch. The variable RPB is the logarithm of the rural population per bank branch. Time-series data on the number of branches of depository institutions in both rural and urban areas were provided by the national statistical authorities of India, Korea, Nepal, Sri Lanka, Taiwan, and Thailand. The 2SLS pooled time-series estimate for this group of Asian developing countries for the period 1961–1981 is

$$SNY = 0.134(d - \pi^e) + 0.114(TTIN) - 9.682(DR)$$
$$(2.065) \qquad\qquad (6.395) \qquad\qquad (-12.982)$$

$$- 0.016(RPB) + 0.204(\widehat{YG}), \qquad\qquad\qquad (8.5)$$
$$(-5.839) \qquad\qquad (1.961)$$

$$\overline{R}^2 = 0.885$$

where $TTIN$ is the logarithm of the terms-of-trade index. Here a 10 percent reduction in rural population per rural branch increases the national saving ratio on average by 0.16 of a percentage point.

Equation 8.5 suggests that over the period 1961–1981 increased branch proximity was responsible for raising the national saving ratio in these countries by the following percentage points:

India	4.7
Korea	4.1
Nepal	4.1
Sri Lanka	8.6
Taiwan	1.7
Thailand	0.8

Increased proximity of depository institution branches seems to have exerted a substantial influence on national saving ratios by increasing rural saving, most notably in Sri Lanka, over the past two decades. Hans-Paul Burkner (1980, 467) also finds significantly positive coefficients for the real deposit rate and bank branches per 1,000 inhabitants in an estimate of private saving for the Philippines.

As a device for raising saving ratios in the future, the efficacy of branch proliferation must be qualified. Experience shows that indiscriminate branching is no panacea. Expected profitability within the medium term must be the primary criterion for extending rural branch networks. Viability judged on this basis is determined, in turn, by the population and per capita incomes in the proposed catchment area, as well as by branch attributes such as convenient office hours, ease of depositing and withdrawing funds, reliable bookkeeping, the use of local employees, and sufficient autonomy to extend at least some categories of loans without recourse to head or regional offices.

Provided bank employees are not paid substantially higher salaries than the average income of the bank's catchment area, an efficiently run branch could be viable, based on worldwide comparative figures, in a location with as few as 10,000 inhabitants. This would suggest that additional profitable branch expansion could raise the saving ratio in most of these sample countries by at least several percentage points.

My own estimates of the effect of changes in the real deposit rate of interest on national saving ratios are similar to those estimated for several other groups of developing countries (Abe et al. 1977; Brown 1973, 195; Fry 1978, 1979a, 1980a, 1984; Khan 1988). Typically, the estimated real interest rate coefficient in a saving ratio function lies in the range 0.1 to 0.2. However, some investigators find substantially different real interest rate effects. Liang-Yn Liu and Wing Thye Woo (1994, 522) estimate significant coefficients of real interest rates for private saving ratios averaging –1 in cross-section estimates using 17 OECD countries plus Korea and Taiwan. In contrast, Shahid Yusuf and Kyle Peters (1984, 21) produce a real deposit rate coefficient exceeding +1 for Korea over the period 1965–1981. Using the period 1971–1991, Jinsoo Hahn (1994, 30–33) finds that this coefficient has fallen to 0.3 to 0.45 in both national and private saving functions.

Bela Balassa (1990, 114) suggests that measurement error in expected inflation combined with only small changes in nominal interest rates generally bias downwards the estimated interest elasticity of saving. "This was not the case in Korea where large changes in interest rates occurred. As suggested by Shaw, small and reversible changes in interest rates may not affect savings" (Balassa 1990, 114).

Premachandra Athukorala and Sarath Rajapatirana (1993, 25) estimate an interest rate elasticity of private saving of 1.11 in Sri Lanka over the period 1960–1987; here the dependent variable is the natural logarithm of real private saving and the interest rate variable is $\ln(1 + r)$, where r is the weighted average real saving and time deposit rate of interest expressed in proportional rather than percentage form. Sri Lanka is another country in which interest rates were raised substantially as part of a financial liberalization program.

As part of its financial liberalization program, the 12-month time deposit rate in Turkey increased dramatically to 50 percent in 1981, raising the real deposit rate of interest by 18 percentage points. Libby Rittenberg (1988, 119) estimates Turkey's national saving ratio over the period 1961–1985 and produces coefficients of 0.24 and 0.29 for the real deposit rate of interest (using the actual inflation rate rather than any estimate of expected inflation). Merih Celasun and Aysit Tansel (1993, 285) also detect a positive and significant effect of the real deposit rate on private saving in Turkey over the period 1972–1988. When estimating the saving ratio with the real deposit rate and the square of the real deposit rate, Rittenberg (1988, 123) finds that the coefficient of the squared term is negative. This means that a rising real deposit rate increases the saving ratio at a decreasing rate. While an increase in the real deposit rate from −30 percent to −20 percent raises the saving ratio by 5.6 percentage points, an increase from −5 to +5 percent raises the saving ratio by only 1.8 percentage points (Rittenberg 1988, 124).

Jaime de Melo and James Tybout (1986, 573) find that the real interest rate exerted a significantly positive, albeit small (0.083), effect on the saving ratio in Uruguay over the period 1962–1973, but they could detect no effect after financial liberalization occurred in 1973. Mario Lamberte et al. (1992, 146) also detect a significantly positive, but minuscule, time deposit rate coefficient in an estimate of the private saving ratio in Philippines over the period 1972–1988.

Among pooled time-series estimates, Sérgio Leite and Dawit Makonnen (1986, 227) find a positive and significant real interest rate coefficient in a pooled least squares regression of gross domestic saving weighted to correct for heteroscedasticity for the financially repressed economies of Benin, Burkina Faso, Côte d'Ivoire, Niger, Senegal, and Togo over the period 1967–1980. Homogeneity tests were unable to reject the hypothesis that saving behavior is determined in the same way in these six countries that all use a common central bank, Banque Centrale des Etats de l'Afrique de l'Ouest (BCEAO).

Alberto Giovannini (1983b) reestimates the saving function reported in Fry (1978), is unable to find a significant real interest rate effect for a somewhat different regression period, and concludes that my results are not robust. With the 14-country sample used in equations 8.2 and 8.3 for the period 1961–1983, however, the real deposit rate variable yields virtually the same positive and significant coefficient whether it is estimated using actual or expected inflation, and whether or not instrumental variables are applied to the inflation term. Elsewhere, Giovannini (1985, 199–201) suggests that my original estimates for the 1962–1972 period give undue weight to the Korean interest rate reform of the mid-1960s. With the 14-country sample used in equations 8.2 and 8.3, however, both the value and the significance of the real deposit rate coefficient are *increased* marginally when Korea is omitted. Whatever the explanation of Giovannini's results, it cannot be a smaller weight attached to the Korean interest rate experiment.

Kanhaya Gupta (1987) reports pooled time-series estimates of saving functions for a sample of 22 Asian and Latin American developing countries. He finds that pooling across continents is inappropriate. Financial conditions do not affect saving in Latin America but do in Asia. Specifically, the nominal deposit rate of interest and the financial intermediation ratio both exert positive effects on saving in Asian developing countries. Martin Ravallion and Abhijit Sen (1986) question the appropriateness of pooling data even for Asia and criticize the omission of inflation as an independent explanatory variable. In fact, when inflation is included as well as the real interest rate, coefficients of the real interest rate are increased in their estimates.

Nicola Rossi (1988) analyzes the effects of both liquidity or borrowing constraints and real interest rates on consumption behavior over the period 1973–1983 in 49 developing countries which he separates into six regional groups.[1] Low-income countries in each group, defined as those countries currently eligible for International Development Association (IDA) concessional loans, are allowed to take coefficients of the borrowing-constraint proxy (expected disposal income minus current consumption) that differ from those of the richer developing countries in the group. Rossi (1988, 116) estimates expected real interest rates, expected government spending, and expected disposable income using vector autoregressions (VARs) before using a "between-within groups fixed-effects estimator" (2SLS on transformed variables that equal the original variable minus the country and time means plus the total mean, so eliminating the constant and the regional error term).

Rossi (1988, 117) summarizes his results as follows:

> First, the omission of liquidity constraints appears consistently and seriously to bias downward the estimates of the intertemporal elasticity of substitution. Second, where liquidity constraints are substantial (as in regions where the use of IDA resources is common), intertemporal substitution is weak, and very large changes in incentives are necessary to induce postponement of consumption. Third, as expected, low-income countries suffer most from liquidity constraints and therefore react strongly to expected income changes, although there is no clear-cut pattern in the way different countries react to unexpected income

---

[1] Sub-Saharan Africa (Botswana, Burundi,* Cameroon, Ethiopia,* Ghana,* Kenya,* Liberia,* Malawi,* South Africa, Swaziland, Zambia,* Zimbabwe), North Africa and the Middle East (Iran, Jordan, Morocco, Syria, Tunisia), East and South Asia and the Pacific (Fiji, India,* Indonesia, Korea, Malaysia, Pakistan,* Philippines, Sri Lanka,* Thailand), Southern Europe (Cyprus, Greece, Israel, Malta, Portugal, Turkey), Central America and the Caribbean (Costa Rica, Dominican Republic, El Salvador, Guatemala, Honduras, Jamaica, Mexico, Panama), and South America (Bolivia,* Brazil, Chile, Colombia, Ecuador, Paraguay, Peru, Uruguay, Venezuela); * denotes countries currently eligible for International Development Association concessional loans.

shocks. In short, the picture that emergences from the evidence is a highly coherent one in which differences in behavioral responses appear to be linked more to the stage of development of different areas or countries than to unexplained shifts in preferences.

Rossi's (1988, 125) implied short-run real interest elasticities of saving are:

Sub-Saharan Africa	0.25
Middle East and North Africa	1.04
East and South Asia and the Pacific	0.18
Southern Europe	0.18
Central America and the Caribbean	0.37
South America	0.01

The low elasticity for South America is consistent with Gupta's (1987) finding.

To the extent that real interest rates affect the rate of economic growth, the overall impact of financial liberalization on saving ratios will be biased downwards if this indirect effect, as illustrated in Figure 2.1, is not recognized. While Rossi (1988, 117) points out that the omission of liquidity or borrowing constraints also biases the estimated real interest elasticity of saving downwards, he does not discuss the direct effect of borrowing constraints on saving ratios. Rather, Rossi (1988), Nadeem Ul Haque and Peter Montiel (1987), and others have stressed the importance of borrowing constraints as an explanation for the rejection of Ricardian equivalence when government deficits are found to have significant negative effects on national saving ratios.

If financial liberalization or deregulation not only raises real interest rates but also relaxes household borrowing constraints, a positive interest rate effect on the saving ratio could be outweighed by a negative effect produced by easier access to consumer credit. In a study of eight large OECD countries (Australia, Canada, France, Germany, Italy, Japan, the United Kingdom, and the United States), Adrian Blundell-Wignall, Frank Browne, and Stefano Cavaglia (1991, 18–19) find that "aggregate consumption in general seems to be less constrained by capital market imperfections in the 1980s than in the 1970s or 1960s. The conclusion of diminishing liquidity constraints implies that consumption behaviour is increasingly more accurately described by the permanent income theory of consumption." Blundell-Wignall, Browne, and Paolo Manasse (1990, 152–157) present similar evidence for seven of these OECD countries (Australia is excluded) in another paper.

While borrowing constraints appear to explain the rejection of Ricardian equivalence tests and financial liberalization can be used as an explanation for the increasing role of permanent as opposed to transitory income as the appropriate income variable in the consumption function, their effects on the level of saving have only recently been examined. Tamim Bayoumi (1993, 1437–1439) estimates a simultaneous system of household saving functions for 11 regions of the United Kingdom over the period 1971–1988 using three-stage least squares. He estimates that financial deregulation and innovation in the 1980s produced a decline in the personal saving ratio of $2\frac{1}{4}$ percentage points, a finding consistent with the three-period consumption model described in section 6.8. If this model provides the correct explanation for this fall in the saving ratio, one would expect the saving ratio to rise back to its original level gradually as the older generation of borrowing-constrained consumers disappears.

Tullio Jappelli and Marco Pagano (1994, 95–98) use the maximum loan-to-value (LTV) ratios applied to mortgages as well as the beginning-of-period ratio of consumer loans to net national product to measure borrowing constraints in 19 OECD countries. They construct period-average data for 1960–1970, 1971–1980, and 1981–1987 to obtain 50 observations. A 10 percent increase in the LTV ratio reduces the national saving ratio by about 2 percentage points. A 10 percentage point increase in the ratio of consumer credit to net national product at the beginning of each period reduces the national saving ratio by about 3 percentage points. Finally, the rate-of-growth effect is smaller the higher is the maximum LTV ratio, another finding consistent with the model outlined in section 6.8.

Hugh Patrick (1994) suggests that restrictions on bank lending to finance consumption and housing seem to have been particularly effective in promoting saving in Japan, Korea, and Taiwan. Liu and Woo (1994, 523–525) also believe that improved financial intermediation would reduce saving ratios in Japan and Taiwan.

8.3 Investment Ratios

Under conditions of disequilibrium interest rates and credit rationing, the quantity of credit rather than its price determines investment. Several investigators find that the investment ratio is positively related to the availability of domestic credit as measured by the ratio of total or private sector domestic credit to GNP or the change in real total or private sector domestic credit divided by real GNP (Athukorala and Rajapatirana 1993; Blejer and Khan 1984; Dailami and Giugale 1991; Fry 1980a, 1986a, 1993e; Lamberte et al. 1992; Leff and Sato 1980, 1988; Solimano 1989; Voridis 1993). Martin Rama (1990) reviews empirical studies of investment behavior and lists 18 studies, all of which estimate positive coefficients of the credit availability variable.[2]

One 2SLS pooled time-series estimate of the flexible accelerator model developed in section 5.4 (equation 5.9) for 61 developing countries for the period 1961–1975 gives the following result (Fry 1980a, 322):

---

[2] All but one of these studies find significantly positive coefficients.

$$IY = 0.4715 + 0.1234(\widehat{YG}) + 0.1874(FY)$$
$$(2.3169) \quad (1.9952) \qquad (5.0169)$$

$$+ \ 0.0140(\widehat{DCY}) + 0.1036\Delta\log(\widehat{DCY})$$
$$(0.3269) \qquad\qquad (10.3615)$$

$$+ \ 0.0063(PX) + 0.0198(\widehat{P}/P^e) + 0.5222(IY)_{t-1},$$
$$(1.8686) \qquad (3.0328) \qquad\quad (10.1033)$$

$$\overline{R}^2 = 0.68$$

(8.6)

where IY is the ratio of domestic investment to GNP (expressed in current prices), YG is the continuously compounded rate of growth in real GNP, DCY is the ratio of domestic credit to GNP, FY is the ratio of foreign exchange receipts to GNP, PX is the purchasing power of exports or income terms of trade, and $\widehat{P}/P^e$ is the ratio of the endogenous actual price level to the expected price level. The rate of change in the ratio of domestic credit to GNP has a highly significant positive coefficient.

Another estimate of the flexible accelerator model for the sample of 14 Asian developing countries examined in section 8.2 over the period 1962–1983 is reported in Fry (1986a, 66):

$$IY = 0.304(\widehat{YG}) - 0.108(TTG) + 0.100(TTG)_{t-1}$$
$$(5.472) \qquad (-2.205) \qquad\quad (2.120)$$

$$+ \ 0.063(DCPY) - 0.200(RW) + 0.784(IY)_{t-1},$$
$$(2.526) \qquad\quad (-2.640) \qquad (19.133)$$

$$\overline{R}^2 = 0.907$$

(8.7)

where $DCPY$ is credit to the private sector divided by GNP and RW, the world rate of interest, is proxied by the real ex post yield on six-month U.S. treasury bills.

The two private sector credit variables included in equation 5.9 are highly collinear but have virtually the same explanatory power when entered separately in equation 8.7. The ratio of private sector domestic credit to GNP produces a slightly higher correlation coefficient. In both equations 8.6 and 8.7, the domestic credit variables exert a significantly positive influence on the investment ratio.

If the real deposit rate of interest is held below its free-market equilibrium level, the effective (albeit unobservable) real loan rate would decline as the real deposit rate rises, as shown in Figure 2.1 (Fry 1982c). The lower the real deposit rate, the smaller is the volume of saving and hence the higher is the market-clearing loan rate of interest. In such case, the real deposit rate could act as an inverse proxy for the real loan rate and should have a positive impact on the investment ratio (Blejer and Khan 1984, 386). This is indeed the case when the real deposit rate is substituted for $DCPY$ in equation 8.7. Hercules Voridis (1993, 280–281) finds positive real interest rate effects on investment in Greece over the period 1963–1985, a period characterized by financial repression. Mansoor Dailami and Marcelo Giugale (1991, 18) find positive real interest rate effects on private investment ratios in Colombia and India over the period 1965–1985. Prem Laumas (1990b, 384) also estimates a positive coefficient of the real deposit rate of interest in a 2SLS regression of the private investment ratio in India for the period 1954–1975. In contrast, the market-determined U.S. real interest rate has a significantly negative impact on domestic investment in equation 8.7.

Panicos Demetriades and Michael Devereux (1992, 19–21) estimate a positive, albeit insignificant, effect of negative real interest rates on investment in a pooled time-series estimate for 63 developing countries over the period 1962–1990. In contrast, they find a highly significant positive coefficient for a variable that includes the difference between the real U.S. treasury bill rate and the real domestic loan rate. They interpret this result to indicate that, by lowering the real marginal cost of borrowing, financial repression stimulates investment. This argument is based on the model presented by Philip Arestis and Demetriades (1993), in which subsidized credit is always available in a fixed proportion to curb market loans.

Haque, Kajal Lahiri, and Peter Montiel (1990, 552) find a significantly negative, albeit small, coefficient of the real interest rate in a pooled time-series estimate of domestic investment for 31 developing countries over the period 1963–1987. However, the real interest rates used in their study are estimated from other behavioral relationships in the macroeconomic model in order to provide real domestic shadow interest rates used in section 5.2. Sebastián Edwards (1988, 192) also finds a negative effect of the real curb market interest rate as well as a positive effect of the real flow of new loans from the commercial banks in Korea over the period 1969–1983. Since both of these studies use market-equilibrium interest rates, they are consistent with positive coefficients of below-equilibrium real interest rates.

Joshua Greene and Delano Villanueva (1991, 48) find a significantly negative coefficient of the real deposit interest rate in a pooled time-series estimate of private investment ratios for 23 developing countries over the period 1975–1987; the inflation rate also exerts a significantly negative effect on the private investment ratio. This result challenges the findings of positive coefficients and may perhaps be due to the inclusion of 11 Latin American countries in the sample. For example, Andrés Solimano (1989, 15–17) shows that high real interest rates reduced profits which in turn reduced private investment in Chile over the period 1977–1987 (quarterly data). Dailami and Giugale (1991, 18) find a negative real interest rate coefficient in a private investment ratio function for Brazil, but they also find negative coefficients for Korea and Turkey after controlling for credit availability.

In one of the most interesting studies of investment behavior under financial repression, Rittenberg (1991) addresses the issue of regime changes before and after liberalization in the case of Turkey by estimating a switching model over the period 1964–1986. The estimates indicate that investment is constrained by saving, as in Figure 2.1, when the real deposit rate of interest is negative; the interest rate coefficient in the investment function is positive for negative real rates. When real deposit rates are positive, however, a regime switch occurs such that investment is reduced by higher interest rates; the interest rate coefficient is negative for positive real rates (Rittenberg 1991, 160).

While credit availability is clearly an important determinant of the quantity of investment, the effect of real interest rates is not so clear-cut. Chapter 9 presents evidence that real deposit rates of interest exert a positive effect on credit availability in line with the simple banking model sketched in Chapter 1. Hence, while higher real deposit rates stimulate investment by easing credit constraints, they may deter investment by lowering profits.

8.4   Investment Efficiency

If financial intermediaries allocate investible funds more efficiently than other allocative mechanisms, then raising real deposit rates of interest up to the point where interest rates reach their competitive free-market levels will improve the quality of investment. Real interest rates could influence the average efficiency of investment in the ways suggested by Vicente Galbis (1977), McKinnon (1973), and Shaw (1973) illustrated in Figures 2.1 and 2.4. The empirical evidence does indeed suggest that the financial sector plays a role in affecting the average rate of return to either investment or the capital stock. For example, William Branson and Stephen Schwartz (1989, 27) find positive effects of both a financial aggregate (*M2, M3,* and private sector credit, all divided by GDP) and the real interest rate on growth, after controlling for the investment ratio, in growth rate functions for 33 to 41 developing countries over the period 1974–1988.

If average investment efficiency is monotonically related to the incremental output/capital ratio (IOCR) σ, a positive association between the IOCR and disequilibrium real deposit rates would support the efficiency models presented in Chapters 2, 4 and 5. Such an association is indeed found in a sample of 11 Asian developing countries and in Turkey (Asian Development Bank 1985, 48; Fry 1979a; 1981c, 79). One ordinary least squares (OLS) pooled time-series estimate with dummy variables for India, Korea, Malaysia, Nepal, Pakistan, Singapore, Taiwan, and Thailand gives (Asian Development Bank 1985, 48):

$$IOCR = 0.303 + 0.645(d - \pi^e).$$
$$(7.512) \quad (2.385)$$

$$\overline{R}^2 = 0.772$$

(8.8)

For Turkey I use the incremental capital/output ratio (ICOR) rather than the IOCR as the dependent variable (Fry 1979a, 132):

$$ICOR = 2.528 - 24.870(d - \pi^e).$$
$$(5.842) \quad (-3.096)$$

$$\overline{R}^2 = 0.253$$

(8.9)

In both estimates, an increase in the real deposit rate of interest is associated with an increase in the IOCR. In an equation similar to 8.8, Alan Gelb (1989, 20) estimates a coefficient of 0.989 using period-average data for 1965–1973 and 1974–1985 for 34 developing countries and Jacques Morisset (1993, 146) produces a coefficient of 1.206 for Argentina over the period 1961–1982.

One way of analyzing the efficiency-improving role of financial intermediation starts by recognizing the fact that, when real interest rates are negative, there is no incentive to use capital efficiently. Excess capacity is costless, so plants are built with far more capacity than required for immediate production plans. Overtime, shift work, and other measures that increase the effective utilization of plant and machinery are not worthwhile when keeping the capital stock idle is costless.

Under such circumstances, the measured capital stock exceeds the effective capital stock. For example, the effective capital stock might be equivalent to 66 percent of the measured capital stock when the real interest rate is −15 percent. However, the effective capital stock might equal the measured capital stock at a real interest rate of 5 percent. In this example, therefore, the effective capital stock can be expressed as the actual capital stock times $(0.915 + 1.7r)$, where r is the real interest rate expressed in proportional rather than percentage terms. A simple Cobb-Douglas production function embodying this efficiency effect can be expressed $Y = AL^\alpha(\beta K + \gamma r K)^{1-\alpha}$, where Y is output, A is a constant, L is labor, K is capital, r is the real interest rate, and α, β, and γ are parameters.

Statistical analysis of this relationship in 10 Asian developing countries (Bangladesh, India, Indonesia, Korea, Malaysia, Pakistan, Philippines, Sri Lanka, Taiwan, and Thailand) indicates that the effective capital stock is increased significantly by a rise in the real deposit rate of interest towards its competitive free-market equilibrium level. This analysis is based on a seemingly unrelated or weighted-iterative regression of the rate of economic growth on labor force growth, capital stock growth, and capital stock growth multiplied by the real deposit rate of interest using annual data for these 10 countries over the period 1961–1988. The sum of the labor force and capital stock growth coefficients is constrained to 1 (278 observations):

$$YG = 0.256(KG) + (1 - 0.256)(LG) + 0.420(KG) \cdot (d - \pi^e),$$
$$(4.551) (4.551) (4.961)$$
$$\overline{R}^2 = 0.21 \qquad DW = 1.66$$

(8.10)

where KG is the continuously compounded rate of growth in the capital stock and LG is the continuously compounded rate of growth in the labor force. The capital stock is estimated by assuming a capital/GNP ratio of 2.5 in 1960 and cumulating gross real investment annually after depreciating the previous year's capital stock by 5 percent. The labor force is estimated as the population multiplied by $(1 -$ the population dependency ratio), where the population dependency ratio is defined as population under 15 and over 65 divided by the total population. The real deposit rate of interest is the 12-month deposit rate minus the rate of change in the GNP implicit deflator, both continuously compounded.

For the same country sample, I also find a positive and significant relationship between growth attributed to total factor productivity changes and the real deposit rates of interest. Using period-average growth rates and real deposit rates for 1961–1967, 1968–1974, 1975–1981 and 1982–1988, the simple regression of the total factor productivity growth rate on the real deposit rate yields a coefficient for $d - \pi^e$ of 0.14 with a t statistic of 2.05 (Fry 1991a, 31). Both these relationships are consistent with the efficiency-improving role of financial deepening.

A major question remains concerning the relationship between total factor productivity growth rates, on the one hand, and investment efficiency or the rates of return to capital, on the other. Highest total factor productivity growth rates have been achieved by Korea and Taiwan. Did these countries post high rates of return to their capital stocks? Unfortunately, measured rates of return to capital are rarely available. I have however attempted to estimate two measures of the rate of return to capital in Taiwan (Fry 1990a) using a method developed by Arnold Harberger (1978). The first measure is the net productivity of capital, the second is the private after-tax rate of return to private capital.

To illustrate that rates of return to capital in Korea and Taiwan were indeed well above worldwide rates of return two decades ago, Table 8.1 reproduces some of Harberger's (1978, 55) estimates. This table also includes my estimates for Taiwan calculated for the same period and in identical fashion. Table 8.1 shows that rates of return to capital were generally higher in the sample Asian countries than in the sample OECD countries. The rates of return to capital in Korea and Taiwan were about twice the rates found in the other countries. In 1987, I still find high rates of return to Taiwan's capital

Table 8.1. Harberger's Rates of Return to Capital, 1969–1971

Country	Net Productivity of Capital	Private After-Tax Return to Private Capital
Canada	8.4	6.4
Germany	7.1	5.6
Sweden	4.4	3.1
United Kingdom	5.0	4.4
United States	8.5	7.6
Korea	16.3	15.2
Sri Lanka	9.7	6.8
Taiwan	24.2	15.7
Thailand	7.3	10.2

stock: the net productivity of capital in Taiwan is 18 percent and the private after-tax rate of return is 18.6 percent (Fry 1990a, Table 4, 24). From his estimates, Harberger (1978, 54) notes that Korea is "a clear outlier." Not too surprisingly, I find that Taiwan is too. This then provides some support for the use of total factor productivity growth as a proxy for investment efficiency.

A number of studies have examined the efficiency issue from a micro-economic perspective. Richard Sines (1979) tests the Galbis two-sector or McKinnon choice of technique model illustrated in Figure 2.4 by examining a sample of Venezuelan food-processing firms. One group consists of incorporated firms with access to institutional credit, while the other group consists of unincorporated firms without access. Sines finds that total factor productivity is significantly higher for the group of incorporated firms. He then argues that the lack of access to institutional credit prevents the unincorporated firms from adopting modern technologies. Therefore, financial liberalization which provided greater access to institutional credit for business investors would improve investment efficiency.

Using a sample of Colombian manufacturing firms, James Tybout (1983) also finds a significant difference in credit access between large firms that could obtain cheap institutional credit and small firms that were excluded from the institutional credit market. His econometric estimates indicate that credit-constrained small firms invested only when favorable earnings shocks provided funds, while large firms were able to realize their desired investment levels (based on an accelerator model) regardless of earnings. Tybout (1983, 606) concludes: "If small firms, though less capital intensive, cannot realize their notional investment levels, McKinnon's argument that there exists considerable variation in the marginal efficiency of investment across firms is valid for the case of Colombia."

Both Sines and Tybout conclude that their empirical evidence suggests that financial liberalization improves the efficiency of resource allocation. However, they arrive at this conclusion from opposite directions. Sines argues that low productivity in credit-constrained firms in Venezuela is caused by their inability to borrow. Hence, access to institutional credit would enable them to improve their efficiency. In contrast, Tybout suggests that credit-constrained firms in Colombia already have higher marginal efficiencies of investment. Hence, a reallocation of credit from large to small firms would improve the average marginal efficiency of investment. While Tybout provides no direct evidence on the relative efficiency of constrained and unconstrained firms in Colombia, Sines is unable to show that financial liberalization actually improved investment efficiency in Venezuela.

Some empirical work has compared credit allocation across firms before and after financial liberalization. Prior to the 1983 financial reforms, credit allocation in Indonesia favored large firms with political connections, influence, and special relationships with the state-owned banks. John Harris, Fabio Schiantarelli, and Miranda Siregar (1992, 16–17) find that after financial liberalization in 1983 smaller firms increased their investment more than large firms. Their econometric estimates of the investment behavior of 218 firms indicate that small firms became less dependent on internal funds after 1983. They conclude that "[t]he process of shifting from administrative allocations of credit towards market-based allocations has increased borrowing costs, particularly for smaller firms but, at the same time, widened access and finance. The net effect appears to have been positive from the standpoint of investment and rates of profit" (Harris, Schiantarelli, and Siregar 1992, 35–36). Unfortunately, this study suffers from the same lack of direct evidence as Tybout's on the relative efficiency of constrained and unconstrained firms.

Direct evidence on relative efficiencies is provided in a study using panel data for 853 firms in Ecuador. Fidel Jaramillo, Schiantarelli, and Andrew Weiss (1993a, 18–19) suggest that directed credit policies pursued before financial reform in 1986 favored small firms. From 1986, financial resources were redistributed from small and medium-sized firms to larger and older firms. In contrast to the view that small firms are more efficient in Colombia, Jaramillo, Schiantarelli, and Weiss (1993a, 26) find that in Ecuador the larger and older firms are more efficient as measured by how close the firm is to the production possibility frontier for a given quantity of capital and labor. Jaramillo, Schiantarelli, and Weiss (1993a, 26) find that while efficiency and new credit is not correlated in the preliberalization period, the relationship is positive and significant after the financial liberalization. They conclude that "financial liberalization has helped in directing credit to technically more efficient firms" (Jaramillo, Schiantarelli, and Weiss 1993a, 29).

Extending these studies of Indonesia and Ecuador, Schiantarelli, Weiss, Miranda Gultom, and Jaramillo (1994) analyze the effect of financial liberalization in Ecuador and Indonesia on the efficiency of resource allocation using panel data for manufacturing firms. The Indonesian sample consists of 2,992 firms for which cash flow and balance sheet data were collected for the period 1981–1988; financial liberalization was completed in 1984. Similar data were collected for 420 firms for the period 1983–1988 in Ecuador where financial liberalization occurred in 1986. Their efficiency measure is the ratio of the total return on investment divided by the total return that would have occurred had investible funds been allocated to firms in proportion to their share of the capital stock. The results indicate a "large improvement in the allocation of capital after liberalization" in Indonesia (Schiantarelli, Weiss, Gultom, and Jaramillo 1994, 8–9). Similar estimates also indicate that "financial liberalization improved the allocation of investment funds" in Ecuador (Schiantarelli, Weiss, Gultom, and Jaramillo 1994, 14).

Yoon Je Cho (1988, 107) examines the efficiency of credit allocation in Korea over the period 1972–1984 by calculating average costs of borrowing by 68 different manufacturing sectors and the variance of these costs. The results show that average costs were 15 percent in 1972 and then rose steadily from 11 percent in 1973 to 20 percent in 1980 before declining to 14 percent in 1984. The variance of these borrowing costs declined from 43 in 1972 to 21 in 1980 and 6 in 1984. Cho (1988, 107–109) also finds that the difference between borrowing costs of priority and nonpriority sectors was virtually eliminated by 1984. Assuming that firms equate the marginal cost of borrowing with the marginal return on investment, Cho (1988, 108) concludes that the reduction of the disparity in borrowing costs implies "that the allocative efficiency of credit has been improved substantially since the Korean Government adopted its financial liberalization policy."

Sang-Woo Nam (1989, 140) reports evidence on the effects of Korea's directed credit policies. Between the periods 1971–1978 and 1979–1985, the output/capital ratio for heavy and chemical industries supported through directed credit policies only in the 1970s remained constant at 23 percent while other industries (excluding tobacco) posted an output/capital ratio of 28 percent in the period 1971–1978 and 21 percent over the period 1979–1985. Hence, the heavy and chemical industries improved their relative efficiency in the 1980s. Nam (1989, 140) concludes: "Cheap capital in the 1970s led to excessive and inefficient investment in heavy and chemical industries."

While the studies reviewed so far in this section draw inferences about credit allocation from estimation of firm behavior, Tein-Chen Chou (1991, 31–32) assesses the efficiency of resource allocation in Taiwan by estimating bank behavior. The government banks, which have dominated Taiwan's financial system, have been constrained by a variety of portfolio restrictions, including stringent collateral requirements. Until recently, loan officers responsible for bad loans were prosecuted for criminal offenses. Hence, bank behavior was bureaucratic in the extreme. Chou's regression analysis of the determinants of the ratio of bank loans to external funds in particular sectors of the economy indicates that only the sector's fixed assets/total assets and fixed assets/external funds ratios have positive effects, while sales/assets, profit/sales and the industry's growth rate have negative effects. Chou concludes that banks allocate credit solely on the basis of safety factors, not performance, and hence that bank loan allocation in Taiwan is inefficient.

Chou's findings are consistent with data reported by Tyler Biggs (1988, 9–14) indicating a strong bias in Taiwanese bank lending in favor of large firms. Biggs then reports evidence that medium-sized firms had returns to capital 9 percentage points higher than large firms in 1970s. Chou's findings are also consistent with evidence reported by Jia-Dong Shea and Ya-Hwei Yang (1990, 17) that easier access to bank credit for state-owned firms in Taiwan led to more capital-intensive technologies with lower rates of return. They conclude that there was inefficient overallocation of credit to state-owned and large firms by the government-owned banks pursuing a typical set of selective credit and financially repressive policies in favor of both public firms and large private firms.

Examining financial repression at an even more microeconomic level, Paul Seabright (1991a) analyzes investment efficiency in two Indian villages. Using various measures of the return to investment, Seabright (1991a, 65–66) finds that livestock investment financed through a subsidized credit scheme (IRDP) yielded far lower returns than investments not financed with such assistance. Seabright (1991a, 68) concludes: "So there seems to be no reasonable doubt that investments in IRDP cattle have performed worse in both survey villages than investments in similar non-IRDP cattle, even when the substantial element of subsidy is taken into account. This poor performance has meant little more than half of families have benefited at all, and a large number will have been positively harmed unless the outstanding loans are to some extent written off." The main reason for these results lies in the fact that those who were given subsidized loans paid considerably more for the cattle bought. In other words, sellers were able to engage in price discrimination (Seabright 1991b, 339–348).

This collection of microeconometric studies of investment and credit allocation determinants suggests that financial conditions affect the behavior of both banks and firms. Each study provides one or two pieces of a mosaic. The pieces can be combined to present a picture in which financial liberalization improves resource allocation by relaxing financial constraints on firms facing higher yielding investment opportunities. However, they could also be used to create alternative pictures.

8.5   Economic Growth

According to economists of almost all persuasions, financial conditions may affect the rate of economic growth in both the short and medium runs. Tobin's monetary growth model predicts a negative impact of a higher real return on money holdings in the medium run but has nothing to say about the short run. The McKinnon-Shaw school expects financial liberalization (institutional interest rates rising towards their competitive free-market equilibrium levels) to exert a positive effect on the rate of economic growth in both the short and medium runs. The neostructuralists predict a stagflationary (accelerating inflation and lower growth) outcome from financial liberalization in the short run. In the medium run, there is the possibility that the saving ratio will increase by enough to outweigh the negative influence of portfolio adjustments. In practice, neostructuralists, with the possible exception of Edward Buffie (1984), view a dominant saving effect as unlikely.

A simple way of discriminating between the McKinnon-Shaw school and others would be to examine episodes of financial liberalization and see whether or not these were accompanied by higher or lower rates of economic growth. In practice, however, most clear-cut cases of financial liberalization were accompanied by other economic reforms (such as fiscal, international trade, and foreign exchange reforms). In such cases it is virtually impossible to isolate the effects of financial components of the reform package. This is unfortunate, since causality can be inferred when financial conditions have been deliberately and substantially changed, as in the case of a discrete financial liberalization. Examining the association between financial conditions and economic growth over time provides in itself no evidence of causality. With this caveat, the empirical evidence on the association between financial conditions and rates of economic growth can be examined.

The effect of financial conditions on the rate of economic growth in the medium run can be calculated indirectly from the estimated effects of disequilibrium real deposit rates on saving ratios reported in section 8.2 and on investment efficiency reported in section 8.3. Mohsin Khan and Carmen Reinhart (1990, 23) show that there is a strong positive relationship between economic growth and the ratio of private investment to total investment in a sample of 24 developing countries using average data for the period 1970–1979. Since credit availability is an important determinant of private investment, they suggest that the effect of financial conditions on growth may occur through this channel (Khan and Reinhart 1990, 19 and 25).

The effect of financial conditions on economic growth can also be estimated from reduced-form equations. Anthony Lanyi and Rüşdü Saracoglu (1983b, Appendix III) implicitly address the causality issue by dividing 21 developing countries into three groups. Lanyi and Saracoglu give a value of 1 to countries with positive real interest rates, 0 to countries with moderately negative but "not punitively negative" real interest rates, and −1 to countries with severely negative real interest rates. The regression reported by Lanyi and Saracoglu (1983b, Table 4, 29) of the average rates of growth in real gross domestic product (GDP) YG on interest rate policies R for the period 1971–1980 is

Table 8.2. Rates of Economic Growth and Interest Rate Policies in 22 Developing
Countries, 1971–1980

Country	Real GDP Growth
A. Positive Real Interest Rates	
Taiwan	9.2
Singapore	9.1
Korea	8.6
Malaysia	8.0
Philippines	6.2
Sri Lanka	4.7
Nepal	2.0
B. Moderately Negative Real Interest Rates	
Thailand	6.9
Colombia	5.8
Kenya	5.7
Morocco	5.5
Pakistan*	5.4
Greece	4.7
Portugal	4.7
Burma	4.3
South Africa	3.7
Zambia	0.8
C. Severely Negative Real Interest Rates	
Turkey	5.1
Peru	3.4
Zaire	0.1
Ghana	−0.1
Jamaica	−0.7

Source: Lanyi and Saracoglu (1983b, 27)

* 1974–1980

Note: Taiwan is added here to the original sample based on data from national sources.

$$YG = 4.35 + 2.40(R).$$
$$(9.12) \quad (3.64)$$

$$\overline{R}^2 = 0.41$$

(8.11)

Table 8.2 reproduces the Lanyi-Saracoglu classification of their sample of
21 developing countries by interest rate policy and adds Taiwan. Reestimating
the Lanyi-Saracoglu regression with Taiwan included yields

$$YG = 4.451 + 2.592(R).$$
$$(9.474) \quad (4.074)$$

$$\overline{R}^2 = 0.426$$

(8.12)

Lanyi and Saracoglu (1983b, 28–30) conclude that this result

> seems to give some tentative support to the view that, in the longer run, positive real interest rates contribute to the growth of output. One possibility is that the principal effect of positive real interest rates is to raise the quality of investment, thereby increasing the growth rate of output and consequently that of financial saving. Another possibility is that the principal line of causation is, as suggested earlier, from interest rates to financial savings to growth of output. In either case, there does appear to be a relationship between interest rate policy and growth. Because of the administered nature of interest rates in these countries, a reversed direction of causation from either growth of output or growth of financial savings to interest rates has been ruled out in this analysis.

The World Bank (1989) uses the same methodology as Lanyi and Saracoglu for a sample of 34 developing countries. Over the period 1974–1985, the first group exhibited positive real deposit rates of interest, the second group posted moderately negative deposit rates (less than zero but greater than –10 percent), and the third group experienced strongly negative deposit rates (lower than –10 percent on average over this period). Given the fact that deposit rates were fixed by administrative fiat in all the countries posting negative deposit rates, one can argue that these rates are exogenous to the growth process.

The World Bank (1989, 31) presents its results in the tabular form shown in Table 8.3. Clearly, economic growth in the countries with strongly negative real deposit rates was substantially lower than growth in countries with positive real interest rates. Although the investment ratio was only 17 percent higher in the countries with positive real interest rates, the average productivity of investment, as measured by the incremental output/capital ratio, was almost four times higher.

The World Bank (1989, 30) also reports the following regression using period-average data over the periods 1965–1973 and 1974–1985 for 33 developing countries:

$$YG = -0.12 + 0.20(R) - 0.02(D),$$
$$(-2.5) \quad (5.2) \quad (-3.4)$$

$$\overline{R}^2 = 0.45$$

(8.13)

where D is a dummy for the 1974–1985 period.

Several other studies present regression estimates showing positive and significant relationships between the rate of economic growth and the real

Table 8.3. Rates of Economic Growth and Interest Rate Policies in 34 Developing Countries, 1974–1985

Indicator	Positive Real Interest Rates	Moderately Negative Real Interest Rates	Strongly Negative Real Interest Rates
Real interest rate	3.0	–2.4	–13.0
GDP growth rate	5.6	3.8	1.9
M3/GDP	40.3	34.0	30.5
Investment/GDP	26.9	23.2	23.0
Change in GDP/investment	22.7	17.3	6.2
Change in real *M3*/real saving	16.6	8.2	–0.9
Inflation rate	20.8	23.9	50.3

Source: World Bank (1989, 31)

deposit rate of interest (Asian Development Bank 1985; Easterly 1993; Fry 1978, 1991a; Gelb 1989; Polak 1989; Roubini and Sala-i-Martin 1992b). The OLS estimate with country dummy variables of growth on the real deposit rate for pooled time-series data from seven Asian developing countries, 1961–1972, reported in Fry (1978, 470) is

$$YG = 0.033 + 0.405(d - \pi^e).$$
$$(4.761) \quad (3.733)$$
$$\overline{R}^2 = 0.158$$

(8.14)

Another OLS estimate with country dummies on pooled time-series data for 14 Asian developing countries, 1961–1982, reported in Asian Development Bank (1984, Volume II, 70) is

$$YG = 0.044(d - \pi^e).$$
$$(2.305)$$
$$\overline{R}^2 = 0.774$$

(8.15)

The empirical results reported in Fry (1978, 470; 1979a, 132–134; 1980a, 324; 1981c, 87–88) suggest that on average a 1 percentage point increase in the real deposit rate of interest towards its competitive free-market equilibrium level is associated with a rise in the rate of economic growth of about $\frac{1}{2}$ percentage point in Asia. The World Bank (1989, 32) estimate reported above gives a coefficient of 0.20, Gelb (1989, 20) estimates coefficients of 0.20 to 0.26 for his sample of 34 countries, while Jacques Polak (1989, 67) estimates coefficients of 0.18 to 0.27 when regressing the average annual rate of growth in real GDP on the median real interest rate for 40 developing countries. For 53 countries over the period 1960–1985, Nouriel Roubini and Xavier Sala-i-Martin (1992b, 22) also find that countries with real interest rates less than –5 percent in the 1970s experienced growth rates that averaged 1.4 percentage points less than growth rates in countries with positive real interest rates. If the difference is approximately 10 percentage points, the implied interest rate coefficient is 0.14. That Asian developing countries may be more sensitive to real interest rate changes than other groups of developing countries has already been noted.

Khan and Villanueva (1991, 30–31) estimate the effects of real interest rates on growth for 23 developing countries using average data for the period 1975–1987 in equations that control for the ratio of private investment to GDP *IPY*:

$$YGN = -1.13 + 0.25(IPY) + 0.08(d-\pi);$$
$$\quad\;\;(-1.3)\quad (3.4)\qquad\quad (2.4)$$
$$\bar{R}^2 = 0.55$$

(8.16)

$$YGN = -1.997 + 0.184(IPY) + 0.241(XKG) + 0.067(d-\pi),$$
$$\quad\;(-2.36)\quad (2.86)\qquad\quad (3.37)\qquad\quad (2.34)$$
$$\bar{R}^2 = 0.718$$

(8.17)

where *YGN* is the rate of growth in per capita real GDP, *IPY* is the private investment ratio and *XKG* is the rate of growth in exports at constant prices. They conclude that, "after allowing for changes in the rate of private investment, the real interest rate has a significant direct positive effect on per capita growth, suggesting that the direct favorable effects of real interest rates on the efficient use of capital, and thus on factor productivity, outweigh any possible negative impact on the rate of private investment such as found by Greene and Villanueva" (Khan and Villanueva 1991, 30).

Lance Taylor (1983, 122) is unconvinced by the empirical evidence:

> The evidence from a few econometric studies seems to show that the working-capital channel is the one that matters in the short run in developing economies, while traditionally Keynesian responses are more important in the longer run. Proponents of deposit rate increases might draw support from these conclusions since their nostrum works better just under such circumstances. Nonetheless, the situation remains complex—too complex for any simple policy prescription along financial liberalization (or other) lines to be worth serious thought.

However, the additional evidence accumulated over the past decade may have weakened Taylor's skepticism.

José De Gregorio and Pablo Guidotti (1993) claim that real interest rates are not a good indicator of financial repression or distortion. They suggest that the relationship between real interest rates and economic growth might resemble an inverted U curve: "Very low (and negative) real interest rates tend to cause financial disintermediation and hence tend to reduce growth, as implied by the McKinnon-Shaw hypothesis. On the other hand, very high real interest rates that do not reflect improved efficiency of investment, but rather a lack of credibility of economic policy or various forms of country risk, are likely to result in a lower level of investment as well as a concentration in excessively risky projects" (De Gregorio and Guidotti 1993, 11).[3] Hence, De Gregorio and Guidotti abandon real interest rates in favor of domestic credit to the private sector divided by GNP.

In fact, the point made by De Gregorio and Guidotti (1993) holds up well with the data set prepared for the *World Development Report 1991*. Using this data on real interest rates for a sample of five Pacific Basin developing countries (Indonesia, Korea, Malaysia, Philippines, and Thailand) and 11 other developing countries (Argentina, Brazil, Chile, Egypt, India, Mexico, Nigeria, Pakistan, Sri Lanka, Turkey, and Venezuela) for the period 1970–1988, I estimated the relationship between the rate of economic growth YG, the investment ratio IY, the real rate of interest RD, and the rate of growth in exports at constant prices XG in an equation of the form $YG = \beta_1(IY) + \beta_2[IY \cdot (RD + \beta_3) \cdot (RD + \beta_3)] + \beta_4(XG)$. Since the parameter β_3 was not significantly different from zero, although its negative value implies that growth is maximized at some positive real interest rate, I drop it from the estimate reported here. Three-stage iterative least squares estimation gives the following result (297 observations, t statistics in parentheses):

$$YG = 0.164(\widehat{IY}) - 0.237(\widehat{IY \cdot RD^2}) + 0.070(\widehat{XG}).$$
$$(11.541) \qquad (-5.123) \qquad\qquad (12.628)$$

$$\overline{R}^2 = 0.217$$

(8.18)

The overall effect of a rising real interest rate on growth in equation 8.18 is illustrated in Figure 8.1. This figure is produced using the mean values of all the explanatory variables with the exception of the real deposit rate of interest. The mean value of the real deposit rate is zero with a standard deviation of 23 percent. Its minimum value is –83 percent and its maximum value 221 percent. The line C_n denotes two standard deviations below the mean of all negative interest rates in the control group, P_n denotes two standard deviations below the mean of all negative interest rates in the Pacific Basin economies, P_p denotes two standard deviations above the mean of all zero or positive interest rates in the five Pacific Basin economies, while C_p denotes

---

[3]This criticism is based on work by Guillermo Calvo and Fabrizio Coricelli (1992).

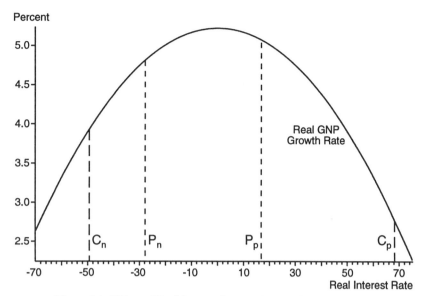

Figure 8.1. Effect of Real Interest Rate on Economic Growth Rate

two standard deviations above the mean of all zero or positive interest rates in the remaining 11 countries. Evidently, real interest rates deviated from their growth-maximizing level far more in the control group countries than they did in the Pacific Basin economies. The annual growth rate in the control group averaged 4.0 percent compared with 6.2 percent in the Pacific Basin economies.

Since real interest rates are strongly negatively correlated with inflation rates, a further question arises as to whether inflation or fixed nominal interest rates constitute the basic problem. Growth rates are negatively related to inflation rates in the medium and long runs (*Asian Development Outlook 1991*, 39; De Gregorio 1992a, 422–423; De Gregorio 1993, 288–290). High inflation is invariably more variable and less predictable than lower inflation. Hence, the negative effects of low real interest rates caused by high inflation rates on economic growth rates may be due more to the increasing volatility and unpredictability of inflation and real interest rates than to their levels. Furthermore, real institutional interest rates may well be strongly correlated with a broader range of financial factors and hence act as a proxy for a more general indicator of financial conditions.

Using maximum loan-to-value (LTV) ratios applied to mortgage loans, Jappelli and Pagano (1994, 100) find that a higher LTV ratio has a significantly negative effect on average rates of growth in GDP per employee in one sample of 25 countries covering the period 1960–1985 and on average per capita real GDP growth rates in another sample of 30 countries also for the period

1960–1985. An increase in the LTV of 10 percentage points raises the growth rate by between 0.25 and 0.35 percentage points. These cross-section estimates indicate that above-average downpayment requirements have increased average growth rates in Korea and Taiwan by 0.9 and 0.7 percentage points, respectively, over the period 1960–1985 (Jappelli and Pagano 1994, 104).

Jappelli and Pagano (1994, 84) conclude:

> If banks ration credit to households while making it available to firms efficiently, capital accumulation and growth will be enhanced. The idea that credit rationing may be selectively directed to households but not firms is not unwarranted as a description of financial intermediation in several OECD economies in the postwar period. It can also be rationalized in view of the difference in regulations and in the intrinsic nature of lending to households and firms, which differs with respect to the average loan size, the pervasiveness of informational asymmetries, and the costs of contract enforcement.

Recent empirical work has tended to resort to far larger data sets than were used in studies before 1990. For example, Ejaz Ghani (1992) estimates growth equations for a sample of 50 developing countries following an approach used by Robert Barro (1991). The initial levels of human capital (as measured by years of schooling) and financial development (as measured by the ratio of total assets of the financial system to GDP or the ratio of private sector credit to GDP) in 1965 yield significantly positive coefficients, while the initial level of per capita real GDP produces a negative coefficient in an equation explaining average growth rates over the period 1965–1989 (Ghani 1992, 17). De Gregorio and Guidotti (1993, 29–30) produce similar results for middle and low-income countries using Barro's data set. Niels Hermes and Robert Lensink (1993) also find that growth in per capita real GDP is positively affected by the ratio of private sector credit to aggregate domestic credit in 14 Latin American countries over the period 1963–1989 using five-year averages for all variables.

Using financial ratios rather than real interest rates, King and Levine (1993a, 1993b, 1993c) examine links between finance and growth in a cross section of 77 developing countries over the period 1960–1989. They construct four financial indicators: (a) liquid liabilities divided by GDP (usually *M2* divided by GDP);[4] (b) domestic assets in deposit money banks divided by domestic assets of both deposit money banks and the central bank; (c) domestic credit to the private sector divided by aggregate domestic credit; and (d) domestic credit to the private sector divided by GDP. King and Levine also construct four growth indicators: (a) average rate of growth in per capita real GDP; (b) average rate of growth in the capital stock; (c) the residual between

---

[4] To obtain mid-year estimates, beginning-of-year and end-of-year values of all financial variables are averaged.

(a) and 0.3 of (b) as a proxy for productivity improvements; and (d) gross domestic investment divided by GDP.

Using bivariate regressions, King and Levine (1993a, 725–727; 1993b, 530) show that each financial indicator is positively and significantly correlated with each growth indicator at the 99 percent confidence level. The same positive relationship is illustrated by dividing the 77 countries into four groups with respect to the growth indicators; countries are divided into those with average per capita income growth above 3 percent, greater than 2 but less than 3, greater than 0.5 but less than 2, and less than 0.5 percent. There are about 20 countries in each group. In each case, the average value of the financial indicator declines with a move from a higher to a lower growth group. Multivariate analysis produces much the same picture (King and Levine 1993c, 180–181).

Since these results fail to address the issue of causality, King and Levine (1993a, 731; 1993b, 532) then examine the impact of the value of liquid liabilities divided by GDP in 1960 on average per capita real GDP growth over the subsequent period 1960–1989. The first regression includes the logarithm of per capita real GDP in 1960, the logarithm of the secondary school enrollment ratio in 1960, and the ratio of liquid liabilities to GDP in 1960. The second regression adds the ratio of government consumption to GDP in 1960, the inflation rate in 1960, and the sum of import and exports divided by GDP in 1960. The third regression adds the index of civil liberties, the number of revolutions, and the number of assassinations. The fourth regression adds country dummies for Sub-Saharan Africa and Latin America. In the first three regressions, the ratio of liquid liabilities to GDP in 1960 is significant at the 99 percent confidence level. In the fourth regression it is significant at the 95 percent confidence level.

Finally, King and Levine (1993a, 733; 1993b, 534; 1993c, 183–185) regress pooled decade averages of the growth indicators on values of the financial indicators at the start of that decade, initial values of other explanatory variables (logarithm of per capita real GDP, logarithm of secondary school enrollment ratio, ratio of government expenditures to GDP, inflation rate, ratio of trade to GDP), and dummy variables for each decade. All initial values of the financial indicators are positive for each growth indicator. For each growth indicator, the initial values of the ratio of liquid liabilities to GDP and the initial ratio of private sector credit to GDP are significant at the 99 percent confidence level. The initial ratio of deposit bank domestic credit to aggregate domestic credit is significant at the 99 percent confidence level in the capital growth and investment ratio equations, at the 95 percent confidence level in the per capita real GDP growth equation, and at the 90 percent confidence level in the residual or efficiency equation. The initial ratio of private sector credit to aggregate domestic credit is not significant in the residual or efficiency equation, but is significant at the 90 percent confidence level in the other three equations.

Jean-Claude Berthélemy and Aristomène Varoudakis (1994) also use a base-year value of financial development, in this case the ratio of *M2* to GDP in 1960, to study growth in a sample of 91 countries. They find a significantly positive effect of the initial money ratio on average growth in per capita real GDP over the period 1960–1985. Using a maximum-likelihood method to produce optimal splits in this country sample, Berthélemy and Varoudakis find that the financial development variable is an important explanatory variable for growth in middle-income countries, but not for growth in industrialized countries or low-income developing countries.

Woo Jung (1986) analyzes causality between financial development and economic growth using Granger-causality tests. He selects 56 countries with a minimum of 15 annual observations each. For high-growth developing countries, Jung (1986, 342–343) finds that causation runs from financial development to economic growth in seven out of eight countries. In a study of 10 developing countries, Demetriades and Khaled Hussein (1993, 18–19) find causality from finance, as measured by the ratio of private sector credit to GDP, to long-run real GDP growth as well as causality from growth to finance in seven countries. Annie Spears (1991, 66) concludes that financial intermediation, as measured by the ratio of *M2* to GDP, causes growth in per capita real GDP in Burkina Faso, Cameroon, Côte d'Ivoire, Kenya, and Malawi. Finally, Anthony Wood (1993, 385–387) finds evidence that the ratio of *M2* to GDP causes real GDP growth in Barbados over the period 1946–1990.

The relationship between the rate of economic growth and disequilibrium real institutional rates of interest has been analyzed using noneconometric methods by a number of other economists. Guillermo Ortiz and Leopoldo Solis (1979, 534) conclude that the slowdown in the rate of economic growth in Mexico was caused in part by financial disintermediation, in turn caused by falling real deposit rates of interest. James Hanson (1979) argues that financial repression in Colombia over the period 1950–1967 reduced the saving ratio and the incremental output/capital ratio, and hence reduced the rate of economic growth. Akiyoshi Horiuchi (1984) dispels the myth that the high rate of economic growth in Japan during the period 1953–1972 was supported by low interest rate policies. Horiuchi (1984, 350–351) shows that both nominal and real discount, deposit, and money market rates were higher in Japan than they were in Britain, Germany, or the United States. After 1972, nominal and real interest rates in Japan fell, as did the rate of economic growth.

8.6 Summary

My interpretation of the empirical work reviewed above is:

- the real interest rate has virtually no direct effect on the level of saving, but may exert an indirect effect by increasing the rate of economic growth;

- if financial deregulation increases the availability of consumer credit, saving declines;

- credit availability is an important determinant of investment in developing countries;

- an increase in the real interest rate towards its normal free-market competitive equilibrium level (probably lying somewhere in the range −5 to +10 percent) is associated with higher growth attributable to improved total factor productivity and increased incremental output/capital ratios;

- less financial repression as measured by a variety of variables is associated with higher rates of economic growth.

Although the last finding has been bolstered recently by investigators who derive a growth equation from an endogenous growth model, this empirical work fails to discriminate between endogenous growth and any other kind of growth. The empirical results are consistent with a Harrod-Domar model in which financial repression lowers the incremental output/capital ratio. However, the bulk of the empirical evidence presented in this chapter is consistent with the McKinnon-Shaw view that financial liberalization increases saving, improves the efficiency with which resources are allocated among alternative investment projects, and therefore raises the rate of economic growth.

Many nonfinancial as well as noneconomic variables, such as the population dependency ratio, exert strong effects on saving and investment ratios, as well as growth rates. There is no intention here to overemphasize the importance of financial variables. However, this book is devoted to the role of finance in the process of economic development. The analysis of the many other determinants of economic development is beyond its scope.

Chapter 9

Empirical Evidence on Transmission Mechanisms and Income Distribution

9.1 Introduction

IF FINANCIAL LIBERALIZATION INCREASES the availability of credit for investment, then the positive effect of credit availability on investment detected in Chapter 8 may constitute an indirect mechanism by which financial liberalization stimulates economic growth. Section 9.2 shows that both money demand (broadly defined to include all types of deposits as well as currency in circulation) and the ratio of domestic credit to GNP are influenced positively and substantially by the real deposit rate of interest. These findings contrast sharply with the low sensitivity of saving behavior to the real deposit rate. One implication is that changes in the real deposit rate of interest cause considerable reallocation of household portfolios while producing only modest changes in the overall sizes of those portfolios.

Various tests of Ronald McKinnon's (1973) complementarity hypothesis are reviewed in section 9.3. On the one hand, several studies find that saving or investment ratios exert a positive impact on money demand. On the other hand, financial conditions affect investment behavior, as already shown in Chapter 8.

The issue of substitutability between curb loans, time deposits, and currency or inflation hedges is examined in section 9.4. Unfortunately, there is only one empirical test of a portfolio model consisting of time deposits, curb loans, and inflation hedges (van Wijnbergen 1982). Van Wijnbergen estimates only one of the three demand functions, that for time deposits. The results indicate greater substitutability from curb loans than from inflation hedges into time deposits after an increase in the time deposit rate of interest. Direct evidence that movements in the curb market interest rate are positively related to time deposit rate changes in Korea and Taiwan also provides some support for the neostructuralist hypothesis that higher time deposit rates reduce the overall supply of credit. None of this evidence is conclusive enough to resolve this issue.

The final section examines the effects of financial conditions on income distribution and economic concentration. The available empirical evidence suggests that financial repression worsens the distribution of income and encourages greater economic concentration.

9.2 Financial Saving and Portfolio Allocation

In the majority of developing economies, direct financial claims, such as stocks and bonds, are unimportant compared with indirect claims, such as demand and time deposits. Financial saving—the process of accumulating financial assets—is, therefore, directed in the main towards claims offered by depository institutions. The financial aggregate generally analyzed consists of currency in circulation, all types of bank deposits (excluding government and interbank deposits), and deposits held in nonbank depository institutions. This measure includes virtually all the financial assets available in the lower-income developing countries and a large proportion of the financial assets offered to the public in most of the higher-income developing countries. It is the growth in the inflation-adjusted or real magnitude of this monetary aggregate, commonly referred to as *M3*, that is used to measure financial saving. The change in these liabilities of the financial system represents the increase in its resources. Hence, the inflation-adjusted growth in *M3* indicates the extent to which financial intermediaries can increase the supply of credit in real terms or in relation to the level of economic activity.

The rate of change in the real stock of financial assets is determined almost exclusively on the demand side. However, the nominal stock of financial assets is determined largely on the supply side. Imbalances between rates of growth in nominal supply and real demand are, of course, reconciled through inflation. The OLS pooled time-series estimate for the sample of 14 Asian developing countries used in Chapter 8 over the period 1961–1983 shows that the rate of change in the real stock of financial assets is influenced by the rate of change in per capita permanent or expected real income $\Delta\log(y/n)^e$, the change in the real deposit rate of interest $\Delta(d-\pi^e)$, and the lagged dependent variable:

$$\Delta\log(m) = 0.928\Delta\log(y/n)^e + 0.847\Delta(d-\pi^e) + 0.414\Delta\log(m)_{t-1},$$
$$(8.578) \qquad\qquad (17.141) \qquad\qquad (10.568) \qquad\qquad (9.1)$$
$$\overline{R}^2 = 0.573$$

where m is per capita real money balances (*M3*).

On average, a 1 percentage point change in the real deposit rate of interest in these 14 sample countries changes the demand for financial assets by 0.8 percent in the short run and 1.4 percent in the long run; Christophe Chamley and Qaizar Hussain (1988, 16, 29, 41) estimate long-run deposit rate coefficients of 0.8 for Thailand (1974–1986), 1.2 for Indonesia (1972– 1985), and 1.9 for the Philippines (1972–1987). These interest rate effects on *financial* saving are substantially greater than interest rate effects on *national* saving. Therefore, an increase in the real deposit rate of interest increases the proportion of saving routed to investment through the financial intermediation channel.

A 10 percentage point increase in the real deposit rate of interest raises the ratio of financial assets to GNP by 4.0 to 6.6 percentage points in the 14 sample economies (depending on the initial ratio of *M3* to GNP). The same interest rate increase raises the ratio of national saving to GNP by about 1 percentage point. This implies that between 75 and 85 percent of the increase in financial saving comes from substitution out of other saving channels, rather than from increases in national saving.

Were the proportions of saving routed to investment through government appropriation, self-finance, and financial intermediation optimal before any increase in real institutional interest rates, the resulting substitution caused by higher real deposit rates would reduce allocative efficiency through excessive use of the financial intermediation channel. To the extent that institutional interest rates are held below their free-market equilibrium levels or that other types of financial repression exist, however, the proportion of saving routed through financial intermediaries will be suboptimal. Not only would an increase in institutional interest rates towards their competitive free-market equilibrium levels improve allocative efficiency due to the ensuing substitution effect, it would also enhance the efficiency with which financial intermediaries allocated the larger real volume of investible funds at their disposal. Empirical tests of the hypothesis that a rise in real institutional interest rates can increase average investment efficiency are reported in section 8.4.

Lanyi and Saracoglu (1983b) analyze the effect of interest rate policies on financial deepening, as measured by the rate of growth in real *M2* money balances $\Delta \log(M2/P)$, where P is the price level. Table 9.1 shows the financial data for the sample countries (with Taiwan added). Replicating the OLS regression, reported by Lanyi and Saracoglu (1983b, 29), of $\Delta \log(M2/P)$ on the interest rate policy index R as defined in section 8.5 with Taiwan included yields

$$\Delta \log(M2/P) = 4.460 + 6.140(R).$$
$$(5.776) \quad (5.873)$$

$$\overline{R}^2 = 0.61$$

(9.2)

Table 9.1. Rates of Growth in Real *M2* Money Balances and Interest Rate Policies in 22 Developing Countries, 1971–1980

Country	Real *M2* Growth
A. Positive Real Interest Rates	
Taiwan	13.9
Malaysia	13.8
Korea	11.1
Sri Lanka	10.1
Nepal	9.6
Singapore	7.6
Philippines	5.6
B. Moderately Negative Real Interest Rates	
Pakistan*	9.9
Thailand	8.5
Morocco	8.2
Colombia	5.5
Greece	5.4
South Africa	4.3
Kenya	3.6
Burma	3.5
Portugal	1.8
Zambia	−1.1
C. Severely Negative Real Interest Rates	
Peru	3.2
Turkey	2.2
Jamaica	−1.9
Zaire	−6.8
Ghana	−7.6

Source: Lanyi and Saracoglu (1983b, 27)

* 1974–1980

Note: Taiwan is added here to the original sample based on data from national sources.

From their evidence reported here and in section 8.5, Lanyi and Saracoglu (1983b, 28) conclude : "The data supports the argument that positive interest rate policies stimulate output growth, and that this stimulus is transmitted mainly through the intermediation of financial asset accumulation." Lanyi and Saracoglu do not resolve the issue of causality. However, Jung's (1986) formal Granger-causality tests show that the predominant direction of causality is from financial conditions to the rate of economic growth.

When held below its equilibrium level, the real deposit rate of interest may affect the investment ratio through the credit availability mechanism discussed in section 5.4 or McKinnon's complementarity process outlined in section 2.4. Empirical results reported in Fry (1981c, 81–84) for 12 Asian developing countries (Burma, India, Indonesia, Korea, Malaysia, Nepal, Pakistan, Philippines, Singapore, Sri Lanka, Taiwan, and Thailand) are consistent with the credit availability effect outlined in section 5.4. The ordinary least squares (OLS) pooled time-series estimates of domestic credit equations in Fry (1981c, 81–84) for the period 1961–1977 are:

$$DCY = \underset{(3.149)}{0.049}(d-\pi^e) + \underset{(3.923)}{0.053}(YNL) + \underset{(17.052)}{0.781}(DCY)_{t-1};$$

$$\overline{R}^2 = 0.95$$
(9.3)

$$DCPDC = \underset{(3.236)}{0.486}(d-\pi^e);$$

$$\overline{R}^2 = 0.85$$
(9.4)

$$DCPY = \underset{(3.204)}{0.036}(d-\pi^e) + \underset{(47.627)}{0.952}(DCPY)_{t-1},$$

$$\overline{R}^2 = 0.97$$
(9.5)

where DCY is the ratio of domestic credit to GNP, YNL is the natural logarithm of per capita real GNP expressed in 1970 U.S. dollars, $DCPDC$ is the ratio of private sector domestic credit to aggregate domestic credit, and $DCPY$ is the ratio of private sector domestic credit to GNP. Elsewhere, I report similar results for seven Pacific Basin developing countries (Fry 1981a, 12).

9.3   McKinnon's Complementarity Hypothesis

McKinnon's complementarity hypothesis has a rise in disequilibrium real deposit rates towards their free-market equilibrium levels increasing investment, in this case by reducing the burden of accumulating the necessary money balances prior to making lumpy investment expenditures. The complementarity hypothesis has been tested several times (Akhtar 1974; B. Fischer 1981; Fry 1978; Harris 1979; Jao 1976; Laumas 1980, 1990a, 1990b; Min 1976; Ram 1982; Vogel and Buser 1976; Yoo 1977). One group of investigators tests the hypothesis by including an investment variable in the money demand function (Akhtar 1974; Fry 1978; Harris 1979; Laumas 1980, 1990a; Min 1976; Ram

1982). Akbar Akhtar (1974, 43), James Harris (1979), and Prem Laumas (1990b, 383) include the investment ratio, whereas Byoung Kyun Min (1976, 21) and I (Fry 1978, 471) include the domestic saving ratio on the grounds that investment financed by foreign saving could hardly generate any finance-motive demand for money. Laumas (1980) and Rati Ram (1982) include the change in next year's investment.

Akhtar, Harris, Fry, and Min apply the money demand function to aggregate data, while Laumas and Ram use a sample of Indian business firms. Akhtar (1974, 50) finds that the investment ratio is positive but insignificant for Pakistan over the period 1951–1970. Harris (1979) runs regressions for five Asian developing countries and finds that only for Taiwan do the estimates consistently support the McKinnon hypothesis. Harris concludes that his results provide only very weak support for McKinnon's complementarity hypothesis. Min (1976, 21) rejects the complementarity hypothesis for Korea over the period 1955–1972.

In a pooled time-series estimate for 10 Asian developing countries over the period 1962–1972, I produce a significantly negative coefficient of the domestic saving ratio in a money demand function (Fry 1978, 473). The two-stage least-squares (2SLS) estimate is

$$\log(m) = -2.129 - 0.752(\widehat{SNY}) + 0.664(YNLE)$$
$$(-4.930)\ (-2.112) \qquad\quad (5.331)$$

$$+\ 1.883(d-\pi^e) + 0.726\log(m)_{t-1}, \qquad\qquad (9.6)$$
$$(8.821) \qquad\qquad (14.230)$$

$$\overline{R}^2 = 0.995$$

where m is the per capita real money stock ($M2$), SNY is the national saving ratio, $YNLE$ is per capita real expected income estimated by polynomial distributed lags on current and past levels of per capita real income, d is the 12-month deposit rate of interest, and π^e is expected inflation estimated by polynomial distributed lags on current and past inflation rates. The *negative* saving ratio coefficient is inconsistent with the complementarity hypothesis.

Laumas and Ram recognize that the finance motive refers to the buildup of money balances in advance of investment expenditures. Therefore, they include the change in next year's investment expenditure as an explanatory variable in their money demand functions. Laumas (1980, 125) reports a significantly positive coefficient on the logarithm of the change in investment between 1964 and 1965, using the logarithm of money balances held by individual firms in 1964 as the dependent variable. Using annual data for 1961–1974, however, Ram (1982, 102) finds significantly positive coefficients for the change in investment using both linear and logarithmic functions in less than half of his estimates.

Another group—Bernhard Fischer (1981), Y. C. Jao (1976), Min (1976),

Robert Vogel and Stephen Buser (1976), and Jang Yoo (1977)—tests the complementarity hypothesis by including real money balances in investment or saving functions. This seems a far less satisfactory test, since money balances and investment ratios are both strongly correlated with per capita real incomes. Furthermore, real money balances can hardly be treated as exogenous. Only Min addresses the exogeneity issue. All investigators except Min find significantly positive coefficients on their chosen monetary variables. Min (1976, 22) finds a significantly negative coefficient on the logarithm of per capita real money balances in a saving function for Korea, 1955–1972. Min uses 2SLS to take account of the endogeneity of real money balances.

Given the econometric problems associated with the investment function approach and the conflicting results of the money demand estimates, one must conclude that the empirical support for McKinnon's complementarity hypothesis and Keynes's finance motive is tenuous at best.

9.4 Time Deposits, Curb Market Claims, and Credit Availability

A key issue in the debate between the McKinnon-Shaw school and the neo-structuralists hinges on the empirical question of whether increased demand for time deposits caused by an increase in the real deposit rate of interest reduces the demand for currency (or inflation hedges) or the demand for curb market claims. Van Wijnbergen uses a portfolio model in which households allocate wealth among curb loans, time deposits, and currency. He estimates the demand for time deposits in real terms TD/P, using a function that includes the real GDP Y, the nominal curb market rate i_c, the time deposit rate i_t, and the inflation rate π, all continuously compounded. Van Wijnbergen's (1982, 156) 2SLS estimate corrected for serial correlation using quarterly data for the period 1964(I)–1978(IV) is

$$\log(TD/P) = 0.36 - 0.89(i_c) + 1.63(i_t) - 0.38(\widehat{\pi})$$
$$ (1.71)\ (-2.42) \quad\ (4.08) \quad\ (-3.51)$$

$$ + 0.02\log(\widehat{Y}) + 0.93\log(TD/P)_{t-1}. \qquad (9.7)$$
$$ (0.53) (42.40)$$

$$\overline{R}^2 = 0.997 \quad \rho = 0.3$$

Van Wijnbergen uses 2SLS to address the potential errors-in-variables problem from using the actual inflation rate as a proxy for the expected inflation rate (which would bias its coefficient downwards).

Van Wijnbergen derives equation 9.7 from a model of household portfolio allocation among curb loans, time deposits, and currency, with real returns on these three assets of $r_c{-}\pi$, $r_t{-}\pi$, and $-\pi$, respectively. Demand for time deposits depends on $i_t-\pi$ and the returns on the two substitute assets:

$$\log(TD/P) = b_1(i_c-\pi) + b_2(i_t-\pi) + b_3(-\pi). \tag{9.8}$$

If all assets are gross substitutes, $b_1 < 0$, $b_2 > 0$, and $b_3 < 0$. This equation can be rearranged

$$\log(TD/P) = b_1 i_c + b_2 i_t + \beta\pi, \tag{9.9}$$

where β equals $-b_1-b_2-b_3$. Equation 9.7 gives values for b_1, b_2, and β. Therefore b_3 equals $-\beta-b_1-b_2$ or $+0.38+0.89-1.63 = -0.36$.

Since the curb rate coefficient is greater than the inflation coefficient, van Wijnbergen concludes that in Korea the elasticity of substitution is higher for curb market loans than for currency. However, van Wijnbergen does not say whether or not the coefficients of the curb market rate and the inflation rate are significantly different from one another.

Korea now reports a quarterly consumer price index starting in 1970 and a deposit rate series starting in 1969. Hence I was unable to replicate van Wijnbergen's estimates. However I have estimated a 2SLS equation for the period 1969(III)–1989(I) using the GDP implicit price deflator instead of the consumer price index:

$$\log(TD/P) = 0.378 - 0.477(i_c) + 0.502(i_t) - 0.087(\widehat{\pi})$$
$$ (1.563)\ (-1.894)\quad (1.571)\quad (-0.833)$$

$$+\ 0.065\log(Y) + 0.906\log(TD/P)_{t-1}. \tag{9.10}$$
$$ (1.396)\qquad\quad (21.292)$$

$$\overline{R}^2 = 0.991 \quad \rho = -0.300$$

A Wald test is unable to reject the hypothesis that the coefficients of the curb market rate and the inflation rate are identical. A second Wald test fails to reject the hypothesis that the sum of the coefficients of the curb market rate, the deposit rate, and the inflation rate equals zero. Given that none of these coefficients is significant at the 95 percent confidence level, these Wald test results are unsurprising.

A major problem, as noted by Wanda Tseng and Robert Corker (1991, 43), is that "in practice, multicollinearity between interest rates implies that only one rate can feasibly be used to measure opportunity cost." Here it is possible to make a virtue out of necessity by recognizing that a complete system of demand equations requires the imposition of adding-up constraints, as demonstrated in section 7.3. If there are only three assets in the portfolio, the relevant constraint is $b_1+b_2+b_3 = 0$ in equation 9.8. With this constraint, equation 9.8 can be rewritten

$$\log(TD/P) = b_1(i_c-\pi) + b_2(i_t-\pi) + (b_1 + b_2)(\pi) \tag{9.11}$$

or

$$\log(TD/P) = b_1 i_c + b_2 i_t. \qquad (9.12)$$

Both van Wijnbergen and Taylor treat currency and inflation hedges as synonymous, even though the nominal return on currency is zero, while the nominal return on inflation hedges is the inflation rate. However, an alternative interpretation of equation 9.7 is possible if inflation hedges are substituted for currency as the third asset in the portfolio. While the real return on currency is $-\pi$, as in equation 9.8, the real return on inflation hedges is zero. In this case, equation 9.8 would be rewritten

$$\log(TD/P) = b_1(i_c - \pi) + b_2(i_t - \pi) \qquad (9.13)$$

or, with nominal returns, as

$$\log(TD/P) = b_1 i_c + b_2 i_t + b_3 \pi. \qquad (9.14)$$

Imposition of the adding-up constraint on equation 9.14 yields equation 9.13. The OLS estimate of equation 9.12 for the period 1969(II)–1989(I) is

$$\log(TD/P) = 0.422 - 0.508(i_c) + 0.513(i_t)$$
$$\qquad\qquad (1.802)\ (-2.465)\qquad (1.579)$$

$$+ 0.093 \log(Y) + 0.875 \log(TD/P)_{t-1}. \qquad (9.15)$$
$$\quad (2.514)\qquad\qquad (23.849)$$

$$\overline{R}^2 = 0.990 \quad \rho = -0.279$$

The implied coefficient of $-\pi$, the real return on currency, is -0.006, suggesting that the elasticity of substitution between curb market loans and time deposits has risen in comparison with the substitutability between currency and time deposits since the period for which van Wijnbergen estimated his time deposit demand equation.

Using inflation hedges as the third asset produces the following OLS results

$$\log(TD/P) = 0.153 - 0.216(i_c - \pi) + 0.529(i_t - \pi)$$
$$\qquad\qquad (0.743)\ (-1.670)\qquad\qquad (3.063)$$

$$+ 0.122 \log(Y) + 0.867 \log(TD/P)_{t-1}; \qquad (9.16)$$
$$\quad (3.547)\qquad\qquad (27.444)$$

$$\overline{R}^2 = 0.992 \quad \rho = -0.351$$

$$\log(TD/P) = 0.257 - 0.328(i_c - \pi^e) + 0.561(i_t - \pi^e)$$
$$\qquad\qquad (1.176)\ (-1.676)\qquad\qquad (3.006)$$

$$+ 0.115 \log(Y) + 0.866 \log(TD/P)_{t-1}, \qquad (9.17)$$
$$\quad (3.162)\qquad\qquad (25.912)$$

$$\overline{R}^2 = 0.991 \quad \rho = -0.331$$

where π^e is expected inflation estimated as a polynomial distributed lag in the time deposit demand function with weights on the current, one-, and two-quarter lagged inflation rates of 0.5, 0.333, and 0.167. Equation 9.17 yields an implicit coefficient for the return on inflation hedges of −0.313, while the implied coefficient for the return to inflation hedges in equation 9.18 is −0.233; 2SLS estimates failed to increase these implicit coefficients. In neither case is substitutability between curb market claims and time deposits significantly different from the substitutability between inflation hedges and curb market claims.

With a required reserve ratio of 25 percent, the curb market coefficient must be three times larger than the currency or inflation hedge coefficient for aggregate loans to fall after a rise in the time deposit interest rate. With a required reserve ratio of 50 percent, however, a curb market coefficient greater than the third asset coefficient is sufficient to reduce aggregate loans when the time deposit rate is increased. Of the four estimates presented above, equation 9.15 supports the neostructuralist position, equation 9.10 is ambiguous, and equations 9.16 and 9.17 reject it for reserve requirement ratios below 50 percent.

Since curb market interest rates have been published regularly in Taiwan, I also examined the demand for time deposits there. Unconstrained estimates with curb market, time deposit, and inflation rates produced meaningless results, probably due to multicollinearity. The estimate of the time deposit equation without the inflation rate yielded negative coefficients for both curb market and time deposit interest rates. Therefore I report just one OLS estimate, equivalent to equation 9.16, for the period 1970(III)–1993(IV):

$$\log(TD/P) = -1.837 - 0.276(i_c - \pi) + 0.760(i_t - \pi)$$
$$(-3.147) \ (-0.956) \qquad\quad (2.527)$$

$$+ \ 0.321 \log(Y) + 0.833 \log(TD/P)_{t-1}. \qquad (9.18)$$
$$(3.373) \qquad\quad (17.669)$$

$$\overline{R}^2 = 0.999 \quad \rho = 0.410$$

Equation 9.18 gives an implicit coefficient for the return on inflation hedges of −0.485. The first Wald test indicates that the sum of the coefficients of $i_c-\pi$ and $i_t-\pi$ are significantly different from zero. This means that the implied coefficient of the return on inflation hedges is significant. A second Wald test shows that this implied coefficient is significantly greater in absolute magnitude than the curb market coefficient. In Taiwan, therefore, there appears to have been greater substitutability from inflation hedges to time deposits than from curb market claims to time deposits after an increase in the time deposit interest rate.

Another way of determining whether or not total credit supply increases or decreases after a rise in the real time deposit rate is to examine the behavior of the curb market rate. If the total real supply of credit declines after an increase in the real time deposit rate of interest, the curb market rate should rise. Unfortunately, there are extremely limited time-series data on curb market rates of interest. Akira Kohsaka (1984) finds that after the Korean interest rate reform of 1965 there was virtually no change in the curb market rate until 1967. Thereafter the curb market rate declined. Due to the 1950 interest rate reform in Taiwan, however, nominal curb market rates fell from 231 percent in 1949 to 181 percent in 1950, and continued to fall to 24 percent in 1964. At the same time, the differential between the curb market rate and the time deposit rate declined substantially, and the rate of economic growth accelerated (Kohsaka 1984, 433).

Kohsaka (1984) states that in the Korean case there was no change in real credit supply in the short run but an increase in real credit supply in the medium run, a possibility explored in a theoretical context by Edward Buffie (1984). In Taiwan's case, the interest rate reform apparently increased total credit immediately. One reason for the different short-run outcomes in Korea and Taiwan is that reserve requirements were raised four times between 1965 and 1967 in Korea to absorb capital inflows from abroad (Ito 1984, 456). The segmented financial market produced cheap foreign credit for large firms but tight domestic credit conditions for firms unable to resort to the foreign markets.

While Korea and Taiwan possess curb markets of a size and scope probably not found in any other developing economies, they also constitute the only developing countries for which time series data on curb market interest rates exist. Figure 9.1 shows "unorganized money market" (UMM) loan rates and 12-month deposit rates in Korea, while Figure 9.2 shows the interest rate on postdated checks and the 12-month deposit rate in Taiwan.[1] In both figures, ρ is calculated as $(i_c - i_t)/i_c$, where i_c is the curb market or UMM interest rate and i_t is the 12-month deposit rate, to indicate the degree of divergence between informal and formal interest rates (Montiel, Agénor, and Haque 1993, 88). In neither country have curb and formal interest rates converged over time, perhaps in large part because financial liberalization has been so limited in both countries.

An econometric examination of the two interest rate series in both countries indicates that all four series are *I(1)* variables and follow a random walk. Using quarterly data for Korea over the period 1969(I)–1989(I), the following two relationships are detected:

---

[1]Data for Figure 9.1 are taken from David Cole and Yung Chul Park (1983, Table 29, 130) and the Bank of Korea's sample surveys. Data for Figure 9.2 are taken from Central Bank of China, *Financial Statistics Monthly: Taiwan District, Republic of China,* various issues.

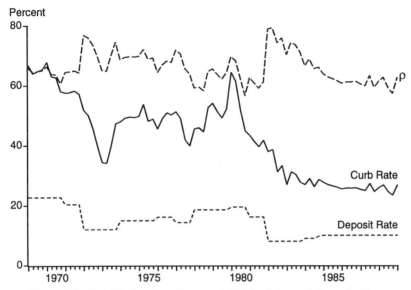

Figure 9.1. Curb Market Loan Rates and 12-Month Deposit Rates in Korea

$$\Delta i_c = -0.408 + 0.577\Delta i_t;$$
$$(-1.043)\ (2.262)$$
$$\overline{R}^2 = 0.050$$
(9.19)

$$\Delta i_c = -0.351 + 0.516\Delta i_{t,t-2} + 0.602\Delta i_{t,t-4}.$$
$$(-0.875)\ (2.034)\qquad (2.370)$$
$$\overline{R}^2 = 0.117$$
(9.20)

Similar estimates using monthly data for Taiwan over the period March 1970 to November 1993 yield:

$$\Delta i_c = 0.021 + 1.045\Delta i_t;$$
$$(0.712)\ (11.792)$$
$$\overline{R}^2 = 0.328$$
(9.21)

$$\Delta i_c = 0.014 + 0.413\Delta i_{t,t-3}.$$
$$(0.407)\ (3.906)$$
$$\overline{R}^2 = 0.117$$
(9.22)

Percent

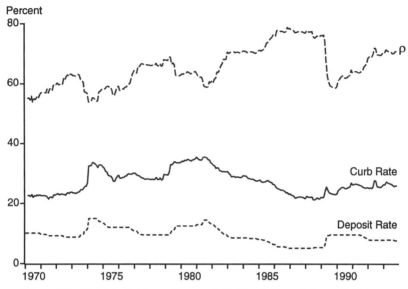

Figure 9.2. Curb Market Loan Rates and 12-Month Deposit Rates in Taiwan

While these estimates suggest that an increase in the 12-month time deposit rate raises the curb market interest rate, there is no evidence of any reverse causation from curb market rates to deposit rates of interest. Changes in curb market rates have been both accompanied and preceded by changes in deposit rates in the same direction. While these results lend support to van Wijnbergen's interpretation of his time deposit estimate, they may not apply to any other developing countries simply because curb markets are so much less prominent elsewhere. Furthermore, since time deposit rates were not set far below their free-market competitive equilibrium levels in either country, these comovements may reflect changes in monetary policies.

9.5   Income Distribution and Industrial Concentration

Very little quantitative work has been conducted on the issue of whether or not financial conditions affect income distribution and industrial concentration. Gilbert Brown (1973, 209), Yoon Je Cho (1984), and James Tybout (1983, 606) produce limited evidence that financial liberalization improves income distribution. Jaime Marquez and Janice Shack-Marquez (1987, 20) find that the concentration of savings deposits in Venezuela over the period 1965–1984 is reduced by higher real deposit rates of interest. Vogel (1984, 141) demonstrates that subsidized credit increased income accruing to the wealthiest 10 percent of the population in Costa Rica from 30.0 to 34.4

percent of total income. Several economists associated with Ohio State University's Agricultural Finance Center have stressed the point that subsidized credit programs invariably discriminate against rather than favor small borrowers (Adams, Graham, and Von Pischke 1984; González-Vega 1976, 1981, 1984a, 1984b; Sayad 1983; Vogel 1984; Von Pischke, Adams, and Donald 1983). Walter Ness (1974, 470–471) finds that Brazil's attempt to stimulate capital market development in the mid-1960s through strong tax incentives to buyers of new equity issues worsened income distribution.

Cho (1984) presents a detailed comparative analysis of Korea and Taiwan. Over the period 1966–1977, institutional finance in Korea was characterized by zero real interest rates and by selective credit policies that channelled subsidized funds to priority sectors. However, Taiwan exhibited positive real institutional interest rates and its selective credit policy was confined to exports. Hence Korea certainly did not liberalize its financial system to anything like the extent that Taiwan did, a point emphasized by Min (1976).

Table 9.2 presents some relevant data for Korea and Taiwan (Cho 1984, 47–49). It shows that industrial concentration has been far higher in Korea than in Taiwan. In 1981 the 20 largest conglomerate firms in Korea produced about 50 percent of the value added in the manufacturing sector. Even the smallest of these Korean conglomerate firms had a gross turnover greater than the combined turnover of the 10 largest firms in Taiwan.

These comparative statistics are consistent with the theory that low interest rate and selective credit policies lead to industrial concentration and to a less equal income distribution. The Gini coefficients indicate that income distribution became less equal in Korea but more equal in Taiwan between 1964 and 1976. Cho (1984, 54) concludes that the low interest rate policy in Korea transferred wealth from small depositors to large borrowers, caused highly capital-intensive production techniques to be chosen, and lowered the demand for labor.

Tybout (1983, 603) finds that the selective credit policy in Colombia favored large firms. Since small firms were borrowing constrained and could not expand, their market price was artificially low. This produced an incentive for large firms with access to cheap credit to take over small firms (Tybout 1983, 606). This is one explanation for the increasing concentration of industry that occurred in both Colombia and Korea.

John Harris, Fabio Schiantarelli, and Miranda Siregar (1994) analyze the effects of Indonesia's 1983 financial liberalization on 2,970 manufacturing firms. Their main findings are that smaller firms became less borrowing constrained after the liberalization:

> The economic reforms had a favorable effect on the performance of smaller establishments. On the financial side, liberalization has helped to reallocate domestic credit toward smaller establishments. Although nominal and real interest rates have risen to very high levels, real returns

Table 9.2. Income Distribution and Industrial Concentration in Korea and Taiwan

Concentration Index	Korea	Taiwan
Average annual percentage growth rate in number of firms, 1966–1977	0.9*	9.6
Average number of employees per firm in 1976	69*	28
Percentage of domestic credit absorbed by largest 100 firms	35	12†
Percentage of domestic credit absorbed by largest 400 firms	49	18‡
Gini coefficient for income distribution in 1964	0.344§	0.381
Gini coefficient for income distribution in 1976	0.360	0.307

Source: Derived from Cho (1984, 47–49)

* Korea collects data only on firms with five or more employees.

† The largest 97 firms

‡ The largest 333 firms

§ 1965

to capital assets remain high and have increased substantially, particularly for small and medium-size exporting establishments.

The overall conclusion that can be drawn from our investigation is that financial reforms have had a significant, positive impact on firms' real and financial choices. The process of shifting from an administrative allocation of credit toward a market-based allocation has increased borrowing costs, particularly for smaller units, but, at the same time, has widened access to finance and decreased the degree of credit market segmentation. From the standpoint of investment and rates of profit, the net effect appears to have been positive. (Harris, Schiantarelli, and Siregar 1994, 42–43)

Jeffrey Nugent and Mustapha Nabli (1992) examine the effect of credit availability, as measured by private sector domestic credit divided by GDP, on the share of manufacturing firms of 100 or more workers in aggregate manufacturing employment after excluding employment in firms with fewer than 10 workers in a sample of 54 countries for 1980.[2] Their regressions show that concentration in manufacturing industries is negatively and significantly affected by credit availability, except in the subsample of 23 industrialized

---

[2] Data availability necessitated using dates between 1970 and 1985.

countries. They conclude: "The heretofore unattained objective of quantifying the effects of the repression (or alternatively development) of financial markets on dualism and the size distribution of manufacturing plants would seem to be attainable. This is important because recent research indicates that size distribution constitutes a key link to income distribution and previously neglected efficiency effects" (Nugent and Nabli 1992, 1495).

9.6 Summary

The first empirical finding reported in this chapter is that the interest sensitivity of demand for financial assets is far higher than it is for national saving. This suggests that institutional interest rates affect portfolio allocation more than they affect the overall size of the portfolio. By substituting financial assets for inflation hedges, household portfolio reallocation can increase the average efficiency of investment and therefore the rate of economic growth in the medium run. Hence this portfolio effect may well be the channel through which the real deposit rate affects the incremental output/capital ratio and growth rate, two of the empirical findings presented in Chapter 8.

The second finding is that curb market and deposit rates of interest in Korea and Taiwan have moved in the same direction over the past two decades. This suggests that curb market claims may be closer substitutes than inflation hedges for deposits in these two countries. This finding can hardly be used to justify financial repression, since real deposit rates were positive in both countries. Indeed, it may indicate that both rates are equilibrium rates and that monetary policy affected both deposit and curb market rates in the same way.

The third finding relates to the effect of financial conditions on the allocation of credit. Specifically, financial repression and the ensuing credit rationing worsen income distribution and increase industrial concentration. The evidence presented in section 9.5 indicates that subsidized credit policies discriminate against rather than in favor of small borrowers.

Chapter 10

Effects of Financial Liberalization on Inflation and Short-Run Growth

10.1 Introduction

VERY FEW ECONOMETRIC ESTIMATES of the short-run effects of stabilization programs that incorporate features of the McKinnon-Shaw financial liberalization strategy exist. This chapter is therefore forced to concentrate on work by van Wijnbergen and myself. I attempt to measure the effects that stabilization programs involving interest rate reform as a key component have on inflation and the rate of economic growth. The regression results reported here cover only Turkey and the 14 Asian developing countries used in Chapters 8 and 9; Turkey makes a particularly interesting case study in view of its interest rate reform in 1980.

Section 10.2 presents my econometric estimates of a monetary model of inflation and short-run economic growth in Turkey. The estimates are then used to simulate alternative monetary policy stabilization strategies. Section 10.3 applies the same model to two samples of Asian developing countries.

Section 10.4 examines van Wijnbergen's (1982) econometric study of the effects of stabilization policies in Korea. Although he mentions policy with respect to the deposit rate of interest, van Wijnbergen simulates only monetary deceleration. Specifically, he simulates the effects of both a one-shot reduction in the money stock and also a continuous decrease in the monetary growth rate on inflation and growth in Korea.

Section 10.5 examines the effects of different monetary policy regimes on both short- and long-run rates of economic growth. This is done by estimating a growth equation on pooled time-series data for 55 countries. Money growth shocks, the variance of money growth shocks, and an indicator of accommodative monetary policy are the explanatory variables used to capture each country's monetary policy regime.

206

10.2   Inflation and Short-Run Growth in Turkey

This section presents an empirical application to Turkey of the simple monetary model developed in section 5.7 (Fry 1980b, 1981a). Although there is a great deal of empirical evidence on the determinants of inflation, there are few estimates of the particular inflation equations derived in Chapter 5 (equation 5.37). In particular, the effects of a change in the real deposit rate of interest on inflation have rarely been subjected to empirical evaluation.

Inflation is explained here by the difference between the rates of growth in per capita nominal money supply and per capita real money demand using a broad definition of money *M2*. Real money demand is determined everywhere by one or more price variables and a budget constraint. The price variable chosen here is the real deposit rate of interest $d-\pi^e$, where d is the nominal 12-month deposit rate of interest continuously compounded, and π^e is expected inflation. This implies that tangible assets used as inflation hedges, rather than bonds, are the dominant substitute asset for broad money. Holdings of nonmonetary financial assets by the nonbank sector were very limited in Turkey throughout the regression period. The budget constraint is per capita real permanent GNP; the rate of change in this variable is denoted *YNGE*. In contrast with the standard way of estimating permanent income, here I estimate expected income growth first, and then adjust last year's actual income level for expected income growth this year. This procedure can be justified by the fact that the rate of growth in GNP follows a random walk.

The first estimate of the inflation equation 5.37 (without the rate of change in the lagged per capita real money stock) is an OLS estimate for Turkey over the period 1950–1977 reported in Fry (1980b, 537):

$$INF = 1.115(MNG) - 2.152(YNGE) - 1.418\Delta(d-\pi)^e,$$
$$(7.493) \qquad (-3.501) \qquad (-3.046)$$
$$\overline{R}^2 = 0.659 \quad DW = 1.92 \tag{10.1}$$

where *INF* is the continuously compounded rate of change in the GNP deflator, *MNG* is the rate of growth in per capita *M2*, *YNGE* is expected growth in per capita real GNP, and $\Delta(d-\pi)^e$ is the expected change in the real deposit rate of interest.

The rate of change in per capita real permanent income and the change in the expected real deposit rate of interest were both estimated as far-end constrained third-order polynomials applied to values of the rate of change in per capita real GNP and the change in the real deposit rate of interest over the preceding six years. Hence the observation period for equation 10.1 is 1943–1977. The estimated weights are:

Variable	t–1	t–2	t–3	t–4	t–5	t–6	t–7
YNG_{t-i}	0.226	0.223	0.202	0.167	0.119	0.062	0.000
$\Delta(d-\pi)_{t-i}$	0.030	0.215	0.274	0.245	0.165	0.071	0.000

I reestimated this equation to include observations for the inflationary surge of 1977–1980. The annualized inflation rate as measured by the wholesale price index hit 119 percent in the first quarter of 1980. During the 1950–1977 period, inflation had never exceeded 30 percent. The 2SLS estimate of the inflation equation in Turkey for the period 1951–1985 is

$$INF = \; 1.096(\widehat{MNG}) - 2.045(YNGE) - 1.641\Delta(d-\pi^e).$$
$$\quad\;\; (18.413) \qquad (-5.096) \qquad (-5.386)$$

$$\overline{R}^2 = 0.826 \quad DW = 1.65$$

(10.2)

This estimate differs hardly at all from equation 10.1. Expected inflation π^e rather than the expected change in the real deposit rate of interest $\Delta(d-\pi)^e$ is used in equation 10.2. Expected inflation is estimated in a semi-logarithmic per capita real money demand function over the period 1950–1985 as a far-end constrained second-order polynomial distributed lag. Expected permanent income growth $YNGE$ is estimated in equation 10.2 itself, also as a far-end constrained second-order polynomial.

The coefficients of the three variables in equations 10.1 and 10.2 all agree with a priori expectations. The coefficient of the rate of change in the per capita nominal money supply is not significantly different from 1. The elasticity of money demand with respect to per capita real permanent income is about 2, a figure comparable with elasticities estimated directly in money demand studies using a broad definition of money. The coefficient of the change in the expected real deposit rate of interest of about –1.5 is also of the same order of magnitude as coefficients estimated for Turkey and other developing countries in money demand functions (Abe et al. 1975, Fry 1978, Fry and Farhi 1979, ch. 4).

My own empirical findings on the relationship between both the short- and medium-run rate of economic growth and the real deposit rate of interest are consistent with the McKinnon-Shaw model. The short-run relationship between growth and the real deposit rate of interest estimated here is based on the Fisherian Phillips curve, with the credit availability effect discussed in section 5.7 (equations 5.38 and 5.39). If higher real deposit rates increase credit availability in real terms, the rate of economic growth should rise in the short run following an increase in the real deposit rate. If, however, higher real deposit rates reduce total credit availability in real terms due to substitution from curb market loans into time deposits subject to the reserve requirement leakage, as the neostructuralists argue, the rate of economic growth should decline.

In the Turkish case, disequilibrium interest rate and exchange control systems imply that real money demand determines to a large extent the real supply of domestic credit because domestic credit is the primary asset backing the monetary liabilities of the banking system. The supply link between credit availability and real economic growth springs from the ratio of credit to output, or from the real rather than the nominal volume of credit, as discussed in section 5.7.

Normal or noncyclical growth YGN is determined by, among other factors, the volume and productivity of investment. Both are affected positively by the real deposit rate $d-\pi^e$ or RD, as discussed in sections 5.7, 8.3, and 8.4. Here, however, I assume that investment raises productive capacity—so moving the transformation frontier outwards—smoothly over time. For industrial countries, the time trend of real GNP may provide a reasonable proxy for the normal or noncyclical component of supply determined solely by productive capacity. For most developing countries, fluctuations in agricultural output must also be taken into account. Year-to-year changes in the level of agricultural output are determined largely by variations in weather conditions. Therefore, they represent exogenous shifts in the production possibility curve.

Trend growth in real GNP in Turkey differed significantly before and after 1962 (Fry 1971, 322), as well as 1977. Therefore, logarithmic trends in real GNP and agricultural output were calculated separately for 1948–1961, 1962–1976, and 1977–1985. Normal supply is defined as trend real GNP plus the difference between actual and trend real agricultural output.

The first application of this expectations-augmented Phillips curve with credit availability effect (equation 5.39) is to Turkey for the period 1950–1977 (Fry 1980b, 540). The 2SLS estimate is

$$YG = 0.865(YGNA) + 0.010(\widehat{PPE}) + 0.120(d-\pi)^e,$$
$$(10.763) \qquad (1.738) \qquad (2.208)$$

$$\overline{R}^2 = 0.828 \quad DW = 2.19$$

(10.3)

where YG is the continuously compounded rate of growth in real GNP, $YGNA$ is trend growth in real GNP adjusted for fluctuations in agricultural output about its long-run trend, and PPE is the actual price level divided by the expected price level. Expected price P^e is $e^{\pi^e} \cdot P_{t-1}$, and π^e is estimated using the polynomial weights for $\Delta(d-\pi)^e$ in equation 10.1.

I also reestimated the short-run growth equation for Turkey to cover the period since 1977. The 2SLS estimate of the growth equation in Turkey for the period 1951–1985 is

$$YG = 0.957(YGN) + 0.009(\widehat{PPE}) + 0.154(d - \pi^e),$$
$$(8.585) \qquad (1.304) \qquad (3.039) \qquad\qquad (10.4)$$
$$\overline{R}^2 = 0.731 \quad DW = 1.95$$

where YGN is trend growth in real GNP unadjusted for agricultural fluctuations.

Equations 10.1 and 10.2 show that an acceleration in nominal money growth raises the inflation rate and so PPE or P/P^e. In turn, an increase in P/P^e raises growth in real GNP, as shown in equations 10.3 and 10.4. This is the standard short-run Phillips curve tradeoff. But when *expected* inflation rises, so reducing both P/P^e and $d - \pi^e$, the growth rate declines. In long-run equilibrium P equals P^e because inflation is fully anticipated. Then only the negative impact of the lower real deposit rate $d - \pi^e$ is felt. With d held constant and below its market equilibrium level, the long-run Phillips curve produces a negative relationship between inflation and growth in a financially repressed economy like Turkey through the real credit supply mechanism, even before the effect of inflation on the saving rate and on the average efficiency of new investment is taken into account.

The inflation and growth equations presented above show that a higher deposit rate of interest reduces inflation and raises the growth rate at the same time. Therefore, an optimal monetary policy must set the nominal deposit rate at its upper bound. An obvious answer would be to abolish all institutional interest rate ceilings. In practice, however, the optimal competitive deposit rate would have to be forced upon Turkey's cartelized and oligopolistic banking system (Fry 1972, chs. 3–4, 6). One way of doing this might be to fix a *minimum* deposit rate and to require banks to satisfy all deposit demand at this rate. This would be sufficient to produce the competitive result, provided loan demand were elastic at rates above the competitive loan rate of interest.

Table 10.1 gives data on actual money growth, inflation, real GNP growth, and the real deposit rate of interest over the period 1975–1985. That the Turkish government recognized the efficacy of financial liberalization in the 1980s is shown by the large increases in the real deposit rate then. The first dynamic simulation in Table 10.1 is a benchmark simulation treating money as exogenous. It shows the benign effects on inflation and growth of the interest rate increases that occurred between 1979 and 1981.

Table 10.1 also illustrates what might have happened had the 12-month deposit rate of interest been held at 9 percent, its rate between 1970 and early 1978. Inflation would have been much higher than it actually was between 1978 and 1982. The simulation forecasts an inflation peak at 99 percent in 1981 and inflation rates of over 50 percent for four years in succession, 1979–1982. It also predicts much lower growth and declining real GNP for the seven years 1979–1985. This simulation suggests that the large increases in deposit

Table 10.1. Dynamic Simulations of Inflation and Growth in Turkey with Exogenous Money, 1975–1985 (Continuously compounded percentage rates of change)

	Actual			
Date	Money Growth	Inflation Rate	Real GNP Growth	Real Deposit Rate
1975	23.8	15.0	7.7	−9.4
1976	22.8	15.5	7.6	−9.0
1977	25.3	21.9	3.9	−10.3
1978	30.2	36.3	2.8	−13.5
1979	40.1	53.7	−0.4	−17.5
1980	49.7	71.2	−1.1	−22.3
1981	57.9	35.0	4.0	−4.4
1982	51.2	24.2	4.5	0.9
1983	32.5	24.6	3.3	0.1
1984	36.2	40.1	6.0	5.2
1985	45.5	36.1	4.9	7.0

	Benchmark Dynamic Simulation			Simulation with Constant Deposit Rate		
Date	Inflation Rate	Real GNP Growth	Real Deposit Rate	Inflation Rate	Real GNP Growth	Real Deposit Rate
1975	15.0	7.7	−9.4	15.0	7.7	−9.4
1976	−4.1	7.5	−3.2	9.4	7.0	−7.2
1977	45.8	0.4	−12.8	27.0	0.6	−10.4
1978	21.3	2.1	−11.1	41.3	1.3	−17.1
1979	26.0	2.7	−7.4	64.4	−0.4	−29.3
1980	47.2	2.6	−7.3	83.7	−2.9	−44.4
1981	16.0	5.1	12.7	99.4	−5.7	−60.6
1982	33.9	6.2	10.8	77.1	−5.6	−66.1
1983	14.6	4.6	10.0	32.1	−5.6	−55.9
1984	3.5	7.4	23.0	39.5	−3.7	−48.7
1985	24.5	7.3	23.1	60.0	−3.7	−48.5

rates were responsible for Turkey's relatively small recession and reasonably rapid recovery after the stabilization program was initiated in 1980. Comparing the benchmark simulation with the counterfactual simulation shows just how substantial the effects of the interest rate hikes in the early 1980s on inflation and growth were.

Accelerated monetary growth had a debilitating effect on the rate of economic growth in Turkey, at least until 1983. Over the period 1951–1985, the simple correlation between money growth and inflation is 0.81. Even the short-run Phillips curve exhibits a negative relationship between inflation and economic growth. Over the period 1951–1983, the correlation between inflation and growth is −0.45, while the correlation between money growth and economic growth is −0.29.

The small-scale macroeconomic model presented above explains the negative correlation between inflation or money growth and economic growth through the effects of the real deposit rate of interest. Over the period 1951–1983, the correlation between the real deposit rate of interest and the rate of economic growth was 0.45. Over the same period, the correlation between inflation and the real deposit rate of interest was −0.81, while between money growth and the real deposit rate it was −0.40. The real deposit rate moved inversely to the inflation rate because nominal rates of interest were adjusted so infrequently. When interest rate adjustments started to be made more frequently after 1983, this negative association disappeared, as did the negative association between inflation or money growth and the rate of economic growth.

The importance attached by the model to the real deposit rate is undoubtedly exaggerated. A government that mismanages one macroeconomic policy instrument is most likely to be following a variety of other growth-inhibiting macroeconomic policies. That the upsurge of inflation in 1984 and 1985 was not accompanied by declining growth cannot be attributed solely to the high real deposit rates of interest in these two years. Realistic changes in deposit rates and rationalization of the taxation of financial intermediation suggest that other government-controlled prices were probably also adjusted in appropriate ways during those years. Previously, rigidities of a variety of key prices such as interest rates and exchange rates made Turkish inflation a very costly affair. Perhaps Turkey has now learned to live with inflation as a far better alternative to pretending that it does not exist.

10.3 Inflation and Short-Run Growth in Some Asian Developing Countries

This section contains the estimates of my model of inflation and growth for a sample of Pacific Basin developing countries. The OLS pooled time-series estimate of equation 5.37 using annual data over the period 1961–1977 for a sample of seven Pacific Basin developing countries—Indonesia, Korea, Malaysia, Philippines, Singapore, Taiwan, and Thailand—reported in Fry (1981a, 13) is

$$INF = 0.930(MNG) - 0.927(YNGE)$$
$$\quad\;\; (33.196) \qquad\quad (-4.359)$$

$$- 0.986\Delta(d-\pi^e) - 0.280(MNKG)_{t-1}, \qquad (10.5)$$
$$(-10.849) \qquad\qquad (-4.303)$$

$$\overline{R}^2 = 0.92$$

where $MNKG$ is the per capita real money stock.

The lag coefficients for the per capita real permanent income growth rate $YNGE$ and expected inflation π^e in equation 10.5 were obtained by applying polynomial distributed lags to the rate of change in per capita real GNP and to the change in the inflation rate in the following first difference semi-logarithmic money demand function:

$$MNKG = a_1 YNGE + a_2\Delta\pi^e + a_3 MNKG_{t-1}. \qquad (10.6)$$

The price level is the GNP deflator. Unconstrained first-, second-, and third-order polynomials were applied in turn to the coefficients of current and past changes in the inflation rate and rate of change in real per capita income for each country. Choices of polynomial degrees and lag lengths were based on the pattern of the lag coefficients, a nonnegativity criterion, and the correlation coefficients. Monotonically declining or inverted U-shaped coefficient patterns were preferred as being more consistent with an a priori assumption about formation of expectations. Sign changes were inadmissible for the same reason—the nonnegativity criterion. Satisfactory results were obtained for all the sample countries with first- and second-order polynomials. The lag coefficient estimates used for the pooled time-series analysis are presented in Table 10.2.

Finally, a comparable OLS estimate of equation 5.37 for the 14 Asian developing countries examined in Chapters 8 and 9 over the period 1961–1983 is

$$INF = 0.895(MNG) - 0.631(YNGE)$$
$$\quad\;\; (44.132) \qquad\quad (-5.313)$$

$$- 0.887\Delta(d-\pi^e) - 0.408(MNKG)_{t-1}. \qquad (10.7)$$
$$(-18.426) \qquad\qquad (-10.823)$$

$$\overline{R}^2 = 0.871$$

The coefficients of the four variables in equations 10.5 and 10.7 all agree with a priori beliefs. The implicit long-run coefficient of the rate of change in the per capita nominal money supply is 1.292 in equation 10.5 and 1.512 in equation 10.7; neither is significantly greater than 1. The implicit long-run income elasticity of money demand is 1.286 in equation 10.5 and 1.066

Table 10.2. Lag Coefficients for Seven Pacific Basin Developing Countries

Country	Order	Permanent Income Lag Coefficients						
		t	t–1	t–2	t–3	t–4	t–5	t–6
Indonesia	1	0.597	0.403					
Korea	1	0.652	0.348					
Malaysia	1	0.300	0.247	0.193	0.140	0.086	0.033	
Philippines	1	0.338	0.662					
Singapore	0	1.000						
Taiwan	0	1.000						
Thailand	2	0.594	0.159	0.247				

Country	Order	Expected Inflation Lag Coefficients						
		t	t–1	t–2	t–3	t–4	t–5	t–6
Indonesia	2	0.326	0.236	0.164	0.109	0.071	0.050	0.046
Korea	2	0.304	0.245	0.190	0.137	0.086	0.039	
Malaysia	1	0.243	0.213	0.182	0.151	0.121	0.090	
Philippines	2	0.187	0.234	0.240	0.206	0.133		
Singapore	1	0.780	0.220					
Taiwan	1	0.994	0.006					
Thailand	2	0.334	0.240	0.166	0.113	0.080	0.068	

in equation 10.7, figures comparable to those produced directly in money demand estimates. The implicit long-run coefficient of the change in the real deposit rate is 1.368 in equation 10.5 and 1.498 in equation 10.7, rather similar to the coefficients estimated in equations 10.1 and 10.2.

A 2SLS estimate of the expectations-augmented Phillips curve with the credit availability effect added, using annual pooled time-series data over the period 1961–1977 for the sample of seven Pacific Basin developing countries reported in Fry (1981a, 14) is

$$YG = 0.390(YGNA) + 0.043(\widehat{PPE}) + 0.049(d-\pi^e).$$
$$(9.139) \qquad (11.403) \qquad (4.257)$$
$$\overline{R}^2 = 0.26$$

(10.8)

The last estimate of the growth equation shown here, using annual data over the period 1961–1977 for a sample of 12 Asian developing economies —Burma, India, Indonesia, Korea, Malaysia, Nepal, Pakistan, Philippines, Singapore, Sri Lanka, Taiwan, and Thailand—is reported in Fry (1981c, 97):

$$YG = 0.521(YGNA) + 0.027(\widehat{PPE}) + 0.034(d - \pi^e).$$
$$(13.627) \qquad (9.419) \qquad (2.926) \qquad\qquad (10.9)$$
$$\overline{R}^2 = 0.44$$

The estimates of the short-run growth rate function presented above produce coefficients of $d-\pi^e$ ranging in value from 0.034 to 0.138. Hence a 10 percentage point increase in the real deposit rate of interest towards its competitive free-market equilibrium level is associated with an increase in the short-run rate of economic growth of between 0.3 and 1.4 percentage points.

This section now presents the simulated outcomes of three alternative stabilization strategies based on the growth and inflation estimates for the seven Pacific Basin developing countries analyzed in Fry (1981a). The monetary authorities of all these countries had at their disposal two independent instruments of monetary policy to confront the inflationary surge of the late 1970s —the rate of growth in the nominal money supply and the nominal deposit rate of interest. There is in practice an upper bound to the deposit rate at its competitive market equilibrium rate (Fry 1980b, 542). The discussion here is based on the assumption that the nominal deposit rate lies below this upper bound.

Equations 10.5 and 10.8 are used to simulate three alternative stabilization policies for a composite economy somewhat resembling the Indonesian economy. The economy starts off in a steady state, with a 20 percent inflation rate that has been stable for the past decade. Expectations of both expected inflation and per capita real income growth are realized. The real deposit rate is −10 percent, the normal real economic growth rate is 7 percent, and the population growth rate is 2 percent. The lag coefficients for expected inflation and per capita real permanent income used for these simulations are:

t–1	t–2	t–3	t–4
0.4	0.3	0.2	0.1

Equation 10.8 can now be solved to yield an actual growth rate of 6.54 percent and per capita real permanent income growth of 4.54 percent. The steady state solution of equation 10.5 gives a stable money supply growth rate of 30.63 percent a year.

The first stabilization strategy reduces the growth rate of the nominal money supply from 30.63 percent to 17.14 percent in year 0 and all subsequent years. This lowers the inflation rate in the new long-run equilibrium to 7 percent and hence raises the real deposit rate of interest from −10 percent to +3 percent, with no change in the nominal deposit rate of interest. The new long-run equilibrium per capita real growth rate increases from 4.54 to 5.18 percent, as shown in Table 10.3.

Table 10.3. Dynamic Simulations of Three Stabilization Strategies in a Composite Pacific Basin Developing Country (Continuously compounded percentage rates of change)

Year	Strategy 1		Strategy 2		Strategy 3		
	Per Capita Real GNP	Price Level	Per Capita Real GNP	Price Level	Per Capita Real GNP	Price Level	Money Supply
−1	4.54	20.00	4.54	20.00	4.54	20.00	30.63
0	4.03	7.45	4.21	−5.37	5.10	18.19	42.47
1	4.30	2.96	4.94	4.25	5.10	17.47	32.24
2	4.72	1.20	5.21	6.76	5.10	16.64	28.65
3	5.14	1.57	5.28	7.23	5.10	15.73	26.95
4	5.45	3.39	5.26	7.15	5.10	14.79	25.76
5	5.57	6.10	5.19	7.00	5.10	13.90	24.73
6	5.51	8.08	5.17	6.95	5.10	13.00	23.72
7	5.37	9.00	5.17	6.96	5.10	12.09	22.71
8	5.21	8.96	5.18	6.98	5.10	11.19	21.71
9	5.09	8.30	5.18	7.00	5.10	10.29	20.71
10	5.05	7.42	5.18	7.00	5.10	9.38	19.71
11	5.06	6.71	5.18	7.00	5.10	8.48	18.71
12	5.11	6.34	5.18	7.00	5.10	7.58	17.71
13	5.16	6.31	5.18	7.00	5.10	6.67	16.71
14	5.20	6.52	5.18	7.00	5.10	5.77	15.71
15	5.22	6.82	5.18	7.00	5.10	4.87	14.71
∞	5.18	7.00	5.18	7.00	5.18	7.00	17.14

The second stabilization strategy also reduces nominal money growth to 17.14 percent but raises the real deposit rate through deposit indexation to 3 percent at the outset of the program in year 0. The third strategy establishes the 3 percent real deposit rate but sets money growth at whatever rate is required to maintain a constant per capita real rate of economic growth of 5.10 percent a year.

The main point to note in the simulation results presented in Table 10.3 and Figures 10.1 to 10.3 is that the first and second strategies both produce a recession. Per capita real GNP growth declines because actual prices fall below expected prices. To some extent, increased credit availability offsets the reduction in supply produced by the expectations effect. Naturally, the credit availability effect is stronger for the second strategy. In this case, real economic growth does not fall so much and picks up faster, despite the fact that higher real money demand actually reduces the price *level* in the second

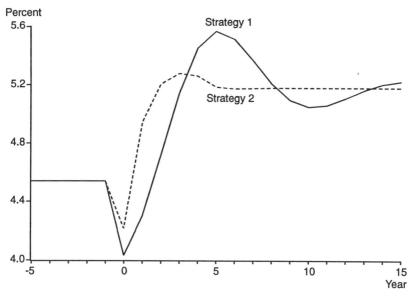

Figure 10.1. Per Capita Income Growth under Stabilization Strategies 1 and 2

strategy. Both economic growth and inflation converge to their new steady state values faster under the second strategy than under the first strategy, as shown in Figures 10.1 and 10.2.

The third strategy maintains a constant per capita real growth rate marginally below its new steady state level. This permits a gradual and smooth reduction in the inflation rate. However, because of the sharp deflationary increase in the real deposit rate in year 0, nominal money growth must *accelerate* initially. Thereafter, nominal money growth falls gradually and smoothly in step with the declining inflation rate.

The strategies of raising the real deposit rate are far more successful than the strategy of reducing money growth alone in achieving both higher real growth and lower inflation. However, once the optimal deposit rate has been fixed, higher nominal money growth always increases inflation as well as real economic growth in the short run but does not affect the latter in the long-run steady state. Conversely, lower monetary growth reduces inflation and real economic growth in the short run but again has no long-run influence on real economic growth. As suggested by Donald Mathieson (1980), optimal policy with respect to nominal money growth could be solved as a dynamic control problem, given policy makers' loss function.

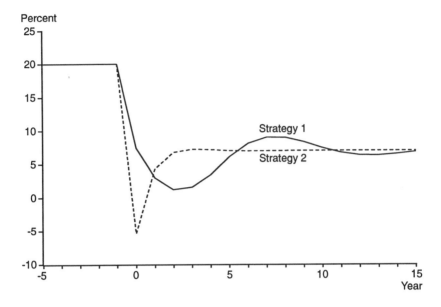

Figure 10.2. Inflation Rates under Stabilization Strategies 1 and 2

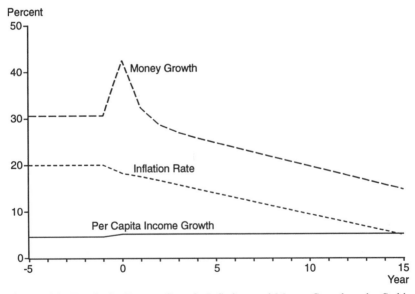

Figure 10.3. Per Capita Income Growth, Inflation, and Money Growth under Stabilization Strategy 3

10.4 Van Wijnbergen's Model of Inflation and Short-Run Growth in Korea

In his quarterly monetary model of Korea estimated over the period 1966–1979, van Wijnbergen (1982) divides the economy into export and nonexport sectors. The export sector faces a perfectly elastic supply of credit at the special export loan rate of interest, while the nonexport sector confronts credit rationing. For the export sector, van Wijnbergen estimates both demand and supply equations. The price of exports, interpreted as the export supply equation, is affected positively and significantly by the special interest rate on export loans (van Wijnbergen 1982, 139). The domestic price level determined by costs of production is affected positively by the nominal curb market rate (van Wijnbergen 1982, 144). Real consumption, investment, and intermediate imports are all affected negatively and significantly by the real curb market rate of interest (van Wijnbergen 1982, 140–143).

Van Wijnbergen's (1982, 146) wage equation is a standard expectations-augmented Phillips curve. Unemployment has a negative effect on the wage rate. Using Okun's law, unemployment itself is determined by the gap between potential and actual output; unemployment and actual output are both seasonally adjusted (van Wijnbergen 1982, 147). Finally, on the real side, potential output is determined solely by the volume of fixed investment and last period's potential output (with a coefficient of 1.03) (van Wijnbergen 1982, 147). Although potential real GNP is given as the dependent variable in this equation, presumably it is actual real GNP with potential real GNP taken as the value of real GNP predicted by the equation.

The financial sector of the model determines the banking system's balance sheet. Van Wijnbergen (1982, 149) specifies a function that determines the nominal amount of inter-office borrowing by Japanese branches in Korea from their parent banks. Inter-office borrowing is influenced positively and significantly by the ratio of the Korean bank lending rate to the Japanese call money rate. The domestic Korean banks also borrow abroad. The real level of foreign borrowing by domestic banks in Korea is affected positively and significantly by the difference between the Korean bank lending rate and the three-month Eurodollar rate (van Wijnbergen 1982, 150).

Domestic and foreign banks supply loans to both the export and nonexport sectors. The nominal supply of bank loans to the nonexport sector is influenced positively and significantly by the difference between the Korean bank lending rate and the Bank of Korea's discount rate. It also rises *pari passu* with these banks' foreign borrowing. The quantity of loans to the export sector is determined by demand, since there is no quantity constraint on the Bank of Korea's rediscount facility for export loans. The real demand for export loans is affected negatively and significantly by the real export loan rate (van Wijnbergen 1982, 152). Direct foreign borrowing by the nonbank private sector is affected negatively by the Eurodollar rate and positively by the curb market rate (van Wijnbergen 1982, 153).

Van Wijnbergen (1982, 154–157) models money demand using James Tobin's portfolio allocation model. The demand for time deposits in real terms is affected negatively and significantly by both the curb market rate and the inflation rate, and positively and significantly by the time deposit rate of interest, as described in section 9.4. The demand for *M1* is affected negatively and significantly by the inflation rate, while the currency/deposit ratio adjusts gradually towards a constant fraction. Private sector assets consist entirely of curb market loans and *M2*. Hence the change in total private sector assets equals the difference between disposable income and private consumption. In van Wijnbergen's model, therefore, all the accumulation of financial assets comes from saving, none from substitution out of tangible assets held as inflation hedges. This assumption conflicts with the empirical evidence reported in Chapters 8 and 9.

Van Wijnbergen's (1982, 158–159) Korean model is completed with an accounting identity for the *M2* money supply which equals net domestic credit to the government plus bank loans to the export and nonexport sectors plus net foreign assets minus other liabilities. Changes in other liabilities are produced in this model solely through the revaluation of net foreign assets due to exchange rate changes. Such revaluations change the Korean currency value of net foreign assets without affecting the money supply.

The curb market interest rate is determined by the equilibrium of *M2* supply and *M2* demand; the demand for *M2* is the sum of the demands for time deposits and *M1*. Van Wijnbergen finds that a rise in the time deposit rate produces greater substitution from curb market loans than from the *M1* component of the money stock into time deposits. Since curb market loans suffer no intermediation leakages from reserve requirements, this pattern of substitution reduces the aggregate supply of domestic credit and hence raises the curb market interest rate in the model. In fact, however, the Bank of Korea's rediscount system allowed the commercial banks to intermediate some of their liabilities at better than one-to-one. By no means was all high-powered money lost to the private sector in practice.

Van Wijnbergen (1982, 159–166) now presents three dynamic simulations of his model. The first is a base run, the second involves a one-shot reduction in the money stock by 5 percent, and the third traces the effects of a continuous reduction in monetary growth by 10 percent each year over a three-year period. This halves the actual monetary growth rate used in the base run. The simulated effect of the one-shot 5 percent money stock reduction is to raise the inflation rate from an annualized rate of 32 percent to 45 percent in the first quarter. Output is reduced in the first quarter by about $\frac{1}{2}$ percent. The substantial increase in the curb market interest rate required to equate money demand and supply raises prices through the markup mechanism and lowers output by deterring both consumption and investment. Van Wijnbergen's model reproduces the increase in velocity of circulation following monetary deceleration that reduces growth in Kapur's model.

The one-shot money supply reduction reduces inflation in the second and third quarters below the base-run rates by 11 and 4 percentage points, respectively. After that, inflation returns to the base-run rates. However, real GNP growth continues to lie below the base-run rate in the second quarter. Indeed, in the second quarter, real GNP lies over 3 percent below its base-run level. The growth rate picks up in the third quarter, and the level of real GNP converges to its base-run level by the fifth quarter. None of these results differs in any substantial way from those produced by McKinnon-Shaw models.

Van Wijnbergen's simulation of a continuously lower monetary growth rate does offer some surprises. The reduction in the rate of monetary growth over three years by 10 percent each year produces a higher inflation rate in the first period, as in the simulation of a one-shot reduction in the money stock. However, subsequent reductions in monetary growth fail to reduce inflation below the base-run rates at any time during this three-year period. Part of the reason for this persistence in the inflation rate is that continuously lower monetary growth holds the level of real GNP below the base-run levels throughout these three years. Lower monetary growth rates also keep the real curb market interest rate above the base-run rates. High curb market rates reduce private consumption slightly and private investment considerably. They also raise velocity of circulation of *M2* by 25 percent at the end of the third year. Both the one-shot reduction and the continuous reduction in monetary growth worsen the balance of payments on current account by reducing domestic supply by more than domestic demand.

The results of van Wijnbergen's dynamic simulation of a continuous reduction in monetary growth are surprising in that he finds prices so sticky or slow to adjust in Korea; the short run spreads itself over at least three years. My own model presented in sections 10.2 and 10.3 above is based on complete price adjustment within a year. Nevertheless, van Wijnbergen and the McKinnon-Shaw school are in complete agreement with the proposition that monetary contraction reduces real GNP growth and can worsen the current account.

All the McKinnon-Shaw models produce an initial decline in the inflation rate, albeit by less than the reduction in monetary growth, whereas van Wijnbergen has an initial rise in the inflation rate from his markup pricing equation. This difference, however, is not so much a matter for major disagreement as for raised eyebrows. Indeed, there is nothing in the dynamics of van Wijnbergen's model per se to which the McKinnon-Shaw school would take strong exception.

The McKinnon-Shaw school parts company with the neostructuralists over the latter's policy prescription to lower the deposit rate of interest at the outset of a stabilization program (van Wijnbergen 1982, 166). The McKinnon-Shaw models show that real credit supply and hence aggregate output can be raised by an increase in institutional interest rates towards their free-market equilibrium levels. As discussed in section 9.4, van Wijnbergen finds that an increase in the time deposit rate reduces credit availability by causing substitution out of curb market loans.

Conclusive resolution of this dispute awaits a comparison of McKinnon-Shaw and neostructuralist models using identical data sets and estimation techniques. My own estimate of equation 5.39 (excluding normal growth) for Korea over the period 1969–1992 gives a positive and significant coefficient for $d-\pi^e$, as well as a positive but insignificant coefficient for PPE:

$$YG = 0.055 + 0.020(PPE) + 0.246(d-\pi).$$
$$(0.507) \quad (0.188) \qquad (2.937)$$

$$\overline{R}^2 = 0.232 \qquad DW = 1.918$$

(10.10)

Here higher deposit rates of interest have a significantly positive influence on the rate of economic growth through the credit availability effect.

10.5 Monetary Policy Regimes and Economic Growth[1]

The only way of estimating both the medium- and long-run effects of discretionary monetary policy on the rate of economic growth is by pooling time-series data across countries. The test presented in Fry and Lilien (1986) and reported here uses 647 observations for 55 developed and developing countries. It is the first appropriate estimate of both medium- and long-run effects of monetary policy on the growth rate.

Country i's rate of growth in GDP in year t is composed of a country-specific long-run or normal growth rate g_i^n and a country-specific cyclical growth rate g_{it}^c:

$$g_{it} = g_i^n + g_{it}^c.$$

(10.11)

Equation 10.12 specifies long-run output growth as a function of country-characteristic dummy variables and a number of variables designed to capture the long-run effects of monetary policy:

$$g_i^n = \alpha_0 + \alpha_1 IND_i + \alpha_2 OILX_i + \alpha_3 DM_i^* + \alpha_4 MVAR_i$$
$$+ \alpha_5 MACC74_i + \alpha_6 DP_i^* + \alpha_7 NDCG_i^*,$$

(10.12)

where IND_i and $OILX_i$ are dummy variables for industrialized and oil-exporting countries. Industrialized countries may experience lower output growth rates ($\alpha_1 < 0$) than developing countries until per capita incomes in developing countries catch up (Barro 1987, ch. 11).

---

[1]This section was written with David Lilien.

The variable DM_i^* is the long-run rate of growth in the money supply, measured as a simple average of the annual *M1* growth rates over the sample period. Money neutrality requires α_3 to be zero. This restriction is tested rather than imposed on the data.

Two other measures of monetary policy are included in equation 10.12. $MVAR_i$ is the variance of money growth shocks (described below) and is a measure of the variability and uncertainty of monetary policy. Constantine Glezakos (1978), Axel Leijonhufvud (1981), and others show that greater uncertainty with respect to the future price level reduces output growth.

The variable $MACC74_i$ is a dummy variable for monetary accommodation of the 1973–1974 oil shock. It takes a value of 1 if the ratio of *M1* to nominal GDP rose between 1974 and 1977. While one would not expect accommodation of a single oil shock to affect the long-run rate of economic growth, one could take $MACC74_i$ to indicate a country's willingness to use monetary policy to accommodate other supply shocks. Few would doubt that monetary accommodation can reduce the negative impact of supply shocks on output growth in the short run. Here, however, the aim is to measure its impact on long-run growth. Since $MACC74_i$ could be an alternative measure of variability in monetary policy, one might expect it to lower the rate of economic growth in the long run.

The period-average inflation rate is DP_i^*. Inflation depresses long-run output growth in the inside-money models of Fry (1980b) and Lee (1980) but increases growth in Tobin's (1965) outside-money model. Since DP_i^* may be determined simultaneously with g_i^n, a reduced-form model in which DP_i^* is omitted is also estimated.

The variable $NDCG_i^*$ is the trend ratio of net government credit to total domestic credit. When government extracts greater seigniorage by increasing the proportion of domestic credit allocated to the public sector, credit availability for the private sector is reduced, as explained in earlier chapters.

Country i's cyclical output growth in period t is a function of both policy shocks and exogenous supply shocks:

$$g_{it}^c = \beta_{i1}DMR_{it} + \beta_{i2}DMR_{it-1} + \beta_{i3}DMR_{it-2}$$

$$+\lambda_{i1}OILDP_t + \lambda_{i2}OILDP_{t-1} + \lambda_{i3}OILDP_{t-2} \qquad (10.13)$$

$$+\theta_1 NDCGR_{it} + \gamma_1 g_{it-1}^c + \gamma_2 g_{it-2}^c,$$

where DMR_{it-j} represents innovations to the time-series process of money growth. It is the residual of country-specific regressions of the money growth rate on its own lagged value and time. This variable is similar to that used by Robert Barro (1978) and others to measure unanticipated money. Since output is measured here as a growth rate, long-run neutrality requires that the sum of the β coefficients equal zero. Short-run neutrality or total policy ineffectiveness implies that each β would equal zero.

Money growth shocks are not assumed to have the same effect in all countries; the βs have i subscripts. Rather, Robert Lucas's (1973) hypothesis that money growth shocks have a smaller impact on real variables in countries where highly variable monetary policy makes the current money growth or inflation rate a poor signal of real disturbances is tested here:

$$\beta_{ij} = \delta_{0j} + \delta_{1j}MVAR_i + \delta_{2j}MACC74_i. \qquad (10.14)$$

Following Lucas (1973), one would expect $\delta_1 < 0$ and $\delta_2 < 0$.

Supply shocks are measured by the rate of change in oil prices $OILDP_t$. Oil shocks can have an impact on oil-exporting countries that differs from their impact on oil-importing countries:

$$\lambda_{ij} = \phi_{0j} + \phi_{1j}OILX_i. \qquad (10.15)$$

Other supply shock proxies, including country-specific changes in the terms of trade, were also tested. The coefficients had the expected signs but were less significant than the oil-price coefficients.

Shocks to the government credit ratio $NDCGR_{it}$ (measured in the same way as DMR_{it}) and lagged output growth rates are also included in equation 10.13. The regressions reported in Table 10.4 are estimates of the equation for real GDP growth g_{it} derived from equations 10.11 to 10.15.[2]

Annual data for 1950–1983 were taken from *International Financial Statistics* (October 1985 computer tape). The country sample consists of all IMF member countries with populations over two million for which complete data sets from 1960 to 1983 are available. In order to reduce noise caused by substantial year-to-year fluctuations in agricultural output, two-year averages of all the raw annual data were taken. Hence variables that are included with zero-, one-, and two-period lags use data spanning six years. Two-year averaging means that this model does not analyze short-run behavior, for which monthly or quarterly data would be needed, but rather medium- and long-run behavior.

Five pooled time-series GDP growth estimates are shown in Table 10.4. Long-run output growth is positively and significantly associated with the average rate of money growth. Neutrality with respect to DM_i^* is rejected at the 99 percent level. The hypothesis that money variability as measured by $MVAR_i$ and $MACC74_i$ reduces long-run output growth is confirmed.

These results must be interpreted with care. While higher money growth rates significantly increase output growth, most countries with high values of DM_i^* have high values of $MVAR_i$ as well.[3] High values of $MVAR_i$ offset

---

[2] Note that Table 10.4 gives standard errors rather than t statistics in parentheses.

[3] See Dwight Jaffee and Ephraim Kleiman (1977) and Dennis Logue and Thomas Willett (1976) on the positive association between the inflation rate and its variability.

Table 10.4. Output Growth Rate Equations

Equation	(10.16)	(10.17)	(10.18)	(10.19)	(10.20)
Variable	Long Run—Variables Are Period Averages				
Constant	0.037 (0.004)	0.027 (0.004)	0.026 (0.004)	0.038 (0.003)	0.043 (0.003)
DM_i^*	0.120 (0.023)	0.125 (0.023)	0.043 (0.021)	0.174 (0.022)	0.081 (0.021)
$MVAR_i$	-0.213 (0.147)	-0.316 (0.145)	-0.330 (0.150)	-0.493 (0.146)	-0.595 (0.155)
$MACC74_i$	-0.007 (0.002)				
DP_i^*	-0.081 (0.011)	-0.077 (0.011)		-0.098 (0.010)	
$NDCG_i^*$	-0.011 (0.004)				
IND_i	-0.007 (0.003)	-0.004 (0.003)	-0.004 (0.003)	-0.005 (0.002)	-0.005 (0.002)
$OILX_i$	0.001 (0.005)	0.002 (0.004)	0.004 (0.005)	0.003 (0.004)	0.005 (0.004)
Variable	Medium Run—Variables Are Annual Observations				
DMR_{it}	0.168 (0.023)	0.161 (0.023)	0.145 (0.024)	0.171 (0.023)	0.152 (0.025)
DMR_{it-1}	0.104 (0.024)	0.097 (0.024)	0.067 (0.025)	0.128 (0.024)	0.101 (0.025)
DMR_{it-2}	-0.035 (0.024)	-0.044 (0.024)	-0.056 (0.025)	-0.011 (0.024)	-0.013 (0.026)
$MVAR_i \cdot DMR_{it}$	-0.012 (0.004)	-0.012 (0.004)	-0.020 (0.004)	-0.011 (0.004)	-0.022 (0.004)
$MVAR_i \cdot DMR_{it-1}$	-0.004 (0.004)	-0.003 (0.004)	-0.007 (0.004)	-0.006 (0.004)	-0.012 (0.004)
$MVAR_i \cdot DMR_{it-2}$	0.006 (0.003)	0.006 (0.003)	0.005 (0.004)	0.003 (0.004)	-0.001 (0.004)
$NDCR_{it}$	0.013 (0.006)				
$OILDP_t$	-0.020 (0.006)	-0.020 (0.006)	-0.027 (0.006)	-0.013 (0.006)	-0.019 (0.006)
$OILDP_{t-1}$	-0.015 (0.006)	-0.014 (0.006)	-0.017 (0.007)	-0.019 (0.006)	-0.026 (0.007)
$OILDP_{t-2}$	-0.003 (0.006)	-0.001 (0.006)	-0.004 (0.006)	-0.006 (0.006)	-0.013 (0.006)
$OILX_i \cdot OILDP_t$	0.027 (0.017)	0.025 (0.016)	0.026 (0.017)	0.029 (0.016)	0.034 (0.018)
$OILX_i \cdot OILDP_{t-1}$	-0.017 (0.017)	-0.018 (0.017)	-0.012 (0.017)	-0.010 (0.017)	0.001 (0.018)
g_{it-1}	0.179 (0.043)	0.210 (0.042)	0.287 (0.043)		
g_{it-2}	0.088 (0.042)	0.113 (0.041)	0.140 (0.042)		
R^2	0.314	0.298	0.245	0.253	0.157

Note: Standard errors are shown in parentheses.

the effects of high DM_i^* on the rate of economic growth. Furthermore, higher inflation produced by higher money growth itself reduces long-run output growth.

There is an important question about the interpretation of $MACC74_i$. A change in the money/nominal GDP ratio between 1974 and 1977 could well be a result of a change in the opportunity cost of holding money rather than a change in monetary policy stance. However, one might interpret it to be a short-run monetary policy indicator, as do Bela Balassa and Desmond McCarthy (1984), for two reasons. First, the change in the money/GDP ratio over this period is strongly correlated with the change in the ratio of net government credit to GDP. Second, similar results are obtained from several alternative measures of monetary accommodation, including the change in the ratio of net government credit to GDP and a dummy variable reflecting the sign of the coefficient of the rate of change in the terms of trade, when used as an explanatory variable in a money growth equation.

The estimates show that inflation and the ratio of net government credit to total domestic credit reduce output growth in the long run. With noninterest-earning required reserves, higher inflation reduces the real return on all forms of money balances. The discriminatory tax on financial intermediation imposed by the reserve requirement increases as inflation and nominal interest rates rise. By reducing the attractiveness of the financial sector's liabilities, the reserve requirement tax reduces the relative size of this sector of the economy. Hence the private sector suffers a credit squeeze in real terms as inflation (and nominal credit expansion) accelerates. When government increases the proportion of domestic credit allocated to the public sector, credit availability for the private sector is again reduced. Suboptimal provision of institutional credit lowers both the quality and quantity of investment, and hence also the rate of growth in output.

Medium-term output growth is positively and significantly affected by money growth and net government credit shocks, as well as lagged output growth rates. Equations 10.19 and 10.20 also show that dropping the lagged dependent variable increases the other coefficient values and their statistical significance somewhat, but reduces the overall fit of the equation.

Output growth is negatively and significantly affected in the medium term by the rate of change in oil prices. The immediate effect of an oil shock in oil-exporting countries is a modest increase in output growth (measured by the sum of the coefficients of $OILDP_t$ and $OILX_i \cdot OILDP_t$). After two years (one period), however, growth is depressed even in oil-exporting countries, as predicted by the "Dutch disease" models.

A positive effect of money-growth shocks on output growth has been found by Barro (1978), Sebastián Edwards (1985), James Hanson (1980), Roger Kormendi and Philip Meguire (1984), and others. Since the sum of the DMR_{it-j} coefficients is significantly positive, neutrality (sum of coefficients equal to zero) is rejected at the 99 percent level in all the equations that include the current and two lagged values of DMR_{it-j} and at the 95 percent level in equations (not shown) containing three lagged values of DMR_{it-j}. The estimates imply that money growth shocks have a permanent effect on the *level* of output.

Lucas (1973) and Kormendi and Meguire (1984) show that the coefficients of money growth shocks in country-specific output growth equations are smaller the greater the variance of the shocks. Here the same phenomenon emerges in a single pooled time-series model. The impact of money growth shocks on output growth is reduced by greater variance of the shocks, as shown by the negative coefficients of $MVAR_i \cdot DMR_{it-j}$. This effect is large enough to turn the implied total coefficient of DMR_{it-j} negative (although not significantly) for several of the high $MVAR_i$ countries in this sample. This means that increasing the money supply can raise output growth in the medium term only when such a policy is used infrequently. A history of accommodation and highly variable monetary policy makes monetary policy totally ineffective in the medium term and, as already noted, leads to reduced output growth in the long run.

Shocks to the ratio of net government credit to total domestic credit increase output growth over and above the indirect effects of such shocks produced by concomitant money growth shocks. Government deficits in most developing countries are financed predominantly by the central and commercial banks. Hence an increased deficit shows up as a shock to the government credit ratio. Since government credit is expanded by increasing money, one might interpret the positive coefficient of the government credit shocks to be pure fiscal stimulus. An increase in government spending can cause a temporary acceleration in output growth.

10.6 Summary

My small-scale monetary model of inflation and short-run growth estimated and simulated in this chapter shows how two monetary policy variables—the rate of growth in the money supply and the deposit rate of interest—affect two target variables, inflation and short-run growth in real GNP. Simulations indicate that monetary policy consisting solely of a deceleration in the rate of monetary growth produces a recession. Van Wijnbergen's simulations of monetary deceleration in Korea show the same negative effects on the rate of economic growth. However, monetary contraction raises the inflation rate initially in van Wijnbergen's model, while reducing it in mine.

The simulations of my model suggest that stabilization policies raising the time deposit rate of interest are superior to policies relying solely on control over the nominal money supply. When the deposit rate is fixed below its equilibrium level, higher deposit rates can *raise* the rate of economic growth by increasing credit availability in real terms while slower monetary growth lowers the inflation rate. Raising the time deposit rate of interest in van Wijnbergen's model reduces economic growth because it reduces the aggregate supply of credit. Unfortunately, van Wijnbergen does not provide a simulation of this interest rate policy.

The oil price increases of 1973–1974 and 1979–1980 reduced output growth in oil-importing countries. The econometric evidence contained in section 10.5 suggests that discretionary monetary policy can be effective in counteracting exogenous shocks to an economy, but only if it is used sparingly. Frequent use of discretionary monetary policy to accommodate exogenous shocks reduces its effectiveness and has a negative effect on economic growth in the long run.

The econometric results in section 10.5 show that money is neutral neither in the medium run nor in the long run. In the short run, the effects of current and lagged money growth shocks on output growth are significantly positive. In the longer run, however, discretionary monetary policy produces a higher variance of money growth shocks. Both this and an indicator of an accommodative monetary policy regime are negatively related to the rate of growth in real GDP.

Monetary accommodation of exogenous shocks, specifically accommodation of the 1973–1974 oil price increase, offsets temporarily the growth-reducing impact of the shock in the medium term. However, accommodation adds noise to the economic environment and reduces output growth in the longer run. Indeed, the monetary accommodation variable performs in virtually the same way as the variance of money growth shocks.

Expansionary fiscal policy has medium- and long-run effects on output growth which are similar to monetary accommodation. Specifically, shifts in the ratio of net government credit to total domestic credit raise output growth. A series of expansionary fiscal policy shocks raise the ratio of net government credit to total domestic credit in countries lacking well-developed direct financial markets. A higher government credit ratio lowers output growth in the long run by starving the private sector of finance for productive investment. This interpretation of the econometric results is inconsistent with the Ricardian equivalence hypothesis.

Chapter 11

Monetary Policies in Pacific Basin Developing Economies

11.1 Introduction

INFLATION WAS ONE OF THE major macroeconomic topic of the 1970s. A decade of accelerating inflation culminated in the double-digit inflation associated with the first oil price shock of 1973–1974. A second worldwide inflationary spurt occurred contemporaneously with the second oil price shock of 1980. Refuting a popularly held view that inflation is now under control, Figure 11.1 shows that inflation in the developing countries accelerated after 1986 and reached a record level in 1990.[1]

Inflation in the developing world accelerated from 21.9 percent in 1976 –1980 to 33.8 percent in 1981–1985, and to 60.6 percent in 1986–1990. In 1990, the average inflation rate in developing countries was 107 percent. The main culprits for the rapidly accelerating developing country inflation rates lie in the developing countries of Europe and the Western Hemisphere. Africa and the Middle East also raised the average worldwide inflation rate during most of the past two decades.

Inflation declined steadily in the industrial countries from 12 percent in 1980 to 3 percent in 1986, although it then rose to 5 percent in 1990. Inflation also fell, albeit somewhat more erratically, in eight developing economies of the Pacific Basin—Indonesia, Hong Kong, Korea, Malaysia, Philippines, Singapore, Taiwan, and Thailand. Over the past two decades inflation in these eight Pacific Basin developing economies mirrored the pattern of inflation in the industrial countries. Although inflation in these eight Pacific Basin developing economies deviated only occasionally from inflation in the

---

[1] Inflation rates are weighted by relative GNPs. Data for Figure 11.1 are taken from *International Financial Statistics*, March 1994 CD-ROM.

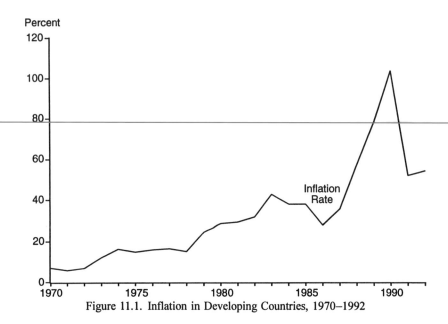

Figure 11.1. Inflation in Developing Countries, 1970–1992

industrial countries, such correspondence is not observed in the rest of the developing world.

Inflation fell in the industrial countries from 9.1 percent in 1976–1980, to 6.3 percent in 1981–1985, and to 3.6 percent in 1986–1990; it also declined in the Pacific Basin economies from 9.0 percent in 1976–1980, to 6.9 percent in 1981–1985, and to 3.6 percent in 1986–1990. The 1974 peak was considerably higher in the Pacific Basin than in the industrial countries, but inflation was subsequently brought down more rapidly (and less painfully) than it was in the industrial countries. The 1980 peak was also somewhat higher in the Pacific Basin than in the industrial countries, but the difference was not dramatic. The anomalous Pacific Basin bulge in 1984 was due solely to the political disruptions that year in the Philippines.

Inflation was below 5 percent in three of the eight Pacific Basin economies examined here in 1990; consumer prices rose by 2.2 percent in Malaysia, 3.4 percent in Singapore, and 4.1 percent in Taiwan. In the remaining economies, inflation was 5.6 percent in Thailand, 6.1 percent in Indonesia, 8.6 percent in Korea, 9.7 percent in Hong Kong, and 12.7 percent in the Philippines. Inflation rates were higher in 1990 than they were in 1986 in all eight economies.

Under the fixed exchange rate system embodied in the Bretton Woods agreement, it was fashionable to blame the United States for the rising trend in worldwide inflation. In developing countries, however, inflation averaging 12 percent over the period 1964–1973 was *lower* in 1970–1972 than it had been in 1964–1966. Since 1975 inflation in developing countries has accelerated in each five-year period, while it has fallen in the United States from 8.9 percent in 1976–1980, to 5.5 percent in 1981–1985, and to 4.0 percent in 1986–1990. Hence, it is difficult to argue that the accelerating inflation in developing countries has been imported from anywhere else.

This chapter addresses three questions about inflation in the larger Pacific Basin developing economies: (a) Has financial liberalization, deregulation, or opening reduced the stability of money demand and inflation relationships? (b) Can these developing economies pursue independent monetary policies? (c) Is inflation lower in these developing economies than it is in other developing countries because of the way in which monetary policy has been conducted?

The developing economies of the Pacific Basin have become increasingly open over the past two decades. In particular, they have liberalized capital account transactions. This financial opening has implications for monetary control: perfect international capital mobility means that these economies would be unable to pursue independent exchange rate and monetary targets. Under a managed exchange rate, a restrictive monetary policy would produce overwhelming capital inflows that would completely negate the restrictive effects.

Although there has been substantial financial opening in the Pacific Basin developing economies, little attention has been paid to the issue of whether or not monetary control has actually been lost. This chapter examines the issue of monetary control by testing econometrically whether or not there have been significant structural changes in both capital inflow and monetary policy behavior over the past three decades. Structural changes in the capital inflow equations are detected roughly when they might have been expected, but monetary control has not been lost. Indeed, the estimates suggest that the monetary authorities in the larger Pacific Basin developing economies have strengthened monetary control over time.

11.2 Demand for Money and Inflation

Hong Kong and Singapore are so open that their exchange rates effectively determine the domestic price level. Hong Kong abolished exchange controls in 1973, Singapore in 1978. The Hong Kong dollar floated from 1974 until a destabilizing speculative run depreciated it to over HK$9 to the U.S. dollar in 1983. Since 1983 it has been pegged to the U.S. dollar at HK$7.80. After allowing it to float from 1973 to 1975, the Monetary Authority of Singapore has pegged the Singapore dollar to a trade-weighted currency basket. From S$3 in 1970, the Singapore dollar appreciated fairly steadily to S$2 to the U.S. dollar in 1981; by 1991 it had appreciated to S$1.77 to the U.S. dollar.

Since 1983 both Hong Kong and Singapore have used the exchange rate as a nominal anchor. Hong Kong pegs definitively to the U.S. dollar to maintain confidence in its currency during the political uncertainty leading up to 1997, while Singapore chooses to appreciate its currency as required to maintain domestic price stability. The tiny size and great openness of these two economies allow the exchange rate to be the dog that wags the tail of domestic prices. Hence, these exchange rate policies ensure that there can be no independent monetary policies in these two economies. Indeed, neither economy has a central bank.

The remaining six Pacific Basin developing economies are considerably less open than Hong Kong and Singapore; the majority of them maintain exchange controls. Hence, exchange rate and monetary policies are distinct and some degree of monetary control may be possible. Since effective monetary control requires a stable money demand, I start by testing whether recent financial innovations have reduced the stability of money demand and inflation functions in Indonesia, Korea, Malaysia, Philippines, Taiwan, and Thailand.

For an overview of money demand and inflation in the Pacific Basin developing economies, I estimated two systems of seemingly unrelated equations with the same slope parameters but different intercepts for each country. Equation 11.1 is a first difference semi-logarithmic money demand function estimated over the period 1962–1990 (Indonesia, 1967–1990; Malaysia, 1963–1990; Taiwan, 1963–1990):

$$\Delta \log(m) = 0.573 \, \Delta \log(y) - 0.437 \, \Delta(\pi)_c) + 0.282 \, \Delta \log(m)_{t-1},$$
$$ (0.141) (0.050) (0.053) \tag{11.1}$$
$$R^2 = 0.531$$

where m is per capita real money (*M2*) holdings, y is per capita real GNP, and π_c is the continuously compounded rate of change in the consumer price index. The figures in parentheses are standard errors.

Equation 11.2 is an unrestricted error-correction model of inflation estimated over the period 1963–1990 (Indonesia, 1966–1990; Malaysia, 1964–1990):

$$\pi = 0.737 \, \Delta \log(M/N) + 0.135(\pi)_{t-1} - 0.059 \log(P)_{t-1}$$
$$ (0.061) (0.055) \phantom{(\pi)_{t-1}} (0.014)$$
$$+ \, 0.074 \log(y)_{t-1} + 0.115 \, \Delta(\pi)_{t-1}, \tag{11.2}$$
$$ (0.022) \phantom{\log(y)_{t-1}} (0.052)$$
$$R^2 = 0.832$$

where π is the continuously compounded rate of change in the GNP deflator, M/N is the per capita nominal money stock (*M2*), and P is the GNP deflator.

Table 11.1. *F* Statistics for Forecast Chow Tests on Money Demand Estimates

Date	Indonesia	Korea	Malaysia	Philippines	Taiwan	Thailand
1980	0.4334	0.5683	3.3097†	0.4431	1.0201	1.9753
	(0.9039)	(0.8244)	(0.0219)	(0.9095)	(0.4801)	(0.1153)
1981	0.5290	0.5895	3.1475†	0.4833	0.7599	1.5625
	(0.8350)	(0.7991)	(0.0250)	(0.8759)	(0.6635)	(0.2105)
1982	0.6169	0.5388	2.9573†	0.5725	0.7675	1.3174
	(0.7613)	(0.8257)	(0.0308)	(0.8005)	(0.6476)	(0.3019)
1983	0.6454	0.4345	3.5316†	0.6304	0.7112	0.8142
	(0.7277)	(0.8841)	(0.0152)	(0.7418)	(0.6789)	(0.6002)
1984	0.7756	0.3701	3.5798†	0.7307	0.5814	0.8662
	(0.6184)	(0.9080)	(0.0149)	(0.6488)	(0.7618)	(0.5506)
1985	0.8841	0.3903	3.7003†	0.4435	0.7134	0.9603
	(0.5315)	(0.8761)	(0.0142)	(0.8405)	(0.6436)	(0.4774)
1986	1.0479	0.3691	4.4455*	0.5601	0.3298	0.8927
	(0.4262)	(0.8637)	(0.0075)	(0.7292)	(0.8887)	(0.5046)
1987	1.2003	0.4123	2.6056‡	0.7073	0.4260	1.0557
	(0.3488)	(0.7978)	(0.0667)	(0.5959)	(0.7881)	(0.4027)
1988	1.4061	0.2920	1.7118	0.9878	0.3459	1.2693
	(0.2754)	(0.8307)	(0.1952)	(0.4167)	(0.7924)	(0.3094)
1989	2.1928	0.0798	0.5122	0.7533	0.5403	1.8681
	(0.1405)	(0.9236)	(0.6061)	(0.4821)	(0.5901)	(0.1771)
SEE	0.0754	0.0837	0.0587	0.0590	0.0545	0.0400
Mean	0.1239	0.1127	0.0757	0.0208	0.1319	0.0462
$\bar{R}^2$	0.5553	0.6092	−0.0404	0.5880	0.5232	0.2481

Probabilities in parentheses
* Significant at 99 percent confidence level
† Significant at 95 percent confidence level
‡ Significant at 90 percent confidence level

Neither of these estimates contains any surprises. Equation 11.1 indicates that money demand responds in the expected way to income and price variables, while equation 11.2 suggests both that inflation is related to the rate of change in the money stock and that a stabilizing error-correction mechanism exists.

To examine the stability of money demand and inflation functions over the past decade, I ran forecast and break-point Chow tests together with four recursive least-squares tests (CUSUM, CUSUM of squares, one-step forecast *F* test, and the recursive coefficient estimates test) on the money demand and inflation equations estimated separately for each economy. Tables 11.1 and 11.2 present the forecast Chow tests for the 1980s; the figures are *F* test

Table 11.2. *F* Statistics for Forecast Chow Tests on Inflation Estimates

Date	Indonesia	Korea	Malaysia	Philippines	Taiwan	Thailand
1980	0.9498	1.6561	0.7623	2.3046‡	0.6998	0.6339
	(0.5444)	(0.2079)	(0.6697)	(0.0909)	(0.7181)	(0.7691)
1981	1.1129	1.6965	0.7162	2.6956‡	0.7023	0.7481
	(0.4409)	(0.1911)	(0.6967)	(0.0535)	(0.7080)	(0.6726)
1982	0.9858	1.8177	0.7853	3.1834†	0.8181	0.9003
	(0.5039)	(0.1586)	(0.6352)	(0.0289)	(0.6103)	(0.5514)
1983	0.5646	1.9748	0.9540	3.8562†	0.9468	0.4554
	(0.7866)	(0.1268)	(0.5085)	(0.0134)	(0.5109)	(0.8674)
1984	0.6799	1.9982	1.0685	4.5034*	1.1381	0.4342
	(0.6872)	(0.1233)	(0.4314)	(0.0070)	(0.3913)	(0.8657)
1985	0.8166	1.5621	1.2922	0.8941	1.2642	0.2907
	(0.5760)	(0.2217)	(0.3189)	(0.5223)	(0.3273)	(0.9327)
1986	0.8473	1.3526	1.5594	0.3854	1.3055	0.3076
	(0.5388)	(0.2904)	(0.2276)	(0.8519)	(0.3079)	(0.9016)
1987	0.7090	0.9812	0.4996	0.3634	1.6518	0.3040
	(0.5983)	(0.4424)	(0.7364)	(0.8314)	(0.2049)	(0.8715)
1988	0.9733	0.6230	0.0336	0.2608	1.3940	0.4274
	(0.4297)	(0.6088)	(0.9915)	(0.8527)	(0.2752)	(0.7356)
1989	1.3746	0.5051	0.0251	0.0324	0.8433	0.5822
	(0.2797)	(0.6109)	(0.9752)	(0.9682)	(0.4450)	(0.5679)
SEE	0.0711	0.0544	0.0469	0.0736	0.0528	0.0391
Mean	0.2913	0.1354	0.0323	0.1080	0.0556	0.0552
$\bar{R}^2$	0.9815	0.4729	0.3336	0.1462	0.1935	0.4977

Probabilities in parentheses

* Significant at 99 percent confidence level

† Significant at 95 percent confidence level

‡ Significant at 90 percent confidence level

statistics with their probabilities in parentheses. Column 1 gives the first year of the prediction period; the first test is on predictions over the 11 years 1980 –1990.

All the tests indicate that the estimates for Indonesia, Korea, Taiwan, and Thailand are stable. In Malaysia, predictive ability of the money demand estimate fails around 1986, while the Philippines' inflation equation fails in 1984. The break-point Chow tests for 1978, 1980, 1982, and 1984 provide similar results. Significant *F* statistics occur for both Malaysia and the Philippines when the break point divides the data set into the periods 1962–1983 and 1984–1990. Both the CUSUM squares and the one-step forecast *F* test also indicate that Malaysia's money demand estimate is unstable in 1986 and that the Philippines' inflation equation is unstable in 1984.

Table 11.3. *F* Statistics for Forecast Chow Tests on Malaysia's Money Demand and Philippines' Inflation Estimates with Critical Years Excluded

Date	Malaysia	Philippines
1980	1.8637	0.2319
	(0.1490)	(0.9856)
1981	1.6755	0.2527
	(0.1903)	(0.9767)
1982	1.4397	0.2827
	(0.2611)	(0.9601)
1983	1.7779	0.3476
	(0.1673)	(0.9177)
1984	1.6690	0.3412
	(0.1959)	(0.9042)
1985	1.5566	0.3412
	(0.2286)	(0.9042)
1986	1.9480	0.2614
	(0.1561)	(0.9277)
1987	1.2464	0.2991
	(0.3270)	(0.8745)
1988	1.9480	0.3509
	(0.1561)	(0.7890)
1989	1.0826	0.3444
	(0.3578)	(0.7130)
SEE	0.0476	0.0456
Mean	0.0504	0.0521
$\overline{R}^2$	0.1091	0.2349

Probabilities in parentheses

Note: Observations for 1986 and 1987 are excluded for Malaysia, observations for 1984 are excluded for the Philippines.

Malaysia's money demand instability was caused by an 18 percent decline in its terms of trade in 1986, which followed a 9 percent decline in 1985. While consumer prices rose by 1 percent in 1986, Malaysia's GNP deflator fell by 10 percent. The Philippines' political upheaval in 1984 explains instability there. In neither case is there any reason to suppose that instability was due to financial innovation, liberalization, or opening. When 1986 and 1987 are excluded for Malaysia and 1984 for the Philippines, no instability is detected by any of these tests. Table 11.3 presents the forecast Chow tests on Malaysia's money demand estimate with 1986 and 1987 observations excluded and the Philippines' inflation estimate with 1984 observations excluded.

11.3   Do Capital Flows Offset Domestic Monetary Policy?

In its most extreme form, the monetary approach to the balance of payments states that central banks in open economies with fixed exchange rates have no ability to affect the nominal money stock. Among others, Bijan Aghevli et al. (1979, 776) and Lorenzo Bini Smaghi (1982) have used this proposition in more moderate form to assert that Pacific Basin developing economies have only a limited degree of monetary policy independence. Even were these developing countries able to pursue independent monetary policies, Michael Connolly and Dean Taylor (1979) find that in general developing countries do not appear to pursue any systematic monetary policy. In this section, therefore, I address the question: Can developing countries, in particular the Pacific Basin developing economies, pursue independent monetary policies?

The two alternative capital inflow equations examined here are embedded in a macroeconomic model designed for a small semi-open developing economy (Fry, Lilien, and Wadhwa 1988). In this economy, the government sets or manipulates the foreign exchange rate and uses domestic credit as its target for monetary policy purposes. The assets available to residents of this country are money M, other domestic assets K, and foreign bonds B.

Net holdings of foreign bonds are negative when foreign borrowing exceeds foreign lending. Some developing countries can borrow abroad by selling dollar-denominated bonds in world financial markets. In practice, developing country bonds are not perfect substitutes for industrial country bonds. Hence, developing countries face a downward sloping demand curve for their bonds on world markets. It is therefore necessary to specify both supply and demand for foreign bonds.

In most developing countries, neither corporate nor government bonds are traded in open markets. Indeed, corporate bonds simply do not exist in many developing countries. Typically, the commercial banks are captive buyers of low-yielding domestic government bonds by virtue of liquidity ratio requirements. Government deficits are financed domestically almost entirely by loans from the central and commercial banks. As a rough approximation, therefore, the budget deficit equals the change in net domestic credit to the government sector ΔDCg plus loans from abroad. Since the nonbank private sector provides virtually no direct lending to the government, there are no domestic bonds in this model.

The capital inflow equation derived here is similar to the quasi reduced-form equation used by Pentti Kouri and Michael Porter (1974, 447–454), Linda Kamas (1986, 471–472), and Daniel Laskar (1983, 317–321). Following Kamas and Laskar, the current account is treated as endogenous, since the full model determines both national saving and domestic investment. My model also recognizes that many developing countries face country-specific risk premia when borrowing abroad.

Table 11.4. The Key Elements of the Capital Inflow Model

$$M = \xi(\overset{+}{y}, \overset{+}{P}, \overset{-}{i_d}, \overset{-}{i_f}, \overset{+}{W}) \tag{11.3}$$

$$M \equiv NFA + DC \tag{11.4}$$

$$DC \equiv DCg + DCp \tag{11.5}$$

$$B = \theta(\overset{-}{y}, \overset{-}{P}, \overset{-}{i_d}, \overset{+}{i_f}, \overset{+}{W}) \tag{11.6}$$

$$B = \omega(\overset{-}{i_f - \epsilon^e}, \overset{-}{\Sigma CA}, \overset{+}{W^*}) \tag{11.7}$$

$$W \equiv M + K + B \tag{11.8}$$

$$CF \equiv -\Delta B \tag{11.9}$$

$$\Delta NFA \equiv CA + CF \tag{11.10}$$

$$\Delta DC = \mu(\Delta NFA, \pi - \pi^*, \pi^o, \Delta DCg) \tag{11.11}$$

Table 11.4 presents the parts of the underlying model that are of immediate relevance. There are three assets: domestic money M, foreign bonds B, and other domestic assets (for example, productive capital, gold, grain, property, or land) K. The nominal returns on these three assets are zero on money, i_f on foreign bonds (as measured by the rate of return in terms of the domestic currency), and i_d on other domestic assets. The market for other domestic assets is not specified, since it can be derived using Walras's law.

The remaining endogenous variables of the model specified in Table 11.4 are real GNP y, the domestic price level P, the return on other domestic assets i_d, the domestic-currency return on foreign bonds (or the domestic-currency cost of borrowing abroad) i_f, exchange rate depreciation ϵ, expected exchange rate depreciation ϵ^e, the country-specific risk premium ρ, net foreign assets NFA, domestic credit DC, domestic credit to the private sector DCp, capital inflows CF, the current account CA, and the cumulated current account ΣCA.[2] The exogenous variables in equations 11.3 to 11.11 are wealth W at the beginning of each period, foreign wealth W^*, foreign inflation (U.S. wholesale price inflation) π^*, the rate of change in the world dollar price of oil π^o, and net domestic credit to the government sector DCg.

Equation 11.3 is a money demand function. Its determinants include both the return on other domestic assets i_d and the domestic-currency return on foreign assets i_f. For net debtor countries, this return consists of the

---

[2] The full model would also treat national saving, domestic investment, the rate of economic growth, terms of trade, income growth attributable to terms-of-trade improvements, the real exchange rate, exports and imports as endogenous. Hence, none of these variables is used as an instrument in the two- and three-stage least-squares estimates reported below.

dollar yield on foreign bonds or the world interest rate i^* plus the country-specific risk premium on foreign borrowing ρ plus the expected exchange rate depreciation ϵ^e; i^* is exogenous, while ρ and ϵ^e are endogenous. Net foreign bond holdings of the majority of the Pacific Basin developing economies examined here have been negative for most of the observation period; they have been net borrowers. For net creditor countries and for countries with such small values of international loans outstanding that no country-specific risk premia apply, however, the return on foreign assets consists of i^* plus ϵ^e.

Equation 11.4 is the money supply function that takes the form of a simplified balance sheet of the consolidated banking system. The liability—money M—is created by banking system holdings of net foreign assets NFA and domestic credit DC. Equation 11.5 decomposes domestic credit into exogenous net domestic credit to the government sector DCg and endogenous domestic credit to the private sector DCp.

Equation 11.6, the demand for foreign bonds (net) B, takes exactly the same form as equation 11.3. For net creditor countries, equation 11.6 simply specifies the factors determining the demand for foreign bonds. If foreign bond holdings are negative, however, this equation determines the level of net foreign indebtedness that the country wishes to incur, given the interest rate on the debt in terms of the domestic currency.

Equation 11.7 uses work by Jonathan Eaton and Mark Gersovitz (1981), Sebastián Edwards (1986), James Hanson (1974), and Jeffrey Sachs (1984) on the determinants of the country-specific risk premium. For net debtor countries, the net supply of foreign bonds becomes a demand for dollar-denominated developing country bonds. This demand is determined by the world nominal interest rate plus the country-specific risk premium $i^*+\rho$. It is not influenced by the expected exchange rate depreciation ϵ^e, because foreign lenders are unaffected by domestic currency depreciation. Since $i_f = i^*+\rho+\epsilon^e$, it follows that $i^*+\rho$ equals $i_f-\epsilon^e$. The net supply of foreign credit is also affected by the size of a country's cumulated current account position ΣCA.[3] In flow terms, this implies that a large current account deficit makes the rest of the world less inclined to lend more to this developing country. Finally, the net supply of foreign bonds is determined by foreign wealth W^*.

This supply function is appropriate only for negative supplies of foreign bonds or net lending by the rest of the world to the developing country. For positive supplies of foreign bonds or net borrowing by the rest of the world from the developing country, supply is infinitely elastic and purchases are determined solely by demand. For net creditor developing countries, equation 11.7 disappears from the model. This implies that the quasi reduced-

---

[3] A cumulated current account deficit equals net cumulated capital inflows minus the stock of net foreign assets. It provides a rough measure of the relative exposure of the rest of the world to the vagaries of this country's economic performance.

form capital flow equation for net creditor countries differs from the capital inflow equation for net debtor countries.

Equation 11.8 indicates that the exogenous wealth at the beginning of each period W can be allocated among money M, other domestic assets K, and foreign bonds B. Equation 11.9 defines the capital account or capital inflows CF as the change in the holdings of foreign bonds (which can of course be negative) ΔB. Equation 11.10 uses the balance-of-payments identity to express the change in net foreign assets ΔNFA as the sum of the current account CA and the capital account CF. Equation 11.11 is the central bank's monetary policy reaction function in which the change in domestic credit ΔDC is determined by the change in net foreign assets ΔNFA, the difference between domestic and foreign inflation $\pi - \pi^*$, the rate of change in oil prices π^o, and the change in net domestic credit to the government ΔDCg.

Combining equations 11.3, 11.4, and 11.10 gives

$$CA + CF + \Delta DC = \Delta[\xi(y,\ P,\ i_d,\ i_f,\ W)]. \tag{11.12}$$

Equations 11.6 and 11.9 produce

$$CF = -\Delta[\theta(y,\ P,\ i_d,\ i_f,\ W)]. \tag{11.13}$$

Equations 11.7 and 11.9 yield

$$CF = -\Delta[\omega(i_f - \epsilon^e,\ \Sigma CA,\ W^*)]. \tag{11.14}$$

Equations 11.12, 11.13, and 11.14 can be solved simultaneously to eliminate the two price variables, the return on other domestic assets i_d and the domestic return on foreign bonds i_f. The derivation of this quasi reduced-form capital flow equation can be illustrated with a simple linear system in which all coefficients take positive values. For expositional simplicity, W and W^* are omitted. For this illustration, equations 11.12, 11.13, and 11.14 take the specific forms:

$$CA + CF + \Delta DC = a_1\Delta y + a_2\Delta P - a_3\Delta i_d - a_4\Delta i_f; \tag{11.15}$$

$$CF = b_1\Delta y + b_2\Delta P + b_3\Delta i_d - b_4\Delta i_f; \tag{11.16}$$

$$CF = c_1(\Delta i_f - \Delta \epsilon^e) + c_2 CA. \tag{11.17}$$

Equations 11.16 and 11.17 can be rearranged in terms of Δi_d and Δi_f:

$$\Delta i_d = CF/b_3 - (b_1/b_3)\Delta y - (b_2/b_3)\Delta P + (b_4/b_3)\Delta i_f; \tag{11.18}$$

$$\Delta i_f = CF/c_1 + \Delta \epsilon^e - (c_2/c_1)CA. \tag{11.19}$$

Substituting equations 11.18 and 11.19 into equation 11.15 gives the quasi reduced-form capital inflow equation:

$$CF = \{-\Delta DC - [1 - (a_3 b_4 c_2 / b_3 c_1) - (a_4 c_2 / c_1)]CA$$
$$+ [a_1 + (a_3 b_1 / b_3)]\Delta y$$
$$+ [a_2 + (a_3 b_2 / b_3)]\Delta P - [a_4 + (a_3 b_4 / b_3)]\Delta \epsilon^e\}$$
$$/[1 + a_3/b_3 + a_3 b_4 / b_3 c_1 + a_4 / c_1].$$

(11.20)

The qualitative effects on capital inflows of all the variables in equation 11.20, except the current account CA, are unambiguous.

In the case of an infinitely elastic supply of foreign bonds for net creditor countries, equation 11.7 disappears and the quasi reduced-form capital inflow equation is derived solely from equations 11.12 and 11.13; equation 11.16 can still be rearranged in terms of Δi_d. Inserting equation 11.18 into equation 11.15 now provides the alternative quasi reduced-form capital inflow equation:

$$CF = \{-\Delta DC - CA + [a_1 + (a_3 b_1 / b_3)]\Delta y$$
$$+ [a_2 + (a_3 b_2 / b_3)]\Delta P - [a_4 + (a_3 b_4 / b_3)]\Delta i^*$$
$$- [a_4 + (a_3 b_4 / b_3)]\Delta \epsilon^e\}/[1 + a_3/b_3].$$

(11.21)

The qualitative effects on capital inflows of all the variables in equation 11.21 are unambiguous.

The linear versions of equations 11.20 and 11.21 scaled by nominal GNP (not wealth) actually estimated here takes the form

$$CFY = \overset{-}{b}_{11} \widehat{DDCY} + \overset{-}{b}_{12} \widehat{CAY} + \overset{+}{b}_{13} \widehat{YG}$$
$$+ \overset{+}{b}_{14} \widehat{INF} + \overset{-}{b}_{15} \widehat{EDEXG};$$

(11.22)

$$CFY = \overset{-}{b}_{11} \widehat{DDCY} + \overset{-}{b}_{11} \widehat{CAY} + \overset{+}{b}_{13} \widehat{YG}$$
$$+ \overset{+}{b}_{14} \widehat{INF} + \overset{-}{b}_{15} IWD + \overset{-}{b}_{15} \widehat{EDEXG},$$

(11.23)

where CFY is the ratio of capital inflows to nominal GNP, $DDCY$ is the change in domestic credit divided by nominal GNP, CAY is the current account ratio, YG is the rate of growth in real GNP, INF is the inflation rate, $EDEXG$ is the expected change in exchange rate depreciation (continuously compounded), and IWD is the change in the 6-month LIBOR (London Inter-Bank Offered Rate) dollar deposit rate (also continuously compounded). The hats denote endogenous variables.

If expectations are formed rationally, the change in exchange rate depreciation estimated by variables known at time $t-1$ can be used as the expected change in exchange rate depreciation. Specifically, the expected change in exchange rate depreciation is the change in exchange rate depreciation estimated separately for each country by ordinary least squares (OLS) using lagged values of the change in exchange rate depreciation, the rate of growth in real GNP, money ($M2$) growth, the gap between domestic and U.S. inflation, the rate of change in oil prices expressed in U.S. dollars, the change in domestic credit as a ratio of nominal GNP and the ratio of capital inflows to GNP.

The offset coefficient is b_{11} in equations 11.22 and 11.23. Its value can lie between 0 and -1. A value of -1 implies that monetary policy is impotent because the private sector reduces its holdings of net foreign assets *pari passu* with any increase in domestic credit. In this case changes in domestic credit, the intermediate monetary policy target for central banks in open economies, have no effect on the money supply.

The changes in income and price in equations 11.12 and 11.13 are converted into the growth and inflation variables in equations 11.22 and 11.23, since first differences of logarithms are used. They exert positive effects on capital inflows through their positive effects on money demand and negative effects on the demand for foreign bonds. The expected change in exchange rate depreciation reduces capital inflows because of an asymmetry between foreign bond demand and supply functions with respect to this variable. A rise in *EDEXG* encourages capital outflows but has no effect on capital inflows. Hence, a rise in *EDEXG* reduces *net* capital inflows in equation 11.22. In combination with the world interest rate, it also deters capital inflows in equation 11.23.

The major problem in using this model arises from its applicability to a fixed exchange rate regime. In a floating exchange rate regime, changes in domestic credit affect the exchange rate rather than capital flows or the net foreign assets of the banking system. The developing countries examined here have certainly manipulated and generally pegged their exchange rates for virtually the entire observation period. To the extent that they have subordinated exchange rate policy to monetary policy, domestic credit expansion would be met in part by a depreciation in the exchange rate and in part by a loss of reserves. Hence, one would detect smaller offset coefficients. In such case, equations 11.22 and 11.23 would be hybrid functions representing a mixture of private sector behavior and policy response. The offset coefficients no longer measure capital mobility alone but capital mobility combined with an exchange rate policy response. Nevertheless, the offset coefficients do indicate the degree of monetary policy independence given the exchange rate regime adopted by the authorities.

The first regression estimates presented in this section use 699 observations from 27 developing countries: Algeria, Argentina, Brazil, Chile, Côte d'Ivoire, Egypt, Ghana, Greece, India, Indonesia, Korea, Malaysia, Mexico,

Morocco, Nigeria, Pakistan, Peru, Philippines, Portugal, Sri Lanka, Taiwan, Tanzania, Thailand, Turkey, Venezuela, Yugoslavia, and Zaire.[4] These countries comprise developing countries with populations over ten million for which there are reasonably good financial data. The data are taken from *World Tables Socio-economic Time-series* (1989, 1990), *International Financial Statistics* computer tape, and national sources for Taiwan. The observation period is 1960–1988, but a full data set for some countries starts only in the mid-1960s.

The regression method is three-stage least squares (3SLS). The 27 individual country equations for capital inflow ratios are estimated as a system of equations with cross-equation restrictions on all coefficients except the intercept. Coefficient equality over countries within a group is imposed in the estimated equation. However, the instruments are allowed to have different coefficients for each country in the first stage of the estimation procedure. The instruments used for the endogenous variables in the capital flow equations are the world real interest rate, world economic growth, the ratio of government sector credit to total domestic credit, *EDEXG,* and lagged values of real GNP growth, money (*M2*) growth, inflation, the change in the ratio of domestic credit to GNP, and the current and capital account ratios. Since the coefficient of *EDEXG* was not significant, this variable is dropped from the estimates reported below.

Table 11.5 gives estimates of two versions of the capital flow equation. In equation 11.24 the Pacific Basin developing economies have the same coefficients as the rest of the sample. The estimated offset coefficient in equation 11.24 is −0.23. The size of this offset coefficient is inconsistent with the assertion that active monetary policy cannot be pursued in a representative developing country. This offset coefficient is considerably smaller than offset coefficients estimated for most industrial countries. For example, Kouri and Porter (1974, 455–456) estimate offset coefficients averaging −0.57 for Australia, Germany, Holland, and Italy, whereas Laskar (1983, 329) reports his preferred offset coefficients averaging −0.64 for Britain, Canada, France, Germany, Holland, Italy, and Japan. However, it is similar to coefficients estimated for a similar group of developing countries by Susan Schadler et al. (1993, 42). Either capital accounts are less open in this sample of developing countries than they are in the industrial countries or exchange rate policies have been more coordinated with monetary policies in these developing countries.

The χ^2 for the Wald test for equation 11.25 indicates that the six Pacific Basin developing economies—Indonesia, Korea, Malaysia, Philippines, Taiwan, and Thailand—are significantly different from the control group.

---

[4]Greece and Portugal are included in this sample, although they are no longer classified as developing countries.

Table 11.5. Capital Inflow (CFY) Estimates for 27 Developing Countries

Variable	Equation 11.24	Equation 11.25
$\widehat{DDCY}$	−0.234	−0.251
	(−24.394)	(−25.288)
$\widehat{CAY}$	−0.760	−0.838
	(−95.144)	(−85.224)
$\widehat{YG}$	0.073	0.063
	(7.163)	(5.820)
$\widehat{INF}$	−0.008	−0.005
	(−2.569)	(−1.387)
Shift Parameters for Pacific Basin Developing Economies		
$\widehat{DDCY}$		0.100
		(6.772)
$\widehat{CAY}$		0.256
		(14.047)
$\widehat{YG}$		−0.021
		(−0.942)
$\widehat{INF}$		0.005
		(0.790)
R^2	0.533	0.540
χ^2 against equation 22		2031

The hats denote endogenous variables.
t statistics in parentheses

Equation 11.25 shows that the Pacific Basin developing economies have a joint offset coefficient of only −0.15, while the offset coefficient for the control group of developing countries is now −0.25. Again, the size of both these offset coefficients are significantly less than one. Capital flows have by no means completely offset monetary policy action in the form of changes in domestic credit. The lower offset coefficient for the Pacific Basin countries may well signify greater coordination of exchange rate and monetary policies rather than lower capital mobility.

The capital inflow estimates suggest that this sample of developing countries can pursue independent monetary policies over the short run. However, even if these capital inflow estimates indicate that asset markets in this sample of developing countries are not perfectly integrated with asset markets in the rest of the world, arbitrage across goods markets requires consistent monetary and exchange rate policies in the medium and long runs if balance-of-payments crises are to be avoided. One distinguishing characteristic of the Pacific Basin developing economies examined here lies in the general complementarity between their monetary and exchange rate policies. Unlike the majority of developing countries, the Pacific Basin developing economies have rarely allowed their currencies to appreciate in real terms solely as a result of domestic inflation. This policy consistency has been rewarded by phenomenal export growth.

For capital inflow behavior in these six Pacific Basin developing economies as a group over the period 1960–1991, I estimate a system of six equations with the same slope parameters but different intercepts for each economy using iterative 3SLS which is, asymptotically, full-information maximum likelihood (Johnston 1984, 486–492):

$$CFY = -0.127 \widehat{DDCY} - 0.580 \widehat{CAY} + 0.134 \widehat{YG} + 0.049 \widehat{INF}.$$
$$(-3.494) \qquad (-18.085) \qquad (2.016) \qquad (2.451) \qquad \qquad (11.26)$$
$$R^2 = 0.748$$

The estimation technique corrects for heteroscedasticity across country equations and exploits contemporaneously correlated disturbances. The starting and ending dates are determined by data availability for each economy—Indonesia, 1967–1990; Korea, 1965–1991; Malaysia, 1963–1990; Philippines, 1960–1991; Taiwan, 1964–1991; Thailand, 1960–1990. The instruments used in equation 11.26 and for the remaining regressions reported in this section are $EDEXG$, IWD, π^o, $DDCGY$, $DDCY_{t-1}$, YG_{t-1}, INF_{t-1}, CFY_{t-1}, and CAY_{t-1}; $DDCGY$ is the change in net domestic credit to the government sector divided by nominal GNP. The figures in parentheses are t statistics. The coefficients of IWD and $EDEXG$ were not significant and hence these variables are omitted.

Equation 11.26 indicates that capital inflows to these six Pacific Basin developing economies are affected in the ways predicted by the model. An increase in domestic credit and an improvement in the balance of payments on current account reduce capital inflows, while economic growth and inflation increase capital inflows. The offset coefficient of −0.13 is significantly different from both zero and −1 and is very similar to the offset coefficient of −0.15 derived from equation 11.25 for these six economies. Over the period as a whole, therefore, the monetary authorities of these economies as a group have been capable of monetary control through control over domestic credit expansion.

The χ^2 for the Wald test rejects the hypothesis of coefficient equality for $DDCY$ and CAY in equation 11.26. Therefore, this section now examines separate capital inflow equations for each of these six Pacific Basin developing economies. Specifically, I test whether equation 11.22 or 11.23 is most appropriate for each of these six economies. I also test for any structural changes that might have occurred over the past three decades.

Separate two-stage least-squares (2SLS) estimates for each economy indicate that coefficient equality for $DDCY$ and CAY is rejected for Indonesia, Malaysia, and Thailand, but is accepted for Korea, Philippines, and Taiwan. In the capital flow estimate for the Philippines, neither coefficient is significantly different from zero. The rejection of the equality hypothesis for Indonesia, Malaysia, and Thailand indicates that these economies faced upward sloping supply curves for foreign capital that have been influenced negatively by the size of their current account deficits.

To test for structural change, the regression period must be split. In order to retain some degrees of freedom, potential switch dates near the beginning and end of the regression period are excluded; potential switch dates tested here range from 1970 to 1983. For a structural change that occurred between 1975 and 1976, a dummy variable AD takes a value of one for the period 1960–1975 and a value of zero for the period 1976–1991, while a dummy variable DA takes a value of zero for the period 1960–1975 and one for 1976 –1991. The two dummies are then interacted with all the explanatory and instrumental variables, so doubling the number of variables in the system:

$$\begin{aligned} CFY = {} & b_{10}AD + b_{11}AD \cdot DDCY + b_{12}AD \cdot CAY \\ & + b_{13}AD \cdot YG + b_{14}AD \cdot INF \\ & + b_{20}DA + b_{21}DA \cdot DDCY + b_{22}DA \cdot CAY \\ & + b_{23}DA \cdot YG + b_{24}DA \cdot INF. \end{aligned}$$

(11.27)

The maximum likelihood functions show that the most likely switch for the capital inflow equations are 1975–1976 for Indonesia, 1970–1971 for Korea, 1980–1981 for Malaysia, 1977–1978 for Philippines, 1982–1983 for Taiwan, and 1978–1979 for Thailand. These regime-switching estimates can be used to test for coefficient equality over two separate periods. The results indicate that coefficient equality for $DDCY$ and CAY is now rejected for Indonesia and Malaysia, but is accepted for Philippines, Taiwan, and Thailand. Again, none of the relevant coefficients is significantly different from zero in the capital flow estimate for the Philippines. In the case of Korea, coefficient equality is rejected for the earlier period 1960–1970, but is accepted for the later period 1971–1991. In other words, Korea faced an upward sloping supply curve for foreign capital in the 1960s, but has not since 1971.

The estimates discussed so far enable each economy to be classified on the basis of whether or not it has faced an infinitely elastic supply of foreign bonds or foreign lending. The appropriate choice of equation 11.22 or 11.23 can now be made for each country. In Korea's case, a hybrid is used in which equation 11.22 is used for the earlier years and equation 11.23 for the later period.

Table 11.6.   Speed and Timing of Structural Changes in Capital Inflow Equations
Using Logistic-Switching Model

Economy	Years for Half of Switch	Maximum Likelihood Value of δ	Maximum Likelihood Value of α	Maximum Likelihood Switch Date	F Statistic for Structural Change
Indonesia	1/3	6.592	−501	1976.00	3.04*
Korea	1/3	6.592	−459	1969.63	23.49**
Malaysia	2/3	3.296	−279	1984.65	8.31**
Philippines	2/3	3.296	−280	1984.96	3.97*
Taiwan	0	∞	n.a.	1982–83	10.46**
Thailand	0	∞	n.a.	1978–79	11.40**

* Significant at 95 percent confidence level
** Significant at 99 percent confidence level

The step-switching model discussed above forces the structural changes
to take place instantaneously. The logistic function provides a more general
specification of the switching model (Mankiw, Miron, and Weil 1987). Rather
than requiring the values of AD and DA to move instantaneously from one
to zero and vice versa, the logistic function allows the values of AD and
DA to vary gradually over time. Specifically, DA is now defined to equal
$e^{\alpha+\delta t}/(1 + e^{\alpha+\delta t})$ and AD equals $1-DA$ as before. The parameters α and
δ determine the timing and speed of the regime shift. The logistic curve
has its inflection when t equals $-\alpha/\delta$. At this date, behavior is determined
by an equal mix of old and new regime parameter values. The value of δ
determines the speed with which the switch occurs. In particular, one half
of the adjustment takes place within $(\log 9)/\delta$ years. The step-switching
function is the limit of the logistic function when δ equals ∞.

Maximum likelihood estimation of the logistic switching model is done
in two stages. For a given value of δ, the equations are estimated by 2SLS
with alternative values of α that permit structural changes in the period 1965–
1985. This set of iterations is then repeated for a new value of δ. I tried
nine alternative values of δ ranging from 0.220 to 6.592. Table 11.6 presents
the maximum-likelihood results of this procedure. Table 11.7 gives the corresponding offset coefficients for both the single- and the two-period maximum-
likelihood estimates.

Table 11.7 shows that, over the period as a whole, offsetting capital flows
have not jeopardized monetary control in any of these Pacific Basin developing economies; all the offset coefficients are significantly less than −1 in
absolute magnitude. Table 11.7 also shows that the capital inflow equations'
explanatory powers are increased considerably when structural changes are
permitted. From rather mediocre explanatory power of the single-period es-

Table 11.7. Offset Coefficients and Adjusted Correlation Coefficients for Single- and Two-Period Estimates

| Economy | Single Period | | Two Periods | | |
	Single Offset Coefficient	$\overline{R}^2$	First Offset Coefficient	Second Offset Coefficient	$\overline{R}^2$
Indonesia	−0.265	0.425	−1.410*	−0.302*	0.626
	(−1.674)		(−2.882)	(−2.157)	
Korea	−0.238	0.699	0.123	−0.479*	0.890
	(−1.880)		(1.469)	(−4.814)	
Malaysia	0.152	0.563	−0.254	−1.297	0.836
	(0.482)		(−1.434)	(−1.254)	
Philippines	−0.328	0.296	−0.385	0.455	0.462
	(−1.189)		(−1.459)	(1.323)	
Taiwan	−0.487*	0.704	−0.157	−0.499*	0.903
	(−7.631)		(−1.563)	(−4.570)	
Thailand	0.328	−0.027	−0.072	0.179	0.605
	(1.858)		(−0.480)	(1.054)	

* Significant at 95 percent confidence level
t statistics in parentheses

timates, the regime-switching capital inflow equations provide substantially improved explanatory power. This improvement is most noticeable for Thailand's capital inflow estimate. The three significant offset coefficients for the second period are all significantly less than −1 in absolute terms. However, Indonesia's offset coefficient was not significantly different from −1 in the period before 1976 and Malaysia's offset coefficient in the period since mid-1985 has not been significantly different from either 0 or −1.

My finding of relatively small significant offset coefficients in recent years contradicts the conclusions of recent work on interest rate linkages in the Pacific Basin (Claassen 1992, Faruqee 1991, Fischer and Reisen 1992, Glick and Hutchison 1990, Scholnick 1993). It also challenges the conclusion of Nadeem Haque and Peter Montiel (1990, 11) using an indirect approach that "the degree of openness in developing economies, though it differs across countries, tends to be surprisingly large." Haque and Montiel find that the assumption of perfect capital mobility cannot be rejected for two thirds of their sample of developing countries. Among those countries are Indonesia, Malaysia, and Philippines.

My finding is not inconsistent with that of Helmut Reisen and Hélène Yèches (1991, 30), who conclude that in Korea and Taiwan "the capital account of both countries seems still quite closed, with the possible exception of Taiwan's interbank market in very recent years. Therefore, the authorities in both Korea and Taiwan have continued to enjoy considerable scope for an independent short-term monetary policy."

One explanation for these divergent findings may lie in the fact that bank loans differ substantially from bonds (Fama 1985). Most bank borrowers do not have access to bond markets either at home or abroad. In a sense, therefore, they are captive borrowers from their domestic banking systems. Furthermore, voluntary holdings of bonds by banks in these economies are very limited; bank portfolio substitution is also restricted. Where there are only a few banks, some of which may well be government-owned, implementation of monetary policy can work through a number of well-known nonprice channels (Lin 1991). As Wanda Tseng and Robert Corker (1991, 34) point out, "the use of indirect instruments of monetary control has been hampered by the thinness of monetary and capital markets and by the large domestic financing needs of governments." Hence, the monetary authorities' ability to influence the volume and direction of domestic credit may not have been eroded by increased interest rate linkages in these bond and interbank markets. The monetary authorities simply do not rely on these markets for monetary policy implementation.

Nonprice rationing can ensure that domestic credit targets are met regardless of interest rate movements. Hence, capital flows could well be influenced by relative interest rates in direct financial markets but not to anything like the same extent by the volume of domestic credit supplied by the banking system. Whether or not this interpretation is accepted, I now turn to the implementation of monetary policy in these economies, having established that offsetting capital flows do not make monetary policy impotent in any of these six Pacific Basin developing economies.

11.4   Determinants of Monetary Policy in Pacific Basin Developing Economies

In the previous section I conclude that, due to capital controls, capital market imperfections, nonprice credit rationing of bank loans, or exchange rate flexibility, the six Pacific Basin developing economies can pursue independent monetary policies even though they peg their exchange rates. In this section I address the question: Do they pursue systematic discretionary monetary policies? The monetary policy reaction function, specified as the change in domestic credit scaled by GNP $DDCY$, is designed to discover whether or not monetary authorities in these sample developing countries have pursued systematic monetary policies.

Equation 11.11 in Table 11.4 is the central bank's monetary policy reaction function determining the change in domestic credit. Following the early work on monetary policy reaction functions by Grant Reuber (1964) and Richard Froyen (1974), central bank objectives have typically been taken to include a balance-of-payments target ΔNFA, an inflation target π or an inflation target relative to U.S. inflation $\pi-\pi^*$, where π^* is the rate of change in U.S. wholesale prices, and possibly some response to exogenous shocks such as oil price inflation π^o. Here, an attempt is also made to determine the extent to which the central bank accommodates the credit requirements of the government sector ΔDCg without squeezing private sector credit availability, as discussed in section 5.8.

The monetary policy reaction function is specified for estimation in the form:

$$
\begin{aligned}
DDCY = {}& b_{30} + \overset{-}{b_{33}} \widehat{DNFAY} + \overset{?}{b_{34}} DNFAY_{t-1} \\
& + \overset{-}{b_{35}} \widehat{INFGAP} + \overset{?}{b_{36}} INFGAP_{t-1} \\
& + \overset{?}{b_{37}} DOILPL + \overset{?}{b_{38}} DOILPL_{t-1} + \overset{?}{b_{39}} REXL_{t-1} \\
& + \overset{+}{b_{40}} DDCGY + \overset{?}{b_{41}} DDCGY_{t-1},
\end{aligned}
\tag{11.28}
$$

where $DDCY$ is the change in domestic credit scaled by GNP, $DNFAY$ is the change in net foreign assets of the banking system scaled by GNP, $INFGAP$ is the gap between domestic inflation and inflation in the United States, $DOILPL$ is the rate of change in the dollar price of oil, $REXL$ is real exchange rate expressed in natural logarithms, and $DDCGY$ is the change in net domestic credit to the government scaled by GNP.

In order to compare monetary policy implementation in the Pacific Basin developing economies with monetary policy implementation in a control group of developing countries, I estimate the monetary policy reaction function as a system of 27 country equations by 3SLS with cross-equation restrictions on all coefficients, except the intercept, using 694 observations over the period 1960 –1988 for the same sample of developing countries used for equations 11.24 and 11.25. Instruments for $DNFAY$ and $INFGAP$ are $OILINF$, $OILINF_{t-1}$, $DDCY_{t-1}$, $DNFAY_{t-1}$, $INFGAP_{t-1}$, $DDCGY$, $DDCGY_{t-1}$, U.S. inflation, the world real interest rate, world economic growth, and lagged values of real GNP growth and money ($M2$) growth.

Table 11.8 reports two estimates of the monetary policy reaction function. Both equations show that the monetary authorities in this sample of developing countries do appear to react systematically to changes in several economic variables. The results presented here contrast with those of Connolly and Taylor (1979, 287), who find no evidence that developing countries pursue any systematic monetary policies. They also contrast with estimates of substantial or complete sterilization in industrial countries (except for Switzerland) reported by Jacques Artus (1976, 326), Michael Darby (1983, 307–308), Leroy

Table 11.8. Monetary Policy Reaction Functions ($DDCY$) for 27 Developing Countries

Variable	Equation 11.29	Equation 11.30
$\widehat{DNFAY}$	−0.184	−0.168
	(−14.385)	(−12.912)
$DNFAY_{t-1}$	0.066	0.045
	(5.612)	(3.740)
$\widehat{INFGAP}$	0.090	0.088
	(19.774)	(19.991)
$INFGAP_{t-1}$	−0.015	−0.014
	(−4.059)	(−4.010)
$OILINF$	0.017	0.016
	(6.016)	(6.449)
$OILINF_{t-1}$	0.024	0.032
	(7.431)	(10.973)
$DDCGY$	0.858	0.882
	(81.300)	(86.134)
$DDCGY_{t-1}$	−0.027	−0.033
	(−2.647)	(−3.443)
Shift Parameters for Pacific Basin Developing Economies		
$\widehat{DNFAY}$		−0.245
		(−7.822)
$OILINF_{t-1}$		−0.014
		(−2.754)
$DDCGY$		−0.388
		(−8.812)
$DDCGY_{t-1}$		−0.135
		(−3.177)
R^2	0.766	0.769
χ^2 against equation 11.29		130

The hat denotes an endogenous variable.
t statistics in parentheses

Laney and Thomas Willett (1982, 144–147) and Maurice Obstfeld (1983).

The two sets of policy coefficients in equation 11.30 indicate that the Pacific Basin market economies adopted entirely different monetary policy stances from the other countries in the sample; the χ^2 test for equation 28 is highly significant. Of most importance is the finding that the Pacific Basin developing economies sterilized 41 percent of the increase in net foreign assets

(−0.24 plus −0.17), compared with only 17 percent in the other developing countries. The χ^2 for the Wald test accepts the hypothesis of coefficient equality for *DNFAY* in the same monetary policy reaction function estimated separately for the six Pacific Basin developing economies.

The small sterilization coefficient for the non-Pacific Basin countries may well be due to the fact that some countries in this group actually increased domestic credit when net foreign assets rose. Arturo Porzecanski (1979, 434–435) finds in Mexico and Venezuela that higher net foreign assets led to more rapid domestic credit expansion; I detect the same phenomenon in Turkey (Fry 1988, 90–98). In these countries, domestic credit was increased when foreign exchange receipts rose so that a larger volume of capital equipment and raw material imports could be financed. Rather than contracting domestic credit to sterilize foreign exchange inflows, these central banks reacted by expanding domestic credit to stimulate investment and growth.

The developing countries outside the Pacific Basin accommodated domestically generated inflationary pressures *INFGAP,* the increase in oil prices *OILINF* and the government's credit requirements *DDCGY.* Indeed, these countries contracted domestic credit to the private sector by only 12 percent of the increase in the government's credit requirements (15 percent over a two-year period).

In contrast, the Pacific Basin developing economies sterilized 41 of any increase in the banking system's net foreign assets *DNFAY* and increased domestic credit less than the control group when oil price inflation *OILINF* accelerated. Finally, the Pacific Basin developing economies neutralized two thirds of the effects of the government's credit requirements on the money supply. The monetary authorities of the Pacific Basin developing economies increased aggregate domestic credit by only 33 percent (0.85 plus −0.52) of any increase in the government's credit requirements over a two-year period. This implies a reduction in domestic credit to the private sector equal to 67 percent of the increase in the government's credit requirements.

Equation 11.30 demonstrates that the implementation of monetary policy in this group of Pacific Basin developing economies is significantly different from monetary policy implementation in the other sample countries. These results support Arnold Harberger's (1988, 177) finding that "when East Asian countries deviate from average behavior, they deviate on the side of prudence. Their economic policy was indeed quite different." The estimates reported in this section suggest that inflation in the Pacific Basin developing economies was indeed lower than it has been in other developing countries because of the way in which monetary policy has been conducted.

Separate 2SLS estimates of *DDCY* indicate that regime switches took place in each of the six Pacific Basin developing economies. The maximum likelihood functions show that the most likely switch for the domestic credit equations are 1983–1984 for Indonesia, 1978–1979 for Korea, 1976–1977 for Malaysia, 1983–1984 for Philippines, 1980–1981 for Taiwan, and 1971–1972

Table 11.9. Sterilization Coefficients and Adjusted Correlation Coefficients for Single- and Two-Period Estimates

Economy	Single Period		Two Periods		
	Single Sterilization Coefficient	$\overline{R}^2$	First Sterilization Coefficient	Second Sterilization Coefficient	$\overline{R}^2$
Indonesia	−2.884 (−1.904)	−1.465	−0.075 (−0.209)	−2.808* (−4.604)	0.629
Korea	−0.252 (−0.351)	−0.563	−0.381 (−0.625)	−0.754 (−1.608)	0.604
Malaysia	1.300 (1.328)	−0.598	0.584 (1.003)	−0.738 (−1.628)	0.606
Philippines	0.174 (0.481)	0.686	−0.394 (−1.072)	0.346 (1.684)	0.840
Taiwan	1.861 (1.380)	−3.029	0.558 (0.803)	−1.077* (−3.238)	0.802
Thailand	−2.915 (−0.745)	−1.271	0.496 (0.361)	−1.315 (−1.985)	0.605

* Significant at 95 percent confidence level
t statistics in parentheses

for Thailand. Except in the case of the Philippines, the monetary authorities sterilized capital inflows to a greater extent in the second period than in the first period. The estimated coefficients are given in Table 11.9.

Table 11.9 shows that explanatory power is increased considerably when regime changes are permitted. From negligible explanatory power of the single-period estimates, the regime-switching monetary policy equations provide substantially improved explanatory power. The point estimates of the second-period sterilization coefficients suggest that the monetary authorities in all the economies, except the Philippines, sterilize at least three quarters of any capital inflow. Except in the cases of Indonesia and the Philippines, none of the estimated second-period sterilization coefficients is significantly different from −1.

11.5 Summary

In this chapter I examined three questions relating to monetary policy and inflation in a sample of Pacific Basin developing economies. The major findings are: (a) financial liberalization, deregulation, and opening have not reduced the stability of money demand and inflation functions in the larger Pacific

Table 11.10. Sample Means for Some Key Macroeconomic Variables in 27 Developing
Countries

Variable	Control Group Mean	Pacific Basin Mean	Difference	SE of Difference
INF	0.209	0.128	−0.081*	0.0237
DDCY	0.089	0.060	−0.029*	0.0050
DCG	0.276	0.215	−0.062*	0.0172
DCGR	0.396	0.160	−0.235*	0.0246
YG	0.040	0.067	0.027*	0.0035

INF —	Rate of change in GNP deflator (continuously compounded)
DDCY —	Change in domestic credit/GNP (current prices)
DCG —	Rate of change in domestic credit (continuously compounded)
DCGR —	Net domestic credit to government/domestic credit (current prices)
YG —	Rate of growth in GNP (constant prices, continuously compounded)

* Significant at 99 percent confidence level

Basin developing economies; (b) the monetary authorities of these economies can pursue independent monetary policy despite pegged exchange rates; and (c) inflation has been lower in the Pacific Basin developing economies than it has in a control group of 21 other developing countries because of the way in which monetary policy has been conducted.

Monetary policies pursued by these Pacific Basin developing economies have been much less accommodative and hence less inflationary than policies followed by the rest of the sample countries. Further support for this proposition is provided by the tests of different sample means in Table 11.10. The means of inflation, domestic credit expansion and the proportion of domestic credit expropriated by the government (reflecting fiscal discipline) are all significantly lower in the Pacific Basin developing economies than in the control group of developing countries. In contrast, the rate of economic growth is significantly higher in the Pacific Basin developing economies.[5]

Finally, I examine simple relationships between rates of economic growth, inflation, and the ratio of net domestic credit to the government sector to total domestic credit for the 27 sample countries; Table 11.11 presents these bivariate regression estimates. They yield a significantly negative relationship between growth and inflation and between growth and the government credit ratio. On the other hand, they indicate a significantly positive relationship between inflation and the government credit ratio. The same relationships can be detected when the country means of the same variables are used instead

---

[5]The variance of inflation is also lower in the Pacific Basin developing economies than in the control group.

Table 11.11. Bivariate Relationships between Growth, Inflation, and Government Credit Ratios in 27 Developing Countries

	Dependent Variable			
	YG		*INF*	
Independent Variable	Annual Observations	Country Means	Annual Observations	Country Means
INF	−0.049 (−8.231)	−0.040 (−2.136)		
DCGR	−0.009 (−2.496)	−0.028 (−2.273)		
DCGR			0.081 (3.609)	0.075 (0.573)

t statistics in parentheses

of the annual observations. These results are consistent with the hypotheses that government deficits raise inflation and lower rates of economic growth.[6]

The econometric results and significant differences in means reported here can hardly be used to infer that policy rather than behavioral differences explain the superior economic performance of the Pacific Basin developing economies. However, econometric analysis of the rate of economic growth reported elsewhere (Fry and Lilien 1986) indicates that accommodative, discretionary monetary and fiscal policies have negative effects on economic growth in the long run. Monetary accommodation of exogenous shocks adds noise to the economic environment by increasing the variance of money growth shocks. In the same vein, Harberger (1988) suggests that erratic exchange rate policies in Latin America have reduced export supply elasticities in that part of the world.

The conclusions reached by Fry and David Lilien (1986) combined with results reported here are certainly consistent with the hypothesis that greater monetary discipline in the Pacific Basin developing economies has been one of the factors contributing to the substantially higher rates of economic growth in this region. Nevertheless, the job of linking the results reported here that detect distinctly different monetary policy stances in the Pacific Basin developing economies with work that suggests that these policy differences may explain the distinctly better economic performance in these economies still remains.

---

[6]The variance of inflation also has a significant negative relationship with economic growth.

Chapter 12

Foreign Capital Flows to Developing Countries

12.1 Introduction

FOREIGN CAPITAL FLOWS to developing countries constitute part of the world's saving. Over the past two decades, world saving as a proportion of world income has fallen. A comparison of the periods 1968–1981 and 1982–1988 illustrates this worldwide decline in saving ratios (Aghevli et al. 1990, 9, 36–37): saving in industrialized countries fell from 25 to 20 percent of GNP and developing country saving fell from 25 to 22 percent of GNP. One important reason for the worldwide decline in saving is rising government deficits: up from 2.9 percent in the period 1972–1980 to 4.5 percent in the period 1981–1988 (*International Financial Statistics Yearbooks* 1988 and 1991, 156).

The decline in world saving implies that not every country can maintain its level of domestic investment by increasing foreign capital inflows. Overall, the decline in saving has to be matched by an equal decline in investment. In fact, saving and investment ratios have fallen in all geographical regions of the world since 1982, but least in developing countries of Asia. As world saving has shrunk, so the world real interest rate has risen from 1.5 percent during the period 1970–1980 to 4.8 percent in the period 1981–1991, as illustrated in Figure 12.1. With no signs of a reversal in the declining trend in global saving and the immediate saving-reducing impacts of reunification of Germany, reconstruction of Eastern Europe, and deliberate current account reduction policies being implemented by Japan, Korea, and Taiwan, the costs of foreign borrowing can be expected to rise still higher in the 1990s as the saving curve in Figure 12.1 moves even further to the left.

The decline in foreign capital inflows to developing countries has necessitated structural adjustment in the form of an increase in export earnings or a reduction in import expenditure. The national accounting identities imply that the adjustment has to raise national saving or reduce domestic investment. To

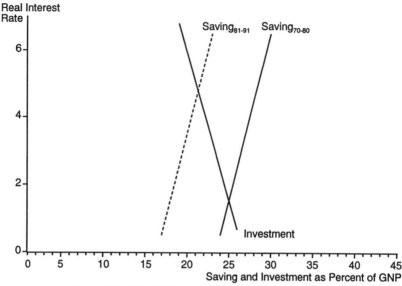

Figure 12.1. World Saving and Investment, 1970–1991

maintain or increase rates of economic growth, the adjustment must take the form of increased exports and increased national saving. Import compression and reduced domestic investment inevitably lower growth rates. However, as Riccardo Faini and Jaime de Melo (1990, 492) note: "With the significant exception of East Asian countries, adjustment was achieved by cutting investment rather than increasing saving." The inevitable effect has been sharp reductions in rates of growth in all parts of the developing world, again with the exception of Asia.

Foreign direct investment (FDI) has become increasingly tempting to developing countries facing declining domestic investment, higher costs of foreign borrowing, and excessive foreign debt. In the aftermath of the debt crisis, FDI has appeared to be a progressively attractive alternative to long-term bank loans as a form of capital inflow to developing countries. Indeed, FDI has been viewed by some as a panacea for declining domestic investment and higher costs of borrowing abroad. Over the past decade, several developing countries have taken measures to attract foreign direct investment. However, the effects have differed widely from one country to another.

Foreign direct investment seems attractive because it involves a risk-sharing relationship with investors from the home country. Such risk-sharing does not exist in the formal contractual arrangements for foreign loans. Foreign direct investment seems particularly attractive when existing stocks are low. Low stocks of foreign-owned capital imply low flows of repatriated profits. Over time, however, success in attracting FDI will increase this coun-

Table 12.1. Foreign Direct Investment Inflows, 1990

Country	$ millions
Industrial Countries	151,970
Developing Countries	32,473
Argentina	2,036
Bermuda	819
Brazil	2,118
Chile	595
China	3,489
Colombia	501
Egypt	947
Hong Kong	783
Indonesia	964
Korea	715
Malaysia	2,902
Mexico	2,632
Nigeria	588
Philippines	530
Saudi Arabia	572
Singapore	4,808
Taiwan	1,330
Thailand	2,376
Turkey	697
Venezuela	451

Source: United Nations, *World Investment Report 1992: Transnational Corporations as Engines of Growth* (New York: United Nations, 1992), Annex Table 1, 312–316

terflow, which could exceed the alternative flow of interest payments in the longer run. Clearly, therefore, the question of the cost of FDI to reduce risk must be addressed in any evaluation of the benefits to be derived from substituting FDI for foreign borrowing. The benefits to the host country will depend on both the size of the package of incentives and disincentives to FDI as well as the extent of other distortions in the economy.

Globally, FDI has increased dramatically over the past decade. However, most of this increase has occurred in the industrial countries. In the developing countries, FDI has been heavily concentrated among a small number of countries. Indeed, Table 12.1 shows that over 90 percent of FDI inflows to developing countries in 1990 were received by only 18 countries. Half of this total flowed to eight Pacific Basin developing economies (Hong Kong, Indonesia, Korea, Malaysia, Philippines, Singapore, Taiwan, and Thailand). Given that neither Korea nor Taiwan has shown strong interest in attracting

FDI, it may seem surprising that these economies feature in Table 12.1. The explanation lies in their superlative investment climates (Fry 1991b).

Before this recent interest in FDI, developing countries borrowed extensively from multinational banks to finance their current account deficits. Therefore, this chapter starts by examining some of the effects of foreign debt accumulation in developing countries. The United States has also been borrowing heavily abroad to finance apparently unsustainable current account deficits. Even in the unemotional language of an international bureaucracy, the IMF refers to these current account imbalances as "large"; it also raises a question about whether they are sustainable (*World Economic Outlook* 1986, 7; 1987, 9; 1988, 1; 1989, 1; 1990, 2). However, several economists claim that the perceived problem is illusory. For example, John Makin (1989, 28) argues that the U.S. current account deficits are sustainable: "After 1987 normal investment flows from greatly enlarged foreign portfolios have created a sustainable net capital inflow to the United States of over $100 billion annually." He derives this figure from an examination of portfolio balances, taking into account desired portfolio diversification in both the United States and the rest of the world.

Paul Masson, Jeroen Kremers, and Jocelyn Horne (1994) also analyze the current account imbalances of Germany, Japan, and the United States; they test for the existence of long-run equilibrium relationships between the net stock of foreign claims and other factors. They find that the ratio of net foreign claims to GNP is cointegrated with the ratio of government debt to GNP and population dependency ratios relative to those in the rest of the world. They also detect short-run feedback effects from the stock of net foreign claims to variables such as domestic absorption, real exchange rates, and real interest rates. These feedback mechanisms act as stabilizers to ensure an eventual return to long-run equilibrium (Masson, Kremers, and Horne 1994).

Population dependency ratios are clearly bounded and have specific values for steady-state demographic equilibrium. A rational government would necessarily keep its indebtedness within some bounds too. Hence, cointegration of the net foreign claim ratio with these two variables implies that it too has some long-run steady-state value. In this steady state, the current account would ensure that net foreign claims changed exactly in proportion to GNP. Such a current account imbalance would be sustainable indefinitely, since it would not change the ratio of net foreign claims to GNP. The Masson-Kremers-Horne analysis corroborates Makin's view: changes in desired stock levels determine the corresponding flows and not vice versa. In other words, if a country wants to increase its level of foreign indebtedness, it runs a current account deficit. To decrease its foreign debt or increase its foreign assets, a country runs a current account surplus.

The policy conclusion of this research is that concern over the balance of payments should not focus on a current account imbalance per se, but rather on the accumulation of an unmanageable amount of foreign liabilities.

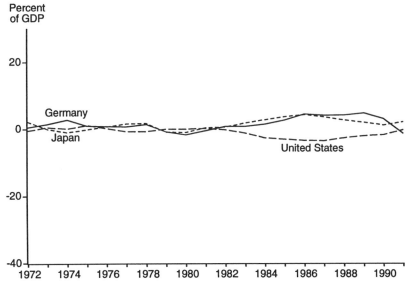

Figure 12.2. Current Account Imbalances in Germany, Japan, and the United States

However, the Masson-Kremers-Horne work suggests that economic forces pull the current account imbalances in Germany, Japan, and the United States towards *sustainable* long-run positions. The same conclusion is reached in related empirical work on the United States by Michael Wickens and Merih Uctum (1993). Since this implies that the stock of net foreign liabilities (as a proportion of GNP) will not rise indefinitely, policy concern is unwarranted; no specific policy actions are required.

Here I address the question of whether this comforting conclusion can also be reached after examining foreign indebtedness in some developing countries. For an answer, I analyze current account behavior and monetary policy implementation in a sample of developing countries. Since the limited observation period prevents the use of the Masson-Kremers-Horne cointegration approach, I use the informal error-correction model developed in Chapter 5.

In this sample of developing countries, annual current account imbalances (as percentages of GDPs) have been far larger than the peak imbalances in Germany, Japan, and the United States. Current account imbalances in most of these countries also fluctuated far more over time than did those in the three largest industrial countries. Figure 12.2 presents the current account imbalances in Germany, Japan, and the United States over the period 1972–1991. For comparison, Figure 12.3 shows current account imbalances in Korea, Venezuela, and Zaire over the same time period. Data for Figures 12.2 and 12.3 come from *International Financial Statistics Yearbooks* (1989–1992). Clearly, current accounts in the three developing countries exhibited much

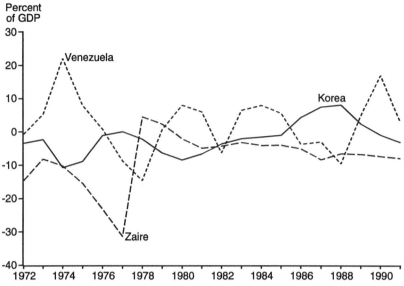

Figure 12.3. Current Account Imbalances in Korea, Venezuela, and Zaire

greater volatility than they did in the three industrial countries. Hence, the existence of self-correcting current account imbalances in developing countries is an important as well as an open question.

Section 12.2 reports two-stage least-squares pooled time series estimates of saving and investment functions in a sample of 28 heavily indebted developing countries, while section 12.3 reports iterative three-stage least-squares estimates of current account and monetary policy equations on pooled time series for a different sample of 26 developing countries. Section 12.4 presents some dynamic simulations to illustrate the finding that certain types of foreign debt accumulation produce destabilizing effects on the current account. Section 12.5 analyzes the effects of foreign direct investment (FDI) on saving, investment, export, and import ratios, as well as the rate of economic growth in a third sample of 16 developing countries.

12.2   Effects of Foreign Debt Accumulation on Saving and Investment Ratios

The first estimates presented in this section consist of saving and investment functions estimated for 28 developing countries that were heavily indebted to the World Bank in 1986. The average ratio of government plus government-guaranteed foreign debt to GNP for these 28 countries was 0.25 over the period 1967–1985. By the end of this period, it had risen to 0.45. The highest end-of-period (1984 or 1985) ratio was achieved by Jamaica (1.28), with Zambia (1.15) and Morocco (0.83) falling in second and third places. The other countries in this sample with debt/GNP ratios over 0.5 in 1984 or 1985 are Chile (0.63), Côte d'Ivoire (0.71), Peru (0.61), Poland (0.59), and Sudan (0.64).

Foreign lenders tend to be more concerned about a country's prospective earnings ability and hence use the debt/*export* ratio. However, economic behavior in the indebted country may well be influenced more by the ratio of debt to total output than to exports. The average debt/export ratio, the ratio used more typically by the multinational lending banks, averaged 1.45 over the period 1967–1985. By the end of this period, it had risen to 2.03. The highest end-of-period debt/export ratio was achieved by Bangladesh (7.72), with Sudan (4.91) and Morocco (3.35) falling in second and third places. The other countries in this sample with debt/export ratios over 2 in 1984 or 1985 are Argentina (2.86), Chile (2.33), India (2.10), Mexico (2.27), Pakistan (2.97), Peru (2.60), and Zambia (2.76). Brazil dropped out of this group with a massive decline in its debt/export ratio from 2.28 in 1984 to 1.98 in 1985 as exports surged.

The empirical results reported here show that, at these levels of indebtedness in these particular countries, an increase in foreign debt actually reduces saving by more than it reduces investment. Hence, the current account deficit worsens as foreign indebtedness rises over time. When foreign indebtedness reaches some critical level, additional capital inflows seem to do more harm than good.

The tendency to overborrow can be countered by macroeconomic policies designed to stimulate saving (or to depress investment). Higher saving (or reduced investment) depreciates the real exchange rate which, in turn, increases exports and reduces imports. Foreign lenders might force a cold-turkey cure on a heavily indebted developing country by cutting off further net capital flows. In such case, the developing country could retaliate by repudiating its foreign debt. Alternatively, the necessary adjustments to saving (or investment) can be undertaken voluntarily and possibly more gradually. In either case, this model indicates that the growth rate should accelerate as the debt burden recedes. None of the alternative policy measures—stimulating exports, compressing imports, and repudiating debt—simulated in Fry (1989a) seems capable of solving these countries' debt problem over the longer run.

The regression estimates presented here use 502 observations pooled from the 28 sample countries. For most of these countries, the regression period is 1967–1985, but there are fewer than 19 observations for some countries. The country sample (dates given when not 1967–1985) is: Algeria, Argentina (1970–1984), Bangladesh (1976–1985), Brazil, Cameroon (1967–1984), Chile (1974–1984), Colombia, Egypt, India, Indonesia, Côte d'Ivoire, Jamaica, Kenya (1970–1985), Korea, Malaysia, Mexico (1967–1984), Morocco (1967–1984), Nigeria (1967–1984), Pakistan, Peru, Philippines, Portugal (1967–1984), Sudan (1967–1984), Thailand, Tunisia, Turkey, Yugoslavia, and Zambia. This country sample was chosen for accuracy and availability of foreign debt data.[1] Even so, consistent foreign debt data going back to the 1960s are confined to government plus government-guaranteed foreign debt.

The regression method is two-stage least squares (2SLS) with country dummy variables. In the light of Jack Johnston's (1972, 414–420) survey of Monte Carlo studies of alternative estimation techniques, the unavoidable presence of measurement and specification errors suggests that the choice of 2SLS is most appropriate in this instance.

Coefficient equality between countries is imposed in both the first and second stage of the estimation procedure. With a maximum of 19 observations per country and 18 variables per equation (19 for the growth rate equation), excluding the country dummies, in the first stage of the two-stage estimation procedure, the validity of pooling the data cannot be tested for each individual country. However, I tested the appropriateness of pooling the Pacific Basin sample countries (Indonesia, Korea, Malaysia, Philippines, and Thailand) with the remaining countries in the sample using an F test. I also applied the same test to the group of Latin American and Caribbean sample countries (Argentina, Brazil, Chile, Colombia, Jamaica, Mexico, and Peru). The F tests indicate that coefficient equality cannot be rejected. Given the data limitations, pooling seems to provide a reasonable characterization of a representative country from this sample.

The saving estimate is:

$$SNY = 0.176(\widehat{YG}) + 0.451(\widehat{TTG})$$
$$(2.404) \qquad (4.491)$$

$$- \ 0.056(RW) - 0.017(DCGR) + 0.071(DETY)$$
$$(-1.484) \qquad (-2.152) \qquad (2.298) \tag{12.1}$$

$$- \ 0.112(DETY)^2 + 0.707(SNY)_{t-1};$$
$$(-3.253) \qquad (22.813)$$

$$R^2 = 0.883 \qquad Q(4) = 1.537$$

Hats indicate the endogenous explanatory variables and t statistics are reported in parentheses below each coefficient estimate. The Box-Pierce Q statistic (for first to fourth order serial correlations) shown below the equation indicates that there is no significant correlation in the residuals.

The national saving ratio SNY is increased by higher growth in real GNP YG and by terms-of-trade improvements TTG. Income growth attributable to terms-of-trade improvements raises the saving ratio by more than income

---

[1] The sample excludes Bolivia, Costa Rica, Ecuador, Uruguay, and Venezuela from the World Bank's group of 17 developing countries classified as heavily indebted in World Bank (1988, 193).

growth attributable to output growth. In a permanent income framework, this is consistent with the perception that terms-of-trade changes are more temporary than output changes. A higher world real interest rate RW and a higher ratio of net government credit to total domestic credit $DCGR$ reduces the national saving ratio, as does higher foreign debt after the debt/GNP ratio $DETY$ exceeds 0.314. The Ricardian equivalence hypothesis with respect to foreign debt is rejected; higher government plus government-guaranteed foreign debt reduces rather than raises national saving ratios in these countries. The domestic investment estimate is:

$$IKY = 0.323(\widehat{YG}) - 0.058(RW) + 0.035(TTL)_{t-1}$$
$$(3.065) \quad (-1.223) \quad (4.429)$$

$$+ 0.033(\widehat{REXL}) + 0.102(DETY) - 0.093(DETY)^2$$
$$(1.728) \quad (2.794) \quad (-2.308) \qquad (12.2)$$

$$- 0.033(DCGR) + 0.029(DCPY) + 0.667(IKY)_{t-1}.$$
$$(-3.845) \quad (0.583) \quad (20.130)$$

$$R^2 = 0.862 \qquad Q(4) = 13.257$$

The Box-Pierce Q statistic again indicates that there is no significant correlation in the residuals.

The domestic investment ratio IKY is raised by faster real GNP growth YG, lagged improvements in the terms of trade TTL, and a higher real exchange rate $REXL$ that makes imported capital goods cheaper.[2] Capital inflows allow domestic investment to exceed national saving, a movement down the investment curve from its intersection with national saving in Figure 5.1. They also stimulate domestic investment by appreciating the real exchange rate, so moving the investment curve itself to the right. A higher ratio of net government credit to total domestic credit reduces the investment ratio, as does a higher foreign debt ratio after the debt/GNP ratio exceeds 0.548. The change in real domestic credit to the private sector $DCPY$ has a positive but insignificant coefficient.

Estimates of a five-equation model which includes these saving and investment functions indicate that capital inflows raise economic growth by allowing investment to exceed saving and by stimulating investment indirectly through the real exchange rate effect (Fry 1989a). However, a rising ratio of foreign debt to GNP eventually has three negative impacts on growth: it reduces the saving ratio, it deters domestic investment, and it lowers the efficiency of investment (Fry 1989a). These negative effects of debt *stock*

---

[2] When the ratio of imports is substituted for the real exchange rate, a higher import ratio also raises the investment ratio.

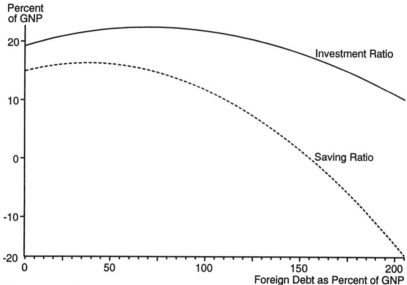

Figure 12.4. Effects of a Rising Foreign Debt Ratio on National Saving and Domestic Investment Ratios

start to outweigh the positive effects of debt *flow* when the debt/GNP ratio reaches about 0.5; this corresponds to a debt/export ratio of about 2.4 for this sample of countries. In fact, debt/GNP ratios ranged from 0.02 to 1.28 in this sample of countries. The problem arises from the lack of any automatic deterrent to continued debt accumulation after its effects turn malign.

Figure 12.4 shows the direct and indirect effects of increasing foreign debt on the national saving and domestic investment ratios (Fry 1989a, Figure 2, 328). These are short-run equilibrium effects, since the values of all lagged endogenous variables are held constant while $DETY$ is increased from 0 to 2. The gap between the saving ratio and the investment ratio increases monotonically as the debt ratio rises. The same result occurs whether the foreign debt ratio is entered linearly or to the third or fourth power with beginning- or end-of-year values in both the saving and investment ratio equations. Whether entered linearly or in quadratic form, the debt/export ratio also produces the same result but has a somewhat lower explanatory power than the debt/GNP ratio in both the saving and investment functions.

That some developing countries have overborrowed (and some lenders have overlent) is certainly not a new finding. Michael Bruno (1985), Richard Cooper and Jeffrey Sachs (1985), Carlos Diaz-Alejandro (1985), Arnold Harberger (1986), and Ronald McKinnon (1991) all provide explanations for why private sectors will borrow more abroad than is socially optimal unless restrained from so doing.

Bruno (1985, 868) and Harberger (1986, 157–158) show that the optimum tariff theory can be applied to the taxation of foreign capital inflows when a country faces a rising supply schedule of foreign loans. In such case, a country's general welfare can be increased by reducing the incentives to borrow abroad through a tax on foreign indebtedness. Bruno (1985, 868) also argues that differential speeds of adjustment justify restrictions on capital inflows during a liberalization program. Cooper and Sachs (1985, 34–35) show that a *laissez faire* policy towards foreign borrowing is justified only under very restrictive conditions. Specifically, the private sector must have rational expectations regarding the possibility of a liquidity crisis, the probability of such a crisis must not be a function of the overall level of foreign debt, the private sector must believe that the government will not bail it out, and the liquidity crisis must not cause a wave of disruptive bankruptcies.

Diaz-Alejandro (1985, 18) and McKinnon (1991) pursue the bailout condition. They argue that government guarantees and deposit insurance combined with inadequate regulation have produced a strong incentive for the multinational banks to overlend to developing countries. In sum, government involvement seems to have affected the foreign borrowing and lending process in a rather predictable way.

12.3 Effects of Foreign Debt Accumulation on Current Accounts and Monetary Policy

Since the current account equals national saving minus domestic investment, the current account expressed as a ratio of GNP must equal the national saving ratio minus the domestic investment ratio. Furthermore, the current account ratio can be explained by the same factors that determine the national saving and domestic investment ratios by substituting equations 5.8 and 5.9 into equation 5.3. Rearranging the variables and simplifying the resulting coefficients gives:

$$CAY = b_{10} + \overset{+}{b}_{11} FLY_{t-1} + \overset{?}{b}_{12} DETY_{t-1} + \overset{?}{b}_{13} DETY^2_{t-1}$$

$$+ \overset{-}{b}_{14} \widehat{DDCY} + \overset{?}{b}_{15} \widehat{TTL} + \overset{?}{b}_{16} \widehat{YG} + \overset{?}{b}_{17} RW \qquad (12.3)$$

$$+ \overset{-}{b}_{18} REXL_{t-1} + \overset{+}{b}_{19} SNY_{t-1} + \overset{-}{b}_{20} IY_{t-1},$$

where FLY is the cumulated current account deficit and $DDCY$ is the change in domestic credit both divided by nominal GNP.[3]

---

[3] The lagged value of $REXL$ is included in equation 12.3 instead of the current value because

The 26 countries in this sample are Algeria, Argentina, Brazil, Chile, Côte d'Ivoire, Egypt, Ghana, Greece, India, Indonesia, Korea, Malaysia, Mexico, Morocco, Nigeria, Pakistan, Peru, Philippines, Portugal, Sri Lanka, Tanzania, Thailand, Turkey, Venezuela, Yugoslavia, and Zaire. These countries comprise developing countries with populations over ten million for which there are reasonably good financial data (Gelb 1989, Hanson and Neal 1986).

These regression estimates use 597 observations for the current account equation and 644 observations for a monetary policy equation. The data for constructing the relevant variables for these 26 developing countries are taken from *World Tables Socio-economic Time-series* (1989, 1990) and *International Financial Statistics* computer tape. The observation period is 1960–1988 but a full data set for some countries starts only in the mid- or late-1960s. Hence, there are too few degrees of freedom for cointegration analysis or even individual country estimation.

The regression method is iterative three-stage least squares (3SLS) which is, asymptotically, full-information maximum likelihood (Johnston 1984, 486–492). I estimate the 26 individual country equations for the current account as a system of equations with cross-equation equality restrictions on all coefficients except the intercept. Hence, the estimates apply to a representative developing country in this sample rather than to any single country. The estimation technique corrects for heteroscedasticity across country equations and exploits contemporaneously correlated disturbances. For the current account estimates, the instruments are the exogenous explanatory variables plus oil price inflation $OILINF$, $DDCY_{t-1}$, TTL_{t-1}, YG_{t-1}, the change in net domestic credit to the government divided by nominal GNP $DDCGY$, and the rate of growth (continuously compounded) in OECD output. Similarly, the 26 individual country equations for the monetary policy reaction function were estimated as a system of equations with cross-equation restrictions on all coefficients except the intercept. Instruments for the domestic credit estimates include the instruments used in the current account estimates plus the change in net foreign assets divided by nominal GNP $DNFAY_{t-1}$, the gap between domestic and U.S. inflation $INFGAP_{t-1}$, $OILINF_{t-1}$, $DDCGY_{t-1}$, lagged money ($M2$) growth, and U.S. inflation.

Since the coefficients b_{19} and b_{20} were almost exactly equal but opposite in sign, I constrain these coefficients to be equal and opposite by substituting the lagged current account ratio for the lagged saving and investment ratios. The estimate with the highest correlation coefficient adjusted for degrees of freedom is (hats denote endogenous variables, t statistics are given in parentheses):

---

the initial specification search found that the coefficient of $REXL_{t-1}$ was significant, while the coefficient of $REXL$ was insignificant.

$$CAY = 0.112\,FLY_{t-1} - 0.081\,DETY_{t-1}^2 - 0.037\,\widehat{DDCY}$$
$$(24.359) \qquad (-17.709) \qquad\quad (-6.888)$$

$$+ 0.019\,\widehat{TTL} - 0.001\,\widehat{YG} - 0.056\,RW$$
$$(10.161) \qquad (-0.093) \qquad (-6.503) \qquad\qquad (12.4)$$

$$- 0.004\,REXL_{t-1} + 0.655\,CAY_{t-1}.$$
$$(-1.895) \qquad\quad (36.199)$$

$$\overline{R}^2 = 0.685$$

This estimated current account equation shows that an increase in the cumulated current account deficit as a ratio of GNP FLY_{t-1} improves the current account ratio significantly. In other words, this stock variable exhibits a stabilizing effect or an error-correction mechanism; current account deficits cumulated in the past improve current account balances in the future, perhaps in the way illustrated in Figure 5.1.

In contrast, however, the ratio of government and government-guaranteed foreign debt to GNP squared $DETY_{t-1}^2$ exerts a significantly negative effect on the current account ratio. Current account deficits financed through this type of foreign debt are not self-correcting. Perhaps because it stimulates capital flight, a rise in the stock of foreign debt of this type worsens the current account and hence accelerates its own buildup.

As anticipated, accelerated domestic credit expansion $DDCY$, higher economic growth YG, an increase in the world real interest rate RW and an appreciation in last year's real exchange rate $REXL_{t-1}$ worsen the current account, while an improvement in the terms of trade TTL improves the current account.

Table 12.2 reports two estimates of the monetary policy reaction function derived in section 5.8. The high t statistics illustrate the considerable efficiency improvement achieved by iterative 3SLS. Equations 12.5 and 12.6 add three variables, FLY_{t-1}, $DETY_{t-1}$, and $REXL_{t-1}$ to those used in equations 11.29 and 11.30. Because Taiwan has been a net creditor country for most of the observation period, it is dropped from this sample of developing countries. Even with these changes, equations 12.5 and 12.6 produce very similar results to equations 11.29 and 11.30. Of most importance is the finding that, in contrast to the other developing countries, the Pacific Basin developing countries controlled monetary expansion by sterilizing most of any increase in net foreign assets and completely neutralizing any increase in the government's borrowing requirement by concomitantly reducing domestic credit to the private sector.

Equation 12.6 indicates that the non-Pacific Basin countries sterilized only 10 percent of any increase in net foreign assets $DNFAY$. The monetary authorities also expanded domestic credit after a depreciation in the real

Table 12.2. Monetary Policy Reaction Functions ($DDCY$) for 26 Developing Countries

Variable	Equation 12.5	Equation 12.6
FLY_{t-1}	−0.071	−0.043
	(−22.241)	(−63.561)
$DETY_{t-1}$	0.082	0.038
	(29.333)	(33.172)
$\widehat{DNFAY}$	−0.221	−0.104
	(−24.068)	(−38.408)
$DNFAY_{t-1}$	0.060	0.147
	(7.046)	(74.902)
$\widehat{INFGAP}$	0.086	0.057
	(35.578)	(78.122)
$INFGAP_{t-1}$	−0.025	−0.004
	(−12.266)	(−6.748)
$OILINF$	0.018	0.011
	(11.713)	(23.579)
$OILINF_{t-1}$	0.016	0.018
	(9.671)	(27.191)
$REXL$	−0.016	−0.024
	(−19.432)	(−74.305)
$DDCGY$	0.732	0.843
	(87.255)	(410.104)
$DDCGY_{t-1}$	0.025	−0.003
	(2.686)	(−1.109)
Shift Parameters for Pacific Basin Developing Economies		
$\widehat{DNFAY}$		−0.665
		(−151.953)
$\widehat{INFGAP}$		−0.042
		(−38.878)
$DDCGY$		−0.577
		(−77.078)
$DDCGY_{t-1}$		−0.239
		(−49.097)
R^2	0.802	0.792

Hats denote endogenous variables.
t statistics in parentheses

exchange rate $REXL$. The reaction function coefficients for the developing countries of the control group suggest that the monetary authorities in this sample of developing countries have generally pursued accommodative monetary policies.

In contrast, the Pacific Basin developing countries sterilized 77 percent (-0.104 plus -0.665) of any increase in the banking system's net foreign assets $DNFAY$ and accommodated domestic inflation $INFGAP$ to a much smaller extent than the control group. The Pacific Basin developing countries also neutralized two thirds of the effects of the government's credit requirements on the money supply. The monetary authorities of the Pacific Basin developing countries increased aggregate domestic credit by only 37 percent (0.843 plus -0.577) of any increase in the government's credit requirements. This implies a reduction in domestic credit to the private sector equal to 67 percent of the increase in the government's credit requirements. In the year after an increase in the government's requirements, however, the Pacific Basin developing countries reduced domestic credit by an additional 24 percent of the government's credit requirements (-0.003 plus -0.239). Over a two-year period, therefore, the monetary authorities in the Pacific Basin developing countries reduced domestic credit to the private sector by 98 percent ($1 - [0.843 - 0.003 - 0.577 - 0.239]$) of any increase in the government's credit requirements. Ishrat Husain (1991, 8–10) suggests that the prudent and conservative monetary policies pursued by the Pacific Basin developing countries explain, in part, why these countries avoided the debt crisis.

For all 26 countries, the monetary authorities' reaction to foreign debt buildup is paradoxical. When the cumulated current account deficit FLY_{t-1} rises, the monetary authorities reduce domestic credit expansion. Hence, the current account is *improved* by an increase in FLY_{t-1}: (a) directly in the current account equation itself; (b) indirectly through its effect in the monetary policy equation. There are, therefore, both behavioral and policy-induced stabilizing influences or error-correction mechanisms at work to reduce an excessive current account deficit to a sustainable long-run equilibrium level.

The reaction of the monetary authorities to a buildup of government and government-guaranteed foreign debt is quite different. Instead of reining in domestic credit expansion, the monetary authorities expand domestic credit. In this case, therefore, the current account is *worsened* by an increase in $DETY_{t-1}$: (a) directly in the current account equation (actually by the increase in $DETY_{t-1}^2$); (b) indirectly through its effect on monetary policy. Both behavioral and policy-induced reactions to increased government and government-guaranteed foreign debt are destabilizing, thereby inhibiting any long-run steady-state equilibrium from emerging.

An increase in government and government-guaranteed foreign debt could cause an increase in domestic credit by increasing the public sector borrowing requirement for debt service. However, this effect is already taken into account by including the public sector's borrowing requirement as a ratio of

GNP $DDCGY$ in the estimated monetary policy equation. When $DDCGY$ and last year's value of this variable are excluded, the estimated effect of government and government-guaranteed debt on domestic credit expansion is more than doubled. It seems, therefore, that the monetary authorities expand domestic credit when $DETY_{t-1}$ increases not only to finance the public sector's increased debt service expenses but also to accommodate the private sector's increased debt service burden or even to facilitate capital flight.

12.4   Dynamic Simulations of Foreign Debt Accumulation

The model I use for dynamic simulation consists of equations 12.4 and 12.5 together with the following two additional equations:

$$FLY = FLY_{t-1}/e^{YG} - CAY;   \tag{12.7}$$

$$DETY = DETY_{t-1}/e^{YG} - CAY.   \tag{12.8}$$

Equations 12.7 and 12.8 adjust the lagged ratios FLY_{t-1} and $DETY_{t-1}$ for GNP growth before adding the current year's current account deficit ratio. Here I assume that government and government-guaranteed foreign debt rises by exactly the amount of the current account deficit. An alternative assumption is that the ratio of $DETY$ to FLY remains constant:

$$DETY = FLY \cdot (DETY_{t-1}/FLY_{t-1}).   \tag{12.9}$$

The simulation model contains four endogenous variables: CAY, $DDCY$, FLY and $DETY$. The remaining explanatory variables in equations 12.4 and 12.5 are treated as exogenous in the simulation model and take their mean last-observation values for the 26 sample developing countries throughout the simulation period. Figure 12.5 presents the benchmark dynamic simulation of this four-equation model from 1989 to 2012. This figure shows the deteriorating current account ratio CAY and the accumulation of government and government-guaranteed foreign debt $DETY$, the cause of the worsening current account in this representative developing country. Using equation 12.9 instead of equation 12.8 produces virtually identical results. This is hardly surprising, given that the mean last-observation value of FLY is 0.52 (52 percent of GNP), while the mean last-observation value of $DETY$ is 0.56.

Whether or not a steady state can be achieved depends on the starting values of the explanatory variables as well as the estimated coefficients. Using equation 12.6 instead of equation 12.5 and exogenous variables calculated from mean end-of-period values for the Pacific Basin developing countries produces convergence to a steady state. Table 12.3 gives the starting values for all the explanatory variables in the current account equation. Column 1 shows the mean last-observation values for the explanatory variables in the 26 sample developing countries. Column 2 shows the minimum change for each

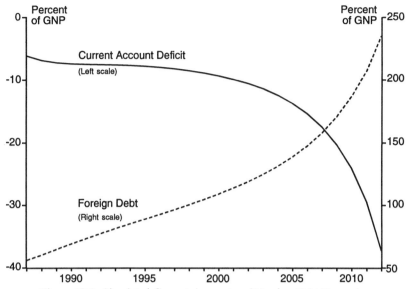

Figure 12.5. Simulated Current Account and Foreign Debt Dynamics

particular variable needed to achieve a steady-state solution. In each case, all other variables take the values given in column 1. By itself, no change in the starting value of FLY_{t-1}, $DETY_{t-1}$, or CAY_{t-1} can produce a steady-state solution. For $DDCY$, TTL, RW, $DDCY$, and $REXL_{t-1}$, the required starting values are unrealistic.

An exogenous improvement of the current account by 1 percentage point and a doubled rate of economic growth constitute the two remaining feasible changes in the explanatory variables that are capable of producing a steady-state solution for the representative developing country. The exogenous improvement in the current account is achieved by increasing the constant in the simulation equation from −0.051 to −0.041. The direct effect of an increased growth rate in equation 12.4 is to worsen the current account. However, by increasing GNP and so reducing $DETY$, its indirect effect improves the current account.

I also ran the simulation model separately for each of the sample developing countries. Here, I use average values for the explanatory flow variables from 1981 to the end of the observation period. For FLY and $DETY$, I use last-observation values. In 15 countries (Argentina, Brazil, Chile, Egypt, Greece, Mexico, Morocco, Nigeria, Pakistan, Peru, Philippines, Portugal, Sri Lanka, Tanzania, and Zaire), the current account deficit explodes at some point. For 11 countries (Algeria, Côte d'Ivoire, Ghana, India, Indonesia, Korea, Malaysia, Thailand, Turkey, Venezuela, and Yugoslavia), however, the simulations converge to a steady state.

Table 12.3. Starting Values of all the Explanatory Variables in the Current Account Equation

	(1)	(2)	(3)	(4)
	Complete Sample		Stable	Unstable
Variable	Actual	Required	Countries	Countries
Constant	−0.051	−0.041	−0.010	−0.082
FLY_{t-1}	0.516	n.a.	0.313	0.906
$DETY_{t-1}$	0.560	n.a.	0.404	0.919
$DDCY$	0.124	−0.165	0.102	0.190
TTL	−0.192	0.358	−0.213	−0.240
YG	0.049	0.096	0.043	0.071
RW	0.040	−0.160	0.040	0.040
$REXL_{t-1}$	−0.353	−3.993	−0.343	−0.491
CAY_{t-1}	−0.062	n.a.	−0.020	−0.126

Columns 3 and 4 of Table 12.3 give the mean last-observation values for the explanatory variables in these two groups (stable and unstable) of developing countries. When the simulation model is run with these sets of values for the explanatory variables, the stable country group produces a steady-state solution, while the unstable country group achieves a current account deficit of 90 percent and a foreign debt ratio of 366 percent of GNP in 2000 before exploding soon thereafter. The difference between these two country groups is illustrated most strikingly by the lagged current account ratio CAY_{t-1}. The unstable country group has a current account deficit of 12.6 percent of GNP in 1988 while the stable group posts a current account deficit of only 2.0 percent of GNP. The differences in FLY_{t-1} and $DETY_{t-1}$ also illustrate the very different past histories of current account deficits in these two groups of countries.

The stable country group pursued less expansionary monetary policies and benefited from somewhat better terms of trade than the unstable group. However, the stable group posted a substantially lower growth rate and a more appreciated real exchange rate than the unstable group. Rather frustratingly, one must conclude that the stable country group simply consists of innately higher savers or lower investors than the unstable group; the difference in the constants is their crucial distinguishing characteristic.

Another way of achieving a steady-state solution is to adjust the coefficients of the model. Specifically, the monetary policy reactions to debt buildup can be strengthened sufficiently to ensure a steady-state outcome from the dynamic simulation. If the coefficients of both FLY_{t-1} and $DETY_{t-1}$ are set

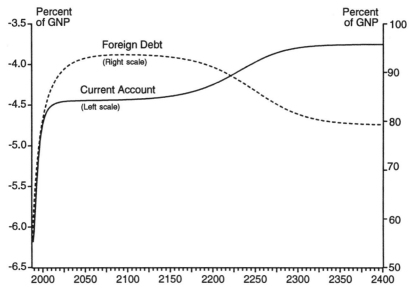

Figure 12.6. Simulation with Tighter Monetary Policy Reaction to Foreign Debt Buildup

equal to -0.167, so replacing the estimated coefficients of -0.071 for FLY_{t-1} and 0.082 for $DETY_{t-1}$ in equation 12.5, a steady-state solution results.

Figure 12.6 illustrates this steady-state convergence when the coefficients of FLY_{t-1} and $DETY_{t-1}$ are both set at -0.167. All other coefficients and starting values of the explanatory variables remain as they are in the benchmark simulation. In the long-run steady state achieved in this case, the current account deficit is 3.75 percent of GNP. With a rate of economic growth of 5 percent (the average last-observation growth rate for the 26 sample countries), foreign debt necessarily converges to 75 percent of GNP.

12.5 Foreign Direct Investment

Virtually all the empirical investigations into the causes and consequences of FDI use single-equation models; the exceptions include the simultaneous two-equation models used by Jungsoo Lee, Pradumna Rana, and Yoshihiro Iwasaki (1986) and Husain and Kwang Jun (1992). Here I estimate the five-equation macroeconomic model developed in Chapter 5 for a sample of 16 developing countries (Argentina, Brazil, Chile, Egypt, India, Indonesia, Korea, Malaysia, Mexico, Nigeria, Pakistan, Philippines, Sri Lanka, Thailand, Turkey, and Venezuela). The results provide some new information on the direct and indirect effects of FDI inflows to this sample of developing countries. They also provide some indicators of the problems to be faced and pitfalls to be avoided by developing countries embarking upon policies to promote FDI inflows.

The regression method is again iterative 3SLS. The instruments are the exogenous explanatory variables plus the lagged FDI ratio, lagged domestic credit expansion divided by GNP, the lagged terms-of-trade index in natural logarithms, lagged growth, the public sector borrowing requirement divided by GNP, the world real interest rate, oil price inflation, and the rate of growth (continuously compounded) in OECD output. The population growth rate is used as an instrumental variable for the growth rate estimates and current rather than lagged terms of trade is used in the trade equations. The estimation period is 1966–1988, except for Brazil (1966–1985), Chile (1966–1984), Indonesia (1967–1888), and Pakistan (1968–1988). For the trade equations, the estimation period is 1965–1988.

Table 12.4 gives three estimates of the investment function with the current FDI ratio and three estimates with the average FDI ratio over the previous five years *FDIYL* instead of the contemporaneous FDI ratio. For the complete sample, the foreign debt ratio reduces the domestic investment ratio, while the rate of economic growth increases it, as anticipated. The domestic credit variable is not significant in this estimate, while the negative coefficient of the real exchange rate suggests that an appreciation in the real exchange rate worsens the investment climate by pricing exports out of world markets. The coefficient of the lagged investment ratio indicates that 30 percent of the adjustment to changes in the explanatory variables occurs in the current year. Hence, the effects of all the other explanatory variables on the domestic investment ratio are 3.3 times greater in the long run than they are in the short run.

The key coefficient, that of the ratio of net FDI inflows to GNP *FDIY*, is significantly negative for the 16 sample developing countries as a group. The inflow of FDI could affect the investment ratio through its influence on the growth rate. When the growth rate is omitted, the FDI coefficients are slightly higher than the coefficients reported in Table 12.4 in all estimates. Hence, total direct and indirect effects of FDI on investment ratios are virtually identical to the direct effects shown in Table 12.4. The negative effect of FDI on the domestic investment ratio in these countries indicates that FDI neither increases domestic investment nor does it provide additional balance-of-payments financing.

Part of the problem may lie in the imposition of coefficient constraints across the entire country sample. Individual country estimates of the investment function indicate that the FDI coefficient is significant only in three countries. It is significantly negative in Chile but significantly positive in Indonesia and Malaysia. This would suggest a strategy of splitting the sample into subgroups. Hence, I estimate each equation for two subgroups—

Table 12.4. Domestic Investment Estimates IY

Variable	All	Pacific Basin	Control
$\widehat{FDIY}$	−0.351	0.853	−0.738
	(−2.344)	(2.983)	(−3.398)
FLY_{t-1}	−0.049	−0.040	−0.024
	(−5.240)	(−2.592)	(−1.738)
$\widehat{DDCY}$	0.010	0.269	0.013
	(0.776)	(3.894)	(0.658)
$REXL_{t-1}$	−0.237	0.169	−0.198
	(−7.011)	(1.212)	(−3.651)
$\widehat{YG}$	0.255	0.330	0.219
	(14.482)	(4.853)	(6.803)
IY_{t-1}	0.703	0.679	0.753
	(30.576)	(12.766)	(21.093)
R^2	0.814	0.866	0.781
No. obs.	358	114	244

Investment with Lagged Foreign Direct Investment

$FDIYL$	0.097	0.117	0.104
	(6.982)	(2.764)	(5.309)
FLY_{t-1}	−0.133	−0.139	−0.099
	(−10.393)	(−3.485)	(−5.751)
$\widehat{DDCY}$	0.039	0.241	0.011
	(3.277)	(3.427)	(0.623)
$REXL_{t-1}$	−0.111	−0.126	−0.207
	(−3.027)	(−0.836)	(−3.752)
$\widehat{YG}$	0.209	0.314	0.198
	(10.038)	(4.534)	(6.457)
IY_{t-1}	0.739	0.763	0.719
	(33.798)	(12.682)	(22.863)
R^2	0.832	0.858	0.798
No. obs.	355	115	240

Note: Hats denote endogenous variables, t statistics are given in parentheses.

five Pacific Basin economies (Indonesia, Korea, Malaysia, Philippines, and Thailand) and a control group of the remaining 11 countries.

In the Pacific Basin, FDI corresponds to capital formation on a one-to-one basis since the coefficient of $FDIY$ is not significantly different from 1. This implies that FDI may not be a close substitute for other forms of capital inflow in these economies. Furthermore, it suggests that FDI does not crowd out or substitute for domestically financed investment. *Ceteris paribus,* it increases the current account deficit by the magnitude of the capital inflow. This conclusion that FDI is not a close substitute for other capital inflows in these Pacific Basin developing economies corroborates the same conclusion reached by Rana and Malcolm Dowling (1990, 92) for a similar sample of Pacific Basin developing economies.

The Pacific Basin economies may differ from the control group because a number of Latin American countries have combined debt-equity swaps with programs of privatization; this has not happened in the Pacific Basin. In these cases, the deliberate aim of attracting FDI was not to increase capital formation but rather to substitute one form of capital inflow for another. The recorded net FDI inflow cancelled part of the country's foreign debt and was used to acquire holdings in the newly privatized industries such as Mexico's Teledyne. While this process of privatization continues, private investors may take a wait-and-see stance before undertaking new investment projects. Hence, the net inflow of FDI may be associated with a degree of uncertainty that clouds the investment outlook and so reduces capital formation. In some cases, however, the process of privatization appears to have improved the investment climate sufficiently to attract some complementary private capital inflows.

Use of FDI in debt-equity swap programs may also have been a last resort measure taken under crisis conditions. Hence, the significantly negative coefficient for the control group may reflect the fact that FDI increased when the investment climate deteriorated in the wake of debt crises. In such case, the foreign debt crises may well have simultaneously reduced domestic investment and increased FDI. If so, higher FDI did not cause the decline in domestic investment but was associated with it since both were caused by some other factor.

In an attempt to pin down the key factors causing such disparate effects of FDI on domestic investment ratios across these two country groups, I interacted the black market exchange rate premium B, the domestic real interest rate RD, the degree of openness (the average ratio of exports plus imports to GNP over the preceding five years) TRL, the investment climate (the average investment ratio over the preceding five years) IYL, and the lagged foreign debt ratio FLY_{t-1} with the FDI ratio $FDIY$. The following estimate includes the three variables whose interactive terms were significant (356 observations):

$$IY = -2.259\,\widehat{FDIY} - 1.411\,\widehat{FDIY} \cdot B + 5.081\,\widehat{FDIY} \cdot TRL$$
$$(-11.135) \qquad (-3.303) \qquad\qquad (16.993)$$

$$- 1.337\,\widehat{FDIY} \cdot FLY_{t-1} - 0.080\,FLY_{t-1} + 0.057\,\widehat{DDCY}$$
$$(-3.317) \qquad\qquad (-10.230) \qquad\quad (6.473) \qquad\qquad\qquad (12.10)$$

$$- 0.327\,REXL_{t-1} + 0.315\,\widehat{YG} + 0.610\,IY_{t-1}.$$
$$(-11.692) \qquad\quad (28.825) \qquad (33.408)$$

$$R^2 = 0.806$$

Evidently, high black market exchange rate premiums and foreign debt ratios produce the negative association between FDI and the domestic investment ratio. If FDI constitutes a last-resort source of external financing during debt and balance-of-payments crises, it may well be associated with a reduction in investment productivity. In a direct test, I find that investment productivity does deteriorate as a country accumulates foreign debt (Fry 1989a). In any event, an open economy with a low black market exchange rate premium (perhaps signifying open capital as well as current accounts) and a low foreign debt ratio experiences a positive association between FDI and the domestic investment ratio.

The bottom part of Table 12.4 presents estimates of the investment function with the average FDI ratio over the previous five years *FDIYL* instead of the contemporaneous FDI ratio. Evidently, lagged FDI is associated with higher domestic investment ratios. These estimates suggest that while FDI deters domestically financed investment in the current period, there is a small degree of intertemporal complementarity. In other words, past FDI stimulates current investment. The combination of contemporaneous substitutability and intertemporal complementarity is proposed by Lazaros Molho (1986a) in the context of firm holdings of real money balances and capital.

Table 12.5 gives the national saving function estimates. For the complete sample, increased foreign debt ratios reduce national saving ratios. However, since FLY_{t-1} reduces the national saving ratio by less than it reduces the domestic investment ratio, a rising debt ratio improves the current account and hence acts as a stabilizer. For each pair of foreign debt coefficients in the saving and investment equations, a rise in the foreign debt ratio increases saving by more than it increases investment, or reduces saving less than it reduces investment. Hence, for both subsamples a rise in the foreign debt ratio exerts a stabilizing influence on the current account.

A higher growth rate raises the national saving ratio as predicted by the life-cycle model. Higher world real interest rates also raise national saving ratios in this sample of countries. The coefficient of the lagged dependent variable indicates that about one third of the adjustment occurs in the current year. Hence, the effects of all the other explanatory variables on the saving

Table 12.5. National Saving Estimates SNY

Variable	All	Pacific Basin	Control
$\widehat{FDIY}$	−0.650	−0.225	−0.237
	(−6.845)	(−0.691)	(−1.270)
FLY_{t-1}	−0.021	0.028	0.023
	(−3.651)	(1.820)	(2.514)
$\widehat{YG}$	0.155	0.379	0.090
	(8.420)	(5.968)	(2.931)
RW	0.122	0.011	0.077
	(3.509)	(0.126)	(1.533)
SNY_{t-1}	0.640	0.892	0.783
	(21.251)	(25.056)	(20.175)
R^2	0.858	0.847	0.847
No. obs.	364	114	250

	Saving with Lagged Foreign Direct Investment		
$FDIYL$	0.052	−0.038	0.038
	(4.053)	(−0.998)	(1.505)
FLY_{t-1}	−0.033	0.058	−0.003
	(−2.925)	(1.702)	(−0.145)
$\widehat{YG}$	0.143	0.373	0.070
	(7.509)	(5.955)	(2.230)
RW	0.080	−0.014	0.102
	(1.821)	(−0.168)	(1.881)
SNY_{t-1}	0.798	0.888	0.781
	(37.067)	(25.534)	(20.097)
R^2	0.856	0.833	0.839
No. obs.	361	115	246

Note: Hats denote endogenous variables, t statistics are given in parentheses.

ratio are about three times greater in the long run than they are in the short run.

The estimate for the entire sample indicates that an increase in FDI reduces national saving.[4] Since its negative effect on the national saving ratio is larger than its negative effect on the domestic investment ratio, FDI inflows to these 16 developing countries have a direct negative impact on the current account. When the growth rate is dropped from the saving estimates, the changes in the values of the FDI coefficients are minuscule. Hence, total direct and indirect effects of FDI on the current account are also negative.

The subsample estimates indicate that the control group is responsible for the negative effect of FDI on national saving for the whole sample. The coefficient of FDI in the Pacific Basin group estimate is not significantly different from zero.

As with the investment function, I interacted the black market exchange rate premium, the degree of openness, the investment climate, and the lagged foreign debt ratio with the FDI ratio in an attempt to detect any systematic influence of these variables on the relationship between FDI and saving behavior. In this case, the degree of openness and the investment climate produce significant interactive term for the complete sample, but only when included in separate estimates (364 observations):

$$SNY = -1.138\,\widehat{FDIY} + 0.869\,\widehat{FDIY} \cdot TRL - 0.016\,FLY_{t-1}$$
$$\;(-4.596)\qquad\;(2.188)\qquad\qquad(-2.895)$$

$$+\;0.114\,RW + 0.176\,\widehat{YG} + 0.653\,SNY_{t-1}. \qquad (12.11)$$
$$(3.268)\qquad(10.426)\qquad(22.297)$$

$$R^2 = 0.862$$

In contrast to the results in the top half of Table 12.5, this approach suggests that a more open economy can anticipate a less negative effect of FDI on its national saving ratio. Per se, therefore, greater openness induces greater positive effects of FDI on both domestic investment and national saving ratios.

An improved investment climate also reduces the negative effect of FDI on national saving ratios, as shown in the following estimate for the complete sample (364 observations):

---

[4] The individual country estimates indicate that FDI inflows have significant impacts in only two countries; the coefficients are negative and significant in Chile and Korea.

$$SNY = -2.126\,\widehat{FDIY} + 5.776\,\widehat{FDIY} \cdot IYL - 0.019\,FLY_{t-1}$$
$$\quad\ \ (-6.892) \qquad\quad (4.900) \qquad\qquad (-3.429)$$

$$+ 0.096\,RW + 0.197\,\widehat{YG} + 0.632\,SNY_{t-1}. \qquad\qquad (12.12)$$
$$\ \ (2.942) \qquad (11.740) \qquad (21.320)$$

$$R^2 = 0.859$$

The bottom half of Table 12.5 gives three estimates of the national saving function with the lagged ratio of FDI. As with the investment function, lagged FDI has the reverse effect to current FDI on the national saving ratio. High FDI over the preceding five year period has a small but significant positive effect on national saving. One possible explanation is that a five-year period of high FDI inflows indicates improved stability of various kinds. Foreign investors have demonstrated confidence in the economy and the same confidence could reduce capital flight and so raise measured national saving.

Estimates of the rate of growth in real GNP YG for the sample developing countries are shown in Table 12.6. Export growth exerts a small positive effect on the growth rate, while higher inflation reduces growth except in the Pacific Basin. The FDI variable in this equation is the ratio of FDI to domestic investment $FDII$ which is substituted for $FDIY$ to avoid multicollinearity with IKY. The variable IKY includes both domestically financed as well as foreign direct investment; it is aggregate capital formation in the economy. Hence, an insignificant coefficient of $FDII$ indicates that FDI does not exert a significantly different effect from domestically financed investment on the rate of economic growth. In the control group, the significantly negative coefficient implies that growth falls when $FDII$ rises.

The bottom half of Table 12.6 substitutes the average FDI ratio over the preceding five years for the ratio of FDI to domestic investment. A sustained period of high FDI inflows is associated with higher economic growth. As in the case of the positive effect of lagged FDI on the national saving ratio, perhaps a five-year period of high FDI inflows indicates improved stability which in turn improves efficiency of resource allocation. It might also reflect lagged demonstration effects and other externalities from FDI on current total factor productivity growth.

Although Table 12.6 suggests that the direct effects of current and lagged FDI ratios on rates of economic growth do not vary across the country groups, I tested a variety of effects interacted with both the FDI variable and with the investment ratio. The first significant interactive term is between the lagged FDI variable and the investment ratio (351 observations):

Table 12.6. Rate of Growth Estimates YG

Variable	All	Pacific Basin	Control
$\widehat{FDII}$	0.010	0.101	−0.126
	(0.419)	(1.805)	(−2.159)
$\widehat{IKY}$	0.239	0.142	0.250
	(23.184)	(8.745)	(20.095)
$\widehat{INF}$	−0.025	0.092	−0.032
	(−4.254)	(4.285)	(−4.601)
$\widehat{XKG}$	0.051	0.162	0.049
	(4.123)	(5.627)	(2.453)
R^2	0.164	0.133	0.150
No. obs.	355	114	241
Growth with Lagged Foreign Direct Investment			
FDIYL	0.036	0.039	0.020
	(6.030)	(1.705)	(1.760)
$\widehat{IKY}$	0.210	0.157	0.223
	(24.100)	(9.360)	(11.282)
$\widehat{INF}$	−0.042	−0.008	−0.030
	(−9.182)	(−0.715)	(−4.460)
$\widehat{XKG}$	0.042	0.184	0.023
	(3.677)	(6.531)	(1.170)
R^2	0.179	0.170	0.155
No. obs.	351	115	236

Note: Hats denote endogenous variables, t statistics are given in parentheses.

$$YG = 0.213\,\widehat{IKY} + 0.137\,\widehat{IKY} \cdot FDIYL$$
$$\quad\;\; (24.182) \qquad (5.382)$$

$$- \; 0.037\,\widehat{INF} + 0.039\,\widehat{XKG}. \qquad (12.13)$$
$$(-8.478) \qquad (3.403)$$

$$R^2 = 0.169$$

This positive effect of lagged FDI on investment productivity may again reflect spillovers from previous FDI on the efficiency of current investment. However, Brian Aitken and Ann Harrison (1992) and Mona Haddad and Harrison (1993) do not detect spillovers from FDI to domestically financed investment in the same industries in their microeconomic estimates of the effects of capital formation owned by foreign firms. Of course, a high and stable inflow of FDI over a five-year period itself reflects a country's macroeconomic management, foreign trade and exchange rate policies, and other factors likely to improve investment efficiency.

One estimate of a function in which growth is determined solely by the FDI ratio, the domestic real interest rate RD, and the export growth rate interacts the real interest rate with FDI in level, quadratic, and cubic form. This permits the real interest rate to exert a non-linear effect on FDI efficiency. For the 16-country sample, the iterative 3SLS estimate is (297 observations):

$$YG = 0.582 \widehat{FDIY} + 0.093 R$$
$$\quad\ (7.599) \qquad\ \ (17.134)$$

$$-\ 9.425\,(\widehat{FDIY} \cdot RD) - 5.965\,(\widehat{FDIY} \cdot RD^2)$$
$$(-12.621) \qquad\qquad\quad (-6.082)$$

$$+\ 2.886\,(\widehat{FDIY} \cdot RD^3) + 0.065\,\widehat{XKG}.$$
$$\quad (5.647) \qquad\qquad\quad\ (13.142)$$

$$R^2 = 0.161$$

(12.14)

Estimates that included both the investment ratio and FDI as a proportion of domestic investment interacted with the real interest rate squared failed to converge.

The overall effect of a rising domestic real interest rate on growth in equation 12.14 is illustrated in Figure 12.7. This figure is produced using the mean values of all the explanatory variables with the exception of the real deposit rate of interest. The mean value of the real deposit rate is zero with a standard deviation of 23 percent. Its minimum value is –83 percent and its maximum value 221 percent. Figure 12.7 shows that the relationship between the domestic real interest rate and growth does indeed resemble an inverted U. Both very low and very high real interest rates reduce growth both directly and through the effects of such interest rates on FDI productivity.

The line P_n denotes two standard deviations below the mean of all negative interest rates in the Pacific Basin economies, C_n denotes two standard deviations below the mean of all negative interest rates in the remaining 11 countries (the control group), P_p denotes two standard deviations above the mean of all zero or positive interest rates in the Pacific Basin economies, while C_p denotes two standard deviations above the mean of all zero or positive interest rates in the control group countries. Evidently, real interest rates deviated from their growth-maximizing level far more in the control group countries than they did in the Pacific Basin economies.

This result is comparable to other estimates of the effect of domestic real interest rates of economic growth. For example, Jacques Polak (1989, 66–70) reports econometric estimates for a sample of forty developing countries over

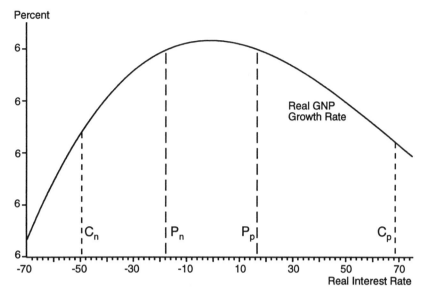

Figure 12.7. Effect of Real Interest Rate on Economic Growth Rate

the period 1965–1985 in which an increase in a negative real interest rate by 10 percentage points raises the rate of economic growth by between 2 and 3 percentage points. He concludes that a reduction in the real interest rate below its equilibrium level by 1 percentage point requires an increase in the investment ratio by 1 percentage point in order to maintain a fixed rate of economic growth. Similar relationships for other country samples are reported in Chapter 8.

Distortion in foreign trade has also received attention. In relation to FDI, Seiji Naya (1990, 298) points out that

> the immiserization literature is of great significance because it illustrates how FDI and other capital flows can lead to suboptimal welfare levels, and even reduce welfare below preflow levels, when recipient industries are protected. In short, since protection will result in non-optimal investment decisions by foreign investors which in turn cause a misallocation of resources, the level of social welfare could easily be lower with foreign investment in a protected industry than without it.

The indicator used here is the black market foreign exchange premium B because of its availability on an annual basis for all 16 sample countries (353 observations):

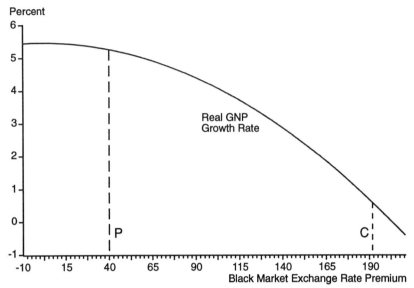

Figure 12.8. Effect of Black Market Exchange Rate Premium on Economic Growth Rate

$$YG = 0.274\,\widehat{FDIY} - 1.331\,(\widehat{FDIY} \cdot B^2) + 0.029\,\widehat{XKG}.$$
$$(1.941)(-2.879)(2.410)(12.15)$$
$$R^2 = 0.175$$

The effect of a rise in the black market foreign exchange premium is illustrated in Figure 12.8. The growth rate is reduced as the black market exchange rate premium rises through its effect on FDI productivity. The mean value of the black market exchange rate premium is 31 percent with a standard deviation of 63 percent. Its minimum value is –10 and its maximum value is 639 percent.

The line P denotes two standard deviations above the mean of all zero or positive black market exchange rate premia in the Pacific Basin economies, while C denotes two standard deviations above the mean of all zero or positive black market exchange rate premia in the control group of countries. Evidently, black market exchange rate premia tended to be considerably higher in the control group than they were in the Pacific Basin economies.

The policy implications that might be derived for developing countries about to embark upon policies to attract FDI are:

- Foreign direct investment can increase capital formation or provide additional balance-of-payments financing but cannot perform both functions at the same time. If FDI is attracted for privatization or debt-equity swap programs, it may provide additional or alternative balance-of-payments support, but it will not accelerate capital formation or economic growth.

• Stimulating FDI through special incentive schemes may simply encourage roundtrip capital flows from the host country. In such case, measured national saving may fall.

• In the presence of financial and trade distortions, FDI can remove from the host country more than it contributes. In other words, it can be immiserizing.

• The most efficacious way of encouraging FDI is to implement policies that generally improve the investment climate. Where domestically financed investment is booming, FDI will seek to participate. Nondiscrimination discourages roundtrip capital flows and reduces the possibilities for immiserization.

• Maximum benefit from FDI can be achieved in open economies that are free of domestic distortions such as financial repression and trade controls. Under such conditions, restrictions on the sectoral location of FDI reduce its growth-enhancing impact.

12.6 Summary

When the World Bank asked me to analyze the effects of developing country foreign debt in 1986, I was convinced that debt crises, like oil crises before them, were more a figment of the international bureaucrats' imagination than an actual problem in the real world. I expected to find self-correcting or error-correcting mechanisms of the kind illustrated in Figure 5.1, posited by Makin (1989), and detected by Masson, Kremers, and Horne (1994), and Wickens and Uctum (1993). My first effort at analyzing these effects changed my mind (Fry 1989a). In that work, some of which is reported in section 12.2, I found that once government and government-guaranteed foreign debt exceeds about 50 percent of GNP, further foreign debt accumulation in the form of government and government-guaranteed debt tends to reduce the total resources available for investment. Capital flight exceeds the additional foreign borrowing and the rate of economic growth falls, both because investment necessarily declines and because investment efficiency also declines under such circumstances (Fry 1989a).

My more recent investigation reported in sections 12.3 and 12.4 extends the earlier work by examining the different effects of alternative types of foreign debt. It also uses a different sample of developing countries. When government and government-guaranteed foreign debt is held constant, an increase

Table 12.7. Direct Effects of Foreign Direct Investment Inflows

Variable	All	Pacific Basin	Control
Domestic investment	neg.	≈ 1	neg.
National saving	neg.	n.s.	n.s.
Exports	neg.	n.s.	neg.
Imports	≈ 1	≈ 1	pos.
Economic growth	n.s.	n.s.	n.s.
Domestic investment (lagged FDI)	pos.	pos.	pos.
National saving (lagged FDI)	pos.	n.s.	n.s.
Economic growth (lagged FDI)	pos.	n.s.	n.s.
Exports (lagged FDI)	pos.	pos.	n.s.
Imports (lagged FDI)	neg.	pos.	neg.

Note: n.s.: not significantly different from zero at the 95 percent confidence level

in net foreign liabilities as measured by the cumulated balance-of-payments deficit produces self-correcting tendencies, possibly through higher effective interest rates which reduce investment and declining wealth which reduces consumption and raises saving. In other words, these results corroborate the Masson-Kremers-Horne (1994) and Wickens-Uctum (1993) findings for the same measure of net foreign indebtedness.

In contrast, when the cumulated balance-of-payments deficit is held constant and government and government-guaranteed debt rises, destabilizing forces are unleashed. Because government and government-guaranteed foreign borrowing has actually financed capital flight in many heavily-indebted countries, its accumulation has failed to produce a self-correcting wealth effect. It has, however, made the accumulation of assets in the heavily-indebted country less and less attractive. Although the private sector response to the buildup of this type of debt is easy to understand, why the monetary authorities fail to invoke a more restrictive monetary policy when such debt accumulates is a question that remains to be addressed by another study.

By analyzing FDI in a macroeconomic framework, section 12.5 throws new light on various channels through which FDI can influence saving, investment, growth, and the balance of payments on current account. Table 12.7 sets out all the direct effects of larger FDI inflows in the three groups of developing economies examined in Fry (1993e). The first empirical finding for a sample of 16 developing countries is that FDI does not provide additional balance-of-payments financing for a preexisting current account deficit. Since FDI is associated with reduced domestic investment outside the Pacific Basin, this implies that FDI is a close substitute for other capital inflows and may also crowd out domestically financed investment. In the Pacific Basin, however, FDI raises domestic investment by the full extent of the FDI inflow. In these countries, therefore, FDI has not been used as a substitute for other types of capital inflows but has increased capital formation and so worsened the current account. Furthermore, in these countries FDI has not crowded out domestically financed investment. By increasing domestic investment in these economies, FDI has increased growth rates.

In examining some other effects, I find that FDI has a significantly negative impact on national saving in this sample of developing countries. One possible explanation is that residents may find that terms and conditions for FDI are more favorable than they are for locally financed investment. Hence, they would have an incentive to remove capital from their country and to bring it back again in the form of FDI. To the extent that these individuals wish to conceal the capital outflow, they will overinvoice imports and underinvoice exports. In such case, an increase in FDI would be accompanied by a reduction in recorded national saving.

The concurrent effect of FDI on exports is negative outside the Pacific Basin. One possible explanation is that FDI accommodates export declines in the control countries. In contrast, however, FDI inflows over the preceding five years are associated with higher export ratios. Given the earlier finding that FDI does not increase aggregate domestic investment outside the Pacific Basin, the strong positive effect of lagged FDI inflows on exports may be caused by a change in the composition of investment. In other words, FDI may crowd out, at least in part, domestically financed investment in countries outside the Pacific Basin. Unsurprisingly, the investment financed by FDI seems to be export-oriented.

An inflow of FDI is strongly associated with a higher import ratio. The immediate effect of FDI, therefore, is to finance a larger import bill. However, FDI inflows over the preceding five years are associated with a significant decline in the import ratio outside the Pacific Basin. In these control countries, FDI seems to have been directed not only into export industries but also into import-substitution activities. In all three country groups, higher lagged FDI inflows improve the current account. In the control group, FDI inflows over the preceding five years raise exports and reduce imports.

Finally, I show that FDI raises the rate of economic growth in the absence of financial repression and trade distortions in the 16 sample developing countries taken together. However, financial repression as measured by the real deposit rate of interest and trade distortions as measured by the black market exchange rate premium can both cause FDI to be immiserizing. When the domestic economy is distorted, FDI inflows are associated with a low or negative growth. When real interest rates are positive, however, FDI can accelerate the rate of economic growth more when restrictions on the sectoral location of this investment are relaxed.

The overall conclusion of section 12.5 on FDI is that both the nature and the effects of FDI flows vary significantly between different regions of the developing world. Outside the Pacific Basin, FDI appears to have been used in large part as a substitute for other types of foreign flows; it has not increased aggregate domestic investment. When the control group countries attracted more FDI inflows, national saving, domestic investment, and the rate of economic growth all declined. Hence, FDI appears to have been immiserizing in these countries. In contrast, the role of FDI in the Pacific Basin has been benign. In these economies, FDI financial flows have not been close substitutes for other types of foreign capital flows.

The superior efficiency of FDI in the Pacific Basin economies reflects not only less distorted financial conditions than in other parts of the developing world but also less distorted trading systems. The outward orientation of the Pacific Basin economies ensures that relative prices cannot diverge too far from world market prices. Under these conditions, there are few possibilities for FDI to find high profits in protected markets.

The favorable investment climates in the developing economies of the Pacific Basin have ensured that FDI flows are readily available without the need for governments to discriminate in favor of this particular form of investment finance. Hence, these economies have avoided the two major pitfalls of FDI, namely, low or negative productivity caused by distortions in the economy and expensive discriminatory incentives provided in the mistaken belief that FDI brings externalities.

Recently, Morris Goldstein, Donald Mathieson, and Timothy Lane (1991, 43) have noted the links between macroeconomic policies that promote domestic saving and capital repatriation on the one hand, and a successful experience with FDI on the other hand:

> At a minimum, domestic fiscal, monetary, exchange rate, and financial policies must be designed to create stable domestic economic and financial market conditions, to provide domestic residents with clear incentives to hold their savings in domestic financial claims, and to ensure that available domestic and foreign savings are used to support productive investment. Stable economic conditions are also important for encouraging foreign direct investment.

It comes as no surprise, therefore, to find a strong positive correlation between the ratio of domestically financed investment to GNP and the ratio of FDI to GNP.

Indeed, inflows of foreign direct and portfolio investment provide good indicators of development performance and potential. Policies aimed directly at stimulating these forms of capital inflows appear to be ineffective or to produce the opposite effects to those desired. The evidence suggests overwhelmingly that policies that promote domestic investment and growth are most likely to stimulate private sector capital inflows in all forms. In summarizing findings similar to those of Venkataraman Balasubramanyam (1984),

Jamuna Agarwal, Andrea Gubitz, and Peter Nunnenkamp (1991, 128) conclude:

> The effectiveness of tax and tariff exemptions as well as related privileges for FDI, some of which are very costly for the host countries, is uncertain at best. They may even result in a vicious circle if privileges granted to foreign investors give rise to hostile feelings against FDI in the recipient countries. The consequences may be a new wave of regulations, intensified efforts to circumvent the restrictions, and finally the retreat of foreign investors. It appears more promising to adhere to the rule: "what is good policy for domestic investors is also good for foreign investors", by creating a stable and favourable general framework for investment. Ad hoc interventions should be kept to the minimum. It is not only the rules and regulations that matter, but also how they are applied in practice. The approval procedure should be fast and transparent as it is a crucial element in the investment decision of foreign companies.

The evidence presented in this chapter is certainly consistent with this conclusion.

In a neoclassical world, intertemporal utility maximization ensures that each household plans its consumption expenditures optimally over its life cycle. Saving or dissaving is simply the residual between that optimal consumption stream and the household's income path. Under such ideal conditions, there are no policy issues. In the real world, however, there are at least three major obstacles to this utility-maximizing outcome: (a) financial market imperfections, often aggravated by government, that distort relative factor prices; (b) misguided fiscal policies, particularly with respect to deficit financing; (d) foreign debt buildup, since each developing country faces an upward sloping supply of foreign saving. This means that unrestrained foreign borrowing can result in a country-specific risk premium that is too high from the social welfare viewpoint. Foreign debt buildup can, and often is, accelerated by financial repression and large government budget deficits. Financial repression also reduces the effectiveness of FDI in the process of economic development.

Part III

Microeconomic and Institutional Aspects of Financial Development

Chapter 13

Financial Institutions, Instruments, and Markets

13.1 Introduction

Ｎｅｏｃｌａｓｓｉｃａｌ ｍｏｄｅｌｓ ｈｏｌｄ ｏｎｌｙ when transaction costs are zero. Ronald Coase (1960) points out that in this case institutions are irrelevant. When transaction costs are positive, however, institutions are important. Indeed, Douglass North (1987, 420) argues both that "the costs of transacting are the key to the performance of economies" and that the industrial countries successfully developed the elaborate institutional structures needed for complex and impersonal exchanges to take place at minimum cost. Without this institutional development, economic growth would have been thwarted. Financial systems constitute one such institutional arrangement for minimizing transaction costs.

This chapter examines some microeconomic and institutional aspects of financial systems. The next section presents the basic principles of financial intermediation. Section 13.3 discusses the problem of defining and measuring efficiency in the context of financial sector activities. Section 13.4 outlines the Gurley-Shaw model of financial development and then examines financial development in the industrial countries and recent financial reform and development in developing countries.

Section 13.5 presents the Stiglitz-Weiss credit rationing analysis and then examines Yoon Je Cho's (1986b) argument that financial liberalization along the McKinnon-Shaw lines is insufficient to maximize allocative efficiency of investible funds. Specifically, Cho stresses the need for equity finance to ensure optimal allocation of investible funds in the presence of information costs about borrowers' riskiness. Cho suggests that, in the absence of an equities market, a government could improve allocative efficiency through selective credit policies. Ben Bernanke and Mark Gertler (1990) dispute the case for investment subsidies. Their model indicates that a move towards

293

the socially optimal level and pattern of investment may be achieved through the taxation of successful projects and deterred by investment subsidies, even when investment is suboptimal. Another strategy examined here is deposit insurance.

The final section of this chapter concentrates on the development of financial instruments and markets, as opposed to financial institutions. Although deliberate measures to develop equity markets have rarely succeeded, markets in short-term debt instruments have sprung up spontaneously in a number of developing countries. Hence this chapter ends with a brief survey of markets in short-term financial instruments which have emerged in developing countries.

13.2   Financial Intermediation

Financial intermediaries perform two major economic functions. First, they create money and administer the payments mechanism. Second, they bring together savers and investors, lenders and borrowers. Financial intermediation is the activity of obtaining funds from lenders to pass on to borrowers. What distinguishes financial intermediaries or financial institutions from all other business enterprises is that their assets consist predominantly of financial claims. On the one hand, financial institutions buy direct financial claims, such as treasury bills, mortgages, and commercial notes, from borrowers. On the other hand, they offer their own indirect financial claims to lenders. Banks offer deposits—passbook entries or deposit receipts that represent claims against the bank. Other financial intermediaries offer insurance, pensions, or bonds. In the case of insurance, the claim or liability is contingent on special conditions—for example, death or an accident. For pensions, the condition is reaching retirement age.

To survive, financial intermediaries must compete successfully with other borrowers to attract lenders, depositors, or savers. With funds thus obtained, they must then compete with other lenders to buy direct claims. In one way or another, financial intermediaries must offer indirect claims that are as attractive as or better than direct claims to lenders, while at the same time competing with lenders to buy direct claims. This is achieved through specialization and by reaping economies of scale in financial transactions, information gathering, and portfolio management.

If lenders had to seek out borrowers and borrowers had to search for lenders, the *net* return to lenders could be substantially lower than the *gross* cost to borrowers. Lenders would subtract search costs, together with any risk premium due to the uncertainty about the borrowers' credit worthiness and any illiquidity factor, from the interest payments in calculating the net return on lending; borrowers would add them to find the gross cost of borrowing. A broker might be able to reduce the wedge between gross borrowing and net

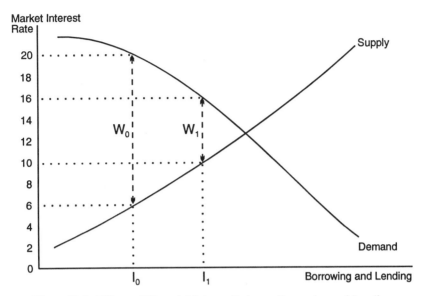

Figure 13.1. Effects of Financial Intermediaries on Borrowing and Lending

lending rates by reducing total search costs. A financial intermediary performs a function similar to that of a broker in reducing search costs through specialization and scale economies. In addition, it may engage in denomination and maturity intermediation to reduce uncertainty for the lender.

Consider the situation in which there are no financial intermediaries. Lending, represented by the supply curve in Figure 13.1, is a function of the net return on savings. The net return is the market interest rate adjusted for risk and illiquidity. For example, from a 12 percent yield on direct claims, lenders might subtract a 2 percent search cost, a 3 percent risk premium, and 1 percent for illiquidity, giving an adjusted yield of 6 percent. Borrowing, represented by the demand schedule in Figure 13.1, is a function of the gross cost of borrowing. Borrowers, for example, might add an 8 percent transaction cost of selling their direct claims to the 12 percent interest cost. In this way, a wedge of 14 percentage points is created between the gross cost of borrowing and the net return on lending. Figure 13.1 shows that the volume of lending and borrowing under these circumstances is I_0.

Financial institutions can reduce this wedge between the gross cost of borrowing and the net return on lending. By providing information as well as denomination and maturity intermediation, financial intermediaries might cut lenders' search cost, risk, and illiquidity premia from a total of 6 to 1 percent. Borrowers' transaction costs could be reduced from 8 to 2 percent. To cover their own costs, financial intermediaries might offer loans at 14 percent and deposits at 11 percent. The wedge between the gross borrowing cost and the net return on lending would thereby be reduced from 14 to 6 percentage points. In this example, borrowing increases as a result of the reduction in the gross cost from 20 to 16 percent. Lending also rises because of the increase in the net return from 6 to 10 percent. Figure 13.1 shows that the volume of borrowing and lending moves from I_0 to I_1.

Higher net returns to lending and lower gross costs of borrowing not only increase lending and borrowing but also raise saving and investment. Figure 13.1 can be reinterpreted as a saving-investing diagram in which saving rises with an increase in the net real return on lending; investing increases with a decline in the gross real cost of borrowing. The more efficiently the financial sector carries out its intermediation role, therefore, the greater the volume of investment will be. More efficient financial intermediation may also increase the average productivity of investment, as suggested by the empirical evidence in Chapter 8. If the market rate of interest in Figure 13.1 is set below its equilibrium level, lending and saving decline. So too, of course, does investment.

Oren Sussman (1993) develops a model in which the reduction in bank operating cost ratios constitutes the essence of financial development. A spatial model permits banks to exploit a certain degree of monopoly power in their districts. As the country develops and its capital stock increases, the market for financial intermediation grows. The number of banks increases and each bank becomes more specialized and efficient over a smaller market share, which implies a smaller geographical area in this spatial model. As the market becomes more competitive and banks become more efficient, the costs of financial intermediation fall.

13.3 Functional Efficiency

James Tobin (1984, 2–3) indicates that there are at least four separate concepts of efficiency by which the financial system can be measured: information arbitrage, fundamental valuation, full insurance, and functional efficiency. Information arbitrage efficiency measures the extent to which it is possible to gain on average from trading on the basis of generally available information. Complete information arbitrage efficiency implies that it is not possible to gain from such trading. Fundamental valuation efficiency measures the degree to which market values of financial assets reflect accurately the present value of the stream of future payments associated with holding that asset. Full insurance efficiency measures the degree to which the financial system offers ways of hedging (insuring) against all possible future contingencies (states of the world). Hugh Patrick (1990, 35) measures financial system efficiency on the basis of three criteria: monetary policy, allocative, and transaction cost efficiency.

Functional efficiency relates to the two main economic functions of the financial sector, administering the payments mechanism and intermediating between savers and investors. It involves risk pooling, resource allocation, general insurance, administering the payments mechanism, and mobilizing saving for investment. As Tobin (1984, 11) points out, "very little of the work done by the securities industry, as gauged by the volume of market activity, has to do with the financing of real investment in any very direct way" in the United States.

Functional efficiency is the focus of this part of the book. Specific pointers for assessing functional efficiency include the soundness of appraisals, perhaps measured by the level of arrears; the resource cost of specific operations; the quality and speed of delivery of services; and the amount of red tape involved, particularly in routine financial transactions such as making a deposit. In examining the practical problems of measuring commercial bank efficiency, Dimitri Vittas (1991b, 48) concludes that "ratios cannot substitute for detailed knowledge and understanding of local conditions and practices."

As already pointed out, financial intermediaries perform two major economic functions in almost all economies. First, they create money and administer the payments mechanism. In most economies today, a central bank or monetary authority issues currency and depository institutions supply deposit money. Financial intermediaries administer a country's payments mechanism by providing currency notes of desired denominations when and where they are wanted and by transferring deposits upon instructions, as for example in the form of a check.

Money's primary function is to act as a medium of exchange. It also serves as a unit of account, a store of value, and a standard of deferred or future payment. Money emerged when and only when its use could reduce transaction costs by more than its cost of adoption. The benefits of money over barter transactions are well known. Less obvious perhaps is that different monies perform their functions more or less efficiently.

Transaction costs are reduced most by a money whose value remains stable over time and which provides an efficient payments mechanism. Inflation erodes several of money's attributes. And money is a less efficient means of payment than it could be if, for example, there is insufficient small change, if notes are so worn out that they disintegrate easily, if counterfeit notes abound, or if deposits cannot be transferred accurately and speedily from one party to another. Even some of the richer developing countries, such as Turkey, do not possess national check-clearing facilities. There, deposit transfer from one part of the country to another is an expensive, slow, and somewhat unreliable procedure. A financial system does not administer its country's payments mechanism efficiently if it has failed to develop a cheap, quick, and safe method for interregional payments. The same point also applies to international payments.

Supplying money and administering the payments mechanism is not costless. Efficiency must therefore be measured in terms of the benefit/cost ratio. The resource cost of a commodity or full-bodied money equals the total value of the money supply. The costs of producing and maintaining fiat paper money rarely exceed 5 percent annually of the value of the notes outstanding. In the main, these comprise the costs of replacing worn-out notes, adding additional notes, and preventing forgery. The costs of supplying and maintaining deposit money are generally far lower.

The resource costs of administering the payments mechanism include the value of resources used up in the process of providing currency of the desired denominations when and where it is wanted and effecting deposit transfers. In running the national check-clearing system in the United States, the Federal Reserve System incurs resource costs greater than the GNPs of several small developing countries. Legal and regulatory constraints in the United States have impeded the introduction of a nationwide electronic funds transfer system, such as the giro used in most European countries, a much more efficient method for transferring deposits than clearing checks.

For various reasons, a country may not possess the most efficient money and payments system, as measured by the highest attainable benefit/cost ratio. The government may be using money issue as a stopgap, inefficient source of revenue. There may be legal or regulatory constraints preventing the adoption of technological innovations such as electronic funds transfer. A country may choose to produce its currency notes domestically for national security reasons, despite lower costs of obtaining notes printed abroad. Similarly, foreign banks may be excluded in favor of domestic enterprises, despite the fact that multinational banks would bring in technical know-how at very low marginal cost, stimulate competition, and facilitate the inflow of foreign capital (Grubel 1977, 357–358). Infant industry, dependency, or nationalistic arguments are often used to justify the deliberate choice of less than maximum economic efficiency.

Inefficiency, however, may be and often is unintentional. For example, when the deposit industry is not behaving competitively, perhaps as the result of economies of scale, the supply and maintenance of deposit money are never as efficient as they could be. In a very small economy, the banking industry may simply be a natural monopoly. More typically, uncompetitive behavior is caused by government regulation.

Two major determinants of functional efficiency are market structure and the regulatory framework under which the financial sector operates. In this context, market structure consists of the degree of competition, concentration, and interlocking control between financial institutions and business enterprises, as well as the degree of specialization within the financial sector. It is influenced by the internal organization and management of the financial intermediaries. These, in turn, are affected by the degree of government ownership and control. The regulatory framework includes regulations imposed both for monetary policy as well as prudential purposes. It also includes the legal environment, the adequacy of commercial law, and the efficiency with which the judicial system makes and enforces legal decisions. There is clearly interdependence between market structure and government intervention. Rondo Cameron (1972, 9) suggests that the two major determinants of banking structure are the demand for financial services and government policy. Chapter 14 is devoted to the structure of financial markets in developing countries, while government intervention in the financial sector is covered in Chapter 15. The next section of this chapter examines financial sector development in theory and practice.

13.4 Financial Sector Development

Functional efficiency is determined in part by financial conditions and the stage of financial development in the country under consideration. The stage of financial development can refer to the evolution of a financial system, to its structural form, to its mode of operations, or to the types of financial claims it offers (Khatkhate and Riechel 1980, 478). Financial conditions include accessibility of branches, variety of products, information collection and dissemination by financial institutions, risk taking, yield and liquidity of indirect claims, as well as population per bank branch and the real deposit rate of interest.

John Gurley and Edward Shaw (1960) provide the following analytical description of the process of financial development. In the first stage, outside money, commodity money, or money backed entirely by government debt appears. Such rudimentary finance constrains the process of economic development: "With no financial asset other than money, there are restraints on saving, on capital accumulation, and on efficient allocation of saving to investment that depress the rate of growth in output and income" (Gurley and Shaw 1960, 13).

In the second stage, direct claims and inside money—money backed by private debt—are introduced. Although direct claims such as bonds and equities were used first as the major source of industrial finance in both England during the industrial revolution and in the United States, indirect claims—liabilities issued by financial institutions, especially deposit liabilities —were the predominant source of investible funds in both continental Europe and the developing countries.

The third stage involves the proliferation of different financial claims issued by different financial and nonfinancial institutions. Both borrowers and lenders find advantages in differentiation and diversification:

> Development of financial techniques creates alternatives to face-to-face loans that increase, for borrowers or lenders or both, the gains from trade in loanable funds.

> There are two principal types of financial techniques. Distributive techniques [information collection and dissemination, including brokerage services] increase the efficiency of markets on which ultimate borrowers sell and ultimate lenders buy primary securities. Intermediary techniques bring financial institutions into the bidding for primary securities in the portfolios of ultimate lenders. Both techniques play a major role in determining the structure of primary securities. (Gurley and Shaw 1960, 123)

The development of modern financial systems in the industrial countries took place in an environment vastly different from that in which developing countries' financial systems have developed. Before the Great Depression, 1929–1933, governments intervened neither in the macroeconomic management of the economy nor in special regulation of the financial sector. As a result, a wide variety of both specialized and general-purpose financial institutions emerged (United Nations 1984, 90). A distinct trend towards universal, general-purpose, or multipurpose banking was stopped by the regulations introduced everywhere in the early 1930s. That trend, however, reemerged again in the 1970s as some of the excess regulatory constraints of the 1930s began to be removed.

The industrial countries exhibited two distinct patterns of financial development. The Anglo-Saxon countries developed commercial banks that supplied short-term finance for trade. Two important principles were self-liquidating paper and arms-length relations with business enterprises. In contrast, the universal or multipurpose banks that developed in eighteenth-century Germany supplied both short- and long-term finance and had close associations with their borrowers (United Nations 1984, 90).

Joseph Schumpeter (1912, 1939) regards banking and entrepreneurship as the two key agents in the process of economic development. Alexander Gerschenkron (1962, 1968) is more specific. He suggests that the more backward the country, the greater the need for banking to supply both capital and entrepreneurship (Cameron 1972, 10–11). Gerschenkron believes that the banking system played a key role at certain stages in the European industrialization process. In Germany, the banking system was the primary source of both capital and entrepreneurship:

> The inadequacy in the number of available entrepreneurs could be remedied or substituted for by increasing the size of plant and enterprise above what otherwise would have been an optimal size. In Germany, the various incompetencies of the individual entrepreneurs were offset by the device of splitting the entrepreneurial function: the German investment banks—a powerful invention, comparable in economic effect to that of the steam engine—were in their capital-supplying functions a substitute for the insufficiency of the previously created wealth willingly placed at the disposal of the entrepreneurs. But they were also a substitute for entrepreneurial deficiencies. From their central vantage points of control,

the banks participated actively in shaping the major—and sometimes even not so major—decisions of individual enterprises. It was they who very often mapped out a firm's paths of growth, conceived far-sighted plans, decided on major technological and locational innovations, and arranged for mergers and capital increases. (Gerschenkron 1968, 137)

Cameron (1972, 20–21) points out that where banks are established by and for industrialists they are more responsive to business demands for medium- and long-term funds. Historical examples include eighteenth-century England, nineteenth-century Russia, and twentieth-century Japan.

The Gerschenkron hypothesis received considerable academic attention in the late 1960s and early 1970s. It was taken up again in 1980 by Deena Khatkhate and Klaus-Walter Riechel (1980) and Patrick (1984) in the form of advocacy for universal or multipurpose banking in developing countries. The first wave of World Bank reports on the financial sectors of developing countries, written in the late 1970s and early 1980s, tended to concentrate on macroeconomic and sectoral issues. At the institutional level, however, the reports favored deregulation and often advocated the adoption of universal banking. For example, a report prepared jointly by the IMF and the World Bank recommends universal banking for the Philippines (World Bank 1980).

More recently, policy advisors have asserted that financial institutions under the control of industrial conglomerates worsen resource allocation. The apparent conflict with the historical experience of Europe lies in the fact that conglomeration in the developing countries is often strongly motivated by the desire to avoid interest rate ceilings and other regulations on lending, such as credit ceilings. In Turkey, for example, volatile financial conditions of the 1970s made it virtually imperative for large industrial groups to obtain their own banks in order to secure minimal credit facilities. Obviously, small businesses without the resources to acquire banks found it increasingly difficult to obtain institutional credit as the large organizations took over the banks for their own purposes.

An important parallel between nineteenth-century Europe and many postwar developing countries lies in the banks' involvement in government finance. Nineteenth-century Austrian banks focused their attentions on financing the government's perennial deficits. The same happened in Italy, Serbia, and Spain. In Serbia, "the privileged position of the government in the capital market, and its penchant for unproductive expenditures—just as that of Austria, Italy, and Spain—made it difficult for the banking system to contribute to industrial development" (Cameron 1972, 21). Banks in Austria, Italy, and Spain took the easy path of lending to finance large government deficits. These examples from nineteenth-century Europe bear more than a passing resemblance to many developing countries today. Government policy and government finance had as large an impact in molding the structure of financial systems in nineteenth-century Europe as they had in the postwar period in developing countries.

Japan's financial development provides a number of interesting lessons. The initial creation and spread of modern financial institutions throughout Japan took place between 1868 and 1910 in an environment characterized by easy entry, no interest rate controls, and general government encouragement. Macroeconomic policy was conducive to rapid financial development because inflation was kept under control.

From 1910 to 1936, Japan's financial system grew and diversified in a relatively free-market environment. Nevertheless, government policy had considerable influence over the structure of the financial system through entry requirements, type of charter (generally for unit banks or specialized financial institutions only), degree of competition, interest rate regulations, and the establishment of government institutions (Patrick 1984, 307). In particular, the government sponsored institutions to finance foreign trade, housing, and agriculture, and for long-term industrial finance. During these two phases from 1868 to 1936, there was considerable financial dualism, with large interest rate differentials between the traditional and modern financial institutions. Gradually, however, the efficiency of the modern financial institutions overpowered the traditional financial sector, and by the start of the postwar period the latter was insignificant (Patrick 1984, 306).

The government abandoned its competitive, market-oriented philosophy in 1937 and proceeded to engage in highly inflationary deficit finance throughout World War II. The number of banks was reduced dramatically from 377 in 1937 to 61 in 1945. Japan emerged from the war with a highly concentrated banking system vastly reduced in real size, substantial direct credit allocation by the government, and a low controlled interest rate policy (Patrick 1984, 316). Financial growth was slow in relation to economic growth due to low real yields on financial assets throughout the postwar period. One important effect of the postwar system was the severe discrimination against small savers and investors. Some degree of financial liberalization has occurred in the 1980s.

Four differences should be borne in mind when comparing the financial systems of most developing countries with industrialized countries' financial systems. First, financial markets are oligopolistic in most developing countries, whereas they are competitive in most industrialized countries, particularly so in the United States.[1] Second, although detailed regulations concerning financial transactions exist in all countries, they are generally enforced much more consistently and effectively in the developed than in the developing countries. The same regulations on paper may be quite different in practice. Third, disintermediation in the developed economies implies substitution from indirect to direct financial claims. In most developing countries, it implies

---

[1] Even in the United States, however, unit banking restrictions in many states and some prohibition against interstate banking reduce the competitiveness of the banking system, at least for consumers and small businesses (Fry and Williams 1984, ch. 7).

substitution from deposits into tangible assets used as inflation hedges. Hence national saving ratios may be unaffected by deposit rate ceilings in industrialized countries but be affected by them in developing countries. Finally, the driving force behind the recent wave of financial innovations and reforms in the industrialized countries may well have been market forces in the face of the worldwide inflationary surge of the 1970s, whereas the ideas of Ronald McKinnon (1973) and Shaw (1973) have had substantial impact in developing countries, perhaps most obviously in the policy recommendations of the IMF and the World Bank.

Compared with changes that have taken place in the financial sectors of most industrialized countries over the past decade, those that have taken place in many developing countries have been minor and hardly constitute reform. In several cases, including Korea, Philippines, and Thailand, financial repression has been reinstated after short-lived attempts at financial liberalization. As a case in point, a number of changes have occurred in the Philippines but, due largely to increasing concentration within the financial system, most observers feel: "Plus ça change, plus c'est la même chose." For example, the interest rate ceilings that were abolished under the interest rate reform appear to have been replaced by a cartel agreement linked to the Manila Reference Rate, which is supposed to be determined competitively in the free market. It is not. Removal of many balance sheet restrictions has produced increased concentration in the Philippine financial system rather than the intended increased competition.

Postwar financial development in developing countries differs in several important respects from financial development in the industrialized countries. First, the pace has been forced in developing countries, with government intervention occurring with increasing frequency. There has been a strong tendency towards increased government ownership of financial institutions in developing countries over the past two decades. Second, concentration is far higher in the banking industry in developing countries now than it was in the industrial countries prior to World War I. For the five member countries of the Association of South East Asian Nations (ASEAN), George Viksnins (1980, Table 6, 23) shows banking concentration in terms of deposits for 1977:

Country	Percentage of Largest Bank	Percentage of Four Largest Banks	Percentage of Ten Largest Banks
Indonesia	26.8	73.1	86.7
Malaysia	19.9	50.3	56.7
Philippines	22.9	39.8	63.7
Singapore	7.7	20.6	27.0
Thailand	33.3	64.6	88.5

Morocco provides a typical example of the lack of competition within financial sectors of developing countries. The Moroccan financial sector is highly concentrated. There is little competition within Morocco's financial sector, due not only to high concentration but also to fixed interest rates and commissions, the need for a license to open any new branch, the selective credit policy that extracts over half the funds raised from deposits for government-directed lending, and the imposition of uniform credit ceilings on each bank. Monetary control through the imposition of credit ceilings throttles competition for deposits.[2] The lack of competition within the Moroccan financial sector is blamed in part for the excessive spreads between average deposit and loan rates, fragmentation of the credit market, poor resource allocation, and the lack of initiative in mobilizing private financial savings.

Morocco's specialized financial institutions do not compete with one another or with the commercial banks because each has its own specialized sector to finance. The same is true of Indonesia, where the financial system is dominated by five state-owned commercial banks and each state bank is responsible for a particular sector (Baliño and Sundararajan 1986, 192–194).

A very similar situation to Morocco's can be found in Thailand. The segmented approach to financial intermediation, combined with highly restrictive entry conditions and interest rate ceilings, has also constrained competition there. Commentators blame this uncompetitive environment for the operational and allocative inefficiencies that emanate from the Thai financial sector.

The same broad picture emerges from examining Brazil's financial system. In Brazil, state financial institutions play a major role, private financial institutions are becoming increasingly absorbed by business conglomerates, financial markets are seriously segmented, and there is a substantial degree of financial layering.[3] Between 1970 and 1976 the number of banks fell from 144 to 69. The typical financial conglomerate includes a commercial bank, an investment bank, and a finance company, as well as insurance and foreign trade companies. They are often connected to industrial conglomerates. This has led to conflicts of interest, undermined competition, and worsened resource allocation. Banks are also linked to industrial groups in Colombia, Turkey, and many other developing countries.

13.5 Allocative Efficiency of Financial Intermediation

When a borrower approaches a lender for a loan, the lender is at an informational disadvantage. The borrower may have spent years working on a

---

[2]Recognizing this, Indonesia abolished its system of monetary control through credit ceilings in June 1983 in order to improve efficiency.

[3]See section 14.4.

project which now requires financing. The lender knows little or nothing either about the project or the borrower. This asymmetric information creates two problems, one before the loan is agreed, the other after the loan has been extended. A response to both problems on the part of the lender is to ration credit. In other words, banks do not necessarily continue to raise their loan rates until supply equals demand. Their profit-maximizing strategy may be to keep their loan rates below that level and to provide borrowers with less than they demand or to turn away some borrowers with no loans at all. This behavior, which has been analyzed by, among others, Udo Broll and Michael Gilroy (1986), Dwight Jaffee and Thomas Russell (1976), Janusz Ordover and Andrew Weiss (1981), Joseph Stiglitz and Weiss (1981, 1983), and Stephen Williamson (1986), is called equilibrium credit rationing.

Adverse selection is the problem that occurs before the loan is negotiated. Lenders want to lend to borrowers with high probabilities of repaying the loans. However, those who are most anxious to borrow usually have riskier projects than the others. Since they have a higher probability of default, banks would prefer not to lend to them. Raising loan rates tends to discourage the type of borrower lenders like, risk-averse borrowers with relatively safe projects. Hence, raising loan rates can cause adverse selection by leaving a smaller pool of borrowers with a higher proportion of riskier borrowers.

An example may help to elucidate this effect. Suppose that two equal-sized groups of risk-neutral investors, *A* and *B*, face two separate types of investment opportunities, *X* and *Y*, each costing $100. Investments in type *X* yield $150 with a probability of 0.8, and zero with a probability of 0.2; the expected return on this investment is 20 percent. Type *Y* investments yield $125 with a probability of 0.96, and zero with a probability of 0.04; these investments also yield an expected return of 20 percent.

All potential investors must borrow 80 percent of their investment costs and cannot provide any collateral apart from the projects themselves. Now suppose that banks charge a loan rate of 15 percent. If *X* investments succeed, group *A* investors repay $80 plus $12 interest to the banks. They make $38 or 190 percent from their equity investment of $20. If *X* investments fail, neither banks nor investors receive anything. Hence the expected return on the equity of group *A* in type *X* investments is $26.40 or 132 percent (190 percent with a probability of 0.8 and –100 percent with a probability of 0.2). Similarly, the expected return on the equity of group *B* in type *Y* investments is $11.68 or 58.4 percent (65 percent with a probability of 0.96 and –100 percent with a probability of 0.04).

Since group *A* investors have higher expected returns to their equity than group *B* investors, despite the fact that *X* and *Y* investments yield exactly the same expected returns, the difference must be explained by different expected returns to the banks. Clearly, lending to group *A* borrowers subjects banks to a much higher default risk than does lending to group *B* borrowers. However, if banks cannot discriminate between groups *A* and *B*, they would lend half their funds to group A and the other half to group B investors all at the same interest rate. In this example, the banks' expected net return on their loan portfolios is 1.2 percent: $100 \cdot [(\$80 \cdot 0.8 \cdot 1.15 + \$80 \cdot 0.96 \cdot 1.15)/\$160) - 1]$.

Banks can increase their net returns by raising their loan rate, but only up to the point at which group B borrowers choose not to borrow and hence decide not to undertake type Y investments at all. Suppose that group B investors can obtain a yield of 3 percent on government bonds if they do not invest in type Y investments. Then they would choose not to borrow at a loan rate exceeding 19.28 percent. At a 19 percent loan rate, banks would make a net return of 4.72 percent on their loan portfolios. At a 20 percent loan rate, however, only group A borrowers would want to borrow and banks would make a net return of −4 percent because of the higher expected default rate. Hence, even if there is excess demand for loans at 19 percent, banks would maximize their net returns by rationing rather than by raising their loan rates. The banks want to include group B investors in their portfolios because of their lower default risk; this provides the incentive for credit rationing.

This adverse selection problem has implications for economic efficiency. The numerical example above could be adjusted so that group A investors faced type X investment opportunities with expected yields lower than those on the type X investments available to group B investors. Nevertheless, returns to equity could easily be higher for group A than for group B investors. Indeed, for this reason, investors with riskier but less productive investments could seek loans at higher interest rates when investors with less risky but more productive investments dropped out of the loan market altogether.

The efficiency problem arises because the interests of the investor cannot be made to coincide with those of the lender when information about riskiness is costly. When the project succeeds, the investor receives the profit while the lender simply gets paid the interest charge. When the project fails, the lender shares the loss with the investor. Under these conditions of asymmetric information, expected profit to the investor rises and expected return to the bank falls as the riskiness of the project increases, even though the project's own expected return remains constant.

Moral hazard is the problem that occurs after the loan has been extended. The basic idea of moral hazard is that individuals do not have the same incentive to look after other people's property as carefully as they look after their own. The term originated in the insurance literature to describe the reduced diligence people take in caring for their own property after it has been insured. In the case of borrowing, borrowers have less incentive to look after borrowed money than they have to look after their own money. The reason for this lies in bankruptcy provisions: the worst outcome for defaulting borrowers is the loss of their equity. They are not thrown in jail, nor do they have to spend the rest of their lives paying off their delinquent debts.

Given that investors can walk away from a failed project and start again on something else, higher loan rates can actually encourage investors to select projects that are riskier than those they would choose were they investing only their own equity funds in them. In other words, they have a decreasing incentive to look after borrowed money carefully and a greater incentive to succumb to the moral hazard of failing to look after it carefully as the cost of borrowed money rises.

For example, suppose again that investors face the choice between two types of investment opportunities, X and Y, each costing $100. In this case investments in type X yield $150 with a probability of 0.8, and zero with a probability of 0.2; the expected return on this investment is 20 percent as before. Type Y investments yield $140.33 with a probability of 0.96, and zero with a probability of 0.04; these investments now yield an expected return of 34.72 percent.

Again all potential investors must borrow 80 percent of their investment costs and cannot provide any collateral apart from the projects themselves and banks charge a loan rate of 15 percent. In this case, expected returns to equity equal 132 percent for both types of investment. Hence, investors would be indifferent between the high- and low-risk investments. Avoiding the moral hazard is costless, so one might assume that investors choose type Y investments with lower risk and higher social returns than type X investments.

The moral dilemma occurs as soon as the interest rate rises above 15 percent. At an interest rate of 20 percent, for example, expected returns to equity in type X investments are 116 percent, while expected returns to equity in type Y investments are only 112.8 percent. The higher interest rate provides an incentive to switch from less risky investments with higher social returns to riskier investments with lower social returns. In contrast, at an interest rate of 10 percent type Y investments yield the higher expected return to equity of 151.2 percent, while type X investments yield an expected return to equity of only 148 percent.

Stiglitz and Weiss (1981) draw on the adverse selection theory developed for labor market analysis to produce a considerably more elegant model of voluntary credit rationing by banks than the one sketched above. However, the basic conclusion is the same: credit rationing is an equilibrium outcome of the unfettered rational behavior of lenders when information costs are significant. Even if there is excess demand for loans at a certain level of interest rates, a lender may find it more profitable to ration credit than to raise the interest rate. In this case, the expected returns of the excluded groups' investments may be higher than the expected returns of the investments of the groups that obtain the loans. Capital is misallocated under such circumstances.

One response to the moral hazard problem is to raise the percentage equity contribution required. It is again easy to construct examples of investments with differing risk-return attributes whose expected returns to equity can be reversed as the equity component is raised. A higher net worth or equity contribution makes the debt contract increasingly incentive compatible by aligning the incentives of the borrower more closely with the interests of the lender. If the lender contributes only a tiny fraction of the investment funds, investors act as if the project were entirely equity financed. Hence, they look after the lender's funds just as carefully as they look after their own. This idea can be extended to collateral requirements (Broll and Gilroy 1986, 365). However, Stiglitz and Weiss (1986) argue that those possessing collateral may constitute lucky risk-taking individuals banks would prefer to avoid.

Bernanke and Gertler (1990) examine the relationship between financial fragility and economic performance. They start with the proposition that "generally, the less of his own wealth a borrower can contribute to the funding of his investment 'project,' the more his interests will diverge from those of the people who have lent to him" (Bernanke and Gertler 1990, 88). They continue by defining financial fragility and its effects on investment:

> We define a *financially fragile* situation to be one in which potential borrowers (those with greatest access to productive investment projects, or with the greatest entrepreneurial skills) have low wealth relative to the sizes of their projects. Such a situation (which might occur, e.g., in the early stages of economic development, in a prolonged recession, or subsequent to a "debt-deflation") leads to high agency costs and thus to poor performance in the investment sector and the economy overall. (Bernanke and Gertler 1990, 88)

Their general point is that higher gearing or leverage procured by businesses to finance investment projects increases the principal-agent problem. In the context of financial development, Cho (1986b) points out that efficient equity markets are as critically important as efficient bank lending to counter adverse selection problems of the kind analyzed by Stiglitz and Weiss (1981).

Adopting the Stiglitz-Weiss analysis, Cho (1986b) argues that financial liberalization emphasizing the abolition of interest rate ceilings and the promotion of freer competition among financial intermediaries overlooks endogenous constraints to efficient credit allocation. Specifically, he suggests that the absence of a well-functioning equities market can prevent the efficient allocation of capital even if the banking system has been liberalized along the lines prescribed by McKinnon (1973) and Shaw (1973).

Suppose that banks could distinguish between different groups of borrowers but not among borrowers within each group. Because banks have imperfect information, they must charge a uniform loan rate to seemingly identical borrowers. At this interest rate, investors choose whether or not to borrow. Among those who decide to borrow, expected profits are higher for those with riskier projects, even though all projects in this group have the same expected yield. Banks unable to discriminate within the group receive a lower return relative to the projects' return when the deviation among borrowers within a group is greater. The gap between the banks' return and the average expected return of the group's project widens as the bank has poorer

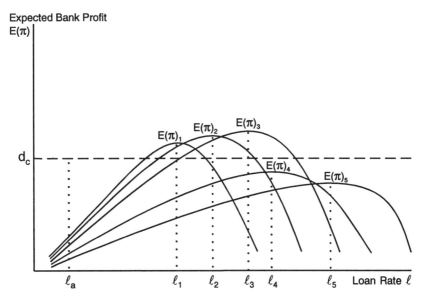

Figure 13.2. Expected Return to Bank Lending as a Function of Loan Rates to Groups of Borrowers

information or screening ability for a particular group. Hence the banks' return from one group can be lower than from another, even if the former faces higher-yielding investment opportunities.

This is illustrated in Figure 13.2, in which the expected return to a bank $E(\pi)_i$ from each group of borrowers i is a function of the uniform loan rate ℓ_i charged to that particular group. Assuming a competitive banking system with no administrative costs, the rate of return from lending is also the deposit rate of interest. Hence the vertical axis represents both the rate of return from lending and the deposit rate of interest. The loan rate lies on the horizontal axis. Higher-numbered groups face higher-yielding investments. The first important point illustrated in Figure 13.2 is that the ranking by investment yield is not identical to the ranking by expected return to the bank.

Now consider allocative efficiency of credit with and without an interest rate ceiling. Suppose that the government has set an administered loan rate at ℓ_a. The bank will prefer group 1 over group 2, group 2 over group 3, and so on. This ranking is completely inefficient, since the productivities of the investments of each group increase with group number. When the ceiling is eliminated, the bank's preference ranking is group 3, group 2, group 1, group 4, group 5. This improves the allocation of credit, but it is clearly still suboptimal. If the competitive deposit rate lies at d_c, groups 1, 2, and 3 will be able to borrow. Groups 4 and 5 will be rationed out, despite the fact that they have the highest-yielding investment projects.

The implication of all this is that abolishing interest rate ceilings on financial intermediation is not alone sufficient to achieve optimal allocation of investible funds when there is imperfect information. Banks would rationally avoid lending to finance new, innovative, and productive investments because of their greater heterogeneity. However, investors might well be able to raise funds in a well-functioning equities market since there are high expected returns on the investments. Cho (1986b) points out that equity finance need not suffer from the adverse selection bias or the moral-hazard problem of debt finance.

Bernanke and Gertler (1990, 111) point out that the key determinant of agency costs is the "insiders' stake," by which they mean "the amount of wealth that insiders (managers, directors, activist shareholders, and others with inside knowledge about the firm) have at risk in the firm." Hence, leverage may be higher without causing financial fragility in systems where banks take equity stakes and participate in the management of their borrowers.

Bernanke (1981, 1983) and Bernanke and Gertler (1989, 1990) argue that bank loans are special because banks provide unique information-gathering services. Costly information about borrowers makes the market for bank loans a customer market. Information asymmetries between borrowers and lenders produce a principal-agent problem. The greater the leverage of the borrower, the less are his interests coincident with the lenders, as shown in the numerical example above. This implies that agency costs (deadweight losses) or the costs of credit intermediation (CCI) rise as leverage increases.

Bernanke and Gertler (1990) show that the positive relationship between leverage and agency costs results in a suboptimal level of investment. The more equity, and hence the lower the leverage ratio in the project, the less the interests of the borrower diverge from the interests of the lender. When the borrower has better information about the project than the lender does, this greater compatibility of interests reduces the agency costs of the investment process and hence raises the level of investment towards its socially optimal level.

In the absence of an equities market, and hence where leverage is typically excessive, a government might be tempted to intervene in an attempt to improve credit allocation. Selective subsidies and taxes could be employed to persuade banks to lend to borrowers with higher-yielding investment projects. In practice, however, governments invariably have less rather than more information than the market about potentially high-yielding investments. Furthermore, selective credit policies have a tendency to be used primarily for political rather than economic ends. Bernanke and Gertler (1990) show that a move towards the socially optimal investment level may be achieved through taxing successful projects. This improves the average quality of investments and hence lowers agency costs. However, investment subsidies are counterproductive, even when the level of investment is suboptimal. Another alternative is to permit banks to take equity positions in business enterprises, as do universal banks (Khatkhate and Riechel 1980).

Yet another possibility is deposit insurance. With perfect information about borrower characteristics, deposit insurance not charged on an actuarial basis can produce inefficient resource allocation due to the conflicting interests of depositors and bank shareholders. The standard deposit insurance scheme is uniform across banks and does not involve higher premiums for banks holding riskier portfolios.

The following numerical example illustrates the effect of deposit insurance. Portfolio X yields 20 percent with a probability of 0.95, and −100 with a probability of 0.05. Portfolio Y yields 42.5 percent with a probability of 0.8, and −100 percent with a probability of 0.2. Both portfolios have an expected return of 14 percent. Suppose a bank has equity capital equal to 10 percent of its loan portfolio (its only assets). Leverage in this case is 10:1. Suppose that the deposit rate of interest (the gross cost of borrowed funds) is 10 percent. If portfolio X is held, the return on bank owners' equity would be 110 percent with a probability of 0.95, and −100 percent with a probability of 0.05. If a $100 portfolio yields 20 percent, it earns $20, from which $9 goes to pay deposit interest. The $10 equity earns $11, or 110 percent. If the loans default (−100 percent return), equity is wiped out. However, −100 percent is the worst that can happen to equity investment in a limited-liability joint stock company. Hence, the expected return on equity for portfolio X is 99.5 percent: 100[0.95($11) + 0.05(−$10)]/$10.

The same calculation can be performed for portfolio Y. The return on equity is 335 percent with a probability of 0.8, and −100 percent with a probability of 0.2. In this case, therefore, the expected return on equity is 248 percent. Clearly, risk-neutral shareholders would prefer portfolio Y to portfolio X. However, portfolio Y is considerably riskier than portfolio X.

In the absence of deposit insurance, depositors would deposit their money in bank A holding portfolio X rather than in bank B holding portfolio Y. For the same 10 percent interest, the risk of deposit loss is 5 percent with bank A but 20 percent with bank B. Uninsured depositors would require a deposit rate of at least 30.6 percent from bank B to offset the higher probability of deposit loss. This higher cost of borrowed funds would reduce the expected return on bank B's equity to 99.5 percent, exactly equal to the expected return on bank A's equity. In other words, without deposit insurance, there is no incentive for a bank to hold a higher-risk loan portfolio if the expected return on that portfolio is the same as the expected return on a lower-risk portfolio.

All this changes with deposit insurance. Depositors are no longer at risk and so are indifferent about holding their money in bank A or bank B, provided both banks offer the same deposit rate and other services. In this case, shareholders are no longer indifferent regarding loan portfolios X and Y. Loan portfolio Y provides a higher expected return to equity than does portfolio X, despite the fact that both portfolios yield the same expected return.

Under competitive private insurance arrangements, however, banks choosing riskier loan portfolios would be assessed higher deposit insurance premiums. Even with a uniform deposit rate, the incentive to choose the riskier loan portfolio with the same expected yield would be offset exactly by the higher deposit insurance premium.

The typical government-sponsored deposit insurance scheme encourages more risk taking than is efficient when probability distributions of the returns on alternative portfolios are known. Shareholders would prefer a riskier loan portfolio even if its expected return were slightly lower than the expected return of a less risky portfolio. However, when banks have imperfect information about borrowers, encouraging risk can *improve* credit allocation, as argued above. So could loan guarantee arrangements supported by central banks or governments (Anderson and Khambata 1985, 366). In practice, however, such schemes have been rather unsuccessful, for reasons explored in section 15.4. Furthermore, the costs of subsidized loan guarantees will be financed through some form of distortionary taxation that could negate any advantage derived from the risk encouragement so financed.

Excessive reliance on debt finance makes business firms vulnerable to exogenous shocks and economic fluctuations. Defaults and bankruptcies resulting from such fragility can be inefficient. Here again the government may be tempted to intervene in an attempt to create a more stable environment. Experience, however, suggests that government intervention more often than not increases rather than reduces uncertainty (Nickell 1977).

McKinnon (1984, 1988, 1991), Frank Veneroso (1986), and Arvind Virmani (1982, 1984, 1985) have also adopted the Stiglitz-Weiss model of credit rationing. McKinnon uses it to explain the disastrous results of financial liberalization programs in Argentina, Chile, and Uruguay. Specifically, McKinnon (1986a, 24–28) argues that, under conditions of macroeconomic instability (characterized by strong positive covariance in default rates of bank borrowers), expectations of government bailouts when outcomes are unfavorable create a moral-hazard problem in bank lending. If the expected government assistance takes the form of both deposit *and* equity insurance, bankers will have an incentive to raise interest rates and to take greater consequent risks than they would under stable macroeconomic conditions.

There has, however, been virtually no discussion of the second-best dilemma that arises when controls in some areas (over interest rates) are dismantled but controls in other areas (asset portfolio limitations) are strengthened. Indeed, Chile may have been following the only set of policies with any theoretical underpinnings when it abolished virtually all controls over every financial activity. Unfortunately, the Chilean government was unable to persuade the private sector that its hands-off policy also implied no bailouts. In fact, credibility in this regard was destroyed when the government stepped in to rescue a failing bank as early as 1977 (Diaz-Alejandro 1985, 8). This is not to say that the Chilean government should not have intervened. Rather, the government might then have introduced a sound system of financial institution supervision in recognition of its inevitable role in that sector of the economy.

13.6 Financial Instruments and Markets

Financial development involves the evolution of financial instruments and markets, as well as financial institutions. Financial instruments or financial claims fall into one of two categories—direct and indirect. Direct financial claims are issued by nonfinancial units. Mortgages, corporate bonds, and treasury bills are direct claims issued by households, business firms, and governments, respectively. Indirect claims, such as deposits and currency notes, are created by financial institutions. Credit money is a financial claim that exists in all economies. These claims are called indirect financial instruments because the depositor or lender supplies funds that are channelled indirectly to ultimate borrowers. In other words, financial institutions intermediate between lenders and borrowers, or between savers and investors. They sell indirect financial instruments, such as deposits, and buy direct claims, such as commercial bills and government securities.

Financial instruments possess several characteristics that differentiate one type of claim from another. These characteristics include the duration of the contract, the marketability and riskiness of the instrument, the level and type of yield, and the kind of issuer. Finer distinctions can be drawn with respect to the rights of the issuer to make an early repayment of the loan (callability), the recourse available to the borrower for demanding premature repayment, the taxability of the yield, and so on. Competition would ensure that disadvantages were balanced by advantages, such as a higher gross yield. Under competitive conditions, a high-yielding financial claim would possess at least one drawback, such as high risk.

In a broad sense, there are as many financial markets as there are financial instruments. There are, however, two distinct types of market. One is the centralized market, such as the stock exchange on which stocks and bonds are traded. The other is the decentralized market, such as the market for deposits. The type of market is itself a differentiating characteristic of the financial instrument.

For every claim in existence, there must be a demand and a supply. In some cases, such as stocks and bonds, demand and supply may interact freely to determine price. In other cases, such as deposits, the prices or yields may be regulated by government. Here, supply and demand may be equilibrated through nonprice competition, such as the provision of checking services at below cost. Alternatively, there may be disequilibrium in this market, necessitating some form of rationing.

There is also a distinction between primary and secondary markets. Markets for newly issued financial claims are primary markets. Markets for "used" financial claims are secondary markets. The existence of an efficient secondary market increases a financial claim's liquidity because a secondary market facilitates liquidation. Financial claims serve the purpose of transferring purchasing power from the buyer to the seller. In the primary market, the transfer takes place from lender to borrower. This transfer increases the aggregate volume of credit and could be used, for example, to finance new investment. In contrast, transactions on secondary markets take place between one lender and another lender. There can be no direct net increase in credit from secondary market activity.

Newly issued and "used" financial claims with identical characteristics are perfect substitutes. Hence, prices of identical new and "used" claims are always the same under free-market conditions. Where secondary markets flourish, they become so large in comparison to primary markets that they actually dominate the price setting process. For example, if demand in the secondary market increases, prices of financial claims rise and their yields fall. Borrowers can then issue new financial claims on the primary markets at lower rates of interest, and borrowing becomes cheaper.

The critical role of financial instruments in the context of economic development is that of facilitating and encouraging both saving and investment by providing efficient means for transferring claims over resources from savers (lenders) to investors (borrowers). Economic policies in some countries have deterred saving and investment to such minuscule levels that concern over financial instruments, or the lack thereof, is pointless until the deterrents to investment are removed. Some prerequisites for successful financial development are discussed in Chapter 19.

Capital formation may be stimulated by increasing the number of financial instruments and markets through which domestic resources can be mobilized; many developing countries possess a very narrow range. Although a greater variety of financial instruments would undoubtedly encourage more financial saving and, under conducive economic conditions, more investment, deliberate proliferation of instruments can soon reach the point of zero marginal return. Elasticities of substitution between alternative financial instruments are generally high. In any search for new instruments, therefore, one criterion for selection would be the extent to which they are bad substitutes for those that already exist. This will also indicate, in some degree, the effect of such innovations on aggregate real demand for financial assets. For this reason, optimal financial development policy may involve only a modest innovation of financial instruments.

There are a number of cases of successful development of particular financial instruments. The International Finance Corporation (IFC) has been a strong promoter of security markets for many years. However, deliberate attempts to develop stock markets have rarely succeeded. U Tun Wai and Patrick (1973, 268–269) conclude:

> With only a few exceptions (for example, in Brazil, India, Malaysia, and Singapore), markets are thin, with little or no trading and with relatively few and insignificant amounts of new public issues by private corporations. With a somewhat larger amount of issue, the market for government debt may appear to be more developed, but its sales are mainly to captive buyers. Information is poor and manipulation is substantial, especially for private issues. The occasional speculative splurges end in a crash that eliminates the nascent public investors, and the market reverts to its lethargic state.

In his 134-page report recommending the establishment of a security market in Bangladesh, Sidney Robbins (1980) devotes two pages to supervision and another two pages to accounting disclosure in a chapter entitled "The Peripheral Areas." Robbins (1980, 118) points out that "there is very little control, Government or otherwise, over security practices in Bangladesh," before stating that "through a training program it is hoped that Bangladesh ... will have a core of personnel capable of staffing an effective supervisory structure ... [which] would parallel the U.S. Securities and Exchange Commission." Robbins (1980, 119–121) then turns to the woeful state of the accountancy profession in Bangladesh. Realism finally raises its ugly head: "It is probably premature to expect any significant changes to take place in financial reporting over the near future." Given these two "peripheral" lacunae, the idea of developing a security market in Bangladesh is risible. At present, not a single financial asset is priced in the free market. Surely, therefore, any financial development program for Bangladesh should start with the development of markets for simpler and shorter-term financial assets such as treasury bills and certificates of deposit rather than equities.

Most developing countries could learn from the experiences of those countries in which flourishing financial markets have developed, invariably spontaneously. For example, the markets for postdated checks in Taiwan (Effros 1971), treasury bills in the Philippines (Emery 1967), and the *financiera* in Mexico illustrate the type of financial instrument which appears relatively easy to develop. The *financiera* is a long-term, fixed-dividend instrument with a competitively high yield. It offers the holder high liquidity because the issuing institution guarantees repurchase at par. The guarantee provides a market-price floor, so counteracting any initial lack of confidence. On the foundations laid by the *financiera,* Mexico is one of the very few developing countries that have managed to develop sound security markets.

13.7 Summary

Financial intermediaries can raise the level of investment by reducing search costs. Therefore, it seems reasonable to advocate the removal of impediments to competitive financial intermediation in order to accelerate the pace of economic development. The McKinnon-Shaw school promotes financial liberalization and nonintervention by government in financial markets to this end. Recent theoretical work on microeconomic aspects of financial intermediation, however, identifies an instance of market failure arising from asymmetric information between borrowers and lenders. Hence, there may be a case for government intervention. Paradoxically, appropriate intervention may well take the form of taxing profitable investments. There may also be a case for government provision of deposit insurance.

Chapter 14

Financial Institutions and Markets in Developing Countries

14.1 Introduction

RECENT EXPERIENCE WITH financial reform and liberalization indicates just how important are the roles of market structure and regulation in determining the outcome of such programs. In particular, cartelized or highly concentrated banking systems have not responded as anticipated to the abolition of interest rate ceilings. Bank associations simply assume responsibility for establishing appropriate interest rates for their members when governments relinquish this function. As pointed out in Chapter 1, financially repressed markets tend to be cartelized or highly oligopolistic in the first place.

In summing up the experience with liberalization policies in the Southern Cone (Argentina, Chile, and Uruguay), Mario Blejer (1983, 441) concludes that

> many domestic markets, given their size and organization, reacted in an oligopolistic manner to the opening of the economy. In the financial market, this situation was particularly notorious. The domestic market displayed a high degree of segmentation, since not all financial agents had the same access to international borrowing, especially before financial institutions specializing in international intermediation were developed. Given the fixed set-up costs and the structure of the domestic banking system, the development of new institutions requires substantial time. In the meantime, borrowers without direct access to international markets must obtain credit from domestic financial intermediaries that can borrow abroad and lend to domestic agents. In such a situation, the domestic interest rate is not determined solely by the foreign interest rate, the expected rate of change in the exchange rate, and any risk premium, but is also strongly influenced by domestic market conditions, including the domestic demand and supply for credit, the structure of the domestic financial system, and the state of inflationary expectations.

317

In Indonesia, David Cole and Betty Slade (1992, 136) report that after interest rate controls on state banks were abolished in 1983 these banks simply continued to behave as before, "still operating in the bureaucratic control mode." The monetary authorities in Malaysia and Thailand have also been frustrated by the sticky response of bank lending rates to changes in market interest rates. Turkey provides one of several examples where bank associations have taken over the interest rate setting function when the monetary authorities relinquished it. In India, the Indian Banks' Association fixed an interest rate ceiling of 10 percent on the interbank call money market rate until May 1989. The basic problem in all these cases has been lack of competition, often sanctioned by government (Haggard, Lee, and Maxfield 1993).

Uncompetitive financial markets have been one of the side effects of government-directed credit policies. In general, specialization within developing country financial sectors has occurred not because of the efficiency inherent in division of labor, but rather as a result of decrees and prohibitions. Far from reducing intermediation costs, specialization produced in this manner has generally raised them. In most developing countries, specialized financial institutions have been established with exclusive franchises for particular financial activities or particular sectors of the economy. On the one hand, this has destroyed any actual or potential competition. On the other hand, it has not achieved the goal of adequate and efficient distribution of credit. All too often, the specialized bank has expropriated scarce resources to finance large and inefficient investments. Other small investment projects have been starved of funds.

One response by the authorities to an uncompetitive and oligopolistic banking system has been to permit and encourage competition from unregulated financial institutions such as finance companies. Examples of this method of stimulating competition can be found in Malaysia, Philippines, Sri Lanka, Taiwan, Thailand, and Turkey. In all cases, however, these two-tier financial systems led to financial crisis, fraud, and scandal. While unregulated finance companies may provide competition to a lethargic banking system, they do not offer a viable alternative to low-risk deposits. In practice, it has proved politically impossible to avoid providing some protection to depositors in failed finance companies.

Other steps taken in several developing countries to stimulate competition include lowering entry barriers, abolishing interest rate ceilings, and privatizing government-owned financial institutions. The last one raises the broad issue of government ownership of financial institutions. As a general premise, government ownership per se produces no special issues of concern, as evinced by widespread government ownership of financial institutions in France, Italy, and Taiwan. Although the government-owned Taiwanese banking system is strongly criticized for bureaucratic procedures and lack of initiative, it has done little damage to the Taiwanese economy because macroeconomic policies together with the roles expected of the public sector financial institutions have been conducive to rapid economic growth. What is clear, however, is that the use of government-owned financial institutions to dispense political patronage or to implement social welfare programs leads rapidly to insolvency.

Bank ownership by conglomerate business groups has also been blamed for lack of competition and inefficient credit allocation. However, this view is challenged by Ben Bernanke and Mark Gertler (1990), who illustrate their analysis with the Japanese experience. Some advocates of universal banking argue that competition can be stimulated by despecializing development finance institutions (DFIs) and commercial banks.

Another puzzle whose answer must lie in institutional or regulatory arrangements concerns the appearance of extremely high real loan rates of interest after financial liberalization measures are introduced. For example, financial liberalization in Chile in the late 1970s and in Turkey in the 1980s resulted in a large spread between deposit and loan rates, as well as extraordinarily high real loan rates. In both countries, real loan rates in the range of 20–35 percent caused serious financial difficulties for business firms.

This chapter, therefore, examines institutional aspects of financial systems in developing countries that may influence the effects of financial policies.[1] Since commercial banks tend to dominate the financial sectors of most developing countries, section 14.2 considers their important role. It also discusses the role of foreign banks and the emergence of Islamic banking. Section 14.5 analyzes the recent move towards universal banking. High intermediation costs, arising in part from high default and delinquency rates, are examined in section 14.3, while financial layering, another cause of high costs, is analyzed in section 14.4. Conglomerates, bank holding companies, and industrial groups are discussed in section 14.6.

The remainder of this chapter covers a potpourri of additional institutional topics—finance companies, financial institution management, shallow bond and equity markets, and interbank money markets. Noninstitutional finance or curb market lending is important in many developing countries. It has received less analytical attention than it deserves because of the lack of data. The penultimate section of this chapter surveys some of the extant literature on noninstitutional finance.

14.2 Commercial Banks

Commercial banks tend to be the first financial institutions to emerge in the process of economic development. They perform the most general functions of providing a payments mechanism and intermediating between lenders and

---

[1] John D. Von Pischke (1991) provides an excellent nontechnical exposition of the roles of finance and financial markets in developing countries.

borrowers. Other financial institutions spring up after banks to offer more specialized intermediary services.

The development of commercial banking in a fair number of countries has been closely interwoven with the problems of public finance. For example, in 1694 the Bank of England was given the privileged status of joint stock company in return for loans to the government; all other banks had to remain as partnerships with unlimited liability. The origins of the Ottoman Bank, established in 1856 to assist the Ottoman Empire in obtaining both foreign and domestic loans, were somewhat similar.

Bank performance in developing countries is often criticized. Yet the criteria on which performance is found unsatisfactory are seldom made explicit. Bank performance, monetary policy implementation, and bank examination are interrelated in various ways. Monetary policy may itself establish at least some performance criteria. It also determines many of the constraints under which banks must operate. Assessing performance and implementing monetary policy both require information on bank activities. For several reasons, not the least of which is inadequate external auditing, monetary authorities may need to check information reported by the banks through some form of bank examination.

Under conditions of perfect competition, bank performance could be assessed very simply on the basis of profitability. Furthermore, such competition would ensure optimal performance from the banking system. It is, therefore, not surprising that most criticisms of banking systems in developing countries spring from the evident lack of competition. Under uncompetitive conditions, particularly where a large proportion of the financial institutions is nationalized, efficiency could be evaluated in terms of: (a) speed and cost of effecting payments; (b) attracting savings; (c) intermediation costs; and (d) allocating investible funds.

For the payments efficiency criterion, several indicators can be used: (a) percentage growth in demand deposits; (b) ratio of clearings to demand deposits; (c) average time taken to cash a check; and (d) average time taken to process accounts. Costs of providing the payments mechanism are difficult to separate from intermediation costs. However, total costs can be adjusted for each bank's particular mix of payments and intermediation. Cost ratio analysis constitutes one tool with which to judge bank performance.

Efficiency of resource mobilization is considerably more difficult to measure than is the efficiency of effecting payments. However, comparative analysis provides some indication of relative efficiency among institutions within a country, as well as between countries.

It is efficiency in allocating funds, however, that poses the greatest measurement problems. Perhaps most important are the criteria on which loan decisions are made. Financially repressive regimes, uncompetitive markets, and banker bureaucracies found in so many developing countries seem to encourage the adoption of the least efficient lending criteria.

An important differentiating characteristic of banking systems in developing countries is the role that foreign banks are permitted to play. In most very small developing countries, such as Bahamas, Barbados, Fiji, Maldives, Saint Lucia, Seychelles, Solomon Islands, and Western Samoa, banking systems are dominated by branches or subsidiaries of foreign commercial banks. Indeed, in 1981, Bahamas, Maldives, Seychelles, Solomon Islands, and Western Samoa possessed no purely domestic commercial banks (Fry 1981d). In contrast, some of the larger developing countries prohibit foreign banks or restrict their activities to specific types of business in specific parts of the country.

The role of foreign banks in developing countries has shown wide variance over the past two decades. In some countries, such as Korea, Philippines (after 1976), and Taiwan, the share of banking business conducted by foreign banks has increased. In many others, particularly those that were formerly colonies, such as Indonesia, Malaysia, and Philippines (before 1976), the share of banking business taken by foreign banks has declined in the postwar period (Pigott 1986, 267).

It is no coincidence to find a strong negative correlation between economy size and the preponderance of foreign banks in a country's financial sector. It reflects the basic fact that there are important economies of scale in the banking industry. These can be exploited by multinational banks even in the smallest economy, provided only that the economy is large enough to support just one bank branch. The critical economy size of a bank branch's viability is much smaller than the cutoff point for a new bank's viability. This is due to the fact that a branch has recourse to head office services, whereas a new bank must set up those services itself within the economy (Fry 1982a).

In a study of banking in OECD countries, Henry Terrell (1986, 301–302) finds that banks in countries that exclude foreign banks earned higher gross margins, had higher pretax profits as a percentage of total assets, and had higher operating costs than banks in countries that permit foreign banks to operate. He concludes that the exclusion of foreign banks reduces competition, so making domestic banking more profitable but less efficient. In the case of developing countries, George Viksnins (1980, 21–22) suggests, "It is certainly tempting to conclude that the superior record of Malaysia and Singapore in financial deepening and their ability to reap the benefits of an appreciating currency in world money markets is in large part due to the competitive discipline provided by a significant number of foreign bank branches."

Islamic banking has grown rapidly over the past two decades in a number of Moslem countries. The main distinguishing characteristic of Islamic banking is the absence of fixed interest rates on deposits or loans (Haque and Mirakhor 1986, Khan 1986, Khan and Mirakhor 1991). Instead, returns from lending are achieved through markup pricing or profit-sharing. With markup pricing for mortgage finance, for example, the bank buys the house and resells it at a far higher price to the borrower. The borrower then has 25 years to repay the price charged by the bank; the loan is considered to be interest-free. Profit-sharing interest-free deposits have achieved considerable popularity in a number of Moslem developing countries. Initially, they have tended to yield returns somewhat higher than fixed-interest deposits (Popiel and Dalla 1984, 12–13). Interest-free banking has the potential for improving efficiency, since it effectively frees institutional interest rates from administrative control. One problem with profit-sharing, however, lies in the prevalence of double book-keeping for tax evasion by business firms in developing countries. It can therefore be difficult for the participating bank to find out the actual profit made by the firm.

14.3 Financial Intermediation Costs

One disappointment with financial liberalization experiments lies in the continued high costs of financial intermediation after the liberalization. Just like the reserve requirement, the costs of financial intermediation drive a wedge between deposit and loan rates that reduces the size of the financial system. Bernanke (1983) defines the cost of credit intermediation as the cost of channelling funds from the original saver or lender to good borrowers. The cost includes screening, monitoring, accounting, and expected losses from bad loans.

When financial intermediaries perform efficiently, domestic resource mobilization through the financial sector is enhanced. In practice, the benefit/cost ratio of a country's financial system cannot be measured directly. There is no direct measurable indicator of total benefits. Therefore, various indirect methods must be used. Other things being equal, unit resource costs of intermediation between savers and investors would be associated negatively with efficiency, provided the total costs of transferring funds from original savers to final investors is calculated here. Costs of financial intermediation might be measured at the micro level by assessing the resource costs associated with lending for new investment from an increase in available funds (from saving). In practice, financial intermediaries' total operating costs—wages, depreciation, intermediate input costs, such as computer expenses and advertising—as a percentage of total earning assets may serve as a reasonable proxy. *Ceteris paribus*, the lower this percentage, the smaller the spreads between net returns to savers and gross costs to investors.

14.3.1 Operating Costs

Costs of financial intermediation refer to the spread between the gross costs of borrowing and the net returns on lending. They can be broken down into borrower, lender, and intermediary costs. If borrower and lender resource costs of such things as information, travel, and time have relatively low variance or vary in a way unrelated to intermediary costs, the spread or wedge between gross borrowing costs and net lending returns varies with transaction costs of the financial intermediaries. These transaction costs consist of administrative costs and default costs. Both can and do vary widely. For example, Delano Villanueva and Katrine Saito (1978, 18) find that the administrative costs of lending to small farmers in the Philippines are approximately triple, and the costs of lending to small-scale industry are double, the costs of lending to large-scale industry. Intermediation costs are higher, the smaller and more risky the loan. The World Bank (1974, 40) finds that just the administrative costs of an efficient agricultural credit institution lending to small farmers equal 7–10 percent of its total portfolio.

The World Bank (1974) compiled the data shown in Table 14.1 on administrative costs for a sample of 29 DFIs and other specialized financial institutions in 24 developing countries. Administrative costs as a percentage of total resources range from 1 for Peru's FONDO to 11 percent for Mexico's ABC. The median administrative cost is 3 percent. Given that most of these institutions do not raise funds directly from ultimate savers, but obtain the bulk of their resources at subsidized interest rates from central and commercial banks, these administrative costs indicate only part of the costs of intermediating between savers and investors. In such case, administrative cost ratios over 5 percent probably indicate serious inefficiencies.

Villanueva and Saito (1978, 20) present evidence showing that rural banks in the Philippines have surprisingly low administrative costs. They interpret this finding as follows:

> One reason for the relatively low administrative costs of rural banks may be the fact that many of them are owned and managed by those who were originally the local money lenders. As a result of a government policy to institutionalize the informal sector, local money lenders were encouraged by the Central Bank to establish rural banks. In such a capacity they could utilize to full advantage their contacts with the local clientele and their knowledge of local conditions and problems. An additional factor may be the rather conservative attitude of rural bankers concerning collateral requirements, and their tendency to rely less on project analysis. It is true that rural banks currently have problems with arrearages, but this is to be expected, given the nature of agricultural lending. In comparison to credit institutions of other LDCs the percentage of overdue loans to total portfolio is not particularly high. Moreover, the relatively low transaction costs of their lending operations do clearly indicate that this kind of institutionalization of the informal sector is a particularly appropriate way of extending credit to the small-scale sector.

14.3.2 Causes of Excessive Operating Cost Ratios

During the Great Depression in the United States, the cost of credit intermediation increased. The banking crises resulted in a reduction in bank credit

Table 14.1. Administrative Costs of Credit Institutions in Developing Countries

Country	Institution	Percentage of New Loans	Percentage of Total Resources
Africa			
Ghana	ADB	10	10
Côte d'Ivoire	CNCA		9
Kenya	AFC		3
Morocco	CNCA	10	3
Senegal	BND		3
Uganda	Co-ops	5	
Asia			
Bangladesh	KTCC	17	10
	BKB		3
India	LDB		3
Indonesia	BIMAS	25	
Jordan	ACC	30	3
Korea	NACF	6	4
Lebanon	BCAIF		3
Malaysia	BPM	20	
Pakistan	ADB		3
Philippines	Rural banks	3.7	3.2
Thailand	BAAC	13	8
Turkey	SCR	5	2
	BAT		6
Taiwan	Farmers' Association		2.5
	Co-op Bank		2.5
	Land Bank		1.5
Latin America			
Brazil	ACAR	10	
Colombia	INCORA	10	7
Costa Rica	BNCR	7	3
Ecuador	DAPC	4	
El Salvador	ABC	16	11
Mexico	FONDO	3	1
Peru	ADO		6

Source: World Bank, "Bank Policy on Agricultural Credit." Washington, D.C.: World Bank Report No. 436, May 1974, Annex Table 13

and a scramble for liquidity. Small firms had to switch from bank credit to trade credit. "In a world with transactions costs and the need to discriminate among borrowers, these shifts in the loci of credit intermediation must have at least temporarily reduced the efficiency of the credit allocation process, thereby raising the effective cost of credit to potential borrowers. If credit flows are dammed up, potential borrowers in the economy may not be able to secure funds to undertake worthwhile activities or investments" (Bernanke 1983, 263, 267). In such case the economy's productive capacity may be constrained. To the extent that credit for working capital is more difficult to obtain, existing productive capacity may also be underutilized. Precisely these two effects have been produced in developing countries when rising inflation has raised intermediation costs and reduced the real stock of bank credit.

James Hanson and Roberto de Rezende Rocha (1986, 51) find no evidence that banking is necessarily more costly in developing countries than in the OECD countries. Other things being equal, therefore, one would expect to find no significant difference in the spreads between average deposit and loan rates in developing and OECD countries. Other things, however, are not equal. Specifically, developing country banking systems are less competitive, are more heavily taxed, and suffer higher loss rates than the OECD banks. Hence spreads tend to be substantially wider. In Uruguay, for example, the spread between average deposit and loan rates remained over 15 percentage points until June 1981 despite reduced required reserve ratios, due to the oligopolistic structure of the banking system (Hanson and de Melo 1985, 926).

Hanson and de Rezende Rocha do find high bank operating costs in developing countries with high inflation rates and little or no competition (Hanson and de Rezende Rocha 1986, 11, 13). Financial repression, which is intensified as inflation rises, raises bank cost ratios by reducing the real size of the banking system and at the same time encouraging nonprice competition, such as the proliferation of bank branches. Implementing selective credit policies also involves substantial administrative costs for the banks (Morris 1985, 69).

In a number of high-inflation Latin American countries, operating costs are also high due to labor contracts. In Uruguay, for example, labor union contracts with all banks contained a clause that employees of any failed bank would be absorbed at the same pay scale in other banks. Work rules also raise operating costs in Argentina, Greece, and Jamaica.

Operating costs as a percentage of *earning* assets can be calculated from balance sheets and income statements that are usually published annually by all financial intermediaries. This particular ratio gives the minimum average spread between deposit and loan rates of interest required to cover inter-mediation costs. Time-series data for one particular country may indicate efficiency trends. For example, I calculate the following operating costs for all commercial banks in Turkey:

Year	Percentage
1967	6.56
1972	7.43
1977	8.54

The comparable figure for all insured banks in the United States for 1976 was 3.39 percent. Operating costs of Turkish banks in 1977 were about two and a half times higher than those of U.S. banks then.

Following the procedure established by Jack Revell (1980) and now accepted as the standard yardstick for cost comparisons, operating costs of Turkish banks as a percentage of *total* assets were 6.6 percent in 1977. By 1980, this figure had risen to 9.5 percent. Given that reserve requirements then were 35 percent for sight deposits and 30 percent for time deposits, the comparable operating cost ratio against *earning* assets must have exceeded 16 percent in that year.

The causes of high and rising bank operating costs in Turkey when compared with bank operating costs in the United States are: (a) interest rate ceilings; (b) an oligopolistic and cartelized financial sector; (c) accelerating inflation; and (d) high and rising reserve requirements.

Deposit rates of interest fixed administratively below their market equilibrium levels encouraged Turkish banks to substitute nonprice for price competition. There has been huge expenditure on advertising and opening new branches. As inflation accelerated in the 1970s (from under 10 percent in every year between 1960 to 1970 to about 100 percent in 1980), the gap between the free competitive market equilibrium deposit rate and the fixed ceiling widened. This produced even higher levels of expenditure on nonprice competition, and hence higher operating cost ratios.

Nonprice competition incurs resource costs, while price competition does not. Interest is a transfer payment involving no resource cost and differs from operating costs for precisely this reason. This distinction would be unimportant from the welfare standpoint were the resource costs of nonprice competition valued at par with deposit interest by depositors. Since this does not seem to be the case, there is resource misallocation when depository institutions are obliged to substitute nonprice for price competition.

Deposit rate ceilings tend to encourage and condone bank cartels. Overt banking cartels for the purpose of setting interest rates exist in, among other countries, Hong Kong and the Philippines. In Thailand, the oligopolistic structure of the banking system has led to extreme downward deposit rate inflexibility because the banks have been anxious not to lose market shares by reducing their rates. Cartels, such as the Turkish bankers' association, tend to raise operating resource costs, so reducing the efficiency of financial intermediation:

> Many observers have remarked that the gap between rates on loans and rates on deposits is excessive in Turkey compared to other countries. High costs would appear to absorb a large part of this gap. Why are costs high? One simple answer is that costs are high because the gap is wide. As both loan and deposit rates are fixed, perfect competition does not exist. Non-price competition in the form of massive advertising expenditure, impressive building, etc., takes place. Furthermore, there is no incentive to be efficient. To exhibit large profits is asking the authorities to step in and reduce the gap. This is the kind of market situation in which tacit collusion to maintain high costs and to keep profits within certain limits would flourish. (Fry 1972, 127)

Accelerating inflation, combined with fixed or sticky nominal deposit rates of interest, reduces real money demand and hence the real volume of resources at the disposal of the banking system. The nominal volume of deposits fails to increase in step with nominal GNP (and perhaps with inflation itself) as inflation accelerates. In contrast, bank operating costs do tend to rise at least as fast as GNP. Hence operating costs as a percentage of earning assets increase. Between 1977 and 1980, the real *M2* money stock in Turkey declined by over 25 percent. Over the same period, however, the number of bank branches increased by more than 15 percent and the number of bank personnel increased by over 10 percent.

A dramatic inflation-induced rise in bank operating costs also occurred in Brazil as inflation there rose from 13 percent in 1952 to 41 percent in 1966. Bank operating expenses as a percentage of bank loans outstanding increased on average from 6 percent in 1952 to 24 percent in 1966 (Christoffersen 1968, 9a, 18a).

Another cause of the positive relationship between inflation and bank operating cost ratios springs from a tendency for aggregate operating costs to rise in real terms as inflation accelerates. In Argentina, for example, accelerating and volatile inflation was associated with a strong increase in liquidity preference. Practically no deposits with maturities of over 30 days were held by 1985. A week is a long time in finance under such volatile conditions. Rolling over deposits and loans on a weekly basis makes the system very costly.

Bank operating costs and the concomitant spread between deposit and loan rates are inordinately high in most developing countries suffering from inflation in excess of about 20 percent. Inflation is the basic problem, bringing it down the only sensible cure.

14.3.3 The Reserve Requirement Tax

Higher reserve requirements raise bank operating costs. Ignoring bank capital and excess reserves, earning assets equal deposit liabilities when required reserves are zero. With a required reserve ratio of 50 percent, however, the same deposit base sustains only half the volume of earning assets. The calculated operating cost ratio against earning assets is doubled, even before the negative effect of a higher reserve requirement on deposit volume is considered. Required reserves impose a tax on financial intermediation. Ignoring resource costs, a 50 percent required reserve ratio ensures that the average deposit rate of interest can be no more than half the average return on earning assets.

As shown in Chapter 7, the reserve requirement tax increases as inflation accelerates. When inflation is zero, earning assets might yield an average return of 4 percent. In such case, the maximum average deposit rate is 2 percent when the required reserve ratio is 50 percent. If inflation rises from zero to 10 percent and earning assets now yield 14 percent, the maximum average deposit rate would be 7 percent. In real terms, the deposit rate has fallen from 2 percent to –3 percent. Without inflation, the reserve requirement imposed an effective tax on deposits of 2 percent. With 10 percent inflation, it imposes an effective tax rate of 7 percent. Depositors are deterred by such a substantial drop in their real return, and real money demand declines. In turn, this raises the operating resource cost ratio, as discussed above.

The payment of interest on bank reserves has received some attention. Robert Hall advocates interest payment on all bank reserves, while Tobin prefers to leave the reserve requirement tax in place and advocates payment of interest only on excess reserves (Suzuki and Yomo 1986). The tax extracted through required reserves can be sizable in practice. Half the Asian developing countries for which data are available imposed required reserve ratios against sight deposits at or above 10 percent in 1981. In the Philippines, the required reserve ratio against both sight and time deposits was 20 percent in that year, while in Taiwan it was 25 percent against sight deposits. In Korea, the required reserve ratio against sight deposits reached 35 percent in 1966. With a rate of interest on loans of 26 percent at that time and no interest paid on required reserves, the maximum average deposit rate that Korean banks could have paid was 16.9 percent, assuming that deposits equalled the sum of loans plus required reserves, that banks incurred no resource costs, and that there were no government subsidies. In fact, the Korean government did subsidize deposit rates of interest.

It is difficult to find any case in favor of a positive discriminatory tax on financial intermediation (Chamley and Honohan 1990, Morris et al. 1990). It is even harder to see how an optimal tax, should it exist, could move exactly in step with nominal interest rates. Indeed, Anthony Courakis's (1984) model presented in section 7.2 indicates that the deposit-maximizing required reserve ratio varies inversely with inflation and hence with nominal interest rates. A number of industrialized and developing countries do pay interest on banks' required reserves. In India, Korea, and Philippines, for example, interest is or has been paid on required but not on excess reserves precisely for the purpose of reducing the reserve requirement tax.

Apparently no country pays interest only on excess reserves or even on total reserves. The main reason for not paying interest on excess reserves is to keep the opportunity cost of holding such reserves as high as possible. Excess reserves are then held at minimum levels, and the money supply multiplier is more predictable. This can be of particular importance in some developing countries in which there are long lags in data collection and compilation (Fry 1979b). A lag of up to six months before money stock estimates are available is atypical but not unknown.

Conventional taxes—interest withholding taxes, stamp duties, transaction taxes, value-added taxes, profit taxes, license fees—levied on financial intermediation all widen the spread between deposit and loan rates of interest. They therefore have exactly the same effect on the real volume of financial intermediation and hence saving and investment as do higher operating costs.

14.3.4 Arrears, Delinquency, and Default Costs

Banks in many developing countries hold a truly alarming volume of nonperforming assets. Frank Veneroso (1986) lists Brazil, Côte d'Ivoire, Mali, Benin, Liberia, and Portugal as countries in which there are widespread payments delays. The issue of arrears is particularly acute for DFIs (Gordon 1983, World Bank 1985, ii). Here, the World Bank (1985, ii) suggests that much of the problem springs from the increasing use of DFIs as tools of development policy. Arvind Virmani (1985, 2) points out that the forced lending requirement used as part of selective credit policies is a recipe for high arrears, the responsibility for which must be assumed by the government.

Felipe Morris (1985, 20) finds that the primary cause of high arrears in India is the rapid expansion of lending in response to government pressures to achieve mandated credit disbursement targets. Morris lists the following causes of high arrears in India: (a) failure to tie lending to productive investments; (b) neglect of marketing and linking credit recovery to the sale of the product; (c) defective loan policies—delayed loan disbursement, too much or too little credit, and unrealistic repayment schedules; (d) misapplication of loans; (e) ineffective supervision; (f) apathy and indifference of bank management with respect to recovering loans; and (g) lack of responsibility and discipline on the part of borrowers.

Yoon Je Cho and Deena Khatkhate (1989, xiii) analyze the problem of nonperforming assets in Indonesia: "The Indonesian financial system also faced the serious problem of a growing volume of bad and doubtful assets in bank portfolios. The main reason for this was the high level of interest rates in relation to the productivity of capital. This had an adverse impact on the corporate sector first and later on the financial sector."

In Asia Wanda Tseng and Robert Corker (1991, 9) find that

> excessive regulations of the banking system during the 1970s (both in
> terms of interest rate and credit controls) had important deleterious ef-
> fects: banks' lending portfolios had been weakened in some countries,
> and nonbank financial institutions, that were in some cases not subject
> to adequate supervision, had grown rapidly. Nearly all of these coun-
> tries (Indonesia, Korea, Malaysia, Nepal, the Philippines, Singapore, Sri
> Lanka, and Thailand) implemented measures to restructure failing fi-
> nancial institutions and to strengthen the supervision of other financial
> institutions.

Default costs are extraordinarily difficult to measure, since accounting
practices regarding nonperforming loans vary from country to country. Typically, however, the true default costs are understated. In Bangladesh, for
example, financial institutions are required for tax purposes to report interest
accrued, whether or not it has actually been received. All DFIs in Bangladesh
are insolvent, yet have taxes assessed on illusory profits every year. In a number of countries, tax regulations specify a maximum percentage of earnings
that can be set aside for loss provisions. The magnitude of default losses
of DFIs in developing countries appears to be extremely serious. The World
Bank (1985, 11) finds that, in general, DFIs make inadequate provision for
loan losses. For its sample of DFIs, the average return on assets would have
been negative had realistic provisions been made for default costs. One third
of the DFIs sampled recently by the World Bank (1985, 12) were unlikely to
survive without radical restructuring.

A partial indication of the delinquency or default problem plaguing DFIs in
most developing countries can be gleaned from data on arrears. World Bank
(1974) figures on arrearages of a sample of financial institutions in developing
countries are given in Table 14.2. The arrears rates range from 2 percent for
Malawi's Lilongwe to 95 percent for Nigeria's FAID. The median arrears rate
is 41 percent. The World Bank points out that even these figures understate
the full extent of the problem because most DFIs treat rescheduled loans as
fully repaid. The new loan is then classified as a performing asset until the
next delinquency. Hence simple bookkeeping can keep down unacceptably
high rates of arrears.

Delinquency rates are high in developing countries for a variety of reasons. Cultural factors undoubtedly play an important role. The concept of
loan repayment is unfamiliar in some countries. When the government is
involved in credit programs, recipients often fail to distinguish loans from
grants. In part this may be because government officials behave, perhaps to
encourage recipients of such loans to extend gratuities, in ways that suggest
the government is providing assistance. As Clive Bell (1990, 301) notes, there
is a "widespread view in rural India that institutional loans are really grants,
because politicians regularly vie with one another in promising, if elected,
to have such debts forgiven." Subsidized credit, of course, does contain a

grant component. Since the grant fraction of a subsidized loan is never made explicit, a borrower can become confused into thinking that all of it is a grant. Government-supervised credit programs in Peru, for example, suffered serious arrearage problems, in part because collateral was not required. Low subsidized interest rates, negative in real terms, themselves provide a strong incentive to postpone loan repayments. Poor asset quality also arises through related lending to firms within a conglomerate, as has happened in Brazil and Chile.

Nonperforming assets are encountered in commercial banks as well as in DFIs. In 1986, about 40 percent of bank loans in Argentina were nonperforming, primarily because of the macroeconomic crisis. Roland Tenconi (1986, 9) estimates that 30 percent of commercial bank loans in Madagascar were nonperforming at the end of 1985. The major cause of the problem there appears to be that public sector enterprises are delinquent. The World Bank (1989, 71–72) lists 33 countries experiencing serious problems of nonperforming assets in their banking systems.

Given its economic success, Korea provides a surprising example of high levels of nonperforming assets in its banking system (Choi 1991, 67–68):

> The "restructuring" (in effect bail-out) episodes, which recurred in 1969–1970, 1972, 1979–1981, and 1986–1988 are an eloquent testimony to the existence of a vicious circle of financial repression produced by the strategic interdependence between the government and big business. To begin with, the "strategic interdependence" between the government and big business has fostered, rather than sanctioned, the weak corporate financial structure of big business. When their highly-leveraged investments come to face financial difficulties for whatever reasons (economic recession, structural depression, etc.), it has never been their problem alone. The related banks have been forced to accumulate bad loans. In this situation, the failure to prevent their bankruptcy would mean the bankruptcy of banks. So the government has been forced to step in to rescue banks and to facilitate industrial adjustment. Unintentionally, the repeated practice of bail-out has only encouraged big business to rely on further indebted growth. The government's compensation of the loss to be incurred by banks only intensified the banks' habitual reliance upon the government.

In the early 1980s, nonperforming assets of the Korean banks constituted 11 percent of total loans and represented 2.6 times their reported net worth. By 1987, nonperforming assets had risen to 20 percent of total bank loans (Park and Kim 1990, 36). Some troubled firms were in declining industries like textiles and plywood, others were in heavy and chemical manufacturing, and others in shipping and overseas construction. In many cases, the Korean government constituted the reason for financial difficulties in the corporate sector. For example, the government embarked upon a policy of developing

Table 14.2. Percentage Loan Delinquency Rates in Developing Countries

Country	Institution	Arrears to Portfolio	Arrears Rate
Africa			
Ethiopia	Wolamo		3
	CADU		50
Ghana	ADB		55
Côte d'Ivoire	BNDA		14
Kenya	GMR	25	33
Malawi	Lilongwe		2
Mali	AFC	51	36
Niger	CNCA	11	29
Nigeria	WSACC	52	80
	FAID		95
Morocco	SOSAP		50
	CNCA	13	5
Sudan	COOP		26
	ABS		13
Tanzania	NDCA	28	50
Tunisia	BNT	66	50
Asia			
Afghanistan	ADBA	37	77
Bangladesh	AB	43	76
India	PCCS	34	7
	PLDB	12	20
Iran	ACBI		44
Jordan	ACC	41	82
Korea	NACF	7	15
Malaysia	BPM	6	21
Pakistan	ADB	36	65
Philippines	Rural Banks	25	24
Sri Lanka	New Credit Scheme	50	41
Thailand	BAAC		50
Turkey	ABT	29	43

Source: World Bank, "Bank Policy on Agricultural Credit." Washington, D.C.: World Bank Report No. 436, May 1974, Annex Table 12

*The arrears rate is equal to 100 minus the repayment rate. Both the percentage of arrears to portfolio and the arrears rate have various shortcomings. For example, most institutions consider rescheduled loans to have been repaid. A low ratio of arrears to portfolio may be misleading when loans are expanding rapidly and are not yet due, particularly if the repayment rate on previous loans is poor.

Table 14.2. Percentage Loan Delinquency Rates in Developing Countries *(Concluded)*

Country	Institution	Arrears to Portfolio	Arrears Rate
Latin America and Caribbean			
Bolivia	Agricultural Bank	1	68
Chile	INDAP	16	60
Colombia	Caj. Agr.	19	
	INCORA	4	16
Costa Rica	BNCR, BCR	35	
El Salvador	ABC	37	81
Honduras	BNF, Sup. Cr.	10	18
Jamaica	ADB	31	10
Peru	Plan Costa	33	

heavy and chemical industries in the late 1970s, coercing the banks to make risky long-term loans (McKinnon 1991, 389).

The Korean government decided to support the troubled firms and persuaded the banks to carry the nonperforming loans on their books as long as they could. Banks had to pump more credit into troubled firms so squeezing credit to healthy firms. After implementing industrial restructuring by providing subsidies so that solvent firms could take over troubled firms, the government rescheduled the nonperforming loans at lower interest rates and additional credit. To avert bank insolvency, the Bank of Korea compensated banks for some of their losses through subsidized rediscounts (Park and Kim 1990, 35–36).

Ronald McKinnon (1991, 389) comments:

> Because of its determination to support the development of heavy industry and Korean contractors undertaking major construction projects in the Middle East and elsewhere, the Korean government coerced the banks into making risky long-term loans, many of which became nonperforming. In the 1980s the Bank of Korea still provided subsidized credit lines (official discounting at below-market interest rates) to various commercial banks to enable them to avoid bankruptcy by keeping these old (1970s) loans on their books. This bad loan syndrome continues to hinder the full liberalization of the Korean financial system despite the successful monetary stabilization.

A similar analysis is provided by Alice Amsden and Yoon-Dae Euh (1993) and Chung Lee (1992).

Government intervention in the form of pressures to achieve mandated credit disbursement targets has also been the main cause of high levels of nonperforming assets in the Indian banking system. Morris (1985, 20) lists the following additional causes of high arrears in India: (a) failure to tie lending to productive investments; (b) neglect of marketing and linking credit recovery to the sale of the product; (c) defective loan policies—delayed loan disbursement, too much or too little credit, and unrealistic repayment schedules; (d) misapplication of loans; (e) ineffective supervision; (f) apathy and indifference of bank management with respect to recovering loans; and (g) lack of responsibility and discipline on the part of borrowers. Some of these problems, which have been identified in many other developing countries, are the result of government intervention.

Veneroso (1986) suggests that the increasing problem of defaults and delinquencies faced by banks in developing countries springs in large part from the fact that bankruptcy is used less frequently than it was. Veneroso attributes the recent rise in nonperforming assets to overinvestment in energy and capital-intensive industries in the early 1980s, borrowing abroad at real interest rates that were negative but are now positive, and borrowing when the real exchange rate was appreciated due to capital inflows. When capital inflows slowed down or stopped, the real exchange rate depreciated and dollar-denominated debt increased in relative magnitude on firms' balance sheets, whether the firms were banks or nonfinancial enterprises.

Most governments are reluctant to allow financial institutions to fail, and developing country governments also tend to bail out large nonfinancial institutions. In the case of government enterprises, some of the worst bank borrowers in Brazil and Portugal, creditors cannot force bankruptcy and may have no legal recourse at all (Veneroso 1986, 9, 19–20).

The crucial problem of arrears lies in the fact that, if financial institutions are to remain solvent, higher default costs must reduce net returns to savers or raise gross costs to successful investors. They create a wedge, just as administrative costs do, between loan and deposit rates of interest. Arrears also reduce banks' flexibility in that credit cannot be redirected towards alternative activities if it is not repaid. Excessive arrears and default rates indicate inefficiency of one kind or another. The financial institution has either financed unproductive investments or failed to press for loan repayment. In either case, financial intermediation is impaired.

High percentages of nonperforming assets constitute one of the most serious problems facing financial systems in developing countries at present. The worst possible policy approach would be to ignore the problem. This would encourage banks to throw good money after bad, so reducing their flexibility even further. The case-by-case approach now being followed by the World Bank with respect to the restructuring of DFIs appears to be the only viable solution (Callier 1991, Faruqi 1993, Long 1990, Roe and Popiel 1990, Sheng 1991).

14.4 Financial Layering

In assessing the efficiency of financial intermediation carried out by specialized institutions, one must measure the resource costs of transferring funds from original savers to final investors. Unit resource costs of individual financial intermediaries may be misleading if (as in India, for example) there is much financial layering. Then unit resource costs of each financial intermediary in the chain must be summed to produce the total intermediation cost.

Administrative costs per individual financial institution tend to be much higher in Indonesia (3.2 to 8.9 percent) and Korea (6 percent for commercial banks [Que 1979, 399]), for example, than they are in India (barely above 2 percent [Bhatt 1978]). Financial layering, however, makes each individual institution's costs additive in the total costs of intermediating between savers and ultimate borrowers. The resulting high costs of financial intermediation in India are discussed in relation to its selective credit policy in Chapter 18.

Financial layering is supported through the preferential rediscount system in Indonesia (Baliño and Sundararajan 1986, 194). A three-tier financial structure exists in Korea, as in India, with county cooperatives borrowing from the National Agricultural Cooperative Federation, which in turn borrows from the government and the Bank of Korea (Bank of Korea 1978, 34). Similar financial layering occurs in the case of fisheries cooperatives (Bank of Korea 1978, 36). Brazil has a two-tier financial structure, with three federal institutions passing on funds to second-stage financial institutions, such as the commercial, investment, and development banks. Comparable instances of financial layering are found in Colombia, Morocco, Thailand, and many other developing countries (World Bank 1974).

The main purposes of financial layering are to direct credit to priority activities and to reimburse the final lender at least partially for the subsidy. Unfortunately, this supply-leading approach has two major drawbacks in addition to its high resource costs. The first problem is that the mechanism works efficiently only to the extent that all base- and middle-tier institutions possess identical lending capabilities. The refinancing mechanism comes into play only after a loan has been extended. Before that, however, expertise is required at the final stage or at the base of the pyramid to assist the borrower in designing the project and preparing the loan application. The base institution also needs expertise in loan evaluation techniques. Evidently such expertise varies greatly from one institution to another and from one region of the country to another in both India and Korea. Hence credit cannot be spread efficiently and equitably. Its allocation is dependent to a large extent on loan officers of differing abilities in the base institutions.

One alternative to financial layering is the adoption of more innovative financial instruments with which the base- or middle-tier financial institutions could raise funds directly from financial markets. Indeed, this would appear to be the only way of increasing the aggregate real supply of loanable funds. Such an alternative, however, cannot be reconciled with the system of credit subsidies existing in almost all developing countries today. Where subsidies are deemed necessary, they might be provided with less distortion directly from the government budget. Chapter 18 discusses, in more detail, this and other issues related to selective credit policies.

14.5 Universal Banking

Universal banks extend term loans, while commercial banks traditionally restrict themselves or are restricted to short-term lending only. In most developing countries today, however, commercial banks are permitted, and in some cases obliged, to devote some of their resources to term lending. At the same time, thrift institutions and investment banks have extended their activities into areas that used to be the exclusive preserve of the commercial banks. Some universal banks may and do take equity interests in business enterprises.

As pointed out in Chapter 13, Alexander Gerschenkron's analysis of the role of universal banking in the process of German industrialization has been translated into recommendations for universal banking for developing countries (Khatkhate and Riechel 1980, 513; World Bank 1980, 74, 80). Virmani (1985, 46) recommends that Korean banks should be allowed to hold equities to help reduce the excessive debt/equity ratios of Korean business corporations. Millard Long (1983, 40) points out that the World Bank recommended the adoption of universal banking in the Philippines but recommended its removal in Brazil and Mexico.

David Gill (1983, 1) opposes universal banking on the following grounds:

> It has been our [IFC] thesis that securities markets in countries which have at least semi-industrialized economies tend to be more efficient, deeper, more liquid and better able to meet the financing needs of firms at lower or fairer transaction costs, where there is mainly specialization of function and a high degree of competition between and amongst securities market firms on the one hand and banking entities on the other, than in those countries where banking entities tend also to dominate the securities markets.

Elsewhere, Gill (1979, 6) finds no evidence that universal banks are more efficient than specialized financial institutions. Indeed, he believes that enforcing specialization probably speeds the pace of security market development (Gill 1979, 11). Gill develops this theme in two other papers:

> Generally, countries with "universal banking," such as Germany and France, have weaker contractual savings institutions and equity markets than countries which separate to some extent banking activities from securities market activities, as in the U.S. and Canada. Bank dominance

can lead to smaller equity markets than otherwise might be the case. (Gill 1986b, 6)

> Some of the developing countries such as Chile and Argentina, which "deregulated" and "liberalized" financial activities five years or so ago, have seen an emergence of the problems the Glass-Steagall Act was designed to prevent. That is, concentration of economic and political power and abuses thereof, at substantial financial and social costs, as is now well recognized. (Gill 1986a, 5)

However, security markets have not developed successfully even with assistance from the IFC in many developing countries that have promoted financial specialization.

Heinz Arndt and Peter Drake (1985, 388) have also questioned the efficacy of universal banking: "The practice of universal banking, or the 'financial supermarket' is not self-evidently a good model and should be assessed critically by monetary authorities." Arndt and Drake reiterate the case for the banking regulations contained in the U.S. Glass-Steagall Act. The Glass-Steagall Act of 1933 prohibited commercial banks in the United States from underwriting or dealing in equities and restricted them to buying only approved debt securities. Commercial banks had to sell their investment banking operations, thus separating the activities of commercial banks from those of the securities business. Andrés Velasco (1986a, 11) points out that the move towards universal banking in Chile increased economic concentration by strengthening the large conglomerate groups. Carlos Diaz-Alejandro (1985) also suggests that the conglomerate groups in Chile severely distorted credit allocation and recommends adoption of legislation similar to the Glass-Steagall Act in the Southern Cone. McKinnon (1986c, 335) also favors the Glass-Steagall provisions. Meanwhile, the provisions of the Glass-Steagall Act have been gradually eroded in the United States. However, universal banking in Côte d'Ivoire, Jordan, and Mexico, as well as conglomeration of financial institutions in Colombia, Kenya, Philippines, and Thailand, does not appear to have been particularly detrimental to resource allocation in these countries.

The efficacy of universal banking is closely dependent on the market structure of the financial system. Oligopolistic banking systems need more rather than less competition from direct financial markets. Unless entry conditions are eased at the same time, a move towards universal banking may well reduce competition within the financial sector by increasing concentration. However, universal banks may alleviate financial fragility created by shallow equity markets and excessive debt/equity ratios by taking equity positions in their client companies. There is, therefore, no universal case for or against universal banking.

14.6 Conglomerates

Gill (1983, 4) states: "Countries such as Chile, Brazil, Mexico, Turkey and Thailand are increasingly focusing on the potentially dangerous interlocking between major corporate and bank interests." The general presumption is that the control of financial institutions by industrial conglomerates results in less efficient resource allocation (Galbis 1986). Diaz-Alejandro (1985, 13–14) makes the same point with respect to conglomerates, bank holding companies, and industrial groups in Argentina, Chile, and Uruguay. Conglomerates that controlled banks in Chile had far higher levels of indebtedness than business corporations that did not. The *grupos* took over most of the large financial intermediaries and used them to mobilize resources for their own activities (Galvez and Tybout 1985, 7). Julio Galvez and James Tybout (1985) find that conglomerates owning banks in Chile had much higher debt ratios than firms that did not own their own banks. The conglomerates (*chaebols*) in Korea are little affected by any tightening of monetary policy because of their strong credit standing outside Korea, as well as their interlocking directorships of associated financial institutions, including finance companies and banks (Skully and Viksnins 1987, 113).

Banking in the Philippines bears some resemblance to banking in Japan in that the private commercial banks are owned predominantly by family-run industrial groups. One former governor of the Philippine Central Bank commented that the average Filipino banker was in the banking business not for banking profits but to finance his other businesses (*Far Eastern Economic Review* 7 April 1978, 80). The banking system has become more concentrated as these industrial groups have increased their importance in the economy (Patrick and Moreno 1985, 315–317). Although there were 33 private commercial banks in 1973, the number had fallen to 26 in 1984, as a result of mergers caused in part by the substantial increases in minimum capital requirements which had been imposed.

The developing country experience of conglomeration conflicts to some extent with the European historical experience. In part, this is because conglomeration in the developing countries is often motivated strongly by the desire to avoid interest rate ceilings and other regulations on lending, such as credit ceilings, that did not exist in Europe. Furthermore, entry into banking in most developing countries is far more restricted than it was in Europe during the industrial revolution.

The developing country experience suggests that interlocking corporate and bank interests can cause serious problems of financial inflexibility and instability. These problems can be particularly serious in developing countries with inadequate bank regulation and supervision as well as tight restrictions on entry into the banking industry.

14.7 Finance Companies

Finance companies have been permitted and encouraged in a number of countries for the explicit purpose of increasing competition within the financial sector. For example, finance companies in Thailand have grown rapidly since the first company was established in 1969. After 1970, the unregulated interest rates on their promissory notes, already above the fixed structure of bank deposit rates of interest, rose even further above these rates as inflation accelerated. Initially, the government hoped that finance companies would provide some healthy competition for the commercial banks without jeopardizing bank solvency.[2] However, the commercial banks took over most of the larger and more successful finance companies. The advent of finance companies in Thailand actually increased the market shares of the bigger banks.

In Thailand, Chile, Sri Lanka, Turkey, and elsewhere, finance companies encouraged deliberately under less stringent or even nonexistent regulatory frameworks have created financial instability due to scandals and insolvencies. The Chilean *financieras* formed in and after 1974 under little control had caused sufficient problems to necessitate the imposition of some supervision in December 1976 (Velasco 1986a). Scandal and bankruptcies hit the Thai finance company sector in 1979. More recently, the Kastelli scandal produced a run on and crash of the newly developed security houses in Turkey.

In Sri Lanka, differential treatment caused serious disintermediation from bank deposits into finance company liabilities. Although Sri Lankan finance companies experienced rising levels of nonperforming assets along with the commercial banks, they are much more aggressive in collecting debts. Since there is no satisfactory legal recourse, somewhat more direct and violent methods have been employed.

Cho (1986a, 14–30) describes Korea's gradual process of liberalization starting in 1980 with the deregulation of nonbank financial institutions. Entry barriers were relaxed and interest rates freed. So far, this gradual process of financial liberalization has raised real interest rates, produced substantial financial deepening (the ratio of *M3* to GDP rose from 0.42 in 1979 to 0.60 in 1984), and reduced the corporate sector's debt/equity ratio. The liberalization has not yet been adversely affected by more scandals or greater instability.

In general, encouraging unregulated finance companies to compete with a regulated and cartelized banking system is a poor solution to the problem of monopoly power. If banks have sufficient political power, as in Thailand, to block entry into banking, they are also likely to be able to prevent or greatly reduce the impact of competition from nonbank financial intermediaries.

---

[2]This fear was generated by the banks themselves to justify the prohibition of new entrants into the Thai banking community over the past two decades.

14.8   Financial Institution Management

Until very recently, World Bank reports on the financial sectors of developing countries provided almost exclusively descriptive material on the financial institutions themselves. Occasionally there was a recommendation for more banker training and advocacy of less government involvement in management decision making. The literature provides a general impression that bankers in many developing countries are too bureaucratic (in the Indian subcontinent) and often ill-trained (in Africa).

The shortage of trained bankers in Guyana is noted:

> It is widely known that within the expatriate banking sector credit assessments and decisions rest largely with the expatriate members of staff. It is not so well known or recognized however that many of these persons by the nature of their training and experience, and sometimes by the lack of it, are ill equipped in large measure for the business of credit evaluation in a developing economy.
>
> The indigenous banks, especially when they recruit staff from the expatriate banks, also suffer from limitation of relevantly skilled manpower. Consequently, it is not surprising that, in a situation where there are sufficient alternative opportunities for the safe and profitable deployment of funds within and outside the economy, banks, indigenous and expatriate, avoid the new and "riskier" areas and stick to export crops, the distributive trades, large firms, and personal loans. (Bourne 1974, 119–120)

Poorly qualified personnel also staff the state banks in Indonesia. Some of the Indonesian banks that do not conduct foreign exchange business suffer severely from weak management. In Brazil banks tend to be small and inefficient family concerns with nepotistic management, comparable to some banks in the United States in the 1940s. The 1986 crisis caused the Brazilian banks to fire 80,000 bank employees and to close many of their branches.

Bank lending in East Africa is described as follows:

> The present method is to look first at the securities offered, secondly at any additional securities which can be obtained, thirdly at how short the period to maturity is, fourthly at the commissions to be received in connection with the granting of credit, fifthly at the standing of the would-be borrower, sixthly at the amount and seventhly at the project. (Pauw 1970, 249)

Diaz-Alejandro (1985, 13) finds a very different management problem in the countries of the Southern Cone:

> The new financial institutions in the Southern Cone attracted fresh entrepreneurs and stimulated the creation of new conglomerates and economic

groups. While new entrepreneurial blood has an attractive aura, experience indicates that such venturesome animal spirits are better channeled toward non-financial endeavors, where the disciplining threat of bankruptcy could be more credible.

Many developing countries are thought to suffer from an insufficient supply of medium- and long-term credit, in part due to lack of project appraisal expertise in the financial sector. Indeed, this was one of the main reasons for the establishment of DFIs. When DFIs failed to solve the problem, policy advisors turned to the commercial banks. In part, advocacy of universal banking was a response to the perceived shortage of term financing (World Bank 1980, 70–80).

The inverted term structure of institutional loan rates of interest, so frequently encountered in developing countries, deters discretionary long-term lending. Term finance is bound to remain in short supply wherever the authorities invert the term structure of institutional loan rates of interest. However, overdraft or short-term loans constitute close substitutes for term loans. Typically, overdraft lending is equivalent to a variable rate loan of indefinite but medium-term maturity. In practice, therefore, the absence of institutional term lending may not be such a major problem as perceived by many policy advisors.

Poor management pervades all sectors of developing economies. In the financial sector, low civil service pay scales, political interference in management decisions of the nationalized financial institutions, and regulatory systems that discourage innovation by permitting only prescribed activities rather than everything not proscribed all contribute to weak management. Perhaps the entry of foreign banks is the fastest way of improving management expertise in the financial sectors of developing countries that prohibit foreign bank entry at present.

14.9   Undeveloped Bond and Equity Markets

The 35 security markets that exist in the developing countries have generally played only very minor roles in domestic resource mobilization. Antoine van Agtmael (1984, 1) believes part of the reason for this is that "the need for equity as a cushion against adverse developments was often overlooked." McKinnon (1988, 401–409) stresses the point that the absence of open security markets in developing countries throws too much risk on bank-based capital markets. The lack of direct financial markets may also cause higher intermediation costs. Maxwell Watson et al. (1986, 10) conclude from recent capital market liberalization and innovation in the OECD countries that "intermediation costs have been sharply reduced by the substitution for bank credits of direct transactions in securities, by reduced commissions, and by increased competition."

Long (1983, 31) blames high inflation for both the inadequate provision of term finance and the failure of direct financial markets to develop in many developing countries. For example, as inflation accelerated in Turkey between 1978 and 1981 the debt/equity ratios of a sample of large business corporations there rose from 3.2 to 5.7 as the equity market dried up. The same point is made by Edward Shaw (1973, 1975) and by U Tun Wai and Hugh Patrick (1973, 274–276).

Low interest rate policies, often pursued to keep the cost of government borrowing down, ensure that direct financial markets cannot develop (Wai and Patrick 1973, 283). For example, no bonds were issued in Indonesia for the simple reason that many bank loan rates were set below the corresponding deposit rates of interest. Under such circumstances, business firms borrow from the banks at rates lower than those at which they could sell any bonds. Wai and Patrick (1973, 283–284) conclude:

> An essential condition for an effective capital market is that prices be determined freely by interaction of forces determining demand and supply. Yet the low interest rate policy pursued by governments in many LDCs conflicts with the principle and practice of freely determined market prices for securities, notably for bonds.
>
> The moral is that the development of capital markets requires freedom from government attempts to control interest rates in that market.

Hang-Sheng Cheng (1980, 45) points out that

> a well-developed secondary market presupposes a high degree of financial sophistication, based on generally accepted accounting standards, knowledgeable investment-advisory services, efficient communication networks, and reasonable regulatory authorities to enforce the rules of the game. Generally speaking, such preconditions do not exist in developing nations.

Five bottlenecks to capital market development have been detected in Turkey: (a) weak accounting and auditing; (b) interlocking ownership and control of banks and business corporations; (c) lack of nonbank financial intermediaries to support capital market activities; (d) inadequate secondary market; and (e) inadequate supervisory mechanisms. Weak auditing is also a problem in Morocco. Philip Wellons, Dimitri Germidis, and Bianca Glavanis (1986, 23) also recognize that "the absence of a competent accounting profession can threaten the best of schemes" to promote venture capital and equity financing.

Drake (1986, 122) pinpoints regulatory problems: "Legislation and regulatory practices have not been adequate to ensure clean markets in most countries of the [Asian] region." In Sri Lanka, for example, equity markets have remained shallow, in part because dividends are low. The principal owners take out profits in the form of exorbitant directors' salaries. There is clearly an urgent need for a better regulatory framework to protect minority shareholders in Sri Lanka. The same phenomenon is observed in Greece (Molho 1986b, 484) and Colombia.

Another reason for the nondevelopment of direct markets is subsidized indirect markets. For example, the inverted pattern of deposit and loan rates that existed in Indonesia during the 1970s for priority borrowers removed any incentive to issue bonds (Drake 1986, 103). Lending by DFIs at subsidized interest rates retarded capital market development in Sri Lanka. Morris (1985, 23–25) points out that in India the cost of issuing equity is at least 7 percent of the sum raised and that fiscal policy is biased against equity finance. Veneroso (1986) suggests that government intervention itself encourages debt rather than equity deepening. One way of reversing this bias is for governments to reduce their propensity to make good private losses.

Benito Legarda (1986, 6) and van Agtmael (1984, 2–9) argue that many developing countries discriminate against direct financial markets through tax policies that favor deposit interest income over dividends and that effectively tax equity income twice, first as business profit and then as personal income. In Morocco, for example, a 25 percent withholding tax is imposed on dividends, while bearer certificates of deposit are tax-exempt. Taxation or the threat thereof may also discourage corporations from opening their books. Government intervention in the form of unfunded national insurance and social security schemes discourages private insurance and pension funds, which could otherwise develop to invest in equities.

Gill (1986a) finds another cause for undeveloped capital markets, namely financial liberalization and deregulation. Liberalization that strengthens banks by, for example, permitting universal banking, may weaken equity markets, according to Gill, because bankers have greater resources with which to lobby for political support than do stockbrokers. Oligopolistic banking systems have a strong incentive to stifle any potential competition from bond and equity markets. However, Drake (1986, 124) concludes that financial liberalization is "most likely to foster the flotation and trading of both corporate and government securities." Clearly, financial liberalization in the form of the abolition of interest rate ceilings is a prerequisite for security market development. But financial liberalization that results in greater monopoly power for the banks may well impede such development.

The "perils" of overleverage are recognized by Wellons, Germidis, and Glavanis (1986, 7). Legarda (1986, 1) concurs that "until recently, risk capital, financial markets and non-banking financial institutions were largely ignored because they were supposed to be irrelevant in the savings mobilization process. The emphasis was on intermediation, with scant attention (if any) to the possibility of over-intermediation, i.e., excessive debt relative to equity."

The IFC advocates fiscal incentives to encourage equity market development, as does the World Bank on occasion (in Nigeria, for example). In contrast, Drake (1986, 124) ends his survey of security markets in Asia with the conclusion that the viable stock exchanges in Hong Kong, Malaysia, and Singapore evolved without government assistance, while fiscal incentives in Korea did not generate significant new capital. Peter Wall (1981) states that fiscal incentives are much less important than broader political and economic conditions.

Developing countries have had ample experience with financial instability due to excessive debt/equity ratios in recent years. Equity market development, however, is one of the long-term aspects of economic development in general. There are no quick-fix remedies at hand (Dailami and Atkin 1990).

14.10   Interbank Money Markets

There are few well-functioning interbank money markets in developing countries. Yet efficient monetary policy implementation and domestic resource allocation necessitate interbank borrowing and lending. Without an efficient way of lending among themselves, banks may be affected differentially by the same monetary policy measure. The speed of responses to monetary policy actions may also depend in part on the efficiency of the interbank money market. Reasons for nondevelopment include: (a) taxation of all financial transactions, making very short-term overnight borrowing and lending totally uneconomical; (b) central bank discount facilities that provide inexpensive and unlimited loans to banks in need of funds; (c) interest rate ceilings that prevent banks from negotiating terms of interbank loans; and (d) insufficient penalties for shortfalls in required reserves, as was the case in Turkey.

The interbank money market in the Yemen Arab Republic is impeded by reserve requirements imposed on such borrowed funds. In Turkey, bankers regard borrowing from another bank as a sign of weakness. In Thailand, money market development was impeded by four factors: (a) the commercial code, which did not define certificates of deposit as negotiable instruments; (b) stamp duties and withholding taxes applied to all borrowing (except at call); (c) interest rate ceilings; and (d) the captive market for government securities (Wilson 1986, 311).

Interbank borrowing and lending can improve both resource allocation and the effectiveness of monetary policy. Interbank money markets are needlessly deterred by explicit and implicit taxation, which raises virtually no revenue, precisely because even relatively low tax rates stifle the development of such short-term financial markets.

14.11   Indigenous Financial Institutions

In his survey of research on indigenous financial institutions, Jürgen Holst (1985, 126–127) points out that the informal financial sector has been subject to criticism for decades. Critics claim that its performance is bad or insufficient in virtually all respects. In recent years, however, an increasing number of experts have begun to evaluate the costs and benefits of informal financial institutions in a more objective manner in terms of responsiveness to the needs of savers and borrowers, economic efficiency, use of market power in setting interest rates and the allocation of resources.

Among others, Dale Adams (1991), Tim Besley, Stephen Coate, and Glenn Loury (1990), Frits Bouman (1990), Germidis, Denis Kessler, and Rachel Meghir (1991), Prabhu Ghate et al. (1992), Erhard Kropp et al. (1989), Gilberto Llanto (1990), Peter Montiel, Pierre-Richard Agénor, and Nadeen Ul Haque (1993), Hans Dieter Seibel (1989b), Seibel and Uben Parhusip (1992), and James Thomas (1992, 1993a, 1993b) have provided just such objective analysis in recent years.

Indigenous, informal, or unorganized finance abounds throughout the developing world. The informal institutions do, however, take different forms and perform different functions in different parts of the world. In Asia, indigenous financial institutions such as the curb market in Korea, the finance companies in India, and chit funds in Thailand tend to engage in a considerable volume of business and trade finance for even large-scale enterprises. In Africa, the predominant form of indigenous financial institution is the rotating savings and credit association, called *ekub* in Ethiopia, *djanggi* in Cameroon, *tontine* in Benin, *chilemba* in Malawi, Uganda, Zambia, and Zimbabwe, and *esusu* from Zaire to Liberia (Holst 1985, 122). Here indigenous financial institutions are used to finance household consumption or investment, or very small-scale business enterprises. Rotating credit associations, called chit funds in India and Thailand, are also common throughout Asia (Nayar 1984).

Ghate et al. (1992, ch. 2) classify informal finance into four categories. Intermittent lenders, such as friends and relatives, account for a considerable share of informal finance in most Asian developing countries; intermittent lending also takes place between firms. A second category of informal finance consists of professional moneylenders, pawnbrokers, indigenous bankers, and finance companies that make untied loans. The third category is tied credit, such as trade credit. Landlords who lend to their tenants can also be included in this category. The fourth category is group finance where individuals pool their savings for distribution among the group's members.

In the broadest, albeit necessarily incomplete, survey of indigenous financial institutions in developing countries, Wai (1977, 301) reports that 55–60 percent of the demand for noninstitutional credit is for purely productive purposes, a finding that differs from the commonly held belief that high-interest informal lending is invariably used to finance consumption expenditure.

Wai (1977, 293) finds that indigenous finance grew in real terms during the 1950s and 1960s, but not as fast as modern banking:

Unorganized money markets in most developing countries in the fifties were larger than the organized money markets. By the seventies this pattern had changed and the organized money markets in many countries became more important than unorganized money markets. (Wai 1977, 291)

In some countries, such as India and Korea, this was due to deliberate attempts by the government to suppress the indigenous financial system. Elsewhere, it was the result of the absorption of indigenous banks into the modern financial sector, as happened with the rural banks in the Philippines. In other cases, such as Japan in the first half of this century, it was due to the general process of economic development and the economies of scale in modern banking.

Indigenous banks in India used to provide a full range of banking services. With the development of modern banking, however, indigenous banks transformed themselves into specialized financial institutions serving sectors not well-served by the modern banks or providing services not offered by modern banks. Indigenous bankers in India now fall into one of three categories: full-service banks taking deposits and extending loans, commercial financiers lending primarily their own funds, and brokers bringing together borrowers and lenders (Timberg and Aiyar 1984, 43–44).

Finance corporations in India bear close resemblance to the full-service indigenous banks there. Typically, finance corporations are partnerships regulated under the Indian Partnership Act of 1932. They accept nonchecking deposits, offering deposit rates considerably above those offered by the modern banks (Nayar 1982, 1984). Average deposit rates offered by finance corporations and commercial banks in March 1980 are shown in Table 14.3 (Nayar 1984, 59). Finance corporations make loans by discounting trade bills and postdated checks. Some finance corporations run chit funds.

Thomas Timberg and C. V. Aiyar (1984, 44, 54) find four characteristics that explain why indigenous banks exhibit lower transaction costs than modern banks. First, indigenous bankers know their clients better than commercial banks. This reduces information costs. Second, administrative costs are lower for indigenous banks than for modern banks because their employees are paid less (and are less educated), the establishment is less elaborate, and the paperwork simpler. For example, continuous checking of employees for fraud is unnecessary, since most indigenous banks are very small. Third, indigenous bank interest rates are not regulated and can therefore adjust fully to market forces. Nonprice competition is thereby kept down to an optimum level. Fourth, indigenous banks are not subject to the reserve requirements that are imposed on modern banks.

Table 14.3. Average Deposit Rates of Interest in Indian Finance Corporations and Commercial Banks, March 1980

Deposit Type	Finance Corporations	Commercial Banks
Savings deposits	7.19	5.00
Under 1 year	9.16	5.50
1 year	13.03	7.00
2 years	14.44	7.00
3 years	16.81	7.00
4 years	17.70	8.50
5 years	18.91	8.50
10 years	–	10.00
3-year cash certificate	19.17	7.72
5-year cash certificate	20.32	10.46

Administration and default costs as percentages of earning assets for indigenous banks in India are (Timberg and Aiyar 1984, 56):

Banker	Administration	Default Loss	Total
Shikarpuri	4.5	1.0	5.5
Gujerati (Bombay)	2.5	0.5	3.0
Chettiars	3.1	1.5	4.6
Rastogi	3.5	1.5	5.0

These transaction cost percentages are substantially lower than those of the modern financial institutions discussed in section 14.3. Despite the evident efficiency of these indigenous banks, however, regulations have recently been proposed to limit their scope.

Most indigenous banks in urban India serve prosperous enterprises operating in traditional markets. The bulk of indigenous bank credit finances trade and industry in the form of working capital. Except in the intercorporate call market, indigenous bank lending rates are higher than modern bank loan rates, as might be expected. Noninterest costs of borrowing from the modern banks are substantial, whereas they are virtually nonexistent in borrowing from indigenous banks. Somewhat surprisingly, however, Timberg and Aiyar (1984, 48) find that funds from indigenous banks take longer to procure than funds from modern banks (when they were available).

There is a thriving indigenous part of the financial system in Thailand (Cole, Chunanuntathum, and Loohawenchit 1986, 152–153). Many moneylenders, among whom are rich farmers, live and operate in rural areas. Lending cattle is common, and borrowers pay back loans in cash or kind. A widespread form of noninstitutional lending in Thailand is the rotating credit association, or *pia huey*. This method of borrowing is now so popular that in the past few years several companies were formed to operate rotating credit associations. The recent increase in time deposits resulting from the higher real institutional deposit rates produced by declining inflation has, however, been attributed in part to the absorption of some of these noninstitutional markets into the institutional sector.

Indigenous financial institutions normally charge higher explicit loan rates than modern financial institutions. Nevertheless, it is far from clear that gross costs of borrowing from indigenous banks are greater than the gross costs of borrowing from modern banks. Zia Ahmed (1982, 135) presents a unique comparative study of borrowing costs, based on survey results. He finds that 84 percent of rural credit in Bangladesh is supplied by indigenous money-lenders. He estimates that the gross cost of borrowing from such moneylenders averages 86 percent a year. The gross cost of borrowing from commercial banks, however, averages 108 percent annually in rural Bangladesh. There are sizable noninterest costs of bank borrowing, which include travel, enter-tainment, bribes, and the opportunity cost of time involved in securing the loan. Part of the explanation for the high gross cost of bank borrowing in rural Bangladesh lies in the extremely small size of the average loan.

The term structures of gross borrowing costs from indigenous and com-mercial banks in Bangladesh differ considerably. The gross cost of bank borrowing drops sharply as the maturity of the loan increases, since a large proportion of the cost consists of front-end transaction costs. This creates a strong incentive to postpone repayment (Ahmed 1982, 139). Hence all mod-ern domestic financial institutions in Bangladesh suffer from serious levels of arrears (Ahmed 1982, 65). In contrast, the bulk of the gross cost of in-digenous borrowing is the interest cost. Therefore, the term structure of loans from indigenous banks does not slope downwards. Since the marginal cost of lengthening the maturity of a loan from indigenous banks is always positive in real terms, there is little or no incentive to postpone repayment unnecessarily.

Ghate et al. (1992, ch. 11) find little evidence that informal lenders reap monopoly profits. Relatively high interest rates are explained by opportunity cost, risk premium, and transaction costs. This explanation is consistent with the successful experiments with small-scale formal lending. In Indonesia, for example, the Badan Kredit Kecamatan (BKK) was established in 1972 with capital provided by the Central Java provincial government to make small-scale loans. The BKK had more than 500 branches and had made over seven million loans by the early 1990s.

Richard H. Patten and Jay K. Rosengard (1992) note that problem loans constituted less than 10 percent of the BKK's loan portfolio and the cumulative sum of overdue loans represented about 2 percent of the cumulative amount loaned by the early 1990s. Survey results indicate that BKK loans helped borrowers expand their businesses. This positive effect on borrowers occurred despite or even because of the fact that loan rates ranged from 2 to 4.8 percent *per month;* the BKK has been profitable. With inflation averaging under 10 percent annually over the past decade, these interest rates are relatively high in real terms. However, initial political objections to such high interest rates were overcome by advertising them in monthly form.

The success of the BKK can be attributed to its adherence to the fundamental principles of banking. It responded to market demand based on client characteristics, needs, and priorities. It established a clear market niche among its competitors. It engaged in financial intermediation between savers and investors, ensuring that interest rate spreads were sufficient to cover operating costs and loan writeoffs. Being able to attract savings has been essential for the BKK to expand and to become a viable financial institution. This would have been impossible had loan rates been restricted to those typically offered by commercial banks. Small-scale lending is not cheap, but BKK borrowers had investment opportunities with high enough yields to enable rapid repayment of interest and principal, leaving their businesses larger and more profitable in the longer run.

The link between indigenous and modern financial markets is closer in some countries than in others. Wai (1977, 306) concludes that the increased supply of finance from modern financial institutions has generally reduced indigenous bank lending rates. This finding refutes the neostructuralist hypothesis that curb market rates would rise in the aftermath of the financial liberalization and development program advocated by the McKinnon-Shaw school. Timberg and Aiyar (1984, 52) find that indigenous bank rates in India are affected positively by modern bank lending rates. Curb rates in Korea also appear to reflect general credit conditions (Cole and Park 1983, chs. 4, 5). In both these cases, however, the positive association is between two free-market interest rates, not an administratively fixed real deposit rate and the real curb market rate. Indeed, one would expect a rise in institutional rates towards their equilibrium levels to have an effect on curb market rates opposite to that of a rise in these equilibrium rates themselves.

Holst (1985, 141) concludes his survey of indigenous financial institutions in developing countries as follows:

> The conventional views on the performance of the informal financial sector need to be revised in the light of the empirical evidence. The performance of informal institutions is definitely commendable in the following respects:
>
> (a) Moneylenders, indigenous bankers and savings and credit associations respond remarkably well to their customers' short-term financing needs and cover also rural areas where the density of formal institutions is still low. Borrowers appreciate in particular their flexible procedures and the locational conveniences;
>
> (b) The efficiency of these institutions in terms of transaction costs (costs related to the default risk and administrative costs) appears to be quite

favorable. In many cases, costs tend to be lower than that of formal institutions, in particular, in dealing with small farmers and small businesses;

(c) Although in many cases the primary reason for joining a savings and credit association may be the desire to gamble, in the last analysis the strict requirements of regular contributions tend to improve members' savings habits.

The urban curb markets in Korea and Taiwan appear to be considerably more important for business finance than are curb markets in most other developing economies. In Taiwan, curb markets provided 48 percent of loans to private businesses in 1964. Although this ratio fell to 27 percent in 1973, it was back at 48 percent in 1986 (Lee and Tsai 1988, Table 9, 51). The curb market is also of considerable importance for business finance in Korea (Cole and Park 1983). In other developing countries, curb markets or informal credit arrangements appear to be used more to meet the demands of rural and unincorporated businesses and households rather than those of modern industries.

Tyler Biggs (1991, 182) argues that the Taiwanese government supported the curb market through the Negotiable Instruments Law enacted in the 1950s. This law made it a criminal offense to fail to honor a postdated check. Hence, curb market loans could be secured against checks dated three, six, or twelve months in the future since the law also prohibited banks from cashing checks before their due date. The loan would constitute the discounted value of the check. Initially, the postdated check might have been issued to a supplier or subcontractor. With endorsement, the holder of a postdated check could then discount it in the curb market. Checks might circulate several times and hence acquire several endorsements before their due dates.

> The penalty [for writing a bad check] was tough: Failure to redeem a postdated check could result in as many as two years in prison. And the law was vigorously enforced. The law specifically made all endorsers equally responsible for redeeming checks with the issuer. Government agencies policed the system, keeping records on bad check cases and referring malefactors to the courts for prosecution. (Biggs 1991, 182, 185)

A similar law supports the use of postdated checks as promissory notes in Korea.

Biggs (1991, 189–190) assesses the effect of this curb market as follows:

> Emergence of a large and thriving curb market has been enormously important to Taiwan's industrial development for at least four reasons. First, the curb market complemented the formal credit market by providing information-intensive, efficient credit facilities, what Scitovsky has called the "small loans" function of the curb market. Second, the curb market helped to mobilize domestic savings by offering high returns

(although riskier) on investable funds. Third, the presence of an active curb market increased the "fungibility" of financial resources by offering an alternative market-determined interest rate on investment funds: the "safety valve" function of the curb market. Fourth, many curb market transactions facilitated business dealings ("contracting modes") between heterogeneous firms.

Another crucial role of the curb market is to reduce the moral hazard problem of deposit insurance and bank bailouts. The riskier lending business goes to the curb market which is completely unprotected but does not jeopardize the payments system. Not only does free access to the curb market ensure that the opportunity cost of capital to all firms, both large and small, in Korea and Taiwan approximates the competitive free-market interest rate, but the absence of deposit insurance ensures that real interest rates do not rise to unsustainable levels. Curb markets in Korea and Taiwan appear to respond particularly flexibly to the rapidly changing product mix in their small-scale manufacturing sectors.

14.12 Summary

Commercial banks dominate financial sectors of most developing countries. Their performance has substantial influence on the overall efficiency of domestic resource mobilization and allocation. In many developing countries, bank performance is characterized by inefficient lending criteria, a reflection of both weak management and government interference. One empirical study indicates that the extent to which foreign banks are excluded or restricted provides a reasonable prediction of the overall efficiency of the banking system in that country. This chapter explored one of the consequences of inefficient lending criteria, namely high delinquency and default rates.

Until quite recently, most developing country governments and donor agencies generally viewed financial development in terms of increasing the number of specialized financial institutions, such as agricultural and industrial development banks. In general, the results have been disappointing. Some specialized financial institutions have performed far less efficiently than the commercial banks that were criticized for their nondevelopmental behavior in the first instance. Furthermore, the proliferation of specialized financial institutions has created financial layering, which in turn has increased intermediation costs because specialized financial institutions have generally been unable to raise resources directly from savers.

The approach towards financial sector development has now changed. The World Bank's (1980) financial sector report on the Philippines provides an example of the World Bank's change in emphasis with respect to financial sector development. The new stance favors despecialization, the promotion of competition, and a broader view of financial development. This new view is articulated more forcefully in a policy paper on financial intermediation. The major recommendation of this report is that "an important objective of future Bank operations should be the development of an efficient, robust and competitive financial system" (World Bank 1985, iv). Specific measures to achieve these aims include promoting a variety of financial intermediaries and institutions offering a range of financial services, supported by a reliable financial information system, a legal framework ensuring the enforceability of financial contracts, and regulatory and supervisory systems that ensure the stability of the financial system. Similar policy objectives are advocated by two staff members of the IMF (Khatkhate and Riechel 1980, 505).

The old view that curb market lending hampers economic development by facilitating consumption and reducing saving and investment has also been challenged. Both neostructuralists and the McKinnon-Shaw school show how curb markets can play a productive role in the development process. The evidence surveyed in this chapter supports the new view.

Financial sectors in many developing countries do not intermediate efficiently between savers and investors. One reason is financial repression, but other important reasons are market structure and management performance. Cartelized or oligopolistic banking systems jeopardize financial liberalization because bank associations step in to set interest rates when government agencies stop doing so. Weak management results in delinquency and default rates high enough to indicate inefficient resource allocation. Financial liberalization cannot by itself rectify the problem. There now seems to be sufficient evidence to indicate that financial development programs must address the issues of market structure and management performance in order to succeed.

Chapter 15

Government Intervention in the Financial Sector

15.1 Introduction

GOVERNMENT INTERVENTION IN A COUNTRY'S financial sector takes many forms, some benign, some debilitating. Many of today's banking regulations in industrial countries, particularly in the United States, are a legacy of the Great Depression (1929–1933). They are designed to maintain the stability and solvency of a system made inherently unstable by the practice of fractional reserve banking. Regulations that deterred competition have been dismantled within the past decade or so. Over this period, there has been a wave of financial liberalization in both industrial and developing countries.

Typically, governments have intervened in the financial sectors of developing countries to influence the allocation of credit, with the objective of accelerating economic development. This chapter starts with a general survey of the effects of the more popular forms of government intervention on the efficiency of the financial sector, using examples mainly from Asian developing countries. This is followed by sections covering specific forms of intervention that impair the efficiency of the financial system. Section 15.3 examines the effects of discriminatory taxation of financial intermediation. Section 15.4 discusses credit and exchange rate guarantee schemes. Section 15.5 analyzes the general case for bank nationalization before reviewing specific evidence on the performance of government-owned financial institutions in a sample of developing countries. Section 15.6 covers government promotion or ownership of specialized financial institutions established to service particular sectors of the economy.

The chapter then turns to two benign areas of government intervention—deposit insurance and bank supervision. Although there is some disagreement over the effects of deposit insurance on the efficiency of the financial system, there is little dispute over the need for adequate supervision of financial institutions. The chapter concludes with a brief discussion of some legal problems faced by institutional lenders in a number of developing countries. In many of them, providing a conducive legal framework for financial intermediation would improve efficiency by reducing transaction costs far more than any other type of government intervention.

15.2 Government Regulations and the Efficiency of the Financial Sector

In most countries bank regulation has two objectives. The first is the protection of depositors; the second is stronger monetary control. In many developing countries there is a third objective of bank regulation, namely the allocation of credit on the basis of planning priorities.

The belief that government should intervene to protect depositors springs from a perceived externality—one bank failure involving losses to depositors may encourage depositors in other banks to withdraw their funds. If enough depositors want their money back at the same time, not even the strongest and most efficient bank in the world can meet the withdrawals. This is a basic feature of fractional reserve banking. One bank failure can snowball and bring with it an epidemic of bank failures. Fear of the disruptive consequences of a wave of bank failures is the basis for government intervention to reduce the chances of this happening (Bryant 1987, chs. 6–9). One method is deposit insurance; another is government commitment that no bank will ever fail.

The Economist (1982b, 6) notes in a survey of finance in the Far East that "governments in the fastest growing developing countries since 1945 have placed themselves at the center of the economic stage by controlling the financial system. Savings are allocated to those industries earmarked for growth according to co-ordinated investment plans." Typically, however, financial policies in developing countries have neglected the role of the financial system in mobilizing domestic resources. Accelerating inflation and rising nominal interest rates in international markets during the 1970s produced a widening gap between real returns on domestic and foreign financial assets in most developing countries, due to the pervasiveness of administratively fixed institutional rates of interest in these countries. The World Bank (1985, 2) concludes that "if domestic savers had been paid as much in real terms as countries paid to foreign lenders and the expansion in credit kept in check—in particular loans to public enterprises—more resources could have been mobilized domestically and needs for foreign funding would have grown more in line with the debt servicing capacity of the countries."

John Bilson (1984, 55) concurs:

> The outstanding recent success stories in the national economic sweepstakes—Hong Kong, Japan, Korea, and Singapore, for example—have

all experienced very high savings rates in comparison with other countries. One role for a financial system is to ensure that citizens do have an incentive to save and that the savings are used efficiently and productively. Any policy which leads to large and unstable inflation rates invariably encourages unproductive savings in real goods. An effective monetary system must be able to assure those who hold money that its real value will be preserved. Furthermore, the real assets sacrificed in exchange for money should also be used effectively to promote development, particularly of small businesses that are likely to be the most important sources of employment and growth in income.

Unfortunately, government regulation of financial systems in developing countries has more frequently retarded than promoted economic development. The Asian success stories are atypical. Government policies in these economies have generally been well-formulated and well-executed. The objective of regulation has been clear—economic growth. In other developing countries, however, the situation in England during the industrial revolution is more apposite:

> At almost every point at which banking and monetary policy might have been used constructively to promote economic growth, the authorities either made the wrong decision or took no action at all. The monopoly of the Bank of England, the gross inefficiency of the Mint, the restrictions on small notes, the Resumption Act of 1819, the piecemeal and half-hearted reforms of 1826 and 1833, and, finally, the Act of 1844 itself, are all cases in point. Paradoxically, however, the very obstacles placed in the way of a rational banking and monetary system stimulated the private sector to introduce the financial innovations necessary for realization of the full benefits of the technical innovations in industry. (Fortunately for England, the law was sufficiently loose and its administration sufficiently lax that the obstacles to innovation were not insurmountable.) Among these financial innovations were the country banks themselves, the issues of token money and "shop notes," from which many of them grew, and the use of bills of exchange and checks as currency. Without these or similar devices it is scarcely conceivable that English industrial progress would have been either so rapid or so far-reaching. With them, innovating entrepreneurs gained control over real productive services in true Schumpeterian fashion. The financial system that developed to provide them, though not the best that could be imagined, did respond to the needs and demands of the times. (Cameron et al. 1967, 58–59)

Monetary policy is implemented in a substantial number of developing countries through the imposition of credit ceilings. Typically, a ceiling is set on the volume of loans each bank can provide. Excess bank funds can be used either to repay loans from the central bank, so reducing the cash base, or as excess reserves, so raising the reserve/deposit ratio. Hence, lowering credit ceilings reduces the money supply by reducing the cash base or by raising the reserve/deposit ratio (and so lowering the money supply multiplier).

Credit ceilings reduce efficiency in two ways. First, they limit all banks equally, even those that are most efficient at lending or those that have the most dynamic entrepreneurs as their clients. Hence credit ceilings impose an uneven rationing criterion because of the customer-market nature of bank credit. Second, credit ceilings reduce efficiency by destroying competition for deposits. Once the ceiling is reached, extra deposits represent idle cash reserves and so are not wanted. Banks stop making efforts to attract deposits and to provide good service to existing depositors. Alternatively, they may reduce deposit rates of interest. The overall effect of credit ceilings is to increase the spread between gross costs of borrowing and net returns to lenders. Indeed, credit ceilings deliberately reduce financial intermediation. Indonesia and Korea both abolished direct credit controls on individual banks in the early 1980s in order to improve the efficiency of financial intermediation.

Reserve requirements, credit controls, and binding loan rate ceilings impose private costs on deposit suppliers. They do not incur resource costs. Hence private total costs of supplying deposits will exceed the resource or social costs, and the supply of deposit money will be suboptimal. In practice, the main welfare costs of deposit and loan rate ceilings spring not from their effects on the supply of deposits but rather from their impact on financial intermediation between savers and investors.

15.3   Discriminatory Taxation of Financial Intermediation

Financial intermediation is subject to both explicit and implicit taxes that are not applied to other sectors of the economy and are therefore discriminatory. Implicit taxes consist in the main of reserve requirements and forced portfolio investments at below-market interest rates. In 1983, for example, reserve requirements averaged 75 percent in Argentina and 58 percent in Mexico (*World Financial Markets* April–May 1986, 5). High reserve requirements also constitute a major impediment to increased flexibility in the Jamaican banking system.

The World Bank (1985) recommends the reduction of reserve requirements in order to improve the efficiency of financial intermediation. However, Robert Myers, Hafez Ghanem, and Licia Salice (1986, 18) argue that

> there is usually more than one combination of reserve requirements and
> inflation rates that would cover a given level of budget deficit. At the
> moment, economists have no tools that would enable them to determine
> a preferred combination. This implies that Bank advice to reduce reserve
> requirements in many cases may be a recipe for higher inflation, unless
> the deficit is reduced.

Frederick Berger (1980) and James Hanson and Roberto de Rezende Rocha (1986, 5, 10) show that taxes and reserve requirements on financial intermediation provide negative effective protection to the domestic financial system. Financial intermediation is therefore encouraged to move abroad. *World Financial Markets* (April–May 1986, 8–9) points out that

> nonresident deposits in the United States are free of U.S. taxes and, if interest earnings on such deposits are undeclared in Latin America, as often is the case, they are effectively free of tax altogether. Other than on passbook savings, however, interest on deposits in Latin American financial institutions is generally taxed at source—and the applicable tax rates have tended to go up in recent years. Only in Brazil, prior to this year's abolition of indexation, did tax rates apply solely to the return above inflation.

To remove this distortion, discriminatory taxes, including the reserve requirement tax, have to be abolished, or foreign capital inflows must be subject to the same reserve requirements as are domestic financial institutions (Hanson and de Rezende Rocha 1986, 10). In many developing countries, discriminatory taxation of financial intermediation reduces the flexibility of the system by reducing significantly the funds available to the banks for discretionary lending.

15.4 Credit and Exchange Rate Guarantee Schemes

Bank concentration on financing traditional economic activities such as trade, together with the perceived shortage of credit for small- and medium-sized enterprises, has led a number of developed and developing countries to experiment with credit guarantee schemes. By guaranteeing 75–80 percent of the loan for fees of 1 to 4 percent, governments have attempted to persuade commercial banks to extend more loans to small new business enterprises. Jacob Levitsky and Ranga Prasad (1986, 11) conclude from their survey of credit guarantee schemes that the main problem is how to induce private commercial banks to participate in such schemes. The evidence on whether or not credit guarantee schemes actually work in practice is ambiguous.

By not guaranteeing 100 percent of the loan, credit guarantee schemes save themselves from disaster. At the same time, however, this feature ensures that voluntary participation by private commercial banks is insignificant in practice, precisely because the schemes apply specifically to high-risk lending.

Many developing country governments provide borrowers of foreign currency with exchange rate guarantees or insurance. Exchange rate insurance in Argentina was responsible in large part for chronic overborrowing, as firms substituted dollar debt for peso debt. After the reforms had been abandoned in 1981, real interest rates on dollar debt with exchange rate insurance turned highly negative. Continued borrowing abroad contributed to the ensuing balance-of-payments crisis (Petrei and Tybout 1985, 965).

Exchange rate guarantees provide a no-risk bet for foreign exchange borrowers. They subsidize foreign borrowing most just when such borrowing should be restrained—when expectations of devaluation rise. Forward markets and direct equity investments from abroad offer preferable alternatives.

15.5 Government-Owned Financial Institutions

Ask a private banker to summarize the basic aim of his bank and he will probably reply: "Primarily to make profits for our shareholders." Ask management of a public sector financial institution the same question and the answer might be something like this: "Primarily to promote economic development." In many countries, however, private banks have tended to promote economic development as a by-product of profit maximization much more successfully than government banks. There are two major reasons for this. First, private banks tend to be better managed than government banks, in many cases due to the inability of government banks to offer competitive salaries to attract or retain good bank managers. But even good managers cannot manage efficiently when political interference in such matters as staffing is endemic. Second, government banks are typically obliged to implement development policies, such as selected or directed credit programs, that hinder economic development. Private banks have more incentive and opportunity to evade such regulations and directives that misallocate resources.

The case for bank nationalization goes back to the writings of Marx and Friedrich Engels, both of whom advocated the centralization of credit in the hands of the state through a single national bank with an exclusive monopoly (Podolski 1973). Lenin was also a keen proponent of bank nationalization and monopolization: "Even before he took power, Lenin envisaged the banking system as becoming the backbone of the socialist state's administrative apparatus. Nationalization of private banking and establishment of a government monopoly of all foreign exchange transactions were among the first economic measures taken by the Bolshevik government in 1917" (Garvy 1968, 19). None of these political thinkers foresaw the technical difficulties involved in the process of nationalization and amalgamation.

The technical difficulties have, however, constituted the main reason why socialist governments in all Western European countries except Portugal have not fully nationalized their banking systems. The Norwegian Labor government backed down from its bank nationalization scheme after it realized how "extremely complicated the whole matter is, both from a legal, technical and political point of view. It would entail a new set of banking laws, new thinking on credit management and on monetary and credit policy" (Helgesen 1974, 103).

Back in Russia, the banks were duly nationalized in 1918. The unforeseen difficulties then encountered were such that by 1921 "the monetary system of the economy had ceased to exist" (Podolski 1973, 20). It was not until 1931 that the Soviet banking system was operating satisfactorily and could be used effectively as a mechanism for economic planning through the concept of control by the ruble, "a microeconomic control calculated to check or influence behaviour of individual enterprises" (Podolski 1973, 12).

The early Yugoslavian experience illustrates the difficulties of running an efficient centralized and nationalized banking system (Goldsmith 1975, World Bank 1975). Dimitri Dimitrijevic and George Macesich (1973, 51) conclude that "the principal deficiencies in the financial institutions came from their administrative character and strong government influence." In the Yugoslavian reforms of 1965 and 1966 banks were given far more autonomy and responsibility for domestic resource mobilization and allocation (Dimitrijevic and Macesich 1973, 52). When the need is felt, new banks in Yugoslavia are now established at the instigation of socialist enterprises, which themselves subscribe the initial capital. In this case, a full circle has been completed from nationalization of banks in order to separate them from industrial conglomerates to which they were subservient back to the principle that banks must be responsive primarily to the needs of business and hence must be creatures of the industrial class.

One of the features of banking systems that motivated bank nationalization in Eastern Europe—monopoly—can also be found in Western Europe and in many developing countries. Monopoly power has even been detected in the United States. The East Coast financial establishment was frequently held responsible for the high cost of credit in the Western states throughout the nineteenth century. Monopoly power certainly existed in Portugal. There the pre-1974 governments protected the country's financial-industrial cartel from external competition, so ensuring minimum innovation and responsiveness to financial demands of enterprises excluded from the inner circles. Most of Portugal's financial system was nationalized in March 1975.

In a contribution to the debate over bank nationalization in Britain, James Robertson (1974, 36) asserts that government regulation and sanction have been to blame in large part for uncompetitive and unresponsive banking. Close links between financial and other forms of business enterprise are not necessarily undesirable in themselves. But when these links are combined with the cartelization of a sizable section of the economy (encouraged or condoned by the government), the financial sector is unlikely to perform its role efficiently.

Eastern European countries have decentralized and are gradually privatizing their banking systems. Recent reforms in China involve the split-up of the People's Bank of China into a number of separate banks. In order to specialize in foreign exchange operations, the Bank of China became independent from the People's Bank in 1978. In 1979, the Agricultural Bank of China was restored and the China International Trust and Investment Corporation was established. The China Investment Bank was established in 1981, and the Industrial and Commercial Bank of China was established to take over the commercial activities of the People's Bank in 1983 (Weicai 1986, 232).

Early reforms in Eastern Europe provide another indication of the problems inherent in nationalized financial systems: "The need to reduce the volume of overdue loans is a recurrent theme in the financial periodicals and official statements" (Garvy 1968, 81). Many of the problems of government-owned DFIs arise from political interference. Korea recognized the almost inevitable temptation for political interference in loan disbursement and so finally denationalized commercial banks in the early 1980s. The General Banking Act was revised in 1982 to give more autonomy to the denationalized banks with respect to management decisions (Lee 1986, 138).

Nationalized commercial banks and DFIs are fairly prevalent in developing countries. Morris (1985, viii–ix, 19) identifies the following particular problems of the predominantly government-owned financial system in India: (a) proliferation of financial institutions; (b) low resource mobilization by DFIs; (c) low profitability of commercial banks due to overstaffing, high delinquency rates, risky priority sector lending, and low capitalization ratios; (d) reduced flexibility of banks to undertake discretionary lending; (e) increased administrative requirements for loan processing; (f) reduced scope for financial institutions to allocate credit on the basis of economic criteria; (g) reduced autonomy of top management in the larger financial institutions; (h) poor quality of field staff; and (i) weak management and supervision. One observer claims that government-owned financial institutions in Venezuela are simply there to buy votes. Another observer comments that the performance of state-owned banks is highly correlated with general civil service performance. Brazil possesses an excellent bureaucracy and good state-owned banks. The Banco de Brasil provides an example of a well-managed financial institution not subject to political corruption. A less satisfactory state of affairs is found in Venezuela and the Philippines.

After nationalization, efficiency in the Mexican banking system decreased considerably. Morale fell, as did salaries. Top jobs went to political appointees. Hence many Mexican banks no longer possess experienced top management. Credit approval is slow and inefficient, due in part to corruption. Personnel turnover is high and training programs are weak. The Sri Lankan nationalized banks have lost most of their well-trained and experienced bank officials to the private banks. State banks in Indonesia exhibit poor profitability and low efficiency. The state banks employ regular civil service personnel, who are badly paid and underqualified. Overstaffing is endemic.

Roland Tenconi (1986, 1–14) points out that the completely nationalized banking system in Madagascar suffers from lack of autonomy, lack of competition, and overstaffing. The Malagasy banking system faces serious solvency problems because the nationalized banks have been directed to lend to public sector enterprises that are now unable or unwilling to repay their loans. Exactly the same is true in Bangladesh (Hanson and Neal 1985, 89).

In Argentina, public sector financial institutions in the form of the provincial banks which hold one quarter of total commercial bank assets have caused a number of problems: (a) the provincial governments owning these banks have used them extensively to finance their own deficits; (b) nonperforming assets in the portfolios of the provincial banks constitute a much higher percentage of net worth than they do in private commercial banks' portfolios; (c) the central bank rediscount facility is largely preempted by the provincial banks; (d) distress borrowing by some provincial banks has contributed to the exorbitantly high real interest rates; (e) as fear of bank failures increased in the 1980s, deposits were transferred from private to provincial banks; and (f) the provincial banks are not automatically subject to central bank directives. Even when they are, as in the case of reserve requirements, these banks have simply failed to comply. In general, Argentine provincial banks have jeopardized the soundness of the private commercial banks through unfair competition.

The three remaining public sector banks in Bolivia are insolvent. The Banco Agricola de Bolivia, founded in 1946, has become insolvent several times. This bank is used primarily to address social problems in rural areas; its percentage of nonperforming assets is concomitantly high. The Banco del Estado (BANEST), also insolvent, suffers from serious operating inefficiencies, inadequate controls, and a high proportion of nonperforming assets. After its establishment in 1970, the BANEST competed effectively (albeit inequitably) with private commercial banks thanks to its ability to guarantee foreign loans, hold specially low reserve requirements, and obtain ready access to central bank rediscounts. As is so often the case, the basic problem in Bolivia springs from political interference. Many of the loans and guarantees made by the BANEST in its role as a development bank were made under political pressure for projects of dubious developmental benefits, either social or economic, but with substantial benefits for the recipients.

In Brazil, state financial institutions play a major role, while private financial institutions are becoming increasingly absorbed by business conglomerates. There, public sector financial institutions provide 50 percent of all loans to the private sector, many of them under selective or directed credit programs. Despite reasonable internal efficiency of federally owned financial institutions, financial markets are segmented, financial institutions are layered, and resources are misallocated as a result of these policies. Provincial banks in Brazil are tapped to finance election campaigns. After elections, these banks are invariably in critical condition.

Banks were nationalized in Costa Rica to implement selective credit policies in the late 1940s. Nationalized banks have a monopoly over deposits of less than six months maturity and thereby control 90 percent of total bank assets. As in Argentina, government banks in Costa Rica preempt the central bank's rediscount facility. They are not subject to any maximum leverage ratio. In the absence of deposit insurance for the private banks, government banks attract deposits because their deposits are automatically guaranteed by the government.

The three state banks in Ecuador provide 31 percent of total credit and investments of the financial system, excluding the central bank. Selective credit policies and interest rate ceilings have severely reduced the size of the financial system in relation to gross national product in recent years.

The majority of Peru's financial system is nationalized. The largest bank, Bank of the Nation, holds 28 percent of total assets, while other government-owned financial institutions hold 45 percent. The state banks were established to implement selective credit policies; Peru's financial sector suffers from considerable financial segmentation with many specialized financial institutions.

Problems of public sector financial institutions take two forms. The first consists of internal management problems, often the result of political interference or the lack of expertise and incentives. The second consists of external environmental problems created by the policy milieu in which public sector financial institutions are expected to operate. As a general premise, government ownership per se produces no special issues of concern, as evinced by widespread government ownership of financial institutions in France, Italy, and Taiwan. It is certainly the case, however, that Taiwanese banks are strongly criticized for their bureaucratic procedures and lack of initiative. That the publicly owned Taiwanese financial sector has done little damage to the Taiwanese economy lies in the fact that macroeconomic policies together with the roles expected of the public sector financial institutions have been conducive to rapid economic growth.

The worst combination is bad management facing bad macroeconomic policies. Specifically, when public sector financial institutions are obliged to pursue selective or directed credit policies that have social or political objectives, problems are compounded. Weak management combined with policy directives to lend on noneconomic criteria is a recipe for insolvency. Experience suggests that nationalized banks perform best when faced with competition from private banks and private direct financial markets. Management autonomy and competitive pay scales are also crucial prerequisites for successful nationalized banking. Complete nationalization invariably reduces financial sector efficiency and flexibility.

15.6   Specialized Financial Institutions

Practically all developing countries possess specialized public sector financial institutions such as DFIs. Deena Khatkhate and Klaus-Walter Riechel (1980, 505) provide a clear description of the rationale generally used to justify the promotion of specialized financial institutions in developing countries:

> In developing countries, demand for even basic financial services has often not yet been appropriately articulated. In such situations, it appears

desirable to generate through official intervention such special sources of supply that can meet socially desirable, albeit partially dormant, private demand. For this purpose, developing countries have often established new specialized financial institutions to satisfy the previously unmet demand. Operations of such institutions are generally insulated from competition by appropriate legislation and are even given substantial subsidies. Such actions are often defended by arguments that resemble those employed in the infant industry advocacy.

The World Bank (1980, 50) describes the proliferation of specialized financial institutions in the Philippines as follows:

> When it was observed that commercial banks made little effort to penetrate the countryside and to supply financial services to its residents, a system of rural [unit] banks was set up (1952). When a rising demand for medium and long-term development finance was felt in the early years after World War II, development institutions such as the Development Bank of the Philippines (1947) and a number of private development banks (1959) were created or encouraged. Recognition of unfulfilled credit needs of small-scale industries led to the creation of the National Cottage Industries Bank (1963). The perceived shortage of financial services in the Muslim provinces of Mindanao prompted the establishment of the Amanah Bank (1963). More often than not new financial institutions were "tailor-made" in the sense that the legal framework within which they operated reflected fairly rigidly the need—as perceived by the legislators—for additional financial services by particular types of potential customers. This approach to the organization of the financial sector has essentially prevailed to date.

Exactly the same pattern of financial development has been detected in Peru, where new financial institutions were created to carry out each change in policy emphasis. Legislation and other regulations specified the types of activities each financial institution in the Philippines could conduct. For example, rural banks were severely restricted as to borrowers and purposes for which loans could be made.

The proliferation of specialized financial institutions in the Philippines led to serious fragmentation and segmentation of the credit market. There was little competition among financial institutions, intermediation costs were high, and allocation was inefficient. In recognition of these problems, some reforms were implemented in July 1980 to remove or at least to reduce certain functional distinctions between commercial banks and the specialized financial institutions. These measures formed part of a World Bank–sponsored program to rationalize the Philippine financial system, to improve the efficiency of financial intermediation, and to increase domestic resource mobilization.

Evidently the World Bank viewed the promotion of specialized financial institutions in Indonesia as appropriate, despite its rather different assessment in the Philippines. Khatkhate and Delano Villanueva (1978, 982) also criticize the proliferation of specialized financial institutions: "The evidence is strong that the specialized institutions are no panacea for solving the basic problem of credit allocation."

Almost all developing countries possess specialized financial institutions in the form of DFIs or development banks. Invariably, these specialized financial institutions have been established to attract foreign resources, to mobilize domestic savings (in part by developing capital markets), and to allocate investible funds efficiently. The record of the past 30 years suggests that DFIs have attracted foreign resources effectively, have failed completely to mobilize domestic resources, and have a mixed (and deteriorating) record in allocating funds to productive investment projects. In general, DFI efforts at promoting the development of capital markets have been disappointing (Gordon 1983, 16–24).

Very few DFIs have become self-supporting, autonomous financial institutions capable of mobilizing resources entirely on commercial terms. This is partly because DFIs have often been required to make loans at low rates of interest, frequently negative in real terms. About one third of the DFIs in developing countries are now in serious financial difficulties, due in the main to large percentages of nonperforming loans. The problem of arrears increased substantially with the worldwide recession and deteriorating terms of trade for developing countries in the early 1980s. By the end of 1983, almost half the DFIs in developing countries had more than 25 percent of their loans affected by arrears. One quarter of these DFIs suffered arrearages of over 50 percent (World Bank 1985, 11). The World Bank (1985, ii) concludes, however, that "the current problems of DFIs relate in part to their basic approach to finance, the limitations of their management and frequently their inability to follow sound business practices." One particular problem identified is the financing of risky investments solely with debt.

The World Bank has been the leading supporter of DFIs in developing countries over the past three decades or so. Its original model was a privately owned institution in which strong technical expertise in project appraisal would be developed. Since the 1950s, however, there has been a trend towards state ownership of DFIs; the majority of them are now state-owned. The World Bank resisted this tendency for a while, but began lending to government-owned DFIs in 1968. According to David Gordon (1983, 19–20), government-owned DFIs have had a poorer record than privately owned DFIs in terms of domestic resource mobilization and allocation. Political factors influence lending to a greater extent in government-owned than in private DFIs. The World Bank (1985, ii) states:

> The DFIs were in the 1970s increasingly viewed and acted as tools of development policy, channelling resources to publicly promoted or owned enterprises and to priority sectors which commercial lenders were unwilling to finance. The managements of DFIs that were heavily dependent on government resources and operated in highly regulated financial

markets were unable to make lending decisions based on independent assessments of business risks and profits. In addition, the intermediaries' spreads often did not reflect the true costs and risks involved in long-term lending to higher risk projects.

In the 1970s a number of DFIs extended their activities into merchant banking, brokerage and underwriting, money market operations, and leasing. Indeed, DFIs as well as commercial banks have moved in the direction of universal banking (Gordon 1983, 39–41).

Carlos Diaz-Alejandro (1985, 7) points out that in Latin America

> the development banks created to solve one form of perceived market failure (lack of long term credit for socially profitable non-traditional activities) had led to another, i.e., a segmented domestic financial market in which some obtained (rationed) credits at very negative real interest rates, while non-favored borrowers had to obtain funds in expensive and unstable informal markets. Public controls over the banking system typically led to negative real interest rates for depositors. "Financial repression" became an obstacle to domestic savings and their efficient allocation, and financial intermediation languished.

A major inherent problem with virtually all specialized financial institutions in developing countries springs from the fact that they are established to lend to those that existing financial institutions—the commercial banks—have avoided. By and large, commercial banks choose not to lend when the perceived risks are too high. Hence specialized financial institutions are set up deliberately to lend to high-risk borrowers. However, they are not compensated for assuming higher risks with higher loan rates. Invariably, therefore, the specialized financial institution set up to support a problem sector of the economy itself becomes a problem institution. Furthermore, priority sectors delineated for special financial assistance rather infrequently embrace the new innovative entrepreneurs spearheading economic development. Indeed, one priority group in India consists of sick firms. One day they may get their Sick Bank.

15.7 Deposit Insurance

Deposit insurance was introduced first in the United States in 1934. It has undoubtedly achieved its primary objective, the prevention of bank panics. Milton Friedman and Anna Schwartz (1963, 434–442) claim that deposit insurance has contributed much more to monetary stability in the United States than the establishment of the Federal Reserve System. It is hardly surprising, therefore, to find almost unanimous advocacy for deposit insurance in developing countries by the IMF, the World Bank, and other policy advisors (McKinnon 1991). The Central Banking Department of the IMF has advised on the establishment of deposit insurance schemes in several developing countries, including Chile, the Dominican Republic, Panama, and Trinidad and Tobago.

The two important questions concerning deposit insurance in developing countries are: (a) Has deposit insurance facilitated domestic resource mobilization? (b) Has deposit insurance decreased the efficiency of domestic resource allocation? Diaz-Alejandro (1985, 4) outlines the academic objection to deposit insurance: "Like any other insurance scheme, deposit insurance is vulnerable to moral hazard consequences, i.e., it induces depositors to think that 'one bank is as good as another,' and leads bank managers to undertake riskier loans." In such case, bank supervision must be used to prevent overly risky bank lending.

Deposit insurance does appear to have prevented runs on the banks in Argentina and Chile. Conversely, inadequate deposit insurance has been blamed for the 1982 run on the banks in Turkey. Under the highly inflationary conditions there, insurance of principal only and the possibility of having deposits in insolvent banks frozen for up to three years made deposit insurance almost worthless. Nevertheless, one of the benefits of an *explicit* deposit insurance scheme is to convince depositors that they do *not* have 100 percent cover.

Ronald McKinnon (1993, 84–91) emphasizes the adverse selection problem that arises with deposit insurance when inflation is high and unstable. When macroeconomic instability causes positive correlation between returns on alternative bank-financed projects, banks may no longer seek to reduce adverse selection through credit rationing. If deposit insurance protects depositors, banks may choose riskier lending strategies when macroeconomic instability produces strongly correlated outcomes. This is because favorable outcomes produce large bank profits, while unfavorable outcomes resulting in massive bank losses are borne mainly by the deposit insurance agency. Hence, instead of lowering the loan rate to reduce adverse selection when instability increases, banks may have an incentive to raise it. When banks operate under such conditions of macroeconomic instability and deposit insurance protects depositors, effective prudential regulation and supervision is imperative. A second-best solution may be to impose a ceiling on loan rates of interest.

Samuel Talley and Ignacio Mas (1992, 330–331) conclude that the extent of moral hazard caused by implicit deposit protection schemes (IDPSs) or explicit deposit insurance schemes (DISs) depends on

> (1) whether protection is extended to bank management and shareholders, and (2) the feeling of safety imparted to depositors. Insofar as DISs operate through a set of established rules, they can completely eliminate the expectation of managers and shareholders that they will benefit from the insurer's actions. Because such options are not ruled out in IDPSs, these systems are likely to result in greater moral hazard on the part of bankers. It seems likely that the conversion [from IDPS to DIS] would

result in less moral hazard on the part of the bankers, but more moral hazard on the part of the depositors.

However, Talley and Mas (1992, 334) then suggest that there is no point in setting up explicit deposit insurance systems unless countries

> (1) have at least a fairly stable banking system, (2) have an effective prudential regulation and bank supervision system, and (3) exhibit a willingness to adequately fund a DIS and give it the necessary government backup support that may be required to get the system through a period of stress. In our judgment, there probably are relatively few developing countries that now meet these conditions.

There has been increasing recognition that prudential regulation and supervision is a key prerequisite for financial stability. In their absence, financial systems are prone to financial crises, as witnessed by Chile, which experienced high real interest rates in the 1980s: "These incredibly high interest rates on peso loans represented, in large part, the breakdown of proper financial supervision over the Chilean banking system. Neither officials in the commercial banks themselves nor government regulatory authorities adequately monitored the creditworthiness of a broad spectrum of industrial borrowers" (McKinnon 1991, 383).

Over the past decade, weak supervision and government guarantees of deposits permitted the banks in Argentina to assume imprudent risks. Distress borrowing developed among producers of tradable goods as the real exchange rate became increasingly overvalued. The moral-hazard problem in Argentina was caused not only by implicit deposit insurance but also by implicit equity insurance. The lack of clear policies on the part of the central bank created expectations that bank shareholders would not suffer large losses. Because explicit or implicit deposit insurance is a form of government subsidy to indirect finance, it increases "the appetite for debt," leading to greater financial fragility (Veneroso 1986, 36).

Deposit insurance also has ramifications on the international front. Vihang Errunza and Joseph Ghalbouni (1986, 229) argue that it throws more risk onto the international financial markets. McKinnon (1991) believes that deposit insurance is responsible for the entry of banks into the riskier long-term international financial markets. John Cuddington and Gordon Smith (1985, 8) suggest that the high proportion of net international capital flows routed through financial institutions over the past decade is due to deposit insurance and expectations of government bailouts. Heinz Arndt and Peter Drake (1985) and McKinnon (1991) advocate regulations that would get banks out of the long-term international capital market.

Had deposit insurance actually increased the average riskiness of bank lending, one would expect to observe higher real loan rates of interest after the introduction of deposit insurance. The issue is murky because deposit insurance is frequently implicit rather than explicit. Nevertheless, a comparison of real bank lending rates before and after 1934 both in the United States and elsewhere does not indicate any significant rise. Indeed, the worldwide negative real loan rates of interest in the 1970s lead to the opposite conclusion.

Extraordinarily high real loan rates are observed when a substantial proportion of a country's banks have zero net worth or bank managements believe that shareholders as well as depositors are implicitly insured by the government. Velasco (1986b, 4) comments that "in a high-indebtedness situation even a small firm starts to behave strategically: if it alone defaults on its loans and/or declares bankruptcy, it will be penalized; if many firms do it at once, then the costs to each are likely to be much smaller. It then becomes rational to borrow and wait, in the hope that mounting debts will force large numbers of firms into default."

Like financial liberalization, deposit insurance works well when banks are regulated and supervised effectively. Deposit insurance per se does not guarantee an appropriate solution to financial crises, as witnessed by Venezuela and Colombia (Morris et al. 1990, 78–79). Success necessitates complementary systems to detect and confront banking problems when liquidation is not desirable. Given the prerequisite of adequate bank supervision, however, deposit insurance has been highly effective in maintaining financial stability.

15.8 Bank Supervision

In 1973, the new Chilean government auctioned off the nationalized banks to the private sector with little concern over the banking credentials of the new entrants (Diaz-Alejandro 1985, 8). Furthermore, Mauricio Garcés Larrain (1986, 7) points out that "a portion of the problem arose from the fact that many of these institutions had been purchased by their owners with a loan, to repay which it was necessary to resort to the funds of the same institutions purchased." Vittorio Corbo (1985, 905) blames bad banking practices for the collapse of eight financial institutions in Chile that had to be rescued by the central bank; they were renationalized in 1983. McKinnon (1991, 373) blames inadequate supervision: "The failure to exercise proper supervisory control over the banking system ... became an important contributing factor to the ultimate breakdown of Chile's otherwise well-designed program of economic liberalization." Ghanem (1986, 8, 30) suggests that bank failures in the Philippines were also due to both mismanagement and inadequate supervision.

Corbo and Jaime de Melo (1985a, 864) state that Chilean "banks in difficulty raised interest rates to attract new deposits, which they used to cover operating losses." One observer finds that Latin American banks in general seem to have a penchant for throwing good money after bad. This phenomenon is caused, in part, by the absence of clear rules on delinquency and default. Bad loans do not have to be written off in any systematic fashion.

Hence banks engage in competitive window dressing to keep up appearances. At the root of the problem lies the lack of sound regulation. The lack of adequate regulations defining nonperforming assets is also a problem in Bangladesh and Sri Lanka. In contrast, Korean banks hardly ever write off bad loans. The occasional scandal there is dealt with promptly by the central bank leading a rescue operation with financial assistance from the other commercial banks. To a certain extent, supervision can substitute for regulations, as it does in Britain. Clearly, regulations cannot replace supervision.

In comparing Asian and Latin American experiences, McKinnon (1991, 380) notes:

> In Asian countries like Korea and Taiwan, regulatory authorities have been more consistently cautious than their Latin American counterparts about decontrolling (fully liberalizing) the activities of commercial banks —for which the state is necessarily the lender of last resort. Bank loan portfolios have been more carefully monitored (not always benevolently), and competition in the money markets has typically been limited by state-set standard deposit and loan rates.

McKinnon's views, which echo those of Arnold Harberger (1988), are consistent with the empirical findings on monetary policies in Pacific Basin countries reported in section 11.4. Nevertheless, Michael Skully and George Viksnins (1987, 107) claim that Korean banks are inadequately supervised. In any event, adequate bank regulation and supervision are crucial prerequisites for both financial stability and flexibility (Polizatto 1990).

15.9 Legal Environment for Financial Intermediation

Legal problems in the financial sector take two forms. First, there is the issue of the legal framework under which financial institutions operate. In this connection, Khatkhate and Riechel (1980, 513) comment that

> conflict of interest situations and the prevalence of excessive market power require legislation, like antitrust laws, oriented toward tackling these problems directly rather than indirectly through a narrowing of the range of activities a financial institution can cover. The possibility that such unsavory practices may recur should not be taken as a pretext to devise a straightjacket of banking legislation that would destroy the responsiveness, flexibility, versatility, and the dynamism of the financial system.

Second, banks have difficulties securing loans and in obtaining legal redress in the event of nonpayment in many developing countries. For example, there are serious legal problems associated with financial intermediation in Indonesia. New laws are required to enable owners to establish clear titles to both movable and immovable property, and also to allow lenders to take collateral and to collect debts more easily. The Central Banking Department of the IMF has helped a number of developing countries to draft legislation and regulations that improve debt collection.

Under the Debt Recovery Act, the government banks in Sri Lanka cannot seize property of other government-owned enterprises. Hence they are unable to secure loans to state enterprises. In any case, Sri Lankan banks are hampered by slow court procedures; it can take five years to obtain a court order for the seizure of collateral of private parties.

Perhaps one of the most extreme cases of an inadequate legal environment for banking was found in Afghanistan in the 1960s and early 1970s. By 1971, not only had the volume of credit measured at constant prices that was extended to the private sector declined considerably over the past decade, but the variety of loans had also contracted. The United Nations (1970, 106) comments on the difficulties of debt collection: "The banks are reluctant to widen their range of borrowers or to extend credit facilities to industry and agriculture, owing to inadequate protection under existing laws."

The legal problems arose in the main from the influence borrowers continued to exert over the disposal of their collateral, slow and inefficient court procedures, the political and social influence of the borrower, incompetent court officials, and corruption. By the early 1970s, all the government-owned financial institutions had exhausted their resources and were essentially insolvent due to the high percentages of nonperforming assets on their books.

In the course of collecting a number of case histories of problematic loans, the following pattern seemed to emerge (Fry 1974, 144–145):

1. A loan was granted against collateral consisting of shares in a few specified joint stock companies, jewelry, or a real estate mortgage. Unsecured loans were also extended in a few cases.

2. The loan was not repaid on the due date. After negotiation, an extension was usually granted.

3. The bank finally decided to act upon the security. In the case of import finance, this should have been routine and straightforward because the documents needed for customs clearance of all bank-financed imports were supposed to go directly to the financing bank. Unfortunately, customs clearance without the necessary documents was possible through the judicious distribution of relatively small amounts of baksheesh. Even when goods were held up at customs houses, no fixed period after which they became the bank's property was specified in any law or regulation. In the case of other secured loans, the borrower could insist on a minimum price and even the timing of any sale. The transfer of equities also required the borrowers' approval. Land titles were often nonexistent. In practice, expropriation and resale of land were

virtually impossible. Potential buyers of expropriated land were easily dissuaded from bidding.

4. In the few instances where a case reached the courts, decisions were influenced through baksheesh, social pressure, or political influence. The banks hardly ever received satisfaction from the courts.

In most developing countries, banks try to avoid legal recourse precisely because legal systems tend to be unsupportive. Under such circumstances, banks are bound to be more cautious and less flexible over extending loans to new and untested clients.

15.10 Summary

Government intervention in the country's financial system is endemic in both industrial and developing countries. The justifications are generally perceived externalities and market failures. In relatively few developing countries, however, has government intervention been benign. Vested interests have ensured that entry barriers are maintained and competition from direct markets is suppressed. Many developing country governments have overtaxed the financial system through high reserve requirements, directed credit programs, and inflation. Government intervention, taking the form of ownership and control of commercial banks and specialized financial institutions, has led to high levels of nonperforming assets.

Although government intervention in financial sectors of developing countries appears to have increased during the postwar period, bank prudential supervision has typically remained inadequate. Part of the reason is undoubtedly the difficulty in recruiting qualified staff to government regulatory and supervisory agencies. Another serious lacuna in a number of developing countries is the legal framework under which financial intermediaries operate.

Public sector financial institutions in developing countries fail to promote economic development when they are used to implement misguided development strategies or noneconomic goals entirely. Using them instead of public works as a means to alleviate unemployment, for example, removes responsibility for any measure of efficiency from bank management. Paying subsistence-level salaries based on civil service pay scales to top management of public sector financial institutions is another recipe for incompetence and inefficiency.

Once internal barriers to efficiency are removed, development policies require attention. Even good management cannot avoid the inevitably high proportion of nonperforming assets produced when loans are extended to priority sectors of the economy on noneconomic criteria by order of politicians or government planners. The financial system does indeed lie at the heart of a capitalist system. Interference with its activities in the form of directed credit policies and other such bureaucratic interventions simply impedes the creation of wealth. Redistribution of this wealth is another matter and can never come before its creation in the first place.

Part IV

Monetary and Financial Policies in Economic Development

Chapter 16

Macroeconomic Environment and Macroeconomic Policies

16.1 Introduction

GENERAL MACROECONOMIC CONDITIONS have substantial impact on the financial sector and the pace of financial development. Ronald McKinnon (1973, 77–79) and Edward Shaw (1973, 119–120) both emphasize low and stable inflation as a part of, as well as a prerequisite for, financial development. Inflation rose and became more volatile almost everywhere in the 1970s. During the 1980s it continued to do so in many developing countries. Variable and so necessarily unanticipated inflation produces portfolio shifts towards short-term instruments, such as currency and sight deposits. The liquidity premium rises, so making longer-term instruments less attractive to their issuers (Ness 1972, 235–237; Shaw 1975, 9). Furthermore, "monetary policy that adds to the risk of money holding drives risk aversion demand to physical wealth, consumption or foreign assets" (Shaw 1973, 61).

Capital markets disintegrate in times of high and variable inflation. For the same reason, their establishment and development under such conditions are impossible (Wai and Patrick 1973, 280). In Argentina, for example, accelerating inflation has virtually eliminated the demand for time deposits with a maturity over 30 days and driven down the ratio of the broadest measure of money (*M4*) from 35 percent of GDP at the end of 1980 to $12\frac{1}{2}$ percent of GDP in mid-1985.

A reasonable degree of price stability is possibly the most crucial prerequisite for effective and efficient domestic resource mobilization and allocation through the financial sector. The inflationary surge of the early 1970s had subsided by 1976 in the industrial countries and by 1978 in the oil-exporting countries. Inflation fell much less in the developing countries that do not export oil (hereafter referred to as non-oil developing countries), continuing at a rate in excess of 20 percent until 1980, when it accelerated to 32.3 percent. Inflation peaked at over 100 percent in 1990.

James Hanson and Craig Neal (1985, xiii) state that the success of financial liberalization programs depends on appropriate domestic fiscal, monetary, exchange rate, commercial, and trade policies. They also comment that "negative real [interest] rates are generally not a problem, in and of themselves, but a symptom of much larger problems: that the whole macroeconomic framework—monetary, fiscal, exchange rate and tariff policies, as well as the interest rate—are out of line" (Hanson and Neal 1985, xv).

McKinnon (1991, 380–381) also stresses price stability as a prerequisite for successful financial liberalization:

> Both Asian governments [Korea and Taiwan] first sought monetary (price-level) stabilization together with some financial deepening, before fully liberalizing the capital market activities of commercial banks. In contrast, the failed liberalizations during 1977–82 in the Southern Cone of Latin America—not only in Chile, but also in Uruguay and in Argentina—were all characterized by rather complete deregulation and privatization of the commercial banks while inflation remained high and unstable.

Price stability, fiscal discipline, and policy credibility may well be the three key factors explaining Asian successes and Latin American failures in financial reforms over the past three decades (Caprio et al. 1994).

The next section analyzes the worldwide upsurge of inflation in the 1970s. Although inflation fell in the industrialized countries during the first half of the 1980s, it continued to accelerate in the developing countries. Hence this section explores possible common causes of accelerating inflation in the developing countries. The empirical findings suggest that inflation in these countries is predominantly homegrown. Monetary instability is an endemic problem in the developing countries. Since the early 1970s, monetary policy in these economies has been used with increasing frequency to counteract exogenous shocks. The invariable side effect has been higher inflation.

Section 16.3 analyzes the causes of recent financial instability and crises in developing countries. It links the macroeconomic aspects of financial liberalization covered in Parts I and II with the microeconomic issues explored in Part III. Finally, section 16.4 reviews the trends in macroeconomic and financial sector policy advice that developing countries have received over the past two decades.

16.2   Worldwide Inflation

Since a reasonable degree of price stability is possibly the most crucial prerequisite for effective and efficient domestic resource mobilization and allocation through the financial sector, this section concentrates on the causes and effects of the recent inflationary surge in developing countries. Worldwide inflation (measured as a weighted average using GDPs in U.S. dollars as weights) averaged 3.5 percent annually in the 1950s, 4.2 percent in the 1960s, and 10.4 percent in the 1970s. The secular acceleration in inflation was more pronounced in the developing than in the industrialized countries. On average, inflation has risen in every region of the world and in every group of countries over the past two decades. It has also shown greater variability—between country groups, within country groups, within individual countries, between components of consumer price indices, and among relative prices of individual commodities. The increased variability that was concomitant with higher average inflation is not coincidental. The model developed by Dennis Logue and Thomas Willett (1976) shows that higher inflation will be more variable and hence less predictable.

The overall picture of inflation in the developing countries over the past two decades is one of secular upward drift. Higher inflation has been accompanied by greater variance. Inflation in the developing world accelerated from 21.9 percent in 1976–1980 to 33.8 percent in 1981–1985, and to 60.6 percent in 1986–1990. In 1990, the average inflation rate in developing countries was 107 percent. In comparison, inflation declined steadily in the industrial countries from 12 percent in 1980 to 5 percent in 1990.

In addition to the increasing divergence between inflation in the industrial and developing countries, average inflation rates also diverged between groups of developing countries (semi-industrial, primary producing, populous South Asian, least developed, and oil-exporting), among developing countries within each group, and within each country. Furthermore, relative commodity prices exhibited greater variability in the 1970s than they had in the 1960s (Cline 1981, 16). In this case, variability is synonymous with unpredictability, since inflation is not determined solely by past values of observable variables. Economic activity, therefore, takes place in an increasingly uncertain world.

Uncertainty causes economic inefficiency because the allocation of investible funds can be optimal only if all agents correctly estimate the same real rate of interest in making their decisions involving the intertemporal allocation of resources. Inflation uncertainty, however, increases the dispersion of *expected* inflation. Dwight Jaffee and Ephraim Kleiman (1977, 301) find that there is indeed a strong positive relationship between the standard deviation and the average rate of inflation *expected* by survey respondents. A greater dispersion of expected inflation rates necessarily raises the dispersion of ex ante real rates of interest. Some investors view the real interest rate as relatively high, while others view it as relatively low.

On the basis of a cross-section analysis of 40 developing countries, Constantine Glezakos (1978, 179) concludes that "price instability, regardless of the price expectations model used for its estimation, has significant negative effects on income growth." One explanation for this empirical finding is that inflation uncertainty reduces investment efficiency, as suggested by Axel Leijonhufvud (1981). Stanley Fischer (1981, 34) finds that the greater inflation uncertainty accompanying a rise in the inflation rate in the United States from zero to 10 percent imposes a welfare cost of about 0.3 percent of GNP and increases unemployment by 2 percentage points. In many developing countries, the cost is likely to be greater due to the greater number of rigidities imposed on relative and absolute price movements by government regulation.

Since inflation accelerated everywhere in the 1970s, it seems reasonable to search for one or more common causes of the explosion in aggregate demand. The start of such an inquiry is an attempt to separate changes in annual rates of inflation into common and country-specific components. Using 20 observations from 1961 to 1980 on inflation in each of the 53 developing countries for which complete data sets are available, the change in the inflation rate was regressed on time and country dummies. The correlation coefficient of 0.02 indicates that there were no general worldwide movements in inflation rates. Actual percentage point changes in inflation varied too widely among the developing countries for any common trends to be detected. They also fluctuated too widely within each country over time for the country-specific effects (the country dummies) to be significant.

When developing countries that suffered acute inflation (averaging over 80 percent annually for at least three years) and chronic inflation (averaging over 20 percent annually for at least five years) are dropped from the sample of 53 developing countries analyzed above, the correlation coefficient increases to 0.251. The time dummies now contribute 0.246, leaving only 0.005 attributable to the country dummies. In other words, 25 percent of the variation in changes in inflation rates within this subset of developing countries is "explained" by common causes. Even for this group of developing countries, however, the explanation for the bulk of inflation rate changes must be sought elsewhere. Using a latent-variables model, Edgar Feige and Kenneth Singleton (1981) also find that a substantial proportion of the variation in inflation rates is due to country-specific disturbances.

There is still considerable dispute over what are the relevant country-specific disturbances responsible for inflation. The main lines of contention are drawn between cost-push and demand-pull explanations. The cost-push explanations have maintained support, despite vigorous attack on both theoretical and empirical grounds (Lipsey 1979, 289–290; Parkin 1980). Phillip Cagan (1979, 18) explains the appeal of cost-push theories:

> Empirical studies have long found that short-run shifts in demand have small and often insignificant effects, and that, instead, costs play a dominant role. The most common form of this evidence is a statistical regression of price changes on changes in unit wage and material costs and on a proxy for demand shifts. The latter variable usually has a small, and often statistically insignificant, regression coefficient, while the cost variables are highly significant and account for most of the total correlation.

There is, however, an explanation for this relationship in terms of a demand-pull theory of inflation. Final goods are typically produced under conditions of virtually constant marginal costs. Hence an increase in demand for finished goods and services produces an expansion in output but little or no price change. Subsequently, the derived demands for raw materials and labor rise. Since these are not constant-cost or elastic supply markets, prices of raw materials and wages increase—*before* prices of finished goods and services. Now marginal costs of final goods go up and hence higher costs are passed on; final goods' prices rise *after* those of labor and raw materials. Clearly, however, the initial cause of inflation in this case is excess demand rather than higher costs. The latter are dependent on the former (Cagan 1979, 18–23).

Whatever the areas of disagreement, there is general agreement within the economics profession that inflation cannot be sustained without monetary accommodation. Inflation will stop, possibly at an unacceptable cost in terms of forgone output, if a country's money supply is controlled. In general, however, developing countries have failed to implement successful anti-inflationary policies. Indeed, the World Bank (1985, 2) states that "neglect of domestic monetary and credit policies in many of these countries in the 1970s led to inflation at home and excessive borrowing abroad; this in turn forced severe retrenchment in the 1980s."

There has been no secular decline in developing countries' inflation rates. Furthermore, the majority of developing countries that had initiated stabilization programs abandoned them before inflation was eliminated. Indeed, the inflation rate tended to return to, if not exceed, its previous peak. Attempts to reduce inflation generally produce a recession because the initial decline in inflation is unexpected. If expected inflation exceeds actual inflation, entrepreneurs interpret the price shortfall to reflect a decline in the real demand for their products. Production is cut back and unemployment rises. At this point, the stabilization program may be abandoned on the grounds that it is not worth the cost. The cost in terms of lower or even negative economic growth can be avoided if inflation expectations can be brought down in step with the actual inflation rate or if counteracting measures can be taken to stimulate production. Credibility of monetary policy announcements is probably the single most important factor in determining the speed with which expectations adjust to actual inflationary experience, as exemplified by Taiwan's experience. The worst traumas of stabilization policies have been suffered by those countries least capable of implementing the appropriate macroeconomic policies. Credibility is strained at the outset, and scepticism is vindicated when the attempt is abandoned.

A few developing countries reduced inflation rates substantially without a concomitant large deceleration in the rate of economic growth. This group includes Israel in the mid-1950s, Korea in 1964–1966, and Turkey in 1959–1960 and 1979–1981 (Krueger 1981, 92). Two policy measures appear to be capable of sustaining or even increasing the rate of economic growth while monetary deceleration is reducing the inflation rate. The first is trade liberalization, provided an increase in imports can be financed by foreign credits until exports pick up: "Another way to view the importance of foreign credits during the stabilization period is to recall that increased flows of imports simultaneously liberalize the regime faster than would otherwise be possible (except with recession) *and* are deflationary in that they absorb excess aggregate demand" (Krueger 1981, 113).

Trade liberalization reduces import prices and raises export earnings. To the extent that imports are predominantly manufactured goods and exports are largely agricultural products, trade liberalization raises the relative price of agricultural products. At the same time, however, the overall inflation rate may well be falling. Trade liberalization as part of a stabilization policy that includes appropriate monetary deceleration has been effective in the few countries that have tried it, not only in curbing inflation but also in raising the relative price of exportables (Krueger 1981).

The second policy measure that seems capable of sustaining or stimulating economic growth while monetary deceleration is bringing down the inflation rate is financial liberalization. In particular, abolishing ceilings on institutional interest rates or raising them to levels nearer their competitive, free-market equilibrium levels can reduce the price level by increasing money demand while simultaneously raising the rate of economic growth by increasing the real supply of credit. When deposit rates are fixed, accelerated monetary expansion that raises inflation decreases real money demand. This decline in real money demand is matched by reductions in real domestic credit or net foreign assets. Under these conditions, accelerating inflation invariably produces a credit squeeze in real terms. The supply of working capital dries up, and utilization of the existing capital stock is thereby reduced. Sections 8.2 and 8.3 contain econometric evidence consistent with the claim that financial liberalization has been successful as an anti-inflationary policy in Turkey and in some Asian developing countries.

Inflation can be reduced by reducing the rate of growth in the nominal supply of money or by increasing the rate of growth in real money demand.[1] Raising real deposit rates increases real money demand. This lowers the price level and at the same time expands the real size of the banking system, so stimulating economic growth by loosening the credit squeeze. The growth-enhancing impact of higher real deposit rates through the credit availability effect may well outweigh the growth-reducing impact of a lower ratio of actual to expected price, as shown in Chapter 10.

---

[1] Sheila Page (1993) provides a thorough treatment of the practical aspects of implementing monetary control in developing countries.

A marginal reserve requirement scheme of the kind proposed elsewhere (Fry 1979b) can be substituted for the standard required reserve system to remove the tax imposed by required reserves and at the same time to strengthen monetary control. The central bank faces the problem of achieving a target rate of growth in the money stock. By definition, the money stock M equals $H(1+cd)/(rd+cd)$, where H is the cash base or high-powered money created by the central bank, cd is the ratio of currency in circulation to all deposits included in the definition of money, and rd is the ratio of reserves held by the banking system to deposits. This relationship can also be expressed $M = mH$, where m is the money supply multiplier and equals $(1+cd)/(rd+cd)$. If m is constant or predictable, control over H implies control over M.

The central bank can make the money supply multiplier m constant by adopting the following scheme:

1. The central bank imposes a uniform required reserve ratio on all monetary deposits.

2. The central bank imposes a 100 percent reserve requirement on government deposits held in commercial banks. These reserves are not counted as reserve assets or included in the definition of the cash base. This particular reserve requirement ensures that banks do not have to hold any excess reserves to meet possible withdrawals of government deposits.

3. The central bank creates special Z deposits included in the definition of the cash base and in the definition of reserve assets to be owned only by deposit-taking institutions and held with the central bank. The central bank pays a deposit rate of interest on special Z deposits equal to the risk-adjusted net yield on other bank assets.

4. The central bank imposes a 100 percent reserve requirement on any bank's deposit growth that exceeds x percent a month. All those reserves not needed to satisfy the ordinary uniform required reserve ratio would be held in the special Z deposits. Any bank that failed to achieve x percent deposit growth would have to withdraw an amount equal to the entire shortfall minus the required ordinary reserves from its special Z deposit. Special Z deposits can be negative, in which case an overdraft rate higher than the cost of deposit money is charged.

This arrangement makes the money supply multiplier constant. Hence the central bank increases the cash base by x percent a month to achieve a target monetary growth rate of x percent a month. Banks have no incentive to hold any excess reserves because special Z deposits, together with ordinary required reserves, automatically meet 100 percent of any deposit withdrawal. Only in this situation are required reserves the most liquid bank asset. Penalties are needed to ensure that banks maintain the minimum legal levels of required reserves. However, it is important to note that a reserve shortfall cannot occur as a result of a deposit withdrawal, since this is covered by the transfer from special Z deposits to ordinary deposits held at the central bank. This transfer increases ordinary reserves by exactly the amount needed to maintain the minimum required reserve ratio after a deposit withdrawal.

The system can be introduced using any base date for which monetary data are available for the calculation of deposit growth. The base date can be changed at regular or irregular intervals to redistribute special Z deposits and, if desired, to change the aggregate volume of special Z deposits. A change in the aggregate volume of special Z deposits produced in this way will alter the money supply multiplier. However, the money multiplier's new constant value can easily be calculated before any change in the volume of special Z deposits.

Flexibility at the expense of control can be introduced to any desired degree through the severity of the penalties for reserve shortfalls, the length of the averaging period used to calculate reserve requirements, and the width of the band around the target cash base growth rate. The higher the penalties and the shorter the averaging period, the tighter the control over the money supply at any point in time.

This scheme effectively separates the cash base into two components, only one of which is high-powered money. The components of the cash base transform themselves into one another in such a way as to ensure constancy in the money supply multiplier. Specifically, the high-powered money component falls appropriately when the public's currency demand rises and increases by exactly the amount required to keep the money stock constant when the public's currency demand falls. The two important attributes of this scheme are the sterilization of variations in the public's currency demand and the discouragement of excess reserves in the banking system.

The attractive return on special Z deposits encourages deposit-taking institutions to compete for deposits. In this respect, the system avoids the drawback of credit ceilings; uniform credit ceilings penalize efficient deposit taking. Efficiency in lending is not impaired because financial institutions can compete for the fixed supply of loanable funds through an interbank money market. Efficiency in lending can also be stimulated through criteria for allocating the central bank's rediscount or overdraft facilities.

This scheme stabilizes the money supply multiplier and so fixes the relationship between the cash base and the money stock. If the cash base can be controlled, then so can the stock of money.

16.3   Financial Crises and High Real Interest Rates

Ralph Bryant (1987, 109) suggests that potential fragility and instability are endemic characteristics of financial markets, in part because "confidence in financial institutions is a fragile thing." History is indeed replete with examples of financial panic and collapse in both industrial and developing countries.

Several countries that have liberalized their financial systems subsequently experienced financial crises (Sundararajan and Baliño 1991). Particularly in Latin America, financial repression was substituted for financial crash (Diaz-Alejandro 1985). The financial crises that struck a number of developing countries in the 1980s raise two important issues. The first is whether financial crises are the inevitable price of financial liberalization.[2] The second issue concerns appropriate and effective prudential regulation and supervision of the financial system as concomitants to explicit or implicit deposit insurance. It has become increasingly apparent that sound prudential regulation and supervision are essential to counter the pervasive moral hazard problems resulting from deposit insurance.

In a number of developing countries, changes in the cost of credit intermediation have been far greater in 1980s than the changes that occurred during the Great Depression in the United States. One cause has been financial liberalization in the presence of inadequate prudential supervision and regulation. Problems were triggered by exogenous shocks of various kinds —financial opening, recession, and changes in real exchange rates, terms of trade, internal terms of trade, real interest rates, nominal interest rates, and other relative prices.

Newly liberalized financial sectors subject to inadequate prudential supervision and regulation have magnified the impact of these exogenous shocks by accommodating distress borrowing. In this way, banks in these countries compound the problem of insolvency in the real sectors of the economy. Because distress borrowers push real interest rates to levels at which virtually no economic activity can be profitable, solvent businesses start to face liquidity crunches which then force them to borrow at rates which they know are unmanageable. Hence, the accommodation of distress borrowing propagated more insolvency.

Manuel Hinds (1988, 27–28) offers the following explanation of this snowball effect:

> Faced with immediate bankruptcy, both bankers and their debtors give priority to their survival over other, longer-term objectives, including profitability. Debtors borrow at interest rates higher than the long-term profitability of their real assets, even if they have no clear idea of how they are going to repay their debts. Bankers refinance bad debtors because failing to do so would force them to increase their write-offs. Furthermore, bankers lend almost exclusively to bad debtors because, to remain liquid, they raise deposit interest rates to levels that the more solvent borrowers are not willing to pay.

---

[2]Interestingly, instability caused by fraud in Korea's unorganized money market over the period 1982–1984 produced an outcry *for* financial liberalization.

As one example, the Philippines liberalized interest rates and encouraged universal banking in the early 1980s. Initially, real interest rates rose only slightly. However, the fiscal deficit increased from 0.2 percent of GNP in 1978 to 4 percent in 1982, inflation accelerated, and devaluation followed. By 1984, there was a general loss of confidence in the domestic economy. In that year, the government launched a stabilization program, which included sales of high-yielding bills by the central bank. To maintain their deposit bases, the other financial institutions raised interest rates to 20 percent in real terms. The resulting financial distress in the corporate sector, combined with poor management, political corruption, and inadequate prudential supervision and regulation, produced financial crisis.

Jaime de Melo, Ricardo Pascale, and James Tybout (1985) point out that initially the Uruguayan financial liberalization in 1977 did not produce high real interest rates. Real loan rates remained negative until 1980 and rose sharply to levels above 10 percent only in 1981. Hence financial liberalization was not itself responsible for the subsequent excessively high level of real interest rates. Indeed, Mario Blejer and José Gil Diaz (1986, 602) find that the main variables affecting the real interest rate in Uruguay over the period 1977–1982 were changes in prices of traded goods and foreign interest rates. Monetary and nominal exchange rate policies had only minor effects.

Hinds (1986, 3–4) pinpoints the following common features of recent financial crises in developing countries: heavy foreign borrowing followed by devaluation, inward-looking development strategies, expansionary macroeconomic policies, overvalued exchange rate, financial and regulatory policies that concentrate the supply of credit in the hands of a small number of borrowers linked to the banks, and inadequate regulation and supervision of financial institutions. Frank Veneroso (1986, 5) suggests that widespread financial distress was caused by overinvestment in energy- and capital-intensive industries. These investments were financed towards the end of the 1970s by borrowing abroad at low real interest rates. When real interest rates rose after 1981, these industries were unable to repay their loans. Uruguay's massive devaluation in 1982 hit dollar borrowers so hard that the government had to intervene in several banks (Hanson and Neal 1985, 158). In the case of a large adjustment to the real exchange rate, it is almost irrelevant whether the banks or their borrowers bear the exchange rate risk. In the one case, the banks are affected directly, while in the other case they are affected indirectly by the inability of their borrowers to repay their loans.

Both trade and financial liberalization create acute portfolio problems because relative prices change substantially in the process of such liberalizations. Hence weak firms become insolvent. In practice, however, problems arising from such liberalization experiments have been containable and therefore temporary. For example, neither trade nor financial liberalizations created financial crises in Chile or Uruguay. Their financial systems had recovered from liberalization before financial crises occurred.

In the absence of direct financial markets (equity and bond markets), financial institutions will absorb too much risk and business enterprises will rely excessively on debt finance. Direct financial markets cannot compete with the subsidized indirect markets (operated by financial institutions). The main source of subsidy is explicit or implicit deposit insurance (McKinnon 1991, Veneroso 1986). Another source of subsidy is a low interest rediscount facility provided by the central bank. In many developing countries, taxation and regulatory practices discriminate against equity finance. However, Hanson and Roberto de Rezende Rocha (1986, 5) suggest that discriminatory taxation of financial intermediation also increases the financial sector's instability by driving intermediation into the informal, less regulated, and hence less taxed parts of the market.

Concerned only with the widespread existence of institutional interest rates held below their free-market equilibrium levels, advocates of financial liberalization failed to recognize that interest rates might rise too high under certain conditions when freed from controls (Veneroso 1986). One problem in the Southern Cone countries was that they liberalized while inflation was still high and unstable (McKinnon 1991). Another problem lay in the absence of adequate prudential regulation; deposit insurance promoted adverse risk selection by the banks (Diaz-Alejandro 1985, Galvez and Tybout 1985, McKinnon 1991). Millard Long (1983, 41) stresses the point that regulatory reform must be cautious and that financial liberalization requires stronger rather than weaker prudential regulations.

Carlos Diaz-Alejandro (1985) claims that in Chile there was no investigation into new entrants' banking credentials after denationalization, nor was there any supervision until 1981. Deposit insurance, neglect of prudential regulations, new entrants with no banking experience, and concentration through conglomerate takeovers combined to cause extreme indebtedness and financial fragility. Andrés Velasco (1986a, 59) pinpoints an almost identical set of market failures: moral hazard, adverse selection, oligopolistic pricing, implicit government guarantees, lack of portfolio supervision, and interlocking ownership and lending. Velasco (1986a, 58) points out that the conservatively managed Banco del Estado as well as various foreign banks survived Chile's financial crisis intact.

Velasco (1986a) suggests that financial sector instability in Chile contributed to the general state of macroeconomic instability. The financial crisis undermined credibility in the government's stabilization policy because the public anticipated an inflationary bailout of the insolvent financial institutions. The concomitant expected devaluation spurred capital flight (Velasco 1986a, 85). As Diaz-Alejandro (1985, 11) points out, the Chilean government had to make good on contingent liabilities in the form of implicit deposit and equity insurance by printing more money. Veneroso (1986) argues that financial instability resulting in financial institutions that are paralyzed by defaults and delinquencies impedes economic recovery.

High real loan rates of interest are both causes and effects of financial instability. McKinnon (1988, 397–400) finds that the high real loan rates in Chile reflected lending practices that were unsound and improperly supervised. Arnold Harberger (1985) believes that bad loans were rolled over and distress borrowing created a false demand for credit.

Deposit insurance in combination with prudential supervision ended recurrent financial crises in the United States. The long history of banking in no way indicates that deposit insurance causes financial instability. Unregulated and unsupervised financial systems, however, are indeed prone to crises, with or without deposit insurance.

Large interest rate differentials adjusted for expected exchange rate depreciations appeared in Latin America even when exchange risk was virtually nonexistent. The spread between LIBOR adjusted by devaluation and domestic lending rates was never less than 30 percentage points in Argentina during 1978–1979, 23 percentage points in Uruguay in 1979–1980, and 29 percentage points in Chile in 1980. The causes were the unexpected appearance of opportunities for high capital gains, for example, through price freezes which led to stockpiling, the rise in the real value of assets (speculative euphoria), nonmonetization of public enterprise deficits, and consumer credit booms. These were followed by a false or distress credit demand from losers.

Even after financial liberalization, dollar interest rates adjusted for preannounced devaluations were much lower than domestic currency rates in the Southern Cone countries. This encouraged excessive borrowing abroad. Vittorio Corbo and de Melo (1985b) suggest that this phenomenon was a result of policy inconsistencies. In Argentina and Uruguay, government deficits were too large; in Chile, the problem was backward wage indexation. The basic cause of these high spreads was undoubtedly lack of credibility in announced stabilization and liberalization policies. They do not themselves constitute a problem but are a symptom of the basic credibility problem facing (for good reason) almost all Latin American governments.

The real return on Baa corporate bonds in the United States rose from an average of 4 percent over the period 1955–1980 to 10 percent during the years 1981–1985 (Hanson 1986, 1). Real interest rates rose to much higher levels in Argentina, Chile, Colombia, Philippines, Turkey, and Uruguay. For example, the 30-day ex post real loan rate of interest in Chile averaged 39 percent in 1981 and 35 percent in 1982. These rates were down from 64 percent in 1976 (McKinnon 1988, 399).

Hanson and de Rezende Rocha (1986) find that very high real interest rates usually reflect one or more of the following: high and variable inflation, large government deficits, an overvalued exchange rate, and a high proportion of nonperforming loans in the banking system. Elsewhere, Hanson (1986, 3–11) also blames large spreads between deposit and loan rates for high real loan rates of interest. Hafez Ghanem (1986, 10–13) lists increased government borrowing, tighter monetary policy, and excessive taxation of financial intermediation (high required reserves and forced purchases of agrarian reform bonds) as the main causes of a 30 percent ex post real lending rate in the Philippines at the beginning of 1986. Very high real interest rates are usually accompanied by low national saving ratios, high external indebtedness, and capital flight.

The exceptionally high real interest rates observed recently in the Southern Cone countries and in Turkey after financial liberalization constitute a new phenomenon. Veneroso (1986, 17) concludes that in all cases the high real interest rates were caused by distress borrowing in conjunction with deposit insurance. Aristóbulo de Juan (1991b) explains how and why bank management deteriorates during banking crises. The lack of adequate regulation over banking practices led to undue risk taking on the part of the banks. When nonperforming assets rose, the banks raised deposit rates to attract more funds to pay interest on existing deposits (Corbo 1985, 909; Corbo and de Melo 1985a; De Melo, Pascale, and Tybout 1985; Diaz-Alejandro 1985; Fernandez 1985; Petrei and Tybout 1985). In Argentina, "each financial institution closed by the Central Bank was offering the highest interest rates in the market" at the time of its closure (Fernandez 1985, 886).

Extraordinarily high real loan rates appear when a substantial proportion of a country's banks have zero net worth or bank managements believe that shareholders as well as depositors are implicitly insured by the government. The exceptionally high real interest rates produce an epidemic effect: the false credit demand by distress borrowers puts upward pressure on interest rates, which in turn drags down other firms (Corbo and de Melo 1985a). The supply of funds is made available because of explicit or implicit deposit insurance. Demand rises because of firms' expectations that the government will eventually bail out nonfinancial as well as financial enterprises. When net worth is zero, firms have every incentive to gamble on a government bailout in the future. The end result is financial and economic paralysis.

Financial distress results in reduced investment and worse resource allocation through the distressed financial sector. When nonperforming loans rise, banks have less resources for new lending. Furthermore, banks often extend more loans to large firms unable to repay their old loans in an attempt to conceal their own losses, a practice known as "evergreening." In this way, loan demand rises, real interest rates increase, and investment declines. Attempts to lower interest rates by government decree in Argentina, Bolivia, and Yugoslavia made matters worse by accelerating inflation and capital flight. The ensuing disintermediation and lower demand for domestic financial assets compounded the banks' difficulties (World Bank 1989, 74–75). An alternative solution, which is likely to accelerate bank insolvency, is to stop banks from continuing to lend to insolvent borrowers. Clearly, preventing bankruptcy at all costs is highly inefficient.

In general, excessively high real institutional interest rates signal unsound lending in which banks throw good money after bad to enable borrowers to meet their interest payments. The solution is better regulation and supervision. Indeed, the typical response to these financial crises has been to strengthen prudential regulation and supervision, as well as to bring all financial institutions under a uniform regulatory framework. In Malaysia, for example, all financial institutions now come under the Banking and Financial Institutions Act, 1989. Experiments with two-tier financial systems have been abandoned as governments realized that it was impossible in practice to avoid bailing out insolvent financial institutions so that they could repay their depositors. Behind virtually all financial crises that have occurred in the past two decades lies the critical issue of explicit or implicit deposit insurance because it affects the behavior of both depositors and bankers.

Ben Bernanke and Mark Gertler (1989) point out that recessions are typically associated with a high incidence of financial distress—defaults, bankruptcies, and failures—and a general deterioration in firms' balance sheets. Since borrowers' collateral or equity interest is procyclical, agency costs fall during booms and rise during recessions. For this reason, Bernanke and Gertler conclude that changing financial conditions themselves aggravate swings in economic activity:

> Agency costs of undertaking physical investments are inversely related to the entrepreneur's/borrower's net worth. As a result, accelerator effects on investment emerge: Strengthened borrower balance sheets resulting from good times expand investment demand, which in turn tends to amplify the upturn; weakened balance sheets in bad times do just the opposite. (Bernanke and Gertler 1989, 28)

Alan Blinder (1987) makes a similar point that, because bank credit is supplied in a customer market, monetary policy can affect economic activity by changing the stringency of credit rationing. Blinder (1987, 334) concludes that his model of credit rationing is generally unstable. Credit restriction reduces supply by more than it reduces demand. Tighter monetary policy can produce excess demand, rising prices, and hence a smaller volume of credit in real terms.

16.4   Macroeconomic and Financial Sector Policy

Policy advice on financial aspects of economic development has been influenced by its fair share of intellectual fads and fancies. In some areas, prognosis has come full circle. One general impression from a review of recent reports of the Asian Development Bank, the IMF, and the World Bank is the ease with which policy advisors embrace the latest academic idea. Another impression is that the results of policy experiments in financial sectors of developing countries have rather frequently been at variance with the theory on which the policy advice was supposedly based.

The main intellectual bases for financial sector analysis and policy advice over the past 15 years are those propounded by McKinnon (1973) and Shaw (1973). Other important academic influences include Alexander Gerschenkron's (1962, 1968) examination of the role of banks in German economic development and Joseph Stiglitz and Andrew Weiss's (1981) analysis of credit rationing, which draws heavily on the adverse selection theory of labor markets. Noticeable by its absence is reference to the academic literature on prudential regulation and supervision (Benston 1973; Guttentag and Herring 1982; Havrilesky and Boorman 1980, 475–545; Peltzman 1970), despite the increasing attention paid by policy advisors to microeconomic and institutional problems over the past decade.

The World Bank's policy stance on financial sector issues has changed dramatically over the past two decades. As a promoter of development banks since the 1950s, the World Bank favored the establishment of specialized DFIs to meet credit needs not supplied by the commercial banks. Although its original model was a private sector development bank run on quasi-commercial principles, it did little to resist the trend towards nationalization that occurred in the 1960s and 1970s. By 1985, however, the World Bank (1985, ii) was expressing concerns over this trend.

The World Bank shifted its emphasis away from institution building, often within a nationalized framework, towards more reliance on market forces within a systemwide approach to finance. Prior to 1978, the World Bank commissioned only very few comparative studies of financial systems in developing countries. Since then, many financial sector studies have been conducted with the objective of developing broader-based lending programs. Towards the end of the 1970s and during the 1980s, therefore, the World Bank began to replace project loans with apex and structural adjustment loans aimed at the development of entire financial sectors of developing countries.

The first wave of World Bank financial sector reports written in the late 1970s and early 1980s stressed macroeconomic and sectoral issues such as price stability, abolition of interest rate ceilings, rationalization or elimination of directed credit programs, and discriminatory taxation of financial intermediation. Such taxation occurs either directly through transaction taxes, loan and deposit rate taxes, and stamp duties, or indirectly through reserve requirements, forced investments in low-yielding government bonds, and minimum provisions of subsidized credit to priority (high-risk) sectors of the economy. Hanson and Neal (1985, vii) state that

> the financial sector policy advice most often given developing countries is to maintain positive real interest rates, i.e., nominal interest rates in excess of inflation. This recommendation is now beginning to give way to concerns for increased market-orientation in the full range of financial sector policies. As opposed to simply a mechanical insistence on positive real interest rates, the market oriented perspective stresses, among other things, the need to reduce the size of subsidies passed

through the financial sector and to increase the reliance on interest rates
for the mobilization and allocation of resources, paying attention not
only to the real levels of rates, but to the need for differentials which
reflect differences in risk, maturity and cost.

Sections on institutional aspects of the financial sectors being analyzed were
brief in the extreme. To be fair, these early reports often stated that bank
regulation and supervision needed improvement. However, that was about as
far as such recommendations went.

After the disastrous results of financial liberalization experiments in Latin
America and increasing financial fragility worldwide, the second wave of
World Bank financial sector reports from about 1983 devotes much more
attention to microeconomic, institutional, and regulatory issues. There is also
more recognition of macroeconomic stability, particularly fiscal responsibility,
as a prerequisite for successful financial development (Hanson and Neal 1985,
35).

There has, however, been virtually no discussion of the second-best dilemma that arises when controls in some areas (over interest rates) are dismantled but controls in other areas (asset portfolio limitations) are strengthened.
Indeed, Chile may have been following the only set of policies with any
theoretical underpinnings when it abolished virtually all controls over every
financial activity. Unfortunately, the Chilean government was unable to persuade the private sector that its hands-off policy also implied no bailouts. In
fact, credibility in this regard was destroyed when the government stepped in
to rescue a failing bank as early as 1977 (Diaz-Alejandro 1985, 8).

In its financial sector policy paper, the World Bank (1985, i) concludes
that financial repression reduces the national saving ratio:

> In retrospect, it appears that had countries given more attention to their
> domestic financial systems, paid domestic savers as much in real terms
> as they paid to foreign lenders, and held in check the expansion in credit
> —in particular loans to public enterprises—more resources could have
> been mobilized domestically and countries' needs for foreign funding
> would have grown more in line with their debt servicing capacity.

The World Bank (1985, iii) also states: "Financial policies in most countries
discouraged domestic mobilization and encouraged borrowing abroad."

The belief in the efficacy of financial policies to affect national saving
ratios probably springs from the Taiwanese and Korean experiences with interest rate reforms in the 1950s and 1960s. However, the more recent financial
liberalizations in Latin America were not accompanied by any increase in national saving ratios (Diaz-Alejandro 1985, 14). Existing econometric studies
do not support the view that financial liberalization has any substantial impact
on the level of national saving.

If capital flight takes place illegally through underinvoicing exports and
overinvoicing imports, it reduces national saving as measured in the national

income accounts. Hence, if financial liberalization reduces illegal capital flight, this would appear in the national accounts as an increase in measured national saving. Conversely, if financial liberalization does not raise measured national saving ratios significantly, neither can it be expected to deter illegal capital flight.

The World Bank's official position is slightly puzzling, given that Long (1983, 16), the World Bank's own financial sector guru, points out that a rise in the real deposit rate of interest to its competitive market equilibrium level simply raises the demand for financial assets to an optimal stock level. This is a one-time adjustment and does not necessarily affect the annual flow of saving. In fact, financial liberalization has had very little impact on saving ratios. This may well imply that financial liberalization cannot deter or reverse capital flight.

If financial repression deters national saving by more than it deters domestic investment, it then follows that financial repression will lead to higher levels of international indebtedness in open economies. It also follows that if financial repression reduces average investment efficiency, it will raise the ratio of foreign indebtedness to GNP. However, the assumption that financial repression deters saving by more than it deters investment is not supported by the available empirical evidence (Fry 1986a, 66–67). The World Bank's (1985, i) conclusion that financial liberalization reduces foreign borrowing because it raises national saving ratios ignores the salutary effect of financial liberalization on domestic investment rates. Indeed, there appears to be no causal relationship between financial repression and foreign debt problems in developing countries.

In practice, it has been financial liberalization rather than financial repression that has been associated with excessive capital inflows from abroad (in Argentina, Korea, Chile, and Uruguay), presumably because liberalization stimulates investment more than it stimulates saving. These massive capital inflows overvalue the exchange rate and so depress exports. Michael Bruno (1985, 868) concludes that capital inflows after liberalization "can be disastrous for a country's budding export industry." Excessive capital inflows also jeopardize monetary control (McKinnon 1973).

McKinnon (1991, 390–397) states that appropriate policy towards capital inflows during financial liberalization should include: (a) fixing domestic interest rates in line with the preannounced exchange rate depreciation and not letting them rise too high, as happened in the Southern Cone countries; (b) indexing wages to a forward-looking exchange rate depreciation *tablita*; (c) abolishing government exchange rate and repayment guarantees for foreign borrowing; (d) regulating short-term capital inflows tightly; and (e) persuading the IMF and World Bank not to bribe developing countries into trade and financial liberalization programs, since bribes taking the form of capital inflows are themselves harmful to the liberalization effort.

Financial liberalization could well stimulate investment more than it stimulates national saving. This implies that foreign borrowing would rise. Capital inflows require some regulation to ensure that they do not disrupt export industries. In themselves, however, they do not constitute a foreign debt *problem*, with Korea providing a good example.

16.5 Summary

Inflationary macroeconomic policies have prevented effective and efficient domestic resource mobilization and allocation through the financial sectors of many developing countries over the past two decades. Since the early 1970s, monetary policy has been used with increasing frequency to counteract exogenous shocks. Such policy accelerates inflation with each application. Nevertheless, a few developing countries have reduced inflation substantially without incurring recession through trade and financial liberalization.

Higher and more volatile inflation in developing countries has been accompanied by increased financial instability and crises. Recent episodes of financial instability have been characterized by extraordinarily high real loan rates of interest. Such rates were caused by distress borrowing in the absence of adequate bank supervision. With expectations of eventual government bailouts, financial institutions continued to throw good money after bad even though the prospects of repayment were slender at best.

Given the experience of financial repression followed by financial crash, advice on macroeconomic and financial sector policy has changed rather rapidly as experience grew. The 1970s' enthusiasm for unfettered financial markets and complete deregulation has been replaced by a more cautious approach. Experience certainly suggests that the Asian developing countries that ignored the euphoria of Western economists over financial liberalization and continued on their own gradual paths towards financial development were right. The Latin American developing countries looking for another quick-fix solution to their economic malaise were again disappointed in the outcomes of radical financial liberalization programs.

Chapter 17

Central Banks and Deficit Finance in Developing Countries

17.1 Introduction

Traditional texts on central banking generally list the following functions of the central bank: (a) regulating the issue of currency and controlling the quantity of money and credit for monetary policy purposes; (b) acting as banker to the government; (c) acting as banker to the commercial banks, including lender-of-last resort; (d) managing the country's international reserves (De Kock 1974, 14; Morgan 1943, 1). Together with any regulatory responsibilities, these activities are normally considered monetary activities. As the Radcliffe Committee (1959, 276) recognized, however, "monetary policy is now so inextricably connected with the Government's fiscal operations and with the management of debt" that these activities have an important fiscal content.

The relationship between central banks and governments has received some attention (Majumdar 1974, Mittra 1978, Skanland 1984). Until recently, however, central banks' fiscal activities and fiscal aspects of monetary operations have generally been ignored. Most governments expect to benefit financially from the monopoly privilege over fiat money that they grant to their central banks. There are numerous examples of abuse of this monopoly to extract an inflation tax in addition to seigniorage revenue.

In recent years, a number of governments have required their central banks to undertake various fiscal activities. This chapter reviews the fiscal activities that governments in a sample of 26 developing countries have obliged their central banks to undertake. In the main, these activities fall under five categories: (a) collecting seigniorage; (b) imposing financial restriction; (c) implementing selective credit policies; (d) undertaking foreign exchange operations at nonmarket-clearing prices; and (e) providing implicit or explicit deposit insurance at subsidized rates and recapitalizing insolvent financial in-

393

stitutions. Not all central banks engage in all these activities, but some central banks perform additional fiscal activities such as collecting taxes and running food procurement programs.

Central banks in some countries generate revenue equal to the government's explicit tax revenue. Fiscal activities of central banks on the revenue side include collecting seigniorage through the issue of currency and the imposition of reserve requirements, demonetizing currency notes of particular denominations, forcing unfavorable conversions of old for new currency after a currency reform, setting interest rate ceilings on financial assets that compete with government bonds, requiring import predeposits, administering multiple exchange rate systems in which exporters are obliged to sell their foreign exchange earnings to the central bank at lower prices than some importers can buy foreign exchange from the central bank, as well as collecting miscellaneous fees (Robinson and Stella 1988, 22–23). Central bank profits and losses can also be affected by revaluations of foreign exchange assets and liabilities.

On the expenditure side, fiscal activities of central banks include allocating subsidized credit to agriculture and export sectors and to development finance institutions through selective credit policies, providing explicit or implicit deposit insurance and bailing out insolvent financial (or even nonfinancial) institutions when necessary, and providing exchange rate subsidies or guarantees, particularly for debt service and essential imports. Interest rate ceilings imposed and enforced by central banks constitute both taxes and subsidies. The taxes are imposed on depositors/lenders, who subsidize "preferred" borrowers.

Specialized government agencies exist to spend money on particular sectors of the economy. The ministry of agriculture spends money to promote agriculture, the ministry of transport spends money on roads, while the ministry of health spends money to promote the country's health. Although these ministries responsible for different sectors of the economy may collect some revenue, typically this takes the form of user fees rather than taxes. The central bank in its position at the apex of the financial sector, however, not only spends money on its sector but also collects taxes from it. Typically, the tax revenue collected by the central bank from the financial sector exceeds its expenditure on that sector. In this as well as in other respects, therefore, central banks play a unique role in public finance.

Central banks collect revenue in forms that closely resemble conventional taxes. The inflation tax is a well-known example. However, these revenues differ from conventional taxes in a number of important respects: (a) they do not appear in tax codes, nor do they appear in the government's budget; (b) tax rates are not specified and, in some cases, can be estimated only after the revenue has been collected; (c) until very recently, only the inflation tax had been analyzed as a tax on the standard criteria of economic efficiency, administrative simplicity, flexibility, political responsiveness, and fairness.

This chapter focuses on central bank fiscal activities in part because they are so large and yet so well concealed. In addition to any objections on the basis of principles of public finance, obliging a central bank to meet a range of fiscal expenditures undermines not only any independence but also monetary policy objectives. To the extent that they involve expenditures, fiscal activities reduce central bank profits or even produce losses. If central bank losses are not met from government budget appropriations, they must eventually lead to an expansion in central bank money and the abandonment of any monetary policy goal of price stability. As this chapter shows, central banks do not possess any miraculous widow's cruse. Governments can tap central bank profits directly or indirectly (with different side effects); they cannot, however, have their cake and eat it.

17.2 The Central Bank's Balance Sheet

17.2.1 The Conventional Approach

To illustrate the magnitude of the resources generated from a central bank's monopoly over fiat money, I start with the standard textbook presentation of a central bank's balance sheet:

Assets		Liabilities	
Gold and foreign exchange	5	Currency in circulation	10
Government securities	16	Banks' deposits	15
Loans to the banks	4		
		Net Worth	0

The numbers in this balance sheet are percentages of GNP and represent balance sheet figures of central banks in low-inflation developing countries. Published figures of central bank net worth are typically less than $\frac{1}{2}$ percent of GNP; hence, rounding produces a net worth of zero. This representative central bank makes a profit or collects seigniorage by virtue of the fact that it earns interest on its assets but pays no interest on its liabilities of currency in circulation and banks' deposits. The sum of currency in circulation and bank deposits with the central bank is defined as reserve money. In fact, some central banks do pay interest on banks' deposits and transfer seigniorage revenue to their governments through low-interest loans rather than through profit remittance.

This balance sheet understates the true value or net worth of the central bank. In the first place, reserve money is not a central bank liability in the sense that central banks are no longer obliged to redeem their notes. Notes are liabilities of the central bank only in the sense that the central bank is responsible for replacing worn notes and, in some countries, detecting forgery. There are virtually no costs of a similar nature attached to the bank deposit component of reserve money. In the second place, the central bank may exploit its monopoly privilege over note issue. Whatever its value, this monopoly power is clearly an asset rather than a liability.

17.2.2   The Present Value Approach

Consider a zero-growth economy in which the central bank is required to maintain price stability. Annual costs of maintaining currency in circulation generally fall below 1 percent of the nominal value of notes outstanding. For example, the annual cost of currency maintenance incurred by the Bank of England is roughly one third of one percent of the outstanding note issue. With an interest rate of 5 percent, the present value of the future stream of note maintenance costs is therefore unlikely to exceed 20 percent of the face value of notes issued. The present value of bank deposit maintenance costs is virtually zero; any costs actually incurred could easily be charged to depositors. Hence, the textbook central bank has a small value of liabilities compared with its assets. For this illustration, I assume that central bank assets represent claims on the private sector and all earn the market interest rate of 5 percent. In such case, the balance sheet calculated on the basis of the present value of future income streams is:

Assets		Liabilities	
Interest-earning assets	25	Currency maintenance	2
		Net Worth	23

The market value of this central bank, which is obliged to keep the money stock constant in order to maintain price stability in a stagnant economy, is 23 percent of GNP. Assets yield an income of 1.25 percent of GNP each year and maintenance of the currency issue costs 0.1 percent of GNP. The net worth figure is the value of the monopoly over reserve money or the present value of seigniorage less the present value of currency maintenance. The value of this monopoly right is constrained by the restrictions imposed on the supply of reserve money; in this case, the condition that there should be no inflation. With no economic growth, there can be no increase in the supply of reserve money.

Now consider the situation in an economy growing at an annual rate of 2 percent with unit income elasticity of demand for reserve money. In this case, the central bank will be able to increase its holdings of interest-earning assets by 2 percent a year through the issue of new money. Growth in assets of 2 percent a year can be deducted from the 5 percent interest rate; the rising streams of incomes and expenditures are equivalent to constant streams discounted at 3 percent. The present value of the net income stream (1.15

percent of GNP) is now $38\frac{1}{3}$ percent of GNP, the net worth of the central bank in this growing economy. For the particular case in which the rate of economic growth equalled the interest rate, the present value of the net income stream would be infinite; the rate of growth in revenue exactly offsets the discount factor. In the normal case (S. Fischer 1989, 16), the appropriate discount factor exceeds the rate of growth in reserve money demand and the present value of the reserve money monopoly, and hence the net worth of the central bank, is finite.

These net worth figures approximate the prices which a government could obtain by selling its central bank with the constraint that any private owner would be obliged to maintain price stability. One alternative to the *price* stability constraint imposed on the supply of reserve money might be the weaker restriction of *inflation* stability. In other words, changes in the supply of reserve money must not produce accelerating or unanticipated inflation. In this case, maximum net worth or sale price is achieved at the revenue-maximizing inflation rate. Typical money demand estimates show that the revenue-maximizing inflation rate would produce seigniorage revenue in the range of 5 to 10 percent of GNP.

With a revenue-maximizing inflation rate of 20 percent a month, reserve money could have fallen from 25 to 3 percent of GNP. On a monthly basis, therefore, reserve money would represent 36 percent of the month's GNP, 14 percent in currency and 22 percent in bank deposits with the central bank. The assets held by the central bank still equal the face value of reserve money and earn a nominal return of i. The nominal interest rate i, expressed as a proportion rather than a percentage, is defined as $i = (1 + r) \cdot (1 + \pi) - 1$, where r is the real interest rate and π is the inflation rate. A real annual interest rate of 5 percent is equivalent to 0.41 percent a month. Hence, the central bank's assets now yield a nominal return of 20.49 percent a month, producing revenue equal to 7.376 percent of monthly GNP.

With zero economic growth, real reserve money and real assets of the central bank would remain constant over time, as would the central bank's real seigniorage income. This constant real income stream can therefore be discounted by the monthly real interest rate of 0.41 percent to produce a present value of 1810 percent of monthly GNP, which is equivalent to 150.87 percent of annual GNP. In this case, the present value of the monopoly over reserve money is equal to about half the wealth in the country. The balance sheet calculated on the basis of the present values of these future income and expenditure streams is:

Assets		Liabilities	
Interest-earning assets	150.87	Currency maintenance	0.24
		Net Worth	150.63

The fact that currency maintenance costs are bound to be higher at an inflation rate of 20 percent a month than they are under price stability is ignored here. This stable inflation restriction is suboptimal from the viewpoint of both total government revenue and social welfare maximization. The Tanzi effect causes government revenue from sources other than the inflation tax to fall in real terms as inflation rates accelerate (Tanzi 1977, 1989). Hence, some inflation rate below the rate which maximizes the central bank's net worth would maximize total government revenue in real terms for any given tax structure. The socially efficient inflation rate as a component of an efficient tax structure could be another alternative objective for which the central bank's money printing monopoly could be suitably constrained. The main point is that a central bank in the pristine shape of the one illustrated in this example constitutes a large asset under any circumstances.

17.3   The Extent of Central Bank Fiscal Activities

17.3.1   How Fiscal Activities Can Change a Central Bank's Balance Sheet

Not only are central bank fiscal activities large and well concealed, they are also extremely difficult to quantify. Even at a conceptual level, several issues emerge. For example, difficulties arise over the measurement of contingent liabilities, as in the case of deposit insurance or loan guarantee programs. Other problems at this level involve the central bank's accounting conventions, which differ from those of the central government, and the valuation of foreign currency-denominated claims. The most fundamental problem of all concerns the distinction between fiscal and monetary activities. Central banks may make or lose money in their open market operations conducted solely for monetary policy purposes. In effect, someone is taxed when the central bank makes a profit, while someone is subsidized when it makes a loss. Because central banks do not aim to maximize profits, even under some constraint such as price stability, the distinction between monetary and fiscal activities is blurred. Therefore, estimating the magnitude of a central bank's fiscal activities inevitably involves the formulation and application of accounting conventions that are unique to central banking.

Central banks in many developing countries administer selective or directed credit policies designed to channel credit to priority sectors, groups, or regions at subsidized rates of interest. The objectives are to stimulate investment in priority activities and, frequently, to redistribute income and wealth. The subsidy can be distributed through differential rediscount rates and ratios or by portfolio constraints on the commercial banks. Many central banks use part of their seigniorage revenue to subsidize rediscount rates. In its 1987 annual report, the Banco de Portugal (1988, 50) shows in its profit-and-loss accounts that interest rate subsidies represented 50 percent of reported profits that year.

Monopoly over foreign exchange transactions is a source of central bank revenue in many developing countries. Exporters are obliged to surrender their foreign exchange earnings to the central bank, which is the sole supplier of foreign exchange to importers. Foreign exchange can be sold to importers at a far higher price than foreign exchange is bought from exporters. Recently, however, some central banks have made huge losses from foreign exchange activities when the timing of domestic currency receipts has been divorced from the timing of foreign exchange payments.

Over the past decade, a number of developing countries have substituted explicit deposit insurance schemes for implicit insurance. To the extent that the insurance premia (zero where the scheme is implicit) do not cover the risks, the central bank provides a subsidy to the banking industry. Since the subsidy takes the form of a contingent liability for the central bank, the outlays tend to be very uneven. When the central bank recapitalizes an insolvent financial institution, it acquires the substandard assets of the failed financial institution at prices above the market-clearing prices. In some instances, the costs of bank bailouts have constituted a substantial fraction (over 10 percent) of GNP, as exemplified in the case of Chile.

Many central banks have incurred expenses by implementing selective credit policies, offering foreign exchange guarantees, and bailing out insolvent financial institutions. These activities have absorbed seigniorage revenue and hence have reduced profits which would otherwise have accrued to the government. A number of central banks have posted overall losses. By acquiring interest-bearing liabilities as well as substandard assets in the course of undertaking these fiscal activities, central banks have reduced their net worth calculated for any stable inflation rate. Their balance sheets have changed rather dramatically from the ones illustrated in section 17.2. Many central bank balance sheets have also been impaired through interest-free or subsidized loans to the government. In the steady state, however, the extraction of seigniorage revenue through low-interest loans or the transfer central bank profits are equivalent.

A central bank burdened with fiscal activities can hardly aspire to the same degree of independence from government as one which has not been required to assume such activities. Furthermore, fiscal activities are likely to jeopardize monetary policy designed to maintain price stability. Where fiscal expenditures exceed seigniorage revenue consistent with a stable price level, maintenance of price stability necessitates annual government appropriations to keep the central bank afloat, as is now happening in Chile.

17.3.2 Seigniorage

Granting monopoly privilege in return for a fee or a profit share became an increasingly common source of government revenue from the fifteenth to the eighteenth centuries. Some governments held monopolies over mineral resources, others chartered joint-stock companies with monopoly rights (Webber and Wildavsky 1986, 261, 287). Carl Shoup (1969, 285) notes that

> governments operate monopolies in the production or distribution of liquor or tobacco products, or, less frequently, salt or playing cards. Certain forms of gambling are monopolized for the same purpose, notably the lottery. In one country the monopolies return only a modest profit as such, but serve as evasion-proof tax collectors. Other government monopolies, notably the post office, railroads, telephone, telegraph, and radio and television are more commonly drains on the government fisc than contributors to it.

As a means of raising revenue, Shoup (1969, 288) regards monopoly favorably in a comparison with excise taxes on the same industries.

Monopoly over currency issue, in the form of coinage, is typically reserved for the government itself. In 1694 the Bank of England was established with the right to issue loans and print banknotes in return for a loan of £1.2 million to the government; the money was needed to finance the war against France. In 1697 the Bank of England increased its loan to the government in return for a monopoly of chartered banking in England and the privilege of limited liability for its shareholders. The sale of privileges to the Bank continued throughout the eighteenth century (Dowd 1989, 118–119). The origins of the Ottoman Bank, established in 1856 to assist the Ottoman Empire in obtaining both foreign and domestic loans, were somewhat similar. The grant of monopoly as a source of government revenue has fallen into disuse. Nevertheless, a number of countries still maintain monopolies, such as liquor production and distribution, in part for revenue purposes. Monopoly over currency issue, however, is still almost universal.[1]

The analytically intriguing aspect of the inflation tax lies in the ability of the central bank to raise the tax *rate* by expanding the currency issue. A faster rate of growth in currency issue raises the inflation rate which, in turn, raises nominal interest rates. Hence, the opportunity cost of holding currency in the form of interest forgone rises. From the fiscal perspective, an increase in currency issue of $1 can be treated analytically as $1 borrowed. Implicit tax revenue is raised by the 100 percent tax on the interest. This tax revenue shows up as profits in the central bank. The financing item—$1 increase in currency issued—has no net effect on the income statement. The central bank uses the $1 to purchase an interest-earning asset. An increased resort to

---

[1] Panama, which uses U.S. dollars, is the familiar exception; Kiribati uses the Australian dollar.

this form of financing, however, leads to a higher tax rate. Whether it leads to more or less tax revenue in the long run depends, of course, on whether or not the inflation rate is initially above or below its revenue-maximizing rate.

One approach to measuring seigniorage is based on a cash flow basis—the increase in reserve money made available as a residual budgetary financing item (Fischer 1982). The fiscal approach, however, treats seigniorage in terms of tax base and tax rate (Bailey 1956, Friedman 1971, Phelps 1973):

> As in the usual tax theory, the revenue from the inflation tax is simply the excess of the consumer's price over the producer's price (that is, price including tax less marginal cost) *times* the amount produced and purchased—just like the revenue from any other sort of tax. Hence, in the case where liquidity is costless, it is equal to the money rate of interest times real cash balances. (Phelps 1973, 70)

Under competitive conditions, currency issuers would be forced to spend any excess profits on improving the attractiveness of their currencies. The competitive equilibrium is one in which all currencies yield a rate of return equal to the market interest rate less a small amount to compensate for the cost of note production and replacement (Girton and Roper 1980).

To provide some orders of magnitude, I examine a sample of 26 developing countries. The country sample consists of Algeria, Argentina, Brazil, Chile, Côte d'Ivoire, Egypt, Ghana, Greece, India, Indonesia, Korea, Malaysia, Mexico, Morocco, Nigeria, Pakistan, Peru, Philippines, Portugal, Sri Lanka, Tanzania, Thailand, Turkey, Venezuela, Yugoslavia, and Zaire. Here I define the tax rate on reserve money as the current inflation rate as measured by the consumer price index; the tax rate on bank reserves is adjusted for any interest paid. The tax base is the geometric average of beginning- and end-of-year values of currency in circulation plus bank reserves.

The two differences between the inflation tax on currency and the inflation tax on bank reserves are: (a) reserves held almost exclusively as deposits in the central bank involve infinitesimal maintenance costs; and (b) some interest may be paid on such deposits. In this sample of developing countries, the range of interest paid on required reserves runs from zero to 7.3 percent after monetary correction (indexation) in the case of Brazil's 20 percent reserve requirement against saving deposits. In Brazil's case, the tax on these required reserves must be zero or negative at all rates of inflation. Clearly, where indexation is not applied and where nominal interest rates (if any) are sticky, the tax rate on required reserves rises with inflation.

In Table 17.1, an approximate measure of the inflation tax revenue is expressed as a percentage of GNP and as a percentage of the government's current revenue. Where possible, data are provided for 1984. As a percentage of GNP, seigniorage provides a small source of tax revenue in most of the sample countries. However, where it does produce an above-average amount, it contributes a proportionally larger amount of government revenue. On

Table 17.1. Seigniorage Revenue and Central Bank Profits in 26 Developing Countries, 1984

	Seigniorage Tax Revenue		Central Bank Profit	
Country	Percentage of GNP	Percentage of Government Current Revenue	Percentage of GNP	Percentage of Government Current Revenue
Algeria	1.59	n.a.	n.a.	n.a.
Argentina [4]	7.43	46.49	0.41	n.a.
Brazil [1]	2.45	9.09	0.80	2.98
Chile [4]	0.85	2.66	0.01	0.04
Côte d'Ivoire	0.44	1.45	n.a.	n.a.
Egypt	7.50	16.69	n.a.	n.a.
Ghana [1]	0.74	6.17	0.30	2.48
Greece [5]	3.13	8.72	0.02	n.a.
India [6]	0.98	7.57	0.05	n.a.
Indonesia [6]	0.65	6.17	0.58	n.a.
Korea [3]	0.11	1.39	−0.08	−1.02
Malaysia [3]	0.12	0.50	0.97	3.96
Mexico	7.18	41.88	n.a.	n.a.
Morocco [5]	1.67	6.79	0.49	n.a.
Nigeria [3]	0.94	5.05	0.64	3.46
Pakistan [2]	0.48	2.58	0.53	2.82
Peru [1]	8.67	58.05	1.30	8.67
Philippines	2.38	22.09	n.a.	n.a.
Portugal [5]	5.25	14.58	0.32	n.a.
Sri Lanka [2]	0.79	3.43	1.10	4.78
Tanzania [7]	3.14	18.55	1.02	n.a.
Thailand [3]	0.21	1.27	0.14	0.81
Turkey [3]	2.55	13.92	0.04	0.22
Venezuela [6]	1.50	5.68	0.35	n.a.
Yugoslavia	9.77	132.79	n.a.	n.a.
Zaire [2]	3.03	16.08	−0.19	−1.02

Source: *International Financial Statistics,* various issues, and *World Tables Socio-economic Time-series* (1989, 1990)

[1] 1985   [2] 1986   [3] 1987   [4] Central bank profits, 1986   [5] Central bank profits, 1987
[6] Central bank profits, 1988   [7] Seigniorage, 1985; central bank profits, 1987.

Note: Central bank profit combines issue and banking department accounts and includes transfers to the government.

average, a 1 percentage point increase in the inflation tax in relation to GNP corresponds to an increase in the inflation tax in relation to government current revenue of 8 percentage points.

From the banks' viewpoint, required reserves constitute a forced acquisition of an asset on which all interest is taxed away. Under competitive conditions, banks pass the reserve requirement tax on to depositors and borrowers, the incidence depending on relative demand elasticities, in the form of lower deposit rates and higher loan rates, as shown in Chapter 7. Fiscal analysis of this tax is simplified for a small country in which businesses can borrow from the domestic banks or abroad at the world interest rate; in other words, the demand for bank loans is perfectly interest elastic. In this case, the incidence of the reserve requirement tax is borne entirely by depositors. Similarly, currency holders bear the inflation tax on their currency holdings.

17.3.3 Financial Restriction

Issuing currency and noninterest-earning bank reserves in the form of deposits held at the central bank is clearly the main monetary activity of all central banks. It is well recognized that this monopoly is also a source of government revenue. Monetary and fiscal aspects of the monopoly power are inextricably intertwined. The objectives of monetary control conflict with any fiscal objective requiring an issue of reserve money in excess of the amount appropriate for monetary stability. Incompatible aims of monetary and fiscal aspects of issuing reserve money are invariably resolved in favor of the fiscal exigencies, at least in the short run. Thereafter, fiscal reform as part of a stabilization program may attempt to reduce or eliminate the conflict. There are, however, a variety of measures that enable more revenue to be raised without jeopardizing monetary stability. These measures, termed financial restriction in Chapter 2, are generally administered by the central bank.

Central banks in many developing countries administer selective or directed credit policies designed to channel credit to priority sectors, groups, or regions at subsidized rates of interest. The objectives are to stimulate investment in priority activities and frequently to redistribute income and wealth. The subsidy can be distributed through differential rediscount rates and ratios or by portfolio constraints on the commercial banks.

In countries where there are virtually no markets for direct financial claims, the tax derived from financial restriction can be estimated using domestic credit as the tax base and the difference between the parity-adjusted world interest rate and the average domestic rate on the components of domestic credit as the tax rate. An approximate estimate is generally possible in countries which impose interest rate ceilings on all institutional interest rates. In Turkey, for example, lending interest rates were held at least 20 percentage points below world rates in 1979. With domestic credit averaging TL715 billion, the financial restriction tax was TL143 billion or 6.5 percent of GNP. Clearly, this was also the value of the interest rate subsidy to borrowers.

Subsidies in selective credit programs involve not only a lower loan rate but frequently a higher risk of default. The subsidy therefore includes not only the difference between the world market interest rate and the domestic loan rate but some additional risk premium. Part of the cost of that subsidy is included in the cost of bailing out insolvent financial institutions.

From the fiscal approach, financial restriction and selective credit policies implemented by the central bank can be decomposed into tax and subsidy components. The tax is imposed on depositors in addition to the reserve requirement tax to the extent that banks are forced to use their own resources to acquire nonreserve assets that yield net returns below the world market interest rate. The subsidy exceeds the tax to the extent that low-interest rediscount facilities are used to offset part of the cost of low-interest loans.

Alberto Giovannini and Martha de Melo (1993) calculate the tax revenue from financial restriction in the form of holdings of government bonds at yields below the world market rate. For the 16 countries in Table 17.2 for which seigniorage tax revenues are presented in Table 17.1, the average tax revenue from financial restriction is 1.9 percent of GDP. This can be compared with the average tax revenue from seigniorage for these 16 countries of 2 percent of GNP.[2] In broad terms, therefore, it appears that financial restriction is as important a source of government revenue in developing countries as is the inflation tax.

17.3.4 Foreign Exchange Operations

A central bank's foreign exchange activities may also involve both tax and subsidy elements. Foreign exchange is so undervalued in some developing countries that provision of foreign exchange at the official rate is tantamount to a gift. If the central bank does not make a loss in managing undervalued foreign exchange, the cost must be borne by exporters. Hence, even with a single exchange rate, the central bank could be imposing taxes and providing subsidies. Given the plethora of distortions that accompany substantial exchange rate disequilibrium, calculation of effective tax and subsidy rates is virtually impossible.

Central banks in most developing countries act as the sole repository of the country's legal foreign exchange reserves. This enables the central bank to administer multiple exchange rate practices under which importers of nonessential goods may pay higher prices for foreign exchange than importers of capital equipment and other high-priority items. Exporters of traditional exports may receive a lower price for their foreign exchange earnings than

---

[2] The observation periods and denominators differ, so the figures are not strictly comparable.

Table 17.2. Revenue from Financial Restriction in 22 Developing Countries

Country	Period	Percentage of GDP	Implicit Tax Rate	Percentage of Total Central Government Revenue
Algeria	1974–1987	4.30	10.08	11.42
Brazil	1983–1987	0.48	13.45	1.57
Colombia	1980–1984	0.24	22.43	2.11
Costa Rica	1972–1984	2.33	25.11	12.76
Greece	1974–1985	2.53	15.94	7.76
India	1980–1985	2.86	10.81	22.38
Indonesia	1976–1986	0.00	23.27	0.00
Jamaica	1980–1982*	1.38	7.32	4.74
Jordan	1978–1987	0.60	7.18	2.40
Korea	1975–1987	0.25	5.98	1.36
Malaysia	1974–1981	0.12	1.76	0.31
Mexico	1984–1987	5.77	45.81	39.65
Morocco	1977–1985	2.31	16.07	8.89
Pakistan	1982–1983	3.23	25.29	20.50
Panama	1977–1987	0.69	4.36	2.49
Papua New Guinea	1981–1987	0.40	5.56	1.90
Philippines	1975–1986	0.45	11.95	3.88
Portugal	1978–1986	2.22	15.36	6.93
Sri Lanka	1981–1983	3.40	14.53	19.24
Thailand	1976–1986	0.38	4.29	2.57
Tunisia	1978–1987	1.49	13.20	4.79
Turkey	1980–1987	2.20	55.49	10.89
Zaire	1974–1986[†]	0.46	62.29	2.48
Zimbabwe	1981–1986	5.50	20.30	19.13
Average		1.82	18.24	8.76

Source: Alberto Giovannini and Martha de Melo, "Government Revenue from Financial Repression," *American Economic Review*, 83(4), September 1993, Tables 1, 3, 959–960

* 1981 omitted
[†] 1981–1983 omitted

exporters of nontraditional goods. Such a multiple exchange rate system involves taxes and subsidies whose net effect may be either to increase or decrease central bank profits.

In general, serious central bank losses have arisen only when the timing of domestic currency receipts has been divorced from the timing of foreign currency payments. One feature of the foreign debt problem in a number of developing countries is that debt service payments have been made to the central bank in domestic currency but the central bank has not simultaneously made the corresponding payments in foreign exchange. In the interim, the central bank assumes the foreign exchange liabilities. In this and other ways, foreign exchange liabilities of central banks in a number of developing countries have risen above their foreign exchange assets. Servicing these foreign exchange liabilities eats into seigniorage revenue. The subsidy consists of accepting payment in domestic currency at a nonmarket-clearing exchange rate.

One example of central bank foreign exchange losses is the Central Bank of Turkey's foreign exchange risk insurance scheme. The Central Bank absorbed the foreign exchange rate risk by passing on foreign exchange loans to borrowers in domestic currency at an interest rate averaging 29.7 percent over the period 1984–1988, 15 percentage points below the average annual rate of depreciation of the Turkish lira over the same period. In 1988, the subsidy involved in this foreign exchange scheme represented 0.6 percent of GNP. The buildup of foreign exchange liabilities was not matched by the acquisition of assets of equal value.

Venezuela initiated a similar foreign exchange rate guarantee scheme in 1983. Registration of private external debt was completed in 1986, just prior to a 93 percent devaluation of the bolivar from Bs 7.50 to Bs 14.50 to the U.S. dollar in December 1986. The Venezuelan authorities maintained a rate of Bs 4.30 for registered private sector debt service and Bs 7.50 for "essential" imports. The switch from central bank profit on foreign exchange operations in 1986 to losses in 1987 represented 3.2 percent of GDP. In Venezuela's case, the central bank's profits and losses from foreign exchange operations are consolidated with the central government's accounts.

17.3.5 Deposit Insurance and Recapitalizing Insolvent Financial Institutions

Over the past decade, a number of developing countries have adopted explicit deposit insurance schemes. However, to the extent that the insurance premia (zero where no explicit deposit insurance exists) do not cover the risk, the central bank provides a subsidy to the banking industry. Since the subsidy takes the form of a contingent liability for the central bank, the outlays in the form of recapitalizing insolvent financial institutions tend to be very uneven. The central bank has not borne the costs of recapitalizing insolvent financial institutions in all countries. In any event, however, the costs have often been a relatively high fraction (over 10 percent in Chile) of GNP.

17.3.6 Implications for Amalgamating Central Bank Losses and Operational Fiscal Deficits

Vito Tanzi, Mario Blejer, and Mario Teijeiro (1988) show why the conventional measurement of fiscal deficits can give a misleading indication of fiscal stance in times of inflation. *Ceteris paribus,* higher inflation-induced nominal interest payments increase the fiscal deficit. However, the inflation premium in the higher nominal interest rate simply compensates the lender for erosion of principal. Under inflationary conditions, an interest payment is, in real terms, part interest and part repayment of the principal or amortization. The inflation premium in the nominal interest rate is principal repayment or amortization, since it matches the reduced real value of the financial claim, while only the real interest rate constitutes income to the recipient.

If individuals do not mistake principal repayment for income, there should be no macroeconomic impact of a higher recorded fiscal deficit caused solely by higher inflation-induced nominal interest payments, provided the tax system is inflation-neutral. However, if the tax system is not neutral, the higher nominal interest payments will raise tax revenue in real terms and so could make lenders worse off. Whether lenders are worse off when inflation and nominal interest rates rise depends on whether nominal interest rates rise by sufficiently more than the rise in inflation to compensate lenders for the extra tax payments. In countries with open capital accounts, this Darby effect (Darby 1975) is unlikely to occur to the full extent necessary to compensate domestic lenders for the increased taxes.

Given the misleading signals on fiscal stance that can be provided by the conventional fiscal deficit, the operational fiscal deficit has been proposed as an alternative. Tanzi, Blejer, and Teijeiro (1988, 12) explain that the operational fiscal deficit is defined as the conventional deficit minus the part of interest payments that simply compensates lenders for inflation. In other words, the operational deficit substitutes real for nominal interest payments in the calculation of the fiscal deficit. Because the inflation component of nominal interest payments is equivalent to amortization of debt, it should be excluded, as is conventional debt amortization, from the fiscal deficit. Teijeiro (1989, 10) points out that "the generation of a financing need is a *necessary* condition for an expense to be considered as deficit determining, but it is not sufficient; a presumption that the expense will not be reinvested in the capital markets but rather spent is also required. Amortization payments are *always* assumed to be reinvested, even when they involve a capital loss/gain."

The government deficit, whether conventional or operational, reflects the difference between government revenue and expenditure to be met by government borrowing, including direct borrowing from the central bank. Revenue from the inflation tax is deliberately excluded from estimates of both the conventional and operational deficits and is treated as a financing item. Suppose, for example, that the central bank simply lends to the government at zero interest through money creation. In such case, the central bank's profit will be zero at any inflation rate and the entire transfer of funds to the government from the central bank will be treated as a financing item. In a growing economy, the central bank could make positive transfers to the government without producing inflation. In this case, seigniorage accrues directly to the government.

In contrast, suppose that the central bank does not lend to the government but buys private sector claims at market interest rates through money creation. At zero inflation, the central bank's profit would be exactly equal to the noninflationary transfer that could have taken place in the previous example. In fact, for any steady-state inflation rate, the central bank's profit would be exactly the same as the transfer to the government in the previous example.

The difference lies in the fact that when the central bank's profit is remitted to the government, it is usually added to other sources of government income without adjustment. In other words, the entire profit is treated as revenue and not as a financing item. Under inflationary conditions, however, part of the central bank profit constitutes revenue from the inflation tax. Since any interest payments by the government to the central bank net out in consolidation, the inflation component of interest earned by the central bank on its holdings of private sector claims must be subtracted from the conventional profit transfer to ensure that the inflation tax is treated as a financing item. The adjusted central bank profit figure reverts to seigniorage revenue in the absence of inflation.[3]

Central bank revenue from its holdings of private sector claims rises as inflation and nominal interest rates rise. For any given level of fiscal expenditure undertaken by the central bank, the central bank's profitability will depend on the extent to which it exploits its monopoly over reserve money. Until the central bank exploits this monopoly to the full, incipient central bank losses can be reduced or eliminated through higher inflation. A balance sheet situation that causes a loss when prices are stable may produce a profit at some positive inflation rate.

In discussing the appropriate adjustment to the conventionally measured government deficit for central bank losses, David Robinson and Peter Stella (1988, 25) argue that, when a central bank posts a profit that it transfers to the government, any fiscal expenditures by the central bank are fully reflected in the government's deficit. *Ceteris paribus,* higher fiscal expenditures by the central bank lower central bank profits and hence raise the government deficit. Robinson and Stella (1988, 25) then state that when a central bank makes a loss "central bank losses are not fully transferred to the fiscal deficit and an asymmetry exists." They argue, therefore, that central bank losses should be

---

[3]For consistency, the inflation component of interest revenue from claims on the private sector held by other parts of the public sector should also be subtracted from public sector revenue in calculating the operational deficit.

added to the government deficit to restore symmetry. Paul Collier and Jan Willem Gunning (1991) make a similar point in the case of a nationalized banking system.

While this adjustment is appropriate for the conventionally measured government deficit or public sector borrowing requirement, a different approach is required for an appropriate adjustment to the operational deficit. Restoring symmetry in the accounting treatment of central bank profits and losses with respect to the government deficit, as proposed by Robinson and Stella (1988, 25) in the context of zero inflation, is not the appropriate solution for calculating the operational deficit under inflationary conditions. Amalgamating central bank losses with the operational deficit regardless of the inflation rate produces a misleading result. However, Robinson and Stella (1988) concentrate on the appropriate adjustment in a zero-inflation setting and are not concerned with the issue of appropriate adjustment in high-inflation countries.

By convention, the inflation tax component of seigniorage revenue is excluded from government revenue. This implies adding *gross* rather than *net* fiscal expenditures by the central bank to the government deficit and subtracting only the noninflationary component of seigniorage revenue (central bank revenue in the absence of inflation). This ensures that deficit finance includes all the inflation tax. This procedure is consistent with the measurement of the operational fiscal deficit proposed by Tanzi, Blejer and Teijeiro (1988, 12); it also echoes the net worth approach proposed by Willem Buiter (1983).

17.4 The Concept of Central Bank Insolvency

When its net worth is negative at all stable inflation rates, one might say that a central bank is insolvent. A central bank is insolvent, in this sense, when it can continue to service its liabilities only through *accelerating* inflation. In other words, the central bank has reached a situation in which survival is no longer possible in a steady state. Given this definition, I disagree with Robinson and Stella's (1988, 23) conclusion that "there is no reason why a central bank cannot continually make losses and have a persistently negative net worth. Therefore, unlike other public sector entities, central bank losses need not be funded."

Central bank solvency can be evaluated by recalculating the central bank's balance sheet at the revenue-maximizing inflation rate. Currency in circulation is valued as a liability only at the discounted annual costs of printing and replacing notes and, where appropriate, detecting forgery. Noninterest-earning deposits at the central bank take a value of zero. At the other extreme, foreign loans borrowed at market rates retain their full face value as liabilities; so too do domestic liabilities that are fully indexed and pay the market rate of interest. Other domestic assets and liabilities with fixed interest rates require adjusted balance sheet entries which will be lower than their face values depending on the maturity of the claim and difference between the coupon rate and the market interest rate consistent with the revenue-maximizing inflation rate.

Net worth is simply the difference between assets and liabilities when all assets and liabilities are given their market values as calculated by the future streams of receipts or payments discounted at the market rate of interest consistent with this stable inflation rate. If assets exactly equal liabilities and net worth is zero, the central bank can survive only by using the entire increase in reserve money to service its liabilities. In such case, the central bank's profit will be zero and there will be nothing left over to finance any government deficit. If net worth is negative, the insolvent central bank has to issue reserve money at an ever accelerating rate of growth.

All this is based on the unrealistic assumption that the central bank has no commitment to finance ongoing government deficits. If, however, the central bank is on the verge of insolvency and the government requires additional financing, accelerating inflation is the inevitable outcome. On the other hand, an insolvent central bank could conceivably be supported indefinitely through transfers from a government budget surplus. In practice, therefore, the central bank's financial position is not independent of the government budget. Hence, a commitment to finance government deficits should be treated as a central bank liability of some estimated present value.

The essential point of this accounting exercise is to demonstrate that seigniorage revenue can be spent by the central bank or by the government but not by both at the same time, a fact that some governments appear reluctant to acknowledge. Several governments have transferred fiscal activities to their central banks precisely to reduce their own deficits. Some central banks are burdened with expensive fiscal activities and yet their governments still expect these central banks to finance their deficits. In Argentina and Yugoslavia, for example, the result has been rapidly accelerating inflation, which surprised some onlookers because government deficits appeared to be relatively modest.

17.4.1 Central Bank Net Worth under a Foreign Debt Burden

The case of Argentina shows that central bank insolvency is no academic curiosity. In 1982, the Central Bank of Argentina assumed the domestic debt and a large proportion of the external debt of the public sector. Subsequently, large government deficits were financed by the Central Bank virtually free of interest and the Central Bank borrowed abroad to provide additional government financing. Private sector foreign debt payments were made to the Central Bank but the Central Bank failed to remit these payments in foreign exchange. It therefore assumed these foreign exchange liabilities in addition to the public sector debt. The Central Bank's operating losses were almost 5 percent of GDP in the first half of 1985.

For the purposes of this illustration, suppose that the Central Bank of Argentina had acquired Argentina's entire foreign debt by the end of September 1989. On 30 September 1989, the value of *M1* (equivalent to noninterest-bearing reserve money in Argentina's case) was ₳1,221 billion which represented 2.8 percent of GDP expressed at an annual rate (*Carta Economica*, 6/7(79), December 1989). Hence, GDP at the end of September 1989 was ₳43,600 billion, expressed at an annual rate, or ₳3,633 billion over the month itself. On the same date, the Central Bank of Argentina owed ₳3,300 billion in very short-term domestic claims bearing market interest rates (7.6 percent of GDP). The foreign debt valued in domestic currency at an exchange rate of ₳650 to the dollar was ₳36,400 billion (83 percent of GDP). Total interest-bearing liabilities of the Central Bank would therefore have been ₳39,700 billion (91 percent of GDP) at the end of September 1989.

Miguel Kiguel and Pablo Andrés Neumeyer (1989) estimate demand for money functions for Argentina using Phillip Cagan's (1956) money demand function, $M^d/P = a \cdot y \cdot e^{-\alpha \pi^e}$, where M^d/P represents the desired holdings of real money balances, y is real GDP expressed at a monthly rather than an annual rate, π^e is expected inflation, and a and α are parameters. This equation can also be expressed in terms of desired holdings of money balances as a proportion of GDP, $M^d/Y = a \cdot e^{-\alpha \pi^e}$, where Y is nominal GDP. Using monthly data for the period 1979–1988, Kiguel and Neumeyer estimate values of about 1.02 for a and 5 for α. The coefficient for α can be compared to Cagan's estimates for other hyperinflations: 8.55 for Austria, 5.46 for Germany, 4.09 for Greece, 8.70 and 3.63 for Hungary, 2.30 for Poland, and 3.06 for Russia (Cagan, 1956, 43). With zero economic growth (constant y), the revenue-maximizing inflation rate in the steady state (when inflation is constant and equals expected inflation) is $1/\alpha$, in this case 20 percent per month. The revenue produced from this inflation as a proportion of GDP is $(M/Y) \cdot \pi$, in this case 0.075 (7.5 percent of GDP).

The monthly real interest rate on Argentina's foreign exchange liabilities is 0.6 percent. Using this rate and again assuming a zero rate of economic growth, the present value of the Central Bank's monopoly is 1250 percent of monthly GDP or ₳45,417 billion (104 percent of GDP expressed in annual terms), somewhat greater than the total liabilities of ₳39,700 billion. On this basis, therefore, the Central Bank would still be solvent. This does not imply that inflation is the best way of maintaining solvency; default or recapitalization might be preferable in terms of social welfare.

17.4.2 A Dynamic Simulation of Central Bank Foreign Debt Service

Another approach to this problem is to conduct a dynamic simulation of the inflationary process caused by the Central Bank of Argentina's hypothetical cash flow requirements. For this, I combine the Kiguel-Neumeyer money demand estimate with elements of a dynamic model developed by Marcelo

Table 17.3. Central Bank Debt Service Model in Continuous Time

$$dM/dt = d \cdot P. \tag{17.1}$$

$$\mu = (1/M)(dM/dt). \tag{17.2}$$

$$\pi = \mu + \lambda(\ln m - \ln m^d). \tag{17.3}$$

$$m^d = a \cdot y \cdot e^{-\alpha \pi^e}. \tag{17.4}$$

$$d\pi^e/dt = \beta(\pi - \pi^e). \tag{17.5}$$

$$P = P_0 \cdot e^{t\pi}. \tag{17.6}$$

$$m = M/P. \tag{17.7}$$

Giugale (1989). This model is presented in Table 17.3. Equation 17.1 shows that reserve money M is expanded solely to service the central bank's debt, where d is the constant real debt service and P is the price level. Nominal debt service $d \cdot P$ equals the real interest rate r times the nominal debt D. With purchasing-power parity, the rate of change in the nominal value of debt rises in step with inflation π. The nominal value of debt service also rises in step with inflation, given the fixed real interest rate. Equation 17.2 defines the rate of growth in the nominal money stock μ. In equation 17.3, inflation is caused by money growth μ and also by disequilibrium in the money market: $\pi \equiv (1/P)(dP/dt)$ and $m \equiv M/P$. Excess money supply in real terms raises the inflation rate above the rate of growth in the money stock, while excess real money demand reduces the inflation rate. This specification is used by Kiguel (1989, 151). Money market disequilibrium can be justified on the basis of a buffer stock model (Laidler, 1984).

Equation 17.4 is the standard Cagan money demand function in which the demand for money balances in real terms is a function of real GDP y and expected inflation π^e. I use Cagan's adaptive expectations mechanism defined in equation 17.5; the change in expected inflation is a function of the difference between the actual inflation rate and expected inflation rate. Equation 17.6 defines the price level P, while equation 17.7 defines the real money stock m.

In a zero-growth steady state, the money market is in equilibrium ($\ln m^d = \ln m$), expectations are realized ($\pi^e = \pi$), and y is constant. Money market equilibrium therefore can be expressed

$$m = a \cdot y \cdot e^{-\alpha \pi}. \tag{17.8}$$

The financing requirement also provides a relationship between the real money

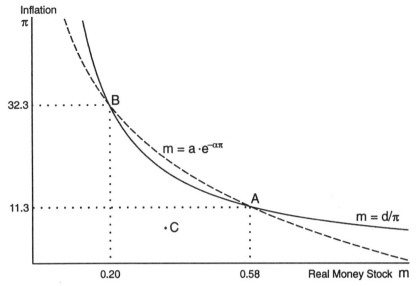

Figure 17.1. Equilibria in Central Bank Debt Service Model

stock and inflation. Differentiating the real money stock M/P or m with respect to time gives $dm/dt = (dM/dt)/P - m\pi$. Substituting equation 17.1 into this expression gives $dm/dt = d - m\pi$. Since dm/dt is zero in the steady state, the equilibrium financing condition implies:

$$m = d/\pi. \qquad (17.9)$$

With a equal to 1.02 and α equal to 5, the equilibrium real money stock as a proportion of monthly GDP at different inflation rates given by equation 17.8 is plotted in Figure 17.1.[4] The equilibrium money market condition is given by the curve labelled $m = a \cdot e^{-\alpha\pi}$. With r set at 0.006, the debt service requirement as a proportion of monthly GDP was 0.06556 at the end of September 1989. This debt service requirement is used to trace out equation 17.9 for different inflation rates in Figure 17.1. The constant real debt service requirement is given by the curve labelled $m = d/\pi$; a higher inflation rate (the tax rate) requires a lower real money stock (the tax base) to yield the same real revenue. The range of inflation rates between A and B are those steady-state inflation rates which produce more revenue than required. At A and B, revenue equals the amount required to service the debt. With suitably selected values for β and λ, A is a stable equilibrium while B is unstable.

---

[4]This diagrammatic presentation is similar to the one used by Lynne Evans and George Yarrow (1981).

Table 17.4. Model of Central Bank Debt Service in Discrete Time

$$M = M_{t-1} + d \cdot P. \tag{17.10}$$

$$\mu = (M - M_{t-1})/M_{t-1}. \tag{17.11}$$

$$\pi = \mu_{t-1} + \lambda(m_{t-1} - m_{t-1}^d)/m_{t-1}^d. \tag{17.12}$$

$$\pi^e = \pi_{t-1}^e + \beta(\pi - \pi^e) \tag{17.13}$$

$$m^d = a \cdot e^{-\alpha\pi^e}. \tag{17.14}$$

$$P = P_{t-1} \cdot (1 + \pi). \tag{17.15}$$

$$m = M/P. \tag{17.16}$$

I use the discrete-time version of the model presented in Table 17.4 to analyze the Central Bank of Argentina's debt servicing obligations. For this dynamic simulation, I assume that real GDP remains constant over time. To ensure that A is a stable equilibrium, I assign a value of 0.1 to both β and λ. The simulation result shown in Figures 17.2 and 17.3 indicates that the dynamic model does not converge to a constant inflation rate. Similar results are obtained when a rational expectations ($\pi^e = \pi$) version of the model with money market disequilibrium and an adaptive expectations version with money market equilibrium ($m_{t-1}^d = m_{t-1}$) are simulated. In both variations, the hyperinflation explodes more rapidly.

At the end of September 1989, the real money stock represented 34 percent of GNP, well below the equilibrium level consistent with the September monthly inflation rate of 7 percent. The simulations therefore start at point C in Figure 17.1. Inflation accelerates too rapidly for the real money stock to increase sufficiently to reach the $m = d/\pi$ curve between A and B, as shown in the scatter diagram of Figure 17.3.

In fact the austral collapsed in 1990, sooner than indicated by this model because the government required additional funds from the Central Bank to finance its ongoing deficit. In 1991, however, the Argentine government initiated fiscal reform and a stabilization program that has so far been highly successful.

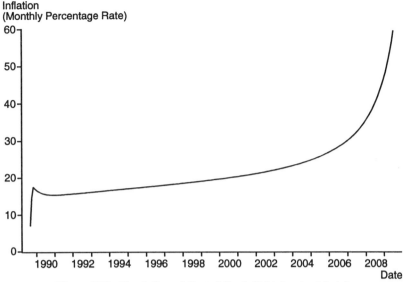

Figure 17.2. Simulation of Central Bank Debt Service Model

17.5 Fiscal Activities of Central Banks from the Optimal Taxation Perspective

17.5.1 Seigniorage

Edmund Phelps (1973) considers the inflation tax using the optimal taxation framework of Peter Diamond and James Mirrlees (1971a, 1971b). Phelps treats money as a consumer durable; it provides useful liquidity services. Hence, real money balances appear in the utility function. Government revenue has to be collected through the imposition of distortionary taxes; lump-sum taxes are ruled out by assumption. Using a static model in which the alternative source of government revenue is a tax on labor, Phelps shows that taxes on both liquidity and labor will be optimal unless the compensated labor supply curve is perfectly inelastic. In the absence of cross-substitution effects, optimal taxation necessitates the imposition of taxes such that all items are reduced in the same proportion (the Ramsey rule). The more inelastic the demand for liquidity, the higher is the optimal inflation tax for any given total government revenue requirement.

Christophe Chamley (1985) extends the analysis of the optimal inflation tax in the presence of distortionary taxes using a dynamic model with money in the utility function. The general result is that the optimal inflation tax is approximately where the interest elasticity of money demand equals the excess burden of other taxes. Chamley shows that when the excess burden of

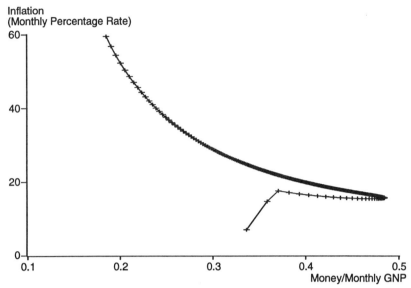

Figure 17.3. Inflation and Real Money Balances in Central Bank Debt Service Model

other taxes tends to infinity, the government maximizes revenue from money creation. Here the interest elasticity of the demand for money is -1. Were lump-sum taxation feasible, no inflation tax should be collected and inflation would equal $-r$, where r is the real interest rate (Chamley 1985, 44).

Kent Kimbrough (1986) obtains an entirely different result by treating money as an intermediate good. Money no longer appears in the utility function but in the budget constraint; money is an intermediate good that helps consumers economize on "shopping" time. Kimbrough follows Diamond and Mirrlees (1971a, 1971b) to show that optimal taxation involves levying distortionary taxes only on final consumer goods, not on intermediate goods. Hence, the inflation rate should be set such that the nominal interest rate is zero, as proposed by Milton Friedman (1969).

None of these models appears to have much policy relevance in the real world. For the general application of general equilibrium and optimal tax models, Alan Tait (1989) presents a long list of practical problems. For the particular case of the inflation tax, three difficulties seem of paramount importance. First, the optimal tax models rely on the assumption that each tax is levied without any costs of administration or compliance (Tait 1989, 17). In practice, the inflation tax can be levied at virtually no cost, whereas costs of collecting most other taxes are considerable. Second, no consideration is given to the interaction of inflation and real revenue collected from other taxes due to lags in tax collection (Tanzi 1977, 1989). In practice, higher inflation may reduce the real revenue obtained from other taxes. Third, inflation creates distortions over and above the tax distortion. For example, maturities of financial claims decrease as inflation accelerates. As a result, the number and cost of financial transactions rise. Higher inflation is always more variable; the increased uncertainty worsens the efficiency in allocating investible funds.

17.5.2 Financial Restriction

Giovannini and de Melo (1993) present an analytical framework which can be used to analyze financial restriction from the tax efficiency standpoint. Identical consumer-investors use their endowments in period one to purchase the consumption good as well as domestic and foreign financial assets. The domestic financial asset is high-powered money. The government spends only in period one and finances its expenditure by borrowing abroad and at home from the central bank. Holdings of foreign financial assets are restricted. This restriction can be modelled as a tax equivalent to τ on interest income. The tax is levied on the value of assets in period two. This tax enables the government to pay a lower net-of-tax interest on its domestic liabilities, since the world rate of interest is unaffected by the tax. In other words, the government effectively discourages purchase of foreign assets by reducing their net return.

The consumer now maximizes utility from consumption in both periods and from government expenditure in period one, subject to the budget constraint, in which interest earned on currency, deposits and foreign bonds is reduced by the tax. The government chooses the level of government expenditure that maximizes consumer utility. Giovannini and de Melo (1993) compare this tax setup with one in which income taxes are levied in both periods. The optimal tax structure is to equalize the marginal distortions from income tax in each period and to eliminate the interest rate tax. This is an application of the Diamond-Mirrlees's (1971a) production efficiency theory which shows that investment decisions should be allowed to maximize income at world prices. Otherwise, suboptimal investment decisions will lower total resources available for both government expenditure and consumption.

17.5.3 Foreign Exchange Taxes and Subsidies

Multiple exchange-rate practices can be analyzed in the same way as trade tariffs and subsidies. Indeed, as Rudiger Dornbusch (1985, 9) points out, "they are no different from a set of tariffs or taxes. Thus anything that could be achieved by these multiple rates could, administrative issues aside, be accomplished in precisely the same way by taxes and/or subsidies." Dornbusch (1985, 10–11) concludes: "A tax-subsidy scheme administered through multiple exchange rates is just as efficient or inefficient as the equivalent system of trade taxes or subsidies. Both as a means of raising general revenue and as an instrument for achieving particular objectives of allocation or distribution trade taxes are almost always second or third best instruments. Their use, as a *permanent* system, would have to be justified by administrative and/or political feasibility or convenience rather than on any intrinsic optimality."

Is there any evidence that multiple exchange-rate systems are easier to administer than equivalent trade taxes and subsidies? Where foreign exchange controls exist in any case, administering multiple exchange rates may well be cheaper than administering trade taxes and subsidies. In practice, however, multiple exchange rates are not used as substitutes for trade taxes; they coexist with occasional inconsistencies (Lizondo 1985, 24).

17.6 Summary

Fiscal analysis tends to concentrate on flow variables. It is therefore natural to examine central bank fiscal activities using income statements. Hence, one may be tempted into believing that effects of such activities are confined to the income period under review. The balance sheet approach used here shows how central bank fiscal activities can have a permanent effect on the central bank's profitability. A government may use its central bank to bail out a failed financial institution by buying financial assets at greatly inflated values. For any given inflation rate, it makes no difference in present value terms whether the government or the central bank provides the funds. What the government saves today it loses in the future through the reduced profits of its central bank. The balance sheet approach illustrates this proposition in terms of the reduced net worth of the central bank.

Since their invention, central banks have served as a source of government revenue. Indeed, the central bank is the goose that lays the golden eggs. The free-range goose, conducting conservative monetary policy with a fair degree of independence, produces golden eggs worth less than 1 percent of GNP (most OECD countries). The battery-farm goose, bred specially for intensive egg-laying, can produce golden eggs in the form of an inflation tax yielding 5 to 10 percent of GNP (Mexico, Peru, and Yugoslavia in the 1980s). The force-fed goose can produce revenue of up to 25 percent of GNP for a limited period before the inevitable demise of the goose and collapse of the economy (Chile in the early 1970s). All three forms of central bank geese have been sighted since the 1920s.

In several developing countries, central banks are no longer profitable despite high inflation. As a general rule, central bank profits are well below the amount implied by calculations of seigniorage revenue. The difference is far larger than any conceivable expenditure on normal central banking activities, such as maintaining the quality of the note issue. Even the most extravagant expenditure on salaries and staff benefits could account for only a small fraction of this discrepancy. In fact, the lion's share of the difference is due to the impairment of central banks' balance sheets by the acquisition of substandard assets and of liabilities not matched by assets of equal value. Many central banks have acquired substandard assets through preferential rediscount policies and by bailing out insolvent financial institutions. They have also acquired liabilities not matched by assets of equal value in accepting domestic currency payments for foreign debts when not possessing the corresponding foreign exchange. These central bank geese have expired under a costly burden of fiscal and quasi-fiscal activities.

When a central bank is solvent, its profits can supplement government revenue. When a central bank is insolvent, the government will eventually have to transfer resources in the opposite direction. In other words, the government will have to remove at least part of the fiscal burden previously placed on the central bank. The only alternative is to declare bankruptcy and for the central bank to default on its liabilities. Even when it comes to the central bank's money monopoly, there is still no such thing as a free lunch.

Chapter 18

Interest Rate and Selective Credit Policies

18.1 Introduction

THERE IS PERHAPS no set of prices over which governments throughout the world have exerted more direct or indirect control than institutional interest rates. Interest rate policies pursued in developing countries are typically designed to achieve one or more of the following objectives: (a) efficient allocation of investible funds; (b) effective domestic resource mobilization; (c) cheap credit for the government sector; and (d) macroeconomic stability. While governments have focused on nominal interest rates, control over real interest rates has been an elusive goal. Figure 18.1 shows the distribution of 597 real interest rate observations that occurred in the range −30 to +30 percent in 34 developing countries over the period 1970–1988 analyzed by Alan Gelb (1989). The data are taken from the *World Development Report 1991* data diskettes. Although these rates cluster around zero, there is considerable dispersion in both directions.

This chapter assesses the actual effects of interest rate policies followed in a sample of 11 Asian developing countries that provides considerable heterogeneity. The country sample—Bangladesh, India, Indonesia, Korea, Malaysia, Nepal, Pakistan, Philippines, Sri Lanka, Taiwan, and Thailand—represents market-based Asian developing countries for which a reasonably comprehensive data set was available. Tables 18.1 and 18.2 present some basic comparative data for these Asian countries.

18.2 Level and Structure of Deposit Rates of Interest

This section compares the level of real 12-month deposit rates of interest and the maturity structure of nominal deposit rates across the sample countries. It also examines movements in these rates over the period 1961–1988. Here the real 12-month deposit rates are calculated by subtracting the continuously

420

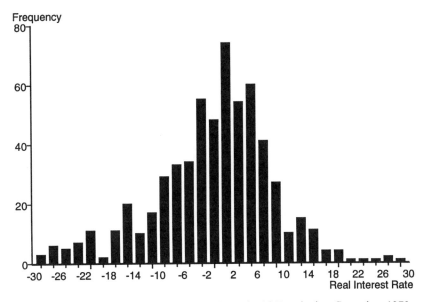

Figure 18.1. Distribution of Real Interest Rates in 16 Developing Countries, 1970–1988

Table 18.1. Basic Economic Indicators for 11 Sample Asian Developing Countries

Country	Per Capita Income Index 1970 (U.S. = 100)	Per Capita Income in 1989 (U.S. dollars)	Population Growth Rate 1979–1989	Rate of Growth in Real Per Capita Income 1979–1989
Bangladesh	3.99	180	2.4	1.0
India	6.06	350	2.1	3.5
Indonesia	5.12	470	2.1	3.1
Korea	13.20	3910	1.2	6.7
Malaysia	17.30	2050	2.7	2.6
Nepal	4.44	180	3.0	1.0
Pakistan	9.08	370	3.0	3.0
Philippines	9.93	680	2.4	–0.5
Sri Lanka	9.53	440	1.5	2.4
Taiwan	20.40	6730	1.4	6.4
Thailand	9.26	1160	2.0	4.6

Source: Income indices for 1970 (United States equals 100) are taken from Irving B. Kravis, Alan W. Heston, and Robert Summers (1978), other variables from *Asian Economic Outlook 1990* and *Key Indicators of Developing Asian and Pacific Countries*, 21, July 1990.

Note: Growth rates are continuously compounded rates of change.

Table 18.2. National Saving, Domestic Investment and Economic Growth in 11 Sample
Asian Developing Countries

Country	National Saving Ratio		Domestic Investment Ratio		Rate of Growth in Real GNP	
	1979–84	1984–89	1979–84	1984–89	1979–84	1984–89
Bangladesh	4.4	5.0	11.1	9.0	3.2	3.5
India	20.3	20.2	23.5	23.7	5.5	5.7
Indonesia	23.1	28.2	29.6	30.2	5.2	5.2
Korea	24.1	32.8	31.8	31.1	5.9	9.9
Malaysia	29.2	30.2	35.6	29.3	6.1	4.6
Nepal	12.0	11.7	17.5	20.4	3.1	4.9
Pakistan	14.6	16.3	17.1	17.2	7.0	5.0
Philippines	22.0	16.2	27.6	16.2	0.8	3.1
Sri Lanka	13.7	11.2	29.4	23.5	4.7	3.2
Taiwan	32.2	35.0	27.9	20.4	7.1	8.6
Thailand	21.1	23.1	25.9	26.0	5.8	7.5

Source: *Asian Economic Outlook 1990* and *Key Indicators of Developing Asian and Pacific Countries,* 21, July 1990

Note: Growth rates are continuously compounded rates of change.

compounded expected inflation rate π^e from the continuously compounded deposit rate d. The expected inflation rate is estimated from the continuously compounded rate of change in the implicit GNP deflator π, the only consistent, though far from perfect, price index available for all the sample countries for the entire period. Expected inflation is estimated by applying polynomial distributed lags to the inflation rate in money demand functions estimated separately for each country. Since continuously compounded deposit and expected inflation rates are used, the real deposit rate is measured correctly as $d-\pi^e$. Table 18.3 presents period-average real deposit rates for the sample countries. These data were used in section 8.4 to show the positive and significant relationships between real deposit rates of interest, the rate of economic growth, and total factor productivity growth.

During the 1960s, real interest rates tended to remain fairly stable in all the sample countries except Indonesia. They fell dramatically in 1973 and 1974 as worldwide inflation accelerated, remaining negative in most countries for the rest of that decade. With possibly the least domestic disturbance combined with a liberal foreign exchange regime, Thailand mirrors worldwide movements in real interest rates since 1961.

Table 18.4 shows that in 1980 or thereabouts the term structure of deposit rates of interest rose steeply in most of this sample of Asian countries.

Table 18.3. Real Deposit Rates of Interest in 11 Asian Developing Countries, 1961–1988 (Annual average continuously compounded rates)

Country	1961–1967	1968–1974	1975–1981	1982–1988
Bangladesh	–0.85	–7.88	–3.19	2.33
India	–2.91	–2.46	0.07	1.13
Indonesia	–	–1.21	–5.80	7.57
Korea	–0.28	1.58	–2.58	5.13
Malaysia	4.94	2.01	1.79	5.37
Nepal	–4.40	–0.62	4.04	3.36
Pakistan	0.23	–2.33	–1.55	2.96
Philippines	–0.21	–4.22	–0.16	–0.32
Sri Lanka	2.45	–4.52	0.27	4.08
Taiwan	9.01	0.34	2.88	5.48
Thailand	5.03	1.24	1.52	7.67

The striking exceptions are Malaysia and Singapore. In three countries with uncompetitive, state-owned banking systems—Burma, India, and Nepal—the term structure rises most steeply, from 1, 4, and 4 percent on 3-month deposits to $2\frac{1}{2}$, 7, and 12 percent on 12-month deposits. The more competitive and unregulated the banking system, such as that in Malaysia, Philippines, Singapore, and Thailand, the flatter the term structure of deposit rates. For example, 12-month deposits in Nepal, Philippines, and Thailand all earn 12 percent. However, three-month deposit rates in these countries were 4, $10\frac{1}{2}$, and 9 percent, respectively, around 1980.

Term structures of deposit rates that are fixed by administrative decision —the case in all countries except Hong Kong, Malaysia, Philippines (since August 1980), and Singapore—have been altered at various times. India provides a typical example. In June 1977, the rate of interest on five-year deposits was held at 10 percent, while rates on all shorter maturities were lowered. The Reserve Bank of India explained that these adjustments were designed to rationalize the interest rate structure. The changes in deposit rates were made to "smoothen" the spread between rates on short- and long-term fixed deposits. However, this term structure was rationalized again in March 1978, when three- and five-year deposit rates were reduced by $\frac{1}{2}$ and 1 percentage point, respectively. Changes occurred once again in September 1979. Table 18.5 shows the March 1978 and September 1979 term structures of deposit rates of interest in India. Evidently the 1979 rationalization steepened slightly the term structure of deposit rates of interest.

The term structure of deposit rates was already steeply rising in India before the additional, albeit small, tilt was introduced in September 1979. This indicates neither strong liquidity preference nor high marginal rates of

Table 18.4. Term Structure of Time Deposit Rates of Interest

Country	Date	Maturity (months)					
		0–1	3	6	9	12	24–36
Bangladesh	11/80	10.00	12.00	13.00	–	14.00	15.00
Burma	11/77	–	1.00	1.50	–	2.50	3.50
Hong Kong	9/80	6.50	–	8.90	–	10.40	–
India	9/79	2.50	4.00	4.50	5.50	7.00	8.50
Indonesia	3/78	3.00	–	6.00	–	9.00	12.00*
Korea	11/80	12.30	14.80	16.90	–	19.50	28.40†
Malaysia	2/80	5.25	5.50	5.75	6.00	7.00	–
Nepal	7/78	–	4.00	9.00	–	12.00	13.00
Pakistan	6/77	8.50	9.00	9.50	–	10.50	11.00
Philippines‡	12/79	9.00	10.50	11.00	–	12.00	13.00
Singapore	3/80	7.52	8.79	8.80	–	8.56	–
Sri Lanka	4/80	12.00	–	–	–	20.00	22.00
Taiwan	8/79	9.00	9.50	10.25	11.25	12.50	12.50
Thailand	6/80	8.00	9.00	10.00	–	12.00	13.00

Source: Central bank and monetary authority publications

Notes: "Date" refers to the date on which this term structure was established.
* This rate applied to large deposits. Small deposits received 15 percent.
† This rate applied to special subsidized workmen's wealth accumulation deposits.
‡ A single ceiling of 14 percent was adopted in August 1980.

time preference because the term structure is imposed purely from the supply side. What it does approximate, however, is a monopolist's profit-maximizing strategy through product differentiation (Fry 1981b).

The problem can be viewed as one of minimizing the cost of generating a target real money demand. Given the inflation rate and the real money demand target, interest costs will be minimized by paying zero or low nominal rates on current and short-term time deposits, for which there are no close substitutes, and higher rates on longer-term time deposits, for which closer substitutes in the form of tangible assets used as inflation hedges do exist. To stabilize the aggregate real money demand in the face of volatile inflation, the nominal interest rates on longer-term time deposits must be adjusted continuously in step with changes in inflationary expectations. In other words, the real deposit rate on long-term deposits has to be held constant. Therefore, the higher the expected inflation rate, the more tilted the term structure has to be.

Whether the appropriate real interest rate on long-term deposits is negative, positive, or zero depends on the volume of real money demand to be generated. In a growing or potentially growing economy, the basic objective of accelerating economic growth would necessitate positive real long-term time deposit rates in order to maximize the real supply of domestic credit, the main asset backing the deposit liabilities of the financial intermediaries.

Table 18.5. Term Structure of Time Deposit Rates of Interest in India, 1978 and 1979

Maturity	March 1978	September 1979
Current	0	0
Savings	4.5	5.0
15–45 days	2.5	2.5
46–90 days	3.0	3.0
3–6 months	4.0	4.0
6–9 months	4.5	4.5
9–12 months	5.0	5.5
1–3 years	6.0	7.0
3–5 years	7.5	8.5
Over 5 years	9.0	10.0

From another viewpoint, a greater inflation tax is levied on current and short-term time deposits, for which there are no close substitutes, while a smaller tax is extracted from deposits for which closer substitutes do exist. Monopolistic product differentiation designed to tap consumer surplus, in this case from depositors, is analyzed in section 7.3. The tax is used in most of this sample of countries as one source of credit subsidy for priority sectors. It is also absorbed in high administrative costs of the uncompetitive financial sectors found in virtually all these countries.

Monopolistic product differentiation of deposits is most evident in Korea. The following variety of deposit types exists there:

Demand Deposits	Time Deposits
Ordinary checking	Ordinary
Personal checking	Special household
Passbook	Multiple maturity
Temporary	Negotiable certificates
Money in trust	Savings
	Installment savings
	Notice
	Mutual installment
	Housing installment
	Workmen's wealth accumulation
	Children's savings stamps

In addition, deposits are subject to a variety of fiscal incentives—exemptions, deductions, credits, and lower tax rates on interest income. A fiscal subsidy is provided for saving by lower-income workers. This produces an effective net return of 38 percent on long-term workmen's wealth accumulation deposits.

Similarly, household, farmer, fisherman, and student deposits receive up to 4 percentage points more interest than the standard rate. Holders of housing installment deposits get priority for buying government-built apartments and houses.

The plethora of differentiated deposits offering differential deposit rates of interest illustrates well the technique of tapping consumer surplus. This technique seems to be used as a deliberate element of interest rate policy in all the sample countries except Hong Kong, Malaysia, Philippines (since 1980), and Singapore. In Hong Kong, Malaysia, and Philippines, however, bankers' cartels appear to exploit the same technique in the interests of profit maximization. Only in Singapore does the term structure of deposits fail to exhibit a tilt consistent with a monopolist's cost-minimization or profit-maximization solution.

There are, of course, a variety of other financial assets in addition to bank deposits which are available to savers in most of the sample countries. In India, for example, approved state-sponsored institutions (such as state electricity boards, rural housing boards, cooperative processing and marketing societies, and state road transport corporations) offer rural debentures yielding 12 percent, which are exempt from both income and wealth taxes. They can be bought by and transferred to individuals only. Product differentiation is introduced through the provision of a one-year lockup period, during which the debenture is nontransferable and ineligible as collateral for a bank loan, as well as the absence of any government guarantee. This financial instrument was designed deliberately to ensure that resources for market borrowing programs of central and state governments and their agencies were not impaired. For urban savers, less attractive—five-year, nonnegotiable, $10\frac{1}{2}$ percent yield—national development bonds are available.

At the least controlled end of the scale in India are company shares, debentures, and deposits. Interest rate ceilings are imposed—11 percent on preference share dividends, $10\frac{1}{2}$ percent on long-term debenture yields, and 16 percent on deposits issuable to a maximum maturity of three years. Larger companies can attract two- and three-year deposits at 3 to 4 percentage points above commercial bank deposit rates (10 to 11 percent).

Detailed regulation of financial assets and their returns in India typifies the situation in those developing countries that implement comprehensive selective credit policies or expropriate a large proportion of domestic credit for the public sector. Regulations on nondeposit financial claims similar to India's are found in Burma, Indonesia, Nepal, Pakistan, and Sri Lanka. In Sri Lanka, for example, a business transactions tax applies only to nondeposit financial claims, and there are legislative bottlenecks preventing the development of an effective capital market. These countries have detailed selective credit policies or high seigniorage ratios. Conversely, some form of negotiable certificate, bankers' acceptance, or promissory note, whose market yield is uncontrollable, exists in Hong Kong, Korea, Malaysia, Philippines (since

1981), Singapore, Taiwan, and Thailand. Relatively free capital movements characterize Hong Kong, Indonesia, Korea, Malaysia, Philippines, Singapore, Taiwan, and Thailand. At least some domestic interest rates in all these countries are influenced by the level of and movements in international rates.

Governments of all the South Asian countries in the sample appear to behave as if they were subject to two conflicting objectives. On the one hand, they are anxious to mobilize domestic resources by offering attractive returns to savers. On the other hand, they wish to finance their own considerable borrowing requirements as cheaply as possible. Furthermore, these governments clearly believe, as do the governments of Indonesia and Korea, that priority groups, sectors, and regions of the country need cheap credit.

These objectives may indeed conflict when the subsidies for government and other priority borrowers are paid by holders of financial assets. A proportional tax on all financial assets to be spread proportionally among borrowers would have no effect at all, provided that interest rates adjusted upwards by exactly the amount of the tax/subsidy. Free-market interest rates would make such an adjustment automatically. Were controlled interest rates not adjusted similarly, the quantity of financial assets demanded (lending) would fall.

The two objectives need not conflict, however, when the tax on financial asset holders is levied as a poll tax or in the form of any alternative intramarginal tax that tapped only consumer surplus. Section 7.3 suggests that the monopolistic price discrimination in terms of the present structure of asset yields on financial claims in the countries of South Asia may well be capable of tapping consumer surplus without reducing aggregate demand in real terms for financial assets. Unfortunately, the rigidity of the structure of nominal institutional interest rates produces demand fluctuations *pari passu* with changes in inflationary expectations. However, indexation of just one long-term financial asset could introduce the necessary flexibility in effective nominal rates to allow the existing system to tap consumer surplus without reducing real aggregate financial asset demand in the face of rising inflationary expectations. Such indexation could be achieved by inflating the principal by the GNP deflator, the consumer price index, or an exchange rate index once a quarter or twice a year and paying the announced interest rate on the new inflated sum.

18.3   Institutional Lending Rates of Interest

Institutional loan rates of interest are not constrained by legal ceilings in Hong Kong, Korea, Malaysia, and Singapore. However, loan rate schedules are fixed in Korea by the Bankers' Association under close government supervision and seem to be regulated in Malaysia by a banking cartel. Nevertheless, there appears to be some recognition of the need for differential risk premia in the loan rate structures in all four countries. Risk and cost differences explain most of the variations in lending rates in Hong Kong, Malaysia, and Singapore. However, preferential rediscount facilities produce subsidized loan rates for priority borrowers in both Korea and Malaysia. A subsidized or concessional rate is defined here as an interest rate set below the effective market rate facing the specific borrower.

Loan rate ceilings but limited rate differentiation characterize loan rate policies of Philippines, Taiwan, and Thailand. In these three countries, as in Korea and Malaysia, interest rates on export loans are heavily subsidized. In the main, loan rate subsidization is implemented in all five countries through differential concessional rediscount facilities.

In South Asia, Indonesia, and effectively in Korea as well, loan rates of interest have been administratively determined on various nonrisk, noncost criteria. Again India typifies these systems. Here institutional lending rates are differentiated, as are margin requirements, and collateral percentages on a variety of criteria:

1. *Size:* Small banks in India may charge 1 percent more than large banks (19 versus 18 percent) on their advances. Small farmers can borrow up to Rs 2,500 (rupees) at 11 percent, irrespective of maturity. Special provisions are also available for artisans, village and cottage industries, tiny sector units, and small vendors/traders, especially in urban and metropolitan centers. Loan rates also differ for bank advances in the size ranges Rs 0 to Rs 100,000, Rs 100,000 to Rs 500,000, Rs 500,000 to Rs 20 million, and above Rs 20 million. Large loans are "discouraged."

2. *Maturity:* Regular short-term advances in India carry interest rates of 18 to 19 percent. Advances to preferred categories are lower, at $12\frac{1}{2}$ percent. Term loan rates of interest range from 8 to $15\frac{1}{2}$ percent. By definition, all term lending is preferred.

3. *Source:* In India, interest rates for a given type of loan may vary depending on the source of funds. Hence, for example, state financial corporations charge 1 percentage point less on loans refinanced by the Industrial Development Bank of India. Different rates may, of course, also be quoted by different financial institutions. For example, a commercial bank may provide an industrial project loan at $12\frac{1}{2}$ percent, while the Industrial Development Bank provides similar loans from its own resources at 11 percent.

4. *Group:* Artisans, farmers, small entrepreneurs, and technicians in India are favored groups to whom credit is provided at concessional rates. Small farmers can borrow from the commercial and cooperative banks at $9\frac{1}{2}$ percent, large farmers at $10\frac{1}{2}$ percent. Sick units under the agreed nursing programs also form a group eligible for concessional terms. The Indian government is the most favored group. The long-term

government bond yield averaged 5.87 percent in fiscal years 1978/79 and 1979/80. Government borrowing is sheltered from competition through the 34 percent statutory liquidity ratio, which all commercial banks are obliged to maintain.

5. *Sector:* Normal priority sectors in India can generally obtain advances at the minimum lending rate of $12\frac{1}{2}$ percent. Export and food procurement credit is extended at 11 percent. Borrowing to finance inventory purchases of "sensitive" commodities (such as sugar, pulses, vegetable oils, and oilseeds) has been discouraged to varying degrees through margin requirements that have been changed with some frequency. Recently, banks have been required to ensure that they were not financing antisocial hoarding of and speculation in such commodities. In Korea, a 50 percent capital gains tax has been imposed to deter real estate speculation. Most countries with negative real loan rates have also adopted antihoarding legislation. Of course, the problem of socially unproductive inventory accumulation or speculation is a direct consequence of negative real institutional interest rates. Such activity cannot yield a private profit when real interest rates are positive.

All long-term lending in India is priority lending, but some activities or groups are more favored than others. Thus, for example, the normal loan rate of interest for projects financed by the Industrial Development Bank is 11 percent, but there is a soft loan rate of $7\frac{1}{2}$ percent for jute, cement, engineering goods, sugar, and cotton textiles.

6. *Region:* Borrowers in backward districts of India receive loans at interest rates below those charged to borrowers in forward districts. For example, the Industrial Development Bank lends to units in backward districts at $9\frac{1}{2}$ percent, compared with the normal project rate of 11 percent. Some state financial corporations have more than two regional distinctions. However, the rural/urban distinction is the most popular.

Nonpriority borrowers in India have been increasingly rationed out of the institutional credit market because of the proliferation of preferred categories of borrowers. Aggregate domestic credit expansion in nominal terms is determined to a large extent by quantitative ceilings. Food and export credit is exempt from these controls. Indeed, refinancing is available for 30 percent of any food procurement credit which exceeds a preset minimum. The same system applies to export credit and credit to small farmers. Here incentives are provided for credit expansion.

In September 1979, loan rates on normal credit in India were raised, additional credit ceilings were imposed, and existing ceilings were tightened. For some normal borrowers the effective institutional lending rate is infinite; they are completely rationed out. Furthermore, alternative sources of funds have been suppressed. Borrower protection legislation has dried up noninstitutional lending, particularly in rural areas. In addition, normal companies have had their nonbank public borrowing limited to 35 percent of their paid-up capital and free reserves. The credit market has been segmented more and more over the past two decades. This is a typical concomitant of selective credit policies, the topic of section 18.5.

18.4   Deficit Finance and Interest Rate Policy

Government deficits for the world as a whole averaged 3.36 percent of gross domestic products (GDP) during the period 1977–1981; that percentage rose to 5.04 percent in the period 1981–1986 (*International Financial Statistics Yearbook* 1989, 156). The main consequence for the world as a whole has been a substantial increase in real interest rates, as government borrowing has competed with the private sector for a declining volume of world saving.

Table 18.6 shows that since 1979 government deficits as a percentage of GNP have declined in Bangladesh, Korea, Malaysia, Sri Lanka, Taiwan, and Thailand, but have risen in India, Indonesia, Nepal, Pakistan, and Philippines. While inflation rates fell in all these developing countries except Bangladesh, inflation rates fell more and averaged considerably less in those countries with declining budget deficits than they did in those countries with rising budget deficits. The relationship between government deficits and inflation in the Asian developing countries is no coincidence.

A public sector deficit necessarily competes directly or indirectly for scarce investible funds, unless the country faces unlimited foreign borrowing opportunities. For a given level of government deficit, therefore, concern must be with its impact on the aggregate supply of funds. A higher government deficit, in conjunction with a typical mix of other government policies that discourage saving, can reduce the total available pool of investible resources as well as appropriating a larger amount of the dwindling pool, thus doubly squeezing private investment. Appropriate policies, however, can improve both aggregate domestic resource mobilization and allocation, although inevitably crowding out some private investment.

A number of Asian developing country governments, particularly in South Asia, want to keep the cost of their borrowing low for budgetary reasons. Of the 11 Asian developing countries in Table 18.6, India has been to greatest lengths to minimize the costs of its borrowing. To further this aim, the government sets all bank interest rates and controls the country's securities markets in several ways. To finance its deficit at low interest rates, the government has more than doubled the banks' required reserve ratio over the past decade; the liquid assets ratio has also been increased to 38 percent of total deposits. To thwart competition which might raise market interest rates, the Indian government sets a ceiling of 14 percent on the yield offered on nonconvertible debentures sold by private companies. Insurance companies

Table 18.6. Overall Government Budget Balance and Inflation in a Sample of 11 Asian Developing Countries

Country	Government Surplus/Deficit as Percent of GNP		Inflation Rate	
	1979–1984	1984–1989	1979–1984	1984–1989
Bangladesh	–6.9	–6.2	10.8	11.0
India	–4.2	–5.3	10.0	7.8
Indonesia	–4.0	–5.7	10.9	5.9
Korea	–2.2	–0.3	11.4	4.1
Malaysia	–14.0	–7.8	5.7	1.4
Nepal	–7.8	–9.5	10.4	10.3
Pakistan	–5.9	–7.0	8.8	5.8
Philippines	–2.3	–2.7	17.9	9.9
Sri Lanka	–15.6	–11.4	15.7	8.1
Taiwan	–0.2	0.1	7.4	1.3
Thailand	–3.5	–1.1	8.0	3.4

Source: *Key Indicators of Developing Asian and Pacific Countries*, 21, July 1990; *Asian Economic Outlook 1990;* and *International Financial Statistics*, various issues

and provident funds are obliged to hold 25 percent of their assets in low-yielding government bonds and an additional 45 percent of their assets in approved public sector securities.

In Korea, Nepal, and Sri Lanka, government securities or their equivalent are sold at yields below market rates to captive buyers. In Korea, banks have been forced to buy monetary stabilization bonds issued by the Bank of Korea with a coupon rate of $12\frac{1}{2}$ percent at times when secondary market yields have ranged between 13 and 17 percent. In Nepal, the central bank buys the majority of government securities. In Sri Lanka, the Provident Fund and National Savings Bank are forced to purchase low-yielding government bonds.

In fact, the social cost of a government deficit is in no way related to the cost of servicing domestically held national debt. The latter is simply a transfer payment. Cheap finance means that the holders—direct and indirect —of government bonds receive a lower return than they otherwise would. They will, therefore, have less incentive to hold such debt voluntarily. In order to make government debt relatively more attractive without increasing its cost, governments frequently introduce measures to make private debt less attractive. The most obvious measure is a ceiling on the interest rate payable on private financial claims. Policies of this kind are termed financial restriction in Chapter 2. In general, they reduce total financial saving, appropriate a larger proportion of the smaller available supply of domestic credit and distort resource allocation.

An alternative method of financing a government is resort to the inflation tax. With accelerating inflation, financial restriction turns into financial repression. Deliberate reliance on revenue from inflation makes little economic sense under any conditions. First, higher inflation tends to reduce revenue in real terms from other taxes because of lags in tax collection. Second, high and volatile inflation retards economic growth (Harberger and Edwards 1980, 31–33; Killick 1981, 7; Thirlwall 1974, 70). One explanation for the negative association between inflation and growth over the long run lies in the fact that a strategy of raising substantial revenue from inflation imposes a crippling credit squeeze in real terms on the private sector. Due to this credit squeeze and the fact that high inflation is inevitably more volatile and hence less predictable, investment declines. The available empirical evidence suggests that in most developing countries inflationary finance tends to become inordinately costly in terms of forgone economic growth when it produces annual inflation rates in excess of 20 percent. As the exception to prove this general rule, Korea posted inflation rates in the range 10–30 percent combined with high growth over the period 1974–1980. Nevertheless, Korea's high growth rate became even higher after its inflation rate was reduced in the 1980s.

There is a strong association between the proportion of domestic credit absorbed by the government sector and the inflation rate. In one study, Arnold Harberger (1981, 40) finds that developing countries suffering from acute inflation (over 80 percent annually for at least three years) had a ratio of government to total domestic credit of 47 percent. His sample of developing countries suffering from chronic inflation (over 20 percent for at least five years) exhibited a ratio of 32 percent, while the control group had a ratio of 25 percent. Harberger interprets these findings as support for the hypothesis that government deficits are typically the underlying cause of acute and chronic inflation. However, they may also indicate one of the effects of inflation. Undoubtedly causality is circular: domestic credit expansion to finance a government deficit creates inflation which, in turn, reduces the real size of the banking system, so raising the proportion of government credit in the declining total.

In any event, the policy implication is the same. The international evidence suggests that this vicious circle can be avoided, provided government sector borrowing requirements from the banking system do not exceed about 25 percent of total domestic credit. Given this rule of thumb, Table 18.7 signals danger for Bangladesh, India, Nepal, Pakistan, Philippines, and Sri Lanka. Real per capita income growth in these six countries averaged 1.7 percent annually over the period 1979–1989, while in the remaining five Asian developing countries it averaged 4.7 percent. This evidence suggests

Table 18.7. Seigniorage in a Sample of 11 Asian Developing Countries

Country	Percentage of Domestic Credit to Public Sector, December 1979	Percentage of Domestic Credit to Public Sector, December 1989	Percentage of Central Bank Assets in Total of Central and Commercial Bank Assets, December 1989
Bangladesh	62	27	24
India	40	48	33
Indonesia	38	-2	29
Korea	9	1	24
Malaysia	-5	6	20
Nepal	52	54	54
Pakistan	49	44	37
Philippines	16	10	25
Sri Lanka	54	55	41
Taiwan	6	1	27
Thailand	24	7	21

Source: *International Financial Statistics*, various issues

that sustained government deficits, which are generally associated with high proportions of domestic credit allocated to the public sector, are unconducive to economic growth.

18.5 Directed Credit Programs and Financial Restriction

There are six major categories of selective credit instruments—subsidized loan rates for priority sectors, differential rediscount rates, direct budgetary subsidies, credit floors, credit ceilings, and proliferation of specialized financial institutions. Tables 18.8 and 18.9 show their use in the 11 sample Asian developing countries in 1980 and 1990.

The most common selective credit technique in this group of countries is subsidized loan rates for priority sectors. The governments of all the sample Asian developing countries set relatively low loan rates of interest for priority sectors.[1] The main problem, of course, is how to persuade the commercial banks to lend to such sectors at these low rates.

One way of solving the problem is to use differential rediscount rates, the second selective credit technique listed in Tables 18.8 and 18.9. Financial institutions are compensated partially, or fully, or even overcompensated for

---

[1] Over the past decade, however, the scope of priority sector lending has been reduced substantially in several Asian developing countries.

Table 18.8. Selective Credit Instruments in 11 Sample Asian Developing Countries, 1980

Country	Subsidized Loan Rates for Priority Sectors	Preferential Rediscount Rates	Direct Budgetary Subsidies	Credit Floors	Credit Ceilings	Proliferation of Specialized Institutions
Bangladesh	Yes	Yes		Yes	Yes	Yes
India	Yes	Yes		Yes	Yes	Yes
Indonesia	Yes	Yes	Yes	Yes	Yes	Yes
Korea	Yes	Yes		Yes	Yes	Yes
Malaysia	Yes	Yes		Yes		
Nepal	Yes	Yes		Yes	Yes	Yes
Pakistan	Yes	Yes	Yes	Yes	Yes	
Philippines	Yes	Yes	Yes	Yes	Yes	Yes
Sri Lanka	Yes	Yes	Yes		Yes	
Taiwan	Yes	Yes				
Thailand	Yes	Yes		Yes		

Source: Central bank and government publications

lending at subsidized rates of interest to priority borrowers when they rediscount priority loans at the central bank on concessional terms. Hence most priority credit may actually be provided by the central bank. This method can and often does jeopardize control over the cash base, as in Korea. It is the only technique that can be used without direct interest or credit allocation controls.

An extensive selective credit policy implemented through the rediscount mechanism is likely to be accompanied by high required reserve ratios designed to reduce the commercial banks' own funds available for discretionary, nonpriority lending. In such case, the central bank's assets will probably constitute a relatively large proportion of the total assets of the financial sector as a whole. Table 18.9 shows that all 11 Asian developing countries still use the preferential rediscount technique, although its scope has been reduced in Indonesia, Korea, Taiwan, and Thailand. Taiwan uses no other selective credit technique.

The third method of implementing selective credit policies is direct budgetary subsidy. In Indonesia, Pakistan, Philippines, and Sri Lanka, negative differentials between priority loan and deposit rates of interest were financed by explicit budget appropriations in 1980. Due to oil revenue in Indonesia, this technique has been used to a greater extent there than it has in Pakistan, Philippines, or Sri Lanka. In the latter three countries, budget subsidies were confined to a small proportion of priority loans—small, interest-free loans to farmers in Pakistan and loans to the government in Sri Lanka. In 1989 Pak-

Table 18.9. Selective Credit Instruments in 11 Sample Asian Developing Countries, 1990

Country	Subsidized Loan Rates for Priority Sectors	Preferential Rediscount Rates	Direct Budgetary Subsidies	Credit Floors	Credit Ceilings	Proliferation of Specialized Institutions
Bangladesh	Yes	Yes		Yes		Yes
India	Yes	Yes		Yes		Yes
Indonesia	Less	Less		Yes		Yes
Korea	Less	Less		Yes	Yes	Yes
Malaysia	Yes	Yes				
Nepal	Yes	Yes		Yes		Yes
Pakistan	Yes	Yes		Yes	Yes	
Philippines	Yes	Yes	Yes	Yes	Yes	Yes
Sri Lanka	Yes	Yes		Informal	Yes	
Taiwan	Less	Less				
Thailand	Yes	Less				

Source: International Monetary Fund, central bank, and government publications

istan's interest-free loans to farmers were abandoned in favor of low-interest loans.

Credit floors constitute the fourth method used to implement selective credit policies in eight of the 11 sample Asian developing countries. The monetary authorities set minimum proportions of total credit or total deposits that must be lent by the banks to specific priority borrowers. In India 40 percent of bank loans are allocated to priority sectors. In 1989, policy-directed loans constituted 38 percent of deposit money bank (DMB) lending in Korea (Park 1990, 45A). The national banks in Indonesia are obliged to make 20 percent of their loans to small- and medium-sized industries. The Nepalese commercial banks must use at least 8 percent of their total deposit liabilities for lending to priority sectors. In the Philippines 15 percent of banks' loan portfolios must be devoted to the rural sector. Credit allocation is conducted informally in Sri Lanka through moral suasion. Medium business banks in Taiwan are required to lend 70 percent of loans to small- and medium-sized enterprises.

The fifth method of implementing selective credit policies is to set credit ceilings either on nonpriority lending or on the aggregate volume of loans. Overall credit ceilings are usually promulgated in conjunction with exemptions for priority loans or credit floors for priority sectors. Credit ceilings were used in eight of the sample Asian developing countries in 1980. In some of these countries (such as India and Indonesia), the incentive for a commercial bank to extend subsidized credit sprang in the main from the ceiling imposed on normal lending. A subsidized loan may have been a more profitable asset than excess cash reserves. However, delinquency and default have plagued priority lending operations, particularly in Bangladesh, India, Indonesia, Korea, and Nepal. Table 18.9 indicates that global credit ceilings have become unfashionable; they are now set only in Korea, Pakistan, Philippines, and Sri Lanka. Even though bank interest rates were deregulated in 1988, Korean DMBs are still subject to quantitative ceilings on lending and loan rates have been maintained artificially low and stable (Park 1990, 43). In Sri Lanka global credit ceilings were imposed in May 1989 (Aries 1990).

The sixth and final method of implementing selective credit policies is heavy reliance on specialized financial institutions. This technique is used in six of the sample Asian developing countries. Funds are extracted from nonspecialized depository institutions through high reserve requirements to be channelled to priority sectors on concessional terms by government-owned specialized financial institutions. Proliferation of such institutions has been taken furthest in India, Korea, and Philippines. Financial layering and market segmentation appear to have been the main effects. In these countries, higher required reserve ratios seem to have reduced the total supply of loanable funds in real terms.

Among them, India, Indonesia, Korea, Philippines, and Thailand provide good examples of all six methods of implementing selective credit policies. Since the nationalization of 14 large Indian banks in July 1969, the share of priority lending in total commercial bank credit has risen rapidly from virtually nil. In September 1979, 35 percent of bank credit consisted of loans for priority sectors, 8 percent for exports, 6 percent for sick industries, and 11 percent for term loans. The interest rate increases at that date covered only 40 percent of bank loans. Sixty percent was exempt because of its priority status. Given the large increases in required cash and liquidity ratios, the reduction to the present required minimum of 40 percent of bank loans to priority sectors still leaves very limited resources with which the Indian banks can make discretionary loans.

The structure of India's financial system can be understood only within the context of India's selective credit policy. Even then, institutional arrangements constitute a "dense and confusing web" (Datey 1978, 2). The aggressive pursuit of selective credit policies or credit planning has produced extensive financial layering in India, Indonesia, Korea, and Philippines, as well as in many African countries. Instead of raising funds from a common pool of loanable funds, each financial institution has its own special sources of funds earmarked for special uses (McKinnon 1980, 106–110).

In India's agricultural sector, for example, there are some 123,000 active primary agricultural cooperative societies (PACSs), covering 40 million members. These PACSs borrow funds from central cooperative banks (CCBs). In turn, CCBs raise funds from deposits and refinancing facilities of the Agricultural Refinance and Development Corporation (ARDC). The ARDC is financed by the Reserve Bank of India, the World Bank, and the Indian government. All this layering decreases rather than increases the total real volume of funds available. This is because about 7 percent of total available resources in India are absorbed in administrative costs (Datey 1978, ii), despite the fact that each individual financial institution displays relatively low intermediation costs (Bhatt 1978). The total direct costs of institutional agricultural credit average about 19 percent. Farmers pay about 12 percent. Therefore, all administrative costs are covered by direct government subsidies. Furthermore, the loans supplied by the Indian government to the ARDC are provided on concessional terms in the first instance.

Provision of these subsidies increases the Indian government's own borrowing requirements. Hence the net real volume of funds available for productive investment is reduced by the higher resource costs of implementing the selective credit program. Of course, to the extent that priority loans are subsidized from the government budget rather than by depositors, the gross real supply of domestic credit will not be affected. However, depositors heavily subsidize the government's own borrowing. Lower deposit rates reduce the gross real supply of funds.

Selective fiscal policy complements India's selective credit policy. Hence, for example, the ARDC was exempted from income taxes and surcharges for five years, the intention being to pass on the benefits in the form of cheaper credit for small irrigation and land development projects. Another example of complementary fiscal policy is the regulation allowing commercial banks to claim tax deductions on bad debt provisions for rural branches.

India's selective credit policy is well-illustrated by the history of the Karnataka State Financial Corporation. It began in 1959, offering loans at a single interest rate of 7 percent. Then the Industrial Development Bank of India (IDBI) was established in 1964. The IDBI offered refinancing facilities to the Karnataka State Financial Corporation on concessional terms. The IDBI's concessional rates were passed on to borrowers whose loans had been refinanced. Hence refinanced loans were provided at a lower interest rate than loans financed from the Corporation's own resources. Then the government introduced and elaborated its selective credit policy in the early 1970s. By 1976 the Karnataka State Financial Corporation had the complicated structure of lending rates shown in Table 18.10 (Simha 1976, 194–195). All these rates were reduced by 3 percentage points for prompt loan repayment. Thus the Corporation had to choose for each borrower one of these 12 rates, depending on location, activity, and source of funds.

Priority borrowers in India expropriated an increasing share of domestic credit at least until 1980. The government then replaced priority private-sector borrowers as the main beneficiary of cheap bank credit. At the same time, the aggregate real supply of credit has been reduced because of the lower interest rates on these loans. Nonpriority borrowers, therefore, have been

Table 18.10. Rates of Interest on Loans Provided by the Karnataka State Financial Corporation in 1976

		Not Refinanced	Refinanced
1.	For Bangalore		
	a. Small-scale industry	15.0	14.0
	b. Other industry	16.5	15.5
	c. Technicians	14.0	13.0
2.	For other forward districts		
	a. Small-scale industry	14.5	13.5
	b. Other industry	16.0	15.0
	c. Technicians	13.5	12.5
3.	For backward districts		
	a. Small-scale industry	13.5	12.0
	b. Other industry	14.0	12.5
	c. Technicians	13.0	11.0
4.	Transport operators	17.0	15.5

doubly squeezed. The overall reduction in the aggregate real supply of credit appears to have had an adverse effect on investment. T. Venkatachalam and Y. Sarma (1978, 82) conclude their study of the determinants of investment in India: "The impact of interest rates is mild compared to the important role played by the quantum of funds available."

Thomas Timberg and C. V. Aiyar (1984) estimate that informal credit markets in India provide credit equal to at least 50 percent of institutional credit at interest rates somewhat above the commercial banks' normal advance rate. Transaction costs of financial intermediation through the noninstitutional markets are lower than those of the formal banking system. Yet the Indian government has tried to suppress the noninstitutional credit system because it does not channel funds in accordance with the Plan: "Government policy aimed partially at channeling funds into the regulated financial sector—and partially at protecting savers and borrowers—has led to measures of repression which have disaggregated [segmented] this informal market from the regulated one" (Timberg and Aiyar 1984, 44). The result is that "the increases in transaction costs occasioned by artificially channeling funds into the formal market may cause a net decrease in available funds, and retard economic activity" (Timberg and Aiyar 1984, 43).

Until recently, five government-owned commercial banks were responsible for the allocation of 80 percent of total domestic credit in Indonesia. Despite their commercial bank status, they all specialized to some extent in specific economic sectors. There were 19 short-term loan categories—seven loan rates of interest (ranging from 9 to 21 percent), three rediscount rates (from 3 to 6 percent), and eight proportions of a loan eligible for rediscount (from 25 to 100 percent). The system of credit rationing existing in Indonesia, which prevailed until 1983, was introduced in 1974 when there was a major shift from interest rate to administrative allocation of credit. A pronounced feature of Indonesia's selective credit policy was the inversion of deposit and loan rates of interest. Budget appropriations were made to cover the negative interest rate spread. Increasingly, Indonesia's selective credit policy has been used to subsidize *pribumi* enterprises. *Bumiputera* enterprises are now the main beneficiaries of Malaysia's directed credit policies.

Korea's selective credit policy is implemented by a variety of state-owned financial institutions: the DMBs and the specialized financial institutions such as the Korea Exchange Bank, Medium Industry Bank, Citizens' National Bank, Korea Housing Bank, National Agricultural Cooperatives Federation, Central Federation of Fisheries Cooperatives, Korea Development Bank, Export-Import Bank of Korea, National Investment Fund, Land Bank of Korea, and Korea Development Finance Corporation. About 50 percent of bank loans were policy loans to priority borrowers extended at the government's direction in 1980; this figure is now around 40 percent (Park 1990, 45A). General lending guidelines set out by the Monetary Board in 1958 have been replaced increasingly by specific directives to DMBs and the specialized financial institutions. The directives require these financial institutions to allocate not only government funds but also their own resources to sectors, subsectors, and even to individual projects or firms. Such detailed intervention by the government has had a serious effect on the efficiency of financial intermediation in Korea. Transaction costs and delinquency rates are high. The denationalization of financial institutions that occurred in the early 1980s was due in part to the recognition that the selective credit policy implemented through state-owned financial institutions had created serious inefficiencies.

The scope of the Philippines' selective credit policy was expanded until the early 1980s, in the main through the proliferation of specialized financial institutions. A major effect was the increasing fragility of the financial sector. For example, both the Philippine National Bank and the government-owned Development Bank of the Philippines failed as a result of large percentages of nonperforming assets on their books. These high percentages of bad loans were caused partly by the banks' roles in implementing the government's selective credit policy, partly by weak management, and increasingly during the Marcos era by political interference.

Until 1984 the Central Bank of the Philippines offered a variety of rediscount terms and conditions depending on the nature and purpose of the loan being discounted. In December 1979 the basic rediscount rate was raised from 9 to 11 percent, while that applied to traditional export finance was increased from 4 to 6 percent. By May 1983 the rediscount rate for traditional exports had been raised to 8 percent, but nontraditional exports could obtain rediscounts at 3 percent. Eighty percent of the loan values could be rediscounted at these rates. Rediscount ceilings for each facility were set for each financial institution. Although differential rediscount rates were discontinued in March 1984, the selective credit policy was still implemented through a floor requirement that 25 percent of any increase in bank loans must go to the agricultural sector. Alternatively, banks could hold central bank certificates of indebtedness to meet this requirement (Patrick and Moreno 1985, 355–356). This floor has been changed to a minimum of 15 percent of lending to the rural sector. All selective credit policies in the Philippines are currently slated to be phased out.

The Philippines' selective credit policy is also implemented through specialized financial institutions such as the rural banks, which are given government assistance to lend to small farmers, the mortgage banks, the Development Bank of the Philippines, the private development banks, and the National Cottage Industries Bank. The specialized banks hold about 20 percent of the total assets of the financial system.

The Philippines is noteworthy for its use of specialized financial institutions for implementing its selective credit policy. The World Bank (1980, 50) describes the proliferation of specialized institutions that has taken place during the postwar period: the Development Bank of the Philippines in 1947, rural banks in 1952, private development banks in 1959, the National Cottage Industries Bank and the Amanah Bank in 1963. In all cases, the institutions were established to meet the particular credit needs—as perceived by the government—of specific sectors or groups. The specialized institutions were specifically prohibited from using their resources for purposes other than those prescribed by the enabling legislation.

Legislated specialization of this kind has produced considerable fragmentation of financial markets, preventing adaptation to changing demands, in particular the demand for longer-term finance. Rural banks are particularly restricted as to borrowers and purposes for which loans are made (World Bank 1980, ii). When the Minister of Finance was convinced that such forced specialization raised intermediation costs, curtailed competition, and produced allocative inefficiencies, the financial reforms of 1980 were introduced.

Thailand's selective credit policy was implemented through concessional loans extended by all government-owned financial institutions to priority borrowers, differential interest rates, a sectoral credit floor for agricultural lending, reserve and liquidity requirements, and, until August 1984, overall credit ceilings. In conjunction with specific directives and moral suasion, the liquidity requirements oblige the commercial banks to channel funds at below-market rates of interest to the Bank for Agriculture and Agricultural Cooperatives and to the Government Housing Bank. In 1989 the scope of the preferential rediscount facility was substantially reduced and concessional loans are now extended only to small borrowers.

Directed, selective, or sectoral credit policies are common components of financial restriction. The techniques employed to reduce the costs of financing government deficits discussed in section 18.4 can be and are used to encourage private investment in what the government regards as priority activities. Interest rates on loans for such approved investment are subsidized. The costs of the subsidies are met by depositors who receive lower deposit rates of interest, by unsubsidized borrowers who pay higher free-market loan rates, and by taxpayers as a result of lower central bank profits. Selective credit policies necessitate financial restriction, since financial channels would otherwise develop expressly for rerouting subsidized credit to uses with highest private returns. For selective credit policies to work at all, financial markets must be kept segmented and restricted.

Selective credit policies or directed credit programs reduce the financial system's flexibility while increasing its fragility. There is no evidence that they improve the economic efficiency of resource allocation. Portfolio constraints reduce the funds available for discretionary bank lending both directly and indirectly by reducing the attractiveness of deposits.[2] They also increase the fragility of the financial system by forcing financial institutions to increase their risk exposure with no compensating return. Directed credit programs are partly responsible for the alarming volume of nonperforming assets on the books of many financial institutions in the Asian developing countries.

International donors have inadvertently compounded financial sector problems in some of the Asian developing countries, such as Sri Lanka, by circumventing domestic financial systems altogether or by pursuing their own selective credit policies through differential interest rate subsidies. Recently, however, awareness of the damaging side effects of aid operations has increased, in part due to the greater emphasis by international donors on program and structural adjustment lending, as opposed to project aid.

The World Bank (1989, 70) concludes that financial difficulties in most developing countries are "rooted in the international shocks of the 1980s and their domestic aftermath and in the policies that governments have pursued over the past thirty years." Specifically, selective or directed credit policies were a major cause of financial distress in developing countries. James Hanson and Roberto de Rezende Rocha (1986, 5) suggest that discriminatory taxation of financial intermediation also increases the financial sector's instability by driving intermediation into the informal, less regulated, and hence less taxed parts of the market.

---

[2] Savers always have the option of using unproductive tangible assets as inflation hedges.

18.6   Objectives of Selective Credit Policies

In general, there are six internal inconsistencies in the objectives of selective credit policies. The first is that they attempt to encourage lower-yielding investments through interest rate subsidies vis-à-vis higher-yielding investments that are not subsidized. Economic growth, however, warrants encouragement of the highest-yielding, most efficient investments. Lowest-yielding investments must be placed at the bottom of the list. The usual counterargument is that private and social returns are not the same. Hence the selective credit policy can encourage investments with high social returns even if private returns are relatively low. In fact, development plans in most developing countries seem to have favored through import licenses as well as selective credit policies investments with relatively low social returns and high domestic resource costs.[3] It is not at all clear from the available evidence that planners have identified investments with high social but low private returns. Even if they had, it can be argued that interest rate subsidy is itself an inefficient inducement because it distorts factor prices.

The second inconsistency in the aims of selective credit policies is that they typically involve a downward sloping term structure of loan rates. With neutral inflationary expectations, free markets would normally produce a rising loan rate term structure, reflecting time and liquidity preferences and risk aversion—the standard asymmetry exploited by financial intermediaries. Selective credit policies set low long-term rates of interest to encourage enterprises to take risks in the form of long-term investments. They may, however, reduce the aggregate supply of credit in real terms and bias factor prices in favor of capital and against labor. As a result, the smaller volume of investment that can be financed is likely to be less efficient.

The third inconsistency lies in the inversion of deposit and loan rates of interest. Under competitive conditions, financial institutions would be unlikely to offer deposits with higher interest rates than their lowest loan rates of similar maturity. The fungibility of financial capital ensures that some borrowing can and does (in Indonesia, Korea, and Pakistan) take place at priority loan rates for the express intention of building up deposits yielding a higher return. Clearly this thwarts completely the objective of the selective credit policy. It merely raises the resource costs of financial intermediation between savers and investors.

The fourth inconsistency of selective credit policies is that, if successful, they reduce the demand for labor by distorting factor prices. Negative real loan rates of interest for priority borrowers give an extraordinary price signal. The message is that this priority credit is not just a free good, but actually has

---

[3]For the Indian case, see Jagdish Bhagwati and Padma Desai (1970, 4–6) and Bhagwati and T. N. Srinivasan (1975, 191, 214–226).

negative value like rubbish. The result is to encourage highly capital-intensive production techniques for any given product, products and processes that are necessarily capital-intensive, and investments with zero or negative returns. As the Indian government knows to its cost, negative real institutional interest rates also encourage unproductive hoarding.

Suppose that an entrepreneur can borrow at a real interest rate of −15 percent, provided that he puts up 10 percent of the capital in the form of equity and that he engages in a specific economic activity. This entrepreneur plans to refine sugar and borrows Rs 900 million to build the refinery. Now it turns out that he actually buys Rs 1 billion worth of refined sugar over the year and puts it through the refinery. He loses 5 percent of the original sugar, and the process costs 5 percent in terms of fuel, manpower, and depreciation. The social loss involved in this economic activity is 10 percent. However, the nominal return on the entrepreneur's own investment of Rs 100 million is 35 percent. Had he simply spent his Rs 100 million on hoarding sugar, his nominal return would have equalled the inflation rate. Hence he has a strong incentive to engage in a socially wasteful investment, provided that the inflation rate in this particular case is less than 35 percent. At this inflation rate the nominal return on his Rs 100 million equity of 35 percent is exactly offset by inflation, leaving a zero real return.

This example illustrates the behavior of a private entrepreneur interested only in his own well-being. However, when prices are distorted sufficiently it is all too easy for state enterprises or the government itself to engage unwittingly in exactly the same type of economic activity. To date, shadow pricing has apparently failed to identify high-yielding investment opportunities, particularly in Bangladesh, Burma, India, Philippines, and Sri Lanka. Greater concern over the efficiency as opposed to the quantity of investment is undoubtedly becoming increasingly urgent in most developing countries.

That selective credit policies with negative real lending rates do reduce output in practice is exemplified by the following example from India (Bharadwaj 1979, 282–291):

> The agricultural support prices and procurement policies have encouraged speculative stocking holdings in agricultural commodities, first, by making such speculation safe as a one-way bet and, secondly, by putting sufficient liquidity into their hands to finance such operations.
>
> It is possible that to a certain extent capital may already have been diverted from productive into nonproductive uses like speculative trading, and stockpiling of inventories of scarce materials. Such an investment may appear attractive when easy credit is available through public institutions ... and there persists a general inflationary trend.

The World Bank estimates real economic rates of return to small-scale investments in India shown in Table 18.11. Evidently there do seem to be simple, small-scale, high-yielding investment opportunities in India. Selective credit policies have failed to exploit them.

Table 18.11. Rates of Return to Small-Scale Investments in India

Type of Small-Scale Investment	Annual Percentage Yield
Pumpset (1.4 hectares)	52
Pumpset (0.8 hectares)	45
Dugwell and pumpset (1.4 hectares)	30
Dugwell and pumpset (2.11 hectares)	Over 50
Dugwell deepening	29
Borewell and pumpset	Over 50
Shallow tubewell	Over 50
Land development	46
Citrus	30
Mechanized fishing vessel	45
Poultry	49
Dairy	48
Average	46

The fifth inconsistency of selective credit policies is that the objectives of selective credit policies must discourage saving and so reduce the aggregate real supply of investible funds. Selective credit policies invariably keep both deposit and loan rates of interest below their market equilibrium levels. Hence the aggregate real supply of investible funds is held below its equilibrium level.

Low deposit rates as a concomitant of selective credit policies reduce aggregate real money demand. The consolidated balance sheet of the banking system indicates that this decline must be matched by a fall in real domestic credit or net foreign assets. The main effect in the less open developing countries of South Asia seems to have been a reduction in the aggregate real supply of credit. Foreign exchange controls and the relatively small volume of international trade ensure that capital flows and hence net foreign assets are not highly responsive to the differential between domestic and foreign interest rates. Indeed, it is this inelasticity that enables these countries to pursue independent interest rate policies in the first place.

Priority borrowers in India have expropriated an increasing share of domestic credit. At the same time, this has reduced the aggregate real supply of credit because of the lower interest rates on these loans. Nonpriority borrowers, therefore, have been doubly squeezed. The overall reduction in the aggregate real supply of credit appears to have had an adverse effect on investment. Venkatachalam and Sarma (1978, 82) conclude their study of the determinants of investment in India: "The impact of interest rates is mild compared to the important role played by the quantum of funds available."

Finally, selective credit policies provide precisely the wrong signals to private sector institutional lenders. Their incentive is to lend first at the normal rate, last at a subsidized rate. Even if compensation is provided through the rediscount mechanism, administrative costs and delays may well make such recourse unattractive.

Perhaps the most telling indictment of selective credit policies is their tendency, as for example in the Philippines, to reduce the supply of credit to sectors of the economy believed to be of highest priority and in most need of financial assistance. Cheap credit that is unavailable is no consolation. Furthermore, the cost of credit is rarely the main constraint to productive small-scale investments. In sum, it is far from "obvious" that "selective credit policies should constitute an integral part of the overall economic strategy for development" (Khatkhate and Villanueva 1978, 980). Rather, they seem to be an ideal recipe for reducing both the quantity and quality of productive investment. In other words, they appear to reduce rather than to increase the efficiency of resource allocation by financial intermediaries.

Selective credit policies tend to be based on two premises: planners know best what investments should be undertaken, and credit allocation can ensure that those and only those investments are undertaken. The performance of several Asian developing economies that rely heavily on public sector investment (Bangladesh, Burma, India, Nepal, and Sri Lanka) over the past two decades throws doubt on the first assumption. The second is belied by the fact that financial capital is fungible (Bitros 1981). Overt relending is a well-documented phenomenon. Of greater significance, however, is the fungibility of financial capital. A farmer receives subsidized credit for a pumpset that he would have bought in any case and uses his own resources thereby released to install air conditioning in his home. Since the air conditioning would not have been purchased in the absence of the subsidized credit, one must conclude that this loan financed air conditioning rather than the pumpset. It is ironic that, to the extent that this kind of fungibility exists, the inefficiencies of selective credit policies outlined above are actually mitigated.

The fungibility of financial capital is well-illustrated by the long history of housing finance in the United States. For many years it has been government policy to encourage the production of housing by increasing the availability of mortgage credit. Availability is increased by government purchase of mortgages through federal agencies. It is reduced again through the bond financing of the mortgage purchases. By itself, this activity of draining funds from one part of the pond to pump back into another part has been futile (Jaffee and Rosen 1978, 933).

Government action and initiative in spreading amortization, lengthening terms, mortgage insurance, and subsidies have had substantial impact on the mortgage market. "The most notable changes are growth in the number and size of specialized thrift institutions that buy mortgages and in the proportion of mortgages to total liabilities of financial institutions" (Meltzer 1974, 764). However, this has had no effect on housing. The ratio of housing to total assets of nonfarm households in the United States has remained virtually constant at 25 percent throughout this century.

What has happened is that the ratio of mortgage debt to housing has risen from about 10 to 40 percent. The ratio of mortgage debt to total liabilities also rose substantially. Cheaper mortgage debt was substituted for more expensive (less subsidized) forms of borrowing. The only conclusion that can be drawn here is that specific liabilities do not finance specific assets. Asset composition and "asset purchases are independent of the form in which credit is made available" (Meltzer 1974, 769). Much of the increase in mortgage debt in the United States has actually financed the purchase of securities. Similarly, most rural credit programs in developing countries have failed to produce dramatic increases in the stock of productive physical capital in rural areas.

The composition of spending is affected in part by the relative prices of the goods and services being bought. Subsidized mortgages in no way affect the relative price of housing. However, they do affect the relative costs of borrowing to buy a house vis-à-vis borrowing to buy something else, or vis-à-vis a cash purchase of the house. They will therefore influence the way in which houses and all other purchases are financed. Subsidized mortgages encourage people to finance a larger proportion of the purchase of a house and a smaller proportion of the purchase of other things on credit. Overall, subsidized mortgages do not affect the stock of houses or even the volume of construction, except in the short run. This is because (a) the subsidy for one person must be a tax on someone else; (b) money channelled through one particular financial institution must come from another institution or market; and (c) financial resources are fungible.

One of the most deleterious effects of loan rate ceilings is that they deter risk taking by financial intermediaries. When they are binding, loan rate ceilings eliminate the possibility of charging differential risk premia. Hence riskier borrowers and riskier projects are rationed out without regard to their expected rates of return. Figure 18.2 shows two interdependent markets— less risky and riskier loans. A loan rate ceiling at r_0 produces a supply curve of S_{B_0} for less risky loans and S_{A_0} for riskier loans. The supply of less risky loans is q_0, while the supply of riskier loans is zero.

The abolition of loan rate ceilings shifts both supply curves. The supply of less risky loans is reduced at each rate of interest because there is some substitution into riskier loans. The supply of riskier loans at each rate of interest is also reduced, since ceiling abolition produces a higher rate for less risky lending. The equilibrium result, however, is that the actual quantities of both less risky and riskier loans are increased from q_0 to q_1 for the former, and from zero to q_2 for the latter.

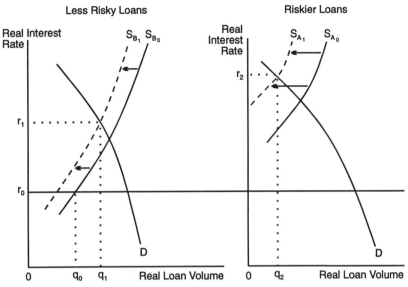

Figure 18.2. Riskier and Less Risky Loan Markets

The nationalized financial institutions in India, Indonesia, Korea, and Nepal have been directed to take risks and to extend small loans without regard to compensating returns. The repayment of such loans is actually insured by a loan guarantee fund in Indonesia. Small loans tend to be more expensive to administer than larger loans. For example, the overall cost —including expected delinquency and default costs—of providing credit to small farmers in India averages $2\frac{1}{2}$ percent more than the cost of providing credit to large farmers. Consequently, smaller farmers are subsidized to a greater extent than large farmers, even with a uniform loan rate. The result of completely disregarding risk has been serious levels of delinquency and default in the loan portfolios of the public sector financial institutions in most developing countries, as shown in section 14.3.

Hugh Patrick (1990, 39) focuses on the way in which financial repression can create moral hazard:

> Financial repression—the gap between market clearing and regulated ceiling interest rates—creates tremendous moral hazard problems. Bank credit has to be rationed, at below-market rates. The rents thus created are huge. (For example, if rationed credit amounts to 50 percent of GNP and the interest rate gap is 10 percent, credit rents amount to 5 percent of GNP per year.) Who receives this rent: the borrower, the purchasers of credit—subsidized output (through lower prices), the lending institution, the loan officer, politicians and/or government bureaucrats? The possibilities for corruption are great, and the temptation high. Occasional

scandals do suggest corruption in financial allocation has been of some significance in all three countries [Japan, Korea and Taiwan].

Mohammad Ahmed (1988, 33–34) discusses the problem of 'financial looting' that arises under selective or directed credit policies. The investor gets back his equity plus profits through overinvoicing by the investor's subsidiaries supplying machinery and engaged for construction. Financial looting enables funds to be diverted to high-yielding investments in nonpriority sectors. Andrew MacIntyre (1993, 124) makes the following comments on Indonesia's directed credit policies: "Ultimately, however, it is not so much the extent of state intervention in credit markets that is remarkable but rather the ad hoc, uncoordinated, and largely inefficient manner in which it has taken place."

18.7 Summary

The Asian developing countries surveyed in this chapter pursued active interest rate policies for most of the period 1961–1990. In the main, these policies involved setting the entire structures of institutional deposit and loan rates of interest. The deposit rate structures in the majority of the sample countries suggest that these countries' governments deliberately used product differentiation to tap consumer surplus. Loan rates are differentiated on a variety of criteria, including ethnic origins of the borrower. Loan rate structures are designed to support the selective or sectoral credit policies that are followed in most of these sample countries.

The objectives of interest rate policies can be achieved, if they can be achieved at all, only through real as opposed to nominal interest rates. However, the authorities have invariably made adjustments to nominal institutional interest rates too little, too late. Hence real rates of interest have generally moved inversely with the inflation rate. The next chapter examines the issue of what, if any, objectives of interest rate policies can be achieved in the context of selective credit policies.

Selective credit policies invariably produce the opposite results to those intended. That governments continue to pursue them is explained largely by the political pressures exerted by vested interests created by these policies in the first place. The Asian developing countries pursuing selective credit policies most vigorously—Bangladesh, India, and Nepal—tend to be those recording the lowest rates of economic growth. Selective credit policies and financial layering have simply failed to improve domestic resource mobilization and allocation.

Selective credit policies have certainly increased the fragility of financial systems in developing countries. Governments have tended to ignore the effects of selective credit policies on the solvency of the financial institutions through which they are implemented. Often the problem is hidden by creative accounting. In a number of countries, however, the situation has reached such a critical magnitude that it can no longer be swept under the carpet. The solution is far from obvious or easy.

If the real concern is the distribution of income and wealth, as it evidently is in India, Indonesia, Malaysia, Pakistan, and Philippines, credit subsidies are no remedy. The evidence indicates that subsidized credit actually makes the distribution of income and wealth more unequal in developing countries (Adams, Graham, and Von Pischke 1984, González-Vega 1981, 1984b). This is simply because wealthier individuals have greater access to the cheap credit.

There is no evidence that selective credit policies and the expensive institutional structure established to implement them have produced any benefits in terms of increased productivity. C. Datey (1978, 25) poses the question as to whether agricultural productivity in India has risen despite, rather than because of, the system of agricultural credit. For most developing countries, Datey (1978, 30) concludes that "the presumed cost-benefit ratio for society as a whole must be negative in most cases, for it is rare to find a situation in which subsidies for agricultural credit have resulted in any significant increase in productivity."

The same indictment of selective credit policies implemented through a proliferation of specialized financial institutions layered one upon another applies also to Indonesia and Korea. The rate of economic growth in Indonesia actually declined in 1973–1979 compared to 1968–1973, despite a substantial increase in the investment ratio. As several observers have concluded, Indonesia's economic problem was not an insufficiency but rather a misallocation of resources. Selective credit policies and financial layering have failed to improve matters.

The poorer Asian developing countries have been particularly reluctant to abandon directed credit policies despite the increasing evidence that these policies have hindered rather than promoted development efforts. Part of the difficulty in abandoning these policies lies in the vested interests that directed credit policies have created. In part, however, it may also lie in a lack of understanding on the part of policy makers of the negative indirect as well as direct effects of directed credit programs.

Chapter 19

Policies for Financial Development

19.1 Introduction

LOW ADMINISTERED INSTITUTIONAL INTEREST rates are endemic in developing countries. Even where financial development programs have been initiated in some Asian countries, interest rates have rarely been freed immediately or completely to find their free-market equilibrium levels. In the Latin American countries (and Turkey) that abolished interest rate ceilings, however, rates rose to disruptively high levels in real terms. The efficacy of complete and immediate interest rate liberalization as part of a stabilization package now seems dubious. Bank supervision and some degree of price stability seem essential prerequisites for the success of financial liberalization (Villanueva and Mirakhor 1990).

Interest rate ceilings distort the economy in three ways. First, low interest rates produce a bias in favor of current consumption and therefore reduce saving. Second, potential lenders may engage in relatively low-yielding direct investment instead of lending to finance higher-yielding investments by depositing money in a bank. Third, bank borrowers able to obtain all the funds they want at low loan rates will choose relatively capital-intensive projects.

Deposit and loan rate ceilings tend to worsen the distribution of income. First, most of the economic rent goes to large borrowers rather than small savers/lenders when deposit and loan rates are held well below their market equilibrium levels. Income distribution is likely to worsen most where the borrowing firms are predominantly family-owned companies. Second, capital-intensive production methods encouraged by low interest rates reduce demand for labor. Hence wages of unskilled labor fall. Duality created by the inefficient small-scale direct investments on the one hand and large-scale investments that are too capital-intensive on the other creates greater dispersion in wages. In practice, bank loans become concentrated in the hands of a small number of large and well-established customers. Greater economic concentration tends to reduce economic efficiency.

Selective or directed credit policies are almost as common as interest rate ceilings. Indeed, the differentiation of interest rate levels for different sectors of the economy is possible only under a system of interest rate ceilings. Selective credit policies or directed credit programs reduce the financial system's flexibility while increasing its fragility. There is no evidence that they improve the economic efficiency of resource allocation. Indeed, the portfolio constraints imposed by directed credit programs reduce the funds available for discretionary bank lending both directly and indirectly by reducing the attractiveness of deposits. They also increase the fragility of the financial system by forcing financial institutions to increase their risk exposure with no compensating return. Directed credit programs are partly responsible for the alarming amount of nonperforming assets on the books of many financial institutions in developing countries.

The main reasons for the lack of change in the financial sectors of most Asian developing countries over the past two decades appear to be the oligopolistic structure of their financial markets, the concomitant political power of the large banks, and the governments' desire to manipulate the financial system to finance its own expenditures at low interest cost, as well as investment in priority sectors of the economy (Haggard, Lee, and Maxfield 1993).

Policy measures taken to deal with fiscal exigencies have often negated financial reforms and retarded financial development. Discriminatory taxes of one type or another have been imposed on financial intermediation. High reserve requirements, obligatory holding of government bonds by financial institutions, and deposit and loan rate ceilings represent a selection of the measures frequently used as fiscal devices that have repressed financial development. Financial systems cannot achieve their full potential unless governments are prepared to compete for investible funds on an equal footing with private sector borrowers.

In most developing countries, however, the financial sector plays a major role in mobilizing domestic resources and allocating them to investment projects. Over the past two decades, developing countries have tended to assign a larger role to private initiative in the development process, implying that a larger proportion of investment is to be undertaken by the private sector. At the same time, many of these developing countries are trying to increase their investment ratios in order to raise their growth rates. In the face of contracting net inflows of external resources, national saving ratios must be raised and more emphasis placed on economic efficiency in resource allocation. It has therefore become increasingly important to assess the potential role of improved financial intermediation in the process of economic development. To accelerate the rate of sustained economic growth, the financial sector must mobilize domestic resources effectively, allocate them efficiently to finance new productive economic activities, and at the same time maintain macroeconomic stability.

Over the past three decades, developing country governments have expressed repeatedly a commitment to improve the mobilization and allocation of domestic resources through their financial sectors. To this end, they have made various changes in the structure and operations of their financial systems under the rubric of financial development, liberalization, or reform. The experience of these efforts has been disappointing in the extreme. In some cases, notably in Asia, changes have been very modest compared with changes that have taken place in financial sectors of most industrialized countries over the past two decades. "Good-bye financial repression, hello financial crash" is the verdict of Carlos Diaz-Alejandro (1985) on the Latin American experiments over the past two decades. Among other countries in this region, Argentina, Colombia, Brazil, Mexico, and Uruguay have instituted and then abandoned quite radical financial liberalization programs. Banking has flourished and collapsed in rapid succession.

The driving force behind recent financial innovations and reforms in the industrialized countries has been market pressures. The market is so distrusted in the majority of developing countries that market pressures are virtually nonexistent. In these countries, the ideas of Ronald McKinnon (1973) and Edward Shaw (1973) have had more impact, perhaps most obviously and effectively in the policy recommendations of the IMF and the World Bank. However, the implementation of such recommendations has been cautious or reluctant in all but a few developing countries; the exceptions lie in Latin America.

A common feature of all the models in the McKinnon-Shaw framework is that the growth-maximizing deposit rate of interest is the competitive free-market equilibrium rate. The competitive free-market equilibrium deposit rate of interest may be raised, so increasing the real supply of credit and hence the rate of economic growth, without affecting the loan rate by reducing reserve requirements or by paying a competitive interest rate on required reserves. The policy implications of these models are that economic growth can be increased by abolishing institutional interest rate ceilings, by abandoning selective or directed credit programs, by eliminating the reserve requirement tax, and by ensuring that the financial system operates competitively under conditions of free entry. Where competitive conditions cannot be achieved immediately, minimum deposit rates may be imposed to simulate the competitive outcome.

The dynamic models developed within the McKinnon-Shaw framework illustrate the benign effects of interest rate policy as a stabilization device starting from a situation of financial repression. Although the McKinnon-Shaw models find no benefit from financial repression under any conditions, there is a double advantage in initiating financial liberalization as part of a stabilization program. It avoids or at least ameliorates the contractionary effects of deflation produced solely through monetary deceleration (Fry 1980b, Kapur 1976a).

Available econometric evidence indicates that national saving ratios may be affected positively by the real deposit rate of interest. Even when this effect is statistically significant, however, its magnitude is not large enough to warrant great policy significance. As a device for increasing saving, the real deposit rate is subject to an upper bound at its competitive free-market equilibrium level (perhaps in the range of 0 to 5 percent). Hence only in countries where the real deposit rate is negative by a considerable margin can there be much scope for increasing saving *directly* by raising the deposit rate. This also implies that raising the real deposit rate of interest is unlikely to deter *illegal* capital flight to any substantial extent. Furthermore, John Cuddington (1986) finds that exchange rate overvaluation is the main economic determinant of *legal* capital flight.

The small amount of empirical evidence on branch proximity suggests that increased branch proximity has raised national saving ratios substantially (by 1 to 5 percentage points over a 20-year period) in six Asian developing countries for which data were available (Asian Development Bank 1985, Table 5, 45). Increased proximity of depository institution branches seems to have exerted a substantial influence on national saving ratios by increasing *rural* saving, most notably in Sri Lanka, over the past two decades.

As a device for raising saving ratios in the future, the efficacy of branch proliferation must be qualified. Experience shows that indiscriminate branching is no panacea. Expected profitability within the medium term must be the primary criterion for extending rural branch networks. Viability judged on this basis is determined, in turn, by the population and per capita incomes in the proposed catchment area, as well as by branch attributes such as business hours, ease of depositing and withdrawing funds, reliable bookkeeping, the use of local employees, and sufficient autonomy to extend at least some categories of loans without recourse to head or regional offices.

Econometric estimates suggest that an increase in the real deposit rate of interest towards its competitive free-market level is associated with a substantial increase in investment productivity, as measured by the incremental output/capital ratio. The effect of financial liberalization on the rate of economic growth in the medium run can be calculated indirectly from the estimated effects of real deposit rates on saving ratios and on investment efficiency. It can also be estimated directly from reduced-form equations of the growth rate. Estimates for a sample of 14 Asian developing countries show positive and significant relationships between the incremental output/capital ratio and the real deposit rate of interest and also between the rate of economic growth and the real deposit rate of interest (Asian Development Bank 1985, 10–11, 48–49).

Even as the econometric evidence showing significantly positive relationships between financial variables and rates of economic growth has grown, I have become increasingly cautious over its interpretation. These quantitative measures of financial conditions may well be proxies for the general state of an economy's financial conditions. If real deposit rates have been negative over substantial periods of time and if no efforts have been made to extend branches of depository institutions into rural areas, financial conditions in general are likely to be unconducive to domestic resource mobilization. Raising real deposit rates of interest and proliferating bank branches in rural areas do not in themselves constitute a general program of financial development. Hence it may well require more comprehensive financial reform and development to produce the effects on saving behavior and investment efficiency that quantitative variables alone are estimated to yield.

Indeed, this interpretation reconciles the quantitative evidence from large cross-country sample data, such as that presented by Robert King and Ross Levine (1993a, 1993b), with the disappointing results of financial liberalization experiments. If the banking system expands rapidly after financial liberalization, there are likely to be acute shortages of trained personnel in the financial sector. Even a short visit makes one immediately aware of the considerable investment in human capital now being undertaken to achieve the objective of establishing Bangkok as a regional financial center for Indochina. Obviously expertise cannot be acquired overnight.

Improved financial intermediation involves more than just the removal of discriminatory taxes and interest rate distortions, and adjustments to other policies directly affecting the operation of the financial sector. First, macroeconomic stability is essential. Second, a sound regulatory framework and effective bank supervision are imperative. Third, some institutional reforms are urgently needed in many developing countries. For example, many developing countries possess highly inefficient financial institutions with neither the incentive nor the expertise to improve domestic resource mobilization and allocation. More specifically, training and financial incentives are woefully inadequate in a number of countries. State-owned banks operated by civil servants with secure tenure offer numerous examples of poor performance. In large part, however, institutional reforms must address the overwhelming problem of nonperforming assets.

19.2 Prerequisites for Successful Financial Development

Experience suggests that there are at least two prerequisites for successful financial liberalization—macroeconomic stability and adequate bank supervision. Price stability, fiscal discipline, and policy credibility may well be the three key factors explaining Asian successes and Latin American failures over the past three decades.

High and variable inflation destroys existing financial markets and prevents potential financial markets from developing. Containing inflation requires monetary control and fiscal discipline. Macroeconomic stability also necessitates consistent macroeconomic policies, in particular monetary and exchange rate policies.

Price stability and fiscal discipline go hand in hand. With moderate understanding of macroeconomics at the policy level, implementation is reasonably straightforward in many developing countries. In some countries, however, there is no understanding of macroeconomics at the policy level. Turkey's two bouts of inflation in the postwar period were due, in my opinion, to a total lack of understanding of the money supply process (Fry 1980b). Turkey has now introduced economic expertise into its economic policy-making process.[1] Policy makers in the high-inflation Latin American countries undoubtedly know enough economics. There the problem is political will. Elsewhere, however, technical problems of implementing monetary policy still exist.

Some developing countries have lost control over their money stocks at one time or another. First, it is essential that policy makers possess at least an elementary understanding of the effect of money on prices. Second, monetary statistics must be available without undue lag. Third, the implementation of a noninflationary monetary policy must be feasible. In practice, feasibility hinges on the government's borrowing requirements. Hence fiscal discipline is a crucial prerequisite for monetary stability.

Once fiscal discipline has been achieved, successful monetary policy implementation should be feasible. It requires some understanding of the basic instruments of monetary policy and how they affect the target variables. The traditional objectives of monetary policy are stable prices, full employment, and rapid economic growth. Unfortunately, these targets are invariably incompatible with one another. Indeed, it is usually impossible to achieve more than one objective with one instrument of policy. Price stability is the correct objective or target of monetary policy, since monetary policy is unable to achieve any other objective, except possibly in the very short run. The indicator selected to judge the successfulness of monetary policy might be the GNP implicit price deflator. A small-scale macroeconomic model and financial programming can be used to estimate the appropriate average rate of growth in the money supply consistent with price stability. Given that high variance in monetary growth rates reduces the rate of economic growth over the medium run, monetary policy should aim to keep monetary growth rates from year to year within a moderate range (perhaps within 5 percentage points) (Fry and Lilien 1986).

Central banks in most industrial countries use open market operations to affect the cash base. Open market operations by central banks in developing countries are usually impossible; most developing countries do not possess functioning open financial markets on which trading can take place.

---

[1] Prime minister Tansu Çiller was a colleague in the Economics Department at Bogaziçi University and former central bank governor Rüşdü Saracoglu was one of my first students at the Middle East Technical University in 1967.

In practice, therefore, monetary control must be exercised through reserve requirements and the rediscount mechanism.

Typically, central banks in developing countries use their rediscount facilities to support the government's selective or directed credit policy. The rediscount mechanism cannot be used for monetary control when its use is preempted for financing priority activities at subsidized interest rates. The rediscount mechanism is clearly an inappropriate instrument for achieving selective credit policy objectives because of the repercussions on the money stock.

Even when rediscounts are used for monetary control purposes, central banks in developing countries tend to allocate the facility on a nonprice basis. Instead of setting a rediscount rate and supplying all bank demands at that fixed rate, central banks generally set a below-market rate and ration the excess demand that is generated. The same control can be achieved more efficiently by auctioning a fixed volume of rediscounts. The market rate of interest for the rediscount facility on offer would equate demand with the fixed quantity supplied.

A simpler and more efficient mechanism to the rediscount system is a central bank overdraft facility. Instead of scrutinizing each bill presented for rediscount, the central bank could provide an overdraft facility for each bank. The total volume of overdrafts could again be fixed and auctioned off to the deposit-taking institutions.

Monetary policy discussed so far is for a closed economy or an economy with a freely floating exchange rate. However, all developing countries are open economies and virtually none of them has a freely floating exchange rate. Monetary and exchange rate policies must therefore be coordinated. An inflation-induced appreciation in the real exchange rate prices exports out of the world market and lowers the price of imports relative to domestic goods. The balance of payments on current account moves into deficit. Eventually, a balance-of-payments crisis occurs when the country can no longer borrow abroad to finance imports in excess of exports. Hence macroeconomic stability necessitates consistent monetary and exchange rate policies to ensure that inflation-induced real exchange rate appreciation is avoided. More rapid monetary expansion may require more frequent exchange rate changes through the adoption of a crawling peg or a freely floating exchange rate system. In one way or another, exporters and potential exporters must be convinced that domestic inflation will not raise domestic costs above the world prices of their products.

Hong Kong provides an extreme example of the link between monetary and exchange rate policies in an open economy. The Hong Kong dollar is pegged at a fixed price to the U.S. dollar. With virtually no current or capital account controls, Hong Kong cannot pursue any independent monetary policy. The currency board system operated by the Exchange Fund ensures that the money stock in Hong Kong is determined solely by the demand for money.

In this way, Hong Kong imports the effects of U.S. monetary policy. Higher monetary growth that raises domestic prices in the United States raises prices in Hong Kong. In turn, higher prices increase the demand for money in Hong Kong. Finally, the increased money demand puts upward pressure on domestic interest rates, which attracts a flow of foreign exchange into Hong Kong. The Exchange Fund ensures that this foreign exchange is converted into Hong Kong dollars, so increasing the supply of money in Hong Kong at the fixed exchange rate.

The fixed exchange rate and passive monetary policy are consistent. Provided that transactions on both current and capital accounts are unimpeded, domestic inflation cannot diverge widely from inflation in the country or countries to which the exchange rate is pegged. Furthermore, the accommodative monetary policy also ensures that the domestic currency never becomes overvalued in the foreign exchange markets. Estonia has followed Hong Kong in adopting a currency board system based on the deutsche mark with the same results.

A consistent alternative for Estonia, Hong Kong, and other highly open economies is an active monetary policy and a freely floating exchange rate. In such case, monetary policy sets the money stock and money demand determines domestic prices and the exchange rate. When an active monetary policy is pursued under a fixed exchange rate system, excessive monetary expansion overvalues the domestic currency and the real exchange rate appreciates.

In an open economy, interest rate and exchange rate policies must also be consistent with each other. Under a definitively fixed exchange rate, domestic interest rates should not deviate far from interest rates in the country or countries to which the domestic currency is pegged. Under crawling or floating exchange rates, domestic interest rates must compensate for expected currency depreciation. In such case, the domestic nominal interest rates should exceed interest rates abroad by the extent of the anticipated currency depreciation. Unless savers are assured that the real returns on domestic financial assets are equivalent to real returns on financial assets abroad, savers will transfer their savings abroad. But experience indicates that where the real interest rate at home *exceeds* the real interest rate abroad by a significant margin, macroeconomic policies are usually inconsistent or the banking system is inadequately supervised.

Political will, political stability, and consistent macroeconomic policies are all needed for policy credibility. Fixing the exchange rate without fixing the fiscal deficit is a recipe for disruptive capital flight. Chile's experience shows that even the most radical financial liberalization followed by inordinately high domestic real interest rates cannot deter capital flight when the domestic currency becomes seriously overvalued (Cuddington 1986).

Even after capital account and financial liberalization, dollar interest rates adjusted for preannounced devaluations were much lower than domestic currency rates of interest in the Southern Cone countries during the late 1970s and early 1980s. This encouraged excessive borrowing abroad. Vittorio Corbo and Jaime de Melo (1985b) suggest that this phenomenon was a result of policy inconsistencies. In Argentina and Uruguay, government deficits were too large; in Chile, the problem was backward wage indexation. Diaz-Alejandro (1985) pinpoints the buildup of contingent liabilities (taking the form of deposit insurance and implicit guarantees to foreign lenders) against the government budget in Chile.

The basic cause of these high spreads was undoubtedly lack of credibility in the announced stabilization and liberalization policies. High spreads have not been observed in Asia. They do not themselves constitute a problem but are a symptom of the basic credibility problem facing (for good reason) almost all Latin American governments.

Credibility can rarely be induced overnight. One currency reform per generation may be swallowed, but hardly more. There is also the problem of contagion. If the Cruzado Plan fails, then even the soundest Austral Plan is thrown into suspicion. For some countries, macroeconomic stability may be wishful thinking. What then? Should they simply maintain financial repression?

Although some readers of his 1973 book may have assumed otherwise,[2] McKinnon (1986b, 326) states that "successful liberalisation is not simply a question of removing all regulations." Certainly the IMF and the World Bank recognize that a prerequisite for successful financial liberalization is strong bank supervision. Financial liberalization involving substantial increases in real rates of interest is bound to produce some casualties. Indeed, this must happen if resource allocation is to be improved by the liberalization. Supervision is needed to ensure that weak financial institutions are detected early and liquidated or merged in an orderly fashion before their managements start engaging in perverse behavior (Ponzi-type lending) of the kind observed in Chile. There exists, however, no analytical framework dealing with the relationship between financial liberalization and financial regulation for prudential and monetary control (Darity and Horn 1986).

Regulation and supervision are the areas in most urgent need of further research. Indeed, these are possibly the fields in which future work on financial sector problems in developing countries could bear most fruit. First, there is the tricky theoretical issue of the relationship between financial liberalization and adequate regulation, which revolves around the theory of the second-best. Then there are the practical problems of differentiating appropriate from inappropriate regulations, delineating appropriate regulatory frameworks, and examining on a case-by-case basis the most suitable supervisory systems to enforce the regulations (Caprio et al. 1994, Stiglitz 1994, Sundararajan and Baliño 1991, Tseng and Corker 1991).

---

[2]For example, Ralph Bryant (1987, 126).

Because inappropriate regulations and inadequate supervision have been the norm, a strong current of academic opinion favors minimalist government intervention in a country's financial sector. For example, Rondo Cameron (1972, 19, 25) concludes his historical essay:

> If a banking system is to be effective in contributing to industrial capital formation, the government must assure minimal conditions of both financial and political order and refrain from random *ad hoc* interference that increases uncertainty for long-range investment planning.

> Where banking was left most free to develop in response to the demand for its services, it produced the best results. Restrictions on freedom of entry almost always reduce the quantity and quality of financial services available to the economy, and thus hinder or distort economic growth. Competition in banking, on the other hand, acts as a spur to the mobilization of idle financial resources and to their efficient utilization in commerce and industry.

Cameron does not elaborate on the minimum conditions of financial order.

After surveying the performance of financial sectors in developing countries, Millard Long (1983, 41) draws conclusions similar to those of Cameron:

> The financial systems of many countries appear to be over-regulated, with the result that the systems are stagnant, inefficient, and uncompetitive, and there is little provision for the orderly entry of new firms and the exit of old firms. In several countries, an overhaul of the regulatory framework seems to be in order.

Again, Long is not forthcoming on the issue of precisely how the regulatory framework should be overhauled. After 1973, the Chilean authorities evidently believed in virtually no regulations or supervision.

Recent scandals on Wall Street as well as the Savings and Loan crisis show that, even in one of the most highly regulated countries in the world, supervision of the financial sector has not been vigilant enough. Although detailed regulations concerning financial transactions exist in all countries, they are generally enforced much more consistently and effectively in the developed than in the developing countries. Regulations that appear the same on paper may be quite different in practice.

Most developing countries do not possess or cannot attract sufficient expertise to staff an effective bank supervision office, much less a securities commission. Government regulatory agencies generally offer salaries that are far too low to attract, let alone retain, staff qualified to undertake effective supervision of financial institutions. This bottleneck may suggest that the best financial development programs for most developing countries would involve institutions and instruments whose transactions are the most transparent and hence easiest to supervise. In general, financial development programs should start with the development of markets for simple short-term financial assets such as treasury bills and negotiable certificates of deposit (NCDs) rather than equities. Together with oligopolistic market structures, this supervisory problem militates against the promotion of universal banking.

Although there is still debate over the need for or desirability of bank examination, some form of audit, examination, or inspection is essential in virtually all developing countries for both monetary policy implementation and the evaluation of nationalized banks' performance. Since most central banks act, in effect, as deposit insurance agencies, bank inspection is also mandatory for prudential purposes (Stiglitz 1994). Examination for all three purposes requires more than a standard audit. Specifically, some qualitative analysis of a bank's loan portfolio must be undertaken.

The dearth of audit skills in most developing countries suggests that some might follow industrial countries such as Belgium, Denmark, France, Germany, and Holland in the use of external auditors. In particular, the Belgian system merits serious consideration. Each bank in Belgium must appoint an auditor chosen from a list maintained by the Banking Commission. The auditor is paid by the bank but is generally responsible to the Banking Commission. The auditor must follow the rules established by the Banking Commission. These cover his need to be consulted before certain actions are taken by the bank, his duty to check the bank's reports (including statistical returns) to the Commission, his duty to inform the Commission of any irregularity by the bank, and his duty to report regularly to the Commission on the state of the bank. The auditor makes regular sample audits and reports on the bank's general policies and the adequacy of the bank's systems and organization, including its internal control system. The auditor is also required to countersign all the statistical and other returns made by the bank. Regular rotation of auditors is used as a means of checking the auditors.

19.3   Monetary Policy Techniques for Financial Development

Some techniques with which monetary policy is implemented retard financial development, while others promote it. Global credit ceilings are perhaps the greatest deterrent to financial development. On the other hand, open treasury bill auctions and the promotion of secondary markets, particularly interbank money markets, encourage financial development. Experience indicates that learning-by-doing with market-determined interest rates in short-term financial markets is the only viable way in which active and stable long-term securities markets can be developed.

Perhaps most instructive in this regard have been the recent adoption of market-based monetary policy techniques in France, Germany, and Italy over the past decade or so. Despite the different objectives of monetary policy, the techniques of monetary policy implementation in the four largest European Union (EU) countries are now remarkably similar. Over the past five years, convergence in monetary policy implementation techniques has been striking. Essentially, each central bank creates continuous incipient liquidity shortages. The continuous drain of liquidity through the repayment of short-term credit facilities provided by them enables these four central banks to accommodate liquidity shortages at an interest rate of their choosing.

The range of instruments used to alleviate liquidity shortages in these EU countries varies somewhat between countries, but most instruments are common to all. To traditional open market operations in government securities have been added repurchase agreements, dealings in commercial paper and certificates of deposit, sales of central bank bills and foreign exchange swaps as instruments of monetary policy. At present, short-term interest rates play a key role in monetary policy implementation in all four EU countries. Britain, France, and Italy use interest rates as the main instrument for influencing their exchange rates, while Germany uses them to achieve its monetary targets and its ultimate goal of price stability.

Prior to 1983, Indonesia's monetary authorities used global credit ceilings as the main instrument of monetary policy. In 1983 direct credit controls were replaced by open market operations and the rediscount window. At the same time the selective credit policy was reduced in scope quite substantially. To date, however, Indonesia has failed to develop a viable money market because its lacks adequate legal, regulatory, and tax systems. Accounting has been pinpointed as a particular weakness that plagues financial development in Indonesia.

Experiments with market-based monetary policy implementation in the form of treasury bill auctions and open market operations have also occurred to varying extents in other Asian countries. In Korea and Sri Lanka, however, the monetary authorities still display a certain distrust of market forces by their penchant for intervening when market-determined interest rates rise too high. The evidence indicates that market-based monetary policy techniques promote financial development.

19.4 Extent, Sequencing, and Timing of Financial Liberalization

Despite frequent reference to its financial reforms of 1964, Korea set low real interest rates for all financial institutions throughout the 1960s and 1970s (Min 1976). In 1980, the government raised interest rates, maintaining real interest rates in the range of 5 to 10 percent throughout the 1980s. The ratio of *M3* to GNP rose rapidly from 49 percent in 1980 to 94 percent 1987 (World Bank 1989, 126). Korea's rate of economic growth increased from 7.0 percent annually over the period 1975–1980 to 9.2 percent annually over the period 1980–1989.

Although interest rate policy may be responsible in part for Korea's phenomenal growth rate during the 1980s, financial liberalization cannot be given much credit. To be sure, some competition was encouraged through deregulation of nonbank financial institutions, relaxing entry barriers to foreign banks, and privatizing the domestic commercial banks. Nevertheless, Yung Chul Park (1990, 2, 30) concludes: "After almost ten years of liberalization attempt, however, Korea's financial sector is still under rigid and pervasive government control and largely remains closed to foreign competition. Despite numerous and often confusing reform measures, deregulation of the financial sector has been slow, uneven, and most of all limited in scope and degree." Although Korea's curb market has recently shown signs of decline, its existence testifies to the modest scope of financial liberalization to date.

In Taiwan, recent measures of financial liberalization have included the move to a managed float from a pegged rate of exchange against the U.S. dollar in 1978, permission for every adult to buy $5 million each year for capital account outflows in 1987, deregulation of institutional interest rates starting in 1980, and the beginnings of open market operations in 1979 (Lee and Tsai 1988, 12–22). The ratio of *M2* to GNP has increased since 1981. Stable prices and positive real interest rates, except in 1973–1974 and 1979–1980, as well as rapid growth in per capita income, have been responsible for the rapid rise in this financial ratio. At first blush, therefore, one might conclude that Taiwan's financial liberalization has been extensive. This conclusion would, however, be erroneous.

When Taiwan stopped pegging its exchange rate to the U.S. dollar in July 1978, only appointed banks were allowed to trade in the foreign exchange market. Furthermore, their foreign exchange exposure was severely limited. Although regulations were relaxed somewhat in 1980 and again in 1984, the foreign exchange market is still less than well-developed (Lee and Tsai 1988, 15).

Over 75 percent of loans from financial institutions come from domestic commercial and medium business banks. Crucial to an understanding of the impact of financial liberalization and reform of Taiwan's financial system on monetary control is the fact that nearly all the domestic banks are owned by the government.[3] Furthermore, half of these banks were established as specialized banks to service particular sectors of the economy with little or no competition from other financial institutions. Hang-Sheng Cheng (1986a, 148) concludes that "virtually free from competition ... banks are generally run as bureaucracies, with bank directors as well as senior management all appointed by the government, carrying out government policy directives." Indeed, *The Economist* (1982a, 10) commented: "Newspapers in Taiwan report regularly on the arrest and punishment of bank officials who make bad

---

[3] The exceptions are two small private banks and one small joint venture bank.

loans. All but three banks are owned by the government, and bankers are forbidden to do anything as immoral as to take risks." Previous government policies combined with the constraints on bank lending, including stringent requirements for collateral, have prevented the banking system from becoming a significant direct source of long-term investment financing (Economist Intelligence Unit 1982, 15). Not surprisingly, small-scale businesses have had very little access to institutional credit.

Although some foreign banks have been permitted to set up branches since 1965, their activities are restricted with respect to both operations and locations:[4] "Foreign bankers too have been kept on a short leash in Taiwan. The bargain between the authorities and the bankers is familiar: foreign banks are allowed to do those pockets of business which the locals cannot do well, in return for lending plenty of money to the country's big international borrowers" (*The Economist* 1982a, 10). Specifically, foreign banks may not accept time deposits of over six months' maturity, nor may they open more than one branch in Taipei and Kaohsiung.

The government has made some effort to develop a capital market, but it has failed to achieve any net transfer of funds from the household sector to the business sector; dividend payments have exceeded the value of new and rights issues. The stock market is still used to a considerable extent for speculation rather than investment, as evinced by the speculative spurge of 1988–1989. The corporate bond market is virtually nonexistent.

One indication that financial liberalization in Taiwan must have been modest in scope comes from the flow-of-funds accounts. Private business enterprises borrowed 52 percent of their funds from financial institutions and 48 percent from curb markets in 1964. Although the ratio of curb market to total borrowing fell to 27 percent in 1973, it was back at 48 percent in 1986 (Lee and Tsai 1988, Table 9, 51). Evidently, any financial liberalization that has taken place has not eroded the curb market. It is also interesting to note that the spread between the post-dated check loan rate and the 12-month deposit rate of interest has not decreased since 1973.

From the cautious pace of financial liberalization in Korea and Taiwan, one might draw two tentative conclusions. First, full-blown financial liberalization is not a prerequisite for spectacular economic growth. Second, the crucial financial variable is the real interest rate. In both Korea and Taiwan real interest rates were positive during most of the 1980s and were maintained reasonably close to free-market levels. Obviously, however, further inferences about the optimal extent, sequencing, and timing of financial liberalization require a deeper study into the nature of financial liberalization experiments in Korea and Taiwan as well as in the other Asian developing countries.

---

[4]Until recently, foreign banks were permitted to establish branches only in Taipei and Kaohsiung. From one foreign bank branch before 1965, the number had grown to 37 in January 1994.

The lessons of experience suggest that analytical work failed to pinpoint at least two prerequisites for successful financial liberalization—macroeconomic stability and adequate prudential supervision and regulation of the banks. The disastrous experiments with rapid financial liberalization in Latin America raise questions of prerequisites for and sequencing of successful financial liberalization programs. McKinnon (1993, 4) insists that fiscal control must precede financial liberalization. If the government continues to run a large deficit, financial liberalization will simply accelerate inflation as the tax base is eroded; the 1977 experiment with financial liberalization in Israel provides a good example (Sussman 1992). As shown in section 19.2, high inflation is inimical to financial development. Expenditure of the entire public sector that includes provincial governments, state-owned enterprises, and particularly the central bank must be brought under reasonable control to prevent runaway inflation from reversing the positive effect of financial liberalization.

Rapid expansion of lending by newly liberalized banks has resulted in just as high levels of nonperforming assets as did directed credit policies under financial repression. Most banking systems simply lack the expertise needed to make good commercial judgments. In any case, they cannot acquire more of such expertise at the moment financial liberalization occurs. Hence, prudential regulation and supervision are doubly imperative at the outset of financial liberalization to curtail the worst excesses of inexperienced and untrained bankers (Villanueva and Mirakhor 1990, Vittas 1992).

Recent experience with financial reform and liberalization also indicates just how important are the roles of market structure in determining the outcome of such programs (Adhikary 1990, Bisat, Johnston, and Sundararajan 1992, Caprio et al. 1994). In particular, cartelized or highly concentrated banking systems have not responded as anticipated to the abolition of interest rate ceilings. Bank associations simply assume responsibility for establishing appropriate interest rates for their members when governments relinquish this function. Financially repressed markets tend to be cartelized or highly oligopolistic in the first place. Therefore, some attention must be devoted early in the financial reform to promoting competition. One way of achieving this is through the issue of relatively small-denomination treasury bills and bonds with competitive yields.

Coordination between financial and balance-of-payments liberalizations should ensure that capital accounts are not liberalized until after financial stability and market-determined domestic interest rates have been established (McKinnon 1993, 9–10). Experience suggests that premature capital account liberalization may on the one hand stimulate capital flight and hence raise effective real domestic interest rates but on the other encourage disruptive capital inflows as happened in Korea in the 1960s and Chile in the 1970s.

Rudiger Dornbusch and Yung Chul Park (1987, 432–433) question the desirability of capital account liberalization at any stage in the liberalization process:

The overriding characteristic of private capital flows, without much exaggeration, is that capital tends to come when it is unnecessary and leave when it is least convenient. As a result it tends to increase the variability of real exchange rates and introduces avoidable macroeconomic instability. One cannot escape the impression that Korea, under the impact of abundant external capital, might lose its competitive exchange rate, overborrow, and ultimately become once again a problem debtor. Korea's investment ratio is more than 30 percent of GNP. There is little to suggest that capital imports are necessary because capital is in short supply.

On the one hand, less liberal capital account policies in both Korea and Taiwan appear not to have been costly in terms of forgone growth (Moreno 1994). On the other hand, Donald Mathieson and Liliana Rojas–Suárez (1993) point out that capital controls have been increasingly ineffective and conclude that capital account liberalization can be beneficial provided consistent macroeconomic and financial policies are pursued. Indonesia is frequently cited as a country which successfully liberalized capital account transactions well before financial liberalization (Cole and Slade 1992, Fischer 1992).

Price stability, fiscal discipline, and policy credibility may well be the three key factors explaining Asian successes and Latin American failures with financial liberalization experiments over the past three decades. After a lengthy survey of financial systems and development, however, the World Bank concludes that there are, in fact, four key prerequisites to success: macroeconomic stability, fiscal discipline, improved legal, accounting and regulatory systems for the financial sector, and a tax system that does not discriminate excessively against finance (World Bank 1989, 1). The evidence presented in support of this conclusion is, in my view, overwhelming. Nevertheless, much still needs to be learned about successful and unsuccessful financial liberalization experiments. Although agreement has now been reached on the prerequisites for successful financial liberalization, there exists very little analysis on the optimal extent, sequencing, and timing of financial liberalization.

19.5 A Path through the Minefield

First and foremost on the list of urgent financial policy reforms for effective and efficient domestic resource mobilization in most developing countries is a solution to the high proportion of nonperforming assets in the asset portfolios of many financial institutions. The crucial problem of nonperforming assets lies in the fact that, if financial institutions are to remain solvent, higher default costs must reduce net returns to savers or raise gross costs to successful investors. They create a wedge, just as administrative costs do, between loan and deposit rates of interest. Arrears also reduce banks' flexibility in that credit cannot be redirected towards alternative activities if it is not repaid.

Excessive arrears and default rates indicate inefficiency of one kind or another. The financial institution has either financed unproductive investments or failed to press for loan repayment. In either case, financial intermediation is impaired.

High percentages of nonperforming assets constitute one of the most serious problems facing financial systems in developing countries at present. The worst possible policy approach would be to ignore the problem. This would encourage banks to throw good money after bad, so reducing their flexibility even further. The case-by-case approach now being followed by the World Bank with respect to DFIs is the only viable remedy. Repetition of this problem can be prevented only by abandoning directed credit programs. Institutional reforms should also be aimed at this issue. Resource allocation by the financial sector must be based solely on the criterion of economic efficiency. Joseph Stiglitz (1990) suggests that peer monitoring can provide a partial solution. Borrowers are obliged to join groups, in which each member co-signs the loans of others. Since all members of a group meet each other's financial obligations, there is a strong incentive to monitor other members of the group. "Peer monitoring is largely responsible for the successful financial performance of the Grameen Bank of Bangladesh and of similar group lending programs elsewhere" (Stiglitz 1990, 351).

In many developing countries, decision making in the banking sector is highly centralized, particularly in the case of state-owned financial institutions. For these institutions, the primary objective appears to be support of the government's development (or political) plan rather than efficiency. The branch banking systems typically found in developing countries are characterized by rigid procedures, expensive staffing patterns, high pay scales, and extensive delays. In general, decentralization enables financial institutions to be more responsive to local conditions as well as to improve efficiency. State-owned financial institutions tend to exhibit the greatest inefficiencies within developing countries' financial sectors. Performance is frequently criticized, but the criteria on which performance has been found unsatisfactory are seldom made explicit.

The first task here is to set out clearly the objectives of the state-owned banks. The fundamental aim of a nationalized banking system might be the efficient operation of a payments mechanism and the mobilization of private savings for productive investment. Efficiency could then be evaluated in terms of (a) speed and cost of effecting payments; (b) attracting savings; (c) intermediation costs; and (d) allocating investible funds.

A number of indicators can be used for the payments efficiency criterion: (a) percentage growth in demand deposits; (b) ratio of clearings to demand deposits; (c) average time taken to cash a check or withdraw funds from an account; and (d) average time taken to process other banking transactions. A comparison of rates of growth in demand deposits among the banks would indicate which banks were perceived to offer the most efficient service for demand deposits. The ratio of clearings to demand deposits also indicates payments efficiency, since those intending to use their deposits more actively for payments will tend to choose banks that provide the best payments service. Bank branches could be sampled to measure the average time taken to cash a check, to withdraw funds from an account, and to process other types of banking transactions. There is, for example, ample evidence to suggest that the substitution of a teller for a cashier system speeds up cash withdrawal very considerably.

Performance can also be judged on the basis of ratios of personnel costs and total operating costs to total assets. However, costs can always be reduced at the expense of service provided. Hence, it is also important to compare earnings, growth in earnings, cost/income ratios, and profits.

Efficient resource mobilization is more difficult to measure than is the efficiency of effecting payments. Attracting saving might be measured by percentage changes in total or time deposits. It is, however, in measuring the efficiency of allocating investible funds that almost insuperable measurement problems arise. First, banks need to prepare statements on their lending policies that must include some discussion of risk taking. Banks must also have policies dealing with loan losses and assessing the performance of individual loan officers. It is essential that such policies recognize and support reasonable risk taking and state clearly that resulting losses do not necessarily reflect adversely in the assessment of a loan officer's performance.

Performance criteria for efficient allocation of funds should also include the time taken to process loan applications of various types. This may also be reflected in loan growth. Perhaps most important are the criteria used by the bank in making its lending decisions. New lending policies must reverse the traditional policies fostered by financial repression, oligopoly, and banker bureaucracy, which concentrate on collateralized short-term loans to finance traditional trading activities.

The second most urgent financial policy reform concerns interest rate policy. Holding interest rates low by administrative fiat to encourage investment does not work because it discourages financial saving, the source of investible funds. With a cartelized banking industry, abolishing interest rate ceilings is unlikely to achieve the optimum result either. Indeed, it may not even produce higher real institutional interest rates. In the light of the recent experiences of Argentina, Chile, Sri Lanka, Turkey, and Uruguay with excessively high real loan rates of interest, continued government intervention in the determination of institutional interest rates may well be the best interim policy until price stability is achieved and bank supervision and competition within the financial sector are adequate. As with monetary policy, however, an administered interest rate policy should select an appropriate objective and not be hampered by pursuit of several incompatible aims.

Possibly the most appropriate objectives of interest rate policy in developing countries are the efficient mobilization and allocation of domestic resources. Efficiency of both the mobilization and allocation of saving is maximized when institutional interest rates are set at their free-market equilibrium levels and discriminatory taxes on financial intermediation are removed. Since most financial systems in developing countries are oligopolistic, the competitive solution may well have to be imposed. Provided adequate bank supervision is in place, there is probably little point in attempting to set loan rates of interest; they can so easily be evaded through compensating deposits. Instead, the monetary authorities might set deposit rates at levels that approximate the competitive free-market rates. Specifically, banks might be required to offer indexed six- or 12-month deposits with a modest (perhaps 3 percent) real return.

One way of stimulating rather than simulating a competitive interest rate solution is for the government to issue treasury bills and bonds with attractive yields. Typically, government securities in developing countries are held only by financial institutions as part of their required liquidity ratios and by business firms required to hold them in order to bid on government contracts. Yields on government securities are so low that voluntary holdings are nonexistent. The appropriate interest rate structure, however, applies equally to the government and the private sector. Indeed, if the government is unwilling to compete in this way, financial development is doomed.

The sale of government securities with attractive yields could start with fixed-price sales at post offices. The next stage would be auction sales at which direct investors as well as dealers and brokers might bid for securities. This scheme has the double advantage of ensuring that both the government as well as the banking system offers competitive returns to savers. An experiment along these lines in Turkey succeeded in raising real deposit rates of interest by 20 percentage points in 1981. The rate of economic growth accelerated sharply in that year.

Efficient domestic resource mobilization and allocation involve lowering the gross costs of borrowing or investing as close as possible to the net returns to lending or saving. The spread between gross borrowing and net lending rates must cover the costs of financial intermediation. It also covers taxes of various kinds. Discriminatory taxes on financial intermediation generally consist of reserve requirements (including directed credit quotas) and withholding taxes on interest income. They may also involve stamp duties on financial transactions and even taxes on loan interest.

Required reserves impose a discriminatory tax on financial intermediation because they incur an opportunity cost in the form of forgone interest that could otherwise be earned on these assets. The tax can be removed either by abolishing required reserves or by paying a competitive interest rate on them. Abolishing required reserves does not vitiate monetary control, but does raise the money supply multiplier. A marginal reserve requirement scheme of the kind proposed elsewhere (Fry 1979b) can be substituted for the standard required reserve system to remove the tax and at the same time to strengthen monetary control.

Selective credit policies go hand in hand with interest rate policies. The defects of low interest rate policies are compounded by selective credit policies that differentiate and subsidize interest rates charged to particular categories of borrowers. The most obvious disadvantage of selective credit policies is that capital rather than labor is subsidized. Where an economic activity is deemed worthy of subsidy, a fiscal subsidy that subsidizes the use of labor by at least as much as it subsidizes the use of capital must be preferred. Fiscal subsidies have the added advantage that they must be budgeted; financing through a consumption tax would probably be least distortionary. The cost of interest rate subsidies is usually concealed and ignored. Abandoning directed credit programs must constitute one of the first steps of any sensible financial development program. If the government is too weak to take this step, it may well be too weak to implement any well-conceived macroeconomic policy.

Markets in which interest rates are freely determined by the interaction of supply and demand are few and far between in the developing world. The monetary authority can offer education in and experience with the market determination of interest rates in a few easy stages. Logical progression in financial development programs is crucial. It is important to start the process by introducing short-term financial assets with no risk other than a small amount of interest risk. Prices must be determined in the market through the free interplay of demand and supply. Since 1984 Indonesia has provided some excellent examples of how to introduce and develop markets in short-term financial claims. Bank deposits are a bad example because their price does not change. Treasury bills, central bank NCDs, and interbank money markets are good examples. After experience has been gained in these simple, low-risk, transparent markets, then and only then does it makes some sense to turn to equity market development. To start, central banks could establish an interbank money market in developing countries that do not already possess such a market. The main function of an interbank money market is to enable financial institutions to hold desired reserve levels on a day-to-day basis.

In the first instance, the interbank money market deals in only one maturity, overnight lending. The market opens at the previous day's interest rate. Initial orders are placed by the banks' brokers. If demand exceeds supply, the interest rate is raised by a constant fraction (typically one eighth) of a percentage point. If supply exceeds demand, the interest rate is lowered. New orders are placed at the new interest rate. The interest rate continues to be adjusted in this way until the demand/supply imbalance is eliminated or reversed. The final interest rate is that which minimizes the imbalance. The central bank itself can meet any difference between demand and supply at that rate.

Trading is now over, with the interest rate and each institution's trading position established. Two lists are then drawn up. The first documents the final trading positions; it is then used to debit and credit appropriately the institutions' accounts with the central bank. The second list documents the sums for repayment on the following day. It constitutes the opening clearing balance for each institution at the next day's clearing.

An interbank market of this kind not only enables financial institutions to hold whatever level of reserves they desire at the equilibrium interest rate but also provides an important indicator for monetary policy purposes. In general, however, the interest rate established in an overnight interbank market will lie between the central bank's rediscount rate (since banks can repay the central bank rather than lend at less than this rate on the interbank money market) and the penalty rate for reserve shortfalls (since it would be cheaper to pay the penalty than a higher rate in the interbank market to avoid the shortfall).

Second, central banks wishing to promote financial development could develop a treasury bill market. The development of such a market would provide some salient competition with the banking system. Negotiable treasury bills with short maturities of 30, 60, and 180 days could be sold by the central bank on behalf of the government. These bills might be sold at auction once a week. The amount to be sold (and possibly also a reservation price below which sales would not be made) would be announced by the central bank during the preceding week. Bids for treasury bills would be placed prior to the actual auction. The bids might take the form of quantities to be bought at prices ranging from the reservation price to the face value of the bill in standard increments. At the time of the auction, the bids would be totalled and the ruling price would be the lowest at which supply exceeded or equalled demand. A small quantity of bills would therefore be unsold after each auction.

The central bank could also establish an open market for the resale of treasury bills. Initially the central bank might offer to repurchase treasury bills, using some formula with which to calculate an offer price. By establishing a physical marketplace and by offering to buy at a price somewhat unattractive to potential sellers, the central bank could attract other buyers, including dealers and brokers, into the market.

Another instrument in which initial experience with market determination of interest rates can be gained is the NCD. It can serve three purposes. First, NCDs stimulate competition among the issuing banks. Second, they lengthen the maturity of banks' liability portfolios, so enabling them to increase their medium- and long-term lending activities without undue interest rate risk. Third, trading in NCDs produces a simple market in which experience with market determination of interest rates can be gained with minimum trauma.

Conditions of supply of NCDs are critical. Clearly, if NCDs are issued on tap at a fixed price with the same fixed guaranteed repurchase price, they will be indistinguishable from savings deposits. The market price would be tied rigidly to the redemption price, and no trading would occur. The ideal solution is sale by auction. Provided the dividend is sufficiently attractive, the market price can be kept above the floor at which banks guarantee repurchase.

Then, provided supply is regulated in one way or another, market trading at prices above the price floor will take place.

The central bank might also offer special NCDs that could be bought only with foreign exchange. Auctions could be held once a week, with quantities supplied determined by some prearranged formula designed to meet a given target for the volume of foreign exchange inflows over a year. What return has to be offered to produce this inflow is, of course, determined in the market.

International donors have inadvertently compounded financial sector problems in many developing countries by circumventing domestic financial systems altogether or by pursuing their own selective credit policies through differential interest rate subsidies. Recently, however, awareness of the damaging side effects of aid operations has increased, in part due to the greater emphasis by international donors on program and structural adjustment lending, as opposed to project aid. Clearly, the first role for donor agencies in financial development is to resist the temptation to provide loans on concessional terms. Grants should be grants and loans should be loans on commercial terms.

19.6 Summary

The past 20 years have witnessed an explosion of research into the effects of financial repression and financial liberalization on economic performance in developing countries. Econometric tests suggest that financial conditions influence the rate of economic growth by affecting the quality rather than the quantity of investment. The recent theoretical emphasis on the productivity rather than the volume of investment not only accords with the empirical findings but also provides an explanation in terms of endogenous growth. Only in the 1990s has financial structure been incorporated into endogenous growth models at the theoretical level. These theoretical developments open up potentially rich avenues for future empirical research.

Theoretical work relating financial conditions to macroeconomic stability has come at a particularly opportune time for practical application to financial instability in many developing countries. Although there is a vast literature describing financial distress and collapse in developing economies, this has lacked a unifying theoretical framework. Hence, it has been unable to suggest a general strategy for reforming financial systems so that they can dampen rather than magnify fluctuations in the real sectors. Again, the theoretical advances in the areas of agency costs, adverse selection, and moral hazard open up possibilities for cross-country comparative studies focusing on the ways in which alternative financial arrangements address these critical problems in practice.

The principal-agent problem inextricably associated with bank lending suggests that equity participation by banks in their borrowers may not create quite the conflicts of interest that have been assumed among advocates of the Anglo-Saxon banking system. Given high information costs of risk assessment in developing countries, universal banking has particular attractions. Nevertheless, experience also highlights the importance of vigorous, albeit regulated, competition in the financial sector. Universal banking can reduce competition if it is not carefully overseen and uncompetitive financial systems exhibit high costs of credit intermediation. Such costs are also raised by inflation and various regulatory arrangements such as high reserve requirements. Perhaps the biggest contributor to high costs of credit intermediation, at least over the long run, is the high proportion of nonperforming assets that banks in developing countries typically hold. Because of the importance of credit intermediation in the growth process, further analysis of methods to reduce costs of credit intermediation in developing countries is still needed.

Disruptive financial crises have occurred in several developing countries in the past two decades. These crises have been linked to high real interest rates caused by distress borrowing. This relatively new phenomenon has itself been linked to deposit insurance of either implicit or explicit form. Because deposit insurance can lead to moral hazard, its presence necessitates strengthened prudential regulation and supervision of banking systems in developing countries. Indeed, it may be that in the absence of the capacity to improve prudential regulation and supervision, financial liberalization would best be delayed. Further research on the effects of alternative deposit insurance and alternative prudential regulation and supervision schemes is clearly warranted.

The way in which the macroeconomic environment impinges on the efficient working of financial institutions and financial markets in developing countries affects the outcome of financial liberalization and reform programs. If the necessary macroeconomic reforms for optimal financial development have not been implemented, a second-best financial liberalization program may perform better than a model program designed in a vacuum. Hence a clear understanding of the outcomes of financial liberalization and reform programs under alternative macroeconomic settings is necessary for the design of the most appropriate program for a particular circumstance. This, therefore, constitutes the subject of a second research effort. The experiences of Argentina, Chile, Korea, Mexico, and Turkey may provide useful pointers here.

Finally, financial system fragility or instability may be related to particular forms of government interference with and regulation of the financial sector (for example, interest rate ceilings, selective credit policies, reserve requirements, and segmentation of financial markets). The third thrust of new research, therefore, should analyze the differential effects of government regulations on the financial sector's ability to withstand exogenous shocks.

Bibliography

Names that include "de," "le," "van," or "von" are listed under these particles.

Abayaratna, G. M. 1990. *Capital Adequacy and Banking Risks in the SEACEN Countries.* Kuala Lumpur: South East Asian Central Banks Research and Training Centre.

Abbott, Graham J. 1985. "A Survey on Savings and Financial Development in Asian Developing Countries." *Savings and Development,* 9(4): 395–419.

Abe, Shigeyuki, Maxwell J. Fry, Byoung Kyun Min, Pairoj Vongvipanond, and Teh-Pei Yu. 1975. "The Demand for Money in Pakistan: Some Alternative Estimates." *Pakistan Development Review,* 14(2, Summer): 249–257.

————. 1977. "Financial Liberalisation and Domestic Saving in Economic Development: An Empirical Test for Six Countries." *Pakistan Development Review,* 16(3, Autumn): 298–308.

Adams, Dale W. 1988. "The Conundrum of Successful Credit Projects in Floundering Rural Financial Markets." *Economic Development and Cultural Change,* 36(2, January): 355–367.

————. 1991. "Taking a Fresh Look at Informal Finance." In *Financial Systems and Development in Africa.* Edited by Philippe Callier. Washington, D.C.: World Bank, EDI Seminar Series, 29–42.

Adams, Dale W, Douglas H. Graham, and John D. Von Pischke, eds. 1984. *Undermining Rural Development with Cheap Credit.* Boulder, Colo.: Westview Press.

Adhikary, Ganesh P. 1990. *Deregulation in the Financial System of the SEACEN Countries.* Kuala Lumpur: South East Asian Central Banks Research and Training Centre.

Agarwal, Jamuna P., Andrea Gubitz, and Peter Nunnenkamp. 1991. *Foreign Direct Investment in Developing Countries: The Case of Germany.* Tübingen: JCB Mohr Paul Siebeck, Kieler Studien 238.

Agénor, Pierre-Richard, and Peter J. Montiel. 1994. *Development Macroeconomics.* Princeton: Princeton University Press, forthcoming.

Aghevli, Bijan B., James M. Boughton, Peter J. Montiel, Delano Villanueva, and Geoffrey Woglom. 1990. "The Role of National Saving in the World Economy: Recent Trends and Prospects." Washington, D.C.: International Monetary Fund, Occasional Paper 67, March.

473

Aghevli, Bijan B., and Mohsin S. Khan. 1977. "Inflationary Finance and the Dynamics of Inflation: Indonesia, 1951–72." *American Economic Review,* 67(3, June): 390–403.

———. 1978. "Government Deficits and the Inflationary Process in Developing Countries." *International Monetary Fund Staff Papers,* 25(3, September): 383–416.

Aghevli, Bijan B., Mohsin S. Khan, Prabhakar R. Narvekar, and Brock K. Short. 1979. "Monetary Policy in Selected Asian Countries." *International Monetary Fund Staff Papers,* 26(4, December): 775–824.

Ahmed, Mohammad. 1988. "Financial Repression in the LDCs: A Survey of Issues and Reappraisal." *Pakistan Journal of Applied Economics,* 7(1, Summer): 19-41.

Ahmed, Zia U. 1982. "Transactions Costs in Rural Financial Markets in Bangladesh." Charlottesville: University of Virginia, Ph.D. thesis.

Aitken, Brian, and Ann Harrison. 1992. "Does Proximity to Foreign Firms Induce Technology Spillovers? Evidence from Panel Data." Cambridge, Mass.: Massachusetts Institute of Technology, July.

———. 1994. "Do Domestic Firms Benefit from Foreign Direct Investment? Evidence from Panel Data." Washington, D.C.: World Bank, Policy Research Working Paper 1248, February.

Akhtar, M. Akbar. 1974. "The Demand for Money in Pakistan." *Pakistan Development Review,* 13(1, Spring): 40–54.

Akyüz, Yilmaz. 1991. "Financial Liberalization in Developing Countries: A Neo-Keynesian Approach." Geneva: United Nations Conference on Trade and Development, Discussion Paper No. 36, March.

Aleem, Irfan. 1990. "Imperfect Information, Screening, and the Costs of Informal Lending: A Study of a Rural Credit Market in Pakistan." *World Bank Economic Review,* 4(3, September): 329–349.

Alm, James, and Robert Buckley. 1992. "Financial Repression, Welfare Costs, and Implicit Tax Revenues: Case of Turkey." Washington, D.C.: World Bank.

Amsden, Alice H., and Yoon-Dae Euh. 1993. "South Korea's 1980s Financial Reforms: Good-bye Financial Repression (Maybe), Hello New Institutional Restraints." *World Development,* 21(3, March): 379–390.

Anand, Ritu, and Sweder van Wijnbergen. 1989. "Inflation and the Financing of Government Expenditure: An Introductory Analysis with an Application to Turkey." *World Bank Economic Review,* 3(1, January): 17–38.

Anderson, Dennis, and Farida Khambata. 1985. "Financing Small-Scale Industry and Agriculture in Developing Countries: The Merits and Limitations of 'Commercial' Policies." *Economic Development and Cultural Change,* 33(2, January): 349–371.

Arestis, Philip, and Panicos O. Demetriades. 1992. "Investment and 'Financial Repression': Theory and Evidence from 63 LDCs." Keele: Keele University, Department of Economics, Working Paper No. 92–16, December.

———. 1993. "Financial Liberalisation and Economic Development: A Critical Exposition." In *Money and Banking: Issues for the Twenty First Century. Essays in Honour of Stephen F. Frowen.* Edited by Philip Arestis. Basingstoke: Macmillan, 287–303.

————. 1994. "The Ethics of Interest Rate Liberalisation in Developing Economies." In *Financial Decision-Making and Moral Responsibility.* Edited by Stephen F. Frowen and F. P. McHugh. London: Macmillan, 176–191.

Aries Group. 1990. *A Study of Securities Market Institutions: Sri Lanka.* Manila: Asian Development Bank, January.

Armijo, Leslie Elliott. 1993. "Brazilian Politics and Patterns of Financial Regulation, 1945–1991." In *The Politics of Finance in Developing Countries.* Edited by Stephan Haggard, Chung H. Lee, and Sylvia Maxfield. Ithaca: Cornell University Press, 259–290.

Arndt, Heinz W. 1982. "Two Kinds of Credit Rationing." *Banca Nazionale del Lavoro Quarterly Review,* (143, December): 417–425.

————. 1991. "Saving, Investment and Growth: Recent Asian Experience." *Banca Nazionale del Lavoro Quarterly Review,* (177, June): 1–13.

Arndt, Heinz W., and Peter J. Drake. 1985. "Bank Loans or Bonds: Some Lessons of Historical Experience." *Banca Nazionale del Lavoro Quarterly Review,* (155, December): 373–392.

Arrow, Kenneth J. 1953. "Le rôle de valeurs boursières pour la répartition la meuilleure des risques." *Econométrie,* 11: 41–48. ["The Role of Securities in the Optimal Allocation of Risk Bearing." *Review of Economic Studies,* 31(2, April), 1964: 91–96.]

Artus, Jacques R. 1976. "Exchange Rate Stability and Managed Floating: The Experience of the Federal Republic of Germany." *International Monetary Fund Staff Papers,* 23(2, July): 312–333.

Asian Development Bank. 1984. *Domestic Resource Mobilization through Financial Development.* Manila: Asian Development Bank, Economics Office, February.

————. 1985. *Improving Domestic Resource Mobilization through Financial Development.* Manila: Asian Development Bank, Economics Office, September.

Askari, Hossein. 1991. *Third World Debt and Financial Innovation: The Experiences of Chile and Mexico.* Paris: Organisation for Economic Co-operation and Development.

Athukorala, Premachandra, and Sarath Rajapatirana. 1993. "Liberalization of the Domestic Financial Market: Theoretical Issues with Evidence from Sri Lanka." *International Economic Journal,* 7(4, Winter): 17–33.

Atiyas, Izak. 1989. "The Private Sector's Response to Financial Liberalization in Turkey: 1980–82." Washington, D.C.: World Bank, Country Economics Department, PPR Working Paper WPS 147, January.

Atje, Raymond, and Boyan Jovanovic. 1993. "Stock Markets and Development." *European Economic Review,* 37(2–3, April): 632–640.

Bailey, Martin J. 1956. "The Welfare Cost of Inflationary Finance." *Journal of Political Economy,* 64(2, April): 93–110.

Balassa, Bela. 1989. "Financial Liberalization in Developing Countries." Washington, D.C.: World Bank, PPR Working Paper WPS 55, September.

————. 1990. "The Effects of Interest Rates on Savings in Developing Countries." *Banca Nazionale del Lavoro Quarterly Review,* (172, March): 101–118.

Balassa, Bela, and F. Desmond McCarthy. 1984. "Adjustment Policies in Developing Countries, 1979–83: An Update." Washington, D.C.: World Bank, Staff Working Paper No. 675, November.

Balasubramanyam, Venkataraman N. 1984. "Incentives and Disincentives for Foreign Direct Investment in Less Developed Countries." *Weltwirtschaftliches Archiv,* 120(4): 720–735.

Baliño, Tomás J. T. 1991. "The Argentine Banking Crisis of 1980." In *Banking Crises: Cases and Issues.* Edited by Venkataraman Sundararajan and Tomás J. T. Baliño. Washington, D.C.: International Monetary Fund, 58–112.

Baliño, Tomás J. T., and Venkataraman Sundararajan. 1986. "Financial Reform in Indonesia: Causes, Consequences, and Prospects." In *Financial Policy and Reform in Pacific Basin Countries.* Edited by Hang-Sheng Cheng. Lexington, Mass.: D. C. Heath and Co., Lexington Books, 191–219.

Banco de Portugal. 1963. *Report of the Board of Directors for the Year 1962.* Lisbon: Banco de Portugal.

———. 1988. *Report of the Directors for the Year 1987 (Abridged Version).* Lisbon: Banco de Portugal.

Bank Negara Malaysia. 1989. *Money and Banking in Malaysia.* Kuala Lumpur: Bank Negara Malaysia.

Bank of Korea. 1975. "A Study of Interest Elasticity of Private Savings in Korea." *Bank of Korea Monthly Review,* 29(9, September): 39–50.

———. 1978. *Financial System in Korea.* Seoul: Bank of Korea.

———. 1983. *Financial System in Korea.* Seoul: Bank of Korea.

Barnes, Guillermo. 1992. "Lessons from Bank Privatization in Mexico." Washington, D.C.: World Bank, Country Economics Department, PPR Working Paper WPS 1027, November.

Barrett, Rodney J., Malcolm R. Gray, and J. Michael Parkin. 1975. "The Demand for Financial Assets by the Personal Sector of the UK Economy." In *Modelling the Economy.* Edited by George A. Renton. London: Heinemann, 500–532.

Barro, Robert J. 1978. "Unanticipated Money, Output, and the Price Level in the United States." *Journal of Political Economy,* 86(4, August): 549–580.

———. 1987. *Macroeconomics,* 2d ed. New York: John Wiley and Sons.

———. 1991. "Economic Growth in a Cross Section of Countries." *Quarterly Journal of Economics,* 56(2, May): 407–443.

———. 1992. "World Interest Rates and Investment." *Scandinavian Journal of Economics,* 94(2): 323–334.

Baumol, William J. 1952. "The Transactions Demand for Cash: An Inventory Theoretic Approach." *Quarterly Journal of Economics,* 66(4, November): 545–556.

Bayoumi, Tamim A. 1993. "Financial Deregulation and Household Saving." *Economic Journal,* 103(421, November): 1432–1443.

Beckerman, Paul. 1986. "The Consequences of 'Upward Financial Repression.'" *International Review of Applied Economics,* 1(2): 233–249.

Bell, Clive. 1990. "Interactions between Institutional and Informal Credit Agencies in Rural India." *World Bank Economic Review,* 4(3, September): 297–327.

Bencivenga, Valerie R., and Bruce D. Smith. 1991. "Financial Intermediation and Endogenous Growth." *Review of Economic Studies*, 58(2, April): 195–209.

————. 1992. "Deficits, Inflation, and the Banking System in Developing Countries: The Optimal Degree of Financial Repression." *Oxford Economic Papers*, 44(4, October): 767–790.

————. 1993. "Some Consequences of Credit Rationing in an Endogenous Growth Model." *Journal of Economic Dynamics and Control*, 17(1–2, January–March): 97–122.

Benston, George J. 1973. "Bank Examination." New York: New York University, Graduate School of Business Administration, Institute of Finance Bulletins 89–90, May.

Bentham, Jeremy. 1787. *Defence of Usury.* London: T. Payne & Sons.

Berger, Frederick E. 1980. "Financial Programming and the Future Role of the Central Bank of Chile." Washington, D.C.: Organization of American States, January.

Bernanke, Ben S. 1981. "Bankruptcy, Liquidity, and Recession." *American Economic Review*, 71(2, May): 155–159.

————. 1983. "Nonmonetary Effects of the Financial Crisis in the Propagation of the Great Depression." *American Economic Review*, 73(3, June): 257–276.

Bernanke, Ben S., and Mark Gertler. 1989. "Agency Costs, Net Worth, and Business Fluctuations." *American Economic Review*, 79(1, March): 14–31.

————. 1990. "Financial Fragility and Economic Performance." *Quarterly Journal of Economics*, 55(1, February): 87–114.

Berthélemy, Jean-Claude, and Aristomène A. Varoudakis. 1994. "Convergence Clubs and Growth: The Role of Financial Development and Education." Paris: OECD Development Centre, January.

Besley, Tim, Stephen Coate, and Glenn Loury. 1990. "The Economics of Rotating Savings and Credit Associations." London: Centre for Economic Policy Research, CEPR Discussion Paper No. 443, August.

Bhagwati, Jagdish N., and Padma Desai. 1970. *India: Planning for Industrialization.* London: Oxford University Press.

Bhagwati, Jagdish N., and T. N. Srinivasan. 1975. *Foreign Trade Regimes and Economic Development: India.* New York: National Bureau of Economic Research, distributed by Columbia University Press.

Bharadwaj, Krishna. 1979. "Towards a Macroeconomic Framework for a Developing Economy: The Indian Case." *Manchester School of Economic and Social Studies,* 47(3, September): 270–302.

Bhatt, Vinayak V. 1978. "Interest Rate, Transactions Costs and Financial Innovations." Washington, D.C.: World Bank, Domestic Finance Study No. 47, January.

————. 1988. "On Financial Innovations and Credit Market Evolution." *World Development,* 16(2, February): 281–292.

Biggs, Tyler S. 1988. "Financing the Emergence of Small and Medium Enterprise in Taiwan: Financial Mobilization and the Flow of Domestic Credit to the Private Sector." Washington, D.C.: U.S. Agency for International Development, Employment and Enterprise Development Division, Employment and Enterprise Policy Analysis Discussion Paper No. 15, August.

————. 1991. "Heterogeneous Firms and Efficient Financial Intermediation in Taiwan." In *Markets in Developing Countries: Parallel, Fragmented, and Black.* Edited by Michael Roemer and Christine Jones. San Francisco: International Center for Economic Growth, 167–197.

Bilson, John F. O. 1984. "The Process of Balance of Payments Adjustment." In *Adjustment, Conditionality, and International Financing.* Edited by Joaquin Muns. Washington, D.C.: International Monetary Fund, 34–57.

Bisat, Amer, R. Barry Johnston, and Venkataraman Sundararajan. 1992. "Issues in Managing and Sequencing Financial Sector Reforms: Lessons from Experiences in Five Developing Countries." Washington, D.C.: International Monetary Fund, WP/92/82, October.

Bisignano, Joseph. 1991. "Banking Competition, Regulation and the Philosophy of Financial Development: A Search for First Principles." London: London School of Economics, Financial Markets Group.

Bitros, George C. 1981. "The Fungibility Factor in Credit and the Question of the Efficacy of Selective Credit Controls." *Oxford Economic Papers,* 33(3, November): 459–477.

Blanchard, Olivier Jean, and Stanley Fischer. 1989. *Lectures on Macroeconomics.* Cambridge, Mass.: MIT Press.

Blejer, Mario I. 1983. "Liberalization and Stabilization Policies in the Southern Cone Countries: An Introduction." *Journal of Interamerican Studies and World Affairs,* 25(4, November): 431–444.

Blejer, Mario I., and José Gil Diaz. 1986. "Domestic and External Factors in the Determination of the Real Interest Rate: The Case of Uruguay." *Economic Development and Cultural Change,* 34(3, April): 589–606.

Blejer, Mario I., and Mohsin S. Khan. 1984. "Government Policy and Private Investment in Developing Countries." *International Monetary Fund Staff Papers,* 31(2, June): 379–403.

Blejer, Mario I., and Silvia Sagari. 1987. "The Structure of the Banking Sector and the Sequence of Financial Liberalization." In *Economic Reform and Stabilization in Latin America.* Edited by Michael Connolly and Claudio González-Vega. New York: Praeger, 93–107.

Blinder, Alan S. 1987. "Credit Rationing and Effective Supply Failures." *Economic Journal,* 97(386, June): 327–352.

Blinder, Alan S., and Joseph E. Stiglitz. 1983. "Money, Credit Constraints, and Economic Activity." *American Economic Review,* 73(2, May): 297–302.

Blomstrom, Magnus, Robert E. Lipsey, and Mario Zejan. 1992. "What Explains Developing Country Growth?" Cambridge, Mass.: National Bureau of Economic Research, NBER Working Paper No. 4132, August.

Blundell-Wignall, Adrian, and Frank Browne. 1991. "Macroeconomic Consequences of Financial Liberalisation: A Summary Report." Paris: Organisation for Economic Co-operation and Development, OECD Department of Economics and Statistics Working Paper No. 98, February.

Blundell-Wignall, Adrian, Frank Browne, and Stefano Cavaglia. 1991. "Financial Liberalisation and Consumption Behaviour." Paris: Organisation for Economic Co-operation and Development, OECD Department of Economics and Statistics Working Paper No. 81, March.

Blundell-Wignall, Adrian, Frank Browne, and Paolo Manasse. 1990. "Monetary Policy in the Wake of Financial Liberalisation." Paris: Organisation for Economic Co-operation and Development, OECD Department of Economics and Statistics Working Paper No. 77, April.

Bolnick, Bruce R. 1987. "Financial Liberalization with Imperfect Markets: Indonesia during the 1970s." *Economic Development and Cultural Change*, 35(3, April): 581–599.

———. 1988. "Evaluating Loan Collection Performance: An Indonesian Example." *World Development*, 16(4, April): 501–510.

Boskin, Michael J. 1978. "Taxation, Saving, and the Rate of Interest." *Journal of Political Economy*, 86(2, ii, April): S3–S27.

Bouman, Frits J. A. 1979. "The ROSCA: Financial Technology of an Informal Savings and Credit Institution in Developing Economies." *Savings and Development*, 3(4): 213–225.

———. 1989. *Small, Short and Unsecured: Informal Rural Finance in India*. New Delhi: Oxford University Press.

———. 1990. "Informal Rural Finance." *Sociologia Ruralis*, 30(2): 155–173.

———. 1994. "ROSCA and ASCRA: Beyond the Financial Landscape." In *Financial Landscapes Reconstructed: The Fine Art of Mapping Development*. Edited by Frits J. A. Bouman and Otto Hospes. Boulder, Colo.: Westview Press, forthcoming.

Bouman, Frits J. A., and K. Harteveld. 1976. "The Djanggi, A Traditional Form of Saving and Credit in West Cameroon." *Sociologia Ruralis*, 16(1–2): 103–119.

Bourne, Compton. 1974. "The Political Economy of Indigenous Commercial Banking in Guyana." *Social and Economic Studies*, 23(1, March): 97–126.

Boyd, John H., and Edward C. Prescott. 1986. "Financial Intermediary-Coalitions." *Journal of Economic Theory*, 38(2, April): 211–232.

Branson, William H., and Stephen Schwartz. 1989. "Financial Markets and Investment Efficiency." Princeton: Princeton University, Department of Economics, September.

Brock, Philip L. 1982. "Monetary Control during an Economic Liberalization: Theory and Evidence from the Chilean Financial Reforms." Stanford: Stanford University, Ph.D. thesis.

———. 1984. "Inflationary Finance in an Open Economy." *Journal of Monetary Economics*, 14(1, July): 37–53.

———. 1989. "Reserve Requirements and the Inflation Tax." *Journal of Money, Credit and Banking*, 21(1, February): 106–121.

Broll, Udo, and Michael B. Gilroy. 1986. "Collateral in Banking Policy and Adverse Selection." *Manchester School of Economic and Social Studies,* 54(4, December): 357–366.

Brown, Gilbert T. 1973. *Korean Pricing Policies and Economic Development in the 1960s.* Baltimore: Johns Hopkins University Press.

Bruno, Michael. 1985. "The Reforms and Macroeconomic Adjustments: Introduction." *World Development,* 13(8, August): 867–869.

Bryant, Ralph C. 1987. *International Financial Intermediation.* Washington, D.C.: Brookings Institution.

Buffie, Edward F. 1984. "Financial Repression, the New Structuralists, and Stabilization Policy in Semi-Industrialized Economies." *Journal of Development Economics,* 14(3, April): 305–322.

———. 1991. "Credit Rationing and Capital Accumulation." *Economica,* 58(231, August): 299–316.

Buiter, Willem H. 1983. "Measurement of the Public Sector Deficit and Its Implications for Policy Evaluation and Design." *International Monetary Fund Staff Papers,* 30(2, June): 306–349.

Burkett, Paul. 1986. "Interest Rate Restrictions and Deposit Opportunities for Small Savers in Developing Countries: An Analytical View." *Journal of Development Studies,* 23(1, October): 77–92.

———. 1987. "Financial 'Repression' and Financial 'Liberalization' in the Third World: A Contribution to the Critique of Neoclassical Development Theory." *Review of Radical Political Economy,* 19(1, Spring): 1–21.

———. 1989. "Group Lending Programs and Rural Finance in Developing Countries." *Savings and Development,* 13(4): 401–417.

Burkett, Paul, and A. K. Dutt. 1991. "Interest Rate Policy, Effective Demand, and Growth in LDCs." *International Review of Applied Economics,* 5(2): 127–153.

Burkett, Paul, and Robert C. Vogel. 1992. "Financial Assets, Inflation Hedges, and Capital Utilization in Developing Countries: An Extension of McKinnon's Complementarity Hypothesis." *Quarterly Journal of Economics,* 107(2, May): 773–784.

Burkner, Hans-Paul. 1980. "Savings Mobilization through Financial Development: A Study of Saving in the Philippines." *Philippine Economic Journal,* 19(3–4): 451–482.

———. 1982. "The Portfolio Behaviour of Individual Investors in Developing Countries: An Analysis of the Philippine Case." *Oxford Bulletin of Economics and Statistics,* 44(2, May): 127–144.

Cagan, Phillip. 1956. "The Monetary Dynamics of Hyperinflation." In *Studies in the Quantity Theory of Money.* Edited by Milton Friedman. Chicago: University of Chicago Press, 25–117.

———. 1979. *Persistent Inflation: Historical and Policy Essays.* New York: Columbia University Press.

Callier, Philippe. 1984. "Growth of Developing Countries and World Interest Rates." *Journal of Macroeconomics,* 6(4, Fall): 465–471.

————. 1990. "Informal Finance: The Rotating Saving and Credit Association—An Interpretation." *Kyklos*, 43(2): 273–276.

————, ed. 1991. *Financial Systems and Development in Africa.* Washington, D.C.: World Bank, EDI Seminar Series.

Calvo, Guillermo A., and Fabrizio Coricelli. 1992. "Stagflationary Effects of Stabilization Programs in Reforming Socialist Countries: Enterprise-Side vs. Household-Side Factors." *World Bank Economic Review,* 6(1, January): 71–90.

Cameron, Rondo, ed. 1972. *Banking and Economic Development: Some Lessons of History.* New York: Oxford University Press.

Cameron, Rondo, Olga Crisp, Hugh T. Patrick, and Richard Tilly. 1967. *Banking in the Early Stages of Industrialization: A Study in Comparative Economic History.* New York: Oxford University Press.

Caprio, Gerard, Jr., Izak Atiyas, James A. Hanson, and Associates. 1994. *Financial Reform: Theory and Experience.* New York: Cambridge University Press, forthcoming.

Caprio, Gerard, Jr., and Lawrence H. Summers. 1993. "Finance and Its Reform: Beyond Laissez-Faire." Washington, D.C.: World Bank, February.

Cardoso, Eliana A. 1992. "Deficit Finance and Monetary Dynamics in Brazil and Mexico." *Journal of Development Economics,* 37(1–2, November): 173–197.

Cargill, Thomas F. 1992. "A Comparative Study of Financial Liberalization Policies: Japan and Korea." Reno: University of Nevada, Department of Economics, July.

Carmichael, Jeffrey. 1982. "Money and Growth: Some Old Theorems from a New Perspective." *Economic Record,* 58(163, December): 386–394.

Carter, Michael R. 1988. "Equilibrium Credit Rationing of Small Farm Agriculture." *Journal of Development Economics,* 28(1, February): 83–103.

Cavallo, Domingo F. 1977. "Stagflationary Effects of Monetarist Stabilization Policies." Cambridge, Mass.: Harvard University, Ph.D. thesis.

Celasun, Merih, and Aysit Tansel. 1993. "Distributional Effects and Saving-Investment Behaviour in a Liberalizing Economy: The Case of Turkey." *METU Studies in Development,* 20(3): 269–298.

Chah, Eun Young, Valerie A. Ramey, and Ross M. Starr. 1991. "Liquidity Constraints and Intertemporal Consumer Optimization: Theory and Evidence from Durable Goods." Cambridge, Mass.: National Bureau of Economic Research, Working Paper No. 3907, November.

Chamley, Christophe. 1985. "On a Simple Rule for the Optimal Inflation Rate in Second Best Taxation." *Journal of Public Economics,* 26(1, February): 35–50.

————. 1991. "Taxation of Financial Assets in Developing Countries." *World Bank Economic Review,* 5(3, September): 513–533.

Chamley, Christophe, and Patrick Honohan. 1990. "Taxation of Financial Intermediation: Measurement Principles and Application to Five African Countries." Washington, D.C.: World Bank, Country Economics Department, PPR Working Paper WPS 421, May.

————. 1993. "Financial Repression and Banking Intermediation." *Savings and Development,* 17(3): 301–308.

Chamley, Christophe, and Qaizar Hussain. 1988. "The Effects of Financial Liberalization in Thailand, Indonesia, and the Philippines." Washington, D.C.: World Bank, WPS 125, October.

Chandavarkar, Anand G. 1971. "Some Aspects of Interest Rate Policies in Less Developed Economies: The Experience of Selected Asian Countries." *International Monetary Fund Staff Papers*, 18(1, March): 48–112.

————. 1985. "The Non-Institutional Financial Sector in Developing Countries: Macroeconomic Implications for Savings Policies." *Savings and Development*, 9(2): 129–140.

Chang, Doug, and Woo S. Jung. 1984. "Unorganized Money Markets in LDCs: The McKinnon–Shaw Hypothesis versus the van Wijnbergen Hypothesis." Nashville: Vanderbilt University, Department of Economics, Working Paper 84–W21, June.

Charemza, Wojciech W., and Subrata Ghatak. 1992. "Financial Liberalization: The Case of Sri Lanka." Leicester: University of Leicester, Department of Economics, January.

Cheng, Hang-Sheng. 1980. "Financial Deepening in Pacific Basin Countries." *Federal Reserve Bank of San Francisco Economic Review*, (Summer): 43–56.

————, ed. 1986a. *Financial Policy and Reform in Pacific Basin Countries.* Lexington, Mass.: D. C. Heath and Co., Lexington Books.

————. 1986b. "International Financial Crises, Past and Present." *Federal Reserve Bank of San Francisco Economic Review*, (4, Fall): 13–23.

————, ed. 1988. *Challenges to Monetary Policy in Pacific Basin Countries.* Boston: Kluwer Academic Publishers.

Cheng, Tun-jen. 1993. "Guarding the Commanding Heights: The State as Banker in Taiwan." In *The Politics of Finance in Developing Countries.* Edited by Stephan Haggard, Chung H. Lee, and Sylvia Maxfield. Ithaca: Cornell University Press, 55–92.

Cho, Yoon Je. 1984. "On the Liberalization of the Financial System and Efficiency of Capital Accumulation under Uncertainty." Stanford: Stanford University, Ph.D. thesis.

————. 1986a. "The Effects of Financial Liberalization on the Development of the Financial Market and the Allocation of Credit to Corporate Sectors: The Korean Case." Washington, D.C.: World Bank, March.

————. 1986b. "Inefficiencies from Financial Liberalization in the Absence of Well-Functioning Equity Markets." *Journal of Money, Credit and Banking*, 18(2, May): 191–199.

————. 1988. "The Effect of Financial Liberalization on the Efficiency of Credit Allocation: Some Evidence from Korea." *Journal of Development Economics*, 29(1, July): 101–110.

————. 1989. "Finance and Development: The Korean Approach." *Oxford Review of Economic Policy*, 5(4, Winter): 88–102.

————. 1990. "McKinnon-Shaw versus the Neostructuralists on Financial Liberalization: A Conceptual Note." *World Development*, 18(3, March): 477–480.

Cho, Yoon Je, and Thomas Hellmann. 1993. "Government Intervention in Credit Markets in Japan and Korea: An Alternative Interpretation from the New Institutional Economics Perspective." Washington, D.C.: World Bank, July.

Cho, Yoon Je, and Deena Khatkhate. 1989. "Lessons of Financial Liberalization in Asia: A Comparative Study." Washington, D.C.: World Bank, Discussion Paper No. 50, April.

Choi, Byung-Sun. 1991. "Government, Financial Systems, and Economic Development: The Case of Korea." Seoul: Seoul National University, Graduate School of Public Administration, October.

———. 1993. "Financial Policy and Big Business in Korea: The Perils of Financial Regulation." In *The Politics of Finance in Developing Countries.* Edited by Stephan Haggard, Chung H. Lee, and Sylvia Maxfield. Ithaca: Cornell University Press, 23–54.

Chou, Tein-Chen. 1991. "Government, Financial Systems and Economic Development in Taiwan." Taipei: National Chung-Hsing University, Institute of Economics, October.

Christensen, M., and M. Paldam. 1990. "Some Further International Evidence on Output-Inflation Tradeoffs: The Lucas Variability Hypothesis Reexamined." *Weltwirtschaftliches Archiv,* 126(2): 222–238.

Christoffersen, Leif E. 1968. "Interest Rates and the Structure of a Commercial Banking System under Inflationary Conditions: A Case Study of Brazil." Washington, D.C.: World Bank, Economics Department Working Paper No. 26, October.

Chung, Bo-Yung. 1988. "The Development and Problems of the Korean Financial System." *International Journal of Development Banking,* 6(2, July): 27–34.

Claassen, Emil-Maria. 1992. *Financial Liberalization and Its Impact on Domestic Stabilization Policies: Singapore and Malaysia.* Singapore: Institute of Southeast Asian Studies.

Cline, William R. 1981. "Real Economic Effects of World Inflation and Recession." In *World Inflation and the Developing Countries.* By William R. Cline and Associates. Washington, D.C.: Brookings Institution, 10–51.

Coase, Ronald H. 1960. "The Problem of Social Cost." *Journal of Law and Economics,* 3(1, October): 1–44.

Cole, David C. 1988. "Financial Development in Asia." *Asian-Pacific Economic Literature,* 2(2, September): 26–47.

Cole, David C., Supote Chunanuntathum, and Chesada Loohawenchit. 1986. "Modelling of Financial Markets in Thailand." In *Pacific Growth and Financial Interdependence.* Edited by Augustine H. H. Tan and Basant Kapur. Sydney: Allen and Unwin, 144–162.

Cole, David C., and Yung Chul Park. 1983. *Financial Development in Korea 1945–1978.* Cambridge, Mass.: Harvard University, Council on East Asian Studies, distributed by Harvard University Press.

Cole, David C., and Hugh T. Patrick. 1986. "Financial Development in the Pacific Basin Market Economies." In *Pacific Growth and Financial Interdependence.* Edited by Augustine H. H. Tan and Basant Kapur. Sydney: Allen and Unwin, 39–67.

Cole, David C., and Betty F. Slade. 1992. "Financial Development in Indonesia." In *The Oil Boom and After: Indonesian Economic Policy and Performance in the Soeharto Era*. Edited by Anne Booth. Singapore: Oxford University Press, 77–101.

———. 1993. "How Bank Lending Practices Influence Resource Allocation and Monetary Policy in Indonesia." Harvard: Harvard University, Harvard Institute for International Development, Development Discussion Paper No. 444, April.

Collier, Paul, and Jan Willem Gunning. 1991. "Money Creation and Financial Liberalization in a Socialist Banking System: Tanzania 1983–88." *World Development*, 19(5, May): 533–538.

Connolly, Michael B., and Dean Taylor. 1979. "Exchange Rate Changes and Neutralization: A Test of the Monetary Approach Applied to Developed and Developing Countries." *Economica*, 46(183, August): 281–294.

Cooper, Richard N., and Jeffrey D. Sachs. 1985. "Borrowing Abroad: The Debtor's Perspective." In *International Debt and the Developing Countries*. Edited by Gordon W. Smith and John T. Cuddington. Washington, D.C.: World Bank, March: 21–60.

Corbo, Vittorio. 1985. "Reforms and Macroeconomic Adjustments in Chile during 1974–84." *World Development*, 13(8, August): 893–916.

Corbo, Vittorio, and Jaime de Melo. 1985a. "Overview and Summary." *World Development*, 13(8, August): 863–866.

———, eds. 1985b. "Scrambling for Survival: How Firms Adjusted to the Recent Reforms in Argentina, Chile, and Uruguay." Washington, D.C.: World Bank, Staff Working Paper No. 764, November.

Corsepius, Uwe, and Bernhard Fischer. 1988. "Domestic Resource Mobilization in Thailand: A Success Case for Financial Deepening?" *Singapore Economic Review*, 33(2, October): 1–20.

Courakis, Anthony S. 1981a. "Banking Policy and Commercial Bank Behavior in Greece." In *Competition and Regulation in Financial Markets*. Edited by Albert Verheirstraeten. London: Macmillan, 220–263.

———. 1981b. "Financial Structure and Policy in Greece: Retrospect and Prospect." *Greek Economic Review*, 3(3, December): 205–244.

———. 1984. "Constraints on Bank Choices and Financial Repression in Less Developed Countries." *Oxford Bulletin of Economics and Statistics*, 46(4, November): 341–370.

———. 1986. "In What Sense Do Compulsory Ratios Reduce the Volume of Deposits?" In *The Operation and Regulation of Financial Markets*. Edited by Charles A. E. Goodhart, David Currie, and David T. Llewellyn. London: Macmillan, 150–186.

Crichton, Noel, and Charles de Silva. 1989. "Financial Development and Economic Growth: Trinidad and Tobago, 1973–1987." *Social and Economic Studies*, 38(4, December): 133–164.

Cuddington, John T. 1986. "Capital Flight: Issues, Estimates, and Explanations." *Princeton Studies in International Finance*, (58), December.

Cuddington, John T., and Gordon W. Smith. 1985. "International Borrowing and Lending: What Have We Learned from Theory and Experience?" In *International Debt and the Developing Countries.* Edited by Gordon W. Smith and John T. Cuddington. Washington, D.C.: World Bank, March: 3–17.

Currie, David, and Michael Anyadike-Danes. 1980. "Interest Rates, Inflation and Growth in Financially Repressed Economies." London: Queen Mary College, Department of Economics, May.

Dailami, Mansoor, and Michael Atkin. 1990. "Stock Markets in Developing Countries: Key Issues and a Research Agenda." Washington, D.C.: World Bank, Country Economics Department, Policy, Research and External Affairs Working Paper WPS 515, October.

Dailami, Mansoor, and Marcelo Giugale. 1991. "Reflections on Credit Policy in Developing Countries: Its Effect on Private Investment." Washington, D.C.: World Bank, PRE Working Paper WPS 654, April.

Darby, Michael R. 1975. "The Financial and Tax Effects of Monetary Policy on Interest Rates." *Economic Inquiry,* 13(2, June): 266–276.

————. 1983. "Sterilization and Monetary Control: Concepts, Issues, and a Reduced-Form Test." In *The International Transmission of Inflation.* By Michael R. Darby, James R. Lothian, et al. Chicago: University of Chicago Press for the National Bureau of Economic Research, 291–313.

Darity, William, and Bobbie L. Horn. 1986. "Some Repressed Difficulties with the Case for Financial Reform in LDCs." Chapel Hill: Department of Economics, University of North Carolina. Southern Economic Association Meeting in New Orleans, 23–25 November.

Dasri, Tumnong. 1990. *The Reserve Requirement as a Monetary Instrument in the SEACEN Countries.* Kuala Lumpur: South East Asian Central Banks Research and Training Centre.

Datey, C. D. 1978. "The Financial Cost of Agricultural Credit: A Case Study of Indian Experience." Washington, D.C.: World Bank, Staff Working Paper No. 296, October.

De Grauwe, Paul. 1987. "Financial Deregulation in Developing Countries." *Tijdschrift voor Economie en Management,* 32(4): 381–401.

De Gregorio, José. 1992a. "The Effects of Inflation on Economic Growth: Lessons from Latin America." *European Economic Review,* 36(2–3, April): 417–425.

————. 1992b. "Liquidity Constraints, Human Capital Accumulation and Growth." Washington, D.C.: International Monetary Fund, August.

————. 1992c. "Savings, Growth and Capital Markets Imperfections: The Case of Borrowing Constraints." Washington, D.C.: International Monetary Fund, December.

————. 1993. "Inflation, Taxation, and Long-Run Growth." *Journal of Monetary Economics,* 31(3, June): 271–298.

De Gregorio, José, and Pablo E. Guidotti. 1993. "Financial Development and Economic Growth." Washington D.C.: International Monetary Fund, July.

De Juan, Aristóbulo. 1991a. "Does Bank Insolvency Matter? And What to Do About It?" Washington, D.C.: World Bank, EDI Working Paper 340/053.

De Kock, M. H. 1974. *Central Banking*. New York: St. Martin's Press.

De la Fuente, Angel, and José Maria Marin. 1993. "Innovation, 'Bank' Monitoring and Endogenous Financial Development." Barcelona: Universidad Autónoma de Barcelona, Instituto de Análisis Económico, September.

De Long, J. Bradford, and Lawrence H. Summers. 1991. "Equipment Investment and Economic Growth." *Quarterly Journal of Economics*, 56(2, May): 445–502.

De Melo, Jaime, Ricardo Pascale, and James R. Tybout. 1985. "Uruguay 1973–81: The Interplay of Real and Financial Shocks." Washington, D.C.: World Bank, Staff Working Paper No. 696, December.

De Melo, Jaime, and James R. Tybout. 1986. "The Effects of Financial Liberalization on Savings and Investment in Uruguay." *Economic Development and Cultural Change*, 34(3, April): 561–587.

De Rezende Rocha, Roberto. 1985. "Costs of Intermediation in Developing Countries: A Preliminary Investigation." Washington, D.C.: World Bank, October.

Deaton, Angus S. 1990. "Saving in Developing Countries: Theory and Review." In *Proceedings of the World Bank Annual Conference on Development Economics 1989*. Edited by Stanley Fischer and Dennis de Tray. Washington, D.C.: World Bank, 61–96.

———. 1991. "Saving and Liquidity Constraints." *Econometrica*, 59(5, September): 1221–1248.

———. 1992. "Household Saving in LDCs: Credit Markets, Insurance and Welfare." *Scandinavian Journal of Economics*, 94(2): 253–273.

Debreu, Gerard. 1959. *Theory of Value: An Axiomatic Analysis of Economic Equilibrium*. New York: John Wiley.

Demetriades, Panicos O., and Michael P. Devereux. 1992. "Investment and 'Financial Repression': Theory and Evidence from 63 LDCs." Keele: University of Keele, Department of Economics, Working Paper 92–16, December.

Demetriades, Panicos O., and Khaled Hussein. 1993. "Financial Development and Economic Growth: Cointegration and Causality Tests for 12 Countries." Keele: Keele University, Department of Economics Working Paper Series No. 93/15, November.

Diamond, Douglas W. 1984. "Financial Intermediation and Delegated Monitoring." *Review of Economic Studies*, 51(3, July): 393–414.

Diamond, Douglas W., and Phillip H. Dybvig. 1983. "Bank Runs, Deposit Insurance, and Liquidity." *Journal of Political Economy*, 91(3, June): 401–419.

Diamond, Peter A., and James Mirrlees. 1971a. "Optimal Taxation and Public Production. I: Production Efficiency." *American Economic Review*, 61(1, March): 8–27.

———. 1971b. "Optimal Taxation and Public Production. II: Tax Rules." *American Economic Review*, 61(2, June): 261–278.

Diaz-Alejandro, Carlos. 1985. "Good-Bye Financial Repression, Hello Financial Crash." *Journal of Development Economics*, 19(1–2, September–October): 1–24.

Dimitrijevic, Dimitri, and George Macesich. 1973. *Money and Finance in Contemporary Yugoslavia*. New York: Praeger.

Dollar, David. 1992. "Outward-Oriented Developing Economies Really Do Grow More Rapidly: Evidence from 95 LDCs, 1976–1985." *Economic Development and Cultural Change,* 40(3, April): 523–544.

Doner, Richard, and Daniel Unger. 1993. "The Politics of Finance in Thai Economic Development." In *The Politics of Finance in Developing Countries.* Edited by Stephan Haggard, Chung H. Lee, and Sylvia Maxfield. Ithaca: Cornell University Press, 93–122.

Dooley, Michael P. 1986. "Country-Specific Risk Premiums, Capital Flight and Net Investment Income Payments in Selected Developing Countries." Washington, D.C.: International Monetary Fund, DM/86/17, March.

———. 1988. "Capital Flight: A Response to Differences in Financial Risks." *International Monetary Fund Staff Papers,* 35(3, September): 422–436.

———. 1990. "Comment". In *Taxation in the Global Economy.* Edited by Assaf Razin and Joel Slemrod. Chicago: University of Chicago Press for the National Bureau of Economic Research, 74–78.

Dornbusch, Rudiger. 1985. "Multiple Exchange Rates for Commercial Transactions." Washington, D.C.: World Bank, CPD Discussion Paper No. 1985–23, March.

Dornbusch, Rudiger, and Yung Chul Park. 1987. "Korean Growth Policy." *Brookings Papers on Economic Activity,* (2): 389–444.

Dornbusch, Rudiger, and Alejandro Reynoso. 1989. "Financial Factors in Economic Development." *American Economic Review,* 79(2, May): 204–209.

Dowd, Kevin. 1989. *The State and the Monetary System.* Hemel Hempstead: Philip Allan.

Drake, Peter J. 1986. "The Development of Equity and Bond Markets in the Pacific Region." In *Pacific Growth and Financial Interdependence.* Edited by Augustine H. H. Tan and Basant Kapur. Sydney: Allen and Unwin, 97–124.

Drazen, Allan. 1981a. "The Permanent Effects of Inflation on Development and the Choice of Production Technique." In *Development in an Inflationary World.* Edited by M. June Flanders and Assaf Razin. New York: Academic Press, 211–232.

———. 1981b. "Inflation and Capital Accumulation under a Finite Horizon." *Journal of Monetary Economics,* 8(2, September): 247–260.

Dutton, Dean S. 1971. "A Model of Self-Generating Inflation: The Argentine Case." *Journal of Money, Credit and Banking,* 3(2, May): 245–262.

Easterly, William R. 1993. "How Much Do Distortions Affect Growth?" *Journal of Monetary Economics,* 32(2, November): 187–212.

Eaton, Jonathan, and Mark Gersovitz. 1981. "Debt with Potential Repudiation: Theoretical and Empirical Analysis." *Review of Economic Studies,* 48(2, April): 289–309.

Economist, The. 1982a. "Taiwan: A Survey." *The Economist,* 31 July.

———. 1982b. "Now for the Next Miracle . . . Finance in the Far East: A Survey." *The Economist,* 13 November.

Economist Intelligence Unit. 1982. *QER: Taiwan, Annual Supplement.* London: Economist Intelligence Unit.

Edwards, Sebastián. 1985. "Are Devaluations Contractionary?" Cambridge, Mass.: National Bureau of Economic Research, Working Paper No. 1676, August.

————. 1986. "The Pricing of Bonds and Bank Loans in International Markets: An Empirical Analysis of Developing Countries' Foreign Borrowing." *European Economic Review,* 30(3, June): 565–589.

————. 1988. "Financial Deregulation and Segmented Capital Markets: The Case of Korea." *World Development,* 16(1, January): 185–194.

Edwards, Sebastián, and Mohsin S. Khan. 1985. "Interest Rate Determination in Developing Countries: A Conceptual Framework." *International Monetary Fund Staff Papers,* 32(3, September): 377–403.

Effros, Robert C. 1971. "The Problem of Postdated Checks in the Republic of China." *International Monetary Fund Staff Papers,* 18(1, March): 113–135.

Emery, Robert F. 1967. "The Successful Development of the Philippine Treasury Bill Market." *Central Bank of the Philippines News Digest,* 19(24, 13 June): 2–7.

Errunza, Vihang R., and Joseph P. Ghalbouni. 1986. "Interest Rates and International Debt Crisis." *Banca Nazionale del Lavoro Quarterly Review,* (157, June): 225–245.

Evans, J. Lynne, and George K. Yarrow. 1981. "Some Implications of Alternative Expectations Hypotheses in the Monetary Analysis of Hyperinflations." *Oxford Economic Papers,* 33(1, March): 61–80.

Faini, Riccardo, and Jaime de Melo. 1990. "Adjustment, Investment and the Real Exchange Rate in Developing Countries." *Economic Policy: A European Forum,* (11, October): 491–519.

Faini, Riccardo, Giampaolo Galli, and Curzio Giannini. 1993. "Finance and Development: The Case of Southern Italy." In *Finance and Development: Issues and Experience.* Edited by Alberto Giovannini. Cambridge: Cambridge University Press, 158–214.

Fama, Eugene. 1985. "What's Different about Banks?" *Journal of Monetary Economics,* 15(1, January): 29–39.

Farhadian, Ziba, and Robert M. Dunn. 1986. "Fiscal Policy and Financial Deepening in a Monetarist Model of the Balance of Payments." *Kyklos,* 39(1): 66–83.

Faruqee, Hamid. 1991. "Dynamic Capital Mobility in Pacific Basin Developing Countries: Estimation and Policy Implications." Washington, D.C.: International Monetary Fund, WP/91/115, November.

Faruqi, Shakil, ed. 1993. *Financial Sector Reforms in Asian and Latin American Countries: Lessons of Comparative Experience.* Washington, D.C.: World Bank, EDI Seminar Series.

Fazzari, Steven M., and Michael J. Athey. 1987. "Asymmetric Information, Financing Constraints, and Investment." *Review of Economics and Statistics,* 69(3, August): 481–487.

Fazzari, Steven M., R. Glenn Hubbard, and Bruce C. Petersen. 1988. "Financing Constraints and Corporate Investment." *Brookings Papers on Economic Activity,* (1, August): 141–206.

Feder, Gershon. 1982. "On Exports and Economic Growth." *Journal of Development Economics,* 12(1–2, February–April): 59–73.

Feige, Edgar L., and Kenneth J. Singleton. 1981. "Multinational Inflation under Fixed Exchange Rates: Some Empirical Evidence from Latent Variable Models." *Review of Economics and Statistics,* 63(1, February): 11–19.

Feldman, David H., and Ira N. Gang. 1990. "Financial Development and the Price of Services." *Economic Development and Cultural Change,* 38(2, January): 341–352.

Fernandez, Roque B. 1985. "The Expectations Management Approach to Stabilization in Argentina during 1976–82." *World Development,* 13(8, August): 871–892.

Financial Times. 1992. "Financial Times Survey: Korean Financial Markets." *Financial Times,* 18 November.

————. 1993. *Banking in the Far East, 1993: Structures and Sources of Finance.* London: Financial Times.

Fischer, Bernhard. 1981. "Interest Rate Ceilings, Inflation and Economic Growth in Developing Countries." *Economics,* 23: 75–93.

————. 1988. "Domestic Capital Formation, Financial Intermediation and Economic Development in Peru." *Savings and Development,* 12(4): 321–342.

————. 1989. "Savings Mobilization in Developing Countries: Bottlenecks and Reform Proposals." *Savings and Development,* 13(2): 117–131.

————. 1992. "Financial Deregulation in an Open Developing Economy: Lessons from the Indonesian Experience." Hamburg: HWWA–Institut fur Wirtschaftsforschung, HWWA Report No. 110.

————. 1993. "Success and Pitfalls with Financial Reforms in Developing Countries." *Savings and Development,* 17(2): 111–134.

Fischer, Bernhard, and Helmut Reisen. 1992. *Towards Capital Account Convertibility.* Paris: OECD Development Centre, Policy Brief No. 4.

Fischer, Stanley. 1979a. "Anticipations and the Nonneutrality of Money." *Journal of Political Economy,* 87(2, April): 225–252.

————. 1979b. "Capital Accumulation on the Transition Path in a Monetary Optimizing Model." *Econometrica,* 47(6, November): 1433–1439.

————. 1981. "Towards an Understanding of the Costs of Inflation: II." *Carnegie-Rochester Conference Series on Public Policy,* (15, Autumn): 5–41.

————. 1982. "Seigniorage and the Case for a National Money." *Journal of Political Economy,* 90(2, April): 295–313.

————. 1989. "The Economics of the Government Budget Constraint." Washington, D.C.: World Bank, PPR Working Paper WPS 224, May.

Fisher, Irving. 1930. *The Theory of Interest as Determined by Impatience to Spend Income and Opportunity to Invest It.* New York: Macmillan.

Fitzgerald, Bruce, and Terry Monson. 1989. "Preferential Credit and Insurance as Means to Promote Exports." *World Bank Research Observer,* 4(1, January): 89–114.

FitzGerald, E. V. K. 1993. *The Macroeconomics of Development Finance.* Basingstoke: Macmillan.

Frenkel, Jacob A., and Assaf Razin. 1986. "The International Transmission and Effects of Fiscal Policies." *American Economic Review,* 76(2, May): 330–335.

Friedman, Milton. 1969. "The Optimum Quantity of Money." In *The Optimum Quantity of Money and Other Essays*. By Milton Friedman. Chicago: Aldine, 1–50.

————. 1971. "Government Revenue from Inflation." *Journal of Political Economy*, 79(4, July–August): 846–856.

Friedman, Milton, and Anna J. Schwartz. 1963. *A Monetary History of the United States, 1867–1960*. Princeton: Princeton University Press for the National Bureau of Economic Research.

————. 1982. *Monetary Trends in the United States and the United Kingdom: Their Relation to Income, Prices, and Interest Rates, 1867–1975*. Chicago: University of Chicago Press for the National Bureau of Economic Research.

Fries, Steven M., and Timothy D. Lane. 1993. "Transforming the Financial Structure in Emerging Market Economies." Washington, D.C.: International Monetary Fund, IMF-World Bank Conference on Building Sound Finance in Emerging Market Economies, June.

Froyen, Richard T. 1974. "A Test of the Endogeneity of Monetary Policy." *Journal of Econometrics*, 2(2, July): 175–188.

Fry, Maxwell J. 1971. "Turkey's First Five-Year Development Plan: An Assessment." *Economic Journal*, 81(322, June): 306–326.

————. 1972. *Finance and Development Planning in Turkey*. Leiden: Brill.

————. 1973. "Manipulating Demand for Money." In *Essays in Modern Economics*. Edited by Michael Parkin. London: Longman, 371–385.

————. 1974. *The Afghan Economy: Money, Finance and the Critical Constraints to Economic Development*. Leiden: Brill.

————. 1978. "Money and Capital or Financial Deepening in Economic Development?" *Journal of Money, Credit and Banking*, 10(4, November): 464–475.

————. 1979a. "The Cost of Financial Repression in Turkey." *Savings and Development*, 3(2): 127–135.

————. 1979b. "Monetary Control When Demand for Cash Is Unpredictable: A Proposal for Stabilizing the Money Multiplier in Portugal." *Economic Journal*, 89(355, September): 636–641.

————. 1980a. "Saving, Investment, Growth and the Cost of Financial Repression." *World Development*, 8(4, April): 317–327.

————. 1980b. "Money, Interest, Inflation and Growth in Turkey." *Journal of Monetary Economics*, 6(4, October): 535–545.

————. 1981a. "Inflation and Economic Growth in Pacific Basin Developing Economies." *Federal Reserve Bank of San Francisco Economic Review*, (Fall): 8–18.

————. 1981b. "Government Revenue from Monopoly Supply of Currency and Deposits." *Journal of Monetary Economics*, 8(2, September): 261–270.

————. 1981c. "Interest Rates in Asia: An Examination of Interest Rate Policies in Burma, India, Indonesia, Korea, Malaysia, Nepal, Pakistan, the Philippines, Singapore, Sri Lanka, Taiwan and Thailand." Washington, D.C.: International Monetary Fund, Asian Department, June.

————. 1981d. "Financial Intermediation in Small Island Developing Economies." London: Commonwealth Secretariat, Commonwealth Economic Papers No. 16.

————. 1982a. "Financial Sectors in Some Small Island Developing Economies." In *Problems and Policies in Small Economies*. Edited by Bimal Jalan. London: Croom Helm, 185–207.

————. 1982b. "Models of Financially Repressed Developing Economies." *World Development*, 10(9, September): 731–750.

————. 1982c. "Analysing Disequilibrium Interest-Rate Systems in Developing Countries." *World Development*, 10(12, December): 1049–1057.

————. 1984. "Saving, Financial Intermediation and Economic Growth in Asia." *Asian Development Review*, 2(1): 82–91.

————. 1985. "Financial Structure, Monetary Policy, and Economic Growth in Hong Kong, Singapore, Taiwan, and South Korea, 1960–1983." In *Export-Oriented Development Strategies: The Success of Five Newly Industrializing Countries*. Edited by Vittorio Corbo, Anne O. Krueger, and Fernando Ossa. Boulder, Colo.: Westview Press, 275–324.

————. 1986a. "Terms-of-Trade Dynamics in Asia: An Analysis of National Saving and Domestic Investment Responses to Terms-of-Trade Changes in 14 Asian LDCs." *Journal of International Money and Finance*, 5(1, March): 57–73.

————. 1986b. "Financial Structure, Financial Regulation, and Financial Reform in the Philippines and Thailand, 1960–1984." In *Financial Policy and Reform in Pacific Basin Countries*. Edited by Hang-Sheng Cheng. Lexington, Mass.: D. C. Heath and Co., Lexington Books, 161–184.

————. 1988. "Money Supply Responses to Exogenous Shocks in Turkey." In *Liberalization and the Turkish Economy*. Edited by Tevfik F. Nas and Mehmet Odekon. Westport, Conn.: Greenwood Press, 85–114.

————. 1989a. "Foreign Debt Instability: An Analysis of National Saving and Domestic Investment Responses to Foreign Debt Accumulation in 28 Developing Countries." *Journal of International Money and Finance*, 8(3, September): 315–344.

————. 1989b. "Financial Development: Theories and Recent Experience." *Oxford Review of Economic Policy*, 5(4, Winter): 13–28.

————. 1990a. "The Rate of Return to Taiwan's Capital Stock, 1961–1987." *Hong Kong Economic Papers*, (20): 17–30.

————. 1990b. "Sri Lanka's Financial Liberalization and Trade Reforms: *Plus Ça Change?*" *International Economic Journal*, 4(1, Spring): 71–90.

————. 1990c. *Current Macroeconomic Policy Issues in Taiwan*. Taipei: Tamkang University Press.

————. 1991a. "Domestic Resource Mobilization in Developing Asia: Four Policy Issues." *Asian Development Review*, 9(1): 15–39.

————. 1991b. "Mobilizing External Resources in Asia: Structural Adjustment and Policy Reforms." *Asian Development Review*, 9(2): 14–39.

————. 1991c. "Foreign Debt Reduction through Improved Domestic Resource Mobilization and Allocation." *Revue d'économie politique*, 101(4, juillet-août): 623–637.

Fry, Maxwell J. 1992a. "Can a Central Bank Go Bust?" *Manchester School of Economic and Social Studies,* 60(Supplement, June): 85–98.

———. 1992b. "Central Banking in Developing Countries." In *The New Palgrave Dictionary of Money and Finance,* Vol. 1. Edited by Peter Newman, Murray Milgate, and John Eatwell. London: Macmillan, 325–327.

———. 1993a. "Monetary Policy Reaction to Foreign Debt Accumulation in Developing Countries." *Manchester School of Economic and Social Studies,* 61(Supplement, June): 60–75.

———. 1993b. "The Fiscal Abuse of Central Banks." Washington, D.C.: International Monetary Fund, WP/93/58, July.

———. 1993c. "Foreign Debt Accumulation: Financial and Fiscal Effects and Monetary Policy Reactions in Developing Countries." *Journal of International Money and Finance,* 12(4, August): 347–367.

———. 1993d. "Inflation and Monetary Policy in Pacific Basin Developing Economies." In *Price Stabilization in the 1990s: Domestic and International Policy Requirements.* Edited by Kumiharu Shigehara. London: Macmillan, 137–164.

———. 1993e. *Foreign Direct Investment in Southeast Asia: Differential Impacts.* Singapore: Institute of Southeast Asian Studies.

———. 1994. "Malaysia's Inverse Saving-Investment Correlation: The Role of Public and Foreign Direct Investment." In *The Economics of International Investment.* Edited by Venkataraman N. Balasubramanyam and David Sapsford. Cheltenham: Edward Elgar, 191–202.

Fry, Maxwell J., and Miriam R. Farhi. 1979. *Money and Banking in Turkey.* Istanbul: Bogaziçi University Press.

Fry, Maxwell J., and David M. Lilien. 1986. "Monetary Policy Responses to Exogenous Shocks." *American Economic Review,* 76(2, May): 79–83.

Fry, Maxwell J., David M. Lilien, and Wilima Wadhwa. 1988. "Monetary Policy in Pacific Basin Developing Countries." In *Monetary Policy in Pacific Basin Countries.* Edited by Hang-Sheng Cheng. Boston: Kluwer Academic Publishers, 153–170.

Fry, Maxwell J., and Andrew Mason. 1982. "The Variable Rate-of-Growth Effect in the Life-Cycle Saving Model: Children, Capital Inflows, Interest and Growth in a New Specification of the Life-Cycle Model Applied to Seven Asian Developing Countries." *Economic Inquiry,* 20(3, July): 426–442.

Fry, Maxwell J., and Raburn M. Williams. 1984. *American Money and Banking.* New York: John Wiley and Sons.

Galbis, Vicente. 1977. "Financial Intermediation and Economic Growth in Less-Developed Countries: A Theoretical Approach." *Journal of Development Studies,* 13(2, January): 58–72.

———. 1979. "Inflation and Interest Rate Policies in Latin America, 1967–76." *International Monetary Fund Staff Papers,* 26(2, June): 334–366.

———. 1981. "Interest Rate Management: The Latin American Experience." *Savings and Development,* 5(1): 5–44.

———. 1982. "Analytical Aspects of Interest Rate Policies in Less-Developed Countries." *Savings and Development,* 6(2): 111–165.

————. 1986. "Financial Sector Liberalization under Oligopolistic Conditions and a Bank Holding Company Structure." *Savings and Development,* 10(2): 117–141.

————. 1993. "High Real Interest Rates Under Financial Liberalization: Is There a Problem?" Washington, D.C.: International Monetary Fund, WP/93/7, January.

Galvez, Julio, and James Tybout. 1985. "How the Financial Statements of Chilean Firms Reflected Stabilization and Reform Attempts during 1977–81." Washington, D.C.: World Bank, January.

Garcés Larrain, Mauricio. 1986. "Treatment of Banks in Difficulties: The Case of Chile." Washington, D.C.: International Monetary Fund, Central Banking Department.

Garvy, George. 1968. *Money, Banking, and Credit in Eastern Europe.* New York: Federal Reserve Bank of New York.

Gelb, Alan H. 1989. "Financial Policies, Growth, and Efficiency." Washington, D.C.: World Bank, Country Economics Department, PPR Working Paper WPS 202, June.

Germidis, Dimitri, Denis Kessler, and Rachel Meghir. 1991. *Financial Systems and Development: What Role for the Formal and Informal Financial Sectors?* Paris: Organisation for Economic Co-operation and Development.

Gerschenkron, Alexander. 1962. *Economic Backwardness in Historical Perspective: A Book of Essays.* Cambridge, Mass.: Harvard University Press.

————. 1968. *Continuity in History and Other Essays.* Cambridge, Mass.: Harvard University Press.

Gertler, Mark. 1988. "Financial Structure and Aggregate Economic Activity: An Overview." *Journal of Money, Credit and Banking,* 20(3, ii, August): 559–588.

Gertler, Mark, and Andrew Rose. 1994. "Finance, Public Policy and Growth." In *Financial Reform: Theory and Experience.* Edited by Gerard Caprio, Jr., Izak Atiyas, and James Hanson. New York: Cambridge University Press, forthcoming.

Gesell, Silvio. 1911. *Die natürliche Wirtschaftsordnung durch Freiland und Freigeld.* Berlin: Freiland-Freigeldverlag. [*The Natural Economic Order.* Translated from the 6th German ed. by Philip Pye. Berlin: Neo-Verlag, 1929.]

Ghanem, Hafez. 1986. "The Philippines: Issues in the Financial Sector." Washington, D.C.: World Bank, CPD Discussion Paper No. 1986–33, June.

Ghani, Ejaz. 1992. "How Financial Markets Affect Long-Run Growth: A Cross-Country Study." Washington, D.C.: World Bank, Country Operations, PR Working Paper WPS 843, January.

Ghatak, Subrata. 1977. "Rural Credit and the Cost of Borrowing: Inter-State Variations in India." *Journal of Development Studies,* 13(1, January): 102–124.

————. 1981. *Monetary Economics in Developing Countries.* London: Macmillan.

Ghatak, Subrata, and Anthony Gyles. 1991. "Money, Prices and Interest Rate with or without Financial Liberalisation in Sri Lanka, 1950–1987: A Transfer Function Analysis." *Indian Economic Journal,* 39(1, July–September): 9–34.

Ghate, Prabhu B., Arindam Das-Gupta, Mario Lamberte, Nipon Poapongsakorn, Dibyo Prabowo, Atiq Rahman, and T. N. Srinivasan. 1992. *Informal Finance: Some Findings from Asia.* Oxford: Oxford University Press for the Asian Development Bank.

Gill, David. 1979. "Some Thoughts on the Implications of Different Financial Institutional Structures on Securities Market Development." Viña del Mar, Chile: Conference on Las Instituciones Financieras en el Mercado de Capitales en Chile, 29 November–1 December.

————. 1983. "Securities Market Structural Issues and Challenges." Toronto: Annual Meeting of the International Federation of Stock Exchanges, 12–14 September.

————. 1986a. "Furthering Securities Market Development." Paris: Eleventh Annual Conference of the International Association of Securities Commissions and Similar Organizations, 15–18 July.

————. 1986b. "Prospects for the Turkish Equity Market." Istanbul: Conference on Turkey and Europe: An Economic and Political Perspective, 6–7 October.

Giovannini, Alberto. 1983a. "Essays on Exchange Rates and Asset Markets." Cambridge, Mass.: Massachusetts Institute of Technology, Ph.D. thesis.

————. 1983b. "The Interest Elasticity of Savings in Developing Countries: The Existing Evidence." *World Development*, 11(7, July): 601–607.

————. 1985. "Saving and the Real Interest Rate in LDCs." *Journal of Development Economics*, 18(2–3, August): 197–217.

Giovannini, Alberto, and Martha de Melo. 1993. "Government Revenue from Financial Repression." *American Economic Review*, 83(4, September): 953–963.

Girton, Lance, and Don Roper. 1980. "The Theory of Currency Substitution and Monetary Unification." *Économie appliquée*, 33(1): 135–160.

Giugale, Marcelo M. 1989. "Real Quasi-Fiscal Deficit, Real Domestic Debt and Inflation under Alternative Macroeconomic Scenarios: A Quantitative Simulation for Argentina 1989–94." Washington, D.C.: World Bank.

Glezakos, Constantine. 1978. "Inflation and Growth: A Reconsideration of the Evidence from LDCs." *Journal of Developing Areas*, 12(2, January): 171–182.

Glick, Reuven, and Michael M. Hutchison. 1990. "Financial Liberalization in the Pacific Basin: Implications for Real Interest Rate Linkages." *Journal of the Japanese and International Economies*, 4(1, March): 36–48.

Gochoco, Maria S. 1991. "Financial Liberalization and Interest Rate Determination: The Case of the Philippines, 1981–1985." *Journal of Macroeconomics*, 13(2, Spring): 335–350.

Goldsbrough, David, and Iqbal Zaidi. 1989. "Monetary Policy in the Philippines During Periods of Financial Crisis and Changes in Exchange Rate Regime: Targets, Instruments, and the Stability of Money Demand." Washington, D.C.: International Monetary Fund, WP/89/98, December.

Goldsmith, Raymond W. 1969. *Financial Structure and Development.* New Haven: Yale University Press.

————. 1975. "The Financial Structure of Yugoslavia." *Banca Nazionale del Lavoro Quarterly Review*, (112, March): 61–108.

————. 1983. *The Financial Development of India, 1860–1977.* New Haven: Yale University Press.

Goldstein, Morris, Donald J. Mathieson, and Timothy Lane. 1991. "Determinants and Systemic Consequences of International Capital Flows." Washington, D.C.: International Monetary Fund, Occasional Paper No. 77, March.

Gonzáles Arrieta, Gerardo M. 1988. "Interest Rates, Savings, and Growth in LDCs: An Assessment of Recent Empirical Research." *World Development,* 16(5, May): 589–605.

González-Vega, Claudio. 1976. "On the Iron Law of Interest Rate Restrictions: Agricultural Credit Policies in Costa Rica and in Other Less Developed Countries." Stanford: Stanford University, Ph.D. thesis.

———. 1981. "Interest Rate Policies, Agricultural Credit and Income Distribution in Latin America." Washington, D.C.: World Bank, Colloquium on Rural Finance, September.

———. 1984a. "Credit-Rationing Behavior of Agricultural Lenders: The Iron Law of Interest-Rate Restrictions." In *Undermining Rural Development with Cheap Credit.* Edited by Dale W Adams, Douglas H. Graham, and John D. Von Pischke. Boulder, Colo.: Westview Press, 78–95.

———. 1984b. "Cheap Agricultural Credit: Redistribution in Reverse." In *Undermining Rural Development with Cheap Credit.* Edited by Dale W Adams, Douglas H. Graham, and John D. Von Pischke. Boulder, Colo.: Westview Press, 120–132.

Gordon, David L. 1983. "Development Finance Companies, State and Privately Owned: A Review." Washington, D.C.: World Bank, Staff Working Paper No. 578, July.

Greenbaum, Stuart I., and Anjan V. Thakor. 1989. "Bank Reserve Requirements as an Impediment to Signaling." *Economic Inquiry,* 27(1, January): 75–91.

Greene, Joshua. 1989. "Inflation in African Countries: General Issues and Effect on the Financial Sector." Washington, D.C.: International Monetary Fund, WP/89/86, October.

Greene, Joshua, and Delano Villanueva. 1991. "Private Investment in Developing Countries: An Empirical Analysis." *International Monetary Fund Staff Papers,* 38(1, March): 33–58.

Greenwald, Bruce C., and Joseph E. Stiglitz. 1989. "Financial Market Imperfections and Productivity Growth." Cambridge, Mass.: National Bureau of Economic Research, NBER Working Paper 2945, April.

Greenwood, Jeremy, and Boyan Jovanovic. 1990. "Financial Development, Growth, and the Distribution of Income." *Journal of Political Economy,* 98(5, i, October): 1076–1107.

Greenwood, Jeremy, and Bruce D. Smith. 1993. "Financial Markets in Development, and the Development of Financial Markets." Rochester: University of Rochester, March.

Grossman, Gene M., and Elhanan Helpman. 1991. "Quality Ladders in the Theory of Economic Growth." *Review of Economic Studies,* 58(1, January): 43–61.

Grubel, Herbert G. 1977. "A Theory of Multinational Banking." *Banca Nazionale del Lavoro Quarterly Review,* (123, December): 349–363.

Gupta, Kanhaya L. 1984a. *Finance and Economic Growth in Developing Countries.* London: Croom Helm.

Gupta, Kanhaya L. 1984b. "Financial Liberalization and Economic Growth: Some Simulation Results." *Journal of Economic Development,* 9(2, December): 25–43.

———. 1986. "Financial Development and Economic Growth in India and South Korea." *Journal of Economic Development,* 11(2, December): 41–62.

———. 1987. "Aggregate Savings, Financial Intermediation, and Interest Rate." *Review of Economics and Statistics,* 69(2, May): 303–311.

Gurley, John G., and Edward S. Shaw. 1955. "Financial Aspects of Economic Development." *American Economic Review,* 45(4, September): 515–538.

———. 1960. *Money in a Theory of Finance.* Washington, D.C.: Brookings Institution.

Guttentag, Jack M., and Richard Herring. 1982. "The Insolvency of Financial Institutions: Assessment and Regulatory Disposition." In *Crises in the Economic and Financial Structure.* Edited by Paul Wachtel. Lexington, Mass.: D. C. Heath and Co., Lexington Books, 99–126.

Gylfason, Thorvaldur. 1993. "Optimal Saving, Interest Rates, and Endogenous Growth." *Scandinavian Journal of Economics,* 95(4): 517–533.

Haddad, Mona, and Ann Harrison. 1993. "Are There Positive Spillovers from Direct Foreign Investment? Evidence from Panel Data for Morocco." *Journal of Development Economics,* 42(1, October): 51–74.

Haggard, Stephan, and Chung H. Lee. 1993. "The Political Dimension of Finance in Economic Development." In *The Politics of Finance in Developing Countries.* Edited by Stephan Haggard, Chung H. Lee, and Sylvia Maxfield. Ithaca: Cornell University Press, 3–20.

Haggard, Stephan, Chung H. Lee, and Sylvia Maxfield, eds. 1993. *The Politics of Finance in Developing Countries.* Ithaca: Cornell University Press.

Haggard, Stephan, and Sylvia Maxfield. 1993. "Political Explanations of Financial Policy in Developing Countries." In *The Politics of Finance in Developing Countries.* Edited by Stephan Haggard, Chung H. Lee, and Sylvia Maxfield. Ithaca: Cornell University Press, 293–325.

Hahn, Jinsoo. 1994. "What Explains Increases in Korea's Saving Rates?" *International Economic Journal,* 8(1, Spring): 23–38.

Hajivassiliou, Vassilis A. 1987. "The External Debt Repayments Problems of LDCs: An Econometric Model Based on Panel Data." *Journal of Econometrics,* 36(1–2, September–October): 205–230.

Hamilton, James D., and Marjorie A. Flavin. 1986. "On the Limitations of Government Borrowing: A Framework for Empirical Testing." *American Economic Review,* 76(4, September): 808–819.

Hanson, James A. 1974. "Optimal International Borrowing and Lending." *American Economic Review,* 64(4, September): 616–630.

———. 1979. "The Colombian Experience with Financial Repression and Incomplete Liberalization: Stagnation, Growth and Instability 1950–1978." Caracas: First International Conference on the Financial Development of Latin America and the Caribbean, February.

————. 1980. "The Short-Run Relation between Growth and Inflation in Latin America: A Quasi-Rational or Consistent Expectations Approach." *American Economic Review,* 70(5, December): 972–989.

————. 1986. "High Real Interest Rates and Spreads." Washington, D.C.: World Bank, April.

Hanson, James A., and Jaime de Melo. 1983. "The Uruguayan Experience with Liberalization and Stabilization, 1974–1981." *Journal of Interamerican Studies and World Affairs,* 25(4, November): 477–508.

————. 1985. "External Shocks, Financial Reforms, and Stabilization Attempts in Uruguay during 1974–83." *World Development,* 13(8, August): 917–939.

Hanson, James A., and Roberto de Rezende Rocha. 1986. "High Interest Rates, Spreads, and the Costs of Intermediation—Two Studies." Washington, D. C.: World Bank, Industry and Finance Series Volume 18, September.

Hanson, James A., and Craig R. Neal. 1985. "Interest Rate Policies in Selected Developing Countries, 1970–1982." Washington, D.C.: World Bank, Staff Working Paper No. 753.

————. 1986. "The Demand for Liquid Financial Assets: Evidence from 36 Developing Countries." Washington, D.C.: World Bank, August.

Haque, Nadeem Ul, Kajal Lahiri, and Peter J. Montiel. 1990. "A Macroeconomic Model for Developing Countries." *International Monetary Fund Staff Papers,* 37(2, September): 537–559.

Haque, Nadeem Ul, and Abbas Mirakhor. 1986. "Optimal Profit-Sharing Contracts and Investment in an Interest-Free Islamic Economy." Washington, D.C.: World Bank, March.

Haque, Nadeem Ul, and Peter J. Montiel. 1987. "Ricardian Equivalence, Liquidity Constraints, and the Yaari-Blanchard Effect: Tests for Developing Countries." Washington, D.C.: International Monetary Fund, WP/87/85, December.

————. 1990. "Capital Mobility in Developing Countries—Some Empirical Tests." Washington, D.C.: International Monetary Fund, Research Department, WP/90/117, December.

Harberger, Arnold C. 1950. "Currency Depreciation, Income, and the Balance of Trade." *Journal of Political Economy,* 58(1, February): 47–60.

————. 1978. "Perspectives on Capital and Technology in Less–Developed Countries." In *Contemporary Economic Analysis.* Edited by Michael J. Artis and A. Robert Nobay. London: Longman, 42–72.

————. 1981. "In Step and Out of Step with the World Inflation: A Summary History of Countries, 1952–1976." In *Development in an Inflationary World.* Edited by M. June Flanders and Assaf Razin. New York: Academic Press, 35–46.

————. 1985. "Lessons for Debtor-Country Managers and Policymakers." In *International Debt and the Developing Countries.* Edited by Gordon W. Smith and John T. Cuddington. Washington, D.C.: World Bank, March, 236–257.

————. 1986. "Welfare Consequences of Capital Inflows." In *Economic Liberalization in Developing Countries.* Edited by Armeane M. Choksi and Demetris Papageorgiou. Oxford: Basil Blackwell, 157–184.

Harberger, Arnold C. 1988. "Growth, Industrialization and Economic Structure: Latin America and East Asia Compared." In *Achieving Industrialization in East Asia.* Edited by Helen Hughes. Sydney: Cambridge University Press, 164–194.

Harberger, Arnold C., and Sebastián Edwards. 1980. "International Evidence on the Sources of Inflation." Chicago: University of Chicago, Department of Economics, December.

Harris, James W. 1979. "An Empirical Note on the Investment Content of Real Output and the Demand for Money in the Developing Economy." *Malayan Economic Review,* 24(1, April): 49–62.

Harris, John R., Fabio Schiantarelli, and Miranda G. Siregar. 1992. "Financial and Investment Behavior of the Indonesian Manufacturing Sector and the Effect of Liberalization: Evidence from Panel Data, 1981–1988." Boston, Mass.: Boston University, Department of Economics, March.

————. 1994. "The Effect of Financial Liberalization on the Capital Structure and Investment Decisions of Indonesian Manufacturing Establishments." *World Bank Economic Review,* 8(1, January): 17–47.

Hastings, Laura A. 1993. "Regulatory Revenge: The Politics of Free-Market Financial Reforms in Chile." In *The Politics of Finance in Developing Countries.* Edited by Stephan Haggard, Chung H. Lee, and Sylvia Maxfield. Ithaca: Cornell University Press, 201–229.

Havrilesky, Thomas M., and John T. Boorman, eds. 1980. *Current Perspectives in Banking: Operations, Management and Regulation.* Arlington Heights, Ill.: AHM Publishing.

Helgesen, H. B. 1974. "Banking: For 'Nationalization' Say 'De-Privatization.'" *Euromoney,* (October): 103–105.

Hemphill, William L. 1974. "The Effect of Foreign Exchange Receipts on Imports of Less Developed Countries." *International Monetary Fund Staff Papers,* 21(3, November): 637–677.

Hermes, Niels, and Robert Lensink. 1993. "The Financial Sector and Its Influence on Economic Growth: Evidence from 14 Latin American Countries, 1963–1989." Groningen: University of Groningen, Institute of Economic Research, Research Memorandum 531, June.

Hettige, Mala. 1992. "Toward Financial Deepening in Sub-Saharan Africa: An Analytical Framework." Washington, D.C.: World Bank, Industry Development Division, May.

Hilferding, Rudolf. 1910. *Das Finanzkapital. Eine Studie über die jüngste Entwicklung des Kapitalismus.* Vienna: Wiener Volksbuchhandlung. [*Finance Capital: A Study of the Latest Phase of Capitalist Development.* Edited with an introduction by Tom Bottomore from translations by Morris Watnick and Sam Gordon. London: Routledge and Kegan Paul, 1981.]

Hillier, Brian, and Tim Worrall. 1994. "The Welfare Implications of Costly Monitoring in the Credit Market." *Economic Journal,* 104(423, March): 350–362.

Hinds, Manuel. 1986. "Draft Paper on Financial Crises in Developing Countries." Washington, D.C.: World Bank, October.

———. 1988. "Economic Effects of Financial Crises." Washington, D. C.: World Bank, Europe, Middle East, and North Africa Department, PPR Working Paper WPS 104, October.

———. 1990. "Outwards vs Inwards Development Strategy: Implications for the Financial Sector." Washington, D.C.: World Bank, EDI Working Papers, 1990.

Hirshleifer, Jack. 1970. *Investment, Interest, and Capital.* Englewood Cliffs: Prentice-Hall.

Hoff, Karla, and Joseph E. Stiglitz. 1990. "Introduction: Imperfect Information and Rural Credit Markets—Puzzles and Policy Perspectives." *World Bank Economic Review,* 4(3, September): 235–250.

Holst, Jürgen U. 1985. "The Role of Informal Financial Institutions in the Mobilization of Savings." In *Savings and Development.* Edited by Denis Kessler and Pierre-Antoine Ullmo. Paris: Economica, 121–152.

Hong, Kyttack. 1985. "Macroeconomic Dynamics in a Financially Repressed Economy." *Journal of Economic Development,* 10(1, July): 169–194.

Hong, Wontack. 1986. "Institutionalized Monopsonistic Capital Markets in a Developing Economy." *Journal of Development Economics,* 21(2, May): 353–359.

Honohan, Patrick. 1989. "An Analytical Approach to the Taxation of the Financial Sector." Washington, D.C.: World Bank, July.

———. 1992. "Financial Sector Failures in West Africa." Dublin: Economic and Social Research Institute, August.

Horiuchi, Akiyoshi. 1984. "The 'Low Interest Rate Policy' and Economic Growth in Postwar Japan." *Developing Economies,* 22(4, December): 349–371.

Husain, Ishrat. 1991. "How Did the Asian Countries Avoid the Debt Crisis." Washington, D.C.: World Bank, PRE Working Paper WPS 785, October.

Husain, Ishrat, and Kwang W. Jun. 1992. "Capital Flows to South Asian and ASEAN Countries." Washington, D.C.: World Bank, International Economics Department, WPS 842, January.

Hutchcroft, Paul D. 1993. "Selective Squander: The Politics of Preferential Credit Allocation in the Philippines." In *The Politics of Finance in Developing Countries.* Edited by Stephan Haggard, Chung H. Lee, and Sylvia Maxfield. Ithaca: Cornell University Press, 165–198.

Ito, Kazuhisa. 1984. "Development Finance and Commercial Banks in Korea." *Developing Economies,* 22(4, December): 453–475.

Ize, Alain, and Guillermo Ortiz. 1987. "Fiscal Rigidities, Public Debt, and Capital Flight." *International Monetary Fund Staff Papers,* 34(2, June): 311–332.

Jaffee, Dwight M., and Ephraim Kleiman. 1977. "The Welfare Implications of Uneven Inflation." In *Inflation Theory and Anti-Inflation Policy.* Edited by Erik Lundberg. London: Macmillan, 285–307.

Jaffee, Dwight M., and Kenneth T. Rosen. 1978. "Estimates of the Effectiveness of Stabilization Policies for the Mortgage and Housing Markets." *Journal of Finance,* 33(3, June): 933–946.

Jaffee, Dwight M., and Thomas Russell. 1976. "Imperfect Information, Uncertainty and Credit Rationing." *Quarterly Journal of Economics*, 90(4, November): 651–666.

James, Christopher. 1986. "Some Evidence on the Uniqueness of Bank Loans." Eugene: University of Oregon, Graduate School of Business, October.

Jao, Y. C. 1976. "Financial Deepening and Economic Growth: A Cross-Section Analysis." *Malayan Economic Review*, 21(1, April): 47–58.

———. 1985. "Financial Deepening and Economic Growth: Theory, Evidence, and Policy." *Greek Economic Review*, 7(3, December): 187–225.

Jappelli, Tullio, and Marco Pagano. 1994. "Saving, Growth, and Liquidity Constraints." *Quarterly Journal of Economics*, 109(1, February): 83–109.

Jaramillo, Fidel, Fabio Schiantarelli, and Andrew Weiss. 1993a. "The Effect of Financial Liberalization on the Allocation of Credit: Panel Data Evidence for Ecuador." Washington, D.C.: World Bank, Policy Research Working Papers WPS 1092, February.

———. 1993b. "Capital Market Imperfections Before and After Financial Liberalization: An Euler Equation Approach to Panel Data for Ecuadorian Firms." Chestnut Hill, Mass.: Boston College, April.

Johansson, Per-Olov, Juha Kähkönen, and Per Lundborg. 1986. "Credit Policies in a Dual Economy: An Analytical Framework." In *A Tribute to Arvi Leponiemi on His 60th Birthday.* Edited by Juha Kähkönen and J. Ylä-Liedenpohja. Helsinki: Acta Academica Œconomica Helsingiensis, series A:48, 49–54.

Johnston, Jack. 1972. *Econometric Methods*, 2d ed. New York: McGraw-Hill.

———. 1984. *Econometric Methods*, 3rd ed. New York: McGraw-Hill.

Johnston, R. Barry. 1991. "Distressed Financial Institutions in Thailand: Structural Weaknesses, Support Operations, and Economic Consequences." In *Banking Crises: Cases and Issues.* Edited by Venkataraman Sundararajan and Tomás J. T. Baliño. Washington, D.C.: International Monetary Fund, 234–275.

Johnston, R. Barry, and Odd Per Brekk. 1989. "Monetary Control Procedures and Financial Reform: Approaches, Issues, and Recent Experiences in Developing Countries." Washington, D.C.: International Monetary Fund, WP/89/48, June.

———. 1991b. "From Good Bankers to Bad Bankers: Ineffective Supervision and Management Deterioration as Major Elements in Banking Crises." Washington, D.C.: World Bank, EDI Working Paper No. 340/047.

Jung, Soo Sik. 1987. "Financial Innovations in Developing Countries: Bank Checks and Currency in Korea." In *Theory and Practice of Economic Development.* Edited by Byung J. Ahn, Soo B. Park, Young I. Chung, Wontack Hong, and Ki J. Jeong. Seoul: Bee Bong Publishing Company, 119–135.

Jung, Woo S. 1986. "Financial Development and Economic Growth: International Evidence." *Economic Development and Cultural Change*, 34(2, January): 333–346.

Jung, Woo S., and Peyton J. Marshall. 1986. "Inflation and Economic Growth: Some International Evidence on Structuralist and Distortionist Positions." *Journal of Money, Credit and Banking*, 18(2, May): 227–232.

Kähkönen, Juha. 1987. "Liberalization Policies and Welfare in a Financially Repressed Economy." *International Monetary Fund Staff Papers*, 34(3, September): 531–547.

Kalecki, Michael. 1939. *Essays in the Theory of Economic Fluctuations*. London: Allen and Unwin.

————. 1971. *Selected Essays on the Dynamics of the Capitalist Economy: 1933–1970*. Cambridge: Cambridge University Press.

Kamas, Linda. 1986. "The Balance of Payments Offset to Monetary Policy: Monetarist, Portfolio Balance, and Keynesian Estimates for Mexico and Venezuela." *Journal of Money, Credit and Banking*, 18(4, November): 467–481.

Kang, Moonsoo. 1992. "Monetary Policy Implementation under Financial Liberalization: The Case of Korea." Seoul: Korea Development Institute, July.

Kapur, Basant K. 1974. "Monetary Growth Models of Less Developed Economies." Stanford: Stanford University, Ph.D. thesis.

————. 1976a. "Alternative Stabilization Policies for Less-Developed Economies." *Journal of Political Economy*, 84(4, i, August): 777–795.

————. 1976b. "Two Approaches to Ending Inflation." In *Money and Finance in Economic Growth and Development: Essays in Honor of Edward S. Shaw*. Edited by Ronald I. McKinnon. New York: Marcel Dekker, 199–221.

————. 1982. "Optimal Stabilization Policies for Less Developed Economies with Rational Expectations." *Pakistan Journal of Applied Economics*, 1(1, Summer): 23–46.

————. 1983. "Optimal Financial and Foreign-Exchange Liberalization of Less Developed Economies." *Quarterly Journal of Economics*, 98(1, February): 41–62.

————. 1985. "Money in Development: Comment." *Southern Economic Journal*, 51(4, April): 1230–1239.

————. 1986. *Studies in Inflationary Dynamics: Financial Repression and Financial Liberalization in Less Developed Countries*. Singapore: Singapore University Press.

————. 1992. "Formal and Informal Financial Markets, and the Neo-Structuralist Critique of the Financial Liberalization Strategy in Less Developed Countries." *Journal of Development Economics*, 38(1, January): 63–77.

Karsten, Ingo. 1982. "Islam and Financial Intermediation." *International Monetary Fund Staff Papers*, 29(1, March): 108–142.

Keller, Peter M. 1980. "Implications of Credit Policies for Output and the Balance of Payments." *International Monetary Fund Staff Papers*, 27(3, September): 451–477.

Keynes, J. Maynard. 1936. *The General Theory of Employment Interest and Money*. London: Macmillan.

————. 1937. "Alternative Theories of the Rate of Interest." *Economic Journal*, 47(186, June): 241–252.

Khan, Ashfaque H. 1988. "Financial Repression, Financial Development and Structure of Savings in Pakistan." *Pakistan Development Review*, 27(4, ii, Winter): 701–711.

Khan, Ashfaque H., and Mushtaq Ahmad. 1985. "Real Money Balances in the Production Function of a Developing Country." *Review of Economics and Statistics,* 67(2, May): 336–340.

Khan, Mohsin S. 1986. "Islamic Interest-Free Banking: A Theoretical Analysis." *International Monetary Fund Staff Papers,* 33(1, March): 1–27.

Khan, Mohsin S., and Nadeem Ul Haque. 1985. "Foreign Borrowing and Capital Flight: A Formal Analysis." *International Monetary Fund Staff Papers,* 32(4, December): 606–628.

Khan, Mohsin S., and Abbas Mirakhor. 1991. "Islamic Banking." Washington, D.C.: International Monetary Fund, WP/91/88, September.

Khan, Mohsin S., and Carmen M. Reinhart. 1990. "Private Investment and Economic Growth in Developing Countries." *World Development,* 18(1, January): 19–27.

Khan, Mohsin S., and Delano Villanueva. 1991. "Macroeconomic Policies and Long-Term Growth: A Conceptual and Empirical Review." Washington, D.C.: International Monetary Fund, WP/92/28, March.

Khatkhate, Deena R. 1988. "Assessing the Impact of Interest Rates in Less Developed Countries." *World Development,* 16(5, May): 577–588.

Khatkhate, Deena R., and Klaus-Walter Riechel. 1980. "Multipurpose Banking: Its Nature, Scope, and Relevance for Less Developed Countries." *International Monetary Fund Staff Papers,* 27(3, September): 478–516.

Khatkhate, Deena R., and Delano P. Villanueva. 1978. "Operation of Selective Credit Policies in Less Developed Countries: Certain Critical Issues." *World Development,* 6(7–8, July–August): 979–990.

Kiguel, Miguel A. 1989. "Budget Deficits, Stability, and the Monetary Dynamics of Hyperinflation." *Journal of Money, Credit, and Banking,* 21(2, May): 148–157.

Kiguel, Miguel A., and Pablo Andrés Neumeyer. 1989. "Inflation and Seigniorage in Argentina." Washington, D.C., World Bank, PPR Working Paper WPS 289.

Killick, Tony. 1981. "Inflation in Developing Countries: An Interpretative Survey." *ODI Review,* (1): 1–17.

Kim, Joong-Woong. 1988. "Economic Development and Financial Liberalization in the Republic of Korea: Policy Reforms and Future Prospects." In *Financial Liberalization and the Internal Structure of Capital Markets in Asia and Latin America.* Edited by Miguel Urrutia. Tokyo: United Nations University, 137–171.

Kimbrough, Kent P. 1986. "The Optimum Quantity of Money Rule in the Theory of Public Finance." *Journal of Monetary Economics,* 18(3, November): 277–284.

King, Robert G., and Ross Levine. 1993a. "Finance and Growth: Schumpeter Might Be Right." *Quarterly Journal of Economics,* 108(3, August): 717–737.

————. 1993b. "Finance, Entrepreneurship, and Growth: Theory and Evidence." *Journal of Monetary Economics,* 32(3, December): 513–542.

————. 1993c. "Financial Intermediation and Economic Growth." In *Capital Markets and Financial Intermediation.* Edited by Colin Mayer and Xavier Vives. Cambridge: Cambridge University Press for the Centre for Economic Policy Research, 156–189.

King, Robert G., and Charles I. Plosser. 1985. "Money, Deficits, and Inflation." *Carnegie-Rochester Conference Series on Public Policy,* (22, Spring): 147–195.

Kiriwat, Ekamol. 1992. "Financial Sector Reform: Thailand." Bangkok: Bank of Thailand, May.

Kitchen, Richard L. 1986. *Finance for the Developing Countries.* Chichester: John Wiley and Sons.

Klein, Benjamin. 1974. "Competitive Interest Payments on Bank Deposits and the Long-Run Demand for Money." *American Economic Review,* 64(6, December): 931–949.

Kohsaka, Akira. 1984. "The High Interest Rate Policy under Financial Repression." *Developing Economies,* 22(4, December): 419–452.

———. 1987. "Financial Liberalization in Asian NICs: A Comparative Study of Korea and Taiwan in the 1980s." *Developing Economies,* 25(4, December): 325–345.

———. 1991. "Financial Development in the Philippines in the 1980s." *Southeast Asian Studies,* 28(4, March): 604–618.

Kormendi, Roger C., and Philip G. Meguire. 1984. "Cross-Regime Evidence of Macroeconomic Rationality." *Journal of Political Economy,* 92(5, October): 875–908.

———. 1985. "Macroeconomic Determinants of Growth: Cross-Country Evidence." *Journal of Monetary Economics,* 16(2, September): 141–163.

Kouri, Pentti J. K., and Michael G. Porter. 1974. "International Capital Flows and Portfolio Equilibrium." *Journal of Political Economy,* 82(3, May–June): 443–467.

Kravis, Irving B., Alan W. Heston, and Robert Summers. 1978. "Real GDP *Per Capita* for More Than One Hundred Countries." *Economic Journal,* 88(350, June): 215–242.

Kropp, Erhard, Michael T. Marx, Ballurkar Pramod, Benjamin R. Quiñones, and Hans Dieter Seibel. 1989. *Linking Self-help Groups and Banks in Developing Countries.* Bangkok and Eschborn: Asian and Pacific Regional Agricultural Credit Association and Deutsche Gesellschaft für Technische Zusammenarbeit.

Krueger, Anne O. 1974. *Foreign Trade Regimes and Economic Development: Turkey.* New York: National Bureau of Economic Research, distributed by Columbia University Press.

———. 1981. "Interactions between Inflation and Trade Regime Objectives in Stabilization Programs." In *Economic Stabilization in Developing Countries.* Edited by William R. Cline and Sidney Weintraub. Washington, D.C.: Brookings Institution, 83–117.

———. 1987. "Debt, Capital Flows, and LDC Growth." *American Economic Review,* 77(2, May): 159–164.

Krugman, Paul R. 1978. "Interest Rate Ceilings, Efficiency, and Growth: A Theoretical Approach." New Haven: Yale University, Department of Economics.

———. 1993. "International Finance and Economic Development." In *Finance and Development: Issues and Experience.* Edited by Alberto Giovannini. Cambridge: Cambridge University Press, 11–23.

Kumar, Ramesh C. 1983. "Money in Development: A Monetary Growth Model à la McKinnon." *Southern Economic Journal*, 50(1, July): 18–36.

Lahiri, Ashok Kumar. 1989. "Dynamics of Asian Savings: The Role of Growth and Age Structure." *International Monetary Fund Staff Papers*, 36(1, March): 228–261.

Laidler, David E. W. 1978. "Money and Money Income: An Essay on the 'Transmission Mechanism.'" *Journal of Monetary Economics*, 4(2, April): 151–191.

————. 1984. "The 'Buffer Stock' Notion in Monetary Economics." *Economic Journal*, 94(Supplement): 17–34.

Lal, Deepak. 1987. "The Political Economy of Economic Liberalization." *World Bank Economic Review*, 1(2, January): 273–299.

Lamberte, Mario B., Joseph L. Lim, Rob Vos, Elizabeth S. Tan, and Maria Socorro V. Zingapan. 1992. *Philippine External Finance, Domestic Resource Mobilization and Development in the 1970s and 1980s*. Manila: Philippine Institute of Development Studies.

Laney, Leroy O., and Thomas D. Willett. 1982. "The International Liquidity Explosion and Worldwide Inflation: The Evidence from Sterilization Coefficient Estimates." *Journal of International Money and Finance*, 1(2, August): 141–152.

Lanyi, Anthony, and Rüşdü Saracoglu. 1983a. "The Importance of Interest Rates in Developing Economies." *Finance and Development*, 20(2, June): 20–23.

————. 1983b. "Interest Rate Policies in Developing Countries." Washington, D.C.: International Monetary Fund, Occasional Paper 22, October.

Laskar, Daniel M. 1983. "Short-Run Independence of Monetary Policy under a Pegged Exchange-Rate System: An Econometric Approach." In *The International Transmission of Inflation*. By Michael R. Darby, James R. Lothian, et al. Chicago: University of Chicago Press for the National Bureau of Economic Research, 314–348.

Laumas, Prem S. 1980. "Some Evidence on Keynes' Finance Motive." *Journal of Development Economics*, 7(1, March): 123–126.

————. 1990a. "Complementarity between Money and Capital in a Developing Country: A Test of Stability." *International Economic Journal*, 4(2, Summer): 87–95.

————. 1990b. "Monetization, Financial Liberalization, and Economic Development." *Economic Development and Cultural Change*, 38(2, January): 377–390.

Laursen, Svend, and Lloyd A. Metzler. 1950. "Flexible Exchange Rates and the Theory of Employment." *Review of Economics and Statistics*, 32(4, November): 281–299.

Le Fort, Guillermo R. 1989. "Financial Crisis in Developing Countries and Structural Weaknesses of the Financial System." Washington, D.C.: International Monetary Fund, WP/89/33, April.

Lee, Chang-Kyu. 1986. "Financial Reform Experiences in Korea." In *Financial Policy and Reform in Pacific Basin Countries*. Edited by Hang-Sheng Cheng. Lexington, Mass.: D. C. Heath and Co., Lexington Books, 137–142.

Lee, Chung H. 1992. "The Government, Financial System, and Large Private Enterprises in the Economic Development of South Korea." *World Development*, 20(2, February): 187–197.

Lee, Jungsoo, Pradumna B. Rana, and Yoshihiro Iwasaki. 1986. "Effects of Foreign Capital Inflows on Developing Countries in Asia." Manila: Asian Development Bank, Economic Staff Paper No. 30, April.

Lee, Tong Hun, and Sil Han. 1990. "On Measuring the Relative Size of the Unregulated to the Regulated Money Market Over Time." *Journal of Development Economics*, 33(1, July): 53–65.

Lee, Yang-Pal. 1980. "Inflation Hedges and Economic Growth in a Monetary Economy." Stanford: Stanford University, Ph.D. thesis.

Lee, Yung-san, and Tzong-rong Tsai. 1988. "Development of Financial System and Monetary Policies in Taiwan." Taipei: Academia Sinica, Institute of Economics. Conference on the Economic Development Experiences of Taiwan, 8-10 June.

Leff, Nathaniel H. 1975. "Rates of Return to Capital, Domestic Savings, and Investment in the Developing Countries." *Kyklos*, 28(4): 827–851.

Leff, Nathaniel H., and Kazuo Sato. 1980. "Macroeconomic Adjustment in Developing Countries: Instability, Short-Run Growth, and External Dependency." *Review of Economics and Statistics*, 62(2, May): 170–179.

———. 1988. "Estimating Investment and Savings Functions for Developing Countries, with an Application to Latin America." *International Economic Journal*, 2(3, Autumn): 1–17.

Legarda, Benito. 1986. "A Philosophy of Financial Market Building." Washington, D.C.: International Finance Corporation, August.

Leiderman, Leonardo, and Mario I. Blejer. 1987. "The Term Structure of Interest Rates during a Financial Reform: Argentina 1977–81." *Journal of Development Economics*, 25(2, April): 285–299.

Leijonhufvud, Axel. 1981. "Costs and Consequences of Inflation." In *Information and Coordination: Essays in Macroeconomic Theory*. By Axel Leijonhufvud. New York: Oxford University Press, 227–269.

Leite, Sérgio Pereira. 1982. "Interest Rate Policies in West Africa." *International Monetary Fund Staff Papers*, 29(1, March): 48–76.

Leite, Sérgio Pereira, and Dawit Makonnen. 1986. "Saving and Interest Rates in the BCEAO Countries: An Empirical Analysis." *Savings and Development*, 10(3): 219–232.

Leite, Sérgio Pereira, and Venkataraman Sundararajan. 1990. "Issues in Interest Rate Management and Liberalization." *International Monetary Fund Staff Papers*, 37(4, December): 735–752.

Lensink, Robert, and Niels Hermes. 1993. "Is There a Long Run Influence of Financial Development on Economic Growth in Latin America?" Groningen: University of Groningen, Institute of Economic Research, Research Memorandum 543, September.

Levhari, David, and Don Patinkin. 1968. "The Role of Money in a Simple Growth Model." *American Economic Review*, 58(3, September): 713–753.

Levine, Ross. 1991. "Stock Markets, Growth, and Tax Policy." *Journal of Finance,* 46(4, September): 1445–1465.

———. 1993. "Financial Structures and Economic Development." *Revista de Análisis Económico,* 8(1, Junio): 113–129.

Levitsky, Jacob. 1986. *World Bank Lending to Small Enterprises: A Review.* Washington, D.C.: World Bank, Industry and Finance Series Volume 16, July.

Levitsky, Jacob, and Ranga Prasad. 1986. "Credit Guarantee Schemes for Small and Medium Enterprises." Washington, D.C.: World Bank, Financial Development Division, July.

Lewis, Jeffrey D. 1992. "Financial Repression and Liberalization in a General Equilibrium Model with Financial Markets." *Journal of Policy Modeling,* 14(2, April): 135–166.

Li, Carmen, and Mahmood Pradhan. 1990. "Inflation, Financial Liberalisation and Bankruptcies in Argentina." In *International Finance and the Less Developed Countries.* Edited by Kate Phylaktis and Mahmood Pradhan. Basingstoke: Macmillan, 98–113.

Li, Kui W., and Michael T. Skully. 1991. "Financial Deepening and Institutional Development: Some Asian Experiences." *Savings and Development,* 15(2): 147–164.

Liang, Ming-Yih. 1988. "A Note on Financial Dualism and Interest Rate Policies: A Loanable Funds Approach." *International Economic Review,* 29(3, August): 539–549.

Lim, Joseph. 1987. "The New Structuralist Critique of the Monetarist Theory of Inflation: The Case of the Philippines." *Journal of Development Economics,* 25(1, February): 45–61.

Lin, See-Yan. 1986. "ASEAN: Financial Development and Interdependence." In *Pacific Growth and Financial Interdependence.* Edited by Augustine H. H. Tan and Basant Kapur. Sydney: Allen and Unwin, 125–143.

———. 1991. "Interaction of Exchange Rate Policy and Monetary Policy: The Case of Malaysia." In *Monetary Policy Instruments for Developing Countries.* Edited by Gerard Caprio, Jr., and Patrick Honohan. Washington, D.C.: World Bank, 131–134.

Lindner, Deborah J. 1992. "Foreign Exchange Policy, Monetary Policy, and Capital Market Liberalization in Korea." Washington, D.C.: Board of Governors of the Federal Reserve System, International Finance Discussion Paper No. 435, August.

Lipsey, Richard G. 1979. "World Inflation." *Economic Record,* 55(151, December): 283–296.

Liu, Liang-Yn, and Wing Thye Woo. 1994. "Saving Behaviour under Imperfect Financial Markets and the Current Account Consequences." *Economic Journal,* 104(424, May): 512–527.

Lizondo, José Saúl. 1985. "Unifying Multiple Exchange Rates." *Finance and Development,* 22(4, December): 23–24, 37.

Llanto, Gilberto M. 1990. "Asymmetric Information in Rural Financial Markets and Interlinking of Transactions through the Self-Help Groups." *Savings and Development,* 14(2): 137–152.

Locke, John. 1695. *Further Considerations Concerning Raising the Value of Money,* 2d ed. London: A. & J. Churchil.

Logue, Dennis E., and Thomas D. Willett. 1976. "A Note on the Relation between the Rate and Variability of Inflation." *Economica,* 43(170, May): 151–158.

Long, Millard. 1983. "Review of Financial Sector Work." Washington, D.C.: World Bank, Industry Department Financial Development Unit, October.

———. 1990. "Financial Systems and Development." Washington, D.C.: World Bank, EDI Working Papers.

Long, Millard, and Dimitri Vittas. 1992. "Changing the Rules of the Game." In *Financial Regulation: Changing the Rules of the Game.* Edited by Dimitri Vittas. Washington, D.C.: World Bank, EDI Development Studies, 43–57.

Lucas, Robert E., Jr. 1973. "Some International Evidence on Output-Inflation Trade-offs." *American Economic Review,* 63(3, June): 326–334.

———. 1976. "Econometric Policy Evaluation: A Critique." *Carnegie-Rochester Conference Series on Public Policy,* (1): 19–46.

———. 1988. "On the Mechanics of Economic Development." *Journal of Monetary Economics,* 22(1, July): 3–42.

———. 1990. "Why Doesn't Capital Flow from Rich to Poor Countries?" *American Economic Review,* 80(2, May): 92–96.

Lundberg, Erik. 1964. "The Financial System of Portugal." Washington, D.C.: International Monetary Fund and World Bank, October.

MacIntyre, Andrew J. 1993. "The Politics of Finance in Indonesia: Command, Confusion, and Competition." In *The Politics of Finance in Developing Countries.* Edited by Stephan Haggard, Chung H. Lee, and Sylvia Maxfield. Ithaca: Cornell University Press, 123–164.

McKinnon, Ronald I. 1973. *Money and Capital in Economic Development.* Washington, D.C.: Brookings Institution.

———. 1974. "Money, Growth and the Propensity to Save: An Iconoclastic View." In *Trade, Stability, and Macroeconomics: Essays in Honor of Lloyd Metzler.* Edited by George Horwich and Paul A. Samuelson. New York: Academic Press, 487–502.

———, ed. 1976. *Money and Finance in Economic Growth and Development: Essays in Honor of Edward S. Shaw.* New York: Marcel Dekker.

———. 1977. "Financial Intermediation, the Foreign Exchanges, and Monetary Control in Chile." Stanford: Stanford University, Center for Research in Economic Growth, September.

———. 1980. "Financial Policies." In *Policies for Industrial Progress in Developing Countries.* Edited by John Cody, Helen Hughes, and David Wall. London: Oxford University Press for the World Bank, 93–120.

———. 1981. "Financial Repression and the Liberalization Problem within Less-Developed Countries." In *The World Economic Order: Past and Prospects.* Edited by Sven Grassman and Erik Lundberg. London: Macmillan, 365–386.

———. 1982. "The Order of Economic Liberalization: Lessons from Chile and Argentina." *Carnegie-Rochester Conference Series on Public Policy,* (17, Autumn): 159–186.

McKinnon, Ronald I. 1984. "Financial Liberalization and the Debt Crisis in LDCs: The International Misregulation of Commercial Banks." Stanford: Center for Research in Economic Growth Memorandum No. 265, October.

———. 1986a. "Financial Liberalization in Retrospect: Interest Rate Policies in LDCs." Stanford: Center for Economic Policy Research Publication No. 74, July.

———. 1986b. "Domestic Interest Rates and Foreign Capital Flows in a Liberalizing Economy." Stanford: Stanford University, Department of Economics. American Economic Association's Meeting in New Orleans, 28–30 December.

———. 1986c. "Issues and Perspectives: An Overview of Banking Regulation and Monetary Control." In *Pacific Growth and Financial Interdependence*. Edited by Augustine H. H. Tan and Basant Kapur. Sydney: Allen and Unwin, 319–336.

———. 1988. "Financial Liberalization in Retrospect: Interest Rate Policies in LDCs." In *The State of Development Economics*. Edited by Gustav Ranis and T. Paul Schultz. Oxford: Basil Blackwell, 386–415.

———. 1991. "Monetary Stabilization in LDCs." In *Liberalization in the Process of Economic Development*. Edited by Lawrence B. Krause and Kim Kihwan. Berkeley and Los Angeles: University of California Press, 366–400.

———. 1993. *The Order of Economic Liberalization: Financial Control in the Transition to a Market Economy*, 2d ed. Baltimore: Johns Hopkins University Press.

———. 1994. "Gradual versus Rapid Liberalization in Socialist Economies: The Problem of Macroeconomic Control." In *Proceedings of the World Bank Annual Bank Conference on Development Economics 1993*. Edited by Michael Bruno and Boris Pleskovic. Washington, D.C.: World Bank, 63–94.

McKinnon, Ronald I., and Donald J. Mathieson. 1981. "How to Manage a Repressed Economy." *Princeton Essays in International Finance*, (145), December.

McLeod, Ross H. 1991. "Informal and Formal Sector Finance in Indonesia: The Financial Evolution of Small Business." *Savings and Development*, 15(2): 187–209.

Majumdar, Bani. 1974. *Central Banks and Treasuries*. Bombay: Vora.

Makin, John H. 1989. "International 'Imbalances': The Role of Exchange Rates." *The AMEX Bank Review: Special Papers*, (17, November): 9–35.

Mankiw, N. Gregory, Jeffrey A. Miron, and David N. Weil. 1987. "The Adjustment of Expectations to a Change in Regime: A Study of the Founding of the Federal Reserve." *American Economic Review*, 77(3, June): 358–374.

Marquez, Jaime, and Janice Shack-Marquez. 1987. "Financial Concentration and Development: An Empirical Analysis of the Venezuelan Case." Washington, D.C.: Board of Governors of the Federal Reserve System, International Finance Discussion Paper No. 300, January.

Marty, Alvin L. 1990. "Money, Financial Repression, and Economic Growth." In *International Finance and the Less Developed Countries*. Edited by Kate Phylaktis and Mahmood Pradhan. Basingstoke: Macmillan, 157–174.

Mason, Andrew. 1981. "An Extension of the Life-Cycle Model and Its Application to Population Growth and Aggregate Saving." Honolulu: East-West Center, January.

————. 1987. "National Saving Rates and Population Growth: A New Model and New Evidence." In *Population Growth and Economic Development: Issues and Evidence*. Edited by D. Gale Johnson and Ronald D. Lee. Madison: University of Wisconsin Press for the National Academy of Sciences, 523–560.

Masson, Paul, Jeroen Kremers, and Jocelyn Horne. 1994. "Net Foreign Assets and International Adjustment: The United States, Japan, and Germany." *Journal of International Money and Finance*, 13(1, February): 27–40.

Mathieson, Donald J. 1979a. "Financial Reform and Capital Flows in a Developing Economy." *International Monetary Fund Staff Papers*, 26(3, September): 450–489.

————. 1979b. "Interest Rates and Monetary Aggregates during a Financial Reform." Washington, D.C.: International Monetary Fund, DM/79/95, December.

————. 1980. "Financial Reform and Stabilization Policy in a Developing Economy." *Journal of Development Economics*, 7(3, September): 359–395.

————. 1982. "Inflation, Interest Rates, and the Balance of Payments during a Financial Reform: The Case of Argentina." *World Development*, 10(9, September): 813–827.

————. 1983a. "Estimating Models of Financial Market Behavior during Periods of Extensive Structural Reform: The Experience of Chile." *International Monetary Fund Staff Papers*, 30(2, June): 350–393.

————. 1983b. "Monetary Reform, Credibility, and the Restarting Problem." Washington, D.C.: International Monetary Fund, DM/83/58, July.

Mathieson, Donald J., and Liliana Rojas-Suárez. 1993. "Liberalization of the Capital Account: Experiences and Issues." Washington, D.C.: International Monetary Fund, Occasional Paper 103, March.

Maxfield, Sylvia. 1993. "The Politics of Mexican Financial Policy." In *The Politics of Finance in Developing Countries*. Edited by Stephan Haggard, Chung H. Lee, and Sylvia Maxfield. Ithaca: Cornell University Press, 230–258.

Mayer, Colin. 1989. "Myths of the West: Lessons from Developed Countries for Development Finance." Washington, D.C.: World Bank, PPR Working Paper WPS 301, November.

Melitz, Jacques, and Christian Bordes. 1991. "The Macroeconomic Implications of Financial Deregulation." *European Economic Review*, 35(1, January): 155–178.

Meltzer, Allan H. 1974. "Credit Availability and Economic Decisions: Some Evidence from the Mortgage and Housing Markets." *Journal of Finance*, 29(3, June): 763–777.

Metzler, Lloyd A. 1968. "The Process of International Adjustment under Conditions of Full Employment: A Keynesian View." In *Readings in International Economics*. Edited by Richard E. Caves and Harry G. Johnson. Homewood, Ill.: Richard D. Irwin for the American Economic Association, 465–486.

Mikesell, Raymond F., and James E. Zinser. 1973. "The Nature of the Savings Function in Developing Countries: A Survey of the Theoretical and Empirical Literature." *Journal of Economic Literature*, 11(1, March): 1–26.

Min, Byoung Kyun. 1976. "Financial Restriction in Korea, 1965–1974." Honolulu: University of Hawaii, Ph.D. thesis.

Mishkin, Frederic S. 1991. "Asymmetric Information and Financial Crises: A Historical Perspective." In *Financial Markets and Financial Crises*. Edited by R. Glenn Hubbard. Chicago: University of Chicago Press for the National Bureau of Economic Research, 69–108.

————. 1992. *The Economics of Money, Banking, and Financial Markets*, 3rd ed. New York: HarperCollins.

Mittra, Sid. 1978. *Central Bank versus Treasury.* Washington, D.C.: University Press of America.

Modigliani, Franco. 1986. "Life Cycle, Individual Thrift, and the Wealth of Nations." *American Economic Review,* 76(3, June): 297–313.

Mohtadi, Hamid, and Harjit Arora. 1988. "Stagflation and Monetary Stabilization Policies in a Disequilibrium Framework: The Case of South Korea." *Journal of Post Keynesian Economics,* 10(4, Summer): 602–617.

Molho, Lazaros E. 1986a. "Interest Rates, Saving, and Investment in Developing Countries: A Re-examination of the McKinnon-Shaw Hypothesis." *International Monetary Fund Staff Papers,* 33(1, March): 90–116.

————. 1986b. "Selective Credit Controls in Greece: A Test of Their Effectiveness." *International Monetary Fund Staff Papers,* 33(3, September): 477–508.

Montiel, Peter J. 1991. "The Transmission Mechanism for Monetary Policy in Developing Countries." *International Monetary Fund Staff Papers,* 38(1, March): 83–108.

Montiel, Peter J., Pierre-Richard Agénor, and Nadeem Ul Haque. 1993. *Informal Financial Markets in Developing Countries: A Macroeconomic Analysis.* Oxford: Basil Blackwell.

Montiel, Peter J., and Iqbal Zaidi. 1987. "Cross-Regime Tests of the Lucas Supply Function in Developing Countries." *International Monetary Fund Staff Papers,* 34(4, December): 760–769.

Moore, Basil J. 1986. "Inflation and Financial Deepening." *Journal of Development Economics,* 20(1, January–February): 125–133.

Moreno, Ramon. 1994. "Exchange Rate Policy and Insulation from External Shocks: The Experiences of Taiwan and Korea, 1970–1990." In *Exchange Rate Policy in Pacific Basin Countries.* Edited by Reuven Glick and Michael Hutchison. New York: Cambridge University Press, forthcoming.

Morgan, E. Victor. 1943. *The Theory and Practice of Central Banking, 1797–1913.* Cambridge: Cambridge University Press.

Morisset, Jacques. 1991. "Can Debt-Reduction Restore Economic Growth in Highly Indebted Countries?" *Revue d'économie politique,* 101(4, juillet-août): 639–666.

————. 1993. "Does Financial Liberalization Really Improve Private Investment in Developing Countries?" *Journal of Development Economics,* 40(1, February): 133–150.

Morris, Felipe. 1985. "India's Financial System: An Overview of Its Principal Structural Features." Washington, D.C.: World Bank, Staff Working Paper No. 739.

Morris, Felipe, Mark Dorfman, José Pedro Ortiz, and Maria Claudio Franco. 1990. "Latin America's Financial Systems in the 1980s: A Cross-Country Comparison." Washington, D.C.: World Bank, Discussion Paper 81, May.

Mourmouras, Alex, and Steven Russell. 1992. "Optimal Reserve Requirements, Deposit Taxation, and the Demand for Money." *Journal of Monetary Economics,* 30(1, October): 129–142.

Mundell, Robert A. 1965. "Growth, Stability, and Inflationary Finance." *Journal of Political Economy,* 73(2, April): 97–109.

Myers, Robert, Hafez Ghanem, and Licia Salice. 1986. "A Review of Policy Proposals in Bank Financial Sector Work." Washington, D.C.: World Bank, Economic Policy Notes, No. CPD–3, February.

Nam, Sang-Woo. 1989. "Liberalization of the Korean Financial and Capital Markets." In *Korea's Macroeconomic and Financial Policies.* Edited by Korea Development Institute. Seoul: Korea Development Institute, 133–171.

―――. 1991. "Korea's Financial Policy and Its Consequences." Seoul: Korea Development Institute, October.

Nascimento, Jean-Claude. 1991. "Crisis in the Financial Sector and the Authorities' Reaction: The Philippines." In *Banking Crises: Cases and Issues.* Edited by Venkataraman Sundararajan and Tomás J. T. Baliño. Washington, D.C.: International Monetary Fund, 175–233.

Nasution, Anwar. 1993. "Reforms of the Banking Sector in Indonesia, 1983–1991." Jakarta: University of Indonesia, Faculty of Economics, April.

Naya, Seiji. 1990. "Direct Foreign Investment and Trade in East and Southeast Asia." In *The Political Economy of International Trade: Essays in Honor of Robert E. Baldwin.* Edited by Ronald W. Jones and Anne O. Krueger. Cambridge, Mass.: Basil Blackwell, 288–312.

Nayar, C. P. Somanathan. 1982. *Finance Corporations: A Study of "Unregulated Banks."* Nungambakkam, Madras: Institute for Financial Management and Research.

―――. 1984. *A Study of Non-Banking Financial Intermediaries.* Nungambakkam, Madras: Institute for Financial Management and Research.

―――. 1986. "Can a Traditional Financial Technology Co-Exist with Modern Financial Technologies: The Indian Experience." *Savings and Development,* 10(1): 31–58.

Ness, Walter L. 1972. "Some Effects of Inflation on Financing Investment in Argentina and Brazil." In *Financial Development and Economic Growth: The Economic Consequences of Underdeveloped Capital Markets.* Edited by Arnold W. Sametz. New York: New York University Press, 228–254.

―――. 1974. "Financial Markets Innovation as a Development Strategy: Initial Results from the Brazilian Experience." *Economic Development and Cultural Change,* 22(3, April): 453–472.

Nichols, Donald A. 1974. "Some Principles of Inflationary Finance." *Journal of Political Economy,* 82(2, March–April): 423–430.

Nickell, Stephen J. 1977. "The Influence of Uncertainty on Investment." *Economic Journal,* 87(345, March): 47–70.

North, Douglass C. 1987. "Institutions, Transaction Costs and Economic Growth." *Economic Inquiry,* 25(3, July): 419–428.

Nugent, Jeffrey B., and Mustapha K. Nabli. 1992. "Development of Financial Markets and the Size Distribution of Manufacturing Establishments: International Comparisons." *World Development*, 20(10, October): 1489–1499.

Nyong, Michael O. 1989. "The Effect of Quality of Management on the Profitability of Commercial Banks: A Comparative Analysis Based on Nigerian Banking Experience." *Developing Economies*, 27(3, September): 286–303.

Obstfeld, Maurice. 1983. "Exchange Rates, Inflation, and the Sterilization Problem: Germany, 1975–1981." *European Economic Review*, 21(1–2, March–April): 161–189.

Odedokun, M. O. 1992. "An Alternative Framework for Estimating Investment and Saving Functions for Developing Countries: An Application to Time-Series Data for Sub-Sahara African Countries." *International Economic Journal*, 6(3, Autumn): 49–74.

Okorie, Aja. 1986. "The Extent of Risk in Commercial Banks' Lending to Agriculture in Nigeria: Some Evidence." *Savings and Development*, 10(4): 409–418.

Okuda, Hidenobu. 1990. "Financial Factors in Economic Development: A Study of the Financial Liberalization Policy in the Philippines." *Developing Economies*, 28(3, September): 240–270.

Olson, Mancur, and Martin J. Bailey. 1981. "Positive Time Preference." *Journal of Political Economy*, 89(1, February): 1–25.

Ordover, Janusz, and Andrew Weiss. 1981. "Information and the Law: Evaluating Legal Restrictions on Competitive Contracts." *American Economic Review*, 71(2, May): 399–404.

Organisation for Economic Co-operation and Development. 1990. "Financial Systems and Financial Regulation in Dynamic Asian Economies." *Financial Market Trends*, (47, October): 17–50.

Ortiz, Guillermo, and Leopoldo Solis. 1979. "Financial Structure and Exchange Rate Experience: Mexico 1954–1977." *Journal of Development Economics*, 6(4, December): 515–548.

Oshikoya, T. W. 1992. "Interest Rate Liberalization, Savings, Investment and Growth: The Case of Kenya." *Savings and Development*, 16(3): 305–320.

Owen, P. Dorian, and Otton Solis-Fallas. 1989. "Unorganized Money Markets and 'Unproductive' Assets in the New Structuralist Critique of Financial Liberalization." *Journal of Development Economics*, 31(2, October): 341–355.

Pagano, Marco. 1993. "Financial Markets and Growth: An Overview." *European Economic Review*, 37(2–3, April): 613–622.

Page, Sheila, ed. 1993. *Monetary Policy in Developing Countries*. London: Routledge.

Park, Yung Chul. 1990. "Growth, Liberalization, and Internationalization of Korea's Financial Sector, 1970–89." Taipei: Academia Sinica. Conference on Financial Development in Japan, Korea and Taiwan, 27–28 August.

———. 1993. "The Role of Finance in Economic Development in South Korea and Taiwan." In *Finance and Development: Issues and Experience*. Edited by Alberto Giovannini. Cambridge: Cambridge University Press, 121–150.

————. 1994. "Korea: Growth and Structural Change of the Financial System." In *Financial Development in Japan, Korea and Taiwan.* Edited by Hugh T. Patrick and Yung Chul Park. New York: Oxford University Press, forthcoming.

Park, Yung Chul, and Dong Won Kim. 1990. "The Behavior and Efficiency of Commercial Banks in Korea." Taipei: Academia Sinica, Institute of Economics. Conference on Financial Development in Japan, Korea and Taiwan, 27–28 August.

————. 1994. "Korea: Growth and Structural Change of the Banking System." In *Financial Development in Japan, Korea and Taiwan.* Edited by Hugh T. Patrick and Yung Chul Park. New York: Oxford University Press, forthcoming.

Parkin, J. Michael. 1980. "Oil Push Inflation?" *Banca Nazionale del Lavoro Quarterly Review,* (133, June): 163–185.

Patrick, Hugh T. 1984. "Japanese Financial Development in Historical Perspective, 1868–1980." In *Comparative Development Perspectives.* Edited by Gustav Ranis, et al. Boulder, Colo.: Westview Press, 302–327.

————. 1990. "The Financial Development of Taiwan, Korea, and Japan: A Framework for Consideration of Issues." Taipei: Academia Sinica, Institute of Economics. Conference on Financial Development in Japan, Korea and Taiwan, 27–28 August.

————. 1994. "Comparisons, Contrasts and Implications." In *Financial Development in Japan, Korea and Taiwan.* Edited by Hugh T. Patrick and Yung Chul Park. New York: Oxford University Press, forthcoming.

Patrick, Hugh T., and Honorata A. Moreno. 1985. "Philippine Private Domestic Commercial Banking, 1946–80, in the Light of Japanese Experience." In *Japan and the Developing Countries: A Comparative Analysis.* Edited by Kazushi Ohkawa and Gustav Ranis with Larry Meissner. New York: Basil Blackwell, 311–365.

Patrick, Hugh T., and Yung Chul Park. 1994. "Concepts and Issues." In *Financial Development in Japan, Korea and Taiwan.* Edited by Hugh T. Patrick and Yung Chul Park. New York: Oxford University Press, forthcoming.

Patten, Richard H., and Jay K. Rosengard. 1992. *Progress with Profits: The Development of Rural Banking in Indonesia.* San Francisco: Institute for Contemporary Studies Press for the International Center for Economic Growth and the Harvard Institute for International Development.

Patterson, Kerry D. 1993. "The Impact of Credit Constraints, Interest Rates and Housing Equity Withdrawal on the Intertemporal Pattern of Consumption—A Diagrammatic Analysis." Reading: University of Reading, Department of Economics, Series A, Vol. VI. 1993/94, No. 272, September.

Pauw, Ernst-Josef. 1970. "Banking in East Africa." In *Financial Aspects of Development in East Africa.* Edited by P. Marlin. Munich: Weltforum-Verlag, 175–258.

Peltzman, Sam. 1970. "Capital Investment in Commercial Banking and Its Relationship to Portfolio Regulation." *Journal of Political Economy,* 78(1, January–February): 1–26.

Pérez-Campanero, Juan, and Alfredo M. Leóne. 1991. "Liberalization and Financial Crisis in Uruguay, 1974–87." In *Banking Crises: Cases and Issues.* Edited by Venkataraman Sundararajan and Tomás J. T. Baliño. Washington, D.C.: International Monetary Fund, 276–375.

Persson, Torsten, and Lars E. O. Svensson. 1985. "Current Account Dynamics and the Terms of Trade: Harberger-Laursen-Metzler Two Generations Later." *Journal of Political Economy,* 93(1, February): 43–65.

Petrei, A. Humberto, and James R. Tybout. 1985. "Microeconomic Adjustments in Argentina during 1976–81: The Importance of Changing Levels of Financial Subsidies." *World Development,* 13(8, August): 949–967.

Phelps, Edmund S. 1973. "Inflation in the Theory of Public Finance." *Swedish Journal of Economics,* 75(1, March): 67–82.

Pigott, Charles. 1986. "Financial Reform and the Role of Foreign Banks in Pacific Basin Nations." In *Financial Policy and Reform in Pacific Basin Countries.* Edited by Hang-Sheng Cheng. Boulder, Colo.: Westview Press, 265–295.

Plosser, Charles I. 1982. "Government Financial Decisions and Asset Returns." *Journal of Monetary Economics,* 9(3, May): 325–352.

Podolski, Tadeusz M. 1973. *Socialist Banking and Monetary Control: The Experience of Poland.* Cambridge: Cambridge University Press.

Polak, Jacques J. 1989. *Financial Policies and Development.* Paris: Organisation for Economic Co-operation and Development.

Polizatto, Vincent P. 1990. "Prudential Regulation and Banking Supervision: Building an Institutional Framework for Banks." Washington, D.C.: World Bank, Development Economics, PPR Working Paper WPS 340, January.

Popiel, Paul A., and Ismail Dalla. 1984. "The Islamization of Pakistan's Financial Sector." Washington, D.C.: World Bank, December.

Porzecanski, Arturo. 1979. "Patterns of Monetary Policy in Latin America." *Journal of Money, Credit and Banking,* 11(4, November): 427–437.

Que, Agustin V. 1979. "Financial System." In *Korea: Policy Issues for Long-Term Development.* Edited by Parvez Hasan and D. C. Rao. Baltimore: Johns Hopkins University Press for the World Bank, 365–403.

Radcliffe Committee. 1959. *Report of the Committee on the Working of the Monetary System (Radcliffe Report).* London: Her Majesty's Stationery Office.

Ram, Rati. 1982. "Further Evidence on Keynes' 'Finance Motive' in Demand for Money." *Atlantic Economic Journal,* 10(4, December): 102–103.

Rama, Martin. 1990. "Empirical Investment Equations in Developing Countries." Washington, D.C.: World Bank, PRE Working Paper WPS 563, December.

Ramsey, Frank P. 1928. "A Mathematical Theory of Saving." *Economic Journal,* 38(152, December): 543–559.

Rana, Pradumna B., and J. Malcolm Dowling. 1988. "The Impact of Foreign Capital on Growth: Evidences from Asian Developing Countries." *Developing Economies,* 26(1, March): 3–11.

———. 1990. "Foreign Capital and Asian Economic Growth." *Asian Development Review,* 8(2): 77–102.

Raut, Lakshmi K., and Arvind Virmani. 1989. "Determinants of Consumption and Savings Behavior in Developing Countries." *World Bank Economic Review,* 3(3, September): 379–393.

Ravallion, Martin, and Abhijit Sen. 1986. "On Some Estimates of an Asian Savings Function." *Economics Letters,* 20(2): 121–124.

Razin, Assaf, and Efraim Sadka. 1989. "Optimal Incentives to Domestic Investment in the Presence of Capital Flight." Washington, D.C.: International Monetary Fund, WP/89/79, August.

Rebelo, Sergio. 1991. "Long-Run Policy Analysis and Long-Run Growth." *Journal of Political Economy,* 99(3, June): 500–521.

————. 1992. "Growth in Open Economies." *Carnegie-Rochester Conference Series on Public Policy,* (36, July): 5–46.

Reisen, Helmut, and Hélène Yèches. 1991. "Time-Varying Estimates on the Openness of the Capital Account in Korea and Taiwan." Paris: Organisation for Economic Co-operation and Development, OECD Development Centre Technical Paper No. 42, August.

Remolona, Eli M. 1982. "Inflation, Debt, and the Reserve Tax: A Theory of Optimal Deficit Finance." Stanford: Stanford University, Ph.D. thesis.

Reuber, Grant L. 1964. "The Objectives of Canadian Monetary Policy, 1949–61: Empirical 'Trade-Offs' and the Reaction Function of the Authorities." *Journal of Political Economy,* 72(2, April): 109–132.

Revell, Jack S. 1980. *Costs and Margins in Banking: An International Survey.* Paris: Organisation for Economic Co-operation and Development.

Ricardo, David. 1817. *On the Principles of Political Economy, and Taxation.* London: John Murray.

Richard, Denis, and Delano P. Villanueva. 1980. "Relative Efficiency of Banking Systems in LDCs: The Philippine Experience." *Journal of Banking and Finance,* 4(4, December): 315–334.

Rittenberg, Libby. 1988. "Financial Liberalization and Savings in Turkey." In *Liberalization and the Turkish Economy.* Edited by Tevfik F. Nas and Mehmet Odekon. Westport, Conn.: Greenwood Press, 115–127.

————. 1991. "Investment Spending and Interest Rate Policy: The Case of Financial Liberalisation in Turkey." *Journal of Development Studies,* 27(2, January): 151–167.

Robbins, Sidney M. 1980. "A Securities Market Development Program for Bangladesh." Washington, D.C.: International Finance Corporation, August.

Robertson, James. 1974. "... the Argument Continues ..." *Bankers' Magazine,* (1559, February): 35–36.

Robinson, David J., and Peter Stella. 1988. "Amalgamating Central Bank and Fiscal Deficits." In *Measurement of Fiscal Impact: Methodological Issues.* Edited by Mario I. Blejer and Ke-Young Chu. Washington, D.C.: International Monetary Fund, Occasional Paper 59, June, 20–31.

Rodrik, Dani. 1990. "Premature Liberalization, Incomplete Stabilization: The Ozal Decade in Turkey." London: Centre for Economic Policy Research, CEPR Discussion Paper No. 402, April.

Roe, Alan R. 1982. "High Interest Rates: A New Conventional Wisdom for Development Policy? Some Conclusions from Sri Lankan Experience." *World Development,* 10(3, March): 211–222.

Bibliography

Roe, Alan R., and Paul A. Popiel. 1990. "The Restructuring of Financial Systems in Latin America." Washington, D.C.: World Bank, EDI Policy Seminar Report No. 25, July.

Roemer, Michael, and Christine Jones, eds. 1991. *Markets in Developing Countries: Parallel, Fragmented, and Black.* San Francisco: International Center for Economic Growth.

Romer, David. 1985. "Financial Intermediation, Reserve Requirements, and Inside Money." *Journal of Monetary Economics,* 16(2, September): 175–194.

Romer, Paul M. 1986. "Increasing Returns and Long-Run Growth." *Journal of Political Economy,* 94(5, October): 1002–1037.

————. 1990. "Endogenous Technological Change." *Journal of Political Economy,* 98(5, ii, October): S71–S102.

————. 1991. "Increasing Returns and New Developments in the Theory of Growth." In *Equilibrium Theory and Applications: Proceedings of the Sixth International Symposium in Economic Theory and Econometrics.* Edited by William A. Barnett, Bernard Cornet, Claude d'Aspermont, Jean J. Gabszewicz, and Andreu Mas-Colell. Cambridge: Cambridge University Press, 83–110.

Rosenzweig, Mark R., and Kenneth I. Wolpin. 1993. "Credit Market Constraints, Consumption Smoothing, and the Accumulation of Durable Production Assets in Low-Income Countries: Investment in Bullocks in India." *Journal of Political Economy,* 101(2, April): 223–244.

Rossi, Nicola. 1988. "Government Spending, the Real Interest Rate, and the Behavior of Liquidity-Constrained Consumers in Developing Countries." *International Monetary Fund Staff Papers,* 35(1, March): 104–140.

Roubini, Nouriel, and Xavier Sala-i-Martin. 1991. "Financial Development, the Trade Regime, and Economic Growth." Cambridge, Mass.: National Bureau of Economic Research, NBER Working Paper No. 3876, October.

————. 1992a. "A Growth Model of Inflation, Tax Evasion, and Financial Repression." Cambridge, Mass.: National Bureau of Economic Research, NBER Working Paper No. 4062, May.

————. 1992b. "Financial Repression and Economic Growth." *Journal of Development Economics,* 39(1, July): 5–30.

Rybczynski, Tadeusz M. 1986. "The Internationalization of the Financial System and the Developing Countries." Washington, D.C.: World Bank, Staff Working Paper No. 788, January.

Sachs, Jeffrey D. 1984. "Theoretical Issues in International Borrowing." *Princeton Studies in International Finance,* (54), July.

————. 1985. "External Debt and Macroeconomic Performance in Latin America and East Asia." *Brookings Papers on Economic Activity,* (2): 523–564.

————. 1986. "Managing the LDC Debt Crisis." *Brookings Papers on Economic Activity,* (2): 397–431.

————, ed. 1989. *Developing Country Debt and the World Economy.* Chicago: University of Chicago Press for the National Bureau of Economic Research.

————, ed. 1990. *Developing Country Debt and Economic Performance*, Vols. 1–3. Chicago: University of Chicago Press for the National Bureau of Economic Research.

St Hill, Rodney L. 1992. "Stages of Banking and Economic Development." *Savings and Development*, 14(1): 5–20.

Saint-Paul, Gilles. 1992a. "Technological Choice, Financial Markets and Economic Development." *European Economic Review*, 36(4, May): 763–781.

————. 1992b. "Technological Dualism, Incomplete Financial Markets and Economic Development." *Journal of International Trade and Economic Development*, 1(1, June): 13–26.

Samson, Michael. 1992. "Financial Repression, Directed Credit Subsidies, and Declining Income: Problem of Optimal Monetary Control." Stanford: Stanford University, November.

Saracoglu, Rüşdü. 1984. "Expectations of Inflation and Interest Rate Determination." *International Monetary Fund Staff Papers*, 31(1, March): 141–178.

Sayad, João. 1983. "The Impact of Rural Credit on Production and Income Distribution in Brazil." In *Rural Financial Markets in Developing Countries: Their Use and Abuse*. Edited by John D. Von Pischke, Dale W Adams, and Gordon Donald. Baltimore: Johns Hopkins University Press for the Economic Development Institute of the World Bank, 379–386.

Schadler, Susan M., Maria Carkovic, Adam Bennett, and Robert Khan. 1993. "Recent Experiences with Surges in Capital Inflows." Washington, D.C.: International Monetary Fund, Occasional Paper 108, December.

Scheinkman, José A., and Laurence Weiss. 1986. "Borrowing Constraints and Aggregate Economic Activity." *Econometrica*, 54(1, January): 23–45.

Schiantarelli, Fabio, Izak Atiyas, Gerard Caprio, Jr., John Harris, and Andrew Weiss. 1994. "Credit Where It Is Due? A Review of the Macro and Micro Evidence on the Real Effects of Financial Reform." In *Financial Reform: Theory and Experience*. Edited by Gerard Caprio, Jr., Izak Atiyas, and James Hanson. New York: Cambridge University Press, forthcoming.

Schiantarelli, Fabio, Andrew Weiss, Miranda Gultom, and Fidel Jaramillo. 1994. "Financial Liberalization and the Efficiency of Investment Allocation." Boston: Boston College, Working Paper in Economics No. 266, May.

Scholnick, Barry. 1991. "Testing a Disequilibrium Model of Lending Rate Determination: The Case of Malaysia." Washington, D.C.: International Monetary Fund, WP/91/84, September.

————. 1993. "Financial Liberalization and Economic Integration." Cambridge: University of Cambridge, Ph.D. thesis.

Schreft, Stacey L. 1992. "Welfare-Improving Credit Controls." *Journal of Monetary Economics*, 30(1, October): 57–72.

Schumpeter, Joseph A. 1912. *Theorie der wirtschaftlichen Entwicklung*. Leipzig: Duncker & Humblot. [*The Theory of Economic Development; An Inquiry into Profits, Capital, Credit, Interest, and the Business Cycle*. Translated by Redvers Opie. Cambridge, Mass.: Harvard University Press, 1934.]

Schumpeter, Joseph A. 1939. *Business Cycles; A Theoretical, Historical, and Statistical Analysis of the Capitalist Process,* 2 vols. New York: McGraw-Hill.

Scott, Maurice FG. 1989. *A New View of Economic Growth.* Oxford: Clarendon Press.

———. 1992. "A New Theory of Endogenous Economic Growth." *Oxford Review of Economic Policy,* 8(4, Winter): 29–42.

Seabright, Paul B. 1991a. "Identifying Investment Opportunities for the Poor: Evidence from the Livestock Market in South India." *Journal of Development Studies,* 28(1, October): 53–73.

———. 1992b. "Quality of Livestock Assets under Selective Credit Schemes: Evidence from South Indian Data." *Journal of Development Economics,* 37(1–2, November): 327–350.

Seibel, Hans Dieter. 1989a. "Finance With the Poor, By the Poor, For the Poor— Financial Technologies for the Informal Sector with Case Studies from Indonesia." *Social Strategies,* 3(2, December): 3–48.

———. 1989b. "Linking Informal and Formal Financial Institutions in Africa and Asia." In *Microenterprises in Developing Countries.* Edited by Jacob Levitsky. London: Intermediate Technology Publications, 97–118.

———. 1991. "Developing the Financial System through Deregulation." *Asia-Pacific Rural Finance,* 4(1, July–September): 30–37.

Seibel, Hans Dieter, and Uben Parhusip. 1992. "Linking Informal and Formal Finance: An Indonesian Example." In *Informal Finance in Low-Income Countries.* Edited by Dale W Adams and Delbert A. Fitchett. Boulder, Colo.: Westview Press, 1–17.

Sengupta, Jati K. 1991. "Rapid Growth in NICs in Asia: Tests of New Growth Theory for Korea." *Kyklos,* 44(4): 561–579.

Servén, Luis, and Andrés Solimano. 1991. "Adjustment Policies and Investment Performance in Developing Countries: Theory, Country Experiences, and Policy Implications." Washington, D.C.: World Bank, PRE Working Paper WPS 606, March.

Shaw, Edward S. 1973. *Financial Deepening in Economic Development.* New York: Oxford University Press.

———. 1975. "Inflation, Finance and Capital Markets." *Federal Reserve Bank of San Francisco Economic Review,* (December): 5–20.

———. 1976. "Portuguese Policy: Repression or Recovery?" In *Portuguese Monetary Problems.* By Maxwell J. Fry. Lisbon: Banco de Portugal, 8–17.

Shea, Jia-Dong. 1990. "Financial Development in Taiwan: A Macro Analysis." Taipei: Academia Sinica. Conference on Financial Development in Japan, Korea and Taiwan, 27–28 August.

———. 1992. "The Welfare Effects of Economic Liberalization under Financial Market." *Academia Economic Papers,* 20(2, ii, September): 697–716.

———. 1994. "Taiwan: Growth and Structural Change of the Financial System." In *Financial Development in Japan, Korea and Taiwan.* Edited by Hugh T. Patrick and Yung Chul Park. New York: Oxford University Press, forthcoming.

Shea, Jia-Dong, and Ya-Hwei Yang. 1990. "Financial System and the Allocation of Investment Funds." Taiwan: Chung-Hua Institution for Economic Research, Occasional Paper No. 9001, December.

Sheng, Andrew. 1989. "Bank Restructuring in Malaysia 1985-88." Washington, D.C.: World Bank, PPR Working Paper WPS 54, September.

————. 1991. "The Art of Bank Restructuring: Issues and Techniques." Washington, D.C.: World Bank, EDI Working Papers.

Shengyuan, Wu. 1988. "Financial System Reform in China." *International Journal of Development Banking*, 6(2, July): 39–42.

Shigehara, Kumiharu. 1991. "Japan's Experience with Use of Monetary Policy and the Process of Liberalization." *Bank of Japan Monetary and Economic Studies*, 9(1, March): 1–21.

Shipton, Parker. 1991. "Time and Money in the Western Sahel: A Clash of Cultures in Gambian Rural Finance." In *Markets in Developing Countries: Parallel, Fragmented, and Black*. Edited by Michael Roemer and Christine Jones. San Francisco: International Center for Economic Growth, 113–139.

Shoup, Carl S. 1969. *Public Finance.* Chicago: Aldine.

Siamwalla, Ammar, Chirmsak Pinthong, Nipon Poapongsakorn, Ploenpit Satsanguan, Prayong Nettayarak, Wanrak Mingmaneenakin, and Yuavares Tubpun. 1990. "The Thai Rural Credit System: Public Subsidies, Private Information, and Segmented Markets." *World Bank Economic Review,* 4(3, September): 271–295.

Sideri, Sandro. 1987. "China's Financial System and Economic Development." *Savings and Development,* 11(1): 77–92.

Sidrauski, Miguel. 1966. "Inflation and Economic Growth." *Journal of Political Economy,* 75(6, December): 776–810.

————. 1967. "Rational Choice and Patterns of Economic Growth in a Monetary Economy." *American Economic Review,* 57(2, May): 535–545.

Simha, Seshadriiyengar L. N. 1976. *Development Banking in India.* Madras: Institute for Financial Management and Research.

Sines, Richard H. 1979. " 'Financial Deepening' and Industrial Production: A Microeconomic Analysis of the Venezuelan Food Processing Sector." *Social and Economic Studies,* 28(2, June): 450–474.

Skanland, Hermod. 1984. *The Central Bank and Political Authorities in Some Industrial Countries.* Oslo: Norges Banks Skriftserie No. 13.

Skully, Michael T., and George J. Viksnins. 1987. *Financing East Asia's Success: Comparative Financial Development in Eight Asian Countries.* New York: St. Martin's Press.

Smaghi, Lorenzo Bini. 1982. "Independent Monetary Policy and Capital Mobility in LDCs: The Case of Malaysia, 1978–1981." Washington, D.C.: International Monetary Fund, DM/82/72, November.

Smith, Adam. 1776. *An Inquiry into the Nature and Causes of the Wealth of Nations.* London: W. Strahan & T. Cadell.

Smith, Roger S. 1990. "Factors Affecting Saving, Policy Tools, and Tax Reform: A Review." *International Monetary Fund Staff Papers,* 37(1, March): 1–70.

Snowden, P. Nicholas. 1987. "Financial Market Liberalisation in LDCs: The Incidence of Risk Allocation Effects of Interest Rate Increases." *Journal of Development Studies,* 24(1, October): 83–93.

Solimano, Andrés. 1989. "How Private Investment Reacts to Changing Macroeconomic Conditions." Washington, D.C.: World Bank, PPR Working Paper WPS 212, December.

Solow, Robert M. 1956. "A Contribution to the Theory of Economic Growth." *Quarterly Journal of Economics,* 70(1, February): 65–94.

Spears, Annie. 1991. "Financial Development and Economic Growth—Causality Tests." *Atlantic Economic Journal,* 19(3, September): 66.

Spellman, Lewis J. 1976. "Economic Growth and Financial Intermediation." In *Money and Finance in Economic Growth and Development: Essays in Honor of Edward S. Shaw.* Edited by Ronald I. McKinnon. New York: Marcel Dekker, 11–22.

Spigelman, David F. 1987. "Macroeconomic Instability of the Less Developed Country Economy when Bank Credit Is Rationed." Stanford: Stanford University, Center for Research in Economic Growth, Memorandum No. 272, July.

Spiller, Pablo T., and Edgardo Favaro. 1984. "The Effects of Entry Regulation on Oligopolistic Interaction: The Uruguayan Banking Sector." *Rand Journal of Economics,* 15(2, Summer): 244–254.

Stiglitz, Joseph E. 1990. "Peer Monitoring and Credit Markets." *World Bank Economic Review,* 4(3, September): 351–366.

———. 1993. "Perspectives on the Role of Government Risk-Bearing within the Financial Sector." In *Government Risk-Bearing.* Edited by Mark S. Sniderman. Norwell, Mass.: Kluwer Academic Publishers, 109–130.

———. 1994. "The Role of the State in Financial Markets." In *Proceedings of the World Bank Annual Bank Conference on Development Economics 1993.* Edited by Michael Bruno and Boris Pleskovic. Washington, D.C.: World Bank, 19–52.

Stiglitz, Joseph E., and Andrew Weiss. 1981. "Credit Rationing in Markets with Imperfect Information." *American Economic Review,* 71(3, June): 393–410.

———. 1983. "Incentive Effects of Terminations: Applications to the Credit and Labor Markets." *American Economic Review,* 73(5, December): 912–927.

———. 1986. "Credit Rationing and Collateral." In *Recent Developments in Corporate Finance.* Edited by Jeremy Edwards, Julian Franks, Colin Mayer, and Stephen Schaefer. Cambridge: Cambridge University Press, 101–143.

Stockman, Alan C. 1981. "Anticipated Inflation and the Capital Stock in a Cash-in-Advance Economy." *Journal of Monetary Economics,* 8(3, November): 387–393.

Stokey, Nancy L. 1991. "Human Capital, Product Quality, and Growth." *Quarterly Journal of Economics,* 56(2, May): 587–616.

Summers, Lawrence H. 1981. "Capital Taxation and Accumulation in a Life Cycle Growth Model." *American Economic Review,* 71(4, September): 533–544.

Sundararajan, Venkataraman. 1985. "Debt-Equity Ratios of Firms and Interest Rate Policy: Macroeconomic Effects of High Leverage in Developing Countries." *International Monetary Fund Staff Papers,* 32(3, September): 430–474.

————. 1986a. "Exchange Rate versus Credit Policy: Analysis with a Monetary Model of Trade and Inflation in India." *Journal of Development Economics,* 20(1, January–February): 75–105.

————. 1986b. "The Debt-Equity Ratio of Firms and the Effectiveness of Interest Rate Policy: Analysis with a Dynamic Model of Saving, Investment, and Growth in Korea." Washington, D.C.: International Monetary Fund, June.

Sundararajan, Venkataraman, and Tomás J. T. Baliño. 1991. "Issues in Recent Banking Crises." In *Banking Crises: Cases and Issues.* Edited by Venkataraman Sundararajan and Tomás J. T. Baliño. Washington, D.C.: International Monetary Fund, 1–57.

Sundararajan, Venkataraman, and Subhash Thakur. 1980. "Public Investment, Crowding Out, and Growth: A Dynamic Model Applied to India and Korea." *International Monetary Fund Staff Papers,* 27(4, December): 814–855.

Sundaravej, Tipsuda, and Prasarn Trairatvorakul. 1989. "Experience of Financial Distress in Thailand." Washington, D.C.: World Bank, PPR Working Paper WPS 283, December.

Sussman, Oren. 1992. "Financial Liberalization: The Israeli Experience." *Oxford Economic Papers,* 44(3, July): 387–402.

————. 1993. "A Theory of Financial Development." In *Finance and Development: Issues and Experience.* Edited by Alberto Giovannini. Cambridge: Cambridge University Press, 29–57.

Suzuki, Yoshio, and Hiroshi Yomo, eds. 1986. *Financial Innovation and Monetary Policy: Asia and the West.* Tokyo: University of Tokyo Press.

Svensson, Lars E. O., and Assaf Razin. 1983. "The Terms of Trade and the Current Account: The Harberger-Laursen-Metzler Effect." *Journal of Political Economy,* 91(1, February): 97–125.

Tait, Alan A. 1989. "Not So General Equilibrium and Not So Optimal Taxation." *Public Finance,* 44(2): 169–182.

Talley, Samuel H., and Ignacio Mas. 1992. "The Role of Deposit Insurance." In *Financial Regulation: Changing the Rules of the Game.* Edited by Dimitri Vittas. Washington, D.C.: World Bank, EDI Development Studies, 321–351.

Tan, Augustine H. H., and Basant Kapur, eds. 1986. *Pacific Growth and Financial Interdependence.* Sydney: Allen and Unwin.

Tanzi, Vito. 1976. "Fiscal Policy, Keynesian Economics and the Mobilization of Savings in Developing Countries." *World Development,* 4(10–11, October–November): 907–917.

————. 1977. "Inflation, Lags in Collection, and the Real Value of Tax Revenue." *International Monetary Fund Staff Papers,* 24(1, March): 154–167.

————. 1982. "Fiscal Disequilibrium in Developing Countries." *World Development,* 10(12, December): 1069–1082.

————. 1989. "Lags in Tax Collection and the Case for Inflationary Finance: Theory with Simulations." In *Fiscal Policy, Stabilization, and Growth in Developing Countries.* Edited by Mario I. Blejer and Ke-Young Chu. Washington, D.C.: International Monetary Fund, 208–237.

Tanzi, Vito, and Mario I. Blejer. 1982. "Inflation, Interest Rate Policy, and Currency Substitutions in Developing Economies: A Discussion of Some Major Issues." *World Development*, 10(9, September): 781–789.

Tanzi, Vito, Mario I. Blejer, and Mario O. Teijeiro. 1988. "Effects of Inflation on the Measurement of Fiscal Deficits." In *Measurement of Fiscal Impacts: Methodological Issues*. Edited by Mario I. Blejer and Ke-Young Chu. Washington, D.C.: International Monetary Fund, Occasional Paper 59, June, 4–19.

Taylor, Lance. 1979. *Macro Models for Developing Countries*. New York: McGraw-Hill.

———. 1981. "*IS/LM* in the Tropics: Diagrammatics of the New Structuralist Macro Critique." In *Economic Stabilization in Developing Countries*. Edited by William R. Cline and Sidney Weintraub. Washington, D.C.: Brookings Institution, 465–503.

———. 1983. *Structuralist Macroeconomics: Applicable Models for the Third World*. New York: Basic Books.

———. 1991. "Economic Openness: Problems to the Century's End." In *Economic Liberalization: No Panacea. The Experiences of Latin America and Asia*. Edited by Tariq Banuri. Oxford: Oxford University Press, 99–147.

Teijeiro, Mario O. 1989. "Central Bank Losses: Origins, Conceptual Issues, and Measurement Problems." Washington, D.C.: World Bank, PPR Working Paper WPS 293, October.

Tenconi, Roland. 1986. "The Malagasy Banking System." Washington, D.C.: World Bank.

Teranishi, Juro. 1990. "Financial System and the Industrialization of Japan: 1900–1970." *Banca Nazionale del Lavoro Quarterly Review*, (174, September): 309–341.

Terrell, Henry S. 1986. "The Role of Foreign Banks in Domestic Banking Markets." In *Financial Policy and Reform in Pacific Basin Countries*. Edited by Hang-Sheng Cheng. Boulder, Colo.: Westview Press, 297–304.

Thirlwall, Anthony P. 1974. *Inflation, Saving and Growth in Developing Economies*. London: Macmillan.

Thomas, James J. 1992. "Whatever Happened to the Urban Informal Sector? The Regressive Effect of 'Double Dualism' on the Financial Analysis of Developing Countries." *Bulletin of Latin American Research*, 11(3): 279–294.

———. 1993a. "The Informal Financial Sector: How Does It Operate and Who Are the Customers?" In *Monetary Policy in Developing Countries*. Edited by Sheila Page. London: Routledge, 227–250.

———. 1993b. "Replicating the Grameen Bank: The Latin American Experience." London: London School of Economics, Department of Economics, April.

Thornton, John. 1991. "The Financial Repression Paradigm: A Survey of Empirical Research." *Savings and Development*, 15(1): 5–18.

———. 1994. "Financial Deepening and Economic Growth: Evidence from Asian Economies." *Savings and Development*, 18(1): 41–51.

Thornton, John, and Sri Ram Poudyal. 1990. "Money and Capital in Economic Development: A Test of the McKinnon Hypothesis for Nepal." *Journal of Money, Credit, and Banking*, 22(3, August): 395–399.

Timberg, Thomas A., and C. V. Aiyar. 1984. "Informal Credit Markets in India." *Economic Development and Cultural Change*, 33(1, October): 43–59.

Tobin, James. 1965. "Money and Economic Growth." *Econometrica*, 33(4, October): 671–684.

————. 1984. "On the Efficiency of the Financial System." *Lloyds Bank Review*, (153, July): 1–15.

————. 1992. "Money." In *The New Palgrave Dictionary of Money and Finance*, Vol. 2. Edited by Peter Newman, Murray Milgate, and John Eatwell. London: Macmillan, 770–778.

Townsend, Robert M. 1978. "Intermediation with Costly Bilateral Exchange." *Review of Economic Studies*, 45(3, October): 417–425.

————. 1983a. "Theories of Intermediated Structures." *Carnegie-Rochester Conference Series on Public Policy*, (18, Spring): 221–272.

————. 1983b. "Financial Structure and Economic Activity." *American Economic Review*, 73(5, December): 895–911.

Tseng, Wanda, and Robert Corker. 1991. "Financial Liberalization, Money Demand, and Monetary Policy in Asian Countries." Washington, D.C.: International Monetary Fund, Occasional Paper 84, July.

Tsiang, Sho-Chieh. 1980a. "Keynes's 'Finance' Demand for Liquidity, Robertson's Loanable Funds Theory, and Friedman's Monetarism." *Quarterly Journal of Economics*, 94(3, May): 467–491.

————. 1980b. "Exchange Rate, Interest Rate and Economic Development." In *Quantitative Economics and Development: Essays in Memory of Ta-Chung Liu.* Edited by Lawrence R. Klein, Marc Nerlove, and Sho-Chieh Tsiang. New York: Academic Press, 309–346.

————. 1989. *Finance Constraints and the Theory of Money: Selected Papers.* Boston: Academic Press.

Tybout, James R. 1983. "Credit Rationing and Investment Behavior in a Developing Country." *Review of Economics and Statistics*, 65(4, November): 598–607.

————. 1984. "Interest Controls and Credit Allocation in Developing Countries." *Journal of Money, Credit and Banking*, 16(4, i, November): 474–487.

————. 1986. "A Firm-Level Chronicle of Financial Crises in the Southern Cone." *Journal of Development Economics*, 24(2, December): 371–400.

Udry, Christopher. 1990. "Credit Markets in Northern Nigeria: Credit as Insurance in a Rural Economy." *World Bank Economic Review*, 4(3, September): 251–269.

Uluatam, F. Aynur. 1973. *Monetary Multipliers and a Self Generating Inflation Model: The Turkish Case.* Ankara: Turkish Republic State Planning Organisation.

United Nations. 1970. *Economic Survey of Asia and the Far East 1969.* Bangkok: United Nations Economic Commission for Asia and the Far East.

————. 1984. "General-Purpose Banks: Their Role in the Mobilization and Conversion of Savings." In *Savings for Development: Report of the Second International Symposium on the Mobilization of Personal Savings in Developing Countries, Kuala Lumpur, 15–21 March 1982.* New York: United Nations, 90–99.

Van Agtmael, Antoine W. 1984. *Emerging Securities Markets: Investment Banking Opportunities in the Developing World.* London: Euromoney.

Van Hoose, David D. 1986. "A Note on Interest on Required Reserves as an Instrument of Monetary Control." *Journal of Banking and Finance,* 10(1, March): 147–156.

Van Wijnbergen, Sweder. 1982. "Stagflationary Effects of Monetary Stabilization Policies: A Quantitative Analysis of South Korea." *Journal of Development Economics,* 10(2, April): 133–169.

————. 1983a. "Interest Rate Management in LDCs." *Journal of Monetary Economics,* 12(3, September): 433–452.

————. 1983b. "Credit Policy, Inflation and Growth in a Financially Repressed Economy." *Journal of Development Economics,* 13(1–2, August–October): 45–65.

————. 1985. "Macro-economic Effects of Changes in Bank Interest Rates: Simulation Results for South Korea." *Journal of Development Economics,* 18(2–3, August): 541–554.

Varoudakis, Aristomène A. 1992. "Financial Development as an Engine of Growth." Strasbourg: Université Louis Pasteur, Bureau d'Economie Théorique et Appliquée, no. 9212, September.

Velasco, Andrés. 1986a. "Liberalization, Crisis, Intervention: The Chilean Financial System, 1975–1985." Washington, D.C.: International Monetary Fund, Central Banking Department, December.

————. 1986b. "Financial Crises and Balance of Payments Crises: A Simple Model of the Southern Cone Experience." Washington, D.C.: International Monetary Fund, Central Banking Department, December.

————. 1991. "Liberalization, Crisis, Intervention: The Chilean Financial System, 1975–1985." In *Banking Crises: Cases and Issues.* Edited by Venkataraman Sundararajan and Tomás J. T. Baliño. Washington, D.C.: International Monetary Fund, 113–174.

Veneroso, Frank. 1986. "New Patterns of Financial Instability." Washington, D.C.: World Bank, February.

Venkatachalam, T. R., and Y. S. R. Sarma. 1978. "An Econometric Analysis of Financial Behaviour of the Private Corporate Sector in India." *Reserve Bank of India Staff Occasional Papers,* 3(2, December): 69–87.

Viksnins, George J. 1980. *Financial Deepening in ASEAN Countries.* Honolulu: Pacific Forum, distributed by University Press of Hawaii.

Villanueva, Delano P., and Abbas Mirakhor. 1990. "Strategies for Financial Reforms: Interest Rate Policies, Stabilization, and Bank Supervision in Developing Countries." *International Monetary Fund Staff Papers,* 37(3, September): 509–536.

Villanueva, Delano P., and Katrine A. Saito. 1978. "Transaction Costs of Credit to the Small-Scale Sector in the Philippines." Washington, D.C.: International Monetary Fund, DM/78/112, December.

Virmani, Arvind. 1982. "The Nature of Credit Markets in Developing Countries: A Framework for Policy Analysis." Washington, D.C.: World Bank, Staff Working Paper No. 524.

————. 1984. "Evaluation of Financial Policy: Credit Allocation in Bangladesh." Washington, D.C.: World Bank, Staff Working Paper No. 672, October.

————. 1985. "Government Policy and the Development of Financial Markets: The Case of Korea." Washington, D.C.: World Bank, Staff Working Paper No. 747, August.

Vittas, Dimitri. 1991a. "The Impact of Regulation on Financial Intermediation." Washington, D.C.: World Bank, PRE Working Paper WPS 746, August.

————. 1991b. "Measuring Commercial Bank Efficiency: Use and Misuse of Bank Operating Ratios." Washington, D.C.: World Bank, PR Working Paper WPS 806, November.

Vittas, Dimitri, ed. 1992. *Financial Regulation: Changing the Rules of the Game.* Washington, D.C.: World Bank, EDI Development Studies.

Vittas, Dimitri, and Bo Wang. 1991. "Credit Policies in Japan and Korea." Washington, D.C.: World Bank, PRE Working Paper WPS 747, August.

Vogel, Robert C. 1984. "The Effect of Subsidized Agricultural Credit on Income Distribution in Costa Rica." In *Undermining Rural Development with Cheap Credit.* Edited by Dale W Adams, Douglas H. Graham, and John D. Von Pischke. Boulder, Colo.: Westview Press, 133–145.

Vogel, Robert C., and Stephen A. Buser. 1976. "Inflation, Financial Repression, and Capital Formation in Latin America." In *Money and Finance in Economic Growth and Development: Essays in Honor of Edward S. Shaw.* Edited by Ronald I. McKinnon. New York: Marcel Dekker, 35–70.

Von Pischke, John D. 1991. *Finance at the Frontier: Debt Capacity and the Role of Credit in the Private Economy.* Washington, D.C.: World Bank, Economic Development Institute.

Von Pischke, John D., Dale W Adams, and Gordon Donald, eds. 1983. *Rural Financial Markets in Developing Countries.* Baltimore: Johns Hopkins University Press for the World Bank.

Voridis, Hercules. 1993. "Ceilings on Interest Rates and Investment: The Example of Greece." *Review of Economics and Statistics,* 75(2, May): 276–283.

Wai, U Tun. 1972. *Financial Intermediaries and National Savings.* New York: Praeger.

————. 1977. "A Revisit to Interest Rates Outside the Organized Money Markets of Underdeveloped Countries." *Banca Nazionale del Lavoro Quarterly Review,* (122, September): 291–312.

————. 1980. *Economic Essays on Developing Countries.* Alphen aan den Rijn: Sijthoff and Noordhoff.

————. 1981. "The Role of Unorganized Financial Markets in Economic Development and in the Formulation of Monetary Policy." Washington, D.C.: International Monetary Fund, DM/81/10, February.

Wai, U Tun, and Hugh T. Patrick. 1973. "Stock and Bond Issues and Capital Markets in Less Developed Countries." *International Monetary Fund Staff Papers,* 20(2, July): 253–317.

Wall, Peter. 1981. "Fiscal Policies for the Development of Equity Markets: A Survey of Country Experiences." Washington, D.C.: International Finance Corporation, IFC–507–A, June.

Watanabe, Kenichiro. 1991. "Financial Reform in Asian Economies and Its Implications." Tokyo: Bank of Japan, International Department, January.

Watanagase, Tarisa. 1992. "Financial Reform: Thailand." Bangkok: Bank of Thailand, Department of Bank Supervision and Examination.

Watson, C. Maxwell, G. Russell Kincaid, Caroline Atkinson, Eliot Kalter, and David Folkerts-Landau. 1986. "International Capital Markets: Developments and Prospects." Washington, D.C.: International Monetary Fund, World Economic and Financial Surveys, December.

Webber, Carolyn, and Aaron Wildavsky. 1986. *A History of Taxation and Expenditure in the Western World.* New York: Simon and Schuster.

Weicai, Wang. 1986. "China's Economic and Financial Reform." In *Financial Policy and Reform in Pacific Basin Countries.* Edited by Hang-Sheng Cheng. Lexington, Mass.: D. C. Heath and Co., Lexington Books, 227–234.

Wellons, Philip, Dimitri Germidis, and Bianca Glavanis. 1986. *Banks and Specialised Financial Intermediaries in Development.* Paris: Development Centre of the Organisation for Economic Co-operation and Development.

White, Kenneth J. 1978. "A General Computer Program for Econometric Methods— SHAZAM." *Econometrica,* 46(1, January): 239–240.

Wickens, Michael, and Merih Uctum. 1993. "The Sustainability of Current Account Deficits: A Test of the US Intertemporal Budget Constraint." *Journal of Economic Dynamics and Control,* 17(3, May): 423–441.

Williamson, Stephen D. 1986. "Costly Monitoring, Financial Intermediation, and Equilibrium Credit Rationing." *Journal of Monetary Economics,* 18(2, September): 159–179.

Wilson, J. Stuart G. 1986. "A Money Market for Thailand?" *Banca Nazionale del Lavoro Quarterly Review,* (158, September): 299–317.

Winters, L. Alan. 1987. "An Empirical Intertemporal Model of Developing Countries' Imports." *Weltwirtschaftliches Archiv,* 123(1): 58–80.

Woo, Wing Thye. 1992. "The Influence of Indonesia's Financial Policies on Its Economic Development." Davis, Calif.: University of California, January.

Wood, Anthony. 1993. "Financial Development and Economic Growth in Barbados: Causal Evidence." *Savings and Development,* 17(4): 379–390.

World Bank. 1974. "Bank Policy on Agricultural Credit." Washington, D.C.: World Bank, Report No. 436, May.

———. 1975. *Yugoslavia: Development with Decentralization.* Baltimore: Johns Hopkins University Press for the World Bank.

———. 1980. *The Philippines: Aspects of the Financial Sector.* Washington, D.C.: World Bank, May.

———. 1985. "Financial Intermediation Policy Paper." Washington, D.C.: World Bank, Industry Department, July.

————. 1988. *World Development Report 1988.* New York: Oxford University Press for the World Bank.

————. 1989. *World Development Report 1989.* New York: Oxford University Press for the World Bank.

————. 1990. "China: Financial Sector Policies and Institutional Development." Washington, D.C.: World Bank, Country Study, December.

————. 1991. *World Development Report 1991.* New York: Oxford University Press for the World Bank.

Yang, Ya-Hwei. 1994. "Taiwan: Growth and Structural Change of the Banking System." In *Financial Development in Japan, Korea and Taiwan.* Edited by Hugh T. Patrick and Yung Chul Park. New York: Oxford University Press, forthcoming.

Yoo, Jang H. 1977. "The Role of Money as a Conduit of Savings and Investment in the UDCs." *Kyklos,* 30(3): 520–525.

Yotopoulos, Pan A., and Sagrario L. Floro. 1988. "The Role of Financial Intermediation in the Mobilisation and Allocation of Household Savings in the Philippines: Interlinks between Organised and Informal Circuits." Paris: OECD Development Centre, May.

————. 1991. "Transaction Costs and Quantity Rationing in the Informal Credit Markets: Philippine Agriculture." In *Markets in Developing Countries: Parallel, Fragmented, and Black.* Edited by Michael Roemer and Christine Jones. San Francisco: International Center for Economic Growth, 141–166.

Yusuf, Shahid, and R. Kyle Peters. 1984. "Savings Behavior and Its Implications for Domestic Resource Mobilization: The Case of the Republic of Korea." Washington, D.C.: World Bank, Staff Working Paper No. 628, April.

Index